Adventuring through the Bible

Bible

A Comprehensive Guide to the Entire Bible

Ray C. Stedman

with James D. Denney

Adventuring through the Bible
Copyright © 1997 Elaine Stedman

Discovery House Publishers is affiliated with RBC Ministries, Grand Rapids, Michigan 49512

Discovery House books are distributed to the trade by Barbour Publishing, Inc., Uhrichsville, OH

Requests for permission to quote from this book should be directed to: Permissions Department, Discovery House Publishers, P.O. Box 3566, Grand Rapids, MI 49501.

Unless indicated otherwise, Scripture quotations are from the *Holy Bible: New International Version,* copyright © 1973, 1978, 1984 International Bible Society. Used by permission of Zondervan Bible Publishers.

Softcover ISBN 1-57293-163-9

The Library of Congress has cataloged the hardcover edition as follows:

Stedman, Ray C.
    Adventuring through the Bible : a comprehensive guide to the entire Bible / by Ray C. Stedman with James D. Denney.
        p. cm.
    ISBN 0-929239-98-9
    1. Bible—Introductions. 2. Theology, Doctrinal—Popular works. I. Denney, James D. II. Title.
  BS445.S66 1996
  220.6'1—dc20

                                                                    96–22598
                                                                    CIP

Printed in the United States of America

05 06 07 08 09 10
SBI
1 2 3 4 5 6 7 8

Contents

PART FOUR: Music to Live By

PART FIVE: The Promises of God

PART SIX: Jesus: The Focus of Both Testaments

Key to Icons

Adventuring through the Bible is designed to be an easy-to-use guide to every book of the Bible. The icons shown here are used throughout the book to help you find key themes, personalities, verses, and applications.

 Theme Identify the important ideas in all sixty-six books of the Bible.

 Personality Find a closeup view of key people.

 Verse Discover the Scripture verse or passage that summarizes and explains, brings hope and comfort.

 Application Learn how to turn biblical principles into life-changing reality.

Part One

A Panorama of the Scriptures

The Goal of God's Word

A nonbeliever once asked a Christian, "Will your God give me a hundred dollars?"

The Christian's reply: "He will if you know Him well enough."

Of course, the riches that God has already made available to us are the riches of His kingdom, the riches of His Word, the riches of His eternal life in a never-ending relationship with Him. But God will indeed give anyone hundreds, thousands, and even millions of dollars—if it serves His purpose and if that person knows Him well enough.

George Müller, as one example among thousands, was a well-known man of prayer and the founder of the world-famous Bristol Orphanages in England. Müller knew God so well that God gave him millions of dollars—money which that good and faithful servant wisely invested in young lives and in building the kingdom of God.

Knowing God is the key. He wants to be your friend. He wants to pour out the riches of heaven upon your life—"good measure, pressed down, shaken together and running over," as Luke 6:38 tells us. But you must get to know Him. And the way you get to know Him is through the pages of Scripture, as interpreted to us by the Holy Spirit.

Notice that all-important linkage: the Scriptures *and* the Spirit—you can't separate the two. The Bible without the Spirit leads to dullness, boredom, and dead, institutional Christianity. The Spirit without the Bible leads to fanaticism and wildfire. We need both the Spirit *and* the Word.

> Knowing God is the key, and the way you get to know Him is through the pages of Scripture, as interpreted to us by the Holy Spirit

ADVENTURING THROUGH THE BIBLE

The importance of
the *entire* Bible

The history and
people of the Bible

The Prophets

The Gospels

The Epistles

Revelation

Moreover, we need the *entire* Bible. For example, the story of humanity before the Fall is necessary that we might know what God made the human race to be and that we might understand the kind of relationship God had in mind when He created the first man and the first woman. The pure, pristine relationship that existed before sin entered the world is precisely the kind of relationship He wants to restore us to now!

We also need to know the lives of the men and women of faith throughout the Bible in order to see how God works in specific situations. What an encouragement these lives are to us! As we read these stories, we see that Abraham, Isaac, Jacob, Joseph, Moses, Joshua, David, Ruth, Isaiah, Jeremiah, Daniel, Mary, Peter, Stephen, Paul, Barnabas, John, and all the others went through the same experiences we do—and they drew upon the same supernatural strength and power that is available to us! We learn that God placed these people in the crossroads of their own times, recording their actions and reactions, so that we might see God's purpose in our own time and so that our actions and reactions might be guided by the lessons of those who went before us. Viewed in this way, the Bible becomes not merely a "religious book," but a practical, relevant guidebook for daily living!

We need to understand the Prophets in order to see how God is working through human history, from beginning to end. As we study what Paul calls "God's secret wisdom, a wisdom that has been hidden and that God destined for our glory before time began" (1 Cor. 2:7), we begin to know God's thoughts, which are not our thoughts, and God's ways, which are far higher than our ways. As our Lord put it, "You have hidden these things from the wise and learned, and revealed them to little children" (Matt. 11:25).

We need to know the Gospels in order to see the perfect life of Jesus Christ—His unique wisdom, His divine power, His human pain, His extraordinary personality, His unparalleled character, and His extravagant love for people. In the Scriptures, we discover the many-faceted richness and depth in the human being who was uniquely the Son of God and the Son of Man.

We need to know the Epistles in order to apply the great truths we learn in the Gospels. Under the inspiration of the Holy Spirit, the writers of the New Testament letters have translated His truths into principles for the most practical daily situations.

Finally, we need to know the book of Revelation, because this world is approaching the hour of crisis. As individuals and as a believing community, we need the assurance that this present darkness shall pass, that the futility and the horrors will be ended, that our bondage will cease, and that Jesus Christ will be manifested in this universe, and He shall reign.

The story of how the Bible came into being is the fascinating story of a miracle of God. In 2 Peter 1:21, the apostle Peter tells us that the Bible was written by men who were moved by the Holy Spirit:

Prophecy never had its origin in the will of man, but men spoke from God as they were carried along by the Holy Spirit.

The Bible clearly transcends all human documents; it is far greater than anything human beings could produce. Despite the tremendous diversity of human authorship and the vast span of time over which it was written, this Book has one message, tells one story, moves to one point, and directs our attention to one Person. It would simply be impossible to take at random any collection of books from literature, put them together under one cover, and have any remotely related theme develop. Such a collection is possible only if behind its many human authors there is one transcendent Author. As Paul wrote to Timothy (2 Tim. 3:16–17):

God's eternal purpose in our lives

All Scripture is God-breathed and is useful for teaching, rebuking, correcting and training in righteousness, so that the man of God may be thoroughly equipped for every good work.

The Bible is not only the story of God and of His Son Jesus Christ. It is also the story of your life and of my life, as well as the story of our race. The Bible explains what we are and how we came to be this way. It illuminates the human condition. It instructs us, exhorts us, admonishes us, corrects us, strengthens us, and teaches us. In this book, God has incorporated all the truths we need to know about ourselves.

How did ordinary human beings—some from the most common callings of life—capture the thoughts and attitudes of God? How did the Holy Spirit lead them in recording the Word of God rather than the mere opinions of human beings? It is a miracle beyond our understanding.

But this we do know: The more we study the truth of the Bible, the more thrilling and compelling it becomes. Like a scientist with a passion for uncovering the secrets of the universe, I am captivated by an intense drive to unfold the wonders of God's Word. After decades of study, I have found that increasing familiarity with this book has only caused it to grow more fascinating, more mysterious, more profound, and more marvelous in its implications and applications to my life.

The more we study the truth of the Bible, the more thrilling and compelling it becomes

This book has survived countless attempts to suppress it and destroy it. It has been preserved and defended for us through the centuries in ways that can only be called providential. Again and again its pages have been stained by the blood, sweat, and tears of martyrs who have spent their very lives to save this book for later generations.

Why has this book been so important to God and His people? What is the Bible's ultimate purpose? What does God want to accomplish by giving us this Book and by sending the Holy Spirit to interpret it and make it real in our lives? The Bible itself gives us the answer. In Ephesians 1:9–12, one of God's human writers, the apostle Paul, makes this amazing Spirit-inspired statement about God's revelation to us in Scripture:

What does God want
to accomplish by
giving us this Book
and by sending the
Holy Spirit to inter-
pret it and make it
real in our lives?

> *He made known to us the mystery of his will according to his good plea-sure, which he purposed in Christ, to be put into effect when the times will have reached their fulfillment—to bring all things in heaven and on earth together under one head, even Christ.*
>
> *In him we were also chosen, having been predestined according to the plan of him who works out everything in conformity with the pur-pose of his will, in order that we, who were the first to hope in Christ, might be for the praise of his glory.*

Astounding! The Creator of the universe, the Lord of space and time, the great starsmith who has fashioned a billion galaxies and thousands of billions of stars, has a purpose for your life and mine, and He has unveiled that purpose in His Word, the Bible! In Ephesians 3:8–12, Paul extends this soul-stirring thought:

> *Although I am less than the least of all God's people, this grace was given me: to preach to the Gentiles the unsearchable riches of Christ, and to make plain to everyone the administration of this mystery, which for ages past was kept hidden in God, who created all things. His intent was that now, through the church, the manifold wisdom of God should be made known to the rulers and authorities in the heavenly realms, according to his eter-nal purpose which he accomplished in Christ Jesus our Lord. In Him and through faith in Him we may approach God with freedom and confidence.*

Probably the clearest declaration of God's eternal purpose for our lives is found in Ephesians 4:11–13, where Paul states that the Lord Jesus, having finished His work on earth through the cross and the res-urrection, ascended to heaven and gave gifts to human beings:

> *It was he who gave some to be apostles, some to be prophets, some to be evangelists, and some to be pastors and teachers, to prepare God's people for works of service, so that the body of Christ may be built up until we all reach unity in the faith and in the knowledge of the Son of God and become mature, attaining to the whole measure of the fullness of Christ.*

That is God's purpose: to bring us to maturity. God wants us to become mature by becoming *like Christ*. All that God has done in human history, all of His works recorded in Scripture, and the entire universe in its physical and moral dimensions have occurred so that you and I might become mature in Jesus Christ. God's purpose for the human race is not some vague, distant, far-off, impersonal goal; it is here, it is now, it is personal, it is clear, and it is profoundly intertwined with our everyday lives. Everything that exists has been brought into being so that you and I might fulfill God's amazing potential and possibilities for us.

And the measure of that humanity is the measure of the stature of the fullness of Jesus Christ.

I used to meet regularly with five high-school-age men. On one occasion I asked them, "Fellows, what is your image of a real he-man?"

"A guy who's really pumped up," said one. "A guy with a lot of muscles."

I knew of one athlete at this young man's school, a fellow with lots of rippling muscles on his body—plus a fair amount of muscle between his ears! "Oh," I said, "you mean like So-and-so?"

Startled, this young man said, "No, of course not! He spends a lot of time on the weight machine, and he has arms and legs like tree trunks—but he's not much of a man."

"Okay," I said, "then I guess muscles aren't a very reliable standard of manhood. So what is it? What do the rest of you think it takes to be a man? Let's make a list."

They all thought some more, then another replied, "Well, I think a real he-man is a guy with guts."

So we wrote down *courage* on our list. The young men did some more thinking and came up with some additional qualities that we added to our list: *consideration, kindness, integrity, purpose,* and so on. Soon, we had quite a long list.

Finally, I said, "You know, fellows, this is amazing! Think of it! You could go anywhere in the world and ask any man, and it wouldn't matter whether he was rich or poor, high or low, black or white or any shade in between. Ask him, 'What does it mean to be a man?' and you would get the same answers you have given on this list! Because all men everywhere want to be men. All women want to be women. The ideal they hold in their hearts is largely the same. There may be small variations in detail but not in the general form. The virtues we have listed are admired everywhere."

The young men nodded thoughtfully, and I continued, "Now, can you name one person who has fulfilled this list of ideals? How about you? Are you fulfilling these ideals?"

God's purpose: to bring us to maturity. God wants us to become mature by becoming *like Christ*

The human ideal

There are two steps toward becoming mature, "attaining to the whole measure of the fullness of Christ" (Eph. 4:13)

1. *Faith*

2. *Knowledge*

"I think I make it about thirty percent of the time," said one.

"No way!" said another. "You wouldn't even make it five percent—and neither do I!"

"Do you know anybody who has accomplished these ideals a hundred percent of the time?" I asked.

Silence and blank expressions. Suddenly, their faces lit up and they said, "Of course! Jesus!"

And they were right. Jesus is God's perfect man, the most flawless and complete expression of manhood and humanity ever to walk the face of the earth.

That is God's ideal for our lives! That is what Ephesians 4:13 tells us: God has planned for us to "become mature, attaining to the whole measure of the fullness of Christ." The steps toward that goal are twofold.

The first step that brings us to this goal is found in the phrase "until we all reach unity in the faith" (Eph. 4:13). *Faith* is the operative word. Faith is always the way by which we actually experience all that God has made available.

The second step that brings us to this goal is "the knowledge of the Son of God"—the *accurate* and *full* knowledge of the Son of God. We cannot achieve maturity in Christ as God intended if we don't know His Son. By knowledge, God does not only mean biblical information, but *personal experience* of Jesus Christ. It is faith, the first step, that leads to knowledge, the second step.

The apostle is careful to make clear that it isn't just my faith or your faith but *our* faith—what he calls "*unity* in the faith"—that brings us to this knowledge. In Ephesians 3, Paul prays that we may come to know with all the saints how high and broad and long and deep is the love of Christ. This means that unless you are in touch with other saints you can't possibly develop as you ought to as a Christian. It is impossible to move to maturity unless we are ready to share truth with each other. We need each other in the body of Christ, and as we fellowship together, share together, worship together, and study God's Word together, we *grow together* in maturity and in the experiential knowledge of the Son of God.

We will investigate this Book, the Bible, together to learn what it means to have a personal relationship with Jesus Christ. As we shall see, the Bible is not merely a collection of sixty-six books written by more than forty human authors over a span of fifteen centuries. It is a single book with a unified theme, a coherent message, and an astonishing relevance to our everyday lives here at the end of the twentieth century.

This one-volume "divine library" is a book of wonderful variety. Its beautiful love stories reflect the tenderest and most delicate of human passions. Its stories of political intrigue and maneuvering rival anything we might read about in today's headlines. Its stories of violence and gore almost make the blood run cold. Its poetic passages soar to the very heights of artistic and emotional expression. It has narratives of intense human drama. Its strange and cryptic passages filled with weird symbols and allegories are difficult to penetrate and comprehend.

Yet one subject dominates and permeates this book: Jesus Christ—Creator, Redeemer, and Lord. We first meet Him as one of the voices at Creation who says, "Let us make man in our image" (Gen. 1:26). His coming is symbolized and foretold throughout the span of the Old Testament. His life is detailed in quadruplicate through the Gospels, and His character is instilled in us throughout the New Testament epistles. Finally, His kingdom is pictured for us and His second coming is described in the book of Revelation: "Come, Lord Jesus" (Rev. 22:20).

From Genesis to Revelation, the Bible is a book about Jesus Christ. In symbol, in story, in marvelous prophetic vision, in simple narrative account, in history, in poetry, in every aspect and dimension of the book, the focus is always on God's Son. He is the secret, the thesis, the unifying thread of the book. In learning about Him, we learn God's plan and pattern for our own lives. We understand our problems and find the solution to those problems reflected in Him. We understand our needs and find the satisfaction of our needs in Him.

One of the most transforming truths found in this book is the truth Jesus spoke in John 10:10, where He said, "I have come that they may have life, and have it to the full." This is not just "good news," it is *great* news! Jesus wants us to know that not only are our sins forgiven by His shed blood, not only are we as Christians on our way to heaven, but we can experience fulfillment, joy, peace, and satisfaction, right here and right now! We don't have to merely struggle through this life making the best of a bad situation, muddling through, falling and failing, doubting and despairing, discouraged and defeated, barely hanging on through life until we finally cross over to the other side and find the release we crave. That's not good news!

The good news God reveals to us in this book is that we don't have to wait until eternity to find eternal life. The wonderful, abundant, eternal life that burned so brightly within Jesus is in our reach right now! We can have what He had, we can possess what He is, right here, right now! As Ian Thomas once said, "We must have what He is in order to be what He was." Once we attain that ideal and become mature in our Christlikeness, then God's purpose for our lives will be fulfilled.

Think of it! Who was this man Jesus? He was the perfect human being. He was God's ideal for humanity. For thirty-three years He lived among us on this pain-wracked, sin-drenched planet, in the very circumstances and under the same pressures we face every day of our

GENESIS THROUGH REVELATION

One subject dominates and permeates this Book: Jesus Christ—Creator, Redeemer, and Lord. In learning about Him, we learn God's plan and pattern for our own lives

The good news

lives. It was under these adverse circumstances that the godly perfection of His character shone with such brilliance and power.

"But," you may say, "I can't do that! I can't become what He was! I can't live a perfect life like the one He lived."

Of course not. But then, in the last analysis, it doesn't really depend on us. We will be what Jesus was when we allow Him to come live His life again through us, when—by simple faith—we take Him at His Word. If we dare to believe Him, moment by moment and day by day, we can allow Him to be what He is in us and through us. This is the good news!

But to do this, we need the Word of God's revelation. We don't come to the knowledge of the Son of God without a learning process, without a conscious commitment to an ever-increasing understanding of His truth. That is why we are adventuring together through this amazing Book.

The view from orbit

What is the "right" way to look at the world?

Most of the time, we see the world with the naked eye. Physicists, however, use expensive particle accelerators to see the world one atom or one electron at a time. Astronauts go out into orbit and look down on the world from a distance, seeing the entire sphere of the world with its continents, seas, and swirling weather patterns. Who has the "correct" view of the world: the physicist, the astronaut, or the naked-eye observer?

Answer: They all do. Each sees the world at a different scale, from a different perspective; each view is valid for its own purpose and in its own way.

Now consider this: What is the "right" way to look at the Bible? Should it be examined minutely, phrase by phrase and verse by verse? Or is a book study—an exhaustive examination of Nehemiah or Ephesians, for example—the right way? Or should we step back and take a wider, more panoramic view, the astronaut's view, surveying the great themes and historical flow of the Bible as if from orbit?

Answer: Each method is equally valid, each offers a different perspective, each serves a different purpose. Our purpose in *Adventuring through the Bible* is to take the wide-angle perspective, the aerial view of the Scriptures. Our survey of the Bible is divided into nine parts:

Part One: A Panorama of the Scriptures
An overview of the Bible, Genesis through Revelation

Part Two: Five Steps to Maturity
The books of Moses, Genesis through Deuteronomy

Part Three: The Message of History
Applying the historical books, Joshua through Esther

Part Four: Music to Live By
Old Testament poetry, Job through the Song of Songs

Part Five: The Promises of God
The prophetic books, Isaiah through Malachi

Part Six: Jesus: The Focus of Both Testaments
Jesus and His Church, Matthew through Acts

Part Seven: Letters from the Lord
Letters to the church, Romans through Philemon

Part Eight: Keeping the Faith
All about faith, Hebrews through Jude

Part Nine: Signs of the Times
The end—and a new beginning, Revelation

With this as our outline, we will journey through all sixty-six books of the Bible, examining its great themes and following the threads of those themes from their beginnings in Genesis to their triumphant conclusion in Revelation. We will probe the grand design of God's revealed Word and discover how each part of the Bible fits together with every other part. We will see the dynamic flow of God's profound revelation to humanity and detect the hand of God's unifying divine authorship behind each book and each human writer.

I encourage you to read through these books of the Bible as we go along. This book is not a substitute for Bible study. In fact, I would rather that you take this book and throw it on a bonfire than use it as a substitute for actually reading and studying God's Word! This book is intended to be opened alongside of, not in place of, the Scriptures.

So join me in the adventure of a lifetime, an adventure of grand discoveries and exciting breakthroughs. Join me as we adventure together through the greatest book of all time!

God Spoke in Times Past

D o you remember where you were and what you were doing on November 22, 1963? Virtually every American who was alive that day can recall with clarity and sadness the moment he or she heard that President Kennedy had been shot and killed in Dallas. If you are too young to recall that day, the nearest equivalent might be January 28, 1986, the day the space shuttle *Challenger* exploded nine miles above the earth killing seven brave astronauts. The emotional aftermath of such an event is one of shock, dismay, and abysmal sorrow. It is as if the sun were suddenly blotted out, and the entire landscape went dark.

If you could magnify that emotional intensity several times over, you might begin to understand how the disciples of Jesus felt in the aftermath of the crucifixion. Luke 24 contains a story of two such disciples walking along the road from Jerusalem to Emmaus. Whenever I read this story I feel a tug inside, a strong wish that I could have been present to witness this event with my own eyes. Even though I believe that since the coming of the Holy Spirit on the Day of Pentecost Christ is more real and available to believers now than when He physically walked the earth, I still would love to have been there to watch what was to take place in the lives of these two downhearted disciples.

It was the day of the resurrection of our Lord, and the countryside was already exploding with the incredible news that Jesus had risen— but few would believe it. Indeed, these two disciples were filled with sorrow and despair. Jesus' death had blotted the sun out of their sky

Jesus and the Old Testament

and they had no idea which way to turn or what to do. As they walked, they talked about their grief. They were intent on their own conversation, and a stranger drew near and began walking with them. The stranger asked, "What are you discussing together as you walk along?" (Luke 24:17).

They stopped and looked at the stranger in amazement. "Are you only a visitor to Jerusalem and do not know the things that have happened there in these days? . . . Jesus of Nazareth . . . was a prophet, powerful in word and deed before God and all the people. The chief priests and our rulers handed him over to be sentenced to death, and they crucified him; but we had hoped that he was the one who was going to redeem Israel. And what is more, it is the third day since all this took place. In addition, some of our women amazed us. They went to the tomb early this morning but didn't find his body. They came and told us that they had seen a vision of angels, who said he was alive. Then some of our companions went to the tomb and found it just as the women had said, but him they did not see" (Luke 24:18–24).

When they had finished speaking, the stranger said to them, "How foolish you are, and how slow of heart to believe all that the prophets have spoken!" (Luke 24:25). Then, Luke tells us, "beginning with Moses and all the Prophets," the stranger—the risen Lord Jesus Himself— "explained to them what was said in all the Scriptures concerning himself" (Luke 24:27). Later on, as they were thinking back over the events of that wonderful incident, they said to each other, "Were not our hearts burning within us while he talked with us on the road and opened the Scriptures to us?" (Luke 24:32).

What was it that caused this wonderful, strange, awe-inspiring sensation of holy heartburn, this divine glow of anticipation that lit again the smoldering fires of faith in their hearts? And don't you just wish that you could have an experience like that? I certainly do!

Well, the source of that strangely warmed experience on the Emmaus road was nothing more nor less than the exposition of the Old Testament in the power and clarity of the Holy Spirit: "Beginning with Moses and all the Prophets, he explained to them what was said in all the Scriptures concerning himself." This is what the Old Testament does: *It points to Christ!* The Old Testament prepares our hearts to receive the One who truly satisfies. That is the discovery made by the disciples on the road to Emmaus. Jesus is not just the object of the New Testament but of the Old Testament as well.

As Jesus once said to the Jewish leaders who opposed Him, "You diligently study the Scriptures because you think that by them you possess eternal life. These are the Scriptures that testify about me" (John 5:39).

In the previous chapter we found that God's purpose in revealing His truth to us through the Bible is to bring us all to maturity as followers of Christ, that maturity being "the whole measure of the fullness of Christ," the complete expression of Jesus Christ in the world. It takes the *entire* Bible, Old and New Testaments, to accomplish this, and it takes the work of the Holy Spirit to open our understanding of Scripture.

In this chapter we will examine the contribution that the Old Testament makes to our maturity in Christ—not in detail, but in an "orbital view" survey. We will gain an overview of the major thrust of the Old Testament so that we can have clear in our minds the part it plays in producing Christlike maturity within each of us.

The Old Testament is deliberately an incomplete book; it never was intended by God to be His last word to the human race. Dr. W. H. Griffith Thomas has suggested that if we were to approach the Old Testament as though we had never read it before and take note of all the remarkable predictions of someone who is coming afterward, we would find that this series of predictions begins in the early chapters of Genesis. As the text moves along, the predictions of this person grow in detail and degree of anticipation until, in the Prophets, they break out in glowing and marvelously brilliant colors, describing in breathtaking terms the One who is to come. And yet, after completing Malachi, the last Old Testament book, we would still not know who this person is. Thus, the Old Testament is a book of unfulfilled prophecy.

An incomplete book

But the mystery of the Old Testament does not end there. Read through the first thirty-nine books of the Bible again and you will notice that an astounding, strange, disturbing stream of *blood* springs forth in Genesis and flows in increasing volume throughout the remainder of this Testament. It is the blood of sacrifices—thousands and thousands of animals whose blood was poured out in a surging tide across the history of Israel. Again and again, the message is hammered home: without sacrifice, there is no forgiveness, no reconciliation. When we close the book again at the end of Malachi, we realize that it is not only a book of unfulfilled prophecies, but of unexplained sacrifices as well.

If we read through the Old Testament a third time, yet another dimension becomes clear: The great Old Testament men and women of God seem to express, again and again, a longing for something more than life offered them, something transcendent, something eternal. For example, Abraham sets out to find the city whose builder and maker is God. The people of Israel were on a pilgrim journey throughout the books of the Old Testament. In Job, in the Psalms, in the books of Solomon, there is the continual cry of thirsty souls longing for something

Jesus alone fulfills
the prophecies,
explains the
sacrifices, satisfies
the longings

that has not yet been realized. So, at the conclusion of this third reading of the Old Testament, we could not help but realize that it is not only a book of unfulfilled prophecies and unexplained sacrifices, but also of unsatisfied longings.

But something wonderful takes place the moment you cross over from the Old to the New Testament. As you open the pages of Matthew, the first words you read are, "A record of the genealogy of Jesus Christ." It is Jesus and Jesus alone who fulfills the prophecies, who explains the sacrifices, who satisfies the longings. The New Testament fulfills the promise of the Old, and we have to acknowledge that we cannot fully appreciate the profound meaning of the New Testament until we have first been awakened by the message of the Old.

Clearly, the Old Testament is a book intended to prepare us for something. The New Testament letter to the Hebrews, of course, ties in closely with the Old Testament themes, and the first two verses of Hebrews catch this idea very beautifully:

> *In the past God spoke to our forefathers through the prophets at many times and in various ways, but in these last days he has spoken to us by his Son.*

There you have the two testaments side by side: "In the past God spoke to our forefathers . . . at many times and in various ways" (the Old Testament), and "In these last days he has spoken to us by his Son" (the New Testament). The completion of the Old is found in the New.

The way the writer to the Hebrews describes the Old Testament is significant: "God spoke . . . at many times and in various ways." Just think of the many times and various ways in which God spoke in the Old Testament. Beginning with Genesis, we have the simple but majestic account of the story of creation, the fall of humanity, and the flood—an account never equaled in all of literature for power and simplicity of expression. Next comes the straightforward narrative of the lives of the patriarchs: Abraham, Isaac, and Jacob. We find the thunderings of the law in Leviticus, Numbers, and Deuteronomy; the true drama of the historical books; the sweet hymns and sorrowful laments of the Psalms; the practical homespun wisdom of Proverbs; the exalted language of the prophets Isaiah and Jeremiah; the touching human tenderness of Ruth, Esther, and the Song of Songs; the vivid, visionary mysteries of Daniel and Ezekiel; and on and on—many and various books, many and various ways of expressing the truth of God.

And *still* it is not complete! Nothing in the Old Testament can stand complete in and of itself. It is all intended as preparation.

As a first year college student, I was inducted into an organization you may have joined yourself. It is an organization with many members, and it is called The Ancient Order of Siam. Looking as ridiculous as possible in our little green skullcaps, a group of us were led into a room where we were subjected to an assortment of indignities. A number of sophomores stood around with paddles in their hands, ready to enforce their commands. We were lined up in a row, and one fellow stood before us and ordered us to follow him in repeating this chant:

Oh wah! . . . Tah goo! . . . Siam!

We dutifully repeated the chant. "Again!" he barked, so we all said it again. "Faster!" he commanded. So we said it faster. Then again, still faster. Then again, and again. Suddenly, we all realized what we were chanting:

Oh, what a goose I am!

Then we were members of the Order of Siam.

Sometimes, the meaning of a thing doesn't emerge until you put it all together. In a far less ridiculous way, a similar experience takes place as we gain the big picture of the Old Testament. Each book of the Old Testament might be likened to a phrase or a syllable. Each book makes its own sound, but it is an incomplete sound. Only by merging all the phrases and syllables together does the overall meaning become clear. A marvelous expression emerges into view—an expression of the fullness of God's Son.

And where do all the phrases and syllables of the Old Testament come together? In the New Testament! That's where all the many Old Testament voices merge into one voice, the voice of the Son of God. At the very end of the New Testament, in the Revelation, the apostle John writes that he saw the Lamb and he heard a voice like the voice of many waters. That voice booms forth, gathering itself out of all the thousands of rivers flowing together in one great symphony of sound: the voice of the Son!

In its incompleteness, the Old Testament is like a collection of syllables and phrases spoken to us by God—wonderful phrases, rich syllables, yet never quite connected and complete. But in the New Testament, these syllables and phrases become one expressive discourse focused on the reality of the Son of God.

You may think, "Why should I spend time on all this preparatory material? Why not skip the Old Testament entirely and go straight to

Many syllables, many phrases, one voice

ADVENTURING THROUGH THE BIBLE

Why not skip the Old Testament entirely and go straight to the New Testament?

the New Testament, the final voice of the Son? I don't need the Old Testament at all." That would be a big mistake! Why? Because you cannot really grasp the fullness and richness of the New Testament without being prepared by the Old. Does that sound like a radical statement? Perhaps, but I don't think it can be successfully challenged. While much of the New Testament is very easy to understand, much of it is built on a foundation of the Old Testament. We will never understand all God has for us in the New Testament until we are prepared by exposure to the Old.

Every successful process requires adequate preparation. Why does a farmer take time and trouble to plow his field for planting? Why doesn't he just take the seed out and sprinkle it over the ground? Some of that seed is bound to find a place in which to take root and thrive. Does the farmer *really* need to spend all that extra time preparing the soil? Yes! Every farmer knows that though the seed is the most important single item in raising a crop, most of it will never take root unless the soil has been adequately prepared!

Why do schoolteachers always start with the ABCs instead of charging right in and teaching Shakespeare? Wouldn't it save a lot of time, money, and effort to simply take the nation's five-year-olds and send them straight to college? Obviously, we cannot educate students this way. Why? Because that's not the way students learn! Without adequate preparation, all the great knowledge in the world, dispensed by the greatest teachers in the world, would wash uselessly over them, leaving them unchanged.

As Paul says in Galatians 3:24, "The law [of the Old Testament] was put in charge to lead us to Christ that we might be justified by faith." Something is lacking in our lives if we try to grasp the reality of Christ without fully grasping the reality of the Ten Commandments. We will never be able to lay hold of all that is in Him unless, like Paul, we have wrestled with the demands of a rigid, unyielding law that makes us say with him, "What a wretched man I am! Who will rescue me from this body of death?" (Rom. 7:24).

For many years I read and taught the book of Romans, including the great liberating, delivering themes of chapters 6 through 8, without truly grasping the core truths of the book. I failed to experience the mighty, liberating power of Romans in my own heart until I had spent some time with the children of Israel in the Old Testament, living out in the wilderness, on the back side of the desert, with the burning desert heat beating down on me, and the pain of a barren, defeated existence throbbing in my soul. After I had seen what God accomplished in the lives of the Old Testament people by delivering them, I was able to understand—for the first time—what God is trying to tell us in

Romans 6, 7, and 8. The "soil" of my heart needed the preparation of the Old Testament in order to receive the "seed" of the New Testament word.

Dr. H. A. Ironside told me a story from his early years of ministry when he was still an officer in the Salvation Army. He was holding evangelistic meetings in a large hall in a major city, and a great number of people were coming every night to hear him. One night, he noticed an alert young man sitting in the rear, leaning forward and listening attentively to everything Dr. Ironside said. The young man returned night after night, and Dr. Ironside wanted to meet him. He tried to catch him before he left the building, but each time the meeting was dismissed, the young man would melt into the crowd and disappear.

One night the young man came in a little late, and the only two seats left in the auditorium were right in the front row. He came down the aisle rather self-consciously and slipped into one of the front-row seats. Dr. Ironside thought to himself, *Ha! You won't escape tonight, my young friend.*

Sure enough, when the meeting was over, the young man turned to go, but the aisle was full. Ironside stepped forward, tapped him on the shoulder and said, "Would you mind if we just sit down here and talk?"

They sat down and Dr. Ironside said, "Are you a Christian?"

"No," said the young man, "I don't think I could call myself a Christian."

"Well, what are you?"

"I really couldn't say. There was a time when I think I would have called myself an atheist. But of late, I just don't think I could say with assurance that God doesn't exist. I guess you could call me an agnostic."

"Well," said Dr. Ironside, "what has produced this change in your thinking?"

The young man pointed to an older man sitting a few seats away. "It's the change in that man right over there."

Dr. Ironside looked and recognized the older man as Al Oakley, who had been part owner of a popular saloon in that city—that is, before he became his own best customer, ending up a skid-row drunk. But Al had experienced an amazing conversion in a Salvation Army jail service, and his life had completely turned around.

"I've known Al Oakley for years," said the young man, "and I know he hasn't any more backbone than a jellyfish. He tried to quit drinking many times but was never able to. Whatever turned his life around must be the real thing. So I've been reading the Bible lately. I can't seem to get anything at all out of the New Testament. But recently I've been reading the book of Isaiah. I've always been an admirer of oratory, and I think

Isaiah slings the language better than anyone! If I could become a Christian by believing Isaiah, I think I would."

So Ironside opened his Bible and said, "I'd like to read you a short chapter from the book of Isaiah. It is about someone who is unnamed in the passage—but when I finish reading, I believe you'll be able to fill in the name."

"I don't know the Bible that well," said the young man.

"I don't think you'll have any problem," said Dr. Ironside. He turned to Isaiah 53 and read:

> *Who has believed our message*
> *and to whom has the arm of the LORD been revealed?*
> *He grew up before him like a tender shoot,*
> *and like a root out of dry ground.*
> *He had no beauty or majesty to attract us to him,*
> *nothing in his appearance that we should desire him.*
>
> *He was despised and rejected by men,*
> *a man of sorrows, and familiar with suffering.*
> *Like one from whom men hide their faces*
> *he was despised, and we esteemed him not.*
>
> *Surely he took up our infirmities*
> *and carried our sorrows,*
> *yet we considered him stricken by God,*
> *smitten by him, and afflicted.*
> *But he was pierced for our transgressions,*
> *he was crushed for our iniquities;*
> *the punishment that brought us peace was upon him,*
> *and by his wounds we are healed.*
>
> *We all, like sheep, have gone astray,*
> *each of us has turned to his own way;*
> *and the LORD has laid on him the iniquity of us all.*

Dr. Ironside continued reading to the end of the chapter, then he turned to the young man and said, "Now, tell me, who was I reading about?"

The young man said, "Let me read it myself." He took the book and began to read rapidly through the whole chapter. Then he suddenly dropped the Bible in Dr. Ironside's hands, and dashed down the aisle and out the door without another word. Not knowing what else to do for the young man, Dr. Ironside simply prayed for him.

The young man didn't return for two nights. Then, on the third night, Dr. Ironside was relieved to see him return. This time there was a different expression on the young man's face as he came up the aisle. Clearly, something had changed in his life. He took a seat in the front row, and when a time of sharing testimonies was announced, the young man stood and told his story.

"I was raised in an unbelieving, atheistic family," he said. "In my school years, I read all the critics and was convinced there was absolutely nothing to this 'Christian' business. But while I was in Palestine, working for the British government, I was exposed to a number of influences that suggested to me that the Bible might be true.

"In Jerusalem, I joined a tourist group that went to visit 'Gordon's Calvary,' the site outside the Damascus Gate where General Charles Gordon believed he had found Golgotha, the skull-shaped hill with the garden tomb nearby. I went up there with this group. We climbed to the top, and while we were there, the guide explained that this was the place where the Christian faith began. It came home to me that this was the spot where, in my mind, the Christian *deception* began. It made me so angry I began to curse and blaspheme. The people ran in terror down the slope, afraid that God was going to strike me dead for blasphemy in such a sacred spot."

At this point, the young man broke down in tears. "You know, friends," he continued, "these last few nights I have learned that the one I cursed on Calvary was the one who was wounded for my transgressions and by whose wounds I am healed."

It took an Old Testament prophecy to prepare this young man's heart for the good news of the New Testament. His experience is a beautiful demonstration of the purpose and power of the Old Testament. The Old Testament was written to set our hearts aflame, to cause our hearts to burn within us in anticipation and longing for the Christ of the New Testament. Truly, the Lord Jesus Christ supplies all our needs, but the Old Testament awakens our hearts to the reality of our need of Him.

No book in all the New Testament asks the kind of deep, soul-searching questions you find in the Old Testament—questions that continue to plague the hearts of men and women today. No place in the New Testament will you find the earnest searchings of the human heart all gathered in one place. In the Old Testament we find expressed all the pain, anguish, and confusion that afflicts the modern soul: Why is there injustice? Why do the wicked prosper? What is our place in the cosmic scheme? How can we find meaning and purpose? Do we just live, laugh, suffer, then die and return to dust? Are we loved? Are we valuable? Or is everything ultimately futile?

> The Lord Jesus Christ supplies all our needs, but the Old Testament awakens our hearts to the reality of our need of Him

> In the Old Testament we find expressed all the pain, anguish, and confusion that afflicts the modern soul

The Old Testament is designed to articulate our deep spiritual hunger, to put life into terms we can see and express, to define the thirst of the soul, so that we can put a finger on our pain, our need, and our desire. How can we recognize the One who satisfies if we haven't identified the sources of our dissatisfaction?

Until we have seen ourselves reflected in the pages of the Old Testament, all we can really know is that we wake up each morning with a hazy sense of emptiness and incompleteness. As a result, we vainly try this and that and the other thing, hoping that *something* will satisfy, and always feel disappointed in the end. So life becomes a continual merry-go-round of pleasure-seeking or money-seeking or relationship-seeking or drug-seeking, which ends only in despair, emptiness, loneliness, or addiction.

For thousands of years, right up to the present moment, people of all cultures and backgrounds have turned to the Old Testament, have read its precious, powerful words, and have said, "That's it! That's me! That's exactly how I feel!" And they have gone on to find the answer for their pain and problems in those pages as well. The Old Testament is the book of human experience. It is designed to graphically, realistically portray us as we are. In the mirror of the Old Testament we see ourselves clearly, and this reflection of ourselves prepares us to listen to the Holy Spirit as He speaks to us through the New Testament.

How poverty-stricken we would be without the Old Testament, yet many Christians, tragically, *choose* to be poor! They ignore the marvelous, preparatory revelation God has given in the Old Testament, so that the rich truths of the New Testament might come alive in our hearts. As we move from the Old to the New Testament in this introductory section of our adventure together, my hope is that you will be challenged and changed in your approach to this great book and that in the years to come, the pages of the first thirty-nine books of your Bible will become as worn, underlined, and treasured as the pages of your favorite New Testament books.

Many Christians *choose* to be poor!

The Old Testament is a living book, a fascinating book, guiding us toward maturity in Christ, preparing our hearts for the good news of the New Testament. May God immerse our hearts in its truths and use it to draw us deeper, ever deeper, into the living reality of His Son.

The divisions of the Old Testament

There are four divisions of the Old Testament, and each of these four divisions is especially designed to prepare us for a relationship with the Lord Jesus Christ. From the story of humanity's origins to the history of Israel to the great Old Testament poetry to the thundering books of prophecy, each section of the Old Testament lays its own foundation of truth. Each division touches our hearts in a subtly different way. Each helps present the coming ministry and person of Jesus in a subtly different light—so that when He is finally revealed at the critical moment in history, we see Him and we say, "Yes! This is the One we have always heard about and read about in the Old Testament!"

Here is a thumbnail guide to the four divisions of the Old Testament:

Fives Steps to Maturity—*The Books of Moses.* These five books take us from our racial babyhood—the origin of the universe and the origin of humanity—and lead us toward maturity through the introduction of sin (and the first gleaming of the plan of salvation), the first judgment of humankind through the Great Flood, the stories of the heroes of faith (Abraham, Isaac, Jacob, and Joseph), the beginnings of the nation of Israel, the captivity and exodus, the leadership of Moses, the introduction of the Law, the wandering in the desert, and right up to the very borders of the Land of Promise.

Genesis means "beginnings," and the book of Genesis opens with the greatest mystery of our existence: our relationship to the universe and to the Creator of our universe. In its stories, we see reflection after reflection of our own human need. Adam and Eve needed a covering for their sins. Noah needed a boat to save him from the waters of judgment. Abraham continually needed God to intervene, to deliver him and supply him with things he lacked. Isaac needed God to prod him to action. Jacob needed a Savior to get him out of the messes he continually made in his life. Joseph needed a deliverer from the pit, from prison, from life's unfairness. The message of Genesis is the message of God's answer to our human need.

Exodus is the story of God's response to our human need. It is the marvelous lesson of His redemptive power in our lives—the story of the first Passover, the parting of the Red Sea, the lawgiving at Sinai. It is the story of human oppression in the land of Pharaoh—and the story of miraculous redemption and deliverance from bondage. The Israelites did nothing to bring about their own salvation. God did it all. That is still how He works in our lives today.

Leviticus is a book of detailed instruction. It is designed to make God accessible to us so that we will be available to God. It begins with the story of the tabernacle, the dwelling place of God. The tabernacle, of course, is a symbol of our lives, the place God ultimately chooses to dwell.

Numbers is the book of the wilderness of failure. The book begins at Kadesh-barnea, at the very edge of the Land of Promise. The people of Israel wander away from that place, losing sight of God's promise to them for forty years. After wandering in barrenness, loneliness, unbearable heat, and blistering sand, haunted mile after mile by defeat, they

THE OLD TESTAMENT

The Books of Moses

Genesis

Exodus

Leviticus

Numbers

finally arrive at the same place where Numbers began—Kadesh-barnea. Numbers is a record of failure—and a warning for our own lives.

Deuteronomy means "second law." It is the story of the regiving of the Law—and the people's recommitment of themselves to follow it. The book closes with the disclosure of the marvelous blessings that await those who pattern their lives after the revealed will of God. So the thread that winds through these five books, beginning with Genesis and leading all the way to the end of Deuteronomy, is that we are advancing, step by step, book by book, toward maturity, toward a living relationship with the living God of the universe.

The Message of History—*Joshua through Esther.* The historical books also make a unique contribution to the preparatory work of the Old Testament. While the first five books of the Old Testament gave us the pattern of God's working in the human race, the next twelve books of history present us with the perils that confront us as we daily walk the walk of faith. These books trace the history of one nation, a peculiar nation with a special ministry—the ministry of representing God to the world and of perpetuating the lineage of the One who will be born the Messiah, the Savior, the Son of God. In the pressures, perils, and failures of Israel, we see the pressures, perils, and failures that beset us today as believers. And in God's loving discipline and His gracious redemption of Israel, we see His work of sanctifying and saving us from our own sin and failure.

The books of history lead us through the battles of *Joshua* as Joshua seeks to obey His Lord and take the Land of Promise. We see the intimidating forces of Jericho, followed by God's miraculous victory. We see the failure of the flesh at Ai and the deception of the Gibeonites. Through it all, we see that Joshua steadily marches onward, relentlessly fighting the battle of faith, never quitting or turning aside from the mission God has assigned him.

In *Judges* we see the cycles of spiritual success and spiritual defeat—and we see God's use of seven special people, the judges of Israel, to bring deliverance to Israel. In *Ruth* we have a wonderful story of faithfulness, set against the backdrop of the failures of Judges. Ruth, an alien woman in the land of Israel, hears the voice of God, obeys, and joins herself to the people of Israel. It is a beautiful story of romance—and of faith.

The books of *Samuel, Kings,* and *Chronicles* tell of the glory years of Israel as a mighty kingdom—and of the tragedies that result when human kings do not obey the King of kings and Lord of lords. These books tell us the stories of King Saul, King David, King Solomon, and on and on—kings who were strong, kings who were weak, wise kings and foolish, righteous kings and evil, great kings and small. Always, it seems, whenever a bad king has led Israel into destruction and disgrace,

Deuteronomy

The historical books

Joshua

Judges

Ruth

Samuel, Kings, Chronicles

the Lord lifts up a man like Hezekiah or Josiah to cleanse the temple, rediscover the book of the Law, and turn Israel back to God.

The books of *Ezra, Nehemiah,* and *Esther* deal with Israel's captivity and restoration. God is always at work in our lives—even in our bondage and pain. He lifts us out of defeat and discouragement and helps us to rebuild the walls of our lives, even as Nehemiah led the rebuilding of the walls of Jerusalem. He enables us to shout in triumph, even amid seemingly hopeless circumstances, just as Queen Esther was able to triumph over her impossible odds. In these twelve books of history, we find yet another facet of God's preparation of our hearts for the long-awaited arrival of the Messiah.

Music to Live By—*Job through Song of Songs.* These are the poetical books that express both the praise and protest of the human heart. *Job, Psalms, Proverbs, Ecclesiastes,* and *Song of Songs* expose our hearts to God, honestly expressing our pain and our longing for God. There is not a single emotion we experience in life that is not explored and expressed in these books. If you want to understand your own experience in life and find a reflection of your own soul in the Scriptures, then turn to these beautiful, powerful Old Testament books.

The Promises of God—*Isaiah through Malachi.* These are the books where God says what He will do. There are seventeen of these books, commonly divided between the "major" prophets and "minor" prophets. They are not major or minor in importance—only in length, the "minor" prophets being much shorter books than the "majors." Whether long or short, all of these books contain powerful, major truths for our lives.

Isaiah is a book of incredible glory and majesty. It promises and predicts in startling detail the life, ministry, and sacrificial death of our Lord Jesus. Isaiah is a book of grace. It tells the story of how we have destroyed ourselves through sin—and how God has intervened and given us the promise of a new beginning. *Jeremiah* and *Lamentations,* by contrast, warn of the absence of God from our lives if we turn our backs on Him. *Ezekiel* begins with a cascading, transcendent vision of God and leads us on a tour of future history, revealing God's promise of intervention in worldwide human events. *Daniel* shows us God's protective power to give us boldness, even when we are in captivity in a hostile, rapidly changing world; Daniel goes on to reveal what God is planning to do through the nations of the world down through the course of history, even beyond our own day.

Hosea is one of the most beautiful books in the Bible, a picture of God's unconditional love toward erring, sinful human beings; it is the promise of God's persistence in pursuing us to bring us redemption. *Joel* is the promise that God can even weave national and individual tragedies

Ezra, Nehemiah, Esther

The poetical books

Job,
Psalms,
Proverbs,
Ecclesiastes,
Song of Songs

The Prophets

Isaiah

Jeremiah,
Lamentations

Ezekiel

Daniel

Hosea

Joel

ADVENTURING THROUGH THE BIBLE

Amos, Obadiah, Jonah

Micah

Nahum

Habakkuk

Zephaniah

Haggai, Zechariah, Malachi

and catastrophes into His eternal plan. *Amos* is the promise that God never relaxes His standards; He continually seeks to bring us to perfection in Him. *Obadiah* is a promise of spiritual victory, as seen in the contrast between Jacob and Esau, spirit and flesh. *Jonah* is the promise of God's patience, and His gracious second chance, as revealed in both the life of Jonah and the repentance of Nineveh.

Micah is the promise of God's pardon, echoing (in shorter form) the themes of Isaiah. *Nahum* promises the destruction of Nineveh; it comes after the story of Jonah and the repentance of Nineveh by a hundred years and demonstrates that God does not change. If we repent once, then lapse back into complacency or disobedience, we can expect to feel the disciplining judgment of God. *Habakkuk* promises that God will ultimately answer our questions and cries for justice in an unjust world. *Zephaniah* is a dark book that promises judgment in "the Day of the LORD."

Haggai promises material restoration if we turn our hearts to God. *Zechariah* is "the Apocalypse of the Old Testament," promising God's management of future events and His preservation of God's people through the time of judgment. *Malachi* promises that God will respond to our need and send us a Savior; it predicts the first coming of Jesus (preceded by John the Baptist), then skips over to the second coming of Jesus, the dawning of the Sun of righteousness.

In a few strokes of the pen, we have sketched the outlines of the Old Testament. In the pages that follow, we will look at some of the details and subtler shadings of God's grand Book of preparation for our lives.

God Has Spoken in These Last Days

There are two ways of learning truth: reason and revelation. People are forever asking which is more important. That is like asking which blade of a pair of scissors is more important or which leg of a pair of trousers is more important. It takes both. In the same way, it is impossible to gather the full, balanced body of biblical knowledge together without relying on both reason and revelation.

Some people throw out reason and attempt to rely on revelation alone. The result is fanaticism. If we decide that our God-given faculty of reason has no value at all, then we will find ourselves behaving irrationally.

I once read of a man who decided that the solution to every problem could be found in the Bible. When gophers began eating the vegetables in his garden, he took his Bible out in the yard and read the gospel of John in the four corners of his property. Somehow, he figured this would solve his gopher problem. It didn't. Reason would suggest that the best way to rid one's garden of gophers would be to set out gopher traps. By attempting to rely solely on revelation without the application of reason and common sense, this man ended up behaving irrationally.

If we throw out revelation and rely on reason alone, the result is equally disastrous. Reason has given us many scientific insights and technological advances, but reason alone has never shown us how to change the human heart; how to end war; or how to eliminate crime, poverty, drug abuse, or racism. In fact, our technological advances have actually

Revelation and reason belong together

**The Word
and the Spirit
together**

rendered the future more dark and frightening. We can never even make a dent in our social and human problems as long as we set aside God's revelation and focus exclusively on reason.

What is revelation?

Revelation is, simply, truth that we cannot know by reason. It is what Paul called "God's secret wisdom, a wisdom that has been hidden" (1 Cor. 2:7). He continued, "None of the rulers of this age understood it, for if they had, they would not have crucified the Lord of glory" (2:8). When he spoke of the rulers of this age, he was not talking about kings and princes, necessarily. He was talking about leaders of human thought in every realm. And he said there is a body of knowledge—a secret, hidden wisdom—that is imparted by God to human beings, but only on certain terms, which none of the rulers with all their cleverness and wisdom could understand. Had they known this, they never would have crucified the Lord of glory.

The religious rulers who demanded the crucifixion of our Lord were a body of learned, clever people who boasted that they, more than anyone else, could recognize truth when they saw it. But when incarnate Truth stood before them, when the Son of God Himself spoke to them, they neither recognized Him nor received His word. They crucified Him because they had thrown out revelation and were clinging only to the power of their own reasoning.

Revelation, in the fullest sense, is really *Scripture interpreted by the Holy Spirit.* We have this Book, which was given to us by God, as Paul declared to Timothy: "All Scripture is God-breathed" (2 Tim. 3:16). Scripture did not originate with human beings. Rather, human beings were the channel through whom God delivered His Word. As Peter wrote, "Men spoke from God as they were carried along by the Holy Spirit" (2 Pet. 1:21). The writers of the New Testament sat down and wrote letters just as we would write them today, expressing their feelings, their attitudes, and their ideas in the most natural and uncomplicated manner. But in the process, a strange mystery took place: the Holy Spirit worked through the New Testament writers to guide, direct, and inspire. In fact, the Spirit chose the very words that would express God's thoughts to human beings.

The marvelous hidden wisdom of God cannot be discovered in a laboratory experiment, yet it is absolutely essential to the kind of life God has always intended us to have. This wisdom is revealed in the Bible—yet it is a wisdom that is inaccessible and worthless to us if we are not instructed by the Holy Spirit. It is possible to know the Bible from cover to cover and to get absolutely nothing from it. You can go to any bookstore and find dozens of books filled with extensive information about the

*Revelation, in the
fullest sense, is
really Scripture
interpreted by the
Holy Spirit*

historical, archaeological, and literary content of the Bible; yet the authors of these books are hardened atheists.

So revelation is not found merely by reading the Bible. The Bible must be illuminated, interpreted, and authenticated in our lives by the Holy Spirit. The Word and the Spirit must act together to bring us to a saving, experiential knowledge of God.

Did you ever wonder why Jesus came to the Jews? Why didn't He come to the Aztecs? or the Chinese? or the Eskimos? There is a simple, commonsense answer to this question: He came to the Jews because they were the nation that had the Old Testament. The Jews, for this reason, were uniquely prepared to receive what God was offering in Christ. Certainly, not all Jews received Him. But for the first few years of its existence, the early church was overwhelmingly a Jewish church. The Jewish nation was qualified to receive the Messiah because it was prepared by the Old Testament to lay hold of Jesus, who was the way to life, truth, and light.

I believe this is why many people today who read only the New Testament can go only so far in grasping the fullness of Jesus Christ. Their hearts are not adequately prepared. Our lives are always shallow and limited if we are trying to grasp something for which we are not quite ready. This is why we need so deeply and continuously the ministry of the Old Testament.

If the Old Testament prepares, then the New Testament fulfills. God designed the New Testament to meet the needs stirred up and expressed by the Old Testament. How does the New Testament meet these needs? By revealing to us the one who is the answer to all our needs. Jesus said, "If anyone is thirsty, let him come to me and drink" (John 7:37). "If anyone eats of this bread [referring to Himself], he will live forever" (John 6:51). "Come to me, all you who are weary and burdened, and I will give you rest" (Matt. 11:28). "Whoever follows me will never walk in darkness, but will have the light of life" (John 8:12). All the needs of the human heart are met in Him.

The New Testament is to be a channel by which the Holy Spirit makes the living Jesus Christ real to our hearts. As we saw in the previous chapter, the New Testament letter to the Hebrews opens with the statement, "In the past God spoke to our forefathers through the prophets at many times and in various ways." In other words, the Old Testament has given us an incomplete message, not the final word. "But in these last days," the passage continues, "he [God] has spoken to us by his Son." The New Testament is the answer to all the yearning that the Old Testament stirs within us.

Another verse in Hebrews sums up the whole New Testament in one brief phrase. In Hebrews 2, the writer states that all the earth was to be subjected to humankind, and that God gave humankind dominion over it. We read in verse 8:

> *In putting everything under him, God left nothing that is not subject to him. Yet at present we do not see everything subject to him.*

That is an accurate assessment of the present situation. As we look around, we do not yet see much of anything in subjection to humanity. This is the problem, isn't it? Why don't things work out the way we think they should? Why is there always a fly in the ointment? Why is it that even our fondest dreams, when they are realized, are never as glorious as we anticipated? Because "at present we do not see everything subject to him." The stamp of rebellion and futility is upon everything we touch. This is the present situation. But the writer goes on:

> *We see Jesus . . . (Heb. 2:9).*

There is the answer! *We see Jesus!* That is the New Testament, the summary of its message to our hearts. We do not yet see everything in subjection. But the story is not ended. The whole tale has not been told. What we do see is the One who will make it possible. We see Jesus. And in the New Testament, He stands out on every page.

The divisions of the New Testament

Every division of the New Testament is particularly designed to set forth the Lord Jesus Christ as the answer to the needs of our lives.

The Gospels are the biographical section of the New Testament. There we learn who Jesus is and what He did. Who is Jesus, as presented in the Gospels? He is the Son of God become human for us. What did He do for us? He submitted to being sacrificed upon the cross. He burst forth from the tomb in resurrection power. He saved us from the penalty for our sins. In the Gospels we discover the mighty secret that the Son of God manifested among human beings, a secret that is nothing less than the most radical principle ever disclosed. I don't hesitate to put it in such strong terms.

The Gospels

There was a time when, in the fullness of my ignorance upon graduating from seminary, I thought the Gospels were hardly worth reading! I had heard that the Gospels were merely the story of the life of Jesus. I knew there was some value in them, but I believed that the most important parts of the New Testament were Paul's epistles. In fact, some of my seminary instructors unwisely reinforced this notion, instructing me to give my attention almost exclusively to the Epistles. They promised that if I would grasp the Epistles, I would be complete and perfect, and I would astonish everyone, including myself.

In time, I found I couldn't grasp the Epistles without the Gospels. I *desperately* needed the Gospels, for as I turned to them and read the life of Jesus Christ and saw Him portrayed in the four magnificent dimensions, I finally discovered the secret that has transformed my own life and ministry. The most radical, revolutionary statement ever presented to the human mind is revealed in the life of Jesus Christ, as recorded in the Gospels. Jesus stated it Himself over and over again in a variety of ways.

For example, Jesus said, "I live because of the Father, so the one who feeds on me will live because of me" (John 6:57). This statement explains the life of Christ—the miracles He wrought, the words He spoke, the power He exercised among human beings. It is the explanation for everything He accomplished, *up to and including the cross and the resurrection.*

Acts gives us the account of the beginning of the church. And the church is nothing more nor less than the body of Jesus Christ today, through which He intends to keep on being who He is, doing what He did. He poured out His physical life in order that He might pour it into a body of people who would express that life throughout the entire planet Earth. The book of Acts is but the simple, straightforward account of how this body began, how it was filled with the Holy Spirit, and how it began to launch out from Jerusalem, out into Judea and Samaria, and far beyond, to the uttermost parts of the earth, setting forth the glory of the life of the Son of God.

The ministry that belonged to Jesus during His earthly life now belongs to His body, the body of believers. It is our task as His followers to open the eyes of the blind, to set at liberty those who are held captive, to comfort those who need comfort, to be conduits for God's transforming, life-changing power in the lives of men and women everywhere.

The Epistles are a series of letters written to individuals and churches in artless, uncomplicated language conveying profound practical truths for Christian living. These letters are amazingly revealing—because, as you know, nothing is as revealing as a personal letter. If I wanted to know what people were like without actually sitting down and talking with them face-to-face, I would try to get some of their letters. These are letters written by human beings—and, through direct inspiration, by God. In them, we find revealed both the personalities of their human writers and of their divine Author.

The Epistles represent a wonderfully varied array of viewpoints. We find God's truth emerging through the personalities of the human writers of these letters. There is Peter the fisherman, always casting his net for the human soul. There is Paul the tentmaker and church builder, always laying foundations and constructing. There is John the net mender; that is what he was doing when Christ first found him. And

John's ministry is one of repairing, restoring, and bringing us back to God's original pattern.

In the letters of the New Testament, we discover the nuts and bolts of the Christian life, and we learn how to allow Jesus Christ to live His life through us. These letters are almost all composed in the same simple pattern. The first part is doctrinal, the second part is practical. The first part sets forth truth, the second part applies that truth to real life.

Truth must be applied. Revelation must be made relevant and real. As the Lord Jesus said, "You will know the truth, and the truth will set you free" (John 8:32). Until we begin to learn who He is and what He does and then apply it in the specific activities of our own lives and hearts, we can read our Bibles for years and years, yet be totally unchanged and untouched by those magnificent truths.

This was vividly brought home to me some years ago at a pastors' conference. Many laypeople think that if anybody exemplifies what the Christian life should be, it is a pastor. It would seem to follow that if you could get a whole group of pastors together, it would practically be heaven on earth! Let me tell you, it isn't that way at all! At this pastors' conference, as at many I have attended, you will find people who are discouraged, confused, soul-sick. In many cases you will find people who are so hurt and defeated that their very faith is hanging by a thread.

One of the speakers at this conference gave an excellent message on Paul's declaration in 1 Corinthians 2:16: "We have the mind of Christ." Then we had a prayer meeting. To my utter amazement and astonishment, pastor after pastor prayed to this effect: "Oh, God, give us the mind of Christ! Oh, if we could just have the mind of Christ!"

Now, what do the Scriptures say? "We have the mind of Christ." What kind of faith is it that prays, "Give me the mind of Christ"? All the marvelous promises of the Scriptures are continually ignored and misapprehended by Christians because we do not believe what they say! We are always asking God for things He already has granted us! He is urging us on, saying, "Help yourself." But we stand there and say, "Oh, if I only had it, what I could do!"

As we adventure through these epistles together, my prayer is that we will listen carefully to the clear, straightforward truths presented therein and that we will take these truths and make them relevant and real in our own lives.

The book of Revelation

Finally, the book of Revelation: This is the only book in the New Testament that deals completely with prophecy. Here, in the form of a vision, God reveals to us not only a slate of future events, but *the reality of who He is now and throughout all ages to come.* Here we read and comprehend the magnificent story of how the kingdoms of this world shall become the kingdoms of our Lord and of His Christ, how He shall reign forever and ever, and how the secret revealed in the Gospels (that the human race is to be inhabited by an indwelling God) enables a great multitude from every tribe and nation on the earth to triumph over sin, death, and hell.

Peace, perfect peace

The message of the New Testament is fundamentally simple. It is the same message that Paul states so simply and eloquently in Colossians 1:27: "Christ in you, the hope of glory." We do not have any hope if we do not have that. If Christ is not active in you, and you have not already begun to experience the mystery of His life being lived in you, then, (1) you are not a Christian, and (2) you have no hope—no hope of glory, no hope of fulfillment, no hope of joy, no hope of eternal love—nothing, zero, zilch! But, thanks to God and His Son Jesus Christ, we have the greatest hope imaginable!

Hymn writer Edward H. Bickersteth puts it beautifully: "Peace, perfect peace." But we cannot grasp the message of this hymn unless we notice its punctuation, because it has a rather peculiar structure. There are two lines in every verse. The first line ends with a question mark. The second line answers the question. The questions all concern life right now, and the answers are aspects of "Christ in you."

Question: "Peace, perfect peace, in this dark world of sin?" Answer: "The blood of Jesus whispers peace within."

Question: "Peace, perfect peace, by thronging duties pressed?" Answer: "To do the will of Jesus, this is rest."

Question: "Peace, perfect peace, with sorrows surging round?" Answer: "On Jesus' bosom naught but calm is found."

Question: "Peace, perfect peace, our future all unknown?" Answer: "Jesus we know, and He is on the throne."

Question: "Peace, perfect peace, death shadowing us and ours?" Answer: "Jesus has vanquished death and all its powers."

These are the questions desperately asked by the sin-sick, pain-wracked human race. And these are the answers found in the New Testament—and notice that each of these answers focuses on the name of Jesus! He is the focus of the New Testament. He is the answer to all our needs.

The Bible itself is a mere instrument, and its purpose is to point us to the living person of Christ. He is the One whose image is embedded in every page of the Bible. The New Testament was written in order that we may see Him—"Christ in you, the hope of glory." We do not yet see everything in subjection to Him, but in the pages of the New Testament, *we see Jesus.*

> The Bible itself is a mere instrument, and its purpose is to point us to the living person of Jesus Christ

PART TWO

FIVE STEPS TO MATURITY

Five Steps to Maturity

T he Jews call the first five books of the Bible "the Law" or (in Hebrew) the "Torah." In Greek it is called the "Pentateuch," from *penta* (five) and *teuchos* (scrolls). Despite the theories of so-called higher critics that the Pentateuch is an unreliable patchwork composed by different writers-editors over hundreds of years, much evidence supports the traditional belief that the author of these books was Moses. These five books demonstrate a unity of theme, content, and style that suggests that they are the work of a single hand.

The opening chapters of Genesis may have been delivered to Moses in a vision or handed down to him in the form of oral traditions. And the closing chapter of Deuteronomy, which records the death and burial of Moses, may well be the work of Moses' successor, Joshua, for it flows seamlessly into the book of Joshua, establishing a stylistic and thematic continuity with the rest of the Old Testament. The grandeur and sweeping scope of the Pentateuch, coupled with its simple and dignified telling of the history of humankind and of the early Jewish people, make a compelling case for belief in Moses' authorship of all five of these books.

The books of the Pentateuch and their principle themes are:

Genesis. The word *genesis* means "the beginning," and this book provides the foundation for all that is to follow, both the Old and New Testaments. Chapters 1 and 2 lay down the origins of the world.

Genesis

Chapters 3 through 5 lay down the origins of the human race and the human condition, the predicament of our race called sin. Here we see both our greatness as creatures made in the image and likeness of God and our tragedy and despair as fallen and sinful creatures who used the power of free will that God gave us to rebel against Him. The first six chapters of Genesis focus on three events that first *shape*, then *shake*, the very foundations of the world:

1. The Creation
2. The Fall of Man
3. The Flood

In chapter 6, the focus of Genesis shifts from three major events to five major people. They are presented to us not as vague historical figures of the past, but as living, breathing, flesh-and-blood personalities with whom we can all relate. This marvelous account preserves accurately for us not only the facts of their lives but the color, depth, and tone of life in their days. They are:

1. Noah
2. Abraham
3. Isaac
4. Jacob
5. Joseph

Exodus

Exodus. At the end of Genesis, the family of Jacob (Israel) has moved to Egypt, where Jacob's son, Joseph, has risen to a position of prominence and power. But as Exodus opens, four centuries have passed, and the children of Israel groan under bondage to a new and cruel Egyptian pharaoh. With this book, the focus shifts to Moses. Exodus recounts the story of Moses' contest of wills with the Egyptian pharaoh, the redemption of Israel in the Passover, the escape of Israel through the parted waters of the Red Sea, and the journey to Mount Sinai, where God gives to the Jewish nation their covenant law. The story of Exodus is the story of Israel's deliverance.

Leviticus

Leviticus. Now that the people of Israel have been delivered, they must be taught how to live as God's chosen people. In Leviticus, God gives Israel a body of regulations, instructions, ritual cleansings, and sacrificial atonements to set His people apart to holy living. The focus of Leviticus is on worship, sanctification, and obedience.

Numbers

Numbers. Having been sanctified, the people of Israel are ready to cross over into the Promised Land—or are they? Just as they are brought to the very brink of their inheritance, their faith falters, their obedience fails. Even God's servant Moses fails and sins. So God judges and disciplines His people, sentencing them to wander in the desert for forty years until the unbelieving, disobedient generation has passed away and a new generation arises—a generation of people who, it is hoped, have learned from the error of their parents. This generation reaches Moab, the gateway to the Promised Land, and there God gives His people instructions for the way they should live as inheritors of this new land.

Deuteronomy. Moses, at the end of his life, passes the baton to his disciple-successor, Joshua, and he delivers a farewell message to the people. It is, in essence, a sermon in which he reminds the people of God's righteousness and faithfulness in the past and points them toward the challenges of the future. He has led and loved the children of Israel, yet they have also been a source of great disappointment, grief, and anger to him. But they are his people, and they are God's people, so he blesses them. Then, from the summit of Mount Nebo, he views the horizon of Canaan, the Promised Land. Finally, he dies and is buried in the land of Moab, and Joshua assumes command of the nation of Israel.

With that background of the first five books of the Bible in view, let's revisit our basic premise: The purpose of God's revelation in Scripture is to stimulate our growth, to make us more mature and complete in Christ. The Bible finds the fulfillment of its function in your life and mine. If it is not producing maturity in our lives, then the Word of God is being wasted, as far as we are concerned. Its whole purpose is to make us effective instruments of God's grace and God's will, so "we will no longer be infants, tossed back and forth by the waves, and blown here and there by every wind of teaching."

Clearly, if these books are to have a maturing, stabilizing effect on our lives, we must incorporate them into our lives, we must read them, we must immerse ourselves in them. But how many of us have actually sat down to read and study these books? How many of us have finished them? Oh, we frequently start off very well in Genesis, with its majestic creation story and its dramatic narratives of the fascinating lives of the patriarchs. And we move on into Exodus, and we get caught up in the tense drama that is played out between Moses and Pharaoh. But then we get to Leviticus, with its strange legal requirements, and we bog down. We never quite get through Leviticus and on into Numbers and Deuteronomy, much less into Joshua.

I'm reminded of a cartoon I once saw in a magazine shortly after the release of the film *The Ten Commandments,* in which Charlton Heston portrays Moses. In the cartoon, two women are walking by a movie theater. The marquee reads, "Now Showing: The Ten Commandments." One woman says to the other, "Oh, yes, I've seen the picture, but I

We bog down
because we read
without vision

As we read these
books with vision,
gaining a pano-
ramic perspective,
we will see the full
sweep, scope, and
stunning impact of
God's message

The book of beginnings

Genesis is rich and
complex in truth
and insight into the
human condition

haven't read the book." Most of us fall into that category. We have seen a great many of the Hollywood versions of Scripture, but we never seem to get around to reading the books.

Why do we bog down? It isn't because the Pentateuch isn't instructive or helpful. In many ways it is the most helpful part of the Bible. My own Christian life has been more greatly strengthened by reading the Pentateuch than perhaps any other portion of Scripture. I think the reason so many of us bog down in these books is because we read them without vision. We don't know why we are reading them. We don't know what to expect from them. We don't know what to look for. We read the text as a simple narrative that sometimes is interesting and sometimes gets complicated, and we fail to probe the text to find out what God is driving at and how He wants to apply its truths in our own daily lives.

Some staggering, marvelous secrets are embedded in these books. That's why, in this study, we are taking the mountaintop view, the orbital view, scanning the layout of the land of the Pentateuch. Though it is important and rewarding to also study these books in close detail, it is easy to miss the main thrust of this passage in a verse-by-verse approach. As we read these books with vision, gaining a panoramic perspective, we will be able to see the full sweep, scope, and stunning impact of God's message to us in the Pentateuch, so that His Word can produce its maturing work in our lives.

We begin with Genesis. Compare the word *genesis* with the word *gene*. A gene is a tiny yet complex chemical component within a chromosome; it initiates and determines the physical unfolding of an individual life. Genesis is much like that gene. It is only one-sixty-sixth of the entire Bible, it is simple, understated, even humble in its style, yet it is rich and complex in truth and insight into the human condition. It initiates and sets the tone for the entire Bible story. It explains why we human beings need a Savior, and as early as Genesis 3:15, it suggests that the line of Adam and Eve will one day produce a Savior who will crush the head of Satan. Genesis is our biblical foundation; without it we cannot fully understand the rest of the Bible.

Genesis is the story of the beginning of our universe, the beginning of the human race, the beginning of sin, the beginning of civilization, and it is a fascinating record of the origins of the physical world that surrounds us. The Bible opens with that majestic, awesome insight:

In the beginning God created the heavens and the earth (Gen. 1:1).

Thus the Bible begins by confronting one of the greatest questions of our existence: the mystery of the universe. Not surprisingly, this is the very theme of science and philosophy today. Our greatest artists, writers, and filmmakers explore this theme. It is a theme frequently revisited in television series, from Carl Sagan's *Cosmos* to the various incarnations of Gene Roddenberry's *Star Trek.* It is here, at the very heart of one of the most fascinating questions of our human experience, that the Bible begins. And it begins with those grand, exalted words, "In the beginning."

Genesis goes on to tell us about ourselves. We human beings, it says, are remarkable creatures who were made to be a reflection of God's mind, an expression of God's love, the instrument of God's plan. The human race is seen in the opening chapters of Genesis in a marvelous faith-love-fellowship relationship with God. Adam, the first man, walks in communion with God, as Genesis 3:8 tells us, in the garden, "in the cool of the day." Rightly translated, this verse should say that God walked in the garden "in the spirit of the day"—that is, in a spirit of understanding and fellowship with Adam. Here we get just a brief glimpse of God's intention for humanity.

Immediately, this sweet communion is shattered by the story of the Fall. Beginning in the third chapter of Genesis, we get the record of the tragedy of disobedience and unbelief. God's Word confronts us immediately with the awful error of faith in the wrong idea—the terrible destruction that comes into our lives when, in blindness and self-willed ignorance, we place our faith in error. It shows us that we are made to be creatures of faith. So here is the story of human failure and fall. It is followed immediately by the story of the failure of the first creation and its eventual destruction in the flood. The rest of Genesis is God's drawing of people in need. It is the story of Abraham, Isaac, Jacob, and Joseph. These are men who experienced great failures, deep hurts, and great successes. Their lives are lessons, given to show us the desperate need in each one's life. We can think of them as four representative types of personality. One of them is like you.

Abraham's story is that of the need for a supplier. Here was a man who always needed somebody to come and deliver something to him that he lacked. He was always short. The modern saying is: "A day late and a dollar short." That is the story of Abraham's life. He was always in need. It is the story of a man whose need was continually being supplied by God.

Isaac was a man who had another kind of need. He never ran short. There is no record of a famine in Isaac's life. But he was in need of a stimulator. He loved to just sit. He needed somebody to motivate him. So God had to prod him repeatedly to get him moving into the place God wanted him to be. Most of us need this kind of stimulation from time to time—or maybe all the time!

Creation

The Fall

The Flood

Abraham

Isaac

Jacob was a man who was in continual need of a bodyguard, a protector. He was always getting himself into trouble. Throughout his life, he needed somebody to come and rescue him from his latest fix.

Then we have the marvelous story of Joseph. How different he was from Abraham, Isaac, or Jacob! So human, so real, yet so admirable! But the story of Joseph's life too is the story of need—the need of a deliverer—not because of his own failure, fault, or sin. In fact, many of his problems seemed to result from his integrity and his commitment to righteous living before God! His is the story of how God continually delivered him, and his story closes the book of Genesis with these words: ". . . in a coffin in Egypt."

Even after his death, Joseph is in need of one last deliverance. His bones lie in a coffin in Egypt, and his final need is to have his mortal remains delivered out of Egypt and taken up to the Promised Land. Here is a symbol of the need of God's people to be delivered from Egypt and taken up to the Promised Land. It is also a symbol of every one of us as believers in Christ whose final hope is to have our own mortality rescued from corruption and taken up to the eternal land God has promised us. Now it becomes clear, from this panoramic view of Genesis, that the whole story of Genesis is a message about the deep need of the human race—your need and mine.

Then we come to Exodus, the story of God's response to human need. It is the marvelous lesson of God's redemption. The whole book revolves around four major incidents: the Passover, the crossing of the Red Sea, the giving of the Law at Mount Sinai, and the construction of the tabernacle. The first two—the Passover and the crossing of the sea—signify the forgiveness and the freedom that God gives. Here we learn that freedom and forgiveness are entirely a gift of God. We have no power to generate freedom or forgiveness by our own efforts.

The first part of the book is the story of how God acted to set His people free. He arranged the marvelous encounters of Moses with Pharaoh and also the great miracles that culminated in the passing over of the angel of death through the land while God protected His people from judgment, as celebrated in the Passover feast. Here is a picture of God at work, setting His people free. They did nothing. They were powerless to liberate themselves. They could only receive freedom.

The crossing of the Red Sea is the story of God's miraculous intervention in setting His people free from bondage. Like a believer passing through the waters of baptism, the people of Israel were brought into a new relationship as they passed through the waters of the Red Sea, walking in the very shadow of death, a valley between two walls of water poised to drown anything in their path the moment the restraining hand of God was removed. When the Israelites emerged on the far shore, they were no longer merely a mob of people; now, for the first time, they were a nation under God.

What did they encounter on the other side of the Red Sea? Mount Sinai and the giving of the Law. The point is clear: When we as human beings are delivered from bondage (whether bondage to an oppressive government or bondage to the oppression of sin), we come under the control of another. The giving of the Law is an expression of God's lordship. The message of Exodus is that a new relationship is begun, a new ownership is entered into. In the New Testament, Paul expresses the fundamental message of Exodus in brief form:

You are not your own; you were bought at a price (1 Cor. 6:19–20).

Just as Passover and the crossing of the Red Sea go together in the life of God's people, so too the giving of the Law and the construction of the tabernacle are inseparable. The pattern of the tabernacle was given to Moses at the same time the Law was given on Mount Sinai.

God designed the tabernacle to be at the center of the camp of Israel. And over the whole camp was the great cloud by day and the fiery pillar by night. This cloud/fire gave evidence of God's presence dwelling among His people. But they could experience His presence only through an intricate system of sacrifices and rituals designed to focus their faith and cleanse their lives.

The construction of the tabernacle was accompanied by an elaborate set of symbols and a rigid set of rules for their use. The symbols teach us that God is absolutely holy and changeless. The tabernacle itself is a picture of God's abiding desire to dwell with His people.

Next we come to Leviticus—the book of the Pentateuch where we are likely to bog down. Leviticus is a book of instruction designed to make God's holiness available to people so that people can be available to God. The theme of Leviticus is access to God.

Leviticus begins with the story of the tabernacle, that wonderful edifice where the presence of God dwelt among the people of Israel. If we could have climbed to a mountaintop and looked out over the wilderness area where the twelve tribes of Israel were encamped, it would have been a strange and wonderful sight to see this vast assemblage spread out on the plains in perfect order and symmetry, each of the twelve tribes in its own assigned place. Walking down the mountain, passing into the camp, we would come through thousands of Israelites until we came to the outer court of the tabernacle.

Entering the great open gate of the tabernacle, we would pass the altar of sacrifice and the brazen laver (bronze washing basin), and would come to the door of the tabernacle itself. Moving through the mysterious and marvelous outer veil, we would come into the Holy Place, where were the showbread, the altar of incense, and the great golden candelabra. Beyond stood the inner veil, and behind that—if we dared to enter—we would find the Holy of Holies. The only article in that room was the ark of the covenant.

It was the mysterious, ominous ark that was the dwelling place of God, with the mercy seat above it and the two cherubim with their wings covering it. There too, in a marvelous way, shone the Shekinah light of God's glory. It was a place of profound holiness—and thus, a place of profound terror for anyone whose heart was not 100 percent pure and righteous. The only one who dared to enter the Holy of Holies and approach the ark was the high priest—and then only once a year with the blood of the goat of atonement. It was the high priest's task to make atonement for the sins of all the people. This is a picture of God's dwelling in the midst of His people, demonstrating how they could have fellowship with Him.

Embedded in the book of Leviticus are three major principles: (1) our need for representation before God, (2) God's adequacy to deliver us from our sins, and (3) our faith in God demonstrated by our obedience to Him. Let's examine each principle in turn.

1. *Representation.* The average Israelite had no right to enter the Holy of Holies. Only the priest could go in, and when he did, he represented the whole nation. By that representation, the nation began to learn the wonderful principle of appropriating the value of another's work. After all, this is exactly what we are asked to do today, isn't it? We are asked to believe that Christ—our representative—died for us and that we died with Him. Here we see the preparatory value of the Old Testament. Here, in the middle of the Pentateuch, God is instructing the people of Israel in their need to have a representative so they can be forgiven and be acceptable to God.

2. *God's adequacy.* Leviticus opens with the institution of five offerings, each one speaking of Jesus Christ in His death for us, each one showing how a basic need of human life is fully met already in what Christ would later do in the New Testament. All of these five offerings, taken together, show us that we will never encounter anything that God hasn't already resolved. He is adequate for all our needs, including our need for deliverance from the bondage of sin and death.

3. *Our obedience.* Jesus' representation of us before God and God's adequacy for our every need become expressed in our lives through our

obedience. Obedience is faith in action, faith in motion, faith acting upon the premise that God's promises are true and His commandments are good and just.

Leviticus is the Old Testament book of instruction, and in many ways it parallels the New Testament book of instruction, Hebrews. If you would like to engage in a fascinating, illuminating Scripture study, I suggest you read Leviticus and Hebrews side by side and compare the teachings of these two instructive books.

In Numbers we arrive in the wilderness of failure. The tragic and circular story of Numbers begins at Kadesh-barnea, right at the edge of the Promised Land. When we get to the end of the book, we are back at Kadesh-barnea again. No progress takes place in this book.

Between the two scenes at Kadesh-barnea are forty years of wandering in a desert. God's original intention for the Hebrews was that they spend forty days between the edge of Egypt and the border of the land. But, because of the unbelief of the people, they were sentenced to forty years of trial, despair, murmuring, barrenness, loneliness, heat, blistering sand, and regret. Throughout those forty years, the people of Israel repeatedly thought back to their captivity in Egypt and talked of their bondage as if it were the good old days! If slavery looked good to them, you can only imagine how barren and defeated they felt in the desert.

We look at the story of the Israelites and we see God's amazing, miraculous deliverance of these people from their Egyptian taskmasters in Exodus; we see the wonderful, detailed instruction they received in Leviticus—and then we have to ask ourselves, "Why did they fail so miserably in Numbers?"

Personally, I cannot understand it, yet I continually encounter this phenomenon not only in others but in myself. How is it that people can read the Bible for years, go to a Bible school, attend a Bible church, listen to the best Bible expositors, attend a weekly Bible study, and then behave as if they hadn't learned anything at all? Yet, it happens.

I particularly recall one woman who clearly had a great knowledge of biblical truth. She had studied the Word for years and years and could answer questions that would stump many theologians and Bible scholars. But she lived in complete defeat. Her faith was absolutely gone. Her family was falling apart. Her behavior was inconsistent with all the biblical truth she had absorbed over the years.

So it was with the Israelites in the book of Numbers. This book is a record of failure, and it serves as a warning to you and me. Yet it is also a testament to God's love and patience. Yes, His people grieved Him, and yes, He disciplined them, but not because He hated them, not because He wanted to destroy them. He still wanted to bring this

The book of the wilderness experience

Numbers is a record of failure, yet it is a testament to God's love and patience

race of people into the beautiful land that He had promised them. So He disciplined the unfaithful generation, and even in their wanderings, even in their ingratitude, even in their complaining, He provided for them with fatherly love and care.

Those of us who find ourselves in a wilderness of defeat following a time of disobedience should take heart and pay attention to the lessons of the Pentateuch. God disciplines those He loves, but He also forgives, provides, and restores. Though Numbers is a book of failures, we know that the success of Israel lies ahead. The book ends with the Israelite nation once more at Kadesh-barnea, at the doorstep of Canaan; their wilderness is behind them now, and the Promised Land lies ahead.

The book of the "second law"

Finally we come to Deuteronomy. The name of the book means "second law," from the Greek *deuter* (second) and *nomas* (law). Deuteronomy begins with a farewell message by Moses. It is, first, a retrospective message, reviewing all of God's love and blessings to the people. It is, second, a recounting of the Law that Moses had already delivered to the people in Leviticus. It is, third, a revelation of the rich blessings that God has in store for those who keep the Law. Why is the Law given a second time in this book?

In the New Testament, the apostle Paul tells us that the Law serves a crucial purpose in our lives: it was, he says, "put in charge to lead us to Christ that we might be justified by faith" (Gal. 3:24). It is when the Law says "thou shalt not" (covet, steal, kill, commit adultery) that we realize our inner hunger to do these very things. We discover our rebelliousness toward any authority that says, "No, you can't." We discover the war that takes place within us: we want to do right, but we are powerless to keep from doing wrong. We are unholy, unrighteous in God's sight. We cannot save ourselves; we desperately need a Savior. If the Law did not shine the light of truth on our sin, we would not recognize our sinful condition. The Law is our teacher; a strict, stern, uncompromising teacher, without compassion, without mercy. It drives us into the arms of our loving Savior, Jesus Christ.

The Law was given to Israel the first time to say, "You are sinful." It was given the second time, after the failure in the wilderness, to say, "You are helpless." God wanted the people of Israel to recognize their complete dependency and helplessness.

When the Law was given the first time on Mount Sinai, the people responded confidently, even smugly, "Everything the LORD has said we will do." But when it was given the second time in Kadesh-barnea, the response of the people was more humble, more subdued, even more

The Law was given to Israel the first time to say, "You are sinful"; it was given the second time to say, "You are helpless"

fearful: "We don't have, of ourselves, what it takes to do this." That was what God wanted to hear: humility and a willingness to live in dependence upon a higher strength than their own. They were then ready to be led into the land.

And who was to lead them? It is profoundly significant that the one who would lead the people of Israel into the Land of Promise was a man named Joshua. "Joshua" is the Hebrew form of a name that you know quite well in its Greek form: "Jesus." That's right! Joshua in the Old Testament had the same name as Jesus in the New Testament. The symbolism is too stark and plain to misunderstand.

When we come to the end of Deuteronomy, we find that at last God has prepared His people for the purpose that He had all along. The five books of Moses were written to bring the people to the very edge of the Land of Promise. Moses could not take them in. Moses represents the Law. As Paul says in Romans 8:3, "What the law was powerless to do in that it was weakened by the sinful nature, God did by sending his own Son." It was Joshua who led his people into the physical Land of Promise, and it is Jesus [Joshua] who leads us into the eternal Land of Promise.

This, then, is the Pentateuch in panoramic perspective. These five books give us the pattern of God's program. You will find the pattern of the Pentateuch stamped upon almost every page of the Bible: five steps, five divisions, a fivefold order.

The number five

The book of Psalms contains five divisions, which coincide exactly with this pattern. So do the five offerings given in Leviticus, the five great feasts that Israel celebrates, and the five sections into which both the Old and the New Testaments are divided. Someone has even suggested that perhaps God, wanting us to remember this, gave us five fingers on each hand and five toes on each foot.

The number five is stamped throughout the Scriptures, and each time it is a repetition of this pattern that God will follow. This is the fivefold pattern that God follows in our lives:

God's fivefold pattern

1. an awareness of our need;

2. a picture of God's activity in moving to meet that need, His response in redemption;

3. instruction in how to live, how to worship, how to approach God;

4. the consequences of our failure and unbelief;

5. an arrival at a place where self-effort ends, where the Law again crushes our self-sufficiency, driving us in helplessness and humility back to the Lord.

It is at this fifth stage where God can truly work. It is there that we say, "Lord, on my own I can do nothing." And God says, "Good, that is right where I want you. Now I can use you. Now I can work through you. Now I can accomplish my purpose through you."

This is the Pentateuch. Without it, the great themes of the rest of the Bible are incomprehensible and opaque to our understanding. With it, we have the key to unlock the deep secrets of the Scriptures. Now that we have gained our orbital view of the Pentateuch, let's move in a little closer and adventure through each of these five amazing books, one by one.

The Story of Faith Begins

Henry Ward Beecher was a prominent U.S. minister in the 1800s. He was once visited by a friend, attorney Robert Ingersoll. The friendship between Beecher and Ingersoll was an odd one, since the attorney had a national reputation as an agnostic and a caustic critic of the Bible. But Beecher never gave up his efforts to convert his unbelieving friend.

During one visit, Ingersoll told Beecher all about a "wonderful" new book he had read by Charles Darwin, and how it explained that everything came into being without God.

"Well, where did human beings come from, according to your Mr. Darwin?" asked Beecher.

"From apes," Ingersoll announced smugly.

"Ah," said Beecher, "and the apes came from?"

"Lower animals," Ingersoll replied. "And the lower animals arose from still lower forms, and on and on, until you go all the way down the chain of life to the one-celled creatures that first formed in the seas."

"And where did the seas come from?" asked Beecher. "And the world itself? And the sun, the moon, and the stars?"

Ingersoll spread his hands. "They just happened. We don't need some mythical deity to explain such things."

Later that evening, Beecher took Ingersoll into his library to show him some new books he had just purchased. Ingersoll's attention was immediately captured by a unique globe on Beecher's desk that depicted the stars and constellations of the night sky. Ingersoll examined the globe closely, trying to find the manufacturer's name so he could buy one for himself. "This is a wonderful globe," he said. "Who made it?"

"Why, nobody made it," said Beecher, grinning ever so slightly. "It just happened."

The book of Genesis, as we shall see, is not very much concerned with *how* things happened. But it is very concerned with *who* made them happen. The opening thrust of the book is bold and unmistakable: The first four words of Genesis make it clear that everything that exists had a divine Author:

"In the beginning God . . . ."

Human inadequacy

In the previous chapter, we scanned the book of Genesis (along with the other four books of the Pentateuch) from an "orbital perspective," examining its outlines and contours. In this chapter, we attach a magnification lens to our camera and zoom in closer.

In our familiarity with the Bible, we sometimes fail to consider what an ancient book Genesis is. The Greek philosopher-historian Herodotus, who lived some 300 years before Christ, is called the father of history. He is the earliest historian whose writings have been preserved for us. Yet Moses, who wrote the first five books of our Bible, was in his grave *over a thousand years* before Herodotus ever saw the light of day. That's how ancient Genesis is.

An ancient book

This book—the book of beginnings—takes us back to the dawn of history, yet its insights are as fresh and timely as this morning's news. So much richness, drama, and understanding of human psychology are captured in Genesis that it is easy to forget how astoundingly ancient it is.

With what other writings of its time can you compare Genesis? If you are familiar with the findings of archaeology, then you know that the ancient columns, slabs, and shards of pottery that have been unearthed over the past couple centuries have given us some insight into the true nature of life in ancient civilizations. From these sources, we can find no ancient writings of other early cultures that come close to Genesis in the liveliness of its human drama, the reality of its human characters, or the richness of its language and description. It is a real book about real people who lived in a real place and time.

A timeless message

But Genesis is not only a book of history. It is a book with a profound message that can be summed up in a single statement: *Human beings are inadequate without God.* That is the whole theme of the book, and as such it strikes the keynote of all subsequent revelation of God. It is a personal message, for we see our own stories reflected in its storyline. You and I can never be complete without God, nor can we ever discover or fulfill the true meaning of life without a genuine personal relationship with an indwelling God. Our inadequacy apart from God is revealed to us by Genesis in three realms:

1. The realm of *natural science:* cosmology (the study of the universe, its origin and makeup), geology (the study of the earth's structure and features), and biology (the study of life in all its manifestations). These natural relationships circumscribe our contact with the physical world around us, yet within them, human beings are seen as inadequate without God.

2. The realm of *human relationships:* sociology, anthropology, psychology, and psychiatry. The beginnings of all these are traced in Genesis, and again humankind is set forth as inadequate to function without a relationship with God.

3. The realm of *spiritual relationships:* theology, soteriology, angelology, and philosophy. In all of these vital areas, the book of Genesis reveals that you and I are totally inadequate apart from God. Here is the outline of the book of Genesis:

The World of Nature (Genesis 1–2)
1. The Creation	1:1–2:25
A. Creation of the world	1:1–2:3
B. Creation of the human race	2:4–2:25

Human Relationships (Genesis 3–5)
2. The Fall	3:1–5:32
A. Temptation	3:1–5
B. Sin	3:6–7
C. Judgment	3:8–24
3. After the Fall	4:1–5:32
A. The first murder	4:1–15
B. The line of Cain	4:16–24
C. The line of Seth	4:25–5:32

Spiritual Relationships (Genesis 6–50)
4. The Flood	6:1–9:29
A. The ungodly human race is judged	6:1–6:22
B. The ark and the flood	7:1–8:19
C. After the flood	8:20–10:32
Noah worships God; God makes a covenant with Noah; the sins of Noah and his sons; the family lines of Noah's sons	
5. The Tower of Babel	11:1–11:9
A. Building the tower	11:1–4
B. Judgment against the builders	11:5–9

6. The life of Abraham   11:10–25:18
   Abraham's history; God's covenant with
   Abraham (Abram); circumcision instituted;
   Sodom and Gomorrah; the faith of Abraham;
   the life of Isaac; the death of Sarah; the death
   of Abraham
7. The life of Isaac   21:1–26:35
   A. Isaac is born   21:1–34
   B. Offering of Isaac   22:1–24
   C. The family of Isaac   23–25
   D. The failure of Isaac   26:1–33
   E. The failure of Esau   26:34–35
8. The life of Jacob   27:1–36:43
   A. Jacob usurps Esau's blessing   27:1–28:9
   B. Jacob's dream   28:10–22
   C. Jacob works to obtain his wives   29:1–30:43
   D. Jacob flees   31:1–55
   E. Jacob returns   32:1–33:20
      Jacob wrestles the angel of the Lord and
      makes peace with his brother
   F. Jacob in Canaan   34:1–35:29
      Jacob's daughter, Dinah, is defiled and
      avenged; Jacob's name is changed to Israel.
   G. The history of Esau   36
9. The life of Joseph   37–50
   A. Joseph's brothers mistreat him   37–38
   B. Joseph is tested   39–40
   C. Joseph interprets dreams   41:1–36
   D. Joseph is exalted over Egypt   41:37–57
   E. Joseph tests his brothers   42–45
   F. Joseph blesses his family   46:1–49:32
   G. The death and burial of Jacob   49:33–50:14
   H. The death and burial of Joseph   50:15–26

Now let's examine each of the book's three divisions in turn.

The world of nature

The first two chapters are primarily concerned with the world of nature. Genesis opens with the greatest material fact in life today: We live in a universe. We exist on a specific set of coordinates in space and time. If we know anything at all about modern science, we are aware that our planet is part of a solar system, which is part of a hundred-billion-star galaxy, which is one among billions of galaxies in a universe that is vast beyond our comprehension. Whenever we look up into the night sky and see the glory of the stars, a sense of awe settles over us and we become aware that we live in a universe.

The Bible opens in a majestic recognition of this fact: "In the beginning God created the heavens and the earth" (Gen. 1:1). What a strange conjunction—to put all the vast heavens on one side and our tiny planet Earth on the other. But the book moves right on to tell us that humankind—what modern science pictures as "man the insignificant," a tiny speck of life clinging to a minor planet at the edge of an unthinkably vast universe—is in fact the major object of God's attention and concern!

Verse 2 tells us that the earth began as a planet covered by an uninterrupted ocean, which was itself wrapped in darkness. It was "formless and empty," that is, featureless and without life. There was no land, no mountain range, no coastline to catch the eye; simply a great world of water, without life. With this picture of the beginnings of the world, science fully agrees. But the revelation of God's Word adds a key factor that many scientists do not acknowledge: the fact that "the Spirit of God was hovering over the waters." God was at work in His universe, interacting with it. Something comes out of nothing. God is moving. The Spirit of God brings light out of darkness, shape out of shapelessness, form out of formlessness, life out of lifelessness.

The earth began as a planet covered by uninterrupted ocean wrapped in darkness

The first step that God took, according to the record, was to create light: " 'Let there be light' and there was light." Light is absolutely essential to life of any sort. With the advent of light, we are now ready for the record of the six days of creation. Each day, except the seventh, includes an evening and a morning and each, except the seventh, records a progressive order of creation. Controversy has raged over whether these are literal twenty-four-hour days or geological ages. This controversy completely misses the point of the Genesis account. It should be clear to anyone upon reading the passage that Genesis does not focus upon the question of time. Important as this may seem to us, it is not God's focus. His focus is to show that, in Creation, He was moving toward a goal through a progression of successive steps that logically succeed one another. Creation does not happen all at once with a snap of His fingers. God chose to accomplish the Creation in stages, and these stages are clearly evident throughout this passage.

The first step God took was to create light

Despite all the knowledge we continue to acquire through space probes, radio telescopes, and the Hubble space telescope, the universe is still a great mystery to us. We know very little about it, and in any direction we choose to go, we soon come to a place where we can go no further. A nuclear physicist once described to me the complexity of the nucleus of an atom, what was once thought to be the most simple and basic building block of matter. Discoveries of new "species" in the "particle zoo" had made the once-simple atom a thing of incomprehensible complexity, organization, and activity. Clearly, many forces and kinds of particles that we have not yet discovered exist within the atom.

Here, at the very outer limits of human knowledge, the very frontiers of human ignorance, the Bible begins to answer the perplexing questions of the scientists: Who or what set the universe in motion? What keeps the universe going? Where did we come from? What, if anything, is its purpose? What is the place of humanity in the cosmic scheme? Why are we here?

Genesis supplies the only answers that fit. It reveals to us that the key to human life and to the mysteries of human existence and the material universe are inextricably bound to the spiritual realm. Without an understanding of God, we cannot understand our universe, ourselves, or our relationship to the world around us. Microscopes and telescopes can give us only a partial view; the spiritual scope of the Bible enables us to complete the picture that science only begins to sketch in for us.

Albert Einstein put his finger squarely upon the inadequacies of science when he said, "Science is like reading a mystery novel." You go down to Barnes & Noble and buy what used to be called a "dime novel" (they cost $29.95 today!), and you take it home, wait until everyone else has gone to sleep, prop yourself up on your pillows, and you read it alone in a darkened room with only a reading lamp for company. In the first chapter are two or three murders, and the whole story soon focuses on one theme: whodunit? Clues appear as you read on. In about the third chapter you've decided that the butler did it. Continuing on, the finger of guilt points more and more to the butler. But then you reach the last chapter in which suddenly all the previous evidence is upset and it wasn't the butler after all. It was the little old lady in tennis shoes who lives on the third floor. Einstein says science is like that. It is always struggling from hypothesis to synthesis, from clue to clue, sometimes running up a blind alley or following a false trail, never seeming to get much closer to the ultimate answer.

The purpose of Scripture; the limits of science

But Genesis starts where science leaves off. This is not a criticism of science, because science was never designed to answer "Why does the universe exist?" The scope of science is intentionally, deliberately limited to certain avenues of inquiry. Genesis answers the "why" question—and, more importantly, the "who" question. Genesis gives answers addressed to faith, not an irrational "leap of faith" but a reasoned faith. The more science learns about the fundamental nature of the universe, the more science seems to agree with the Bible.

Thus the Bible consistently remains true to the most complex discoveries of science while at the same time retaining a simplicity of statement that the most uneducated can understand, even though it is not the intention of the Bible to be a textbook on science. God has deliberately made the physical universe to reveal and manifest an inner spiritual reality. Since the world is made for man, it constantly reflects God's truth to him. This is why Jesus found the world of nature such an apt instrument with which to teach men spiritual realities, as His parables reveal.

Genesis 1:26 shows us that God holds a divine consultation about man, saying, "Let us make man in our image, in our likeness." This divine conversation clearly is the first hint given to us that God consists of more than one person. The key phrase about man in this verse is that he was created in the "image" and "likeness" of God. That image is found not in man's body or his soul, but in his spirit. As Jesus told the woman at the well in Samaria, "God is spirit, and his worshipers must worship in spirit and in truth" (John 4:24).

What is godlike about our spirit? If our spirit is made in the image of God, then it can do things that God can do but no animal can. Three things are suggested throughout Genesis 1 that God alone does: first, God creates; second, God communicates; and third, God evaluates, pronouncing some things good and others not good. It is here that the image of God in man appears. Man can create. Man communicates as no animal can possibly do, sharing ideas that affect others. And man is the only creature who has a moral sense, recognizing some things as good and others as bad, feeling the impact of conscience upon his own actions. Thus, man shares the image of God.

God creates, communicates, evaluates

Chapter 2 finds the man walking in the garden in communion with God, functioning as a spirit living within a physical body and manifesting the personality characteristics of the soul. At this point, God gives him a research project, to investigate the animal world in search of a possible counterpart to himself. God knew that the man would not find what he was looking for, but in the process, the man discovered at least three marvelous truths.

First, he learned that woman was not to be a mere beast of burden as the animals are, because that would not fulfill his need for a helper and companion. Second, he realized that the woman was not to be merely a biological laboratory for producing children. This is what the animals use sex for, but that was not sufficient for Adam's needs. Sex in humankind, therefore, is different from that among the animals. Third, Adam learned that the woman was not a thing outside himself, to be used at the whim of the man and then disposed of. She was made to be his helper, fit for him, corresponding to him, complementing and completing him.

Three truths the man learned about the woman

So, in a remarkable passage, we are told that Adam fell into a deep sleep and God took a rib and from it made a woman and brought her to him. This period of Adam's unconsciousness suggests what modern

Human relationships

Sin is "the ultimate addiction"

psychology confirms, that the relationship of marriage is far deeper than mere surface affection. It touches not only the conscious life, but the subconscious and the unconscious as well.

In chapters 3 through 5, Genesis next examines the realm of human relationships. The human race enters the picture. These chapters trace the story of humanity from Adam through Noah and reveal that the basic unit of society is the family. That pattern has remained absolutely unchanged for ten to twenty thousand years of human history. The family is still the basis of human society. When people ignore that fact and begin to destroy family life, the foundations of a society disintegrate. Why? Because a nation is an extension of the family. The nations of the world are simply large complex family groups!

When a president dies, when an earthquake devastates a city, when hundreds die in a collapsed building, when a space shuttle explodes, what happens? An entire nation mourns! Why? Because, as Americans, we have a common identity, a common bond, a common connection. The more we lose sight of our connectedness as a family-society, the more fragmented and agitated our nation becomes.

These chapters also reveal the failure of human beings in their most basic relationships. People tried to be human without God, and the result was the introduction of the sin principle. Sin is the monkey wrench that has been thrown into the human machinery. It is the reason why we behave in ways that are destructive to ourselves and others— even when we know better and want better for ourselves and others. Keith Miller has called sin "the ultimate addiction," because no matter how much we may want to be free of it, the destructive habit of sin is impossible for us to break in our own power.

As you read these chapters in Genesis, you'll see how Adam rejected God's plan and lost Paradise. You'll see how Cain rejected God and became a murderer; he then went out and founded a civilization that ended in apostasy and the flood. You'll see how, after Noah and his family were spared in the flood, this wise and godly man fell into the snare of sin and alcohol abuse, bringing shame on his family. Later in Genesis, you'll notice how men like Jacob and Lot bring enormous hurt upon themselves and their families. We hear a lot these days about "dysfunctional families," but it is clear, as we read the book of Genesis, that God already wrote the book on that subject.

Genesis 3 explains over one hundred centuries of human heartache, misery, torture, and bloodshed. Remove this chapter from the Bible, and the entire book becomes incomprehensible. But the most striking thing about it is that we find ourselves here. The temptation and the fall are reproduced in our lives many times a day. We all have heard the voice of the tempter and felt the attraction of sin—and we all know the pangs of guilt that follow.

Many biblical scholars feel that the tempter in the garden was not a snake but a "shining one," which is what the Hebrew word for snake means. Snakes were undoubtedly created to represent the punishment that fell upon this being when he brought about the fall of man by his cunning and deceit. It is clearly the devil, in his character as an angel of light, who confronts the woman in the Garden of Eden. His tactic with her is to arouse desire. First he implanted in her heart a distrust of God's love, "Did God really say, 'You must not eat from any tree in the garden'?" (Gen. 3:1). Next, he dares to deny openly the results that God had stated will occur, "You will not surely die" (3:4), he says. Then he clinches his attack with a distorted truth, "God knows that when you eat of it your eyes will be opened, and you will be like God, knowing good and evil." All the devil wishes to do is to leave Eve standing before the fruit that is hanging there in all its luscious fascination, tantalizing her, offering her an experience that she never dreamed would be possible.

Enter temptation—and sin

Now the mind comes into action. Without realizing it, Eve has already experienced an arousing of her emotions so that she longs for the tantalizing fruit before her. Thus, when her mind acts, it can no longer do so rationally. Already the will has secretly determined to act on the facts as the emotions present them and thus the mind can only rationalize. It must twist the facts so that they accord with desire, and the result was that Eve took the fruit and ate.

But there was still hope for the race. Adam had not yet fallen, only Eve. A battle has been lost, but not the war. In the innocent but ominous words, "She also gave some to her husband, who was with her, and he ate it" (3:6), we face the beginning of the darkness of a fallen humanity—what the Bible calls "death" immediately follows.

Death immediately follows

This is followed by banishment from the garden, not, as we so often imagine, to keep them from coming back to the tree of life but, as the text specifically states, "to guard the way to the tree of life" (3:24). There is a way to the tree of life, but it is no longer a physical way. In the book of Revelation, we are told that the tree of life is for the healing of the nations (see Rev. 22:2). It is surely to this that Jesus refers when He says, "I am the way." Spiritually and psychologically (in the realm of emotions and mind) we are to live in the presence of God because a way has been opened back to the tree of life.

Jesus is the way back to the Tree of Life

From the tragic sin of Adam proceeds the criminal sin of Adam's son Cain, who kills his brother Abel out of bitterness and jealousy when Abel's blood offering is accepted over Cain's grain offering to God. From Cain, we trace the beginnings of civilization and especially the part that urban life plays in shaping human society. To Cain is born Enoch, who

Cain kills Abel

builds his city on ground that is yet red with the blood of Abel. The city that Enoch builds contains all the ingredients of modern life: travel, music and the arts, the use of metals, organized political life, and the domestication of animals. It is impressive but built on shaky ground. Violence, murder, and immorality abound as the state rises to replace the family as the focus of human interest. The trend toward urban over rural life is evident and increasing toleration of sexual excess appears.

But in the midst of this deterioration, God has another plan ready. After Abel is slain and Cain is banished by God, Adam and Eve have another son, whose name—Seth—means "appointed." Noah will eventually come out of Seth's line.

Spiritual relationships

The rest of Genesis explores the realm of spiritual relationships. It is the largest part of this book because it is the most important to people. It is the story of the human spirit in relationship with God, told through the lives of five men. If you remember the lives of these five men and what they mean, you will have most of Genesis in the palm of your hand. They are Noah, Abraham, Isaac, Jacob, and Joseph. Genesis reveals in the stories of these men what human beings are always seeking.

Most of us *think* we spend our lives seeking *things*. The popular T-shirt slogan puts it this way: "He who dies with the most toys, wins." But story after story of the final moments of people with the most toys, the rich and famous of this world, show that those who die with nothing to show for their lives but a huge collection of things and toys—castles, cars, fame, wealth, empires—tend to die miserably, clutching at a life that they can no longer grasp, regretting that they have invested their lives in things that don't last. Materialism is bound to disappoint us in the end.

All the restlessness
of our age can be
understood as an
attempt to acquire
the right things in
the wrong way

All the restlessness of our age can be understood as an attempt to acquire the right things in the wrong way. What are the right things? I believe there are essentially three things people want: *righteousness, peace,* and *joy.* But because our understanding is warped by sin, our search for these things gets skewed.

The only
righteousness that
is truly right is the
righteousness of God

Deep inside, we want righteousness, a sense of being right and justified. But instead of seeking the righteousness of God and being justified by faith in the righteous sacrifice of Jesus Christ, we try to justify ourselves! When anyone accuses you of something wrong, what do you do? You start justifying yourself! You make excuses for yourself! That's human nature. Even when we know we are wrong, we want to somehow make it right. But the only righteousness that is truly right is the righteousness of God. That is why we are inadequate apart from Him, and that is why we are complete with Him. His righteousness covers us and justifies us. Only the righteousness of God can truly satisfy our hunger and searching for righteousness.

The second thing we seek is peace. John F. Kennedy once said, "The absence of war is not the same thing as peace." How true! Even when our society has enjoyed so-called peacetime, we have known a sense of national tension, unease, and dissatisfaction. As a people, we are not at peace with each other nor with ourselves. Why? Because we seek it in the wrong places, in the wrong ways. We seek money and a higher standard of living as the key to peace of mind; yet the more we have, the more we want. We never come to a place where we truly know peace. But God gives us, even in uncertain times, a very different and transcendent peace, the peace that passes understanding.

The third thing we all seek is joy. We want a sense of gladness, of happiness, of adventure in life. Tragically, most of us seek our joy-substitute in the form of kicks, highs, and sinful pleasures. The purpose of the last part of Genesis is to introduce us to God, the one of whom the psalmist wrote, "You will fill me with joy in your presence, with eternal pleasures at your right hand" (Ps. 16:11).

Where do we find the true satisfaction of all three of these unseen, almost unconscious, goals of life—righteousness, peace, and joy? Romans 14:17 tells us: "The kingdom of God is not a matter of eating and drinking, but of righteousness, peace and joy in the Holy Spirit." Only God offers these things to human beings, and that is the story of this book.

Our adequacy with God

If Genesis reveals the inadequacies of people without God, it also demonstrates the adequacy and completeness of people with God. That is the great positive message of Genesis.

In the garden before Adam fell, you see Adam as the lord of creation. God has given him dominion. If only we could have known Adam back in the days before the Fall! What a rich personality he must have been. What tremendous power and knowledge he must have had. He knew the world's mysteries and controlled its activities. Humanity can no longer do that. We have the urge to do so, but we cannot.

When we look at the New Testament and read of the miracles of the Lord Jesus' walking on the water, changing the water into wine, stilling the storm with a word, we say to ourselves, "That is God at work." But the Old Testament says, "No, that isn't God; that is unfallen humanity. That is what human beings were intended to be: rulers of the world."

You find it reflected in Psalm 8:4 and 6. Gazing into the heavens, David says, "What is man that you are mindful of him, the son of man that you care for him?" And then he answers his question, "You made him ruler over the works of your hands; you put everything under his

Jesus: what God intended humanity to be

feet." Since the fall, the only human being in whom we have seen these words fulfilled is Jesus. That is why the writer of Hebrews says, "Yet at present we do not see everything subject to him. But we see Jesus . . ." (Heb. 2:8–9).

Genesis reveals that when human beings live with God, they are able to live at peace and in harmony with other human beings. One of the most beautiful stories in this book is that of Abraham's dwelling under the oaks of Mamre with the Canaanites all around him, a race that for many years had been his enemy. But God so worked in the life of Abraham that even his enemies were made to be at peace with him. The story of Abraham closes with the Canaanite tribes coming to him and saying, "You are a mighty prince among us" (Gen. 23:6). So is fulfilled what God says elsewhere, that when a person's ways please the Lord, He makes even that person's enemies to be at peace with him. This is the key. This is the secret of life in all our relationships.

Genesis declares that only human beings in fellowship with God can know supreme happiness

Genesis declares that only human beings in fellowship with God can know supreme happiness—the righteousness, peace, and joy that people always hunger for. Realization comes only as people discover that the indwelling God is the answer to all their needs.

This is revealed in five ways, through the lives of five men:

Noah

Noah is a man who went through symbolic death. That is the meaning of the flood. Noah was surrounded by the flood, he rode upon it, he was preserved through it, he was saved from it. The waters of judgment, the waters of death could not overwhelm him. He was carried into a new world and a new life by His faith in a redeeming God.

Many books have been written depicting what the world might be like after an atomic holocaust. Yet this is virtually the same scenario produced in the days of the flood. Human civilization was destroyed, and Noah and his family were forced to begin afresh on a new earth. Here is a picture of regeneration, of new life. The beginning of life as a Christian is a transition from death into life in Christ, just as Noah passed from death to life in the flood.

Note the numbers associated with the flood. The flood began when the fountains of the great deep burst forth and the windows of the heavens opened up, and the rain continued for 40 days and nights, then ceased. At the end of 150 days the waters began to abate and the ark came to rest on the mountains of Ararat *on the seventeenth day of the seventh month.*

The seventeenth day of the seventh month is exactly the same day of the year when, centuries later, Jesus rose from the dead. After the exodus from Egypt, God changed the beginning of the year from the seventh month (in the fall) to the first month (in the spring) when the Passover was eaten. Jesus rose on the seventeenth day of the first month, which would be the same as the seventeenth day of the seventh month in the old reckoning in this passage in Genesis. Thus, clearly, the emergence of Noah from the ark is intended to be a picture of the new beginning of life that every Christian experiences when he or she enters into the resurrection life of Jesus Christ by the new birth!

Abraham teaches us that we are justified by faith. Here was a man who was far from perfect, yet who lived by faith. Everything Abraham achieved was a result of God's grace, not Abraham's merit or effort. As God led him along and Abraham stepped out in faithful dependence upon the promises of God, he found that God's promises were true. Eight times Abraham's faith was dramatically tried, and eight times he passed the test. If you are ever in a trial of faith, read the life of Abraham. You will find in his life circumstances that are similar to the ones you are going through. Abraham teaches us what it means to be justified, to be the friend of God by faith.

One of the greatest demonstrations of Abraham's faith is his reliance upon God's promise of a coming son, despite Abraham's advanced age. It is at that point in Abraham's walk of faith where we read for the first time in Scripture that marvelous statement, "Abram believed the LORD, and he credited it to him as righteousness" (see Gen. 15:6). It is because of his faith that Abraham was called "God's friend" (James 2:23).

Isaac is a beautiful picture of sonship, what it means to be a child of God. If ever a boy was spoiled and pampered by his father, it was Isaac. He is the darling of his father's heart. I doubt that any message could be more welcome today than the one that is so beautifully exemplified in Isaac: that God loves us, values us, and calls us the darlings of His heart. "Dear friends, now we are children of God," says 1 John 3:2, "what we will be has not yet been made known. But we know that when he appears, we shall be like him." We shall be like Christ.

Jacob was the rascal of Genesis. He was the schemer, the man who thought he could live by his own wits and his own efforts. He went out trying to deceive everybody and ended up being deceived. He troubled his own household by playing favorites, indulging one of his sons over the rest, creating bitterness and resentment among his sons.

Yet, despite all his faults, Jacob is a beautiful picture of sanctification, that marvelous work of God in which we in our folly, attempting to live life in the energy of the flesh, are led into the very situations that drive us to God. Sometimes we give God no choice but to corner us and contend with us until we discover His speaking to us, and we surrender. With our surrender, God is able to take over, and we are able to truly live.

Abraham

Isaac

Jacob

That is what Jacob did at the brook of Peniel. There, knowing Esau was waiting with a band of armed men ready to take his life, Jacob waited alone. There, an angel in the form of a man met him and began to wrestle with him through the long night. As the day broke the angel sought to disengage himself, but Jacob clung with stubborn persistence. The angel touched Jacob's thigh and threw it out of joint, but still Jacob clung in helplessness to the divine messenger, refusing to let go until he was blessed of God. Then the divine being changed the name of Jacob to Israel, which means "he who prevails with God." As the sun rose, Jacob limped off to meet Esau with a totally different attitude in his heart. He no longer feared people but was confident that God would fight his battles for him. Jacob learned the great principle of sanctification: that God was his strength and his refuge and is fully capable of working out all the problems with which he may be confronted.

Jacob's life can be seen in three distinct stages: (1) His early years at home when he was basically a deceiver of others, epitomized by his theft of Esau's birthright. (2) The middle period of his life, when Jacob learns what it is like to be deceived, as illustrated in the story where Jacob labors for seven years to win Rachel as his wife only to be tricked into marrying Rachel's sister Leah first. (3) Finally, Jacob learns to live as a man devoted to the word and will of God, when he wrestles with—and is blessed by—the angel of God.

Joseph

Joseph is a picture of glorification. Joseph is the young man who was loved by his father, Jacob, and mistreated by his brothers. They pounce on him and sell him into slavery, yet even in the chains of a slave, Joseph is exalted by God. His life is a roller coaster of highs and lows: he is given a position of prestige by Potiphar, then cast down into prison by the lies of Potiphar's wife, then is again exalted, taken out of prison, and made an advisor to the pharaoh of Egypt himself! Ultimately, he becomes the second highest leader in the land.

Here, in the life of Joseph, is a symbolic picture of the hope of all believers. What do we look forward to after death? Deliverance from the darkness and pain of this earthly existence, and from the prison house in which we have lived our years—deliverance and exaltation to the very throne and presence of God Himself!

And how did Joseph appropriate God's deliverance and exaltation in his own life? Faith is the only method by which human beings can reach God and appropriate His delivering power. "Without faith it is impossible to please God," says Hebrews 11:6. As you act in faith, it all becomes true. Note that in Joseph's life and in ours, faith does not mean giving intellectual credence to God's promises but stepping out and acting on His promises; when we act in faith, it all becomes true in our experience.

Joseph's character is presented to us with almost unblemished consistency. He is often considered symbolic of Christ, since he was beloved of his father but rejected by his brethren, sold into slavery for twenty pieces of silver, and seemingly died (or so his father thought) and was "brought to life" again as a triumphant king instead of a suffering servant. Like our Lord, he forgave his brothers for their treatment of him and was used to save them from death and preserve the family line.

The thread that runs throughout all fifty chapters of Genesis is that there is a secret to living and that we will never experience completeness of life until we have learned and experienced this secret. The secret is simple—yet so many people in this world tragically miss it. The secret is friendship with God. Without God you cannot understand the world around you. You can't understand yourself or your neighbor or God Himself. You will never have any answers without God. But with Him, everything comes into focus, everything makes sense.

The secret of life

The secret to living is friendship with God

The secret of life is a personal, daily relationship with the living God who was in the beginning, who made the heavens and the earth, who created the human race in His own image, and who wants to have fellowship and a living relationship with the people He has so lovingly created.

This is the first note sounded in the very first chapters of Genesis, and you will see that when we have concluded our adventure through the Bible, it is also the concluding note sounded in the book of Revelation. From beginning to end, the Bible is a love letter to the human race. And we have examined only the first chapter of that love letter.

The Bible is a love letter to the human race

The Design for Deliverance

When God wants to do something *big,* He starts with a baby. That's God's pattern, His modus operandi. He uses the weak things, the simple things, the small things, to confound the great and the wise.

What do we consider to be great historical events? Wars, battles, revolutions, upheavals. We would never think to include the birth of a baby as we consider great historical movements and social changes. We think babies are small and weak and essentially unimportant. God knows better. He knows that it is babies who become the great men and great women who shake the foundations of the world.

In 1809, the whole world anxiously focused on the military exploits of Napoleon Bonaparte. He was the "Stormin' Norman" Schwarzkopf of his day—with a dash of Hitler-like megalomania thrown in! He wanted to conquer the world, and, thanks to his extraordinary military genius, he was well on his way to doing so! The whole world trembled before his towering ambitions and anxiously awaited news reports from the warfront.

Yet, in that same year, 1809, babies were being born all around the world. The world took little note of those babies during the time that Napoleon was making obsolete all the maps of Europe. Yet the seeds of revolutionary change were being planted in that year. The great English poet Alfred, Lord Tennyson was born that year. So was Charles Darwin, whose theory of evolution by natural selection would send a shudder

God uses the small things to confound the great and the wise through the scientific community. Gladstone, who would one day become prime minister of England, was born. And, in a log cabin in Kentucky, so was Abraham Lincoln.

When God wants to change history, He doesn't start with a battle. He starts with a baby. That is God's pattern throughout history, and that is why the book of Exodus opens with the birth of a baby.

God's finger is in evidence at the very beginning of this book, for this is the story of a baby born under the sentence of death, but one whose life was marvelously preserved by God's intervening hand. With a delicate twist of irony that is wonderful to observe, the Holy Spirit of God moves in a beautiful way: Despite the order of Pharaoh to kill all Hebrew male babies in Egypt, Moses is not only saved but is brought right into Pharaoh's household to be raised! Then, piling irony upon irony, God moves Pharaoh to unwittingly hire the baby Moses' own mother to take care of him!

This is the story of a baby born under sentence of death

Such a design is surely one of those delightful expressions of God's humor. If you haven't yet discovered that God has a sense of humor, a great discovery is in store for you. Humorous glimpses appear throughout the Old and New Testaments. I relish biblical accounts of the clever ways in which God adroitly turns the tables and brings a delightful twist out of an evil situation.

Moses grew up in the court of Pharaoh, with access to all the learning opportunities of the Egyptians. He was trained in the best university of the ancient world's greatest empire. He was the foster son of the king himself and every privilege and advantage was his. But when he came of age, God spoke to him and placed upon him the mantle of Israel's deliverer. So Moses went out trying to do God's work in his own strength, and he ended up murdering a man and having to flee into the wilderness.

As you trace the story, you find that Moses left Egypt and herded sheep for forty years in the wilderness. Here, God found him and dealt with him in the remarkable confrontation of the burning bush. God called Moses back to his original task, for which Moses felt completely unprepared. Moses had to learn the same lesson that you and I must learn: To do anything in God's name, we need nothing more than God Himself.

The structure of Exodus

First, let's place Exodus within its context in the Pentateuch. It immediately follows Genesis, the book that reveals the need of the human race. Genesis is about humanity—its creation, its sin, and its groping for God as personified in the lives of Abraham, Isaac, Jacob, and Joseph. Genesis ends with the words "a coffin in Egypt," a phrase that underscores the fact that all you can say about the human race at the end of it all is that we live in the realm of death.

If Genesis is all about humanity, Exodus is all about God. Exodus is God's answer to human need. This book begins with God's activity, and throughout the rest of the book you see God mightily at work. The book is the picture of God's action to redeem us fallen human beings from our need, our sin, our misery, our death. It is a beautiful picture and contains instructive lessons to us of what redemption is, what God has done, what He continues to do, and what He intends to do with our lives.

But Exodus is an incomplete book. The redemption that is begun in Exodus is not completed in this book. To gain the full perspective on God's redemptive story, which is begun in Exodus, you must keep reading through Leviticus, through Numbers, through Deuteronomy, and on into the book of Joshua, which tells the story of Israel's triumphant possession of the Promised Land.

You can understand the story of Exodus by remembering four great events that sum up its great themes:

Four great themes of Exodus

1. The Passover (Exodus 12–13)
2. The crossing of the Red Sea (Exodus 14)
3. The giving of the law (Exodus 19–31)
4. The construction of the tabernacle (Exodus 35–40)

The Passover and Red Sea are but two aspects of one great truth: the deliverance of God's people from the bondage and death. They symbolize the act of a Christian's conversion and regeneration; that is, the deliverance of an individual from the bondage of sin and spiritual death. If you want to know what God did in your life when you became a Christian, study the Passover and the crossing of the Red Sea.

The giving of the Law and the construction of the tabernacle are similarly inseparable. The pattern of the tabernacle was given to Moses when he was on the mountain with God, at the same time that the Law was given. The Law and the tabernacle are inextricably linked, as we shall soon discover.

Here is a structural outline of the book:

The Redemption out of Egypt (Exodus 1–18)

1. Israel multiplies; Moses is born	1–2:25	
2. Moses is called by God	3–4	
3. The redemption of Israel from Egypt	5:1–15:21	
A. Moses opposes Pharaoh	5:1–7:13	
B. The ten plagues upon Egypt	7:14–11:10	
C. The Passover	12:1–13:16	
D. Moses the redeemer leads Israel across the Red Sea	13:17–15:21	
4. Israel is preserved in the desert	15:22–18:27	

The Law and the Tabernacle (Exodus 19–40)

Having briefly outlined the structure of Exodus, let's examine each of the four great thematic strands that form the strong cord of the book.

First theme: The Passover

In Exodus 3 and 4, God comes to Moses, the shepherd and fugitive from justice (he has escaped to the wilderness after murdering an Egyptian), and He calls Moses to fill the role of redeemer of a nation. Speaking to Moses from a bush that burns but is not consumed, God challenges him and instructs him to return to Egypt. At first Moses is reluctant to go. "O Lord," he says, "I have never been eloquent, neither in the past nor since you have spoken to your servant. I am slow of speech and tongue" (Ex. 4:10). God didn't rebuke Moses for his reluctance or his human sense of inadequacy. Instead, He says to Moses, "Who gave man his mouth? Who makes him deaf or mute? . . . Is it not I, the LORD? Now go; I will help you speak and will teach you what to say." Go down to Egypt and I will be your tongue and I will speak through you.

The burning bush

But then Moses says, "O Lord, please send someone else to do it." And *that's* when, as Exodus 4:14 tells us, "The LORD's anger burned against Moses."

At first, Moses was expressing his humble sense of inadequacy. But when God promised to be with him and Moses *still* protested his inadequacy, Moses was really saying, "God, I can't do it—and I don't believe You can do it, either." When Moses challenged God's adequacy to be his strength, God's anger was kindled against him. That is a good point to remember whenever God challenges us to take on a task in His name.

Moses returned to Egypt and immediately came into conflict with Pharaoh. Nothing is more dramatic in all the Old Testament than this tremendous test of wills between Pharaoh and Moses, the representative of Satan and the representative of God. Pharaoh forced God to unleash His mighty power against Egypt. Again and again in this account we read, "Pharaoh hardened his heart."

Ten plagues

There were ten plagues in all: blood, frogs, lice, flies, disease on the animals, boils on people and animals, hail, locusts, darkness, and finally, death of the firstborn sons. It is interesting to note that each of the first nine plagues was directed at one of the gods of Egypt; the target of the tenth was Pharaoh himself, striking Pharaoh's son and all the firstborn sons of Egypt in an attempt to melt Pharaoh's heart of stone. By these plagues, God acted in judgment against the false gods of Egypt and Egypt's evil, hard-hearted king.

Finally, with the tenth plague, Pharaoh's heart was overcome. God's power broke his will. In his grief, Pharaoh relented and allowed Israel to go. During this tenth plague both God's power and love are dramatically revealed—power to punish those who willfully, stubbornly choose to oppose Him and loving provision and protection for those who place their trust in Him. It is during the tenth plague that the beautiful event called Passover, which the Jews still celebrate, takes place.

Through His servant Moses, God commanded the people of Israel to sprinkle blood on the doorposts of their houses and to share a special meal of lamb with unleavened bread—the Passover supper. This event is a beautiful Old Testament foreshadowing of a New Testament truth. Before coming in faith to Jesus Christ, we are simply individuals struggling—without much success—to make our way through life. But after receiving the gift of eternal life through the shedding of His blood upon the "doorposts" of the cross, by partaking of the innocent Lamb and the unleavened bread of His broken and pierced body, we become a part of Him and of every other believer who so partakes.

The Passover is a beautiful picture of the cross of Christ. The angel of death passed over the land, darkening Egypt with the death of the firstborn who were slain. But the Israelites—those who, by a simple act of faith, took the blood of a lamb and sprinkled it on the doorposts and lintels of their houses—were perfectly safe. Then and now, salvation is accomplished by the simple act of faith, a trusting response to God's loving provision of a Savior who has settled our guilt before God. Then and now, the angel of death passes over those who are covered by the blood of the Lamb.

The Passover is a beautiful picture of the cross of Christ

But the Passover is not the whole story. The Passover is never of value until it is linked with the Red Sea experience. The Red Sea experience immediately followed the Passover.

As soon as Pharaoh relented and released the people of Israel, they left the safety of their homes, went out into the wilderness, and walked right to the shore of the sea. They were still in Egypt when they arrived at the sea, and their situation seemed hopeless. Looking behind them, they saw that Pharaoh had once again hardened his heart and was now coming after them with an army. The people began to cry out to Moses and ask him why he had brought them here to die at the water's edge.

Moses' answer is a statement of unswerving faith in God: "Stand firm and you will see the deliverance the LORD will bring you today" (Ex. 14:13). The Israelites, however, assessed their situation with the

Second theme: The Red Sea crossing

gloomy, myopic eyes of sight rather than the far-seeing eyes of faith. But Moses was serene. The Lord had told him to stretch out his rod over the sea, and when he did, the waters rolled back and the people passed through safely between two walls of suspended water. As soon as they set foot on the other side, the waters rolled back into place and their Egyptian pursuers were caught in the deluge and drowned.

The Red Sea experience is not only a historical event; it is also a powerful symbol for your life and mine. It typifies our break with the world, once we have placed our trust in Jesus Christ. Egypt is behind us; the journey to the Promised Land is before us. True, Israel found itself in a wilderness beyond the Red Sea, but they were safely out of Egypt and out of bondage. They had passed through the river of death.

This same river of death rolls between us and the world once we claim Jesus Christ as our Lord. When we pass through a Red Sea experience, when we die to the old life and pass through Christian baptism, taking a stand for Jesus Christ, we divorce ourselves from the bondage and misery of the old life and our old ways. As the apostle Paul tells us, "If anyone is in Christ, he is a new creation; the old has gone, the new has come!" (2 Cor. 5:17).

It is important to note that before the Red Sea experience, the people of Israel were not a nation. They became a nation when they passed through the Red Sea together. That is the meaning of those words from 1 Corinthians 10:2, "They were all baptized into Moses in the cloud and in the sea." By this miraculous baptism, they were transformed from a disorganized mob into a mighty nation, a unit, a body, a fellowship, a society. This powerfully symbolizes the transformation that takes place when we, through faith in Christ, become part of the body of Christ, the church. Through water baptism, we signify that we have died with Christ and that, through Him, we have joined together in a living unit with all other Christians.

Notice the link between the Passover and the crossing of the Red Sea. Both involve faith, but the Red Sea crossing takes faith one step further. The Israelites were essentially passive in their Passover deliverance: they painted the doorposts with blood, they ate their meal, and they waited for God to act. But the crossing of the Red Sea was active, it required obedience, it required a deliberate step of faith.

Today, as in the days of Exodus, true faith requires action and obedience. We cannot remain Passover-passive. We must move ahead as God commands, boldly stepping out, trusting Him to part the waters and lead the way. As we move forward cutting the ties with the bondage of this world, allowing the river of God's judgment to flow between us and the ways of the world, our faith takes on substance and power. That is the moment when God truly dwells in us and moves through us. God cannot complete His work in us and bring us to maturity until we have passed through the Red Sea.

Notice, in Exodus 15, that the first thing they did as they reached the other shore was to break into song. They had not sung in Egypt— that place of bondage, misery, and of unremitting toil. But when they emerged from their "dry baptism" through the Red Sea, they couldn't keep from singing! Real deliverance brings a song.

Preserved in the desert

Immediately after crossing the Red Sea, the Israelites came to the waters of Marah, the place of bitterness. In order to cure these waters, Moses cut down a tree that the Lord had shown him, and he threw it into the water. Thereupon, the water became sweet (Ex. 15:25). The tree symbolizes the cross, the great tree upon which the Lord Jesus was crucified: God's answer to the bitterness of sin and to the bitterness and unhappiness of our past hurts and frustrations.

Manna

Next, the Israelites moved on into the desert. There, manna, the food from heaven, fell to feed and sustain the people. They were instructed to gather this bread from heaven on a daily basis, six days a week (on the sixth day, they are to gather an extra day's supply to carry them through the Sabbath). The people had difficulty obeying God's clear instructions, much as people still do today. We often find it difficult to trust God for His provision and deliverance in the midst of "impossible" situations.

Water from a rock

The people's faith was again tried when they come to a barren, waterless desert. Here again, God patiently met their murmuring and unbelief by providing water from a rock.

The battle against the flesh

In Exodus 17, we come to a battle, symbolic of the Christian's battle with the flesh. The battle against the sin of the flesh is always startling to new Christians. They have experienced the emotional and spiritual high of discovering new life in Christ, and suddenly sin rears its ugly head and they wonder, "What happened?" That's the situation the Israelites faced: They had gone through the glory of the Passover, the Red Sea crossing, the demonstration of God's fatherly love by the provision of the manna. But a shocking realization soon confronted them: Life also required believers to fight battles. Amalek fought with Israel, and God responded by declaring unending war with Amalek (Ex. 17:10).

The apostle Paul stated the nature of the battle that takes place in every Christian: "The sinful nature desires what is contrary to the Spirit, and the Spirit what is contrary to the sinful nature. They are in conflict with each other" (Gal. 5:17). You can never make peace with Amalek, with the sinful desires of the flesh.

In chapter 19, we arrive at Sinai, the place of God's tabernacle and the giving of the Law. These are the third and fourth major themes of Exodus. We will examine these themes individually, and we will see how they are linked together in the flow of this book.

Third theme: The giving of the Law

What is the Law? It is simply a picture of God's holiness, His unrelenting character, and His unchangeability. This is why the giving of the Law is a time of terror, because nothing is more frightening to human beings than the act of squarely facing God's true nature.

The unchangeable nature of God gives wonderful comfort to us, of course, when we think of His love, care, and grace. But it fills us with awe and fear when we think of His holiness, anger, and justice. The Law means that God cannot be talked out of His righteous judgments. God can never be bought off. We cannot get Him to compromise His standards. The Law is the absolute, irrevocable standard of God's character.

Some people think that there are two Gods: an unrelenting Old Testament God and a warm-fuzzy, indulgent New Testament God who winks at our sin. Nothing could be further from the truth! Jesus, in Matthew 5:48, said, "Be perfect, therefore, as your heavenly Father is perfect." Jesus knows that we cannot achieve perfection, we will fail, we will sin; but He also wants us to know that God's standard has not changed. The Law is the Law, and it remains in force in both Testaments, Old and New.

How does God expect us to be perfect? How does He expect us to keep every point of His law without error? Answer: He doesn't. But He has made it possible for our sins to be covered by His perfection. His answer to our imperfection is the fourth theme of Exodus: the tabernacle.

The Law is a picture of God's holiness, His unrelenting character, and His unchangeability

Fourth theme: The tabernacle

On Mount Sinai, the very same mountain on which God gave Moses the Law as a revelation of His character, He also gave the tabernacle, His provision for His dwelling place with the human race and for the covering of human sin.

The camp of Israel was divided up in an orderly fashion, with some of the tribes on the east, some on the north, some on the west, some on the south. Right in the center was the tabernacle. Over the whole camp was the great cloud by day and the fiery pillar by night. This cloud/fire gave evidence of God's presence dwelling among His people. This was made possible only by an intricate system of sacrifices and rituals designed to focus the faith and cleanse the lives of His people, so that they could be brought into His presence.

If you could have gone into the camp of Israel, you would have passed through all the tribes on either side, and at the center of the

The place of the tabernacle: the center of the camp

camp, you would have found the tribe of Levi—the priestly tribe. Continuing to pass among the Levites, you would have come to the tabernacle. At first you would have passed through a great gateway into the outer court where you would have found certain articles—the brass altar and the brass laver. Then you would have come to an inner building with a veil across the entrance, where only priests dared enter: the Holy Place. Behind another veil inside the holy place was the Holy of Holies. The only piece of furniture in it was the ark of the covenant, which was adorned by the cherubim of mercy with their wings touching each other over the ark. Into that place only the high priest could go—once a year and under the most rigid and precise conditions.

The articles in the tabernacle

Now what do the symbols of the tabernacle teach us? Again, the message is that God is absolutely changeless and holy. He can dwell among people only under the most rigid conditions. The trouble with the tabernacle was that it permitted the people to come before God vicariously, only through the priests. Actually, the common people were excluded from God's living presence.

The problem with the Old Testament is not that the Law is inadequate. There is nothing wrong with the Law; it is absolutely good. It remains good and in full force today. The problem was with the tabernacle and the system of sacrifices. They weren't complete. They weren't final. They were a shadow, a symbol, not the reality. That is why, when we come to the book of Hebrews, the whole book is dedicated to teaching us that the Law of God is still unchanged, but our approach to God is different under the new covenant than it was under the old covenant.

In Exodus, only the high priest could enter the sanctuary. But in Hebrews we read, "we have confidence to enter the Most Holy Place" (Heb. 10:19) without fear. Because the blood of Jesus, the perfect sacrifice of the God-Man upon the cross, completes what the blood sacrifices of the Old Testament only symbolized. Through the perfect sacrifice of Jesus, we now have access to the presence of God, which was forbidden to the common people in the days of Moses.

The great message of the book of Exodus is that by means of the cross, God has made it possible for a holy, unchangeable God to dwell with us. The tabernacle is a picture of God's dwelling place with His people. The great truth for us here is that God has completely settled the problem of sin in us—absolutely and completely settled it! Paul says in Romans 8:1, "There is now no condemnation," none whatsoever! We have perfect access to the Father through the Son, and God's indwelling Spirit will never leave us or forsake us. He has taken up His tabernacle in our hearts and lives.

The tabernacle is a picture of God's dwelling place with His people

I think it is tragic that so many Sunday school teachers tell their pupils that a *building* is the house of God. This is simply not true. A building was the house of God in the Old Testament—the tabernacle—but it was a mere shadow. The house of God of the New Testament, of the age in which we now live, is *people,* those who have placed their trust in Jesus Christ. As Paul says in 1 Corinthians 3:16, "*You* yourselves are God's temple" (italics added). So once you are in Christ, you are never out of church! Each of us is a walking tabernacle.

The whole book of Exodus is written to impress upon us a great New Testament truth: the glory of God lives *in* us and *with* us. This truth exalts us, energizes us, and exhilarates us. This truth also places a great sense of responsibility on us. We need to continually remind ourselves that we should walk worthy of the eternal presence that dwells in us. All our actions should be examined in light of the question, "In doing this, will I bring honor or shame to God's walking tabernacle, my body?"

Law and grace — together

Even in the Old Testament, salvation was a matter of God's grace, appropriated by human faith

Sometimes we hear that the weakness of the Old Testament was that Israel was under the law and did not know the grace of God. This is a complete misconception! True, Israel was under the law—but the law was not given to the Jewish people to be their savior. It was given to reveal their sin and to make them aware of the hopelessness of their condition apart from God's redemptive grace. Even in the Old Testament, salvation was a matter of God's grace, appropriated by human faith.

The symbols of Exodus are meant to teach us that, by means of the cross, God now dwells with us. That is why Matthew 1:23 says of Jesus, "The virgin will be with child and will give birth to a son, and they will call him Immanuel—which means, 'God with us.'" God *is* with us, here and now, in a dramatic and powerful way. He has taken up His abode in our hearts. That, brought down to its essence, is the message of Exodus.

Still, Exodus isn't enough. We need to go on into Leviticus and see how this demanding law of God affects us in its effort to correct us and guide our lives. That is where we next turn our attention.

The Way To Wholeness

W hen I first came to the Bay Area of California, I visited a large steel-products factory owned by a friend of mine. He was about to give me a tour when he was called away to deal with a business matter. As I waited for my friend to join me and show me around, I wandered out onto the factory floor and looked around.

My first impression as I stepped into the huge building was one of tremendous clamor. The noise was thunderous! Great machines were pounding away, big trip-hammers were smashing down, and other machines were grinding up metal and spitting out parts. I couldn't even hear myself think.

My next impression was one of mass confusion. People were running here and there paying no attention to one another and getting in each other's way. The machines were all working away with no apparent harmony or connection at all.

Then my friend joined me and we began our tour of the plant. He showed me one area of the factory and explained what they were doing there. He explained the workings of various machines, and he told me what the various workers were doing. We went from department to department, and in each place he explained how all the seeming chaos of the place was actually *controlled* chaos, all carefully planned and executed in order to produce a finished product. Finally, we arrived in the shipping department; there, packaged in glistening shrink-wrap and tucked neatly into cardboard boxes with Styrofoam packing material, was the finished product.

Suddenly, I understood the factory. It was not all "sound and fury, signifying nothing," as I had originally supposed. It all made perfect sense. The noise, the activity, the seeming confusion were all carefully orchestrated to produce the desired effect.

I was no longer confused. Instead, I was amazed and impressed!

The goal of Leviticus

Reading the book of Leviticus can be a lot like visiting a factory without a guide. Coming into this book, you find many strange ceremonies and sacrifices, many odd restrictions, and various other details that seem practically meaningless. But the more you understand of the book of Leviticus, the more these strange details seem to merge and become a complex, cohesive, intricately articulated relationship, moving toward a purposeful goal.

What is that goal? You find it stated clearly in a verse near the middle of the book. If you grasp this one verse, you understand the essence of the entire book: "You are to be holy to me because I, the LORD, am holy, and I have set you apart from the nations to be my own" (Lev. 20:26).

God is saying to the people of Israel, "I have separated you from all the nations around you in order that you might be Mine." When we Christians read this, we must understand that we are the people of God today. What God said to Israel He also says to us, for in the new relationship we have in Jesus Christ there is neither Jew nor Gentile. We are one body in Christ. The promises that appear in picture form in the Old Testament belong also to us who live this side of the cross.

Holiness and wholeness

When the Lord says to the people, "You are to be holy to me because I, the LORD, am holy," many of us have to ask ourselves, *What does that word* holy *really mean?* Most of us associate it with some kind of grimness or solemnity. We think holy people are those who look as if they have been steeped in vinegar or soaked in embalming fluid. I used to think of the word that way. Viewed in that light, the concept of holiness was not at all attractive to me!

But then I came across Psalm 29:2, a verse that speaks of "the splendor of his holiness." I had to ask myself, *What in the world is so splendid about holiness?* When I found out, I had to agree that holiness is indeed a splendid thing.

If you want to get at the meaning of this word, you must go back to its original root. The word *holiness* is derived from the same root as another, much more familiar word: *wholeness. Holiness* actually means "wholeness," the state of being complete. And if you read wholeness in place of holiness everywhere you find it in the Bible, you will be very close to what the writers of Scripture meant. Holiness/wholeness means to have all the parts that were intended to be there and to have them functioning as they were intended to function.

So God is really saying to His people in the book of Leviticus, "You shall be whole, because I am whole." God is complete. He is perfect. There is no blemish in God. He lives in harmony with Himself and knows none of the inner conflict and turmoil that we humans often experience. God is a beautiful person. He is absolutely what a person ought to be. He is filled with joy and love and peace. He lives in wholeness. And He looks at us in our brokenness and says, "You, too, shall be whole."

We long to be whole people. In life, we are continually reminded of our own brokenness, of our lack of wholeness. We know how much we hurt ourselves and each other. We are aware of our inability to cope with life. We sometimes put up a big facade and try to bluff our way through as though we are able to handle anything, but inside, we are running scared. That is a mark of our lack of wholeness.

When man first came from the hand of God, he was whole. He was made in the image and likeness of God. Adam functioned as God intended man to function. But when sin entered the picture, the image and likeness of God was marred and broken. We still have the image, but the likeness is gone.

God has made a decision to heal our brokenness and to make us whole again. He knows how to do it, and He says so: "I am the LORD your God, who has set you apart from the nations" (Lev. 20:24). Our brokenness is rooted in our involvement with the brokenness of our race. Our attitudes are wrong. Our vision of life is distorted. We believe illusions, take them to be facts, and act upon them. So God must separate us. He must break us loose from the bondage of the thought patterns, attitudes, and reactions of those around us. God never forces us to become holy. We become holy only as we *voluntarily* trust God and respond to His love.

As a teenager, I once tried to coax a female deer out of a thicket so I could feed her an apple from my hand. She was wild and scared, but she saw the apple and obviously wanted it. She would venture a few steps toward me, then retreat into the woods, venture forward, then retreat. Then she would come out again, stand still and look around for a minute, then casually graze as if she were indifferent to that apple. I stood perfectly still, holding out the apple, waiting for her to come to me in trust.

Now, it was perfectly possible for that doe simply to walk right up and grab the apple and start eating it. I never would have hurt her or

We long to be whole

God knows how to make us whole

Learning to trust Him

tried to capture her, but she didn't know that. I was there a long time, at least half an hour, trying to get her to come out of the woods. Finally, she came about halfway toward me and stood there with her neck stretched out, trying to muster the courage to reach for that apple. Just as I thought she was going to do it, a car passed nearby and she was gone. I had to eat the apple myself!

That incident strikes me as an apt picture of what God contends with in reaching out toward human beings. It takes infinite patience and love on His part to overcome our fear and doubt, so that we will trust Him to give us what we need. That is why God gave us this book.

He starts us out in spiritual kindergarten. He starts with pictures and shadows, with visual aids, in order to show us what He is going to do someday. All the ceremonies and offerings of the Old Testament are shadows and pictures of Jesus Christ. Christ is as present in the book of Leviticus as He is in the Gospels, but because He is present in symbols and signs, you must look carefully to see His image. Jesus is the focus of Leviticus, and the theme of this book is that God has made His holiness/wholeness available to us through Jesus Himself.

"But," you might say, "the people of the Old Testament didn't know that the pictures and shadows of Leviticus pointed to Jesus!" True, the Israelites did not fully understand that the Old Testament sacrifices and tabernacle pointed to Jesus, but that doesn't matter. People of the Old Testament needed Christ as much as we need Him today. They were hurting and broken and fragmented, just as we are. And Christ was available to them through the symbols and pictures of Leviticus. They met Him through the form of worship that God gave them in Leviticus, and as they placed their trust in God, they came into the same joy and peace that we now have as New Testament believers.

The sacrifices, rituals, and ceremonies of Leviticus are a foreshadowing of Jesus and His saving work, and they can teach us a great deal about how Jesus Christ can meet our needs now

This is why Leviticus is such an important book for us today: Because the sacrifices, rituals, and ceremonies of Leviticus are a foreshadowing of Jesus and His saving work, this book can teach us a great deal about how Jesus Christ can meet our needs now. This is not just a historical book. It is a tremendously practical manual on how to live the Christian life.

The structure of Leviticus

The book of Leviticus falls into two main divisions. The first part (chapters 1 through 17) speaks to human need and tells us how we should approach a holy God. It reveals our inadequacy as a sinful people and sets forth God's answer to that inadequacy.

The second part (chapters 18 through 27) reveals what God expects from us in response, instructing us in how to live holy, sanctified lives, distinct from the world around us. Here is an outline of the book of Leviticus:

How to Approach God (Leviticus 1–17)

1.	Laws regarding offerings to God	1–7
	A. Burnt offering	1
	B. Grain offering	2
	C. Fellowship offering	3
	D. Sin offering	4:1–5:13
	E. Guilt offering	5:14–6:7
	F. Summary of the offerings	6:8–7:38
2.	Laws regarding the priesthood	8–10
3.	Laws regarding purity	11–15
	A. Laws concerning diet	11
	B. Laws concerning childbirth	12
	C. Laws concerning infectious skin diseases	13–14
	D. Laws concerning bodily discharges	15
4.	Laws regarding atonement and sacrifices	16–17

How to Live: Sanctification and Holiness (Leviticus 18–27)

5.	Laws regarding sexual behavior	18
6.	Laws regarding society	19
7.	Penalties for idolatry and immorality	20
8.	Sanctification of the priesthood	21–22
9.	The feasts and laws of worship	23–24
10.	The coming sanctification of the Promised Land	25–26
11.	The laws of consecration of the people and their possessions	27

Part 1: Human need in approaching a holy God

The first seventeen chapters of Leviticus are all about how we, as sinful people, can approach God. They contain four elements that establish human need and reveal what we are like. The first is a series of *five offerings* that symbolize in different ways the offering of Jesus Christ upon the cross for our sins. Perhaps God gave us five fingers on each hand so that we can remember the five offerings:

First element: a series of five offerings

1. the burnt offering
2. the meal offering
3. the peace offering
4. the sin offering
5. the trespass offering

These are all pictures of what Jesus Christ does for us, but they are also pictures of the fundamental needs of human life. They speak of the two essentials for human existence: *love and responsibility.*

We can never be complete if we are not loved or if we do not love. Love is an essential ingredient of life. Nothing harms, distorts, disfigures, or injures a person more than to deny love to that person.

But there is another essential: In order to be whole, in order to have self-respect and self-worth, we must have a sense of responsibility. We must be able to accomplish what is worthwhile. So we need both: love and responsibility.

The second element in the first seventeen chapters is the priesthood. In the Old Testament, the priesthood was comprised solely of the sons of Levi (which is where Leviticus gets its name). But the priesthood takes a new form in the New Testament.

First there is our Lord and High Priest, Jesus Christ, who has pierced the veil of the tabernacle, the Holy of Holies, and given us free access to God the Father. Second is the priesthood of all believers, the body of Christ, where we are all made priests (see 1 Peter 2:5). We love one another, confess to one another, pray for one another, encourage one another, exhort one another, and perform for one another all the functions that, in the New Testament, were performed by the priestly class, the sons of Levi. That is why we need each other in the body of Christ.

The third element that we see in these first seventeen chapters is the revelation of a standard of truth. By this standard we are able to tell the difference between the true and the false, the phony and the real, the helpful and the hurtful, the life-giving and the deadly. Isn't it strange that human beings in their natural condition cannot tell the difference? That is why there are millions of people who are doing things that they think are helpful but that end up to be destructive—and they don't understand why! Because God is loving, He points us to the truth and warns us to avoid the actions that would destroy us.

The fourth and final element that we see in these first seventeen chapters is an opportunity to respond to God. This opportunity is completely voluntary. God never imposes His will on any of us. This opportunity is provided by means of something called "the Day of Atonement." If, when we thoroughly understand our need and God's provision to meet it, we say no to Him, He will let us. But we must recognize that we may never return to the moment of opportunity again. God always gives us a long period of preparation in which He leads us into a full understanding of the choice that He sets before us; but our rejection of Him tends to be progressive, resulting in a gradual hardening of our hearts. Finally, we reach a point where our rejection of Him becomes tragically final.

The second section of the book, chapters 18 through 27, describes the holy, sanctified lifestyle that God makes possible. This section of Leviticus is all about how we should live as obedient people who belong to a holy God. Notice that God does not tell us how we should live until He has first told us about the provision He has made to enable us to approach Him. First, He discusses the power by which we are to act, then He talks about our behavior.

We in the church often get this backward. A great deal of damage has been done to people by insisting that they behave in a certain way without giving them any understanding of the power by which to do so. New Christians and non-Christians are sometimes taught that they must live up to a certain standard before God will accept them. That is totally wrong! That is the deadly, legalistic lie of Satan, designed to keep people away from God's truth and out of God's church. And that is what God endeavors to correct in the book of Leviticus. He wants us to understand that He has first made the provision, and His provision gives us the basis upon which to build a holy lifestyle.

The second part of Leviticus, like the first, is built upon four essential elements. First, there is a need to understand the basis for wholeness, which is blood. Anyone who has read the Old Testament knows that it is full of blood. In fact, a river of blood flows throughout the thirty-nine books of the Old Testament. There are sacrifices upon sacrifices, including sacrifices of bulls, calves, goats, sheep, and birds of all kinds. Why all this bloodshed? Because God is trying to impress us with a fundamental fact: Our sin condition runs very deep and can be resolved only by a death. The death that is pictured in every one of these animal sacrifices is, of course, the death of God's only Son, Jesus Christ.

First element: the blood

The second element that runs through the concluding part of Leviticus is the practice of love in all the relationships of life. The Bible is intensely practical. It is not nearly so concerned with what you do in the tabernacle as what you do in the home as a result of having been to the tabernacle. So this book deals with relationships in the family, among friends, and with society in general. It shows us exactly the kind of love relationship that God makes possible in all these areas of life.

Second element: the practice of love

The third element in this last section is the enjoyment of God— His presence and His power. This section tells us how to live in relationship to God, how to worship God, and how to experience the living presence of God! The most important thing in life is not rituals and laws but an experience of the living God who is behind all the rituals and laws!

Third element: the enjoyment of God

The fourth and final element is the choice that God calls us to make. He makes us aware of the important issues at stake, of how our entire lives hang in the balance, and that a decision is required of us. God shows us that, in the final analysis, the choice is entirely ours. God never says, "I'm going to make you leave your misery." Rather, He says, "If you prefer being broken and don't want to be healed, you can

Fourth element: the choice of life

**The key
theme of
Leviticus**

"You are Mine"

stay right where you are. But if you want life, then this is what you must choose." God never forces His will on us, but He does expect a response. The choice is ours to make.

In closing, we return to the key verse and the key theme of Leviticus, found in Leviticus 20:26 "You are to be holy [whole] to me because I, the LORD, am holy [whole], and I have set you apart from the nations to be my own." It is important to note the verb tense of that last phrase. In our English text, it is in the future tense: "You are to be . . . my own." But the Hebrew language incorporates into this one phrase all three tenses—past, present, and future. It is as if God is saying, "You were mine, you are mine, you shall be mine."

If you pursue this idea throughout the Bible, you can see how true it is. You may know from experience that after you became a Christian, you realized that there was a sense in which you had belonged to God all along. He was active and involved in your life long before you became aware of Him. The apostle Paul expressed this thought when he wrote, "[God] set me apart from birth" (Gal. 1:15). Yet prior to his conversion Paul was a fanatical enemy of Christianity! This is a verification of the amazing love and patience of God, who draws us to Himself even when we oppose Him. "You are Mine," God says to us. "Even though you are against Me, hostile to Me, and fighting Me, you are Mine!"

Then, in the present tense, God looks at us in our brokenness, pain, and imperfection, and He places His loving hand on us and says, "You are Mine, right now, just the way you are. You belong to Me."

Some years ago, a children's service was held at a rescue mission in a city in the Midwest. One of the children who was taking part in the program was a six-year-old boy with a pronounced humpback. As he walked across the stage to give his recitation, it was clear that he was very shy and afraid and very self-conscious about his physical deformity. As he crossed the stage, one of the cruel boys in the audience called out, "Hey, kid, where are you going with that pack on your back!" The little boy stood shaking and sobbing in front of the audience.

A man stood up from the audience, went to the platform, and lifted the sobbing boy in his arms. Then he looked out over the audience. "Who said that?" he asked. No one answered. "I thought so. It takes a real coward to make a remark like that. This boy is my son, and he suffers for something that is not his fault. Whoever you are, you've hurt this boy for no reason whatsoever. But I want everyone here to know that I love this boy just the way he is. He is mine. He belongs to me, and I'm very proud of him."

That's what God is saying to us. He sees our hurt and our brokenness, and He says, "You're *Mine!*"

But that isn't all. Because of His power and wisdom, God also addresses the future, with all the hopefulness and optimism of a loving father. "You will be Mine," He says in the future tense. "You will be healed and made whole. All your blemishes and deformities will be corrected, all your faults will be straightened out, all your sins will be erased, all your tangled relationships unsnarled. You will be whole, for I am whole." That is what this book is about, that is what the Bible is about, and that is what Jesus Christ is about.

From Failure to Victory

A king once lay ill in his bedchamber. He had called for the royal physician to bring him medicine for his ailing stomach. But before the physician could arrive, a messenger arrived with a secret letter, accusing the physician of being involved in a plot to murder the king. "Receive no medicine from the doctor's hand," read the letter. "It will be poison."

The king hid the letter under his pillow just moments before the royal physician arrived with a goblet filled with a medicinal potion. "Trust me, Sire," said the doctor. "This medicine will cure your stomach."

"I do trust you," said the king. Reaching beneath his pillow, he took the accusing letter and handed it to the doctor at the same time he took the goblet of medicine.

"What is this?" asked the doctor, taking the letter from the king's hand.

"Read it," said the king. Then he lifted the goblet to his lips and drank the potion.

The doctor read the letter, then looked up at the king with eyes full of shock and pain. "Your Highness, you must believe me, this letter is nothing but lies! I would never do anything to harm you!"

"I do believe you," said the king, "and I trust you completely—see?" The king held out the goblet. He had drunk every drop. By the next morning, he was completely recovered. The king had demon-strated, in the most dramatic way imaginable, his complete trust in his physician.

Trust is the theme of the book of Numbers. In this book, God dra-matically sets forth what is perhaps the hardest lesson any of us has to learn: our need to trust God rather than our own reason.

In the desert of discipline

The issue of trust is a major struggle for many Christians

We believe we know better than God

The issue of trust is a major struggle for many Christians. The hard-est struggle we have is the same struggle that the Israelites had—the struggle to believe and trust that God is in control, He knows what He's doing and what He's talking about, and He doesn't make mistakes. We struggle to believe that everything that He tells us in His Word is true and that it is for our good.

Again and again, we Christians get into trouble because we believe we know better than God, we are closer to the situation than God, and we had better handle the situation ourselves because we can't trust God to come through for us when we need Him. Proverbs puts it very strongly but accurately: "There is a way that seems right to a man, but in the end it leads to death" (Prov. 14:12). The book of Numbers is a picture of this experience in the life of a believer.

The New Testament counterpart of the book of Numbers is Romans chapter 7, which depicts the unhappy, defeated Christian who is his own worst enemy and who finds himself being disciplined by God because God, the loving Father, loves him and wants the best for him. The Christian in Romans 7 is experiencing what is often called "tough love"—a painful form of love that is designed to produce character growth and maturity. That is also the kind of love portrayed in the book of Numbers.

Numbers is a picture of people who had the faith to follow God out of bondage and slavery but have not yet come into liberty and rest

Numbers is a picture of people who have come out of Egypt but who have not yet reached Canaan. They had the faith to follow God out of bondage and slavery, but they have not yet come into liberty and rest. They have not yet reached the Land of Promise. God loves them, God preserves them in their wanderings, but they are in the desert of disci-pline, not the haven of peace and rest.

Numbers is a book of wanderings. Until the people of Israel learn to trust their God, they must endure the desert of discipline. This tragic book is laden with relevant instruction and warning for our own lives today.

The structure of Numbers

This book falls into three divisions. In the first section, the people of Israel are prepared to inherit the Promised Land, the land of Canaan. In the middle section, the people fail, sin, and are judged; the judgment of God is that this generation must wander in the wilderness and cannot

inherit the Promised Land. In the final section, a new generation is prepared to move into and possess the Promised Land. The book can be
outlined as follows:

**Preparing the People to Inherit the Promised Land
(Numbers 1–10)**

1. The census (numbering) of the people	1
2. The arrangement of the encampment	2
3. The ministry of the priests (the Levites)	3–4
4. The sanctification of Israel (through separation, vows, worship, and divine guidance)	5–10

**The Failure of Israel to Inherit the Promised Land
(Numbers 11–25)**

5. The complaints of the people	11:1–9
6. The complaints of Moses	11:10–15
7. God provides for Moses and the people	11:16–32
8. God chastens the people (plagues)	11:33–35
9. The failure of Moses and Aaron	12
10. The failure and judgment of Israel at Kadesh-barnea	13–14
11. Israel wanders in the wilderness	15–19
A. The offerings	15
B. The rebellion of Korah	16
C. The role of the Levites	17–19
12. The sin of Israel, the failure of Moses	20:1–13
13. Israel at war	20:14–22:35
14. The oracles of Balaam, the false prophet	23–24
15. Israel sins with the Moabites	25

**A New Generation Prepares to Inherit the Promised Land
(Numbers 26–36)**

16. The reorganization and renumbering of Israel	26
17. The appointment of a new leader, Joshua	27
18. The reinstitution of offerings and vows	28–30
19. Military and spiritual preparations for the conquest of Canaan	31–36

The first section of Numbers, chapters 1 through 9, is a picture of
God's provision for guidance and warfare. These are the two critical needs
of Israel in their march from Mount Sinai, where the Law was given, to
the northern wilderness of Paran, at the very edge of the Promised Land,
the land of Canaan. On the way they would need guidance, because this

**God's
provision
for guidance
and warfare**

was a trackless wilderness. Moreover, they would need protection, for the wilderness was occupied by hostile tribes who opposed them every time they turned around.

Is this a familiar picture? We all need guidance to wend our way among the subtle dangers, temptations, and evils of this world. We all need protection from the enemies who surround us, who would defeat us if they could.

This section describes the arrangement of the encampment, including the position of the tabernacle with the tribes on every side, and a numbering of the armed men of Israel. These are pictures for us of the need for defense against the enemies of God. God provides all the strategy and resources necessary to meet every enemy that comes our way. He had ordered the arrangement of the encampment (the tabernacle surrounded by the tribes), and He also provided the cloud over the camp by day and the pillar of fire by night.

These three elements—the tabernacle, the cloud, and the pillar of fire—picture for us the great truth of the indwelling of the Holy Spirit. We have God in our midst. He is able to direct and to lead us through the wilderness of the world by the guidance of the Word. We are led by the cloud and the fire, just as Israel was led, and we are to be obedient to that leading. This is all the potential we need to get us from the place of the law (the knowledge of the holiness of God) to a resting place in the Spirit, which the land of Canaan represents. We have everything we need, just as the people of Israel had all they needed.

Failure!

Rebellion starts with murmuring and complaining

But in chapters 11 through 21, something goes tragically wrong! This tragedy occupies the great central section of Numbers. Here is a description of rebellion and willful disobedience against God. Notice how this rebellion starts: with murmuring and complaining. Whenever you find yourself beginning to complain against your circumstances, consider this: You are on the threshold of rebellion, because rebellion always begins there.

Three levels of complaining

Three levels of complaining mark this part of the wilderness journey:

Level 1: complaint against circumstances

First, the people complained against their circumstances. God had given them manna and quail meat to eat and water to drink, but they complained about the manna and the lack of water. They complained about the meat. They complained about the wilderness itself. Nothing was right, not even God's miraculous provision for their needs.

What do you think manna symbolizes for us today? It typifies the Holy Spirit! The manna tasted like a thin wafer of oil and honey mixture. Oil and honey are both symbols of the Holy Spirit. They were to eat this substance, and it would be enough to sustain the people. It was not enough to satisfy them, because God never intended for them to live so long in the wilderness. He intended for them to move on into the land of Canaan and begin to eat the abundant food there.

But the people got tired of manna. After all, who wouldn't have gotten tired of forty years of oil-and-honey wafers for breakfast, lunch, and dinner? Every day, nothing but manna, manna, manna! First, the people complained; finally, the people rebelled.

Whose fault was it that they rebelled? Not God's! His plan was for the people to possess a land of abundance and endless variety. The people chose to turn their backs on satisfaction and to wander in a dry wilderness with nothing but manna to eat.

When the people complained about a lack of meat, God gave them meat for a month until they were tired of meat. So the people complained that there was too much meat! On and on it went. God provided, the people complained; God provided more, the people complained more. In their murmuring, the one subject the people kept coming back to was Egypt—the land of bondage!

Here is a symbolic picture of a degenerating Christian experience. All the Israelites could think of was the meat, melons, cucumbers, leeks, onions, and garlic of Egypt. Talk about a selective memory! Didn't they remember the backbreaking toil, the slavemaster's lash, the chains of slavery? And what about the land to which God was calling them? They had no thought of Canaan because they had no knowledge of it. They had heard about Canaan, but they had no experience of it.

This murmuring against their circumstances brought about God's judgment. That judgment came in three forms: fire, plague, and poisonous serpents. This is a picture of the inevitable result of whining, complaining, and murmuring as a Christian. When we complain about where God has put us and the kind of people He has surrounded us with and the kind of food we have to eat and all of our other circumstances, we soon discover:

- the fire of gossip, scandal, and slander;
- the plague of anxiety and nervous tension; and
- the poison of envy and jealousy.

Not only did the Israelites murmur against their circumstances, but they continually murmured against the blessing of God. Imagine! They came at last to the edge of the land of Canaan, standing on the very borderline at Kadesh-barnea, and there God said to them, "Send some men to explore the land of Canaan, which I am giving to the Israelites" (Num. 13:2).

The Israelites had sent out spies and had learned that it was a land flowing with milk and honey. The spies had brought back grapes so large that they had to carry them on a stick between the shoulders of two men!

But they also learned that it was a land full of giants, and because of the giants they were afraid to go forward. They thought the giants were greater than God, so they refused to go on into the blessing He wanted to pour out upon them.

So God judged them. They were sentenced to wander in the wilderness for forty years. Because they had refused to move forward and possess God's loving will for their lives, God's inevitable judgment required them to experience the full results of a failure. Only then could they progress in God's program.

Many Christians live the same way, languishing in a miserable, howling wilderness, living on a minimum supply of the Holy Spirit—just enough to keep them going, and that's all. They spend their lives complaining about their circumstances yet still are unwilling to move into the land that God has fully provided for them. You can be sustained in the wilderness, but you will never be satisfied there. That is why the wilderness experience is always marked by a complaining heart and an unending criticism of something or someone.

For Israel, the wilderness experience would not end until a new generation was ready to enter the land. God said to them, "In this desert your bodies will fall—every one of you twenty years old or more who was counted in the census and who has grumbled against me. Not one of you will enter the land . . . except Caleb . . . and Joshua" (Num. 14:29–30). These two men were the only members of the older generation who had demonstrated the faith and trust to move forward and possess the Land of Promise.

There is a powerful lesson here for our own Christian lives. Often, we find that it is not until we come to the end of ourselves, until it becomes clear that we must make a new beginning in our lives, that we are able to allow the Spirit to take over and lead us into our own Land of Promise. This is why so many Christians never seem to find victory until they have a crisis experience followed by a new beginning. God says, "Trust Me," but we resist and resist, so God has to knock all the props out from under us until we have nothing left to cling to but Him. Finally we cry out, "God, I have nothing left but You! You're my only hope!" Then He can say, "Fine. Now you are ready to trust Me. Now I can lead you where I have always wanted to lead you. Now I can bless you as I have always longed to bless you."

A land of death

One of the distinguishing features of Israel's wilderness experience is death. The people wandered in a land of death. Did you ever consider how many Israelites died in those forty years in the wilderness? This book begins with a census of Israel, and it totals 603,000 men—men who were able to go out to warfare, who were at least twenty years old.

Most of them were married, so there must have been a comparable number of women, plus many children, in the camp. Many scholars have estimated the total population at that time to have been well over two million people.

So in the wilderness, during those forty years, roughly 1.2 million people died. That's an average of *eighty-two deaths per day!* The journey in the wilderness was a long, sad funeral march—forty solid years of grief and loss. The wilderness was one huge graveyard. No wonder they had to move so often! This is an Old Testament picture of what Romans warns against: "The mind of sinful man is death" (Rom. 8:6).

The soundtrack of Numbers is the endless babble of murmuring and complaining. First was the murmuring against circumstances. Then the people murmured against God's provision for them. Finally, they murmured against the divinely appointed leadership of Israel, Moses, and Aaron. They complained, "You have gone too far! The whole community is holy, every one of them, and the LORD is with them. Why then do you set yourselves above the LORD's assembly?" (Num. 16:3). They judged themselves by their own standards and rebelled against the properly constituted authority in their midst.

This is another characteristic of defeated Christians! They always think they are holy enough, that they are as holy as they need to be, and they resent anyone else who seems to exercise spiritual or moral authority. They resist any suggestion that they ought to be more than they are. That is what these people did.

God met this attitude with the severest judgment of all. The situation climaxes with the open rebellion of two Israelite priests, Korah and Abiram. These men brought division to the nation of Israel (much as rebellious people continue to divide churches today). When they openly challenged the authority of Moses and Aaron, God said to Moses and Aaron, "Separate yourselves from this assembly so I can put an end to them at once." . . . "Say to the assembly, 'Move away from the tents of Korah, Dathan and Abiram' " (Num. 16:21, 24).

Then God led Moses to say to Israel, "If these men die a natural death and experience only what usually happens to men, then the LORD has not sent me. But if the LORD brings about something totally new, and the earth opens its mouth and swallows them, with everything that belongs to them, and they go down alive into the grave, then you will know that these men have treated the LORD with contempt" (Num. 16:29–30). And as he said the words, the ground opened up beneath Korah and Abiram and all their families, and they went down alive into the pit. Thus, God established His authority

Complaining
subsides when

1. Aaron's rod
grows almonds

2. The brass
serpent saves them
from poisonous
snakes

through Moses by this remarkable judgment. When we rebel against authority, God judges with the utmost severity.

After this judgment, we see an amazing demonstration of the mulish obstinacy of human nature. Murmuring and criticizing is so much a part of who we are as human beings that even after seeing the ground open up and swallow a group of rebels the people continued to complain! The complaining died down only when two things occurred.

First, following the death of Korah and Abiram, all the leaders of the twelve tribes took rods and laid them down before the Lord. One of those rods belonged to Aaron. The next morning, they found that Aaron's rod had grown branches, the branches had blossomed, the blossoms had grown fruit, and almonds hung from the branches. All of this had taken place overnight! Of the twelve rods, only Aaron's blossomed. This is a picture of the resurrection life. God was saying to Israel that the only ones who have the right to bear authority are those who walk in the fullness and power of resurrection life.

Second, when the people murmured about the food, God sent poisonous serpents among them. The people would die without a savior. So Moses cured the effects of the poison by lifting up a brass serpent on a pole. As God directed, all who looked at the serpent were healed. By this symbol, God says to Israel and to us, "The only cure for sin, including the sin of believers, is to gaze again at the cross." In John 3, the Lord Jesus makes reference to this incident and pointed to its symbolic significance in our lives: "Just as Moses lifted up the snake in the desert, so the Son of Man must be lifted up, that everyone who believes in him may have eternal life" (John 3:14–15). The cross utterly repudiates all human endeavor and human worthiness; we are powerless to save ourselves, and we can be saved only on the basis of the resurrection life of Jesus Christ.

Victory at last

Chapter 26 begins the third and last movement of the book. It records the second census taken of the men of war and their families. God gave specific instructions to Moses concerning the division of the land when they came into Canaan.

An interesting incident is related concerning the five daughters of Zelophehad. Left fatherless, they would not have been permitted to receive a share of the real estate when Israel moved into Canaan, according to Middle Eastern cultural norms. Yet these women petitioned and were granted an inheritance in the Land of Promise (27:1–11). In a symbolic way, this incident established the principle that in Christ there is neither male nor female, and it paves the way for the equal and fair treatment of women.

Next, God informed Moses that the time had come for him to die. At Moses' request, God appoints Joshua, the son of Nun, to be his successor (27:18–19). Joshua would not inherit the full authority that Moses exercised, but he would discover the divine will through a high priest.

Following this, God repeated the various offerings and sacrifices to be given at Israel's great feast days, already outlined in the book of Leviticus. Certain exceptions were then made to the general rule concerning vows.

The concluding chapters of the book, from chapter 31 through 36, describe an account of a holy war led by Phinehas the priest against the Midianites, during which Balaam, the false prophet, is also slain. Here also the two tribes of Reuben and Gad and half the tribe of Manasseh unwisely insist on settling on the east side of the Jordan rather than in the proper regions of the Land of Promise. They were permitted to do so only by agreeing to join their brethren in subduing their Canaanite enemies.

After reviewing the route taken by Israel from Egypt to the Jordan and giving directions for the division of the land when the tribes entered it, Moses then assigned certain cities as residences for the Levites, six of which are especially designated as cities of refuge (35:10–15). These cities were for people who had accidentally committed murder, and needed safe places to flee from avengers until their trials could be held.

Historically, the book of Numbers closes where the last chapter of Deuteronomy begins, giving us the account of the death of Moses. Numbers is the record of the failure of the people in their perpetual stubbornness and foolishness, yet it is also the story of the unwearying patience and continual faithfulness of God. Thus it encourages those of us who have often failed in our own spiritual lives, and it shows us that victory is still ours if we hold fast to our trust in God. We have come to learn, as the New Testament declares, that "if we are faithless, he will remain faithful, for he cannot disown himself" (2 Tim. 2:13).

Holy war led by Phinehas against the Midianites

Cities designated cities of refuge

The Law That Brings Deliverance

Deuteronomy is made up of three great sermons delivered by Moses shortly before his death. These were given to Israel while they waited on the east side of the Jordan in the Arabah and after they had been victorious over Sihon, the king of the Amorites, and Og, the king of Bashan. At this time the multitude of Israelites were made up of a new generation who were but children (or yet unborn) when their parents were given the Law from Mount Sinai. Here is an outline of the book of Deuteronomy:

Moses' First Sermon: A Review of What God Has Done for Israel (Deuteronomy 1–4)

1. From Mount Sinai to Kadesh-barnea	1
2. From Kadesh-barnea to Moab	2:1–23
3. The conquest of East Jordan	2:24–3:20
4. Summary: The covenant	3:21–4:43

The first sermon: What God has done for Israel

As the people were about to enter the land of Canaan, it was essential that they thoroughly understand their history. So chapters 1 through 4 give us the first message of Moses, in which he reviewed the journey from the giving of the Law at Mount Sinai until the people reached Moab, at the edge of the Jordan River.

Moses' first task was to recite to the people the wonderful love and care of God, who led them with a pillar of fire by night and the cloud by day and guided them through the trackless desert. He reminded them of how God had brought water from the rock to quench their thirst in a vast and waterless area; how He had fed them with manna that did not fail; and how He had delivered them again and again from their enemies.

Deliverance

In chapter 1, he traced the movement of the people from the giving of the Law at Sinai (also called Mount Horeb) to the refusal of the people to enter the land at Kadesh-barnea. In chapter 2, he reviewed the second movement from Kadesh-barnea to Heshbon, around the land of Edom, and through the wilderness of Moab to their encounter with Sihon, the king of Heshbon. Throughout this passage, Moses emphasized God's continual deliverance of the people from their enemies, despite their unbelief.

Continuing his discourse, Moses reviewed the conquest of the Jordan Valley as far north as Mount Hermon and the decision of Reuben and Gad to settle on the east side of the river. In a note of pathos, he recalled his own eager desire to enter into the land with his people, but he acknowledged God's denial of this privilege. Still, he was permitted to view the land from the top of Mount Pisgah.

Moses closed the historic review, in chapter 4, with an exhortation to the people to remember the greatness of their God and to be obedient from their hearts. He warned also against the danger of idolatry, especially the making of graven images. He concluded the message by setting aside three cities of refuge on the east side of the Jordan for the protection of those who committed involuntary manslaughter.

As we survey this record of God's provision for the people of Israel, we see that God led them out of Egypt, through the wilderness, and right to the brink of Canaan. In their journey, they experienced all the same problems, obstacles, enemies, defeats, and victories that we encounter all through the Christian life. The bondage that the Israelites experienced as slaves of Egypt is the same as the bondage to the world that we experienced before we were Christians. And the land of Canaan, flowing with milk and honey, pictures a life filled with continual victory, which can be ours in Christ. All this is God's way of picturing for us what is happening in our lives.

If you read your Old Testament with this key in hand, it becomes a luminous and very practical book. Every story in it has a direct relationship to your daily life and teaches marvelous lessons. In my own experience, I could not understand the mighty truths declared in the New Testament until I saw them demonstrated in the Old Testament. As these stories come to life for us and we see how they apply to our own experiences, then the New Testament truths that are so familiar to our ears become vibrant, brand-new experiences. Suddenly the world of spiritual truth becomes a world of excitement and adventure!

The second message of Moses covers chapters 5 through 26. This begins with a fresh recital of the Ten Commandments as God gave them to Moses on Mount Sinai. Deuteronomy means "the second [giving of] law." This has more significance than merely being the historical account of the Law's recital for a second time, as we shall see before we finish the book. Deuteronomy is not simply a recital of the journeys of Israel but a divine commentary on the importance of those journeys.

Moses reminded the people that they had promised to hear and to do all that God said. To this God had responded, "Oh, that their hearts would be inclined to fear me and keep all my commands always, so that it might go well with them and their children forever!" (Deut. 5:29). Moses then proceeded to give them the famous Shema, or "Hear, O Israel," which devout Jews still recite to summarize the central feature of their faith—the uniqueness of their God. He admonished them to observe these words and to teach them diligently to their children at every opportunity. This is a great lesson on child rearing: to make the most of teachable moments, using at-hand situations to reinforce family values and beliefs.

Provision

The second sermon: A review of the Law of God

The Shema

Moses then began to review the conditions that they would find in the land and the blessings that would await them there. He especially warned them to beware of three perils: the peril of prosperity, the peril of adversity, and the peril of neglecting to teach their children.

In chapter 7, Moses dealt with the danger that Israel would face in confronting the corrupt nations already in the land. Moses commanded the Israelites to show no mercy to the inhabitants of Canaan but to thoroughly eliminate them so that no vestige of their idolatries and depraved worship should remain to turn the Israelites aside from their worship of Jehovah. Moses reminded the Israelites that they were chosen because the Lord had set His love upon them and that He would be their strength in subjugating nearby nations. Their own prosperity and good health would depend on the faithfulness by which they carried out these instructions.

The danger of corruption

Chapter 8 reminded the people of lessons that God had taught them in the wilderness; how they had been humbled and fed with the manna, so that they might know that "man does not live on bread alone but on every word that comes from the mouth of the LORD" (8:3). These were familiar words to Jesus, who used them to good effect against the tempter in the Judean wilderness centuries later (see Matt. 4:4).

Warning against self-sufficiency

When the people had entered the land and were feasting upon its richness, they were to beware lest they begin to feel self-sufficient and to take credit for all that God had given them. They should not think that their own righteousness caused God to bring them in but remember their persistent stubbornness and their history of continually provoking the Lord to wrath.

Moses then recalled the awesome scene at Sinai, when, in the very face of the demonstration of God's power and might, the people sinned by making the golden calf—this, while Moses was interceding for them for forty days and nights. At that time Moses also received the second tablets of stone and later placed them in the ark of the covenant where they remained.

Love and obedience

In a passage of great beauty and power, Moses reminded the people that God was not asking of them anything but to love Him and to serve Him wholeheartedly, keeping His commandments and statutes for their own benefit. The central emphasis was that "the LORD your God is God of gods and Lord of lords, the great God, mighty and awesome" (Deut. 10:17). Yet His actions toward them were of infinite tenderness and love. As they entered the land, therefore, they were promised rain from heaven to water the earth, grass in the fields for their cattle, and power in their warfare to drive out great nations because the whole land was to become their possession. To remind them of God's love and God's discipline, they were instructed

Promise of provision

to annually recite the blessings on Mount Gerizim and the cursings on Mount Ebal, which faced the site of Jacob's well.

Chapters 12 through 21 constitute a series of statutes and ordinances that were given to the people for their government within the land. They were charged with destroying all the places of worship of the nations then in the land, tearing down their altars and burning their Asherim (phallic symbols). These were clear indications of the foulness of the worship in the land at the time.

God would then indicate, in due season, one place within the land where they were to bring their burnt offerings and sacrifices and there they were to rejoice before the Lord. This was not fulfilled until the days of David and Solomon when the temple was built, though a temporary provision was made when the ark was located at Shiloh.

Further instructions were given regarding the foods they could eat, always avoiding the blood. They were then told how to tell false prophets from true. Even though the false prophet may be a wonderworker, if he should suggest that they go after other gods, the people were to stone him. Even if close friends or relatives should seek to entice them to idolatry, they likewise were to be put to death. Even if a whole city should apostatize and begin to serve other gods, the inhabitants of that city were to be put to the sword, for "you are the children of the LORD your God" (Deut. 14:1).

The dietary laws were restated, as was the tithing that was required for the support of the Levites. The sabbatical years were reiterated as the solution to inequities in economic life and periodic readjustment of the means of wealth. The great feasts of Passover, Unleavened Bread, and Tabernacles were once again required.

Provision was then made for the functioning of judges to decide cases where the law had not specifically spoken, also for the choosing of a king, who could not be a foreigner nor multiply horses nor silver and gold but must carefully walk by the statutes of the Law and keep his heart humble before the Lord his God.

In chapter 18, the great promise was given that "the LORD your God will raise up for you a prophet like me from among your own brothers. You must listen to him" (18:15). In some measure this great prophecy was fulfilled by all the true prophets who would rise later in Israel, but in its ultimate fulfillment the promise looks forward to the coming of Jesus and His Moses-like actions of beholding the face of God and uttering His word to all the people. Jesus perfectly fulfills the Old Testament ideal of priest, prophet, and king.

Again, three cities of refuge were chosen, this time on the west side of the Jordan. Those who were guilty of deliberate murder could find

Offerings and sacrifices

Food

False prophets

Feasts

Judges and kings

A Prophet

Cities of refuge

no sanctuary in these cities, but those who killed accidentally were to flee to them to escape the avenger of blood. Ancient landmarks could not be removed, and truth between one person and another had to be maintained at all costs.

We must remember that the Israelites were being sent into the land not only to gain it for their own possession, but also to act as the instrument of God in exterminating a foul and corrupt people. In view of the warfare this involved, they were charged to keep before them the vision of their God and His power and to eliminate from their armies any whose hearts were occupied with other matters or who were faint-hearted and fearful. Terms of peace were to be offered to every city they attacked, and if they were accepted, the inhabitants were not killed but were put to forced labor. If the terms of peace were refused, the city was to be decimated.

In chapters 22 through 26, we find the various regulations for the life of the people within the land. These rules governed such matters as lost or stolen property, gender identity and transvestism, sexual purity and sanitation, usury, vows, and divorce. Provision was then made for the punishment of theft, but cruel and unusual punishment was strictly forbidden. It was likewise forbidden to muzzle an ox as it tread out the corn—a command that was given spiritual significance by the apostle Paul in 1 Corinthians 9:8–10. The law of the kinsman-redeemer for those left without an heir was again enunciated, and all weights and measures were ordered to be honestly observed.

The second message concluded with Moses' instructions about the way the people were to worship in the new land. They were to bring the firstfruits and offer them to God, with acknowledgments of His provision and grace, and this was to be followed with gifts given to Levites, to strangers, to the fatherless, and to widows. At the conclusion of this second message, Moses gave detailed instructions regarding the impressive ceremony that was to be carried out upon the twin mountains of Gerizim and Ebal. The Ten Commandments were to be given permanent display by being written upon plaster-covered stone monuments, and each year the sons of Rachel and Leah were to recite the blessings upon Mount Gerizim, and the sons of Jacob's concubines were to recite the curses upon Mount Ebal. The curses are detailed in chapter 27 and the blessings summarized in the opening words of chapter 28.

The third sermon: A review of the covenant of God

The third message of Moses, chapters 27 through 31, is a great revelation of Israel's future both in terms of potential blessing and potential cursing. Chapter 28 is one of the most amazing prophecies ever recorded. It is as complete and remarkable in its detail as any other prophecy in all of Scripture because it predicts the entire history of the Jewish peo-

Warfare

Rules and regulations

Worship

ple, even to the time when they ceased to be a nation and were scattered over the face of the earth.

First was the prediction of the Babylonian dispersion, subsequent to the unbelief and disobedience of the people. This occurred eventually under Nebuchadnezzar. Then followed a prediction of their ultimate return to the land and that after several centuries they would again fall into the terrible sin of rejecting the great Prophet whom God would send. A strange nation would come in from the west (the Romans) who would be a hard and cruel people. They would burn the cities of Israel, destroy the inhabitants, and once again disperse them to the ends of the earth.

Israel would then wander for many centuries as a people without a land, but God would at last gather them again for a final restoration. Upon concluding his great prophecy, Moses reminded the people that they stood before the Lord their God, and though they did not completely understand divine government, the things that had been revealed to them about the past were given so that they could walk faithfully before their God in the future. In graphic and vivid terms, he described to them what would result if they turned from the living God to the gods of other nations.

In his closing word, Moses seemed to look far into the future to see the people dispersed in lands of captivity. He reminded them that if they would wholeheartedly return to the Lord, God would forgive their sin, restore their fortunes, and gather them again into the land.

Then Moses uttered the great words that the apostle Paul quoted centuries later in his epistle to the Romans and that reveal the reason why Deuteronomy is called "the second law." Moses said to the people, "What I am I commanding you today is not too difficult for you or beyond your reach" (Deut. 30:11). This speaks of the divine provision by which the demands of the Law might be fully met. "It is not," Moses continued, "up in heaven, so that you have to ask, 'Who will ascend into heaven to get it' . . . beyond the sea, so that you have to ask, 'Who will cross the sea to get it and proclaim it to us so we may obey it?' " (see Deut. 30:12–13); instead, as Moses put it very plainly, "The word is very near you; it is in your mouth and in your heart so you may obey it" (see Deut. 30:14).

In Romans 10:5 Paul wrote that "Moses describes in this way the righteousness that is by the law: 'The man who does these things will live by them.' " Here he quoted the words of Moses concerning the Law given at Sinai and taken from the book of Exodus. Then, in Romans 10:6–9, Paul quoted this very passage from Deuteronomy 30, indicating that it refers to Christ: "The righteousness that is by faith says: 'Do not say in your heart, "Who will ascend into heaven?" ' (that is, to bring

Christ down) 'or "Who will descend into the deep?" ' (that is, to bring Christ up from the dead). But what does it say? 'The word is near you; it is in your mouth and in your heart,' that is, the word of faith we are proclaiming: That if you confess with your mouth, 'Jesus is Lord,' and believe in your heart that God raised him from the dead, you will be saved" (Rom. 10:6–9).

In this quotation from Deuteronomy 30, Paul declared that it is not necessary to bring Christ down from heaven (the Incarnation) or to bring Him up again from the dead (the Resurrection), for this has already been done. It is only necessary that the heart believe and the lips confess that Jesus is Lord and risen from the dead. Thus the second law, which Paul calls "the law of the Spirit of life [in Christ Jesus]," fulfills, by another principle, the righteousness that the Law demands. It is possible, because of this emphasis in Deuteronomy, that the book became Jesus' favorite.

Moses clearly taught these principles to the people of Israel. He constantly reiterated the just demands of God that are expressed in the Ten Commandments. That is the first Law. But, equally, he reminded them again and again of the gracious provision through the sacrifices and offerings by which the life of a living Lord could be their personal possession, enabling them to live at the level that God requires. By keeping God's Word in their mouths and in their hearts, they would be able to do all that God demanded.

As a consequence, Moses concluded his great address by saying, "See, I set before you today life and prosperity, death and destruction" (Deut. 30:15). And with earnest words he pleads with them to choose life "so that you and your children may live and that you may love the LORD your God, listen to his voice, and hold fast to him. For the LORD is your life, and he will give you many years in the land" (Deut. 30:19–20).

Passing the baton

Finally, Moses summoned Joshua, charging him to be strong and courageous. Then God told Moses that the time had come for him to sleep with his fathers and that, in spite of his faithful warnings, the people whom he had led would not fulfill all his solemn predictions, and God would have to discipline the people as He had promised.

Moses was then commanded to write a song that would remain in the memory of the people long after Moses himself had departed. The song deals with the great themes of God's everlasting covenant with Israel, His mercies to them, their failures, the penalties of their disobedience, and the promise of final deliverance. Then Moses offered the people his last benediction, reminding them that "the eternal God is your refuge, and underneath are the everlasting arms" (Deut. 33:27).

The final chapter is undoubtedly added by another hand, perhaps the hand of Joshua, for it recounts how Moses ascended Mount Nebo, and there, with his eyes not dim, with his natural force undiminished, Moses stretched out on the ground and died. The Lord Himself buried Moses in an unknown place in the valley of Moab, and we do not see Moses again in Scripture until we find him on the Mount of Transfiguration along with Elijah the prophet and Jesus the Messiah, talking together about the crucifixion that awaited Jesus at Jerusalem (see Matt. 17:1–13; Mark 9:2–13).

Though the people immediately rallied around Joshua and gave to him the obedience they had shown to Moses, they knew that they would never see anyone like Moses again—a man who spoke to God face-to-face, a man whose deeds were great, terrible, and often miraculous. It was not until the Messiah Himself appeared in the New Testament that Moses' achievements and wonders would be surpassed.

Part Three

The Message of History

The Message of History

Our adventure through the Bible now brings us to the historical books of the Old Testament, Joshua through Esther. We have seen that the great purpose of God's Word and of the Holy Spirit in whose power we understand it is to bring us to maturity in Jesus Christ and to truly reflect His image and His character. God seeks to bring us to maturity in Jesus Christ so that we are no longer children tossed to and fro by every wind of doctrine. He wants us to be able to walk straight and confidently down the path of truth with our heads held high as steadfast followers of God. Through His Word, we are able to discover where we have come from, where we are going, and why we are here.

Each division of the Old Testament makes a unique contribution to our maturity as believers. The Pentateuch lays the foundation for our faith and maturity, telling us who we are: God's image-bearers but fallen, broken by sin, and in need of a Savior. We have explored the foundational truths of the Pentateuch: human helplessness and need, God's answer to that need through His provision of a pattern of worship, the example of Israel's failure and wandering in the wilderness, the encouragement of God's gracious and undeserved provision for Israel, and the second giving of the Law in Deuteronomy that restores and prepares believers to enter the Land of Promise, the place of victory.

The Pentateuch gives us the pattern of God's working; the historical books give us the perils that confront us when we try to walk in faith

Now we are ready to dig into the rich history presented to us in the books of Joshua, Judges, Ruth, 1 and 2 Samuel, 1 and 2 Kings, 1 and 2 Chronicles, Ezra, Nehemiah, and Esther. We will see how these books contribute to the preparatory work of the Old Testament. If the Pentateuch gives us the pattern of God's working, then the historical books give us the perils that confront us when we try to walk in the life of faith. After all, this is what history is for: to serve as a warning to subsequent generations. "Those who do not learn from history," the saying goes, "are doomed to repeat it." The history of Israel includes much that we would be wise *not* to repeat!

Some say that history is "His story," meaning Christ's story. But that is true only in a secondary sense. Christ is in history; however, He is behind the scenes. That is why I love those words of James Russell Lowell:

> *Truth forever on the scaffold,*
> *Wrong forever on the throne,*
> *But God is standing in the shadows,*
> *Keeping watch above His own.*

That is the relationship of God to history. He is behind the scenes.

History is primarily the story of humanity's cycle of failure, the rise and fall of one empire after another, one civilization after another. Great historians, such as Arnold Toynbee, remind us that human history is one cycle of failure after another.

In these historical books of the Bible, we find all of the same lessons that secular history teaches, but they are more condensed, more personal—and we have the added bonus of God's perspective to help us understand them. These books trace the history of one nation, a peculiar nation, a nation with a special ministry. In a symbolic way, these books picture for us the perils, pressures, and problems that confront every Christian believer.

Know your enemies

Every Christian is engaged in warfare. One of the first rules of warfare is: *Know your enemies.* Know who they are. Know where they are coming from. Know their style of attack. Know how they are armed. Know how they are defended. This is true in human warfare, and it is true in spiritual warfare.

No one would be foolish enough to send a submarine against an army entrenched in the mountains. Likewise, Christians cannot rely on randomly chosen spiritual weapons or tactics against the powers of darkness.

We *must* know our enemies. These historical books illuminate our enemies. They show us the perils that beset the life of faith, and they show us how to gain the victory over these perils!

The first of the historical books is Joshua. It begins with a story of victory—Israel's entry into the Land of Promise, the place where God had wanted them to go when He brought them out of Egypt. The Christian life is not only a matter of being called out of a wilderness, it is also a matter of entering into an inheritance, the Land of Promise.

The problem is that many of us are quite content to be brought out of Egypt—the world and its ways of bondage—but we never quite get around to entering into the Promised Land. We have faith enough to leave Egypt, but somewhere during our journey through the wilderness, we falter. We fail to lay hold of the faith that takes us over the Jordan and into the Land of Promise. But in the book of Joshua, we see God's pattern for victory. We see Israel entering into the land. We see Israel's errors and its triumphs. This book traces for us the experience of conquest.

What was the first enemy facing the Israelites as they came across the Jordan River? The imposing city of Jericho, with its tremendous walls—a super fortress of a city. It might have been the first city that this generation of desert nomads had ever encountered. As they looked at it, they saw their own feebleness and the uselessness of their weapons. *How can we prevail over a walled city like this?* they wondered.

Have you ever felt like that? Has anything in your life seemed to you to be an insuperable obstacle? An opponent who always mocked you and baffled you and defeated you? A fortress of arrogant invincibility you feel powerless to overcome? Well, that is your Jericho. The story of the siege of Jericho is symbolic of the world in its assault on the Christian and of Jesus Christ's enabling victory over the world.

The Jericho story is followed immediately by the story of Ai, an insignificant little town, a wide spot in the road that should have been an easy victory for Joshua and his army. Yet Ai handily defeated Israel, sending Joshua's army running. Why? Because sin was in the Israelite camp, and that sin was Israel's Achilles' heel. Until the sin was dealt with, Israel could not defeat Ai.

The story of Ai is symbolic of fleshly sin—its subtlety, its seeming insignificance. We think we can control our tempers and our lusts and our evil thoughts if we simply decide to. But we discover it isn't that easy—and failure to conquer the lusts of the flesh can produce tragic, disastrous defeat.

If you cannot find the perils of your life in the book of Joshua, something is seriously wrong. They are all there. But the theme of the book is set forth for us in chapter 13, verse 1: "When Joshua was old and well advanced in years, the LORD said to him, 'You are very old, and there are still very large areas of land to be taken over.' " The peril that Joshua faced is one we all face from time to time: *the temptation to stop short of complete victory.*

Christ's indwelling empowers *any* believer to experience victory over Satan, and when we experience that victory, it is a glorious and marvelous experience. But somewhere along the line, too many of us back off, settle down, and stop short. We say, "Why go on any further? I know that I have not yet conquered all aspects of sinfulness in the name of Christ, but I have conquered so much. Lord, let me just rest awhile. No more challenges, no more battles, just for a while." Have you experienced this? It is always the first attack of the enemy in times of victory and conquest.

But Jesus said, "Blessed are those who hunger and thirst for righteousness, for they will be filled" (Matt. 5:6). This hunger and thirst must mark our lives. We are never to get over it. Until the war is over and God calls us to a place of rest in the long-awaited Land of Promise, we are on the march, we are on a war footing. We must see the battle through to its conclusion or the battle will be lost.

At the close of the book, Joshua urged the people not to slack off, for they still had a great deal of land yet to possess. He warned them of an attitude of compromise and exhorted them to "choose for yourselves this day whom you will serve. . . . But as for me and my household, we will serve the LORD" (Josh. 24:15). There was never a letdown in Joshua's life, never a willingness to stop the march. He was on the march until the day he died.

In each of the historical books of the Old Testament, we find a unique peril such as the peril Joshua faced, the peril of stopping short before the mission was completed. But in each of these historical books we also find at least one person who gained the victory over that peril, one human being who serves as an example and an encouragement to us. In the book of Joshua, that example is Joshua himself.

Judges and Ruth

Next we come to the books of Judges and Ruth. We will take them together, because the events of Ruth are contemporary with the last part of Judges. While the book of Joshua covers a period of only twenty-five years, Judges covers a period of about three hundred years. The book of Judges is the story of a continually repeated historical cycle: decline, discipline, and then deliverance. Over and over again, God sent judges to the people of Israel to deliver them from recurring bouts with persecution and bondage.

Judges begins with the story of Othniel, the first judge sent to Israel by God. It ends with the familiar story of Samson, the last judge.

There was never a letdown in Joshua's life

The peril of stopping short

Altogether, God used seven judges to deliver the people. In each case, just as God's judge put His people back on their feet, they began to fall again!

Why did the people repeatedly fail? What is the spiritual peril warned about in the book of Judges? We find it stated in Judges 2:11–13:

> The Israelites did evil in the eyes of the LORD and served the Baals. They forsook the LORD, the God of their fathers, who had brought them out of Egypt. They followed and worshiped various gods of the peoples around them. They provoked the LORD to anger because they forsook him and served Baal and the Ashtoreths.

Idolatry! Why? How did they get into this mess so quickly after the tremendous victories of Joshua? How do people suddenly fall from the height of a victorious experience into moral degradation? You find the key to the book in the very last verse, which is also the key to victory or failure in our own lives:

> In those days Israel had no king; everyone did as he saw fit (Judges 21:25).

The peril of well-intentioned blundering

Judges warns us against what we might call *the peril of well-intentioned blundering*. It wasn't that these people did not want to do right. They were simply deluded. Judges doesn't say they did wrong; it says they did what was right *in their own eyes*. But their eyes didn't see clearly. They didn't truly know what was right. This is the terrible peril of dedicated ignorance.

This peril still cripples God's people. Many Christians are weak and defeated because they are suffering from dedicated ignorance. Their dedication is intact. They mean well. I have listened to people, young and old, who recount terrible stories of agony and despair. They say, "I don't know what happened. I started out intending to do right. I thought I was. But something went terribly wrong." They didn't expose themselves to God's truth but went about doing what was right in their own eyes. Inevitably, the result of doing what is right in our own eyes, whether in Old Testament times or in our own day, is a repetitious cycle of failure.

The last chapters of Judges tell of one of the darkest, most terrible times of sexual depravity in Israel's history. Yet it is during this same time frame that the events of the book of Ruth take place—a shining and wonderful little story of faith and faithfulness in the midst of defeat. It is the story of a heathen woman named Ruth who hears the voice of God and leaves friends, home, and family to be with her beloved, believing mother-in-law, Naomi.

This story also features the added attraction of a beautiful romance story in which this young widow, Ruth, meets a rich bachelor with whom she finds true, married love. It is important to note as well that by marrying this young man, Boaz, she joins herself to the line of Christ and becomes one of the historic links God uses to bring His Son, the Messiah, into the world. Ruth is listed in the genealogy of Christ in the book of Matthew:

> Salmon the father of Boaz, whose mother was Rahab,
> Boaz the father of Obed, whose mother was Ruth . . . (Matt. 1:5).

The story of Ruth not only tugs at the heartstrings, but is an integral component of the larger story of Jesus Christ and God's plan of human redemption. It is not only one of the Bible's most delightful stories, but it is also historically and spiritually profound.

1 Samuel

First Samuel is largely the story of two men: Samuel and Saul. In the latter part of the book the early history of David is woven into the story of King Saul. Samuel was the greatest judge Israel ever had. His ministry lasted some forty years. During this time the people were still hungering after something other than God. The great peril of faith set forth in this book is given to us in chapter 8, verse 5. One day the people of Israel came to Samuel and said:

> "You are old, and your sons do not walk in your ways; now appoint a king to lead us, such as all the other nations have."

The peril of legalistic conformity

Now, the problem is that God had called Israel to be unlike all other nations, yet the people of Israel were demanding to be just like all the other nations—ruled by an authority other than God! Here we find *the peril of legalistic conformity,* the desire for outward rule over their lives. Instead of taking responsibility for their own lives and choices, legalists hand over their God-given freedom and liberty to external authorities and rules.

I am continually amazed at how many people don't really want the freedom that God gives us in Christ. They come to me and say, "Don't tell me I have to practice wisdom and discernment in the Christian life. It's too hard to evaluate circumstances and make choices. Just give me a rule. That's what I want. If I just had a rule, then I could satisfy God and I wouldn't have to worry about exercising judgment and making decisions." That is the story of Israel during Samuel's time.

So God allowed the people to choose a king who would make their decisions for them, and the people chose Saul. The story of Saul is one of the great tragedies of the Bible. He was a man of great promise, a handsome man with great abilities. But the lesson of this man's life is *the peril of seeking human favor.*

The defeat of Saul came about as a result of his expedition against the Amalekites. God told him to kill all the Amalekites, but he refused and saved King Agag. Why did he do it? Because he felt this would find him favor in the eyes of the people! So the awful tragedy of Saul's life was the peril of a divided allegiance. He was quite content to serve God as long as it pleased those around him. The secret failure in this man's life was his continual hungering for the affection and honor and favor of other people.

Have you ever discovered this in your life? It is a peril that will ultimately defeat you and bring the same tragic end that Saul finally came to: his kingdom was removed from him, his crown was snatched from his head, and he lost everything except his relationship with God. But in the midst of this grim story, the light of God broke through in the story of Saul's son Jonathan, and David—that marvelous story of the greatest friendship in history.

Then comes 2 Samuel, which links chronologically with the next book, 1 Chronicles, though they are written from quite different viewpoints. These two books center on the story of one man: David, the king after God's own heart.

Whatever David's flaws, we may correctly view him as a symbolic picture of the Lord Jesus Christ, for Jesus Himself used this analogy. David was not only the forerunner and ancestor of Jesus according to the flesh, but in his reign he is a picture of the reign of Christ during the millennium. David experienced a long period of rejection, persecution, and harassment, but during that time of exile he gathered men around him who later became his commanders and officers. Thus, David signifies Christ in His rejection—forsaken by the world but gathering in secret those who will be His commanders and leaders when He comes to reign in power and glory over the earth.

David is also a symbol of each believer. The story of David portrays what happens in a Christian's life as he or she follows God into the place of dominion. Every Christian is offered a kingdom, just as David was offered a kingdom. That kingdom is the believer's own life and it is exactly like the kingdom of Israel. Enemies threaten it from the outside and enemies threaten it from within, just as there were enemy nations beyond and within the boundaries of Israel. The enemies from without represent the direct attacks of the devil upon us. The enemies within

The peril of seeking human favor

2 Samuel and 1 Chronicles

represent those internal enemies of the flesh that threaten to overthrow God's influence in our lives. While David contended with the Ammonites, Jebusites, Perrizites, and other Old Testament enemies, we contend with jealousy, envy, lust, bitterness, resentment, worry, anxiety, and the like. In many ways, these two different forms of enemies operate and attack in the very same ways.

David's story is the most wonderful story in the entire Old Testament, yet there is also an ugly side to the story of David. He became an adulterer and a murderer. It is almost incomprehensible to think of David, God's own man, as having committed these terrible acts. How did his sin start? We find a clue in 2 Samuel 11:1, which tells us:

> *In the spring, at the time when kings go off to war, David sent Joab out with the king's men and the whole Israelite army. . . . But David remained in Jerusalem.*

The peril of a forgotten calling

What was David's peril? I call it *the peril of a forgotten calling*. The result was that he indulged in the lusts of the flesh. David was the king of Israel and Judah. It was his business to be at the head of the army. That is where he belonged. But he forgot his calling. He was staying home and resting while others went into battle. While he was home enjoying himself, he went onto his rooftop and, looking over into his neighbor's yard, saw a beautiful woman taking a bath. The sight did to him what such a sight does to any normal male: He was filled with lust. He indulged his passion and took her, and then, to cover up his sin, he murdered her husband.

The gleam of grace in this story is David's repentance. That is why, despite David's fall, he still can be called a man after God's own heart. The moment he was confronted with his sin, he admitted it and repented, and he accepted God's grace. David offers a wonderful picture of a contrite heart, down on his face before God, crying out his sorrow and repentance over his sin. Out of this experience came Psalm 52, the psalm of a truly repentant heart.

2 Chronicles, 1 Kings, and 2 Kings

We may link 2 Chronicles with 1 and 2 Kings because they cover the same general historical period. These books focus on the stories of two men, Solomon and Jeroboam. Solomon, of course, was the king of Israel who was so renowned for his wisdom and who wrote some of the most beautiful wisdom books of the Old Testament. Jeroboam was the rival to Solomon's son Rehoboam; Jeroboam became king of the northern kingdom, Israel. These books relate the division of the kingdom between Judah and Israel.

The story of Solomon is fascinating—he stepped into his inheritance, being crowned king of Israel even before his father David's death! He came into the kingdom at the height of its glory, and God gave him riches and power. At the beginning of his reign, while still a young man, Solomon chose a heart of wisdom rather than wealth. Along with his wisdom, God gave him power, magnificence, and riches in abundance. But Solomon's misappropriation of these was the seed of his downfall.

In 1 Kings 3:1–3, you find the beginning of the story of the peril that brought him to failure and defeat:

Solomon made an alliance with Pharaoh king of Egypt and married his daughter. He brought her to the City of David until he finished building his palace and the temple of the Lord, and the wall around Jerusalem. The people, however, were still sacrificing at the high places [pagan religious sites], because a temple had not yet been built for the name of the Lord. Solomon showed his love for the Lord by walking according to the statutes of his father David, except that he offered sacrifices and burned incense on the high places.

And as we trace the account, we find that Solomon was seven years in building the temple. But then in 1 Kings 7:1 we read, "It took Solomon thirteen years, however, to complete the construction of his palace." Doesn't that strike you as strange? Seven years building the temple, but thirteen years lavishing magnificence upon his own house! You can see the beginning of the self-centered life and the peril of a love of things. The downfall of Solomon was *the peril of material magnificence,* a heart wooed away from the Lord by a love of things.

The rest of the book is the story of Jeroboam, the rebellion he fomented, and the beginning of the kingdom of Israel. The peril set forth in Jeroboam's life is *the peril of a substitute faith—religious deceit.* In 1 Kings 12:26–28, we read:

Jeroboam thought to himself, "The kingdom will now likely revert to the house of David. If these people go up to offer sacrifices at the temple of the LORD in Jerusalem, they will again give their allegiance to their lord, Rehoboam king of Judah. They will kill me and return to King Rehoboam."

After seeking advice, the king made two golden calves. He said to the people, "It is too much for you to go up to Jerusalem. Here are your gods, O Israel, who brought you up out of Egypt."

I once spoke on the Incarnation, the Virgin Birth, and the glory of the babe in Bethlehem who was God Himself, manifest in the flesh. At the close of the meeting, a woman charged up to the podium and said to me, "Did I understand you to say that the baby of Bethlehem was God?"

"Exactly so," I replied.

"Oh," she said, "I can't believe anything like that! God is everywhere. God is vast and infinite. He fills the universe. How could He be a baby in Bethlehem?"

"That's the glory of the mystery, that God was manifest in the flesh," I said. "You know, there was a time when one of His own disciples took the Lord Jesus by the feet and said to Him, 'My Lord and my God.' Now, do you know more about Him than His disciples did?"

She said, "I was raised in a faith which taught that God is in all the universe, and I simply can't accept this idea."

"What you were taught," I said, "is not what the Bible very clearly teaches. You have been taught a false faith."

Not wanting to hear any more, she turned on her heels and walked away.

This is the peril that deludes and destroys the faith of so many people today. There are many sects, cults, and "isms" that claim to be "Christian," but they teach a substitute faith, a "faith" that opposes the clear teaching of the Bible. That is the kind of deadly, deceitful faith that Jeroboam brought into the nation of Israel. Yet, even in the midst of the spiritual darkness of those days, God's grace came shining forth in the form of a holy and untainted man: Elijah the prophet.

In 2 Kings and the latter part of 2 Chronicles (which are also chronologically linked), we have one rapid-fire story after another chronicling the downfall of one king after another. Many of these kings are murdered by power-hungry rivals. The story of this period in Israel's history (that is, the ten tribes that constituted the northern kingdom) is a story of moral abandonment and abdication.

The irony and the peril of this period in Israel's history is the same dangerous irony and peril we face at the end of the twentieth century: In the mad pursuit of so-called freedom—that is, the total rejection of all standards and restraints—we are actually in danger of sinking into bondage! We often hear words such as, "Oh, I am tired of Christians with all their restrictions and moral rules! I just want to do what I want and go where I please and say what I like and enjoy myself. Then I will be happy." Well, we read the result of such "freedom" in 2 Kings 17:16–17:

The peril of sinking into bondage

They forsook all the commands of the LORD their God and made for themselves two idols cast in the shape of calves, and an Asherah [an idol] *pole. They bowed down to all the starry hosts, and they worshiped Baal. They sacrificed their sons and daughters in the fire. They practiced divination and sorcery and sold themselves to do evil in the eyes of the LORD, provoking him to anger.*

Paul addresses the same condition in Romans 1: People who knew God refused to acknowledge Him or to give thanks. So God gave them up to the most dissolute, depraved, immoral practices. Some in our own society would throw off every restraint of godliness and goodness, and the result in our society would be the same as what took place in ancient Israel: captivity, depravity, and bondage.

The books of Ezra, Nehemiah, and Esther tell the story of the nation in captivity—morally deteriorated, socially disintegrated, economically bereft, completely carried away into bondage. But even in Israel's time of disgrace and captivity, God began to work. After the seventy years of Israel's exile, the prophet Ezra was raised up to lead a group back into the desolate land of Palestine to begin rebuilding the temple.

Ezra, Nehemiah, and Esther

The book of Ezra is the story of a discouraged people who were reluctant to leave captivity. Just as their ancestors looked back longingly to their Egyptian captivity, these Israelites were largely content to remain as captives in Babylon. Only a handful could be persuaded to go back to their homeland. The rest were so blinded that they chose to drift off and lose themselves among the nations of the world. We call them "the ten lost tribes of Israel." No one knows where they are or who they are. They are completely lost. But those who were willing to go back found all the promises of God waiting for them there.

The peril depicted in these three books is *the peril of a discouraged heart.* Sometimes we get into this frame of mind, don't we? We say, "What's the use? I might as well throw it all in and just stay where I am. I know I'm not victorious. I know I'm getting nowhere. I might just as well quit." But the story of Ezra, Nehemiah, and Esther is the story of the triumph of faith in the midst of perils and discouraging circumstances.

The peril of a discouraged heart

In Ezra, a faithful remnant choose to return and build the second temple. In Nehemiah, the people persevere against determined opposition and rebuild the shattered walls of the city. In Esther, we see that God brings about victory in the midst of impossible circumstances. All three books demonstrate that faith is triumphant, even when circumstances seem to predict disaster and defeat.

As you have been reading through this brief survey of the historical books of the Old Testament, you may have recognized in your own life some of the perils illustrated in them. Are you struggling against any of these forces? Then I suggest that you mark the peril you are particularly up against, open the book that deals with that peril, go to your knees, then read it and pray it through with God. Ask Him to speak to you and show you the way of deliverance in the midst of defeat.

That is the purpose of these historical books—to illuminate the pressures and perils that face us in the Christian life so that we can find God's strength and see His leading as He guides us through the maze of darkness and danger, bringing us to a place of safety and rest. May the message of history, contained in these twelve precious books, be a message of help and blessing in your life as we explore them together.

Guidebook to Victory

A be Lincoln was an unknown Illinois prairie lawyer when someone asked him if he had political ambitions. "I will prepare
myself and be ready," the future president replied. "Perhaps my chance
will come." The book of Joshua is the story of another leader who prepared himself and who was ready when his chance came: Joshua, the
son of Nun, the disciple of Moses.

Joshua is one of the two books of the Old Testament that every
Christian should master (the other is Daniel). The messages of both
Joshua and Daniel are primarily designed to help Christians withstand
the first full impact of the battle of the world, the flesh, and the devil.
If you struggle with the deceptiveness and the opposing spiritual forces
of this age, if you want to see a historical demonstration of the spiritual warfare we all face, then these books will be especially important
to you.

Joshua is also an especially important book for those who would
be leaders in the world or in the church. The world urgently needs
righteous, courageous, Christian leaders who can stand up to the pressures and hostility of this world. The leadership model of Joshua is
powerfully relevant and applicable to the world we live in now, at the
threshold of the twenty-first century.

The book of Joshua is packed with practical lessons—challenging concepts to help us grasp the principles of a Spirit-led life. The
key to the book is given to us in the New Testament: "These things

> Joshua is one of the
> two books of the
> Old Testament that
> every Christian
> should master (the
> other is Daniel)

. . . were written down as warnings for us, on whom the fulfillment of the ages has come" (1 Cor. 10:11). The events of Joshua are patterns or metaphors that we can apply to the spiritual battles in our lives today.

The history recorded in the book of Joshua divides into three parts plus a conclusion:

The Entrance into Canaan (Joshua 1–4)
1.	The commissioning of Joshua	1
2.	The spying out of Jericho	2
3.	The crossing of the Jordan	3
4.	The erection of memorials	4

The Conquest of Canaan (Joshua 5–12)
5.	The consecration of the people	5
6.	The central campaign	6–8
7.	The southern campaign	9–10
8.	The northern campaign	11:1–15
9.	The review of the victories	11:16–12:24

The Division of Canaan (Joshua 13–21)
10.	The portion of the two-and-a-half tribes	13
11.	The portion of Caleb	14
12.	The portion of the nine-and-a-half tribes	15:1–19:48
13.	The portion of Joshua; cities of refuge; the Levites	19:49–21:45

Conclusion (Joshua 22–24)
14.	The border dispute	22
15.	The final days of Joshua	23–24

Chapters 1 through 4 concern entering the Promised Land and all that involves. If you are struggling right now with how to enter into a life of victory with Christ, how to move out of the wilderness of doubt, how to settle your restless wanderings and move into the full blessing of the Spirit-led experience, then this section will be especially valuable to you.

Chapters 5 through 12 deal with Israel's conquest of the Promised Land through a series of battles and conflicts as they entered it. Chapters 13 through 21 deal with the division of the land. Chapters 22 through 24, which include many passages from Joshua's own lips, set before us the perils and dangers of the land that we must guard against in order to maintain our position of victory.

Beginning with chapter 1, we see a descriptive picture of the Spirit-filled life and a strong implication that this is a life God intends *every* Christian to live, not just a few "supersaints." In Joshua 1:2, God says to Joshua, "Moses my servant is dead. Now then, you and all these people, get ready to cross the Jordan River into the land I am about to give to them."

This man Joshua has a special significance. His name means "God is salvation," and it's important to note that the names Joshua and Jesus are simply two forms of the original Hebrew name *Yeshua*. To their contemporaries, both Joshua and Jesus were known as *Yeshua*, "God is salvation." This fact underscores a truth we shall later see, that Joshua is in many ways a symbolic forerunner of the victorious Messiah, Jesus the Lord.

The land is given to the people of Israel, just as the life in Christ is made available to us as Christians without any effort on our part. But though the land has been given, it still needs to be possessed. Title to the land is the gift of God; possession of the land is the result of an obedient walk:

"I will give you every place where you set your foot, as I promised Moses" (1:3).

You can have all you that are willing to take. You can have every bit of spiritual life in Christ that you want. God will never give you more than you are ready to take. If you are not satisfied with the degree of your real experience of victory, it is because you haven't really wanted any more.

The land is described as abundant and far-reaching, a land in which you will find all you need in every area of life—"a land flowing with milk and honey," as it was described in Exodus 3:8. The extent of the land is as long and wide as the imagination: "Your territory will extend from the desert to Lebanon, and from the great river, the Euphrates—all the Hittite country—to the Great Sea on the west" (Josh. 1:4).

But possessing the land would not be easy. The way to victory was through the battlefield of spiritual warfare. But the end of that war was never in doubt: "No one will be able to stand up against you all the days of your life. As I was with Moses, so I will be with you; I will never leave you nor forsake you" (1:5).

One of the first things we learn in coming into this place of walking in the Spirit is that although it is a place of conflict, every conflict can end in victory. The Land of Promise is a frontier, and nothing is more exciting than life on a frontier. But it takes courage. There can be

The entrance into Canaan

Joshua and Jesus are two forms of the Hebrew name *Yeshua*, "God is salvation"

"A land flowing with milk and honey"

no drifting aimlessly with the crowd. You are going to have to walk against the current, as the Lord said to Joshua:

> *"Be careful to obey all the law my servant Moses gave you; do not turn from it to the right or to the left, that you may be successful wherever you go. Do not let this Book of the Law depart from your mouth; meditate on it day and night, so that you may be careful to do everything written in it. Then you will be prosperous and successful" (1:7–8).*

Joshua is a book of great promises! The Word of God is our source book of wisdom, guidance, and insight. The more we read it, meditate on it, speak it, and do it, the greater our prosperity and success will be in the way that God leads us.

"Have I not commanded you?" the Lord continues in verse 9. "Be strong and courageous. Do not be terrified; do not be discouraged, for the LORD your God will be with you wherever you go" (1:9). Coupled with God's Word is the presence of God's Spirit. An obedient heart always brings an empowering Spirit.

That is life in the Land of Promise.

Rahab and
the spies

In chapter 2 we have the remarkable and intriguing story of Rahab and the spies that Israel sent out. When these spies came into the house of Rahab, she hid them under some flax drying on the roof. While the men of the city were searching for them, the spies learned a most startling secret from Rahab:

> *"I know that the LORD has given this land to you and that a great fear of you has fallen on us, so that all who live in this country are melting in fear because of you. We have heard how the LORD dried up the water of the Red Sea for you when you came out of Egypt, and what you did to Sihon and Og, the two kings of the Amorites east of the Jordan, whom you completely destroyed. When we heard of it, our hearts melted and everyone's courage failed because of you, for the LORD your God is God in heaven above and on earth below" (2:9–11).*

How long before the spies entered this city had these events taken place? How long had the Canaanites been living in fear of the mysterious wandering nation whose God had led them through the very midst of the Red Sea? Forty years! In other words, for forty years the inhabitants of Jericho had been a defeated foe. Their hearts were melted. They were defeated before the armies got anywhere close. Israel could have gone in at any time and taken the land! Instead, they had pulled back in fear, causing the Lord to sentence them to forty years of wandering in the desert. What a waste!

But before we condemn the Israelites too harshly for their lack of confidence, we should ask ourselves: What opportunity has God set before us that we shrink back from in fear? How long have we been waiting and hesitating to take on that foe whom God has already delivered into our own hands? Have we, in our timidity and lack of confidence, wasted five, ten, or forty years of our own lives, when we could have trusted God and possessed the land He wanted to give us?

Next we read of the spies:

> When they left, they went into the hills and stayed there three days, until the pursuers had searched all along the road and returned without finding them. Then the two men started back. They went down out of the hills, forded the river and came to Joshua son of Nun and told him everything that had happened to them. They said to Joshua, "The LORD has surely given the whole land into our hands; all the people are melting in fear because of us" (2:22–24).

After three days they came back and told this story. Notice the opening verse of chapter 3. On the third day, "early in the morning," they prepared to go into the land. Here is a reminder to us that on the third day, early in the morning, the resurrection took place. And it is in resurrection power that they entered in to take Canaan, symbolizing Christ in His risen life working in and through us to make us victors over all that threatens to hinder or defeat us.

Crossing the Jordan

Between the Israelites and the Promised Land, however, a barrier remained: the Jordan River. This account of the crossing of the Jordan is very similar to the story of the crossing of the Red Sea. In many ways the two crossings picture the same thing: death. Anyone venturing into the Red Sea without the waters having been parted would have faced certain death.

Now, the crossing of the Red Sea is a picture of Christ's death for you and me—when He cuts us off from the world in all its attitudes and ways. In other words, when you became a Christian, you changed your ideas and sense of values. Your baptism was your expression that you were giving up one life for another and that your whole attitude was changed. That was the Red Sea: His death for you.

But the Jordan is a picture of your death with Christ, when all that you are as a fallen son or daughter of Adam comes to an end: your self-reliance, your desire to have your own way. If you cling to your own program, you can have only your own, fallen Adamic life.

But if you want *His* life, you must also adopt His program, which is a program of victory. You cross either the Red Sea or the Jordan River when you accept this principle. Crossing the Jordan is what you do when you let go of your own agenda and say to God, "All right, if this is what You want for me, Lord, this is what it will be. Not my will but Yours be done." That is what happened in the national life of Israel when the people crossed the Jordan and walked into the Land of Promise.

You cross the Jordan the same way you crossed the Red Sea: by obedience and faith. God is saying to Joshua, "In the same way I led Moses to bring Israel through the Red Sea, so I will lead you to bring Israel through the Jordan." The same way! The faith that got you out of Egypt is the same faith that gets you into the Land of Promise. "Just as you received Christ Jesus as Lord," writes the apostle Paul, "continue to live in him" (Col. 2:6).

Was it any harder for Israel to cross the Jordan River than to cross the Red Sea? No, they just walked to the shore, the waters rolled back, and they went right through. The same process. And it is no different to walk into the land. It is simply a matter of believing that God is in you and that what He said about you is true—that He has cut off the old life (as you asked Him to) and He has given you a new basis that will work. You believe it and you act on that basis and say, "Thank You, Lord, for being in me and empowering me to do everything that needs to be done." And you enter the land.

In chapter 4, we see that Israel set up two memorials. One was a pile of twelve stones on the bank of the river, erected as a continual reminder to the people of the principle of faith to which they had now returned after years of wandering in the wilderness. This memorial is representative of the Lord's Supper, which is a continual reminder to us of that principle of life by which we are to live.

The other memorial was a series of twelve stones in the middle of the river that were to be placed where the priests stood while Israel passed over to the other side. The stones were put in place before the waters returned to fill the riverbed. This symbolizes for us the way in which Jesus Christ stays in the place of death long enough for us to relinquish to Christ the control of every area of our lives.

The fall of the fortress city

In chapter 5 we come to the second section, the conquest of the land. What a mighty story it is! As the Israelites contemplated taking possession of the land, they saw the tremendous city of Jericho with its huge walls. While Jericho was the first *visible* obstacle in Israel's pathway, their first *actual* obstacle was not external but internal. They first had to deal with something in their own lives. God never begins His

The faith that got you out of Egypt is the same faith that gets you into the Land of Promise

Two memorials

conquest with the outward problem. You will discover that He always begins with you.

The people of Israel had to do three things before they could destroy the enemy in the land. First, they had to be circumcised. The whole generation that had been circumcised in Egypt had died in the wilderness. A whole new generation had grown up uncircumcised, so when they came into the land, the first act was circumcision. As we know from the New Testament, circumcision is a picture of a surrendered heart—a heart in which the reliance on the flesh has been cut off and put aside—a circumcised heart (Rom. 2:29).

The second thing the people had to do was to celebrate the Passover—the first such celebration since their emergence from the wilderness. The Passover is a remembrance of the night when the Lord and the angel of death passed over the houses of the Israelites back in Egypt. It also symbolizes a thankful heart that looks back to that day of deliverance when Christ became our Passover sacrifice for us.

After their celebration of the Passover came a new food. The manna that had sustained them in the wilderness ceased on the day after they came into the land, and they began to eat its satisfying food. As far as I can discover, the nearest thing that we have to manna today is cornflakes. How would you like cornflakes for breakfast, lunch, and supper every day for forty years? They were certainly tired of "heavenly cornflakes" when they got into the land of Canaan! For forty years they had eaten food that sustained their strength but didn't satisfy. When they came into the land, however, they found satisfying food.

Finally, before their conquest began, Joshua had to plan the strategy for taking the city of Jericho. He must have been a perplexed and bewildered leader. How could he conquer this huge walled city with this inexperienced "army" of people?

He withdrew from the camp and looked out over the city in the moonlight. Suddenly, just a few paces away, he saw a man facing him, sword drawn. Joshua had no idea whether the man's sword was drawn as a threatening gesture or as an offer of assistance. Instinctively, Joshua challenged the stranger: "Are you for us," he asked, "or for our enemies?"

"Neither," the man replied, "but as commander of the army of the LORD I have now come" (Josh. 5:14). In other words, "I haven't come to take sides, I have come to take over. It isn't your job to plan the strategy of battle. That is my job. I have given the city of Jericho into your hands."

Instantly, Joshua knew that this was no mere mortal soldier. He knew that he was in the presence of God's own messenger. In fact, this

JOSHUA

The people of Israel had to do three things before they could destroy the enemy in the land

1. Be circumcised

2. Celebrate Passover

3. Plan the taking of Jericho

A *theophany,* that is, a preincarnate appearance of the Lord Jesus Christ in human form

stranger may have been what theologians call a "theophany," a preincarnate appearance of the Lord Jesus Christ in human form.

The man proceeded to lay out for Joshua the most remarkable battle plan that has ever been arranged. He was to have the people simply march around the city once a day for six days and on the seventh day, seven times; then they would blow a long blast on the trumpets and shout—and the walls would fall down!

Three obstacles, three problems

Three preparations were necessary before engaging in battle, so in this section, we see three major obstacles to be overcome before the land is won. These obstacles picture for us the three types of problems that we confront as we walk the Christian life. The first one is Jericho, a city with walls about three hundred feet thick and sixty feet high, a seemingly insurmountable obstacle.

The city of Jericho symbolizes those problems most frequently occurring at the beginning of our experience of walking in the Spirit when we are confronted by something that has baffled and mocked us for years. Maybe it is a habit that we have had for a long time and have failed to overcome. It may be something that constantly threatens our spiritual lives.

The lesson of Jericho is that the visible obstacle is not the problem; our *attitude* toward it is

An amazing spiritual principle is related to this type of problem. When we follow the strategy outlined here—walk around the problem in the presence of God (represented by the ark), and shout the shout of triumph—then *the walls will fall down*. When there is a complete change of attitude toward an "insurmountable" problem, the problem dissolves into dust. The visible obstacle is not the problem; our *attitude* toward it is.

God had Israel march for seven days. Why that long? Because it took them that long to change their attitude toward Jericho. All that time they were thinking, "What a huge place. How will we ever take this city?" Day after day, while walking around this city, they had time to think about God in their midst, the power that He had already displayed, and what He could do again. Gradually their attitude changed so that on the seventh day they shouted in triumph and the walls fell down. There was nothing to it when they obeyed.

The second obstacle in Israel's path is the little city of Ai. The story of the campaign against Ai begins with the revelation of the sin of Achan. He coveted a forbidden object taken from the defeated city of Jericho, so he took it and hid it among his personal belongings. Later, when the army of Israel went up against the city of Ai—a comparatively weak and unfortified city—Israel was utterly defeated.

Joshua fell upon his face before the Lord and said, "Why did you ever bring this people across the Jordan to deliver us into the hands of the Amorites to destroy us?" (Josh. 7:7). God said to him, "Stand up! What are you doing down on your face? Israel has sinned. . . . I will not be with you anymore unless you destroy whatever among you is devoted to destruction." (Josh. 7:10, 12) Finally, after searching through all the ranks of Israel, they filtered down to Achan and his family, and Achan confessed.

Ai, then, is an instructive and sobering lesson: God expects us to deal completely with our lusts. He expects us to obey Him without rationalizing or compromising with sin. Even a seemingly small sin can have disastrous consequences, so we dare not allow sin to gain a foothold in us.

When the sin of Achan was hidden, Israel was defeated. But the minute this sin was confessed, the army was able to conquer Ai handily. By dealing firmly and decisively with sin in the camp, Israel was able to go into battle unhindered. The key to gaining victory on the battlefield was to gain victory over the inner enemy, the lurking, secret sin within. Once we gain victory over the problems of the flesh, spiritual warfare ceases to be a problem. God is able to act and win the battle for us.

The two battles of Gibeon and Beth-horon signify a third aspect of Satan's special attacks on the believer. The satanic attack pictured in the story of Gibeon is *deception.* The Gibeonites dressed themselves up in old clothes, took old moldy bread and tattered wineskins, and rode emaciated donkeys out to meet Joshua (see Josh. 9:3–27).

They came into the Israelite camp and said, "Your servants have come from a very distant country because of the fame of the LORD your God. For we have heard reports of him: all that he did in Egypt, and all that he did to the two kings of the Amorites. . . . Our elders and all those living in our country said to us, 'Take provisions for your journey; go and meet them and say to them, "We are your servants; make a treaty with us." ' "

The Israelites were suspicious, but the Gibeonites continued, "This bread of ours was warm when we packed it at home on the day we left to come to you. But now see how dry and moldy it is. And these wineskins that we filled were new, but see how cracked they are. And our clothes and sandals are worn out by the very long journey."

Joshua believed them and made a pact with them. When they had signed the treaty, Israel walked over the hill and there was Gibeon! Now, God had previously instructed Joshua to remove all the inhabitants of the land—and that included Gibeon. But Joshua had been taken in by a clever satanic ruse. Even though he had been tricked into signing the treaty, Joshua honored the agreement and spared the Gibeonites. As a result, the Gibeonites became thorns in Israel's side throughout the rest of her history.

> The lesson of Ai is that God expects us to deal completely with our lusts

> The lesson of Gibeon and Beth-horon is that Satan attacks through *deception*

Then comes the account of Beth-horon, where all the kings of the Canaanites banded together and came roaring down in a tremendous league of nations against Joshua—reminiscent of the various times in our own century, such as the 1967 Six-Day War, when various surrounding nations banded together to attack modern Israel. The battle of Beth-horon was a mighty battle, and although Israel was greatly outnumbered, God gave them victory in a most remarkable way: He stopped the sun in the sky, causing the day of battle to last until victory came. This was the famous "long day" of Joshua.

Here is a picture of what happens when the devil comes as a roaring lion in some overwhelming catastrophe that seems to shatter us, to shake our faith, and make us cry out, "God, what is happening to me? Why should this happen to me?" We feel we are being swept off our feet by this terrible, staggering event. But Joshua stood fast in faith, depending on God to work a miracle—and God honored his faith. Proverbs 10:30 tells us, "The righteous will never be uprooted." This is why Paul says in Ephesians that when the enemy comes like this, we are to just stand still, planting our feet on God's promises, and the enemy will be defeated (see Eph. 6:13).

The rest of this section (chapters 11 through 21) deals with the mopping-up operation after the major battles, along with the division of Canaan among the tribes. After the battle of Beth-horon, the land was practically theirs, although individual victories remained to be won. The victories of Caleb, Othniel, and the Josephites and the setting aside of the cities of refuge all contain wonderful lessons on the audacity of faith—boldly taking and using what God has promised.

Three perils

The peril of misunderstood motives

In the last section we learn of three particular forms of peril that beset us in the Christian life. First of all comes the account of the *misunderstood motives* that were ascribed to the Reubenites, the Gadites, and the half-tribe of Manasseh. They built an altar on the wrong side of the Jordan, causing indignation among the other tribes of Israel.

To the other tribes, this was idolatry and disobedience to God's command. So these tribes gathered themselves together and went to make war against their own brethren. When they arrived, all decked out for war, the Reubenites, the Gadites, and the half-tribe of Manasseh were understandably upset. "If we have built our own altar to turn away from the LORD . . . ," they cried out, "may the LORD himself call us to account" (Josh. 22:23).

Then they explained that they were afraid that sometime in the future the Israelites in the land might say to the tribes outside the land, " 'You have no share in the LORD.' " In that case, a good response would be, "If they ever say this to us, or to our descendants, we will answer:

'Look at the replica of the LORD's altar, which our fathers built, not for burnt offerings and sacrifices, but as a witness between us and you' " (22:28).

Does this scene have a familiar ring to it? How many times have you jumped to the wrong conclusion, ascribing wrong motives to your spouse, to a family member, to your pastor, or to another Christian? How many times have other people misjudged, criticized, or wrongly attacked you? It happens all too often in Christian families and in Christian churches. If anything can drive us out of the land of victory, it is controversy over misunderstood motives.

The second peril is *incomplete obedience.* Although the entire land had been given to the people of Israel, they did not possess all of it but left some of it unconquered. Joshua warned the people as he neared the end of his life that the unconquered peoples whom they have permitted to live would always be snares and thorns to them (see Josh. 23:12–13).

The peril of *incomplete obedience*

The final peril that we see in this passage is the peril of *false confidence and pride.* Joshua made a final appearance before the people, challenging them to walk before the Lord their God, saying, "Choose for yourselves this day whom you will serve" (24:15). He is saying: "You think you can go on in a sort of neutral position between following the devil and following the Lord. You can't do it." This is exactly what Jesus said, "No one can serve two masters" (Matt. 6:24). You must serve either God or Satan. You cannot serve both. There is no intermediate ground. Hearing this challenge, the people replied:

The peril of *false confidence and pride*

> *"Far be it from us to forsake the LORD to serve other gods! It was the LORD our God himself who brought us and our fathers up out of Egypt, from that land of slavery, and performed those great signs before our eyes. He protected us on our entire journey and among all the nations through which we traveled. And the LORD drove out before us all the nations, including the Amorites, who lived in the land. We too will serve the LORD, because he is our God" (24:16–18).*

Brave sounding words! But Joshua immediately confronted their bravado, much as Jesus confronted the bravado of Peter when he pledged never to forsake or deny his Lord. "You are not able to serve the LORD," says Joshua in verse 19. Why did Joshua seem to put down his own people just as they are pledging their allegiance to the Lord? Because Joshua understood that the greatest peril Christians face is false confidence.

You may say, "Well, certainly I can do what God wants. I've got what it takes. After all, I know the Scriptures. I have been raised in the right church. I can certainly walk faithfully and honestly before God. Don't talk to me about apostasy, defeat, backsliding, or sin. I *will* serve the Lord!" To this spiritual pride, Joshua responds, "You *are not able* to serve the Lord."

You can never have enough strength to stand by yourself. Your strength comes from an admission of your weakness and your sense of dependence. Only as you are willing to cling to God and His strength can you hope to experience victory. That is why wise old Joshua, near the end of his life, says:

> *"You are not able to serve the LORD. He is a holy God; he is a jealous God. . . . If you forsake the LORD and serve foreign gods, he will turn and bring disaster on you and make an end of you, after he has been good to you" (24:19–20).*

It must have saddened Joshua deeply to hear the people's response, for they said, in effect, "No, Joshua, you don't know what you're talking about. We are going to serve the Lord anyway." Words of spiritual arrogance! Because of the people's attitude, the story does not end with the victories of the book of Joshua. The story continues in the next book, the book of Judges—the book of defeat.

A Panorama
of Defeat

F ew books of the Bible can compare to Judges for color and
intrigue. You wince as you read how Ehud the judge goes to visit
the king in his summer palace and slides his dagger between the king's
fifth and sixth ribs so that the flesh closes around it and the knife cannot be withdrawn. You cringe when Jael drives the tent stake through the
skull of Sisera and pins him to the ground. You bite your fingernails
alongside Gideon as God introduces deep military cutbacks, reducing
Israel's army from thirty-two thousand to three hundred—then sends
this vastly outnumbered miniature army into battle!

Perhaps your heart sinks with mine when Jephthah's daughter
comes out to meet him on his return from battle, and he remembers his
vow to sacrifice to God the first person he meets—and then fulfills that
horrible vow. Perhaps you glory with Samson as he wreaks havoc among
the Philistines, but wonder at his folly in allowing the Philistine
temptress to worm from him the secret of his strength. Doubtless you
turn with revulsion from the story of the Benjaminite perversion that
marks perhaps the blackest chapter in Israel's history.

What kind of books do you like to read? What films and TV shows
are your favorites? Fans of historical romance, military history, soap
operas, conspiracy theories, spy novels, swashbuckling adventure, or
political intrigue will find it *all here in the book of Judges!* This is a fascinating, spellbinding book to read. But from a broader and deeper perspective, Judges is essentially the story of a deteriorating nation—and it

serves as a sober warning against deterioration and decline in our own Christian lives. The structure of Judges follows:

Israel Fails to Complete the Conquest of Canaan
(Judges 1:1–3:4)
1.	The failure of the tribes of Israel	1
2.	The judgment of the tribes	2:1–3:4

The Seven Cycles of Deliverance
(Judges 3:5–16:31)
3.	The judge Othniel	3:5–11
4.	The judge Ehud	3:12–30
5.	The judge Shamgar	3:31
6.	Deborah and Barak	4–5
7.	Gideon defeats the Midianites	6:1–8:32
8.	The judge Abimelech	8:33–9:57
9.	The judge Tola	10:1–2
10.	The judge Jair	10:3–5
11.	The judge Jephtha	10:6–12:7
12.	The judge Ibzan	12:8–10
13.	The judge Elon	12:11–12
14.	The judge Abdon	12:13–15
15.	The judge Samson	13–16

The Depravity of Israel under the Judges
(Judges 17–21)
13.	Israel sinks into idolatry	17–18
14.	Israel sinks into immorality	19
15.	The war between the tribes	20–21

Don't settle for less

Whereas Joshua is a book of victory, Judges is a book of defeat and failure. It is the first in a series of books that sets before us the warnings and danger signals regarding the perils that lie in the path of a believer. The pattern of defeat described in the book of Judges is presented to us over and over again. The key principle that always spelled defeat in the lives of the people of Israel is given to us in the very last verse of the book:

In those days Israel had no king; everyone did as he saw fit (21:25).

These people were not trying to do wrong. They were not rebellious people, bent on frustrating God's will for their lives. At this stage of Israel's history these people were determined to do right—*but they were trying to do what was right in their own eyes.* They succumbed to the folly of consecrated blundering. They were well-intentioned blunderers, intending to do right but ending up all wrong.

I have seen this pattern again and again in my counseling experience. Time after time I have heard people say, "I don't know what went wrong. I tried to do right. I did what I thought was best. But everything seemed to go wrong." This was the problem with Israel in the book of Judges. As the text says, there was no objective authority in their lives. The Lord Jehovah was supposedly their King, but they did not take Him seriously. And when they did not take Him seriously, they ended up taking themselves too seriously. So they did what they thought was right, guided by their own intellects and reasoning—ultimately proving that their ways were not God's ways.

In the first two chapters, we see the pattern of defeat that will repeat itself again and again. Each time God in His grace delivers the people, they slip into yet another cycle of defeat. The tone of defeat is set by these words in chapter 1:

> *Manasseh did not drive out the people of Beth Shan and . . . their surrounding settlements (1:27).*

Israel fails to complete the conquest of Canaan

The tribe of Manasseh failed to obey God's command to drive out all the tribes of the Canaanites. And there are other similar stories of failure:

> *Nor did Ephraim drive out the Canaanites living in Gezer, but the Canaanites continued to live there among them. Neither did Zebulun drive out the Canaanites living in Kitron or Nahalol, who remained among them. . . . Nor did Asher drive out those living in Acco or Sidon. . . . Neither did Naphtali drive out those living in Beth Shemesh, or Beth Anath (1:29, 31, 33).*

That was just the beginning of the story of Israel's defeat. They did not take God seriously about the threat that their enemies posed to them but, instead, moved in among them. God had said that they were to drive out every inhabitant of these Canaanite villages. They were not to mingle with them or have anything to do with them. They were not to marry them.

But when Israel came to some of these villages, instead of mounting armed warfare against them, they went in and investigated the towns. What they saw seemed quite innocuous. The villages did not seem particularly dangerous and the people seemed to be fine people.

So they let them stay in their villages and started another town right next door. They allowed these tribes to retain their villages among the cities and villages of Israel. They settled for less than complete victory.

We read this story, and we think, *How foolish these Israelites were not to obey the commandment of God!* But don't we do exactly the same? Don't we settle for less than complete victory over our sins and bad habits? Don't we say, "Well, yes, I do have a problem with anger (or gossip, or swearing, or impure thoughts, or alcohol, or tobacco), but it's just one little bad habit! I mean, we all need one small vice, don't we?" No! God says that it is these *little* things that we accommodate ourselves to and compromise with that eventually defeat us and destroy us! We cannot afford to settle for anything less than complete victory.

Now look at the next step in this process of decline and defeat. In chapter 2 we see God's grace as He warns them about results of their failure:

> The angel of the LORD went up from Gilgal to Bokim and said, "I brought you up out of Egypt and led you into the land that I swore to give to your forefathers. I said, 'I will never break my covenant with you, and you shall not make a covenant with the people of this land, but you shall break down their altars.' Yet you have disobeyed me. Why have you done this? Now therefore I tell you that I will not drive them out before you; they will be thorns in your sides and their gods will be a snare to you" (2:1–2).

What did Israel do in response?

> The Israelites did evil in the eyes of the LORD and served the Baals. They forsook the LORD, the God of their fathers, who had brought them out of Egypt. They followed and worshiped various gods of the peoples around them. They provoked the LORD to anger (2:11–12).

The next step was open idolatry. The Baals and the Ashtoreths were the gods of the Canaanite tribes. Baal was a male fertility god, Ashtoreth a female fertility god. The Israelites didn't intend to do wrong—at first. They knew that God had commanded them not to bow down before any idols. They knew the Ten Commandments. But they began by compromising with evil, by allowing idolaters to coexist with them in the land God had given them. They didn't intend to get trapped like this, but soon they were doing the unthinkable: partaking in the pagan practices of the ungodly Canaanites.

How did this happen? The Israelites had been farmers in Egypt, and they irrigated their crops; so they weren't used to dry-land farming. After forty years of wandering, they didn't really know how to farm anymore, especially in an arid land without irrigation, and their crops came up poor and scraggly. The Israelites saw the lush grain fields of the Canaanites and asked for advice.

The Canaanites said their abundant crops were a blessing from the fertility gods that they worshiped and welcomed the Israelites to adapt to their ways. Have you ever experienced cultural pressures such as those faced by the Israelites? "If you want to get ahead in this company, you'll have to play the game our way. Come on! Everybody cheats a little! Everybody has a romantic interest on the side! Everyone goes to this kind of movie and that kind of bar! If you expect to be one of us, you'll have to adapt to our ways."

So it was that the Israelites gave in and sank to the level of the people they were commanded to destroy. The Canaanites taught the Israelites how to plant their crops properly, how to fertilize the soil, as well as the proper way to sacrifice to their demonic gods, so the next spring—sure enough!—they found that the crops were wonderful. The Israelites thought, *Hey! There must be something to this fertility god business. We'd better worship these gods after all.* They forsook the God of Israel and bowed down to the Baals and Ashtoreths.

Now what is not recorded here is that these were sex deities and the worship of them involved not only bowing down before stone idols but also engaging in obscene sexual practices. So Israel soon sank into idolatry and gross immorality.

The next step in the cycle is the reinjection of God's grace. The whole pattern is of unutterable human folly in disobeying the simple Word of God. God in His arresting grace puts obstacle after obstacle in the path of these people, trying to warn them about what is happening to them. In chapter 2, we read how God dealt with their disobedience:

They forsook [the Lord] and served Baal and the Ashtoreths. In his anger against Israel the LORD handed them over to raiders who plundered them. He sold them to their enemies all around, whom they were no longer able to resist. Whenever Israel went out to fight, the hand of the LORD was against them to defeat them, just as he had sworn to them. They were in great distress (2:13–15).

Have you ever had the Lord's hand against you? Have you ever sensed that He was against you in everything you did? What you thought you were doing in dedication and sincerity was so opposite to what He had said that you discovered His hand was against you. This is

God demonstrates His anger and His grace

what Israel discovered: Nothing seemed to work out right. They found themselves in bondage. One after another of the tribes around them was allowed to rule over them. These tribes came in and made slaves out of them, year after year after painful year.

Finally, God's grace comes in again for deliverance:

> The LORD raised up judges, who saved them out of the hands of these raiders. Yet they would not listen to their judges but prostituted themselves to other gods and worshiped them. Unlike their fathers, they quickly turned from the way in which their fathers had walked, the way of obedience to the LORD's commands. Whenever the LORD raised up a judge for them, he was with the judge and saved them out of the hands of their enemies as long as the judge lived (2:16–18).

That is why this book is called Judges. Over and over, this pattern is repeated. God raised up Othniel, and then Ehud, and then Shamgar—judge after judge until you come to the last judge, Samson. There were twelve judges altogether, all representing God's intervening grace in attempting to keep these people from the folly of their own senseless disobedience. The perpetual folly is demonstrated by these tragic words:

> When the judge died, the people returned to ways even more corrupt than those of their fathers, following other gods and serving and worshiping them. They refused to give up their evil practices and stubborn ways (2:19).

Thus the book of Judges is nothing but a record of Israel's continuous decline.

**God's
warning
to us**

The lesson of
Judges is that we
must take God
seriously, and we
must take our
enemy seriously

The great lesson of Judges is that we must take God seriously, and we must take our enemy seriously. Jesus Christ has come to save us from our sins, not to help us to comfortably accommodate ourselves to them. He has come to drive those sins and habits out of us. If we do not take God seriously about these so-called little things, then step by step, gradually and imperceptibly, we will move away from God's grace, and we will sink into moral and spiritual collapse.

Occasionally, we hear the story of an outstanding man or woman of God who suddenly, unexpectedly is found to be caught up in dishonest or immoral behavior. A scandal erupts, then widespread disillusionment. People shake their heads in bewilderment and ask, "How could this happen so suddenly? What caused this abrupt change in this person?" I'm convinced that in almost every case, there was nothing sudden about this behavior. Long before this seemingly sudden moral implosion took place, there was a long period of inner deterioration, gradual compromise, secret sins, little sins. They took their toll, day by day, until a major moral collapse became inevitable.

You may be asking yourself, "Is this happening to me? In some area of my life am I saying, 'Lord, this really isn't very important. Why bother me with this little matter? This isn't very important, is it Lord?' " That is a dangerous attitude. If that is your attitude, you are exposing yourself to peril.

Listen to the message of Judges. Read the book carefully. Listen to God's warning-yet-loving voice. If you read it closely, with an open heart, you will make the same discovery I did: The book of Judges is a mirror in which we are able to see ourselves and our condition more clearly. May God give us the courage and the wisdom to take the insights of Judges and apply them personally, so that the image we see in that mirror will look less like that of failed, deteriorating Israel and more like Jesus Christ.

The Romance of Redemption

When Benjamin Franklin was United States ambassador to France, he occasionally attended the Infidels Club, a group of intellectuals who spent most of their time together reading and discussing literary masterpieces. Like so many intellectual snobs, both then and now, the members of this group were largely atheists and agnostics who sneered at the Bible.

On one occasion, Franklin brought in a book and read it before the group. When he was finished, the other members were unanimous in their praise. They said it was one of the most beautiful stories they had ever heard and demanded that he tell them where he had run across such a remarkable literary masterpiece. It was his great delight to tell them that the story was from the Bible, a book they loudly regarded with scorn. Franklin had simply changed the names in the story so that it would not be recognized as a book in the Bible!

The book of Ruth is certainly a literary masterpiece. It is a beautiful story of a touching romance. I wonder how it would be featured in some of our romance magazines today. I can almost see the headline: "How One Woman Found Happiness in the Arms of a Second Husband." It is a book that inflames the imagination because it is entwined with the captivating theme of love, devotion, and true romance.

Yet it must be remembered that the events in this beautiful book take place against the ugly backdrop of the era of Judges. Although

Ruth is a beautiful story in itself, it is the story behind the story—its meaning and significance—that makes this book so valuable for our lives. The book of Ruth is one of those beautiful Old Testament pictures that God has designed to illustrate the dramatic truths of the Christian faith, as expounded in the New Testament. It illustrates the romance of redemption.

The structure of the book is simple:

Ruth, a Woman of Deep Love and Devotion (Ruth 1–2)
1. Ruth's friendship with and devotion to Naomi   1
2. Ruth meets Boaz; Boaz cares for Ruth   2

Ruth's Love Is Rewarded (Ruth 3–4)
3. Ruth's request for redemption   3
4. Boaz marries Ruth; Ruth bears a son, Obed   4

Naomi: A woman bereft

The book of Ruth begins with an introduction of its key characters:

> In the days when the judges ruled, there was a famine in the land, and a man from Bethlehem in Judah, together with his wife and two sons, went to live for a while in the country of Moab. The man's name was Elimelech, his wife's name Naomi, and the names of his two sons were Mahlon and Kilion. They were Ephrathites from Bethlehem, Judah. And they went to Moab and lived there.
>
> Now Elimelech, Naomi's husband, died, and she was left with her two sons. They married Moabite women, one named Orpah and the other Ruth. After they had lived there about ten years, both Mahlon and Kilion also died, and Naomi was left without her two sons and her husband (1:1–5).

Elimelech, whose name means "my God is king," leaves the town of Bethlehem with his wife, Naomi, whose name means "pleasant." Because of famine in the region, they take their two sons, Mahlon and Kilion, and move to the land of Moab. Note that in Bethlehem—the name of which means "the House of Bread"—there was no bread, only famine. The book of Leviticus has already told us that famine indicates a low level of spiritual vitality within a given nation.

In Moab, Elimelech died and his two sons, Mahlon and Kilion, married women of Moab, Orpah and Ruth. After ten years, the two sons also died and Naomi was left with her two daughters-in-law. After the famine was over, Naomi expressed her plans to return to Bethlehem, but she encouraged her two Moabite daughters-in-law to remain in Moab and remarry there. Orpah was unwilling to leave her home for an uncertain life in Palestine, and she decided to take Naomi's advice to stay in Moab. But Ruth refused to stay in Moab and, in a plea of enduring beauty, declared her determination to identify with Naomi's land, people, and faith.

The source of Ruth's devotion and determination is seen in her statement in 1:16: "Your God [shall be] my God." This clearly represents her willingness to leave the idols of Moab for the worship of the living God of Israel.

Boy meets girl—a tender, holy love story

So Naomi and Ruth arrive in Bethlehem at the beginning of the barley harvest with a very uncertain future before them. The invisible, providing, protecting hand of the Lord is apparent in the statement that Ruth went into the fields to glean and "found herself working in a field belonging to Boaz" (Ruth 2:3). This man, a close relative of Elimelech, Naomi's husband, appears in the story as a man of unusual character and sensitivity.

This is a wonderful story of boy meets girl, the kind of romantic story that never goes out of style. Ruth was gleaning in the field and Boaz saw her. He said to his workmen, "Whose young woman is that?" They told him, and Boaz went down to meet Ruth. Now the text doesn't go into detail about their meeting, but if you use your sanctified imagination, you can see that it must have been a bit awkward at first.

She is working away, picking up the grain here and there, and along comes this handsome fellow—evidently a wealthy man by his clothes. She drops her eyes shyly and he shifts nervously from one foot to the other, clearing his throat. Finally, he says, "Shalom." She looks up and says, "Shalom." He goes on to commend her for her kindness to her mother-in-law and especially for her faith in Jehovah, the God of Israel.

Obviously attracted to the beautiful Moabite woman, yet acting always with restraint and dignity, Boaz instructs his workmen to deliberately leave grain in the field for Ruth to glean. To her amazement, Ruth discovers that these workmen are the sloppiest workmen in the whole kingdom of Israel! When she returns to Naomi in the evening with an unexpected abundance, she learns for the first time from her mother-in-law that Boaz is a potential kinsman-redeemer. Thus, at Naomi's instruction she continues gleaning in Boaz's fields throughout the barley and wheat harvests, for approximately three months.

A plan of redemption

At the end of the harvest, after the winnowing of the grain took place, Naomi seized the initiative provided by her relationship with Boaz and advised Ruth of a plan for her redemption. This is what Ruth did: She came to the sleeping Boaz by night and lay at his feet. In doing so, Ruth was following an ancient custom in Israel by which she was symbolically asking Boaz to fulfill the responsibility of a kinsman to marry her and raise up heirs to the deceased Elimelech. She did this so modestly that Boaz commended her for her action. Having clearly fallen in love with her, Boaz eagerly consented to take on the requested responsibility. He had evidently hoped such a situation would occur, for he immediately informed Ruth that a closer kinsman was involved, and his claim had to be settled first.

In the morning he sent her back to Naomi with a generous gift of six measures of barley, and Naomi wisely told her that the matter would surely be settled that day. That same morning, Boaz took his seat at the city gate where the elders gathered for the settling of lawsuits and the judging of other matters brought before them. When the closer kinsman came by, Boaz requested an informal court. When all were seated, he presented his case to the other relative.

Boaz: Ruth's kinsman-redeemer

Boaz declared that Naomi wanted to sell a piece of land that belonged to Elimelech, but if she did so, the next of kin would be responsible to care for the family, since they now would have no property. Seeing the possibility of obtaining a choice piece of property, the first kinsman declared his willingness to assume this responsibility. That's when Boaz played his trump card!

Boaz informed the other kinsman that the land had a marriage encumbrance. According to the custom of that culture, if he bought the property, he would also have to marry the woman who legally encumbered the property. This changed the picture for the first kinsman, since the land would then not belong to him but to any children resulting from his union with Ruth. He decided that he would be better off without the property, and he chose not to take it. To symbolize his decision, in the colorful custom of the East, the man removed his right shoe and handed it to Boaz in the presence of the witnesses. The shoe symbolized his right as owner to set foot upon the land. This right now became Boaz's, and the coast was clear for him to take Ruth as his wife.

The account closes with the birth of a son to Boaz and Ruth, who brought great joy to the heart of his grandmother, Naomi, and grew up to be the grandfather of David, Israel's mightiest king.

Christ: Our kinsman-redeemer

The beautiful little story of Ruth not only provides a link between the days of the judges and the subsequent reign of David, but it symbolizes in the figure of Boaz how Christ, our great Kinsman-Redeemer, overcomes the obstacle of our birth in Adam and takes us to Himself in a union that will produce the fruit of the Spirit to the honor and glory of God. Significantly, the genealogy of Matthew includes Ruth as an ancestress of Jesus the Messiah.

The Flesh and the Spirit

First Samuel is the story of two men, Saul and David. These two people symbolize two principles in the heart of every Christian believer seeking to walk before God: *the principle of the flesh* and *the principle of faith*. Saul is the man of the flesh, the carnal believer. David is the man of faith, the spiritual believer.

In 1 Samuel, we see how these two principles, the principle of flesh and the principle of faith, come into dramatic conflict in our lives. We see in Saul the ruin caused by the will that is set on the flesh. In David, we see the blessing that results from a mind that is set on the Spirit. As Romans 8:6 tells us, "The mind of sinful man is death, but the mind controlled by the Spirit is life and peace."

The fact that both of these men were kings beautifully illustrates the supremacy of the will in human life. When God created the human race, He gave us a completely supreme free will. Even the Spirit of God does not violate it. If we want to say "No" to God, we can. We rule over the kingdom of our lives, just as Saul and David ruled over their kingdoms.

The book actually begins with the story of the man who gives his name to the book. The prophet Samuel is the human expression of God's voice to both Saul and David. The stories of these three men—Samuel, Saul, and David—mark off the three divisions of the book. The first seven chapters give us the life of Samuel. Chapters 8 through 15 present King Saul, the man of the flesh. Then in chapters 16 through 31, David, the man of faith, symbolizes the mind that is set on the Spirit. Here is an outline of 1 Samuel:

Samuel: The judge-prophet

Samuel was the last of the judges and the first of the prophets. The events of this book take place right after Israel has passed through some three hundred years of the rule of the judges. Samuel is God's chosen instrument to close out the realm of the judges and introduce the beginning of the prophetic ministry and the monarchy.

The book opens with the story of a barren woman, Hannah, one of two wives of a man named Elkanah. The other wife had borne Elkanah numerous children, and she taunted and mocked Hannah in her barrenness. Hannah's barrenness is symbolic of the spiritual state of

Israel at this time. The people to whom God personally manifested Himself had fallen into a state of spiritual infertility and barrenness. The priesthood, which God had established along with the tabernacle and the Levitical law, had begun to disintegrate and disappear. The cause for this failure is found in the song Hannah sings after her prayer is answered and she gives birth to a boy, Samuel. In this song, Hannah announces:

> *"Do not keep talking so proudly or let your mouth speak such arrogance, for the LORD is a God who knows, and by him deeds are weighed. The bows of the warriors are broken, but those who stumbled are armed with strength" (2:3–4).*

The rest of the song sets forth God's ability to exalt the lowly and cast down the proud.

In this book we see the eternal conflict between the proud, self-confident heart and the humble spirit that looks to God in utter dependence. This was the problem with Israel. The priesthood was failing not because anything was wrong with the priesthood (which represents the ministry of the Lord Jesus Christ) but because the people refused to bow before the Lord. They refused to come for cleansing. They refused to turn from idolatry. As a result, the priesthood was about to pass out of the picture as an effective means of mediation between the people and God.

At this point we have the account of Samuel's birth and childhood. When Samuel is just a boy, he is brought to the temple and dedicated to God. He becomes the voice of God to Eli the priest and is given a message of judgment. Later he becomes the voice of God to the nation—especially to the two kings, Saul and David.

The first seven chapters tell the story of Israel's fall into decay. The ark of the covenant, the place where God wrote His name and where His presence resided, is taken captive by the Philistines. Eli's priesthood is taken away from him because he did not discipline his sons. And when Eli's grandson is born, his mother names him Ichabod, which means "the glory has departed." Here Israel reaches one of the lowest ebbs in its national history.

Next, we read about the entrance of King Saul. In 1 Samuel 8:4–5, the people demand to have a king like other nations:

Saul: The man of the flesh

> *All the elders of Israel gathered together and came to Samuel at Ramah. They said to him, "You are old, and your sons do not walk in your ways; now appoint a king to lead us, such as all the other nations have."*

The principle of the flesh is at work in the nation of Israel to destroy its fellowship with God and its enjoyment of His blessing. The people of Israel have rejected the authority of God in favor of having the same kind of authority as all the other nations. In other words, the desire of the flesh is to be religious in a manner accepted by the world, to conduct its business as the rest of the world does. You may have seen this principle at work in your church, where people may have wanted to interject worldly business principles into the conduct of the church rather than the principles of Scripture. Instead of relying on the leadership of the Holy Spirit, we often prefer to appoint a committee to plan out a program; then we ask God to bless our program and make it work. The problem is that it is *our* program, not God's.

Someone has said, "Be careful what you ask for—you may get it." Here is a case that proves the saying true: Israel prays for a human king and God gives them one. Samuel was displeased when the people asked for a king, because he knew that this was not God's program. When Samuel prayed to the Lord, the Lord replied:

> *"Listen to all that the people are saying to you; it is not you they have rejected, but they have rejected me as their king. As they have done from the day I brought them up out of Egypt until this day, forsaking me and serving other gods, so they are doing to you. Now listen to them; but warn them solemnly and let them know what the king who will reign over them will do" (8:7–9).*

This is always God's way. If we want something badly enough, He will usually give it to us—even if it is not His perfect will for our lives. The catch is that we must also be ready to face the consequences.

A true story: An eight-year-old child once begged her father for new skates. "The skates I have are too slow!" she said. "All the other kids have fast new ball-bearing skates!" Her father resisted and resisted, but the little girl relentlessly begged her daddy for the faster skates. She even pinned notes to his pillow at night: "Daddy, pretty please with sugar on top, buy me some new ball-bearing skates? Please! Please! Please!"

Finally, this father relented and bought her the new skates. The child gleefully put on the skates, zoomed out onto the sidewalk and disappeared around the corner. The father heard a cry, followed by a sickening thud. He ran around the corner and found his daughter on the sidewalk, unconscious. She had slipped on the faster skates and hit her head. She was taken to the hospital in a coma, and she died before midnight.

Sometimes we beg God for "ball-bearing skates" in our own lives. We think that God is unkind to us when He says "No" to our prayers

again and again. But sometimes a "No" answer is God's blessing to us—
for if we continue to beg Him and He finally says "Yes," we may find
ourselves enduring more tragedy and heartbreak than we ever imagined.
That is the situation of the Israelites when God yielded to their demands
for a king.

The story of Saul is the story of a young man who, like so many
young people today, was living his life without any regard for what God
wanted him to do. He was busy with his father in the donkey business.
How did God reach Saul? He did the obvious thing: He went into the
donkey business Himself! He caused Saul's donkeys to stray, forcing Saul
to set out in search of the donkeys. After a fruitless search, Saul came to
the town where Samuel lived.

In chapter 9, Saul was about to give up and go back home when his
servant said, "Look, in this town there is a man of God. . . . Let's go there
now. Perhaps he will tell us what way to take" (9:6). Saul was not anxious to do this. In fact, he wanted to stay as far from the prophet as possible, because prophets were a very disturbing kind of people. He just
wanted to go home. But the servant prevailed on him to see Samuel, and
to Saul's amazement, Samuel was expecting him.

God had told Samuel the day before to expect a visit from a young
man named Saul. Samuel had a great dinner prepared for Saul and
thirty invited guests. Saul was surprised to learn that he was the guest of
honor. Those troublesome donkeys had gotten him into this and he
wanted to get out of it as fast as possible. Samuel took him aside as they
finished the dinner and announced to him a stunning thing: "Has not
the LORD anointed you leader over his inheritance?" (10:1).

Saul had been out looking for donkeys, but he ended up as the king
of Israel. And he didn't even want the job! In fact, when Saul was on his
way home, he was met by his uncle, who asked what had been happening in his life. Saul said he had gone out looking for the donkeys but had
run into Samuel, who told him that the donkeys were safe at home.
Well, Samuel had told Saul a lot more than that! I doubt that it just
slipped Saul's mind that Samuel had also given him an anointing and a
new commission as king of Israel—but he didn't say a word about that.
Saul was not interested in what God wanted him to do, unless he could
use God for his own purposes.

But Samuel wasn't through. He told Israel that God had listened   Saul is chosen by lot
to their plea and would give them a king, according to their desire.
Samuel called all the people together to cast lots for the choice of a
king. A lot was cast first to see from which tribe God was calling the
king: It was the tribe of Benjamin. Then which family group: It was
the family of Kish. Finally, Saul was selected. The word went out, "Has
the man come here yet?" No one could find him anywhere. Finally, at

the Lord's direction, they found him hiding among the baggage—a likely place to find a king!

Why was he hiding? Was he shy? No, Saul was hiding, according to the account, because he didn't want to be inconvenienced by doing what God wanted. He wanted to live his own life his own way, and he was trying to get away from God's call. Finally, he was crowned king—and he looked the very picture of a king: head and shoulders above everyone else, handsome as could be, a wise young man in many ways, and just.

Saul wins a great victory over the Ammonites

But trouble is brewing up north: The Ammonites are massing for war. Saul sends word to the people of Israel to come together, and to his delight, thirty-six thousand men respond. They march up to the north and utterly destroy the Ammonites in a great victory. Saul begins to feel that maybe serving God is going to be all right after all. Maybe he can use his new appointment for his own glory and advancement.

The next battle he faces is with the Philistines, who aren't merely a tribe but the ancient equivalent of a superpower—heavily armed and very fierce. The Philistines gather a force of thirty thousand iron chariots, six thousand horsemen, and an army too vast to number! When Saul looked and saw this great horde of people advancing, he began to wonder if being king was such a great job after all! He sent out word for more volunteers to fight this new enemy, just as he had when the Ammonites threatened; then he waited. And he waited. Where was the support? Where were the eager young soldiers?

Finally, a thousand people showed up, and then another thousand, and then another thousand. No more came. He compared this pitiful three thousand soldiers with the multitude of the Philistines' tremendous force. Then he sent for the prophet Samuel. In typical fashion, the man of the flesh depends upon his own resources until he gets into trouble; then he calls upon the Lord.

But God was ahead of Saul as usual, and Samuel delayed in coming. While Saul waited for Samuel to arrive, his soldiers began to slip away one by one and return home. His army dwindled from three thousand to two thousand to one thousand and finally to only six hundred men. By this time, Saul was getting desperate, and when Samuel had not come after five or six days, Saul took it upon himself to offer a burnt offering to the Lord. The moment he finished, Samuel came walking up. The old prophet was stern-faced as he asked, "What have you done?"

Saul offers a burnt offering

"When I saw that the men were scattering," said Saul, "and that you did not come . . . , I thought, 'Now the Philistines will come down against me at Gilgal, and I have not sought the LORD's favor.' So I felt compelled to offer the burnt offering" (13:11–12). On hearing this, Samuel said to Saul:

"Now your kingdom will not endure; the LORD has sought out a man after his own heart and appointed him leader of his people, because you have not kept the LORD's command" (13:14).

Here, Samuel prophesied that Saul's kingdom would be taken from him.

Reading on, we find that God gave a great victory through Jonathan's faith and delivered the people from this vast horde of Philistines. When at last the battle was won, Saul built an altar. It is the first altar that we are specifically told King Saul ever built. Here is a man who thinks that the outward marks of faith are all that are necessary. Many believe that way today. *If I go through the external rituals,* they think, *if I belong to a church, recite the creed, sing the hymns, then God will be satisfied.* That is the thinking of a man or woman of the flesh.

But God says that when you act on that basis, your autonomy is inevitably taken away. You no longer have authority in your own kingdom. You become the victim and the slave of an inexorable force that will grind you under its heel and bring you into subjection to it. This is what every man or woman who lives by the flesh sooner or later discovers (see Rom. 6:16).

After Saul builds an altar in his own self-will, God brings him to his knees and gives him one last chance to live by faith instead of by the flesh. At the beginning of 1 Samuel 15, we read:

> Samuel said to Saul, *"I am the one the LORD sent to anoint you king over his people Israel; so listen now to the message from the LORD. This is what the LORD Almighty says: 'I will punish the Amalekites for what they did to Israel when they waylaid them as they came up from Egypt. Now go, attack the Amalekites and totally destroy everything that belongs to them. Do not spare them; put to death men and women, children and infants, cattle and sheep, camels and donkeys.' "*

This was Saul's last chance, because if Saul obeyed this command, he would demonstrate that he was ready to allow the Spirit to do His work against the flesh. In New Testament terms, God was giving Saul a chance to allow God to crucify his flesh and put it to death. The Amalekites are a picture throughout Scripture of the principle of the flesh that opposes the things of God. The Amalekites were a foreign tribe about whom Moses said to Israel, "The LORD will be at war against the Amalekites from generation to generation" (Ex. 17:16). God gave Saul this opportunity to carry out His will and obliterate the Amalekites, but what did Saul choose to do?

Saul attacked the Amalekites all the way from Havilah to Shur, to the east of Egypt. He took Agag king of the Amalekites alive, and all his people he totally destroyed with the sword. But Saul and the army spared Agag and the best of the sheep and cattle, the fat calves and lambs—everything that was good. These they were unwilling to destroy completely, but everything that was despised and weak they totally destroyed (15:7–9).

Weak in whose eyes? I wonder if it wasn't the donkeys that Saul wanted to save. After all, he appreciated farm animals. He probably reasoned, *Why should we destroy these perfectly good animals?* He presumed to find something good in what God had declared utterly bad.

In the New Testament, Paul wrote that we must put off the old nature with its ways of jealousy, perverseness, bitterness, envy, anger, intemperance, selfishness, and the like (Col. 3:9). The mind of the spirit makes no compromise or peace with such things. But the mind of the flesh rationalizes, *Oh, some of this is worth keeping. I can hardly be a real personality if I don't have a hot temper and tell people off once in awhile.* So we presume to find good in what God has declared bad.

The result was that Samuel came to Saul. Saul said, "I have carried out the LORD's instructions" (1 Sam. 15:13). But Samuel said, "What then is this bleating of sheep in my ears? What is this lowing of cattle that I hear?" Saul answered, "The soldiers brought them from the Amalekites; they spared the best of the sheep and cattle to sacrifice to the LORD your God, but we totally destroyed the rest" (1 Sam. 15:15). That is a common excuse, isn't it? We keep something for ourselves, and we pretend to dedicate it to God! The exchange between Samuel and Saul is very instructive for us today:

> [Samuel said], "Why did you not obey the LORD?" . . .
> "But I did obey the LORD," Saul said. . . . Samuel replied: "Does the LORD delight in burnt offerings and sacrifices as much as in obeying the voice of the LORD? To obey is better than sacrifice, and to heed is better than the fat of rams. For rebellion is like the sin of divination, and arrogance like the evil of idolatry. Because you have rejected the word of the LORD, he has rejected you as king" (15:19–23).

No one can walk in authority and freedom as God intended while rejecting the authority of God's Spirit. That is the lesson taught by the tragic story of Saul—the man of the flesh.

David: The man of the Spirit

The story of David, starting in chapter 16, is the story of the man after God's own heart. We can reap tremendous lessons from the account of David, his rejection, and his exile. He was chosen from the eight sons of Jesse. The seven eldest sons passed before Samuel and each one looked—from a human perspective—like a king in the making. But each time, God said through Samuel, "The LORD has not chosen this one." At last came the youngest and the skinniest one of all: David. God put His seal upon him. His choice was not according to outward appearance. God looked instead at David's heart.

David was not set on the throne immediately, as Saul was, but was tested and proved by struggle and adversity. This is the principle that God often follows with the ones who learn to walk by faith. They are put through a time of obscurity, testing, and problems. Everything seems to go against them until at last they recognize the great principle by which God's activity is always carried on: Human beings can do nothing in their own strength but only in complete dependence upon the power of the indwelling God. This is what David learned even as a shepherd boy, so that he could say, "The LORD is my shepherd, I shall not be in want. He makes me lie down in green pastures, he leads me beside quiet waters, he restores my soul" (Ps. 23:1–3).

The most famous of David's various tests was his confrontation with the Philistine giant Goliath. Israel was held in the grip of fear as this towering giant paraded up and down in the zone between the armies, taunting the Israelites. No one dared to face him. When little David came from his flocks to bring food to his brothers, he found the whole camp of Israel plunged into gloom and despair. He came in and asked, "Who is this uncircumcised Philistine that he should defy the armies of the living God?" (1 Sam. 17:26). That is always the outlook of faith. It is never shaken by the circumstances.

Saul receives word about this young man in their midst. Saul asks David what he wants to do. David says, "Your servant will go and fight him." Saul, to be helpful, puts his armor on David. Now Saul was about one and a half feet taller than David, and the armor on the young lad began to clank and get in his way. David tried to move around and couldn't even take a step. Finally he said, "I cannot go in these because I am not used to them." David then went down to the brook and got five smooth stones. Why five? A little later, in 2 Samuel, you will read that Goliath had four brothers. David took five stones because he was prepared to take on the whole family!

David went out with his sling in his hand, let fly, and Goliath fell to the ground with a stone lodged right between his eyes. Then David took Goliath's own sword and cut off his head. This scene reminds us of Hebrews 2:14, which tells us that by His own death the Lord Jesus slew him who had the power of death, the Devil. So David symbolizes Christ—and also the believer who allows Jesus Christ to live His life through him or her.

This event is followed by Saul's great jealousy of David. From chapter 18 on we have the story of Saul's growing persecution of David—an illustration of the principle that Paul declares in Galatians: "At that time the son born in the ordinary way persecuted the son born by the power of the Spirit. It is the same now" (Gal. 4:29).

So Saul persecuted David and tried to kill him. It was during this time that David wrote so many of the psalms, those wonderful songs that speak of God's faithfulness in the midst of distressing and depressing conditions. David was pursued and finally exiled from Saul's presence.

In chapters 21 and 22, we find God's abundant provision for David even in his exile. He is given the very holy bread of the tabernacle. This bread, representing the presence of God, is a symbol of God's deliverance for everyone who looks to Him while undergoing intense stress. To all such people, God gives the hidden bread, the bread from the very table of the Lord Himself. Jesus said, "I am the bread of life," (John 6:35), and, "I live because of the Father, so the one who feeds on me will live because of me" (John 6:57).

In his exile, David the king had a prophet, Gad, and a priest, Abiathar. The resources of these men of God were available to David even though he was hunted like a wild animal. Even greater resources are available to us in our own times of trouble, because we have available to us all the resources of the Lord Jesus Christ (our Prophet, our Priest, and our King).

Twice during this exile period David has the opportunity to kill Saul, and twice he spares Saul. In a remarkable spirit of faith, David waits for God to work out his problems.

The end of the man of the flesh

The end of the book of 1 Samuel brings us to the end of the man of the flesh, Saul. Out of a sense of desperation, he descends to witchcraft in an effort to determine the mind of the Lord after the Spirit of God has departed from him. Although witchcraft was utterly forbidden to the people of God, Saul visits the witch of Endor and tries to get her to call Samuel up. God overrules this and sends not an impersonating spirit, as the witch expects, but the true Samuel. The spirit of the prophet Samuel predicts Saul's doom on the field of battle the next day.

True to the prophecy, Saul and his son Jonathan, David's bosom friend, are slain. Saul's death illustrates Paul's words in 1 Corinthians 3 concerning the works of the carnal believer (the Christian who relies on the flesh rather than the Spirit of God): "If [any man's work] is burned up, he will suffer loss; he himself will be saved, but only as one escaping through the flames" (1 Cor. 3:15). So Saul passes out of history and into eternity—a man whose earthly life and opportunities for serving God are largely wasted. It is an instructive tragedy for us all.

But there are more tales of both glory and tragedy ahead of us. The story of King David continues in the second book of Samuel.

The Story of David

A magazine reporter once paid a visit to a wealthy rancher. "I'd like to do a magazine story on your career as a sheep rancher," said the reporter. "I've heard that yours is a true rags-to-riches tale, and I'd like to share the secret of your success with all my readers."

"Fine," said the rancher. "Be glad to tell you all about it."

"Well," said the magazine reporter, "I understand you own several hundred thousand sheep. Your ranch covers half the county and your net worth is in the millions. Yet I hear that, twenty years ago, you started out with only one sheep."

"Not only that," said the rancher, "but in those days, my wife and I didn't have a roof over our heads or a dollar to our name. All we had was that one sheep. So we sheared it, sold the wool, and used the money to buy another sheep."

"What happened then?"

"The next spring, one of the sheep gave birth to two lambs. Then we had four sheep. We sheared them, sold the wool, and used the money to buy two more sheep. That gave us a total of six sheep."

"So then what happened?" asked the reporter.

"The next spring, we had six more lambs—so now we had twelve sheep to shear. We sold the wool and bought more sheep."

The reporter figured he was really on to something big. Excitedly, he said, "So now we're getting down to it—the secret of your success!"

"That's right," drawled the rancher. "So the next year—"

ADVENTURING
THROUGH THE
BIBLE

King David: The
agony and the
ecstasy

"I know! I know!" the reporter interrupted. "So the next year, you sold more wool and bought more sheep!"

"Nope," said the rancher. "That was the year my father-in-law died and left us fifty million dollars."

King David got his start in much the same way, didn't he? David began with a few sheep—and suddenly, unexpectedly, God exalted him and made him the king over Israel, a man of extraordinary wealth and power. If the story of David were made into a television miniseries, the episode covering 1 Samuel chapters 16 to 31 might be called "King David: The Early Years." Now, in 2 Samuel, we come to the episode called "King David: The Agony and the Ecstasy."

The book of 2 Samuel falls into four simple divisions: Chapters 1 through 5 trace the road to dominion. David began his reign as king over the tribe of Judah; then, seven years later, he was crowned king over all of Israel's twelve tribes.

Chapters 6 through 10 highlight worship and victory; these two elements always go together in God's economy and in the Christian life.

Chapters 11 through 20 record David's failure and God's forgiveness.

Chapters 21 through 24 close the book with an appendix setting forth some of the important lessons that King David learned in the course of his reign. Here is an outline of the entire book:

King David: The Road to Dominion
(2 Samuel 1–5)

1.	David's reign over Judah	1:1–2:7
2.	Ish-Bosheth made king over Israel	2:8–11
3.	David defeats Ish-Bosheth	2:12–4:12
4.	David reigns in Jerusalem over Israel	5

King David: Worship and Victory
(2 Samuel 6–10)

6.	The movement of the ark of the covenant	6
7.	David's covenant with God; he is forbidden to build the temple; God promises David an eternal house	7
8.	David's military victories over the Philistines, Moab, Zobah, and Syria	8
9.	The righteous reign of King David	9
10.	Military victories over Ammon and Syria	10

King David: Failure and Forgiveness
(2 Samuel 11–20)

11.	David commits adultery with Bathsheba	11:1–5

What David represents

Let's consider two ways of looking at the life of David. You may look at him as a representation of Jesus Christ—not only as the forerunner and genetic ancestor of the Lord Jesus, but also, in his reign, as a symbolic image of Jesus Christ in His millennial reign at the end of history. David was rejected and persecuted, as was Christ. During David's exile, he gathered around him men who became his leaders, his commanders, and his generals when he became king. Thus David is a picture of Christ who also was rejected, forsaken by the world, and who secretly gathers those who will be His commanders, generals, and captains when He comes to establish His kingdom and to reign in power and glory over the earth.

1. David is a picture of Christ

But David is not only a picture of Christ. He is also a picture of each individual believer, of you and me. Only as we read from that point of view does the book come alive and glow with truth for us. If you look at these Old Testament books as mirrors, you will always find yourself there.

2. David is a picture of you and me

David's story is symbolic of what happens in a Christian's life as he or she gives it to God. Every Christian is offered a kingdom, just as David was offered a kingdom. That kingdom is the kingdom of your own life, and it is exactly like the kingdom of Israel. Enemies threaten it externally. Enemies threaten to undermine it from within. As we see how God brought David to the place of reigning over his kingdom, we will see how the Holy Spirit works in our lives to bring us to the place of reigning with Christ Jesus.

The first section opens with the death of Saul, the man of the flesh. David learns about Saul's and Jonathan's deaths from a passing Amalekite who boasts that he slew King Saul, took his crown off his head, and brought it to David (2 Sam. 1:10). When we recall that an Amalekite is a descendant of Esau and one with whom God has said He is at war "from generation to generation" (Ex. 17:16), we can regard his tale as essentially a fabrication, for it differs considerably from the account of Saul's death in 1 Samuel. Without a doubt, this man found the dead body of the king, plundered it, and attempted to use it for his own advancement. One lesson taught by this story is how the flesh (symbolized by the Amalekite) can steal away our crowns and seek to glorify itself. David however honors Saul as the Lord's anointed and kills the Amalekite.

In a song of great beauty and power, David, ever the man of faith, extols both Saul and Jonathan as men used by God, despite their weaknesses. The song closes with an eloquent expression of David's sense of loss at the death of his dear friend Jonathan (2 Sam. 1:26).

With Saul dead, David is free to be king over the land. This symbolizes for us the time when we come at last to the full truth of the cross and what the cross means to us. It is the cross of Jesus Christ that puts the old man to death and brings to an end the reign of the flesh, as pictured here by King Saul. When at last it breaks upon our astonished intellect that God truly seeks to crucify the life of Adam in us and raise us with Christ, we stand in the same place that David was at the beginning of 2 Samuel: Our inner "King Saul" is dead. We are free to reign over our own lives.

David rules for
seven years over
Judah

At first David was king over only his own tribe, Judah. For seven years he lived and ruled in the city of Hebron. But while he was king over Judah, a fierce struggle raged between the house of David and the house of Saul. The old flesh dies hard. It doesn't give up its reign easily. A fierce battle rages.

David becomes king
of all Israel

Finally, we read that David comes to the place where he is acknowledged king over all twelve tribes. He is free now to assume his God-given royal prerogatives over the entire land. It is a long and difficult road, but David finally arrives at the place of dominion.

Worship and victory

David attempts to
bring back the ark
of God

Chapter 6 begins the second division of this book. Here we see what happens in David's life when he assumes his full authority within the kingdom. His first concern is to bring back the ark of God. In 1 Samuel we read that the ark had been captured by the Philistine tribes. They had taken it and tried to set it up in their own temple. But when the ark of God stood opposite the grotesque fish god of the Philistines, the fish god could not stand it. The idol fell flat on its face and ended up with a broken neck. The Philistines realized that they couldn't get away with trying to keep the ark of God in their own temple, so they sent it to another city. It remained there until David became king.

When David became king over all twelve tribes, his first concern was to bring the ark of God back from the Philistines into the central life of the nation of Israel. What does this signify? When you first came to the realization that Jesus Christ has the right to be Lord over every area of your life, was it not your desire to put Him squarely in the center of your life? That is what is pictured here in David's desire to bring back the ark. He wants God to have first place in the life of Israel.

David built a brand-new oxcart and set the ark in the middle of it. Then he started back with all the people singing and rejoicing around the ark. It was a time of enthusiastic, sincere devotion to God. But then a terrible thing happened. As the ark was going down the road, the cart hit a rut in the road. A man named Uzzah, standing by the cart, reached out his hand to steady the ark. The moment his hand touched it, the lightning of God struck him and he fell dead.

David didn't know what to do. Of course it cast a pall of tragedy over the whole scene, and all the rejoicing and merrymaking abruptly stopped. This man had died even though his intentions were good; he only wanted to keep the ark from falling to the ground. David was so sick at heart that he turned the oxcart aside, put the ark of God in the first house that was handy, and went back to Jerusalem, bitter and resentful toward the Lord.

This was the first lesson David had to learn. The truth is, it was David's fault that Uzzah had died. Leviticus sets forth very specific instructions on how to move the ark of God. Only the Levites were to do this, and David had failed by not ordering them to do so. He was so presumptuous that he assumed that God was on his side and that he could get away with anything. He just put the ark on an oxcart and started to move it himself—and an innocent man paid the ultimate price. David had to learn the very bitter lesson that sincerity in serving God is never enough. Things must be done God's way in order to accomplish God's will.

I once talked with a young man who, like David, experienced a time of acute resentment and bitterness. This fellow was convinced that God wanted him to carry out a given plan, and he thought that he could foresee exactly how God was going to work. He announced to his friends what God was about to accomplish—but then it all fell apart.

"I can't help feeling God is unfair," this young man later told me. "It seems as if God doesn't back up what He promises." As we talked, it became apparent that he had made some of the same kinds of errors that David had made. He was presumptuous about God's will and tried to carry out God's will in his own way, rather than the way God had laid

Uzzah dies when he touches the ark

Things must be done God's way in order to accomplish God's will out in His Word. If we want to serve God, we must sign onto His agenda and use His methods, not just make our plans and expect God to endorse them. David had to learn this truth, and the death of Uzzah stands as a constant testimony that God will never compromise on this.

The next thing we read in this section is about David's desire to build a temple for God. The ark had been in the tabernacle, a rough old desert tent. So David reasoned with himself, "Here I am, living in a palace of cedar, while the ark of God remains in a tent" (see 2 Sam. 7:2). When Nathan the prophet heard of David's plan to build a house for God, he encouraged David to go ahead with it.

But then God sent a message to Nathan to say that David should not. Why? Because David was a man of war. Only Jesus Christ, or, in Old Testament terms, someone who symbolizes Christ as Prince of Peace, will ever build the temple of God among humanity. David had been the one chosen to represent Jesus as the conquering king over all. God rejected David's plan to build the temple even though it was well-intentioned, sincere, and earnest. From David's response, it seems that he was able to learn the lesson of the death of Uzzah: He praises God and graciously accepts this disappointment and the reversal of his own plans. He agrees that God is right and that the temple should be built by Solomon, his son.

The rest of this section reports David's victories over Israel's enemies, the Philistines and the Ammonites. When God is in the center of David's life, when the king of Israel subjects himself to the King of the universe and His eternal program, nothing can hinder victory. All internal enemies and the external enemies are in complete subjection to the one who walks in a humble, obedient relationship with God.

Moral failure: David's darkest hour

The next major section begins the story of failure in David's life, the black and bitter picture of David's double sin. Chapter 11 begins:

In the spring, at the time when kings go off to war . . . (v. 1).

In some ways, wars were conducted in a more civilized way in those ancient days. Kings waited for good weather before sending their men out to fight and die. It was the spring of the year, and the Lord's agenda called for wars to be fought against the evil, idolatrous nations. It was the season for kings to go forth to battle. So where do we find King David? The text goes on to tell us:

David sent Joab out with the king's men and the whole Israelite army. They destroyed the Ammonites and besieged Rabbah. But David remained in Jerusalem (11:1).

Now we see where the failure begins. David had forsaken his post. He was AWOL—absent without leave—from the Lord's service. To be absent from the place where you belong is to be exposed to temptation, as the text goes on to reveal. What happens next can be told in three simple statements: David saw. He inquired. He took.

Walking on the roof of his house he *saw* a beautiful woman taking a bath. He sent a messenger and *inquired* about her. And then he *took* her. That is how temptation progresses. It follows the same pattern in your life and mine. Temptation starts first with simple desire. There is nothing wrong with the desire. It is awakened in us simply because we are human, but it must be dealt with when it arises. Either it is put away at that point or it becomes an intent. David saw the beautiful woman, desired her, and began to plan a way to take her. He sent and inquired about her. The act followed immediately. Thus did David—the man after God's own heart, the man of the spirit—become involved in the deep, treacherous sin of the flesh.

When it was accomplished, he refused to face the truth. Instead of openly confessing and acknowledging the wrong and trying to make it right, he committed another sin to cover up. This, as we all know from sad experience, begins a descending spiral of progressive sin and cover-up.

David's sin of adultery produced consequences: Bathsheba became pregnant. This was a major problem since Bathsheba's husband, Uriah, had been out on the battlefield (where David should have been!) and could not have gotten his wife pregnant. So David sent for Uriah and tried to trick him. But Uriah, in his simple faithfulness to God—and, ironically, to his king, David—confounded David, refusing to spend the night with his wife.

Finally, David arranged for Uriah to be double-crossed on the battle field. David let the enemy do his dirty work for him. It was one of the most callous, disgusting, dishonorable acts one human being ever perpetrated on another—and we can hardly comprehend how low this man of God had sunk. Moreover, in his sin, David corrupted one of his own generals, making Joab a co-conspirator in this plot against innocent, faithful, truehearted Uriah. Though it was an Ammonite weapon that took Uriah's life, it was as if David himself had plunged it into Uriah's heart. God's verdict on David's act is recorded in 2 Samuel 11:27:

The thing David had done displeased the LORD.

An adulterer. A murderer. An evildoer. And this is the man whom God had chosen to be the ancestor of the Lord Jesus? How could David have done such a thing?

169

But if you want to see what God means when He says that David was a man after His own heart, look at what happens in David's life when God sends Nathan the prophet to him. Nathan approaches David carefully, using the same teaching method that Jesus would later use so effectively: a parable. He tells David the story of a rich man with many flocks of sheep who takes away a poor man's only ewe lamb. When David hears the story, he becomes angry and responds, "The man who did this deserves to die!" (see 2 Sam. 12:1–5).

Now Nathan has him! "You are the man!" the prophet says accusingly.

Immediately, David recognizes the point of this story, and he acknowledges his sin. He no longer tries to justify it or hide it. In fact, it is during this time and because of this situation that David wrote Psalm 51, the psalm of confession and repentance. This is a psalm we should turn to whenever we feel the burden of guilt.

David's restoration

Sin has natural consequences

God is gracious, as we shall see. His grace and forgiveness are so great that He will even restore a person who has committed great sins such as David's. But even though there is forgiveness for all our sin, we must remember that sin has natural consequences, and often those consequences cannot be removed. That is the sad fact David must face in 2 Samuel 12, as the prophet Nathan says to him:

> *"The sword will never depart from your house, because you despised me and took the wife of Uriah the Hittite to be your own."*
>
> *This is what the LORD says, "Out of your own household I am going to bring calamity upon you. Before your very eyes I will take your wives and give them to one who is close to you, and he will lie with your wives in broad daylight" (vv. 10–11).*

That prophecy was literally fulfilled by Absalom, David's son. Nathan goes on:

> [God says] *"You did it in secret, but I will do this thing in broad daylight before all Israel." Then David said to Nathan, "I have sinned against the LORD."*
>
> *Nathan replied, "The LORD has taken away your sin. You are not going to die. But because by doing this you have made the enemies of the LORD show utter contempt the son born to you will die" (12:12–14).*

God forgives David after his confession, and his life is spared—even though the law clearly demands the death penalty in such cases. God restores that inner personal relationship between Himself and David so that David has a sense of peace and freedom from guilt.

Yet God deals with us not only in grace, but also in government. The government of God demands that our deeds, which affect others, carry consequences whether or not forgiveness takes place. So David must face the results of his deeds and, as we learn in the New Testament, God chastens those whom He loves (Rev. 3:19). The baby born of this illegitimate union dies, despite David's pleadings and tears. Moreover, there is trouble ahead in David's home, in his family, and in his kingdom. The New Testament tells us, "Do not be deceived"—that is, don't kid yourself—"God cannot be mocked. A man reaps what he sows. The one who sows to please his sinful nature, from that nature will reap destruction" (Gal. 6:7–8). David is told that he will never again know peace in his house because of his sin.

The rest of this section, chapters 13 to 20, is the working out of this prophecy. In chapter 13 is told the dark story of Amnon, David's son, as he sinned against his own sister, Tamar. This resulted in a black hatred born in Absalom, David's other son, against Amnon. So there in David's own family, among his own sons, is spread the bitter spirit of lust, rebellion, and murder. In all this, King David is utterly helpless. David cannot rebuke his own son because Amnon is simply following in his father's footsteps. Amnon is only committing those sins of passion for which David himself had set the example by taking Bathsheba.

Lust, rebellion, and murder in David's household

Beginning with chapter 15, we read of the treachery and rebellion of Absalom. This handsome, brilliant, gifted, young son of David carefully steals the allegiance of the nation away from King David, drawing men into a conspiracy to unseat David and to take the throne for himself. He is finally so successful that David must flee the city again as an exile. Imagine that! The man whom God has set over Israel as king must now flee like a common criminal—all because of a chain of circumstances leading back to a moment of moral failure: He saw. He inquired. He took. And for years afterward, he paid a heavy price.

Absalom's rebellion

Throughout his troubles, David's heart is humble, penitent, and trusting. David never utters a word of complaint nor ever attempts to blame God. David recognizes that God can still work out the details of his life. Eventually, God restores David to the throne and Absalom is overtaken, conquered by his own vanity. His long hair (which he gloried in) gets caught in the branches of a tree and Joab, David's ruthless general (who also carried out David's order against Uriah), finds Absalom there and kills him.

Joab murders Absalom

In Absalom's death the rebellion is crushed. But that is not the whole story. In chapters 18 through 20, we find the ultimate result of David's sin in the rebellion of Sheba against King David. All of this pain and trouble in David's life stems from David's moral failure. There is no

The appendix

peace for the rest of his reign. He has God's forgiveness, God's grace, God's restoration, and God's blessing, but he continues to reap the circumstantial results of his own folly.

Finally, in chapters 21 through 24, we have the epilogue or appendix to this book. Here are gathered up some of the lessons that King David has learned throughout his forty-year reign. In chapter 21 we find the story of the Gibeonites, which teaches us that the past must be reckoned with. If we have misdeeds in our past that can still be corrected, we have a responsibility before God to go back and set them straight. Many a Christian discovers that the item or money he or she stole in the old life now weighs heavily upon a Spirit-led conscience. Amends must be made, the debt must be paid, because God desires truth in the inward parts. He is not content with mere outward formalities. He wants one's entire life to be right.

In the story of the Gibeonites, David went back and corrected something that happened under King Saul. As Saul's heir to the throne, he had to set it straight. Second Samuel 22:26–27 reproduces the text of Psalm 18, in which David sings:

> *"To the faithful you show yourself faithful,*
> *to the blameless you show yourself blameless,*
> *to the pure you show yourself pure,*
> *but to the crooked you show yourself shrewd."*

David says that God will be to you what you are to Him. If you are open and honest with Him, God will be open and honest with you. If you are crooked and deceitful toward God, He will cause all your circumstances to deceive you and lie to you. If you are pure in heart, you will discover that God brings more of His beauty, purity, and perfection into your own heart and soul. This is what Paul cries out for in Philippians when he says, "Not that I have already obtained all this, or have already been made perfect, but I press on to take hold of that for which Christ Jesus took hold of me" (Phil. 3:12).

David's third sin

The last chapter is the account of David's third recorded sin, the sin of numbering Israel. A plague came upon the people of Israel when David, in his pride, began to rely on his own resources and upon apparent military might, instead of relying upon the power of God. What does this teach us? That our old nature is always there, ready to spring into action the moment we cease to rely upon the Spirit of God. Sin never dies of old age. No matter how long you walk with God, it is still possible to fall. The only thing that maintains the spiritual life is the quiet, day-by-day, moment-by-moment walk in faith.

Sin never dies of old age

It is fitting that the book of 2 Samuel closes with the man after God's own heart turning from his sin and back to the worship of the living God.

How to Lose a Kingdom

F irst Kings is the gripping story of how to lose a kingdom. Like so many Old Testament books, this book is a dramatic and powerful visual aid by which God illustrates many important principles about how we should live. We can see ourselves in the stories and the lives of this book; its truths and insights are aimed at our hearts.

The book of 1 Kings holds the secret of success in reigning over the kingdom of your life. It is the secret of learning to be submissive to God's authority. In other words, you can never exercise dominion over your life unless you first subject yourself to the dominion of God. When you do, He gives you greater freedom and responsibility. If you reject His rulership over your life, then you cannot fulfill your desire to rule your life, and you cannot fulfill the enormous potential God has planned for you. Instead, control of your life will gradually be given over to other forces: to other people, to lusts and desires, to appetites and cravings, to worldly values and worldly pressures. Only by submitting self-will to God's will can we truly be free!

First Kings holds the secret of success in reigning over the kingdom of your life

In the Hebrew Bible, the books of 1 and 2 Kings are combined into one book of Kings. They are aptly named Kings, for they trace the various royal dynasties in Israel and Judah. Throughout these books, the spotlight is always on the king; as the king goes, so goes the nation. When the king walks with God in obedience and humility, God's blessing rests upon the kingdom. There was no such blessing for the

A history of many kings

northern kingdom because it had no godly kings, but in Judah, in the house of David, there was victory and prosperity when godly kings had dominion. The rains came at the right times, the crops grew, the economy flourished, enemies were vanquished, there was peace in the land. When the king walked with God, there was victory and prosperity; when the king disobeyed, there was famine, drought, war, and suffering.

Good kings were always types of Christ, and they included David, Solomon, Hezekiah, Joash, and Jehoshaphat. In the lives of these kings (despite their human failings), we see symbols of the kingly reign of the Lord Jesus Christ. The disobedient kings were types of the Antichrist, the man of sin, the quintessence of human evil who is yet to appear upon the earth.

Here is an outline of the book of 1 Kings:

The Age of Solomon (1 Kings 1–11)

1.	The plot of Adonijah; the anointing of Solomon	1–2
2.	The wisdom and rule of Solomon	3–4
3.	Solomon builds the temple	5–8
4.	The kingdom grows in might and wealth	9–10
5.	The disobedience and decline of Solomon	11:1–11:40
6.	The death of Solomon	11:41–43

A Kingdom Divided (1 Kings 12–22)

7.	Rehoboam and the revolt of the northern tribes	12:1–24
8.	The reign of wicked Jeroboam	12:25–14:31
9.	The reign of Abijam in Judah	15:1–8
10.	The reign of Asa in Judah	15:9–24
11.	Five kings of Israel: Nadab, Baasha, Elah Zimri, and Omri	15:25–16:28
12.	The reign of wicked Ahab in Israel and the miraculous ministry of the prophet Elijah	16:29–22:40
13.	The reign of Jehoshaphat in Judah	22:41–50
14.	The reign of Ahaziah in Israel	22:51–53

As the book opens, we see that God has called aside the nation Israel. He has marked out these people as His own special people. He has made of this little land of Israel an international stage, and He will focus the attention of the world on this tiny piece of real estate, this small but unusual collection of people.

In chapter 1, we find King David upon the throne, and his son, Solomon, is in line to succeed him as king. But one of David's other sons, Adonijah, has different ideas. He is plotting rebellion in order to gain control of the throne even before his father dies. David, learning of this, acts to immediately place Solomon on the throne. So Solomon is anointed king while his father still lives.

This symbolically suggests what the reigning authority in our lives should be: True authority must come by the gift and hand of God. We cannot reign except as we are established by God. When we give ourselves to the authority of God, it becomes His responsibility to bring under control every circumstance and every enemy and every rebellion that would otherwise threaten our reign.

In the second and third chapters, we see Solomon coming to the throne. He rules in power, might, and glory. Solomon's reign marks the greatest extension of the kingdom of Israel and was particularly characterized by a display of outward majesty and power. But in chapter 3, we also find the seeds of defeat. These are crucial to notice:

> *Solomon made an alliance with Pharaoh king of Egypt and married his daughter. He brought her to the City of David until he finished building his palace and the temple of the LORD, and the wall around Jerusalem. The people, however, were still sacrificing at the high places, because a temple had not yet been built for the Name of the LORD. Solomon showed his love for the LORD by walking according to the statutes of his father David, except that he offered sacrifices and burned incense on the high places (3:1–3).*

Here is a man who loves God with all his heart. Solomon begins his reign with a wonderful expression of yieldedness and a desire for God's rule and authority in his life. He follows in the footsteps of his father, David. Nevertheless, he does two little things—seemingly trivial matters—that plant the seeds for the ultimate overthrow of his kingdom.

Two "trivial" matters: seeds for the overthrow of Solomon's kingdom

First, he makes an alliance with the daughter of Pharaoh, the king of Egypt. Throughout Scripture, Egypt is almost always a symbolic picture of the world. Solomon brings this daughter of the world into the central life of the nation of Israel, and Israel, through its king, makes an alliance with the world.

1. His alliance with Egypt by marriage to Pharaoh's daughter

Second, Solomon worships at the high places. In the pagan religions of that day, all the worship and rites were conducted up on the mountaintops. The pagan tribes had erected altars, many of which were the center of very idolatrous and licentious worship. Frequently, the altar was the place where the fertility of sex gods was worshiped in a sexual display. These altars were taken over by the people of Israel and used for the sacrifices to Jehovah.

2. His worship at the high places

Though the ark of God was now in the tabernacle in Jerusalem where David had placed it, Solomon did not present his offerings at the altar in the tabernacle. Instead, he made his offering at the high places. He sacrificed to the God he loved, but he burned those sacrifices on pagan altars.

Outwardly, this young king's rule was admirable and his heart honorable. Nevertheless, one area of his life was not fully committed to God. His fellowship with God was weak. He did not understand that the secret of God's blessing lay in an inner yieldedness to God's will, represented by a worship in strict accordance with His Word and practiced before the ark of the covenant. Solomon's lack of adherence to the Levitical rules regarding worship is the first indication that something is wrong in his life.

Asking for wisdom

Also in chapter 3, we have the account of Solomon's dream, in which God appeared and told him to ask for whatever he wanted. In response, Solomon asks not for riches or for honor but for wisdom:

"Give your servant a discerning heart to govern your people and to distinguish between right and wrong. For who is able to govern this great people of yours?" (v. 9).

A dramatic display of Solomon's wisdom

By beginning his reign in this way, Solomon indicated that he understood what was most important in exercising effective leadership. Solomon's great wisdom was demonstrated in 1 Kings 3:16–28, when he settled a dispute between two women who claimed to be the mother of the same baby. The two women were prostitutes living in the same house, and both had given birth at about the same time, but one baby had died. Each woman claimed the living baby as her own. Solomon was asked to decide whose baby it was.

In a dramatic display of God-given wisdom and insight, Solomon says, "Bring me a sword." Then, laying the baby down before these two women, he says, "Cut the living child in two and give half to one and half to the other." One woman says, "Neither I nor you shall have him. Cut him in two!" But the other woman—the real mother—immediately protests, "Please, my lord, give her the living baby! Don't kill him!"

Solomon had flushed out the imposter—and spotlighted the real mother. This was a powerful demonstration of Solomon's wisdom—and a challenge to today's judges who decide divorce cases, custody cases, and adoption cases by emotionally cutting children in half rather than placing them with people who would truly love and nurture them. Today's courts sorely lack the kind of godly wisdom displayed in Israel during the age of Solomon.

In 1 Kings 4:29–34, we find a commentary on Solomon's great wisdom (my commentary on that commentary is included in brackets):

> *God gave Solomon wisdom and very great insight, and a breadth of understanding as measureless as the sand on the seashore. Solomon's wisdom was greater than the wisdom of all the men of the East* [including all the so-called wisdom of the Orient: the Chinese and Indian], *and greater than all the wisdom of Egypt. He was wiser than any other man, including Ethan the Ezrahite—wiser than Heman, Calcol and Darda, the sons of Mahol* [these were the media pundits of that day]. *And his fame spread to all the surrounding nations. He spoke three thousand proverbs* [we have them recorded in the book of Proverbs] *and his songs numbered a thousand and five* [of those we have only one—Song of Songs]. *He described plant life, from the cedar of Lebanon to the hyssop that grows out of the walls. He also taught about animals and birds, reptiles and fish. Men of all nations came to listen to Solomon's wisdom, sent by all the kings of the world, who had heard of his wisdom.*

What a picture this is of what Paul says in 1 Corinthians, "We have the mind of Christ," and "The spiritual man makes judgments about all things" (1 Cor. 2:15–16). Solomon did not need anyone to teach him, since he already discerned all things. He was able to analyze and understand the workings of the world and the human heart, because he had the wisdom that comes from God.

Solomon made only one request of God—wisdom—and God granted it to him. But Solomon's request contained one slight weakness. He asked for wisdom that he might govern the people. We can only wish as we read that this fine young man had asked for wisdom to govern his own life first. That is where he began to fail. God granted Solomon the wisdom of governance, but He also allowed circumstances in Solomon's personal life that put his wisdom to the test. Along with wisdom, God gave Solomon riches and honor; and it was riches and honor that overthrew Solomon. As Solomon gloried and exulted in the magnificence of his kingdom, pride began to enter his heart; and his pride produced his downfall.

Chapter 4 tells us that the kingdom of Solomon was a well-ordered kingdom. In verses 1 through 19, we see that he delegates authority by appointing eleven princes and twelve governors over the kingdom. By dividing the governance of the kingdom in this way, Solomon ensured that the various levels of government would function in a decent and well-ordered way. Solomon wisely knew that God is not the author of confusion; He does all things decently and in order.

The people prospered and were happy under the wise but firm authority of Solomon, as we read in 1 Kings 4:20:

> *The people of Judah and Israel were as numerous as the sand on the seashore; they ate, they drank and they were happy. And Solomon ruled over all the kingdoms from the River [Euphrates] to the land of the Philistines, as far as the border of Egypt. These countries brought tribute and were Solomon's subjects all his life.*

Here is a picture of Solomon's total control and godly authority over the dominion that God had given him. This is the kind of firm control that God wants all of us to exercise over our own lives.

In chapters 5 through 8, we find the account of the glorious temple that Solomon built. For four hundred years, Israel had been worshipping in the tabernacle—a mere tent! But Solomon fulfilled the dream of his father David, the dream of a permanent and splendid place in which the people of Israel could worship their God.

The glory of the temple

The description of the temple in these chapters conveys a splendor almost beyond imagining. It was built of great hand-quarried stones and imported cedar. The interior was entirely covered with gold. In today's dollars, the structure would have cost not millions but *billions.* The true grandeur of the temple, however, was not the gold but the glory—the Shekinah glory of God that came down and dwelt in the holy place when Solomon dedicated the temple.

The Shekinah glory in the temple

In chapter 10, we have the story, wonderful in its detail, of the visits of the queen of Sheba and the king of Tyre to Solomon and the recognition by the nations of the glory of Solomon's kingdom. Then, suddenly and tragically, we come to chapter 11, where the story of Solomon takes a swift turn for the worse.

The decline and fall of Solomon

The seeds of decline and disobedience that were sown earlier in Solomon's life now begin to sprout:

> *King Solomon, however, loved many foreign women besides Pharaoh's daughter—Moabites, Ammonites, Edomites, Sidonians and Hittites. They were from nations about which the LORD had told the Israelites, "You must not intermarry with them, because they will surely turn your hearts after their gods." Nevertheless, Solomon held fast to them in love. He had seven hundred wives of royal birth and three hundred concubines, and his wives led him astray (1 Kings 11:1–3).*

Solomon's foreign women

This is the same man who, in the book of Proverbs wrote, "He who finds a wife finds what is good" (Prov. 18:22). Apparently, Solomon didn't know when he had too much of a good thing! A thousand wives is 999 wives too many!

Here we see the weakness and failure of Solomon as his heart was turned away from God. Where did Solomon's decline begin? It began with his enjoyment of all the magnificence of his rule. All of this outward magnificence is evidence of God's blessing upon his life, but Solomon's downhill slide begins as his heart is captured by something that God had prohibited. Solomon presents a vivid picture of a principle stated by Jesus in the Sermon on the Mount: "Where your treasure is, there your heart will be also" (Luke 12:34).

I recall the story of a man who enjoyed a tremendous ministry in the pulpit and in many other ways. Suddenly, his ministry collapsed, brought down in shame by charges of immorality. It turned out that for many years there had been an unrighteous, unrepented, unjudged affection in his heart. Outwardly, he was a minister for God; inwardly, immorality and compromise were eating away at the substance of this man's heart and life. Finally, his ministry for God was destroyed. Tragically, this story is replayed again and again in the lives of both ministers and laypeople.

The first step in moral decline always begins with our desires and emotions. What has captured first place in your mind, your desires, and your emotions? If it is not something that God has endorsed, if it is something that God has disallowed, then you have planted the seeds of destruction in your own life just as Solomon planted them in his life. We see the tragic result in the next few verses:

> He followed Ashtoreth [the sex goddess] *the goddess of the Sidonians, and Molech the detestable god of the Ammonites. So Solomon did evil in the eyes of the LORD; he did not follow the LORD completely, as David his father had done.*
>
> *On a hill east of Jerusalem, Solomon built a high place for Chemosh the detestable god of Moab, and for Molech the detestable god of the Ammonites. He did the same for all his foreign wives, who burned incense and offered sacrifices to their gods.*
>
> *The LORD became angry with Solomon because his heart had turned away (11:5–9).*

Chemosh was the hideous image to which the pagan worshipers sacrificed their children in fire. Incredibly, Solomon himself built a place of worship for this grinning, demonic god! As we read through the rest of this chapter, we see that three times in rapid succession, "the Lord raised up against Solomon an adversary."

At the end of this chapter, Solomon "rested with his fathers" and was buried in the city of David—a sudden collapse to the glory and

The first step in moral decline always begins with our desires and emotions

"Solomon . . . did not follow the LORD completely, as David his father had done"

majesty of his kingdom. Even the glory of Solomon's temple proves transitory; though the structure would stand for four hundred years, it would be plundered and stripped of its gold and furnishings only five years after Solomon's death.

A kingdom divided

Jeroboam divides the kingdom and its worship

Chapter 12 begins the second movement in this book: the breakup and decline of the kingdom. Disaster overtakes the kingdom as Solomon's son Rehoboam takes the reigns of government. Jeroboam splits the kingdom, taking the ten tribes of Israel in the north to begin the northern kingdom. There, Jeroboam reintroduces the worship of golden calves—the sin God judged during Israel's trek in the desert (see Ex. 32).

Chapter 14 presents the story of Egypt's invasion and defeat of Israel—the very nation out of which God delivered Israel under Moses! Again, Egypt is a picture of the world and its ways—its wickedness, its folly, its futility, and its foolishness. Most of the treasures that Solomon had amassed during the height of his reign were plundered and carried off.

The account then tells of various kings who come to the throne of Israel—most of them either evil or incompetent, or both. Jeroboam is followed by Nadab, who is followed by Baasha and Zimri. Finally comes Ahab—probably the most evil king Israel ever knew—and his wicked wife Jezebel.

Elijah's ministry to the northern kingdom

The concluding section of the book, beginning in chapter 17, introduces the prophetic ministry, beginning with Elijah. There were other prophets before Elijah, but they did not perform miracles as Elijah did. The prophets who ministered to Judah, the southern kingdom, did no miracles because there God's testimony was still central to the life of the nation. But Israel, the northern kingdom, rejected God's presence and worshiped golden calves instead of Him. The ministry of miracles was a testimony to the people that God was still in their midst and He demanded their attention. God sought to shake them up so that they would see how far they had drifted from Him.

Elijah's ministry is a tremendous revelation of God's dealings with the wayward human heart. First of all, he shut the heavens so that it did not rain for three years. Then he called down fire from heaven upon the sheriffs and others who were sent to arrest him and bring him before the king. These miracles caught the attention of the people and produced at least a degree of repentance. The people understood that God was using a harsh hand, as we human beings sometimes force God to do.

In chapter 18, we come to the judgment against Baal, and the two philosophies in Israel come to a climactic clash on Mount Carmel. There Elijah challenges four hundred priests of Baal to a contest to determine which deity has the power to send down fire from heaven. In a remarkable scene, he taunts them as they slash their flesh and cry out to their god. " 'Shout louder!' he said. 'Surely he is a god! Perhaps he is deep in thought, or busy, or traveling. Maybe he is sleeping and must be awakened' " (1 Kings 18:27).

When the pagan priests have exhausted themselves to no avail, Elijah rolls up his sleeves and goes to work. He repairs the altar of the Lord, which has fallen into disrepair, then he orders four large jars of water to be poured over the bull and the wood upon the altar. He intends to make sure that the demonstration of God's power is not merely spectacular but absolutely astonishing. Then he calls upon God, and God sends down a fire so intense that it not only consumes the sacrifice but the water and the stones of the altar! Once judgment is exercised, the heavens open again and rain pours down upon the land.

This is a picture of what happens in the life of anyone who resists God's rightful rule. In what one writer has termed His "severe mercy," God brings us under His chastening until our stubbornness is broken. Our willful rebellion is ended and we are humbled at last before God. Then the rain of grace can pour once again upon our hearts, bringing good fruit and sweet blessing once more.

In 1 Kings 19 comes an account that I have always found amusing: the story of Elijah's fear of Jezebel. Elijah, this bold, courageous prophet, this rugged man of God who has faced four hundred priests on the mountaintop, is suddenly running in terror from one angry woman! He is so defeated that, as he hides under a juniper bush, he begs God to take his life! But God deals with Elijah according to His amazing grace.

The first thing God does is to put Elijah to bed under the juniper tree and give him a good night's rest. Then God gives him a good square meal, divinely provided by an angel of the Lord. Finally God takes Elijah out on a mountain, and Elijah witnesses all the unleashed fury of nature—an earthquake, a raging fire, a booming thunderstorm. Through this experience, Elijah learns an amazing secret: Jehovah, the Lord God Almighty, is not always to be found in the overwhelming power of nature unleashed. Sometimes His power is most dramatically demonstrated when He moves through the still, small voice of a changed conscience.

The story of 1 Kings is the story of a kingdom lost. Solomon, perhaps the wisest man who ever lived, fell into folly and disobedience and lost a kingdom. After his death, the kingdom was divided in two, and a succession of unwise or evil kings brought nothing but misery to the people of the northern and southern kingdoms.

The book closes with the story of King Ahab, the account of his failure, and his self-centered desire for Naboth's vineyard, which ultimately brings forth God's judgment.

In chapter 22 we learn how God works through apparently accidental circumstances. The two kings of Israel and Judah go out to battle. Ahab, king of Israel, in his satanic cleverness tries to put the king of Judah out in the forefront of battle. Ahab dresses the king of Judah in his own armor so that he might be mistaken for the king of Israel and shot at. But as King Ahab is complimenting himself on how he has tricked the king of Judah into being exposed to danger, we read that an arrow shot into the air (just by chance) by a warrior on the opposite side, finds its way to him and pierces a chink in Ahab's armor, penetrating his heart.

Our God is the God of all circumstances. He is the God whose will is accomplished even through seeming accidents, chance, and coincidence. He is behind all the movements of our lives, and His judgment is accomplished! That is what this account reveals.

Outward circumstances will never dethrone you from ruling your life as God intended from the beginning. Nothing you encounter—pressures, mistreatment, obstacles, accidents—can ever succeed in dethroning you. You can be dethroned and driven into the bondage of the flesh and the devil *only if you allow it,* if you permit some rival form of worship to enter into your heart, leaving no room for God. That rival form of worship may be a habit, an obsession with status and money, a sinful desire or forbidden affection, a self-willed attitude of rebellion, or something else.

If you, like Solomon, allow folly to replace godly wisdom in your life, then your kingdom's days are numbered. But if you make God and His kingdom the single, true desire of your heart, then you will reign forever, and the kingdom of your life will be secure.

A Wasted Life

The first half of 1 Kings was dominated by the story of King Solomon. In the second half, however, a new and towering figure emerges—not a king but a prophet, Elijah. The story continues in 2 Kings, as God repeatedly intervenes in the lives of the kings of Israel in an attempt to reverse the trend of corruption and decay in the kingdom. In addition to the prophet Elijah, God raises up the prophet Elisha. The book of 2 Kings is noteworthy primarily because of the ministries of these two mighty men of God.

It is significant that God never spoke to the nation through a king. The king's role was to govern and to administer justice. The life and the character of the kingdom was a reflection of the life and character of the king.

But when God wanted to speak to the nation, to challenge the nation, to call the nation back to its founding principles, He sent a prophet. Elsewhere in the Old Testament, God sent other prophets to Israel—men such as Hosea, Amos, Joel, Isaiah, and Jeremiah. But the prophets who take center stage in 1 and 2 Kings are Elijah and Elisha.

Here is an outline of the book of 2 Kings:

Second Kings is noteworthy because of the ministries of Elijah and Elisha

God never spoke to the nation through a king

**Further History of the Divided Kingdom
(2 Kings 1–17)**

1. The reign of Ahaziah in Israel   1
2. The reign of Jehoram in Israel   2:1–8:15

**The prophet
Elijah:
Thunderings
of the Law**

Elijah was a rugged outdoorsman who wore haircloth that was bound by a leather girdle. He was a scraggly, mangy-looking character who repeatedly risked his life to confront the king face-to-face. He was bold and faithful, and God protected him. We have already seen in 1 Kings 18 how he challenged the four hundred priests of Baal on top of Mount Carmel and single-handedly defied the power of their abominable false god.

Elijah was a bold, cantankerous character, a dedicated prophet of the law. It was his ministry to bring the thunderings of the law to Israel, to awaken the nation to its shameful condition. His was a ministry of mingled love, fire, and judgment.

At the close of his ministry, Elijah is triumphantly, miraculously caught up into heaven in a chariot of fire, as described in careful detail in chapter 2. When faithful Elisha refuses to leave his great mentor, the mantle of the prophet literally falls upon Elisha and he is promised a double portion of the spirit of Elijah.

The prophet Elisha: Grace and glory

In contrast to Elijah, Elisha's ministry is the ministry of grace and sweetness and glory throughout Israel. Why was this? If you study the narrative carefully, comparing it with the narrative of the four gospels, you will see that these two men together prefigure the double-edged ministry of Jesus Christ—both His thundering truth and His sweet grace.

When the Lord Jesus came to Israel, He found the nation in a state of decay and corruption, as it was when Elijah came to the nation. Herod was on the throne as a vassal of Rome. The high priest's office had gone into the hands of the Sadducees (the rationalists of that day) and they had turned the temple into a place of corruption and commerce. The nation had fallen into dark and bitter times. The Lord Jesus' ministry to official Israel was in the power of Elijah. He began His ministry with a prophetic act: the cleansing of the temple. He made a whip of many cords, then with a voice of thunder and eyes of fire, He drove the corrupt money changers out of the temple, turning over the tables and flinging the merchandise out into the courtyard. But our Lord's ministry to the individual was the ministry of Elisha—the ministry of grace, of winsome sweetness, of compassionate tenderness and helpfulness.

The Lord's ministry to official Israel was in the power of Elijah

The Lord's ministry to the individual was the ministry of Elisha

There is another interesting comparison here: Elisha also seems to symbolize the ministry of the Holy Spirit in the church after the Day of Pentecost. Elisha's ministry begins when Elijah bodily ascends into heaven, just as the Spirit's ministry begins when Jesus ascends into heaven. Elisha's first miracle depicts the ministry of the Holy Spirit: putting salt into the water, causing it to turn sweet. The miracle of the oil that kept flowing continually is another symbol of the Holy Spirit, as is the miracle of the water that suddenly appears in the parched and barren land. There is also the miracle of resurrection when Elisha raises a dead boy to life by laying his staff upon him and breathing on his face. This was not mouth-to-mouth resuscitation but a genuine resurrection! Even when everything looks dead and hopeless, the Spirit conquers death and produces life.

The decline and fall of the kingdoms

The book of 2 Kings traces the continuing decline of these two kingdoms, and Israel, the northern kingdom, is the first to fall. In chapter 17, while under the reign of King Hoshea, Israel is conquered by Assyria's King Shalmaneser and carried away into slavery and captivity:

The LORD warned Israel and Judah through all his prophets and seers, "Turn from your evil ways. Observe my commands and decrees, in accordance with the entire Law that I commanded your fathers to obey and that I delivered to you through my servants the prophets."

But they would not listen and were as stiff-necked as their fathers, who did not trust in the LORD their God. They rejected his decrees and the covenant he had made with their fathers and the warnings he had given them. They followed worthless idols and themselves became worthless. They imitated the nations around them although the LORD had ordered them, "Do not do as they do," and they did the things the LORD had forbidden them to do.

They forsook all the commands of the LORD their God and made for themselves two idols cast in the shape of calves, and an Asherah pole [that is, a sex god]. They bowed down to all the starry hosts, and they worshiped Baal. They sacrificed their sons and daughters in the fire. They practiced divination and sorcery and sold themselves to do evil in the eyes of the LORD, provoking him to anger.

So the LORD was very angry with Israel and removed them from his presence. Only the tribe of Judah was left (17:13–18).

Here is a shocking picture of the human potential for evildoing, and the results of such sin. Here we see evil's infecting the life of a nation that was once dedicated to God; but we also know that evil has enormous power to infect and enslave people, even those who once dedicated themselves to God. We must always be on guard against even the smallest sins and compromises, for they lead to greater sin, to rebellion, to unthinkable acts, and to destruction.

Evil has enormous
power to infect and
enslave people

Hezekiah

Judah's decline and fall was delayed for a while because of a godly and wise king named Hezekiah, who arose in the midst of darkness and led his country for a while into the light. Amazingly, Hezekiah's father had been an ungodly king, and in time, Hezekiah's own son would also become an ungodly king. But Hezekiah himself was a gift of God's grace to the southern kingdom of Judah.

When Hezekiah came to the throne in chapter 18, his first official act was to cleanse the temple. It took the Levite priests sixteen days just to bulldoze all the rubbish and filth out of the temple before they could even begin the act of purifying it for service! That is how corrupt the nation had become.

Next, Hezekiah reintroduced the Passover. He also destroyed the great brazen serpent that the people had been worshiping. This was the very serpent that God had used for their blessing when Moses lifted it up in the wilderness (see Num. 21:8–9), but God had never intended it to become an object of worship. It was merely a symbol of the saving work of Christ, which still lay ahead in history. Hezekiah understood that there was nothing intrinsically sacred about this symbol, and he destroyed it so that it could never again be used for idolatrous worship. Here is an important lesson for us all: Anything, even a God-given blessing in our lives, can become a source of idolatry if we put our trust in the object of blessing (in money, in a job, in a certain religious leader or church), rather than trusting solely in the One from whom all blessings flow!

Manasseh

Hezekiah's life was miraculously extended when the shadow on the sundial turned back ten degrees and he was allowed fifteen more years of life. In those fifteen years, however, he had a son named Manasseh who became one of the worst kings Judah ever had—prompting some to suggest that perhaps Hezekiah lived too long! But it's important to compare Scripture with Scripture to understand the entire story of Manasseh. In 2 Kings 21:1–18, we only see the wickedness of this king. But comparing this account with 2 Chronicles 33:11–13 and 18–19, we find that, after being taken captive in Babylon, Manasseh repented, sought God's forgiveness, and was restored to the throne of Judah, where he reigned wisely for the rest of his days.

Judah is carried to Babylon

So the kingdom declined and finally Judah was carried away by Nebuchadnezzar into Babylon, the symbol of worldly corruption and defilement. For a few years the temple remained in Jerusalem, but eventually it too was stripped and burned. The walls of the city were broken down, and all the people were carried away into captivity. The book closes with Zedekiah, the last king of Israel. The king of Babylon captured Zedekiah, killed his sons before his very eyes, and then destroyed his eyes. Blinded and devastated, he was bound and led away to Babylon.

Zedekiah

Zedekiah was the last king Israel ever had. Later, in the tumult and confusion in Jerusalem during the Passover week when our Lord was crucified, Pilate offered Israel a new king: the LORD Jesus, beaten and bleeding, wearing a crown of thorns. "Here is your king," he said.

But the crowd rejected Him. They meant it when they cried out, "We have no king but Caesar" (see John 19:14–15). Yet it was Caesar's Gentile governor who spoke God's truth to Israel by having this inscription written above the cross: "JESUS OF NAZARETH, THE KING OF THE JEWS" (see John 19:19). The people Israel will never know another moment of genuine prosperity, peace, and blessing—either spiritually or politically—until they see Him whom they have pierced and recognize the King who was sent to them in lowliness as Zechariah prophesied (see Zech. 12:10).

In the end, this book is a picture of a wasted life. The life of the nation of Israel is exactly analogous to the life of an individual Christian. In order to fulfill our potential and become all that God intended us to be, we must build our lives on the foundation laid by Jesus Christ, not a foundation made only with wood, hay, and stubble. Those who, in the secret places of the heart, fail to walk in obedience to the Holy Spirit's prompting will gradually, imperceptibly sink deeper and deeper into corruption. The temple of the human spirit will become darkened and defiled. Eventually, cruelty and rebellion will set in, so that finally the temple of the personality is burned and destroyed.

The apostle Paul tells us that each of us will face a judgment of fire that will reveal our work; the wood, hay, and stubble will be burned, the believer will be saved, "but only as one escaping through the flames" (1 Cor. 3:13–15). The lesson of 2 Kings is that it need not be so. We may be prone to wander, prone to leave the God we love, but God in His mercy continually interrupts the reckless course of our lives, trying to draw our attention to the real issues of life, trying to rescue us from our stubborn and willful ways. Like the two kingdoms, Israel and Judah, we are free to ignore His pleadings. We are free to disobey. We are free to waste our lives.

But one day we shall have to stand naked and without excuse before the One who loves us and gave Himself for us. We will have to bend the knee and confess that we barred Him from the temple of the spirit and robbed Him of His inheritance in the saints. On that day, John says, we shall be ashamed before Him at His coming. May God grant that the lesson of these books may come home to our hearts and, above all, that it may *change our lives.*

David and The Ark of God

T he books of Chronicles cover the same historical era as the books of Samuel and Kings but from quite a different perspective. Much as the four gospels provide four different perspectives and a "quadraphonic" experience of the life of Christ, the books of Chronicles enable us to obtain a "stereophonic" experience of the kingdom period of Israel's history. Just as the purpose, style, and selection of events of John's gospel differ dramatically from those of the other three gospels (the Synoptic Gospels of Matthew, Mark, and Luke), so the purpose, style, and selection of events differs dramatically between the books of Chronicles and the Samuel-Kings histories.

The books of Chronicles center around King David and the temple. The first book focuses on the life and reign of David himself; the second book traces the house of David upon the throne of Judah, the southern kingdom. Israel, the northern kingdom, is almost completely ignored in these books. Why? Because the temple is located in Judah and because David, who is seen as God's king, is the king of Judah.

It is evident that 1 Chronicles was written after the seventy years of Israel's captivity in Babylon. The writer was probably Ezra, the priest, who also wrote the book that bears his name. Ezra was one of the great figures who returned from the Babylonian captivity to reestablish the temple and the worship of God in Jerusalem. Here is an outline of the book of 1 Chronicles:

Genealogies: The Royal Lineage of King David
(1 Chronicles 1–9)

The Reign of King David
(1 Chronicles 10–20)

**Don't
skip the
genealogies!**

The selective character of 1 Chronicles is evident immediately. The first nine chapters are devoted to a long list of genealogies. At first glance, you might think nothing could be more boring than a long list of names; it looks like a phone book! We are tempted to hurry past these lists of names, much like the old Scottish preacher who was reading from the opening chapter of Matthew. Beginning in Matthew 1:2 (KJV), he read, "Abraham begat Isaac; and Isaac begat Jacob; and Jacob begat Judah and his brethren." Then he paused and said, "And they kept on begetting one another all the way down this side of the page and clear on to the other side."

These genealogies, however, are very important to a full understanding of this book, of the history of Israel, and of the entire Old Testament. They are important for two reasons. First, the genealogies help us to ascertain and understand Bible chronology.

Second, the genealogies are carefully selected and constructed to show God's plan in working through human beings to achieve His purposes. The genealogy goes back to the dawn of human history and lists the sons and descendants of Adam: Seth, Enosh, Kenan, Mahalalel. We know Adam had sons named Cain, Abel, and Seth, but here, immediately, Cain and Abel are excluded. They are not mentioned. The whole focus is on the descendants of Seth, for from him eventually came the family of Abraham and the Israelites. Here is the principle of exclusion in action.

Then the line of Seth is traced down to Enoch and to Noah. The three sons of Noah are given: Shem, Ham, and Japheth. But Ham and Japheth are dismissed with just a brief word and attention is focused on the line of Shem. From Shem we trace on down to Abraham and his family. There is this constant narrowing process that then excludes Ishmael, the son of Abraham, and Esau, the brother of Jacob, and focuses on Jacob's twelve sons, who became the fathers of the twelve tribes of Israel. As the genealogy goes on, it selects the tribes of Judah and Levi—the tribes of the king and the priestly line. It traces the tribe of Judah down to David, to Solomon, and then to the kings of the house of David into captivity. The tribe of Levi is traced back to Aaron, the first of the priests, and then to the priests who were prominent in the kingdom at the time of David.

One fascinating incident stands out among these genealogies. It is found in 1 Chronicles 4:9–10, where we read of a man named Jabez:

> *Jabez was more honorable than his brothers. His mother had named him Jabez, saying, "I gave birth to him in pain"* [Jabez means "pain"]. *Jabez cried out to the God of Israel, "Oh that you would bless me and enlarge my territory! Let your hand be with me, and keep me from harm so that I will be free from pain." And God granted his request.*

The fact that this brief story appears in the midst of a "phone book" list of names is significant. It's God's way of spotlighting Jabez and saying, "Pay attention to this man. There is something highly instructive in his story."

In His Word, God often selectively spotlights those who obey Him. And when God excludes a name, when He turns from a line or a family, He generally does so because of their disobedience. Throughout Scripture, we often see God's excluding or dismissing people of high rank, high privilege, and high ancestry—according to human views of such matters—because those people had hearts that were not aligned with God's heart. You can trace this principle throughout this entire genealogy in 1 Chronicles. This principle also sets the pattern for the rest of the book.

In chapter 10, King Saul's life is covered in only a smattering of verses. The reason is given in verses 13 and 14:

> *Saul died because he was unfaithful to the LORD; he did not keep the word of the LORD and even consulted a medium for guidance, and did not inquire of the LORD. So the LORD put him to death and turned the kingdom over to David son of Jesse.*

The rest of 1 Chronicles is about David, the king after God's own heart. The book traces David's life from the moment he is anointed king until his death. David's first act after coming to the place of kingship in Israel is to take over the pagan stronghold of the Jebusites, the city of

Jerusalem—God's holy city. This is the place where God chose to put His name among the tribes of Israel.

Immediately following the conquest of Jerusalem comes a flashback to the time of David's exile and to the mighty men gathered around him there. These were men of faith and passion who were attracted to David by the character he demonstrated. These mighty men who gathered about David and shared his exile eventually became the leaders in his kingdom, symbolizing for us the reign of the Lord Jesus with His saints after returning to earth again. Those of us who share His sufferings now will also share His glory when He comes to establish His kingdom of righteousness.

First Chronicles underscores the importance of the ark of God

This book also dramatically underscores the importance of the ark of God. In chapter 13, we see that David goes down to the Philistine city where the ark has been held captive. He has the ark loaded onto an oxcart and begins to bring it back to Jerusalem. David's unwitting disobedience is recorded for us here. He knew that the law commanded that the ark be carried only by the Levites, but in the exuberance of his joy and his zeal for God's cause, he thought God wouldn't mind if the ark were carried in another way.

But then disaster strikes. One of the men walking alongside the ark, a man named Uzzah, sees the ark totter as the oxen stumbled. Instinctively, he reaches out to steady it. When his hand touches the ark, he is immediately struck dead. David is tremendously shaken by this. His emotions are shaken, and so is his faith.

But as he thinks and prays over this incident, he realizes that this disaster was his fault. He had neglected the word of the Lord. There is no incident from the Old Testament that teaches more clearly the importance of uninterrupted compliance with God's Word, and David is sobered by the lesson that this incident teaches. Afterward, he asks the Levites to bring up the ark according to the law; then the ark is brought back to its rightful place in Jerusalem.

Here is a significant point: The tabernacle had been the home of the ark throughout the Israelite's journey in the wilderness. It had been the central place of worship for Israel during the time of the judges and the reign of Saul. Yet the tabernacle was not located in Jerusalem. It was in the city of Gibeon. One would think that the ark should be returned to that tabernacle, since it had been taken from it. The ark belonged in the Holy of Holies in the tabernacle.

However, when David brings the ark back, he doesn't return it to the tabernacle but to the city of Jerusalem, the city of the king. By his own authority, he sets up a center of worship on the very site where the temple would later be built. Thus he replaces the authority of the priests with the authority of the king. Why? Because David is making a symbolic statement: He is showing that when the king comes, the ark is to be established on a permanent site, not in a tabernacle made of skins and tent poles, but in a temple made of wood and stone and precious metal. Though the temple itself will not be built until Solomon's day, the temple site in Jerusalem symbolizes a new beginning for Israel, a change of government, a change of behavior.

Beginning in chapter 18, where the ark is brought back and placed at the temple site, David's conquest over his enemies throughout Judah is immediately recorded. Chapters 18, 19, and 20 are devoted to King David's victories. These victories symbolically suggest what happens in the heart of the believer if Christ is crowned Lord and King of that person's life.

King David's victories

The only dark picture in the book is in chapter 21. Here is an interlude amid the stories of triumph and glory: the story of David's sin in numbering the people of Israel. Remarkably the double sin of David—his adultery with Bathsheba and his murder of her husband, Uriah—is not recorded here. I believe it is because that sin was David's personal sin as a man, a manifestation of his own weakness and willfulness. It was the personal sin of a man, not the public misconduct of the king.

David's sin in numbering the people

But the sin of numbering the people of Israel was an official act of David's kingly office and an abrupt departure from the principle of dependence upon the strength and glory of God. Why did he number the people? He wanted to glory in the number of people who were available to him as king! He wanted to see his political and military strength!

We see this same problem in Christian circles today when Christian leaders begin to depend on numbers more than on God's leading. One of the great principles that runs through the Bible from beginning to end is that God never wins His battles by majority vote. When we think that the cause of Christ is losing because the number of Christians is decreasing in proportion to the population of the world, we have succumbed to the false philosophy that God wins His battles by numbers. He doesn't need numbers. He needs people who are obedient to His will and His Word.

God doesn't need numbers; He needs people who obey His will and His Word

In the book of Judges we saw that thirty-two thousand men were too many to fight for God under Gideon's command. So were ten thousand. Finally, when Gideon had whittled his force down to a mere three hundred men, God said, "With the three hundred men . . . I will save you and give the Midianites into your hands" (see Judges 7). God always achieves His goals by quality rather than quantity.

As a result of David's departure from this principle and because the whole nation looked to the king as an example, judgment on David was exceedingly severe. A prophet was sent to David (1 Chron. 21:10–17), saying, "I am giving you three options. . . .

"Take your choice: three years of famine, three months of being swept away before your enemies, with their swords overtaking you, or three days of the sword of the LORD—days of plague in the land, with the angel of the LORD ravaging every part of Israel." David did the wise thing. He said, "I am in deep distress. Let me fall into the hands of the LORD, for his mercy is very great."

The angel of the LORD came into the midst of the people and for three days the nation was ravaged by pestilence and plague. David saw the angel with his sword stretched out over the city of Jerusalem, ready to slay there also, but David pleaded with God: "I am the one who has sinned and done wrong. . . . O LORD my God, let your hand fall upon me and my family, but do not let this plague remain on your people." Then God instructed him to buy the cattle and the threshing floor of Ornan and there to erect an altar and worship God. The temple was later built on that site, and the altar was placed where the angel of God stayed his hand from judgment. So the grace of God came even at a time of disobedience and turned the judgment upon David into grace and blessing for the nation.

The mighty warrior and the man of peace

The rest of the book tells of David's passion for the building of the temple. Because he understood that a nation without a focus of worship could never be a nation, he longed to see the temple built. A people without God in their midst will never amount to anything. But David was a man of war, and God wanted a man of peace to rule over the nations of the earth (1 Chron. 22:6–19). So God said to David, "You will have a son who will be a man of peace and rest. . . . He is the one who will build a house for my Name." By this time, David had learned the principle of obedience so well that he accepted God's will, even though it was a great disappointment.

In grace, however, God allowed David to do everything for the temple except actually build it. He drew the plans. He designed the furniture. He collected the materials. He made the arrangements. He set up the order and ritual. He brought down the cedar lumber from Mount Hermon and Mount Lebanon in the north. He dug up the rock and quarried the stones. He gathered in the gold, silver, and iron. He gathered it all together and then the book closes as the anointed Solomon and David reign side by side—a complete picture of the ministry of the Lord Jesus. Christ is both the mighty warrior, David, and the man of peace, Solomon.

What is the message of this book? It is a message about the supreme importance of the temple in our lives—the authority of God.

Over the three great doors of the cathedral in Milan, Italy, are three inscriptions. Over the right-hand door is carved a wreath of flowers and the words, "All that pleases is but for a moment." On the left-hand door is a cross and the inscription, "All that troubles is but for a moment." Over the main entrance are the words, "Nothing is important save that which is eternal." That is the lesson of the book of 1 Chronicles.

God's King in God's House

Tremendous riches are hidden away in the neglected book of 2 Chronicles. As 1 Chronicles was all about King David, 2 Chronicles is all about the house of David. This book follows only the course of the kings of Judah, the descendants of David. Like the first book, 2 Chronicles focuses largely on the temple and presents a picture of God's king walking in the light of God's house. That is the secret of blessing in the kingdom. Here is an outline of the book of 2 Chronicles:

The Reign of King Solomon (2 Chronicles 1–9)

The Kings after Solomon (2 Chronicles 10–36)

**The
construction
of the temple**

The first nine chapters of 2 Chronicles center on the temple. The book opens with a visit of Solomon to the tabernacle in the city of Gibeon. The tabernacle had been the center of God's guidance to the people through the wilderness journey, the days of the judges, the regimes of King Saul and King David. Solomon goes there to make an offering.

But the account immediately shifts from the tabernacle to the temple site that David had bought in Jerusalem. This symbolizes the fact that when the Lord Jesus reigns as king in our lives and we yield to His lordship, we no longer have a relationship with the tabernacle, that impermanent place of worship during our up-and-down, wandering experience. We are now walking in a more permanent relationship in which God's king is ruling and walking in the light of God's house.

In chapter 2, we see that though David planned and provided for the temple, it is being built by Solomon. It was Solomon, as a type of Christ in His role as the Prince of Peace, who was given the honor of actually building the temple. He thus represents the picture that is completed in the New Testament where the Lord Jesus Himself is the builder of the temple of the human spirit.

Solomon's prayer at
the dedication of
the temple

Solomon's prayer in chapter 6 shows that God intended the temple to be a place where the people could be restored from the effects of sin. Whether the people suffered from spiritual failure or the punishment of captivity, they were to remember that if they would pray earnestly and genuinely confess their sin, God would hear them, heal their hearts, and restore them to their rightful place. When Solomon finished his prayer,

God accepts
Solomon's sacrifice

while all the people waited outside in the temple courts, fire came down from heaven and consumed the sacrifice on the altar. Immediately the temple was filled with a cloud of glory so that the priest could not enter. This was the sign that God had accepted the offering and that His presence had filled the house.

**The glories of
Solomon's
kingdom**

Beginning in chapter 9, we have an account of the glories and conquests of the Solomonic kingdom. We are treated to the story of the queen of Sheba's visit. Hollywood versions of this story notwithstanding, this account wonderfully illustrates how God makes His grace known throughout the nations. The Jews, in the days of the kingdom of Israel, weren't sent out into the whole world as we are commanded to do now by the Great Commission (see Matt. 28:19–20). God's grace was displayed by the building of a land and a people so wondrously blessed by God that word spread to the uttermost parts of the earth, and people wanted to come and see for themselves what God was doing in Israel.

This is a picture for us of God's own supreme method of evangelism. Believers everywhere are commanded to live this kind of life, with the Spirit of God inhabiting their individual temples and controlling their wills. When believers walk in obedience to the indwelling Spirit, their lives manifest the victory, rejoicing, blessing, and prosperity of the Lord, so that people can't help but ask, "What is there about these people? I want to know what this is all about!" When the queen of Sheba came to Solomon, she sees:

> . . . the palace he had built, the food on his table, the seating of his officials, the attending servants in their robes, . . . and the burnt offerings he made at the temple of the LORD . . . (2 Chron. 9:3–4).

When she saw all of this, "she was overwhelmed." She said, "Not even half the greatness of your wisdom was told me; you have far exceeded the report I heard" (2 Chron. 9:6). Perhaps you have had a taste of the experience Solomon had, the experience of hearing someone say, "There is something about your life that drew me when I first saw you." It's the experience Peter describes when he says:

> In your hearts set apart Christ as Lord. Always be prepared to give an answer to everyone who asks you to give the reason for the hope that you have. But do this with gentleness and respect (1Pet. 3:15).

This is God's method of evangelism.

The death of Solomon, at the end of chapter 9, is followed in chapters 10 through 36 by the record of Judah's kings up to the time of the Babylonian captivity. Nine of the kings of this period are good kings and eleven are bad. Manasseh, who reigned for fifty-five years on the throne of Judah, started out as the worst king in Judah's history and ended up as one of the best, as God reached him, redeemed him, and restored him. As you read through these accounts, the bad kings reveal the pattern of temptation and evil in a disobedient heart.

A declining standard is evident in this procession of kings. It begins with the infiltration of evil into the kingdom on a rather trivial level.

From Solomon to the Captivity

Rehoboam, the son of Solomon, was unwilling to follow the good counsel of the wise men of his kingdom. He asked the older men, "How would you advise me to answer these people?" They said, "If you will be kind to these people and please them and give them a favorable answer, they will always be your servants." But the young men advised him to say, "My father laid on you a heavy yoke; I will make it even heavier." Rehoboam refused to follow the old men's good counsel. That is all he did. Yet that was the beginning of the progressive evil that was to destroy this kingdom.

A little later, in 2 Chronicles 12:1, you find a further decline in the standards:

After Rehoboam's position as king was established and he had become strong, he and all Israel with him abandoned the law of the LORD.

He turned a deaf ear to what God said. As a result, the kingdom was invaded by the Egyptians. The moment that the king disobeyed the law of God, the defenses of the nation were weakened and the enemies came pouring over the border. It was only by God's grace that the Egyptians were turned back. When Rehoboam humbled himself and returned to God, the Egyptians were repelled.

The next bad king, Jehoram, appears in chapter 21, verse 4:

When Jehoram established himself firmly over his father's kingdom, he put all his brothers to the sword along with some of the princes of Israel.

First, the king refused to listen to good advice. Then he turned a deaf ear to the law. Now, the spirit of jealousy begins to undermine the kingdom. This is immediately followed, as we read in verse 11, by another slide downward:

He had also built high places on the hills of Judah and had caused the people of Jerusalem to prostitute themselves and had led Judah astray.

In one sense, the high places did not yet represent idolatry. They were high hills where the people of Judah worshiped Jehovah, but Jehovah had not told them to worship Him in the high places. He had put His name in the temple and it was there that they were to worship and offer sacrifice. They were worshiping out on the hills because that was where their neighbors and friends were worshiping. They were allowing the pure forms of worship to become contaminated by the surrounding culture, and so their worship of Jehovah was deteriorating. Invasion and disintegration quickly followed. As you read, you find that King Jehoram was immediately afflicted by an invasion from the Philistines, the nation that represented the desires of the flesh.

The next bad king is King Ahaz. In chapter 28, verses 1–2, we read:

> *Ahaz was twenty years old when he became king, and he reigned in Jerusalem sixteen years. Unlike David his father, he did not do what was right in the eyes of the LORD. He walked in the ways of the kings of Israel and also made cast idols for worshiping the Baals.*

Here is the actual introduction of vile, despicable practices of idolatry that were primarily sexual in nature. Judah was increasingly afflicted by these practices. The kings were responsible for introducing them, as we read of King Ahaz (28:3–4):

> *He burned sacrifices in the Valley of Ben Hinnom and sacrificed his sons in the fire, following the detestable ways of the nations the LORD had driven out before the Israelites. He offered sacrifices and burned incense at the high places, on the hilltops and under every spreading tree.*

The pattern is the same. Again, this is followed by invasion:

> *The LORD his God handed him over to the king of Aram. The Arameans defeated him and took many of his people as prisoners (28:5).*

Why are we human beings so prone to emotional afflictions, neuroses, and psychoses? I believe one reason is that we allow the defenses of our own inner temples to be destroyed. We allow some inner idolatry to weaken us and we find ourselves defenseless against these invaders of the spirit: bitterness, anger, depression, frustration, defeat, and darkness.

Throughout this book, the people of Judah suffer under the weight of the wicked practices of their kings. By contrast, the good kings reflect the grace of God in cleansing and restoring, and they bring peace and prosperity to their people. Second Chronicles records five great reformations in Judah as God seeks to arrest the deterioration of the nation and call the nation back to its place of glory and blessing. The first period of reformation was under King Asa, in chapters 14 through 16. In chapter 14, verses 2–3, we read:

> *Asa did what was good and right in the eyes of the LORD his God. He removed the foreign altars and the high places, smashed the sacred stones and cut down the Asherah poles.*

The sexual sign of Asherim involved the worship of the phallus, the male sex organ. Verse 4 continues:

He commanded Judah to seek the LORD, the God of their fathers, and to obey his laws and commands.

The goodness of King Asa was rewarded in the life of the nation. When a massive attack came against Judah with superior numbers from the south, God delivered the nation in a mighty way:

Zerah the Cushite marched out against them with a vast army and three hundred chariots, and came as far as Mareshah (2 Chron. 14:9).

We may be put under pressure at times, but if the heart is obedient to the Holy Spirit's prompting, the defenses are secure against whatever may come. As Isaiah says, "You will keep in perfect peace him whose mind is steadfast, because he trusts in you" (Isa. 26:3). The principle of power is clearly declared when Asa, returning from the battle with the Ethiopians, meets the prophet Oded:

[Oded] went out to meet Asa and said to him, "Listen to me, Asa and all Judah and Benjamin. The LORD is with you when you are with him. If you seek him, he will be found by you, but if you forsake him, he will forsake you" (2 Chron. 15:2).

Is Oded saying that God would forsake a believer so that the believer would be lost? No. The prophet Oded is talking here about being forsaken in the sense of no longer having access to God's power, victory, and ability to stand under stressful circumstances. In order to access the power of God, we must seek fellowship with God. If we forsake Him, how can He possibly impart His power to us? As Paul says in the New Testament, "I press on to take hold of that [resurrection power] for which Christ Jesus took hold of me" (Phil. 3:12). That is the secret of real power.

Five principles of restoration

Each king who leads a reformation in Israel illustrates a different principle of restoration. In Asa we find the first principle of restoration: *the determination to obey the law.*

1. Determination to obey the law

They entered into a covenant to seek the LORD, the God of their fathers, with all their heart and soul. All who would not seek the LORD, the God of Israel, were to be put to death, whether small or great, man or woman. They took an oath to the LORD with loud acclamation, with shouting and with trumpets and horns. All Judah rejoiced about the oath because they had sworn it wholeheartedly. They sought God eagerly, and he was found by them. So the LORD gave them rest on every side (2 Chron. 15:12–15).

Here is a heart that has awakened at last to the fact that it has been drifting into defection and the realization that with defection comes invasion, bondage, and slavery. The way of reformation involved a renewed determination to follow the Lord, to seek Him with a whole heart, which would be sealed by a renewed vow. As a result, the Lord gave them peace and rest.

In the reign of King Jehoshaphat, the next king on the throne of Judah, there is another time of restoration after a time of failure. Jehoshaphat clears the idols out of the land. In 2 Chronicles 17:7–9 the second principle of restoration is set forth: *the ministry of teaching.*

Jehoshaphat

2. The ministry of teaching

> *In the third year of his reign he sent his officials. . . . They taught throughout Judah, taking with them the Book of the Law of the LORD; they went around to all the towns of Judah and taught the people.*

In verse 10, we see the ministry of teaching followed by another reformation and God's blessing of peace:

> *The fear of the LORD fell on all the kingdoms of the lands surrounding Judah, so that they did not make war with Jehoshaphat.*

Later, unfortunately, Jehoshaphat makes an alliance with Ahaziah, the king of Israel, the apostate northern kingdom. Israel and Judah join together in a naval expedition that ends in disaster. It is a moment of weakness in the life of King Jehoshaphat, and it causes the entire nation of Judah to be weakened. As a result, Judah is later attacked by Ammon, Moab, and Edom—all symbolic types of the flesh.

In chapters 23 and 24, we come to the story of King Joash, who illustrates the third principle of restoration: *paying what is owed.* The third restoration of Israel was accomplished by the collection of the temple taxes due from the people:

Joash

3. Paying what is owed

> *Joash decided to restore the temple of the LORD. He called together the priests and Levites and said to them, "Go to the towns of Judah and collect the money due annually from all Israel, to repair the temple of your God. Do it now" (24:4–5).*

Here is something that had been neglected: No one had been paying the costs for repairing the temple, so it had fallen into such disrepair that the doors were actually shut. No sacrifice was being offered in the temple. Joash, realizing this, gathered money to restore the temple. Now if the temple symbolizes the human spirit as a place of worship, restoring and repairing the temple is a picture of the strengthening of the spirit. How? By what we call *restitution,* paying what is owed. It may involve an apology to someone or restoring something wrongfully taken or putting back something that has been wrongfully used. No matter what it may be, this is the principle of restitution and restoration.

Hezekiah

4. The cleansing of the temple

In Hezekiah's reign, chapters 29 through 32, we find the fourth principle of restoration, *the cleansing of the temple.* By the time Hezekiah came to the throne, the nation had fallen on such terribly evil days that the temple had actually been filled with rubbish and filth. There was garbage throughout all the courts. Hezekiah ordered the cleansing of the temple, and the workers found so much rubbish and filth that it took sixteen days to remove it.

At last, when the temple was clean, they restored the worship and celebrated the Passover for the first time since the days of Solomon. What does this represent? It is the cleansing of the temple of our spirits, the putting away of the filth that has accumulated, the turning away from false ideas that have infected our minds, and the return to the cleansing worship of the Lord.

Josiah

In Josiah, the last good king of Judah, we find the fifth and final principle of restoration. By the time Josiah came to the throne, the temple had fallen into complete disuse once again. Josiah set the people to cleaning it up and in 2 Chronicles 34:14 we read:

> While they were bringing out the money that had been taken into the temple of the LORD, Hilkiah the priest found the Book of the Law of the LORD that had been given through Moses.

5. Return to hearing the Word of God

This sounds incredible, but the people had actually forgotten that there was a copy of the Law of Moses in the temple. It had been so neglected in the land that it had been totally forgotten. When the priests went through the temple to clean it, they accidentally found the Law of the Lord, brought it to the king, and read it to him. Hearing the words of the Law, he tore his clothes. He commanded his advisors to inquire of the Lord what he should do:

> The king called together all the elders of Judah and Jerusalem. He went up to the temple of the LORD with the men of Judah, the people of Jerusalem, the priests and the Levites—all the people from the least to the greatest. He read in their hearing all the words of the Book of the

Covenant, which had been found in the temple of the LORD. The king stood by his pillar and renewed the covenant in the presence of the LORD—to follow the LORD and keep his commands (2 Chron. 34:29–31).

So the last principle of restoration is *returning to the hearing of the Word of God.*

But the people had gone a long way down. God's patience was ended. The last chapter of 2 Chronicles gives us the account of the terrible, dark days when Nebuchadnezzar took the city captive and set a puppet king upon the throne. When the puppet king rebelled against Nebuchadnezzar, the Babylonian ruler set the king's uncle on the throne. Finally, he sent a force to Jerusalem to destroy with fire both the rebellious city and the temple.

Contrast this scene of horror with that wonderful scene from the glory days of Solomon's reign: King Solomon, in his royal purple robes, kneeling before the people and praying to the God of heaven. The kingdom is at peace. Solomon's rule extends to the outermost limits of the kingdom promised to Abraham, from the Euphrates River to the River of Egypt. People from all over the world make pilgrimages to Jerusalem to see the glory of God. The fire of God comes down from heaven and the glory of God fills the temple like a cloud.

But at the end of 2 Chronicles, the fire that fills the temple is the fire of judgment and destruction. The temple is ruined, the city is leveled, the people are killed or taken away in chains, the entire land is crawling with enemies and scavengers.

This is the picture that God draws for us of what can happen when the heart walks in disobedience. The book of 2 Chronicles serves as a warning—and an encouragement. Decline and destruction are not inevitable. If we choose obedience and restoration, we can experience the presence of God's glory in the temple of our own inner lives—His peace, His prosperity, His blessing upon our lives. We can experience the wonders of the Solomonic era, the riches of heaven poured into the vessels of our own human spirits; "good measure, pressed down, shaken together and running over," as Luke 6:38 tells us.

Abundance or impoverishment and devastation. The choice is ours.

The Road Back

T he books of Ezra, Nehemiah, and Esther cover the historical period of Israel's captivity in Babylon and the return to Jerusalem. The return to Jerusalem from Babylon involved about fifty thousand Jews, far fewer than the five hundred thousand Jewish war refugees who flooded Israel when the nation was reestablished in 1948, or the 3.5 million Jews who live in Israel today. Yet, though the numbers of Jews returning to Jerusalem after the captivity were small, it was an event of great importance.

In the Hebrew Bible, the books of Ezra and Nehemiah are one book. I am convinced that the events of these two books run parallel to one another, even though most Bible commentators say that the events of Nehemiah chronologically follow the events of Ezra. I believe that a careful study of these two books shows that the events they cover were concurrent.

Ezra is concerned with the building of the temple. Nehemiah is concerned with the building of the city and walls of Jerusalem. The temple was the last structure to be destroyed when the nation fell into captivity. It was the last holdout (if we may put it that way) of the Spirit of God within the nation of Israel. In a symbolic sense, the temple, representing the Spirit, is the last place to be destroyed in an individual's failure to relate to God. It is also the first place where God begins to set about the work of restoration. Therefore the book of Ezra, which deals with restoring the temple, is placed before Nehemiah in the Scriptures. Notice the opening words of this book:

*In the first year of Cyrus king of Persia, in order to fulfill the word
of the LORD spoken by Jeremiah, the LORD moved the heart of Cyrus king
of Persia to make a proclamation throughout his realm and to put it in
writing.*

Compare that statement with these words from 2 Chronicles 36:22:

*In the first year of Cyrus king of Persia, in order to fulfill the word
of the LORD spoken by Jeremiah, the LORD moved the heart of Cyrus king
of Persia to make a proclamation throughout his realm and to put it in
writing.*

The same words exactly! The book of Ezra begins right where
Chronicles leaves off. This strongly indicates that Ezra wrote both books.
Here is an outline of the book of Ezra:

The Restoration of the Temple (Ezra 1–6)

1.	The decree of Cyrus and the first return of the people under the leadership of Zerubbabel	1–2
2.	The building of the temple	3–6

The Restoration of the Nation (Ezra 7–10)

3.	The second return of the people to Jerusalem under the leadership of the prophet Ezra	7–8
4.	Israel strays through intermarriage; Ezra intercedes with God, confessing God's faithfulness and Israel's unfaithfulness	9
5.	Israel repents and is restored	10

**Return,
rebuild, and
restore**

The book of Ezra illustrates for us the work of God in restoring a
heart that has fallen into sin. Restoration can take place on an individual basis, on the basis of a local church, an entire denomination, an
entire city, or an entire nation. Restoration is the work of God that
brings a person or a group of people back from secularism and materialism to true spiritual knowledge and strength. True restoration always follows the pattern depicted here in the book of Ezra.

The book of Ezra
clearly shows the
need for the work
of both king and
priest in accomplish-
ing restoration

The book divides very naturally between the ministries of two
men: Zerubbabel, in chapters 1 through 6, and Ezra, in chapters 7
through 10. Both of these men led the captives of Babylon back to
Jerusalem. Zerubbabel, interestingly enough, was a descendant of
David, an heir of the kingly line. Ezra, descended from Aaron the
priest, is also a priest. The book of Ezra clearly shows the need for the
work of both the king and the priest in accomplishing restoration. The

work of the king is to build (or, in this case, to rebuild). The work of the priest is to cleanse and restore. Both are essential for a restored relationship with God.

Restoration in the individual requires complete surrender to God's Spirit and humble submission to the kingship and lordship of Jesus Christ. Thus, it involves Jesus' ministry as king in our lives. It means recognizing God's right to own us, to direct us, to change us, and to replace our plans with His own.

But restoration also means cleansing. The spirit and the soul are cleansed by our great High Priest who, upon our confession of sin, washes away the guilt and restores us to a place of fellowship and blessedness in His sight. A return from sin is always the work of God's grace, as we clearly see in Ezra 1:1:

> The LORD moved the heart of Cyrus king of Persia.

Verse 5 continues the theme of God's active grace, demonstrated by His moving of people to action:

> The family heads of Judah and Benjamin, and the priests and the Levites—everyone whose heart God had moved—prepared to go up and build the house of the LORD in Jerusalem.

God always takes the initiative. No one, after falling into a sinful experience, would ever come back to Christ unless God brought him or her back. This is indicated so clearly in the case of these Israelites.

In Babylon, the Jews—who began their captivity as slaves—soon became prosperous. They became so prosperous, in fact, that their spiritual values deteriorated and they became lost to materialism. Eventually, many of them became so attached to their material goods that they did not want to go back to Jerusalem even though, as captive subjects of Babylon, they did not enjoy freedom in the land. So when God opened the door to return, many of them refused.

But the Spirit of God stirred up the hearts of some and made them unsatisfied with material prosperity. Mere things will never satisfy the deep-seated cry of the human spirit. When we feel a burning need within us for more than can be satisfied by material things, we should be aware that God the Spirit is stirring us up to return and rebuild the things that lead to spiritual strength.

The Babylonian captivity lasted about seventy years. Then, in 539 B.C. King Cyrus of Persia invaded and defeated the Babylonians. Cyrus issued a decree giving the Israelites their freedom to return to their homeland. So, in chapters 1 and 2, Zerubbabel, the kingly descendant

The first return under Zerubbabel

of David, leads fifty thousand people from Babylon back to Jerusalem.

When the people arrive in Jerusalem, it is the seventh month of the year—just in time for the Jewish Feast of the Tabernacles. This feast (also called the Feast of Ingathering) was the time when Israel dwelt in tentlike booths to remind them of their pilgrim past. Incidentally, this feast looks forward to the eventual regathering of Israel from the vast worldwide dispersion for the Millennium and is the feast mingled with tears of sorrow as the people see the foundations of the temple being relaid.

Their first act is to *build an altar* on the original temple site in the midst of the ruins

Their first act is to *build an altar* on the original temple site in the midst of the ruins. Beneath the open sky, they erect an altar to God and begin to worship and offer sacrifice as the Law of Moses requires. This is significant because the first act of a heart that really desires to restore fellowship after a period of wandering is to erect an altar to God. An altar is always the symbol of ownership. It is both the acknowledgment that God has sole right to us and the symbol of our personal relationship to Him. Therefore, an altar almost invariably involves sacrifice, worship, and praise. In the Old Testament, a sacrifice involved the symbolic death of an animal; in the New Testament, sacrifice means the death of the self, the recognition that "you are not your own; you were bought at a price" (1 Cor. 6:19–20). The experience of sacrifice, worship, and praise brings a restored relationship and the joy of a whole and restored heart.

A man once took time off from work to meet with me and talk about his prayer life. He brought along sheets of paper on which he had written all the things he had been trying to pray about—three or four single-spaced sheets. "I have a great deal of trouble with this," he said. "I find it hard to remember all these things and to go through these lists. It's so mechanical, so empty."

"Why don't you just forget all this," I said. "Just spend your time, for a few prayer sessions anyway, simply praising the Lord."

At first this man was resistant, even resentful. He later told me that he thought, *I took time off work to talk to you, and all you told me was, "Why don't you spend your time praising the Lord?"* He wanted advice in organizing his prayer life to make it more effective and goal-oriented, and I had told him to scrap his lists and goals!

But after he left, he thought about what I had said, and he tried it. Almost instantly, he found that his prayer life was revolutionized! He experienced a sense of restoration, a sense of restored personal communion! That is what God is after. That is why the altar is so important in this work of restoration.

Their second act is to *lay the foundation of the temple.* This work is met with mixed feelings, as we see in Ezra 3:11–13:

*All the people gave a great shout of praise to the LORD, because the foun-
dation of the house of the LORD was laid. But many of the older priests
and Levites and family heads, who had seen the former temple, wept
aloud when they saw the foundation of this temple being laid, while
many others shouted for joy. No one could distinguish the sound of the
shouts of joy from the sound of weeping, because the people made so much
noise. And the sound was heard far away.*

Have you ever felt that way? Have you ever come back to God after
a time of coldness and withdrawal—a period of captivity to sin's
power—with a great sense of joy as His Spirit reestablished the foundations of communion? Yes, there is rejoicing, but also regret for the lost
and wasted years. That mix of emotions is exactly what is portrayed here:
tears of joy mingled with tears of sorrow as the people see the temple
foundation being relaid.

Even in this moment of joy and restoration, however, opposition is
developing, as we see in chapters 4 through 6. A force is at work in every
human heart that bitterly resists the work of God's Spirit. This force
immediately manifests itself here, and it does so deceptively, in the guise
of friendly solicitude and courtesy:

**Opposition
and delay**

*When the enemies of Judah and Benjamin heard that the exiles
were building a temple for the LORD, the God of Israel, they came to
Zerubbabel and to the heads of the families and said, "Let us help you
build because, like you, we seek your God and have been sacrificing to
him since the time of Esarhaddon king of Assyria, who brought us here"
(4:1–2).*

Incidentally, this is the beginning of the Samaritans, frequently
mentioned in the New Testament. These Samaritans approach the Jews
and say, "Let us help you build [the temple] because, like you, we seek
your God and have been sacrificing to him." They come with an open
hand, volunteering to roll up their sleeves and work. That would be a
hard offer for most of us to turn down. It's easy to say no to an enemy
who comes breathing fiery threats, but what do you say to an enemy
who comes saying, "Let me help"? The only way to do so is with a heart
that is obedient to God's Word:

The Samaritans
offer to help

*Zerubbabel, Jeshua and the rest of the heads of the families of Israel
answered, "You have no part with us in building a temple to our God.
We alone will build it for the LORD, the God of Israel, as King Cyrus,
the king of Persia, commanded us" (4:3).*

The Jews decline the
offer

That sounds rude and offensive, but it was not mere capriciousness that made the Jews respond that way. God had commanded Israel not to fellowship with other nations or to engage with them in enterprises concerning the faith. What does this mean? That it was wrong for one nation to intermingle with another? No, this has been distorted and misapplied to unlike situations today. It means simply that God rejects the philosophy of the world in carrying out His work in the world. There is a worldly religion and there is the faith that God gives us, and the two must never be mingled. Worldly religion reflects the spirit of the devil, the god of this age, saying, "Use religion to advance yourself, to achieve self-glorification. Do this for your own glory. Be religious to win admiration, power, fame, or whatever your heart desires." God rejects this principle.

The Samaritans' "friendship" turns to hatred

The genuineness (rather, the lack of it) of the Samaritans' offer is demonstrated by the fact that the Jews' rejection removes all pretense, and the "friendship" that was offered quickly turns to hatred:

> The peoples around them set out to discourage the people of Judah and make them afraid to go on building. They hired counselors to work against them and frustrate their plans during the entire reign of Cyrus king of Persia and down to the reign of Darius king of Persia (4:4–5).

Chapters 5 and 6 relate the story of how successful the opponents were in stopping the work of rebuilding the temple. By deliberately attempting to frustrate the Jews, by mocking them and taunting them, they hindered and discouraged Israel from doing the work that God had commanded. These so-called friends used every means, including legal means, to undermine Israel's authority and right to build. This is what happens whenever someone stands for God. As Paul wrote to the Galatians, "The sinful nature desires what is contrary to the Spirit" (Gal. 5:17). This is what we have here, and the principle was quite successful. The work was stopped for sixteen years and the temple lay half completed, overrun with weeds and grass. Again, worship ceased.

Then God sent two prophets, Haggai and Zechariah. These two men were God's instruments to move the people's hearts. When the people began to turn back to God, He also turned the hearts of the kings, Darius and Artaxerxes, and they issued the decree that resumed work on the temple. Finally the work was finished.

The Jews celebrate the Passover after the temple is completed

In chapter 6 we read that the first thing the Jews did was to celebrate the Passover, marking the beginning of their life under God. In a similar way, renewed fellowship with the living God should bring celebration into your own life. Apart from God, you have nothing to celebrate. Rejoined with God, you enjoy the glory and light of heaven as it shines upon your heart. When you are in fellowship—when the temple of your spirit stands tall and resplendent, filled with the glory of God's presence—then you can bask in the celebration of the joy that God gives you.

The latter part of the book concerns the ministry of Ezra, who led the second return to the land. In chapter 7, we read:

> *This Ezra came up from Babylon. He was a teacher well versed in the Law of Moses which the LORD, the God of Israel, had given. The king had granted him everything he asked, for the hand of the LORD his God was on him (v. 6).*

Wouldn't you like to have that written of you, "the king granted him everything he asked"? What kind of person is this whom a heathen Gentile king regards so highly that he will give Ezra anything he asks? The secret of this man's character is given in verse 10:

> *Ezra had devoted himself to the study and observance of the Law of the LORD, and to teaching its decrees and laws in Israel.*

Ezra is a man of the Word. Therefore, God sent him to Jerusalem to strengthen and beautify the temple. That is the work of the Word of God in our lives: strengthening and beautifying within us the place of fellowship with God:

> *After these things had been done, the leaders came to me and said, "The people of Israel, including the priests and the Levites, have not kept themselves separate from the neighboring peoples with their detestable practices, like those of the Canaanites, Hittites, Perizzites, Jebusites, Ammonites, Moabites, Egyptians and Amorites. They have taken some of their daughters as wives for themselves and their sons, and have mingled the holy race with the peoples around them. And the leaders and officials have led the way in this unfaithfulness" (9:1–2).*

What does this mean? They were simply starting the whole wretched mess all over again! This is what had broken the strength of the nation before! This is what had undermined the power of God among them and finally dispersed the people, broken up the tribes, separated them into two nations, and delivered them into captivity! After seventy years, they hadn't learned a thing!

The flesh never changes. No matter how long you walk in the Spirit, you will never get to the place where you cannot revert to your worst spiritual condition. All it takes is a little inattention, a little straying, a little departure from dependence upon God's Spirit and before you realize it,

No matter how long you walk in the Spirit, you will never get to the place where you cannot revert to your worst spiritual condition you are back in the mire of your old ways. The horrible reality of what his people have done is a shattering experience for the prophet Ezra:

> *When I heard this, I tore my tunic and cloak, pulled hair from my head and beard and sat down appalled . . . . until the evening sacrifice (9:3–4).*

As the book nears its close, Ezra prays to God and confesses the great sin of the nation. In His graciousness, God moves in the hearts of the people. The leaders come in brokenhearted contrition to Ezra and acknowledge their sin. A proclamation is issued. The people assemble together. It is raining, but the people hardly notice as they stand, shoulder to shoulder, many thousands strong in front of the temple, and together they confess their guilt and disobedience.

What happens next is hard for us to accept: The people pledge to put away the wives and children they had acquired outside of God's will. Now this is a hurtful thing, isn't it? It isn't easy. This is what Jesus meant when He said, "If anyone comes to me and does not hate his father and mother, his wife and children . . . he cannot be my disciple" (Luke 14:26). Our relationship with God comes first.

This is a symbolic teaching. God is not saying that we have to divorce and then abandon our children today. Rather, He is saying that we should ruthlessly divorce ourselves from anything that comes from the flesh and hinders our spiritual purity and growth. We must divorce ourselves from our materialism, our lusts and coveting, our ungodly goals and values, our anger and grudges, our habits and sins, all of which are symbolized by these Canaanite tribes in the land.

It was hard for the Israelites to put away their wives and children, but they realized that their only chance of being restored to fellowship with God lay in total, absolute, radical obedience to His Word. Jesus said, "If your right eye causes you to sin, gouge it out and throw it away. . . . If your right hand causes you to sin, cut it off" (Matt. 5:29–30). Be ruthless in these things. Put them away.

That is the road back to holiness, to a completely restored relationship with the One who loves us. The road of obedience is the road back to God.

Rebuilding the Walls

Despite the fact that Nehemiah is not one of the most prominent personalities in the Bible, he was a key player in God's plan for the nation of Israel, and the story of his life is rich in lessons for us today. As you learn more about this great man of faith and godly leadership, I believe you'll be as glad as I was to become acquainted with Nehemiah's story.

The book of Nehemiah falls into two divisions. The first six chapters cover the reCONstruction of the wall, while chapters 7 through 13 deal with the reINstruction of the people. Reconstruction and reinstruction—those two words offer a concise thumbnail sketch of the book of Nehemiah. Here is a more detailed road map of the book:

The Reconstruction of the City Walls (Nehemiah 1–7)

1. Nehemiah prepares for the task   1–2
    A. Nehemiah prays to God   1
    B. Nehemiah asks the king   2:1–8
    C. Nehemiah returns to Jerusalem   2:9–20

2. The rebuilding of the walls   3–7
    A. The restoration of the gates   3
    B. Opposition and persecution   4–6:14
    C. Completion of the reconstruction   6:15–19
    D. The organization and registration of Israel   7

The Reinstruction of the People (Nehemiah 8–13)

3.	Renewal of the covenant with God	8
4.	Reaffirmation of the covenant with God	9–10
5.	Israel obeys the covenant	11–12
6.	Restoration of the people through:	
	A. Separation from the pagan nations	13:1–9
	B. Restoration of worship and the Sabbath	13:10–22
	C. Forbidding of intermarriage with pagans	13:23–31

**Reversed
chronology**

As noted previously, the two books that we know as Ezra and Nehemiah appear as a single book in the Hebrew Bible. Ezra is the story of the building of the temple; Nehemiah is the story of the rebuilding of the city and walls of Jerusalem. Many Bible commentators say that the events of Nehemiah follow the events of Ezra. I believe, however, that the events in Ezra and Nehemiah are parallel, occurring at the same time.

The histories contained in the books of Ezra, Nehemiah, and Esther all occurred during the same general period of Israel's history. They actually appear in *reverse* chronological order in our Bible. In other words, the events in Esther actually occurred before events in Ezra and Nehemiah, when God first began to move the people of Israel out of captivity and back to their own land. The prophet Jeremiah had predicted that Israel's captivity would last seventy years, and the events in Esther mark the middle of that seventy-year period.

Bear with me as I attempt to put the interlocking, interconnecting events of these three books in chronological perspective:

During the captivity, God raised Esther, a young Jewish maiden, to the throne of Persia as queen. Her husband, the king of Persia, is known by various names in these three books, and that might seem confusing at first, but just remember this: King Ahasuerus of Persia is the same king who is called Artaxerxes in the opening chapters of Nehemiah. This king, though he was not a follower of the God of Israel, was moved by God to give the command for Nehemiah to return to Jerusalem to rebuild the city walls. When Nehemiah recounts his meeting with the king in 2:6, one phrase might be overlooked, but I believe it underscores the importance of the queen: "The king, *with the queen sitting beside him*, asked me . . ." (italics added). I believe that queen was Queen Esther, the Jewish woman whom God had raised to a place of prominence and a place of influence with the king.

Why would these different books use different names for the same king? It's because they are not names but titles. Artaxerxes is a title that simply means "the great king"; Ahasuerus is a title meaning "the venerable father." These were not the king's given names. It may be helpful to know that this Artaxerxes/Ahasuerus is the same king who is identified in the book of Daniel as "Darius the Mede." But Artaxerxes in the book of Nehemiah is not the same person as the Artaxerxes in the book of Ezra!

Fortunately, the identity of these kings is not the crucial issue in these books. It is much more important to know who Ezra, Nehemiah, and Esther are—and how God uses them in a mighty way to advance His plan. Each has a unique place in God's blueprint of history, and each has much to teach us about our own place in God's plan. Ezra is God's priest, calling His people back to true worship and fellowship with Him through the restoration of the temple. Esther is an instrument of God's grace, sent to the throne of Persia to move the heart of her husband, the king. Nehemiah is a cupbearer—the king's servant—but he also emerges as a leader of his people. At God's direction, under Queen Esther's influence, the king allows his servant Nehemiah to return to Jerusalem. There, Nehemiah demonstrates godly leadership as the supervisor of God's divine urban renewal project. Some twenty-five years after Nehemiah begins rebuilding the city of Jerusalem, Zerubbabel returns with about fifty thousand captives from Babylon, as recorded in the book of Ezra.

Chronologically, the events in these three books follow this order: Esther, Nehemiah, and Ezra. But God reversed the order of the books, so we have Ezra, Nehemiah, and Esther. Scripture is never concerned only with chronology. It is concerned with the teaching of truth, and the central truth that each book teaches is how to move out of captivity and into your rightful place with God. Each book explores this truth in a different way. Ezra begins with the building of the temple; the theme of this book is that the restoration of authentic worship is the first step on the road back to God. Nehemiah tells the story of the rebuilding of the walls; the theme of this book is that God fulfills our need for security, protection, and strength. The book of Esther reveals God's ultimate purpose for each of us: He uses individual people to achieve His vast, eternal, cosmic plan. He selects a woman from a captive race to become the queen, affecting the course of nations, achieving the plan of almighty God.

That, in a brief survey, is how these three books fit together, like puzzle pieces, forming a picture of God's blueprint for the people of Israel at a significant moment in their history—the moment of their liberation from bondage and their restoration as a worshiping people of God.

A wall is a very symbolic structure. It is more than just a barrier of stone and mortar. A wall is a statement.

The walls of the city of Jericho symbolized the pride and arrogance of that godless city, and that is one reason why God chose to pull them down with nothing but Israel's faith, His own invisible power, and the people's deafening shout. He wanted to show that the arrogance of Jericho was no match for the humility of God's people when it was aligned with the limitless power of God Himself.

The Berlin Wall symbolized not only the division between East and West, but also the misery and despair of people enslaved by communism. One will find no more eloquent statement of the collapse of communism than the photos of the German people tearing down that hated wall.

The fifteen-hundred-mile-long Great Wall of China symbolizes the vast power of the Ch'in Dynasty of the third century B.C. The Great Wall, the largest human engineering project ever built, was erected to defend China from warring tribes of the north. Up to thirty feet high, twenty-five feet wide, with a roadway running along the top and watchtowers spaced at regular intervals, it is a formidable, intimidating structure. It makes a clear statement: "Don't even *think* of invading our land!"

That is what walls usually symbolize: strength and protection. In ancient cities, massive walls were the first, last, and only line of defense. The walls of the city of Babylon, as recounted in Daniel, were about 380 feet thick and over 100 feet high—not as long as the Great Wall of China but much higher and more massive. Given the size of its walls, the Babylonians had every reason to consider themselves safe from attack.

The wall that Nehemiah was called to rebuild around Jerusalem, however, had an even deeper, more spiritual meaning than any of the walls we have just named. The rebuilding of the walls of Jerusalem symbolizes an act all believers should undertake. God calls each of us to rebuild the walls of our lives. What does that mean?

Jerusalem is a symbol of the City of God: God's dwelling place and the center of life for the world. In the New Testament, we see that God's *ultimate* dwelling place is in us, His people. When we rebuild the walls of our individual lives, we reestablish the protection and strength of God in our lives. We all have met people whose defenses have crumbled away. They have become human derelicts, drifting along the streets of our cities, hopeless and helpless, in many cases captive to alcohol, drugs, or a sexual addiction.

But God in His grace will often reach down and take hold of such a person. He will bring that person out of captivity and He will work with that person to rebuild the defenses and strength needed to resist temptation and escape from bondage. The rebuilding of the walls of Jerusalem, the City of God, is a symbolic representation of the way in which the walls of any life, of any local church, of any community, or of any nation, can be rebuilt. It is a picture of the strength, power, and purpose that God wants to rebuild in us as a barrier to sin, discouragement, failure, and destruction.

The text shows us a five-step process that drives Nehemiah's action—a process that is relevant to any life: (1) concern, (2) confession, (3) commitment, (4) courage, and (5) caution.

The first step in the rebuilding process is given in chapter 1: Nehemiah's *concern* about the ruins. While in the citadel of Susa, serving as the king's cupbearer, Nehemiah learns from travelers that Jerusalem's wall is broken down, her gates have been burned, and the few surviving Jews in the region are persecuted in exile. Nehemiah says:

> *When I heard these things, I sat down and wept. For some days I mourned and fasted and prayed before the God of heaven (1:4).*

Rebuilding the walls begins with *concern* over the damage. You will never rebuild the walls of your life until you have first mourned the ruins of your life. Have you ever stopped to compare what God wants to make of your life versus what you have allowed your life to be? Have you examined the potential and possibilities that God has created in you and grieved the potential and possibilities you have already squandered? Like Nehemiah, you have been informed of the desolation and ruin in your history, and a normal and fitting response is to mourn, weep, and pray to God. But don't let your remorse harden into paralysis. Realize, as Nehemiah did, that the desolation that you have discovered is not a cause to give up but a reason to wake up—a call to action and a firm resolve to rebuild.

When Nehemiah hears the report about Jerusalem, he weeps and prays for days, demonstrating his intense concern and burden for God's dwelling place, which has tumbled into ruin. His grief is a necessary first step, but he doesn't stop there. His next act is of *confession*. In chapter 1 we hear Nehemiah's wonderful prayer as he confesses that the nation has forsaken God and that God is just in having disciplined Israel. Fully identifying himself with the sins of his people, Nehemiah says, in part:

> *"I confess the sins we Israelites, including myself and my father's house, have committed against you. . . .*
> *"Remember the instruction you gave your servant Moses, saying, 'If you are unfaithful, I will scatter you among the nations, but if you return to me and obey my commands, then even if your exiled people are at the farthest horizon, I will gather them from there and bring them to the place I have chosen as a dwelling for my Name'" (1:6, 8–9).*

Five steps in the rebuilding process

1. Concern over the damage

2. Confession of sins

These words of confession are followed immediately by *commitment,* as we see in verse 11:

> *"O Lord, let your ear be attentive to the prayer of this your servant and to the prayer of your servants who delight in revering your name. Give your servant success today by granting him favor in the presence of this man."*

Notice that a plan is already forming in Nehemiah's mind even while he is praying. This often happens when we spend time with God in prayer: He speaks to us and gives us insight, ideas, inspiration, and empowerment to solve the very "impossible" problems that we brought before Him through our tears. Here, we see that God has given Nehemiah the beginnings of a plan. By the end of the prayer, Nehemiah has something definite he wants to ask of "this man." What man? The answer is in the last sentence of verse 11:

> *I was cupbearer to the king.*

The king! So here is a man who, out of his concern, after the confession of his heart, *commits* himself to a project. He asks God to begin moving in the king's heart. This is always the process by which we return to the grace of God. We demonstrate concern. Then we confess. Then we commit ourselves to action and ask God to also act in our behalf, because we must face factors over which we have no control. God must arrange those factors in order for us to succeed.

I once heard someone give a testimony at a men's conference. He said that, in the early days of his Christian experience, someone encouraged him to pray about problems that he was having in the workplace— strained relationships with his boss and other employees. He said, "I didn't think praying was the right thing to do at first. I didn't even want to pray for people who were making life difficult for me. But I began to pray for them, almost against my own will, and soon I saw changes in the way these people related to me. Prayer really worked! Looking back, I think we Christians have an unfair advantage over those who don't know the Lord! We have instant access, any time of the day or night, to the One who created the entire universe! How can those who don't know God ever hope to compete with that?"

In this passage, we see that Nehemiah is aware of the limitless power of God to change circumstances that are beyond human control. So he prays about talking to the king. Later, when he goes before the king, the king notices the look of sadness on Nehemiah's face, and he asks why. Remember, as we see in Nehemiah 2:6, that when Nehemiah goes before the king, the king's wife is also present—and this king's wife is none other than Queen Esther, whom the king had selected from among the Jews! This circumstance was part of God's answer to Nehemiah's prayer: In His foreknowledge, He had already arranged to place a Jewish queen on the throne in Susa. Because of his Jewish wife, the king already has a built-in understanding of the Jews' history and a concern for their problems. So the king responds favorably to Nehemiah's plea for permission to return to Jerusalem.

The next step in the program of reconstruction is *courage*. In Nehemiah 2:9–10 we read:

4. Courage

> *I went to the governors of Trans-Euphrates* [the province beyond the Euphrates River] *and gave them the king's letters. The king had also sent army officers and cavalry with me.*
> *When Sanballat the Horonite and Tobiah the Ammonite official heard about this, they were very much disturbed that someone had come to promote the welfare of the Israelites.*

Pay close attention to those names, Sanballat and Tobiah, and the names of the nations they come from, the Horonites and the Ammonites. Whenever you read of the Ammonites, Amorites, Amalekites, Hittites, Jebusites, Perizzites, or any of the other "ites," you have a picture of the enemy of God in the flesh. These various tribes symbolize satanic agency within human beings, causing them to oppose and resist the work, the will, and the ways of God. Sanballat and Tobiah are no different; they are enemies of God and enemies of Nehemiah.

Immediately, we see that courage is necessary to rebuild the walls of God's dwelling place. Whenever someone like Nehemiah says, "I will arise and build," Satan always says, "Then I will arise and destroy." Satan always places roadblocks and obstructions in our way when we start returning to God.

Finally, we see in Nehemiah's program the importance of *caution*. When Nehemiah returns to Jerusalem, in 2:11–16, he doesn't just start putting bricks on top of one another. He doesn't rush out and get all the people excited about building the walls. If he did that, he would fall into the trap of his enemies. The first thing he does is arise secretly at night; he rides alone around the walls of the city and surveys the ruins. He makes careful, cautious plans of exactly what needs to be done.

5. Caution

In the story of Nehemiah, we see that these five steps are fundamental to the task of rebuilding walls, whether they are the walls of a city or the walls of a human life: concern, confession, commitment, courage, caution.

**The
significance
of the gates**

The Lamb of God

Christian witness

Truth

In chapter 3 we learn how Nehemiah went about this task of recon-struction. If the walls of your life are broken down, if your defenses have crumbled so that the enemy is surrounding you on every hand, if you easily fall prey to temptation, then pay special attention to Nehemiah's process of reconstruction.

We learn two things: (1) the people were willing to work, and (2) they immediately became involved and sprang into action. Nehemiah, in his God-given wisdom, set each worker to the task of rebuilding whatever part of the wall was nearest to his own house. That way, each worker had a personal stake in the work!

The rest of chapter 3 centers on the ten gates of the city of Jerusalem. The people were assigned a certain portion of the wall defined by the gates that gave access to the city. As you read through this chap-ter, you find the names of these gates, and each gate has a specific sym-bolic significance. We can draw an important practical lesson from each gate.

The Sheep Gate (3:1–2). This is the gate through which the sheep were brought into the city to be sacrificed at the altar. The Sheep Gate, of course, signifies the Lamb of God, whose blood was shed on the cross for us, and it reveals the principle of the cross. The cross is always the starting place for personal strength. You have to begin by recognizing the principle of the cross; that is, you must utterly cancel out your ego, your own plans, and your self-interest and nail them to the cross of Christ. The cross is that instrument in God's program that puts human pride to death. We cannot save ourselves. Only the Lamb of God, slain for us, can save us. The cross, the Sheep Gate, is the starting place, the source of our strength for the task of rebuilding.

The Fish Gate (3:3–5). What does the name *Fish Gate* suggest to you? Do you remember the Lord Jesus saying to His disciples, "Come, follow me, and I will make you fishers of men" (Mark 1:17)? The Fish Gate suggests the witness of a Christian. Has that gate broken down in your life? Has the wall around the Fish Gate crumbled? Has your wit-ness for the Lord fallen into disuse and disrepair? If so, this gate and its surrounding wall need to be rebuilt and restored, for the Lord Jesus tells us that *every* Christian is to be a witness for Him. If this wall is broken down, the enemy will have an avenue through which to enter your life again and again.

The Old [*Jeshanah*] Gate (3:6–12). This gate represents truth. In many Christians' lives this gate is broken down, and they are no longer resting upon the truth. Truth is always old, settled, eternal; old things provide the base upon which everything new must rest. Somebody has well said, "Whatever is true is not new, and whatever is new is not true." These are the days when old truths are being forsaken—not only in our culture, but frequently even within the church. Many people say that the old truths and values are unnecessary, invalid, and obsolete. But if a thing is true, it is never obsolete. If we allow truth to go by the wayside, we find that the defensive wall crumbles and our enemies can easily gain access to our souls. God's truth will never change; it is eternally true.

The nature of truth is illustrated by the story of a man who went to visit an old musician. He knocked on the musician's door and said, "What's the good word for today?" The old musician said nothing in reply. Instead, he turned and took a tuning fork down from a nearby shelf. He struck the tuning fork against the shelf so that a note resounded through the room.

Then the musician said, "That, my friend, is A. It was A yesterday. It was A five thousand years ago, and it will be A five thousand years from now." Then he added, thumbing over his shoulder, "The tenor across the hall sings off-key. The soprano upstairs flats her high notes. The piano in the next room is out of tune." He struck the tuning fork again and said, "That is A and that, my friend, is the good word for today."

That is the nature of truth. Many voices around us will pretend or presume to speak the truth, but if their "truth" does not conform to the ultimate tuning fork of God's truth, they are out of tune and their truth is a distortion, a falsehood. God's truth never changes. In our churches and our individual lives, we must rebuild the Old Gate of truth.

The Valley Gate (3:13–14). The symbolism of this gate is obvious: It is the place of humility and lowliness of mind. Throughout Scripture, God says that He opposes human pride. He seeks out and lifts up the lowly, the humble, the contrite. Our goal should be to have a humble opinion of ourselves and an exalted opinion of God. The dominant attitude of our age is one of arrogance and pride: "I can do anything I want!" But the attitude God wants to build in us is one of humble dependence upon His infinite resources: "I can do everything through him who gives me strength"! When ego and pride dominate in our lives, our Valley Gate is broken and shattered. Our Valley Gate—our sense of humility before God—is in need of repair.

The Dung Gate (3:14). This gate does not have a very pleasant name, but it serves a necessary function. This is the gate of elimination, the gate where all the rubbish and corrupt things in the city were brought to be flung into the garbage dump in the Hinnom Valley outside of Jerusalem. Our lives need an elimination gate as well. Paul urges us to "purify ourselves from everything that contaminates body and spirit, perfecting holiness out of reverence for God" (2 Corinthians 7:1). We need to daily purge ourselves of secret sin and private corruption. The failure to do so produces misery, spiritual sickness, and even ruined lives.

The Fountain Gate (3:15). The name of this gate reminds us of the words of the Lord Jesus to the woman at the well: "Indeed, the water I give him will become in him a spring of water welling up to eternal life" (John 4:14). This gate was located at the end of the Pool of Siloam. It symbolizes the Holy Spirit, which is the river of life in us, enabling us to obey His will and His Word. Notice that this gate comes immediately after the Dung Gate. After our inner corruption is purged by our active consent, then the cleansing fountain of the Spirit washes us clean.

The Water Gate (3:26). Water is always a symbol of God's Word. It is an interesting coincidence that, in our own nation's history, the term Watergate is etched as a symbol of governmental crisis, scandal, and disgrace. At the Watergate Hotel in Washington, D.C., a presidential administration ran aground, foundered, and sank. Yet, out of that terrible national tragedy, one Watergate figure—a White House attorney named Charles Colson—discovered the Word of God. After confessing his role in the Watergate affair and turning his life over to Jesus Christ, he emerged a changed man, and to this day he is a vital full-time witness for the Word of God.

Note that the Water Gate in Jerusalem did not need to be repaired. Evidently it was the only part of the wall still standing. The text mentions that people lived nearby, but it doesn't mention that the Water Gate needed repair. The Word of God never breaks down. It doesn't need to be repaired. It simply needs to be reinhabited.

The East Gate (3:28–29). This gate faced the rising sun and is the gate of hope. It is the gate of anticipation of the coming day when all the trials of life and the struggles of earth will end, when the glorious new sun will rise on the new day of God. This gate needs to be rebuilt in many of us who fall under the pessimistic spirit of this age and are crushed by the hopelessness of our time.

The Horse Gate (3:28–29). The horse in Scripture is a symbol of warfare or, in this case, the need to do battle against the forces of darkness. "Our struggle is not against flesh and blood," the apostle Paul says, "but against the rulers, against the authorities, against the powers of this dark world and against the spiritual forces of evil in the heavenly realms" (Eph. 6:12). Life is a battle, and each of us is a soldier in a mighty struggle against evil—and we are in this war for the duration!

The Inspection Gate (3:31). This was evidently the place where judgment was conducted. We need to stop and conduct a thorough self-inspection. We need to ask God to sift our consciences, to remove the buildup of toxic sins and bad habits from our lives. Then we will be able to strengthen the protective walls of our souls.

Verse 32 brings us full circle, back to our starting point, the Sheep Gate, the gate of the cross. The cross must be at the beginning and the end of every life. Through these beautiful symbolic gates, the book of Nehemiah has shown us how to rebuild the walls in our lives.

Chapters 4 through 6 show us the opposition that arose as Nehemiah and his people began to rebuild the city walls—principally from a trio of schemers: Sanballat, Tobiah, and Geshem the Arab. The persecution revealed here can be summarized in three words: contempt, conspiracy, and cunning. The enemies heap contempt and mockery on God's activity. When that fails, they hatch a conspiracy, trying to involve the Israelites in a plot that would overthrow this work. When that fails, they try to draw Nehemiah away from his work by a very cunning scheme. But when you come to chapter 6, verse 15, you read this wonderful sentence:

The wall was completed on the twenty-fifth of Elul, in fifty-two days.

Now, that's an amazing record! And Nehemiah goes on to add (6:16):

When all our enemies heard about this, all the surrounding nations were afraid and lost their self-confidence, because they realized that this work had been done with the help of our God.

Reconstruction completed, reinstruction begins

The latter part of the book, chapters 7 through 13, is the story of the reinstruction of the people, following the reconstruction of the wall. The city has been strengthened and fortified; now it is time to strengthen and fortify the people, so that the nation of Israel can remain strong. In chapter 8, we have the great convening of the people by Ezra the priest—an event that is also recorded in the book of Ezra. Notice the steps here. Ezra begins by reading the law among the people (8:5–6):

Ezra opened the book. All the people could see him because he was standing above them; and as he opened it, the people all stood up. Ezra praised the LORD, the great God; and all the people lifted their hands and responded, "Amen! Amen!" Then they bowed down and worshiped the LORD with their faces to the ground.

You will always be encouraged and strengthened when you stop to remember what God has done for you and taught you in the past

What is Ezra doing here? Expository preaching! He is making the Word of God clear to the people, so that the walls of their lives could be strengthened.

After this, the people celebrated the Feast of the Tabernacles, when the people of Israel camped in booths made of tree boughs to remind them that they were simply strangers and pilgrims on earth.

Next came the remembrance of the lessons of the past. In chapter 9,

Ezra offers a tremendous prayer in which he recounts what God has done in the life of the Israelites. You will always be encouraged and strengthened when you stop to remember what God has done for you and taught you in the past.

Following this prayer, the people sign a covenant and agree to do what the law demands. They resolve to take the step of obedience. I can tell you from my own experience as well that you will never be able to retain the strength of God in your life until you are ready to obey Him.

In chapter 11, we find the recognition of gifts among the people. There are the Levites, the gatekeepers, the singers, and various others who ministered in the temple. Similarly, in the New Testament, we are told to discover the gifts that the Spirit has given us and to put them to work. "Fan into flame the gift of God, which is in you," Paul wrote to Timothy (2 Tim. 1:6). If you want to retain your strength, start using the spiritual gifts that God has given you.

In chapter 12, we find the dedication of the walls. The people gather and march around them with instruments, singing and shouting, playing and rejoicing, and crying out with great joy. Nothing will add more to your strength in the Lord than to express and celebrate the joy of the Lord in your life.

The book closes on the theme of resisting evil. You will remain strong if you adopt the attitude of Nehemiah. He was steadfast in saying "No!" to the forces that would destroy what God was doing in his life. Observe what he had to do. In chapter 13, verse 7, having gone back to Babylon and returned to Jerusalem, he says:

> *I learned about the evil thing Eliashib had done in providing Tobiah a room in the courts of the house of God.*

God's priest Eliashib had actually allowed Tobiah, the enemy of God who had opposed Nehemiah, to move right into the temple! What did Nehemiah do? In verse 8, Nehemiah recounts:

> *I was greatly displeased and threw all Tobiah's household goods out of the room.*

He tossed Tobiah out on his ear! And that's not all! He found that the priests had been cheated, so he restored the money that belonged to them. Then he discovered that, throughout the city, people were violating the Sabbath. They were bringing in merchandise and selling it in the streets. In verse 19 Nehemiah says:

> *When evening shadows fell on the gates of Jerusalem before the Sabbath, I ordered the doors to be shut and not opened until the Sabbath was over.*

Nehemiah locked them all out of the city! Then he discovered that some waited outside the doors all night, hoping someone would come out and do a little business. So what did he do then? The answer is in verse 21:

I warned them and said, "Why do you spend the night by the wall? If you do this again, I will lay hands on you." From that time on they never came on the Sabbath.

Then Nehemiah discovered yet another problem! The people were still intermarrying with the forbidden races around them. At this point, Nehemiah became very angry. In verse 25, he says:

I rebuked them and called curses down on them. I beat some of the men and pulled out their hair. I made them take an oath in God's name and said: "You are not to give your daughters in marriage to their sons, nor are you to take their daughters in marriage for your sons or for yourselves."

Was Nehemiah too severe? Shouldn't he have been more tolerant? Shouldn't he have been kinder and gentler? Many leaders today feel it's okay, or even admirable and virtuous, to tolerate evil. "We shouldn't look at everything in such black-and-white terms," they say. "We should recognize that there are shades of gray, that a little compromise is in order." Yes, compromise is sometimes appropriate, but we should never compromise with evil, with the forces that are opposed to God and His Word. That is one of the greatest lessons that the Spirit of God can ever teach us, and Nehemiah had learned that lesson well.

Significantly, the book of Nehemiah closes on the very same note that opens the ministry of the Lord Jesus in Jerusalem. He came into the temple and found it filled with the money changers and merchants who defiled the house of prayer. He made a whip of cords and drove the defilers out of the temple. Jesus was not trying to build a reputation as a kinder and gentler Messiah. He was not interested in tolerating or accommodating those who had defiled God's house. He didn't try to open a dialogue with them. He cleansed the temple, and He did so with obvious anger, with sparks flying from His eyes, yet with complete righteousness and full justification.

Those who have stamped the imprint of God's authority on the pages of history have been those who have been willing to plant their feet, to take a bold stand, and to say "No!" to the forces of sin and evil. Whenever a positive difference has been made for God in the world, it has been made by those who refused to tolerate or compromise with sin, people like John the Baptist, the apostle Paul, the Covenanters, Martin Luther, John Wesley and Charles Wesley, Dietrich Bonhoeffer.

The book of Nehemiah closes on a note of triumph. The walls have been rebuilt. The evildoers have been purged from the city. The people have been reinstructed and renewed within. Strength and vitality surges once more in a city that was once dead and in ruins. Jerusalem has once more become a fit dwelling place for God.

The reconstructed walls of Jerusalem stand once more, bearing witness to the fact that God is alive and active in the lives of His people. When we have reconstructed the walls of our lives, then God will truly live and act through us, and our lives will bear dynamic witness to Him.

The Courage of The Queen

The Holocaust, which took the lives of six million Jews during World War II, is a horror that must never be forgotten. Unfortunately, the Nazi slaughter of the Jews some fifty short years ago is not unique in history. Over the centuries, God's chosen people repeatedly have been marked for extinction by various murdering fanatics. In the book of Esther we encounter one of these Hitleresque extremists, a man named Haman. When he prepares to launch his genocidal assault against the Jewish people, only one thing stands in his way—a Jewish woman named Esther.

The book of Esther is a fascinating little gem in the Old Testament. It is a book rich in drama and emotional power, and there is considerable evidence (despite those who scoff at the Bible as a collection of legends) that Esther is an accurate historical account. The events of Esther take place in the days of Israel's captivity, when the people of Israel were enslaved by Babylon.

Here is an outline of the story of Esther:

The Peril of the Esther, Mordecai, and the Jews
(Esther 1–4)

1. The king selects Esther as his queen   1:1–2:20
2. Haman's plot against Mordecai and the Jews   2:21–4:17

The Triumph of Esther, Mordecai, and the Jews
(Esther 5–10)

Esther is a remarkable book for a number of reasons. For one thing, God is not mentioned anywhere in this book. There is no mention of heaven or hell. It is the kind of story you might find on the bestseller shelves at Barnes & Noble or on the screen at the neighborhood cineplex. Yet here it is in the Bible.

King Xerxes is snubbed by Queen Vashti

The story begins in the same setting as the opening scene of the book of Nehemiah: the royal palace in Susa. It is a time of peace and material blessing. King Xerxes throws a great feast—a six-month long feast—to display the glory, wealth, and power of his kingdom. At one point while he "was in high spirits from wine," the king calls for his servants to bring Queen Vashti to the banquet hall so that her beauty can be displayed. Proud Queen Vashti, however, doesn't want to be put on display, so she snubs the king's order. Angered by her refusal, King Xerxes issues a decree and divorces the queen.

In this storyline, we find parallels to a human life. We were created to be like this king. Each one of us is given a kingdom over which to rule: the kingdom of our souls, which includes the mind, the emotions, and above all, the will—the right to choose. Your body is the capital city of your kingdom. Your empire includes all that you influence, touch, and control. Like a king, your will is seated upon the throne of your kingdom. There is also a hidden member of your life: your inner life, or spirit. That is the deepest and most sensitive part of your being, the part designed to be in touch with God, the place where God Himself is to dwell.

When we meet the king in the book of Esther, we see that he has nothing to do but throw a lavish party to display the glory of his kingdom. In the same way, Adam and Eve, our forebears, had nothing to do but display the glory of God and to rule over the earth. In the book of Esther, the prideful king summoned his beautiful queen Vashti so he could display her before his drunken cronies.

This scene parallels the account of the fall of man, when people chose to assert their own wills against God's revealed will. In the palace of the human spirit, symbolized by Queen Vashti, the God of glory and truth lived. It was there that the human mind, emotions, and will were guided by fellowship with the living Lord, who dwelt in the royal residence of the human spirit. God explained His will to the first two members of the human race. That was His revelation to them, and if they would be obedient to His revealed will, they would fulfill their God-given destiny and utilize the full powers of their unfallen humanity as God originally intended. However, as you know, they set their wills and their reason above God's will and God's revelation. They chose what they wanted to do rather than what God wanted them to do, and with this human choice came the fall.

This beginning of humanity's woes is symbolized for us in the opening chapters of Esther, when the king issues a decree that Queen Vashti must be deposed from the throne. Once issued, this decree became the law of the Medes and Persians; the king could do nothing to reverse it, even though he was lonely and remorseful as a result. In his loneliness, he begins to search for a new queen. The proclamation goes throughout the kingdom to bring the most beautiful young women before him. And one of the young women in this procession is a young Jewish beauty named Esther.

Esther was one of the captives who had been taken from Jerusalem and enslaved in Babylon. With her was her cousin Mordecai. In these two important characters, Esther and Mordecai, we see an important symbolic image. Esther signifies for us the renewed spirit that is given to a person when he or she becomes a Christian, when regeneration takes place and a human spirit is made alive in Jesus Christ. She is under the influence and control of her cousin, Mordecai, who throughout this book is a picture for us of the Holy Spirit. His name means "little man" or "humble man." In his humility, Mordecai is also a symbolic representation of Jesus Christ.

Esther is chosen queen

In chapter 2, Esther, under the guidance of her cousin Mordecai, is brought before the king. King Xerxes instantly falls in love with her and chooses her to be his queen. So Esther is exalted from a place of bondage to the second most honored position in the kingdom. On Mordecai's advice, Esther does not tell the king that she is Jewish. (The king's ignorance of this fact will later become a key detail in the story.)

In this scene you have a picture of what might be called this king's conversion. He receives a new spirit, even though he has no understanding of the Holy Spirit. The king typifies many Christians who have little or no understanding what has truly happened to them at the moment of their conversion. In the background of the story, not always seen but always involved and active, is Mordecai. As he guides the actions of his cousin, Esther, he helps to engineer the wonderful deliverance of the people of Israel.

Chapter 2 closes with the story of Mordecai's discovery of a plot to assassinate the king. Through Esther, Mordecai reports the plot to the king, the conspirators are captured and executed, and Mordecai's deed is recorded in the annals of the kingdom. The importance of this record will soon become clear.

**Enter the
villain**

Chapter 3 introduces us to the villain—a slimy, power-hungry, Hitleresque character named Haman the Agagite. Tracing his ancestry back through Scripture, you find that an Agagite is an Amalekite, and Amalek was a race of people descended from Esau, against whom God said He would make war forever (see Ex. 17:16). King Saul had been ordered to completely eliminate this people, but in his folly he chose to spare Agag, the king of the Amalekites, and thus perpetuated this faithless force in Israel. Throughout Scripture, this tribe of Amalekites represents the human heart's indwelling desire to oppose all that God wants to do. This opposition to God's will is what the New Testament calls "the flesh." Whenever and wherever God's Spirit begins to bring blessing and renewal, this force of opposition arises to oppose the Spirit and—through subtle, crafty schemes—to undermine and undo the work of God. That force of opposition, that will of the flesh, is symbolized in the man called Haman.

Haman rises to a place of prominence, subordinate in power only to the king. He is called a "captain of princes," and his position is much like the one Joseph held under the Egyptian pharaoh: what we might now think of as a prime minister. When Haman learns that Mordecai refuses to bow the knee and pay honor to him like the other nobles of the court, he becomes enraged. Learning that Mordecai is a Jew, he vows to eliminate him from the kingdom—but not Mordecai alone! To repay Mordecai for this perceived insult, Haman hatches a plan "to destroy, kill and annihilate all the Jews." Sound familiar? Tragically, it is all too familiar.

Throughout this account we read how completely Haman was consumed by his hatred of the Jews. Why does he hate this race so much? In Esther 3:8, we get a clue:

> *Haman said to King Xerxes, "There is a certain people dispersed and scattered among the peoples in all the provinces of your kingdom whose customs are different from those of all other people and who do not obey the king's laws; it is not in the king's best interest to tolerate them."*

In other words, Haman is attacking the Jews because they obey a different life principle. Just as the human spirit that is indwelt by the

Holy Spirit is immediately subject to a different rule of living, a different way of thinking, a different demand, so these Jews obeyed a different principle. Whenever you live in a moral, spiritual, upright way, you become a light that highlights the spiritual filthiness and moral decay of the people around you. You stick out like a sore thumb, to use an old expression, and by your very conspicuous righteousness you invite persecution from those whose deeds are evil.

Because the Jews are God's people, living according to God's life principle, Haman hates them—and out of his hate comes a terrible strategy. The central theme of the book from this point on is how God works to get the wrong man out of control and the right man in, and how He uses Esther to bring salvation out of a seemingly hopeless situation. In the stark struggle between good and evil that is portrayed in Esther, we see the struggle of our own lives. Some people wonder why, after becoming Christians, they still have problems and struggles. The reason is simple: The flesh (both our own fleshly will, and the will of God's enemies around us) is continually at work, cleverly and tenaciously opposing all that God wants to do in our lives. We are opposed by the flesh from within and without. Galatians 5:17 clearly explains the dynamics of our ongoing inner struggle:

> *The sinful nature desires what is contrary to the Spirit, and the Spirit what is contrary to the sinful nature. They are in conflict with each other, so that you do not do what you want.*

Haman craftily persuades the king that, for the king's own benefit, he should eliminate these people. A master of the hidden agenda and of political power plays, Haman becomes the power behind the throne, controlling the king like a puppeteer. On Haman's counsel, the king issues an edict to eliminate the Jews from his kingdom—unaware that his own wife, Queen Esther, is Jewish!

In chapter 4, we see God's invisible hand setting events in motion. Mordecai is grieved over the king's proclamation of a coming holocaust. Mordecai's grief parallels the grieving of the Holy Spirit—God's anguish that disquiets and sorrows our own human spirit over our sin. We may not be able to put a finger on it, but we know that something is not right between ourselves and God.

"If I perish, I perish."

Esther finds Mordecai in a state of grief and distress. Not knowing why he is grieved, Esther sends him a change of clothes, hoping that will take care of the problem. Often, when we or someone close to us is in distress, we try to correct the problem with a superficial change. The Band-Aid approach cannot heal a deep and life-threatening illness. The problem of sin concerns not just what we do but what we are, so a more radical treatment is needed—the treatment of a completely changed life, regeneration through Jesus Christ.

Mordecai sends a messenger named Hathach (whose name means "the truth") to convince Esther that she is up against a serious problem. He tells Esther the whole deadly plot of Haman to destroy the Jews. When Esther hears this, she is devastated and doesn't know what to do. Mordecai then advises her to approach the king on behalf of the Jews.

Mordecai has just asked Esther to do a dangerous thing. To appear before the king without being summoned automatically incurs a death sentence—even for the queen. So Esther sends word back to Mordecai, reminding him that to comply with his request could mean her death. Mordecai replies bluntly that Esther should not be naive enough to think she would be spared in Haman's plan to extinguish the Jews nor that she could outwit clever Haman.

Many of us have made the same discovery in our own lives. We tried to defeat some enemy or problem in our lives through our own meager human wisdom instead of relying on God. We have ended up outwitted and outmaneuvered. Only when we come to the end of ourselves and die to our own resources do we become capable of appropriating God's resources. We cannot defeat the flesh by clenching our fists or making New Year's resolutions. We must (as they say in the Christian recovery movement) "let go and let God." That is the truth that Esther faces as she says, resignedly, in Esther 4:16:

> *"Go, gather together all the Jews who are in Susa, and fast for me. Do not eat or drink for three days, night or day. I and my maids will fast as you do. When this is done, I will go to the king, even though it is against the law. And if I perish, I perish."*

**The courage
of the queen**

It is significant that Esther calls upon the Jews to fast for her, three nights and three days. That is the same amount of time Jesus lay in the grave on our behalf.

On the third day, Esther puts on her royal robes and stands in the inner courts of the king's palace, opposite the king's hall, waiting in fear and uncertainty, anticipating with dread what will happen when the king sees her. Here we see the true courage of the queen. Courage is not the lack of fear but the willingness to take a risky, bold step even when we are *filled* with fear and anxiety. As Esther steps forward on this third day, beautifully symbolic of the resurrected life, her overpowering radiance captivates the king's heart.

"What is it, Queen Esther?" asks the king, staring at her transfixed. "What is your request? Even up to half the kingdom, it will be given you" (5:3).

Amazingly, Esther doesn't ask him for anything. Instead, she invites him to dinner that day and says to bring Haman along. Humanly speaking, the smart thing for Esther to have done was to ask the king for Haman's head on a platter! But she doesn't do that. She is operating on God's logic not human logic. In obedience to Mordecai's orders, she waits, she bides her time. In doing so, she is able to accomplish much more than simply destroying Haman. She gives Haman the opportunity to trap himself in his own folly, so that he will be exposed as the evil conniver that he is.

After the dinner, the king again asks the queen what she wants, and she asks them to come back again the next night for dinner. Haman goes out walking on air, thrilled with what has happened. He returns to his wife and sons, telling them in effect, "I knew I was the king's fair-haired boy, but now it looks like I'm the queen's favorite as well! I've got them eating right out of my hand."

Then, filled with pride and arrogance, he goes out and sees his enemy, Mordecai, at the king's gate. When Mordecai, as usual, does not treat Haman with all the bowing and cowering that this little tin god thinks he deserves, Haman is again "filled with rage against Mordecai" (5:9). Haman cannot stand it that Mordecai is unimpressed with his power. Here again, we see that Mordecai symbolizes the Holy Spirit, who is not impressed or intimidated by the arrogance of human flesh. Mordecai's refusal to pay homage eats at Haman's heart, and he says to his wife and friends that, despite all his wealth, power, and honors, he cannot be happy "as long as I see that Jew Mordecai sitting at the king's gate" (5:13).

His wife and friends tell him, in effect, "If Mordecai stands in your way, get rid of him. Erect a gallows seventy-five feet high, then go to the king in the morning and tell the king to hang him!" Isn't that just like the flesh? If anyone or anything gets in your way, just get rid of it.

From a human perspective, all seems lost for Mordecai. But God is taking a hand and moving events in ways that the human mind could never foresee, for that very night, King Xerxes is unable to sleep. So he does what many people do when they have insomnia: He orders some reading material. He orders the annals of the kingdom—a book of memorable deeds—to be brought and read to him (6:1).

In the annals, he hears once again the story of how two of his own guards plotted against his life—and that the conspiracy had been thwarted when Mordecai learned of it and reported it to the king through Esther. The king is reminded who his real friend is. Listening to the story, he realizes that Mordecai has never been properly honored

Esther invites the king and Haman to dinner

Haman cannot stand it that Mordecai is unimpressed with his power

King Xerxes is unable to sleep

for his service to the king. Amazingly (and, of course, through divine timing), Haman chooses that moment to come to the king's court and call for Mordecai's hanging!

When the king learns that Haman has arrived—and not knowing what Haman has in mind—he calls for Haman to be brought to him. When Haman comes into the king's presence, the king asks him for advice: "What should be done for the man the king delights to honor?" (6:6).

Of course, Haman leaps to the wrong conclusion, thinking, *The king must mean me!* So he replies, "For the man the king delights to honor, have them bring a royal robe the king has worn and a horse the king has ridden, one with a royal crest placed on its head. Then let the robe and horse be entrusted to one of the king's most noble princes. Let them robe the man the king delights to honor, and lead him on the horse through the city streets, proclaiming before him, 'This is what is done for the man the king delights to honor!' " (Esther 6:7–9).

So the king says, "Get the robe and the horse and do just as you have suggested for Mordecai the Jew, who sits at the king's gate. Do not neglect anything you have recommended" (Esther 6:10).

Haman must honor Mordecai

Wouldn't you love to have seen Haman's face right then? But what can Haman do? How can he call for Mordecai's hanging now? So he does what the king orders! He goes through with this grinding, humiliating experience. He puts Mordecai, his enemy, on the horse and leads him through the city. Can't you just see him calling out as he goes, "This is what is done for the man the king delights to honor!" All the while, his heart is almost bursting with murderous rage! But the evil heart of flesh will do anything for the sake of survival, even pretend to be religious.

A Christian actor once told me of being in a large New York City church. This church had a young people's band that went around the area holding concerts and giving testimonies. The group used the same vocabulary that evangelicals use, but the thrust of the testimonies was the glorification of the people giving the testimonies, not the glory of God. There was a brassy, glitzy brilliance about the entire production, but it was not genuine. "That's when I learned," the actor concluded, "how the flesh can behave in a religious, pious way, yet still be the flesh." That kind of phoniness is what Haman pictures for us here.

Queen Esther reveals Haman's treacherous plan

The next day, King Xerxes, Haman, and Esther come together, and there, Queen Esther reveals Haman's treacherous plan to destroy the Jews. What's more, Esther identifies with her people and tells the king that she herself is a Jew, threatened with death by Haman's plan. The king is horror-struck. Anguished, he goes out in the garden and paces up and down. It is a drastic thing to kill a prime minister—but it is a drastic evil that Haman has committed. The king knows that there can be no peace in his kingdom until this matter is ended, so he gives the order to hang Haman on the gallows. Haman was hung on the very gallows he had prepared for Mordecai.

The fullness of the Spirit

That same day, King Xerxes gives to Esther the entire estate of Haman, the enemy of the Jews, and Esther confers the estate upon Mordecai. The king also exalts Mordecai to the place of power. This symbolizes the fullness of the Spirit. In chapter 2, the Spirit is received. In chapter 3, the Spirit is resisted. Early in chapter 4, the Spirit is grieved. In the latter part of chapter 4, the Spirit is quenched. Now, in chapter 8, we see the fullness of the Spirit, the exaltation of God symbolized in the exaltation of Mordecai. When Mordecai comes to power, everything begins to change. Instantly another decree goes out, liberating the Jews to destroy their enemies.

The king exalts Mordecai

The Jews are spared

In Esther chapter 8, the Jews are freed from the king's decree of death by the ascendancy of Mordecai, just as in Romans chapter 8 we are freed from the law of sin and death by the power of the Spirit in our lives. One passage in Romans sums up the storyline of Esther: "What the law was powerless to do in that it was weakened by the sinful nature, God did by sending his own Son in the likeness of sinful man to be a sin offering. And so he condemned sin in sinful man, in order that the righteous requirements of the law might be fully met in us, who do not live according to the sinful nature [the Haman-minded flesh] but according to the Spirit [being Mordecai-minded]" (Rom. 8:3–4).

That is the choice we continually face, every day of our lives: Shall we follow the flesh, or the Spirit? Shall we pattern our lives after Haman, or after the life of Esther and the Spirit-led guidance of Mordecai?

Part Four

Music to

Live By

Music to Live By

The third section of the Old Testament consists of five poetical books: Job, Psalms, Proverbs, Ecclesiastes, and the Song of Songs. These books reflect the sorrow and the joy of our lives and our relationships with God. In these books you find the sigh, the exultation, the anger, the contentment, the tears, and the laughter of the human experience. These books are the music of Scripture. They are written in the Hebrew manner of poetry—a form that derives its artistic expression not from rhyming and rhythms but from the structure and restatement of ideas and emotions. Because we are three-dimensional beings, and these five books are bound to our humanity, they reflect the human experience and the human being in all three dimensions: the spirit, the soul, and the body.

Job is the cry of the human spirit, the deep cry of someone who desperately struggles to trust in God when everything in life is crumbling. When suffering reaches such a white-hot intensity that life itself seems senseless, then one's only recourse is to cling to God in faith. Humanity was made to believe in God.

Psalms, Proverbs, and Ecclesiastes join together to express the cry of the human soul. The soul has three aspects—the emotions, the mind, and the will—and each of these books reflects a specific aspect. Psalms is the book of emotions. Proverbs is the book of the will. And Ecclesiastes is the book of the mind, the story of Solomon's philosophical quest for meaning and purpose in life. In these three books, you have the soul's expression of its need, the soul's deep yearning for answers, for refuge, for something to rely on. Just as the answer to the cry of the spirit is *faith,* the answer to the cry of the soul is *hope.*

In the Song of Songs you have the cry of the body, the physical being, for love. Our deepest need as men and women is love. Children cannot grow up whole unless they have love, expressed not only in words, but through affirming eye contact and physical touch. The same is true between marriage partners. This cry of the body for affirming physical connection and love is expressed in the most beautiful love poem ever written, the Song of Songs.

Let's briefly survey each of these books in turn.

Job

The book of Job is a deep and honest protest of the human spirit as it faces apparently purposeless pain and suffering

The book of Job addresses the needs, and particularly the pain and grief, of the human spirit. Job is the oldest book of the Bible and, in many ways, the most profound. It is a deep and honest protest of the human spirit as it faces apparently purposeless pain and suffering. We have not experienced life deeply nor thought about life deeply until we have asked ourselves the questions that Job asks in this book. Job asks the kinds of questions that are asked by more contemporary writers such as Philip Yancey in *Disappointment with God,* or C. S. Lewis in *A Grief Observed.* By immersing ourselves in the book of Job, we learn that God understands our limitations, and He accepts those tough, even angry, questions we bring to Him in our pain.

Psalms

The book of Psalms is divided into five books that parallel the fivefold pattern of the five books of Moses

The Psalms reflect every emotional experience of life. They are divided into five books, each of which—except for the last—ends with the words "Amen and Amen." The fifth division ends with the words "Praise the Lord." In these books you find a fivefold pattern that parallels the fivefold pattern of the five books of Moses, the Pentateuch:

1. In the Pentateuch, Genesis is the book of human need. In the first book of psalms (Ps. 1 through Ps. 41) you have the great expressions of the need of the human heart. This theme reaches its apex in the Twenty-Third Psalm, which begins, "The LORD is my shepherd, I shall not be in want."

2. Exodus is the book of grace and redeeming love. This theme echoes in the second book of psalms (Ps. 42 through Ps. 72). This theme resonates, for example, in Psalm 46, which speaks of God as "our refuge and strength, an ever-present help in trouble."

3. Leviticus is the book of worship wherein humanity is told how to live in close fellowship with the living God. This same note reverberates in the third book of psalms (Ps. 73 through Ps. 89). These psalms are songs of reverence and worship, exalting the majesty of God,

exemplified by the words of Psalm 76: "You are resplendent with light, more majestic than mountains rich with game."

4. Numbers is the book of wandering, of the desert experience, the ups and downs of daily living. Similarly, the fourth book of psalms (Ps. 90 through Ps. 106) is the book of alternating victories and defeats in the experience of life. You will find many joyful songs in this section, but also many Job-like passages in which the psalmist questions and cries out to God in anguish. A typical passage is Psalm 102:1–3:

> Hear my prayer, O LORD;
> > let my cry for help come to you,
> Do not hide your face from me
> > when I am in distress.
> Turn your ear to me;
> > when I call, answer me quickly.
> For my days vanish like smoke;
> > my bones burn like glowing embers.

5. The last book of the Pentateuch, Deuteronomy, is a book of helplessness and dependent obedience. This corresponds to the fifth book of psalms (Ps. 107 to Ps. 150), which sounds a chord of obedience and praise. Perhaps nothing gathers up this theme more beautifully than the well-known words of Psalm 139:23–24:

> Search me, O God, and know my heart;
> > test me and know my anxious thoughts.
> See if there is any offensive way in me,
> > and lead me in the way everlasting.

Countless believers have treasured the Psalms as music to live by. The Psalms lift our hearts and minds to God and bring God down to us so that we can experience true fellowship. Whether your heart is singing or sighing right now, you can turn to the Psalms to find those feelings translated into moving, inspired poetry.

The book of Proverbs is the expression of human intelligence guided by divine wisdom. Here you have the logical, reasonable approach to life—the discovery of the laws of heaven for life on earth. It is a simple book and begins with a magnificent introduction explaining why it was written.

Next, we read a series of discourses on wisdom, given from a father to a son. These fatherly discourses begin with the child in the home, then follow the youth out into the busy streets of the city as he

Proverbs

The book of Proverbs reveals the laws of heaven for life on earth

encounters various circumstances, perils, and temptations of life. These proverbs teach him how to choose and make friends; how to spot and avoid dangers; how to build character and strength.

The fatherly discourses are followed by two collections of proverbs. The first collection, chapters 10 through 24, is made up of proverbs of Solomon concerning godliness. The second collection, chapters 25 through 29, are Solomon's proverbs about relationships; these were copied and preserved by Hezekiah's scribes.

Chapter 30 contains the proverbs of Agur. The very last chapter, Proverbs 31, stands alone, for it was written by King Lemuel and contains proverbs that his mother taught him. Verses 10 through 31 of this chapter contain one of the most magnificent descriptions of a godly wife to be found in literature.

Ecclesiastes

The book of Ecclesiastes reveals the human protest against the monotony and emptiness of life

The title *Ecclesiastes* means "The Preacher." This book is human protest against the monotony and emptiness of life. It is an inquiry into the meaning—or meaninglessness—of life. Ecclesiastes was written by Solomon, a man with unlimited resources and money, someone with complete freedom to spend his time as he wished. Solomon deliberately set himself to answer these questions: "Can life be satisfying apart from God? Can the things found in this world truly fill the human heart?" He questions the satisfaction to be found in acquiring knowledge, in seeking pleasure, in accumulating wealth, in exploring philosophy. In every realm with potential for meaning and satisfaction, he had to conclude, "All is vanity. Everything is in vain."

At this point, you may be thinking, "What a depressing book!" Not at all! because in the final chapter of the book, chapter 12, Solomon places all of life's "vanity" into its proper perspective. In 12:13 he writes, "Now all has been heard; here is the conclusion of the matter: Fear God and keep his commandments, for this is the whole duty of man." But wait! See that word *duty*? Cross it out! It does not appear in the original Hebrew text but was supplied by a translator who missed Solomon's point. Solomon was not saying that fearing (worshiping) and obeying God is our *duty;* he was saying that this is our *purpose in life.* This sums up the reason for our existence.

Knowing and obeying God is the sum total of our satisfaction in life

At the end of the book, Solomon finally stumbles upon a brilliant truth! He has discovered, after years of searching, that nothing can make anyone complete except God. Knowing and obeying God is the sum total of our satisfaction in life. When we worship and obey God, we are whole, we are doing what we were created to do, and we find true satisfaction. Apart from God, everything is vanity, meaninglessness. But when we are in a right relationship with God, then all of life—and even death itself—has meaning. The person who lives and walks with God does not live in vain.

The last of the poetical books is the Song of Songs. It is probably the least understood and most neglected of all the books of the Bible. It is a flagrantly sensuous book about spiritual love, but also a surprisingly candid book about the sexual expression of love between husband and wife. In times past, this book has actually been considered shameful by some religious groups that had an unwholesome view of the human body and human sexuality, as well as an unwholesome view of God's Word. In fact, nothing is shameful about this book nor about the human body. The Song of Songs points us toward a pure and loving expression of our sexuality within the protective, holy enclosure of marriage.

There is no more thrilling sight to a man than the beautiful body of a woman. There is no higher expression of nobility and strength to a woman than the clean, fine body of a man. This book places our God-given bodies and our God-given sexuality in a wholesome perspective.

The Song of Songs places our God-given bodies and our God-given sexuality in a wholesome perspective

The storyline of the book can be confusing, because it is written in several voices—the voice of the Beloved (Solomon), the voice of the Lover (the Shulamite woman), and the voice of the Friends. The Song of Songs is the story of a young peasant woman who unknowingly meets the king of Israel (he is disguised as a peasant shepherd). Later, he reveals himself to her as the king and whisks her away to his palace where they share their love and live happily ever after (perhaps this story was the inspiration for the Cinderella legend!).

But note the deeper meaning to this beautiful book of love poetry. It is a wonderfully symbolic parable of God's redeeming grace toward the human race. The Shulamite woman, the Beloved, represents the followers of God who have been redeemed by His grace. The Lover, the Shepherd, the great King in disguise, manifests His love to her while disguised as a shepherd. He goes away, then returns in His full royal splendor to take the woman away, representing (of course) the Lord Jesus!

This book is also a wonderfully symbolic parable of God's redeeming grace toward the human race

We will explore this rich symbolism further when we examine this book in chapter 28. For now, observe that the Song of Songs is actually two songs in one. On the surface, it is a love song, a beautifully romantic story told in poetic form. Beneath the surface, it is a hymn, a sacred and symbolic retelling of the story of our redemption from sin by our Shepherd and our King, Jesus Christ.

The pages of the poetic section of God's Word are rich, radiant, and fragrant with experiences that touch and transcend our own emotions and experiences. Turn the page with me, and immerse yourself in a story that is incredibly ancient, yet one that encompasses the pain and the passions of contemporary men and women like you and me: the story of Job.

The Hardest Question

J ohnny Gunther was a handsome boy of sixteen when the shadow of brain cancer fell across his life. He majored in math and chemistry at Deerfield Academy and was a straight-A student. During the fourteen months after his diagnosis, he endured two operations. Even after his second operation, he passed the grueling entrance examinations for Columbia University. Two weeks after being accepted to Columbia, Johnny Gunther died.

The character of this brave young man was revealed following the first surgery. The doctors explained the life-threatening seriousness of the boy's condition to Johnny's parents, John and Frances Gunther. "What should we tell Johnny about his condition?" they asked the surgeon.

"He's so bright and so curious about all that's happening to him," the surgeon replied. "He really wants to know everything that's happening to him, so I think we should be honest with him."

The Gunthers agreed.

The surgeon went to Johnny alone in his hospital room and explained to him the seriousness of his brain tumor. The boy listened attentively throughout the explanation, then asked, "Doctor, how shall we break it to my parents?"

Johnny Gunther was a young man with so much promise. Why did such a terrible thing—brain cancer—invade his life? That question echoes the tough, painful questions asked in the oldest book of the Bible, the book of Job.

"Why?"

Senseless suffering
arises from Satan's
continual challenge
to the government
of God

**The
battleground**

Job is poetry, and it is an epic drama not unlike the Greek poetic dramas of Homer, *The Iliad* and *The Odyssey*. But the book of Job is also history. Job was an actual, living person and these events actually happened, but God recounts them for us in this beautiful literary style so that we might have an answer to the age-old, haunting question, "Why does seemingly senseless tragedy invade our lives?" Whenever you find yourself going through pain and trials, whenever you cry out, "Why, Lord?" it is a good idea to open the book of Job. Here is a man who experienced agony, loss, and desolation of spirit beyond our ability to comprehend. Job asks questions of God, seeks answers from God, becomes angry with God—yet he remains faithful, and God brings him through his time of trial.

The ultimate answer to the "Why, Lord?" question is given at the beginning of the book. In the opening scenes of Job, we learn the background of Job's drama—information that Job himself doesn't have. The answer to the great "Why?" question is this: Senseless suffering arises from Satan's continual challenge to the government of God.

As the book opens, we find God meeting with the angels. Among them is Satan, who strides in sneering and swaggering, convinced that self-interest is humanity's only motivator. In the presence of God, Satan asserts that anyone who claims to be motivated in some other way is a phony. In fact, Satan claims he can prove it. God responds by selecting a man named Job to be the proving ground.

On December 7, 1941, a sneak attack on Pearl Harbor in Hawaii brought the United States into World War II. At the beginning of the war between Japan and the United States, it looked as though this conflict would be staged in the middle of the Pacific, around the Hawaiian Islands. But very early in the war, events took a sudden turn and without warning the whole theater of battle shifted abruptly to the South Pacific, an area several thousand miles beyond Hawaii. For the first time, Americans began to hear of islands with strange-sounding names: Guam, Guadalcanal, Wake Island, Luzon, Mindanao, and Bataan. There, in those obscure, out-of-the way corners of the earth, the greatest powers on earth were locked in mortal combat. The islands became the battleground for the great conflict between empires.

This is very similar to what happened in the story of Job. Here is a man going about his business, unaware that he has suddenly become the center of God's attention—and Satan's. Like tiny Guam or remote Wake Island, there is nothing special about Job, but his life becomes a battleground in the cosmic struggle between God and Satan, between good and evil. Job is ground zero, and Satan is about to begin his first major assault.

Here is an overview of this epic story of cosmic warfare that is waged within the mind, body, and spirit of a single human being, the man named Job:

The Losses and Sufferings of Job
(Job 1:1–2:13)

The Conversations of Job and His Three "Friends"
(Job 3–37)

Tragedies piled upon catastrophes

In chapter 1 we see that, one by one, all the props are pulled out of Job's life. Hard on the heels of the first comes each successive tragedy. First, all of Job's oxen are taken by enemy raids, and then his donkey herds are decimated. Next, his sheep are killed in a storm, then Job learns that his great herd of camels—true wealth in the world of the Middle East—are wiped out. Finally comes the most heartbreaking news of all: Job's seven sons and three daughters are together in one home, enjoying a birthday celebration, when a tornado strikes, demolishing the house and killing all of Job's children at once.

Though he is reeling from his losses, Job seeks to respond in faith

Though he is reeling from his losses, Job—a man of great faith and faithfulness to his Lord—seeks to respond in faith. "Naked I came from my mother's womb," he says philosophically, "and naked I will depart. The LORD gave and the LORD has taken away; may the name of the LORD be praised" (Job 1:21).

Satan is taken aback by Job's response. He was sure that the massive assault that he had launched against Job would be more than enough to destroy Job's faith. Job's faith has dealt Satan a stinging setback. So Satan now goes back to God and wants Him to change the rules of the game. Satan has decided to attack Job more directly and petitions God for the right to strike Job's own body. God agrees. Without warning, Job is suddenly stricken with a series of terrible boils.

When I was younger, I experienced within eighteen months a series of boils on my body—no more than two or three at a time, and probably around twenty-five altogether. Since that time, I have had deep sympathy for dear old Job. Nothing is more aggravating than a painful boil that no medication can relieve. You can only grit your teeth and endure the agony until the boil heals of its own accord.

Consider how Job must have felt, being stricken with boils from the top of his head to the soles of his feet. As the pain drags on, his wife's faith succumbs. In Job 2:9, she turns on him and says, "Are you still holding on to your integrity? Curse God and die!" Job has to stand alone, but he is determined to be faithful.

Job's "comforters"

Then comes the final test, when he receives a visit from three of his friends: Eliphaz the Temanite, Bildad the Shuhite, and Zophar the Naamathite. At Job 2:11, the book shifts its focus. We now are no longer looking only at Job but also at his controversy with these three friends. Their conversation occupies the major part of the book.

Initially, Job's three friends seem to respond with genuine empathy. When they first see him, they weep, tear their clothes, and cover themselves with ashes. They hardly recognize Job, so much has he been disfigured by his suffering. For seven days and seven nights, they sit with him, not saying a word, because they see how great his suffering is. If they had simply remained that way, silently present, Job would have felt supported and cared for. But finally they break the silence. They go on and on, talking and arguing, piling pious words and judgment onto Job's suffering, magnifying his pain.

From their limited human perspective, Job's three friends attempt to answer that same haunting question, "Why do senseless tragedies afflict us?" All three come to the same conclusion. With smug, dogmatic certainty, they agree that Job is afflicted because he has committed a terrible sin. So they proceed to argue with him in an attempt to break down his defenses and to get him to admit that they are right. Some comfort they are!

With smug, dogmatic certainty, Job's friends conclude that Job is afflicted because he has committed a terrible sin

Now, it is true that God sometimes uses tragic or painful circumstances to get our attention when we have wandered away from Him. And it is also true that when we violate the laws of God's universe (for example, by taking illegal drugs, engaging in promiscuous sex or gluttonous eating habits), our bodies will have to pay the price in poor health and even intense suffering. But it is also true, as the title of a best-selling book states, that bad things happen to good people. The problem with the argument of Job's three miserable "comforters" is that they stubbornly claim that sin is the *only* possible explanation for the sequence of tragedies in Job's life.

Like a boxer who continues to beat on an opponent who's already down for the count, Job's friends each take three rounds with him. Each presents three arguments, nine arguments in all, and each plays the same tune. They try various approaches. First they try sarcasm and irony. Then they appeal to Job's honesty. Then they accuse him of specific crimes and misdeeds. Finally they act hurt and go away, miffed and sulking. All the while, they attack Job's integrity with the argument that if God is just, then the righteous are always blessed and the wicked always suffer. Therefore, Job's pain is the direct result of Job's sin. It's a tidy, logical explanation—unless *you* are the one who is suffering. In his book *Disappointment with God,* Philip Yancey observes that Christians, like Job's friends, often feel that they must find some hidden spiritual reason behind suffering, such as:

Job's comforters assert that the righteous are always blessed and the wicked always suffer

> "God is trying to teach you something. You should feel privileged, not bitter, about your opportunity to lean on him in faith."
>
> "Meditate on the blessings you still enjoy—at least you are alive. Are you a fair-weather believer?"
>
> "You are undergoing a training regimen, a chance to exercise new muscles of faith. Don't worry—God will not test you beyond your endurance."
>
> "Don't complain so loudly! You will forfeit this opportunity to demonstrate your faithfulness to nonbelievers."
>
> "Someone is always worse off than you. Give thanks despite your circumstances."
>
> Job's friends offered a version of each of these words of wisdom, and each contains an element of truth. But the book of Job plainly shows that such "helpful advice" does nothing to answer the questions of the person in pain. It was the wrong medicine, dispensed at the wrong time.
>
> (Philip Yancey, *Disappointment with God,* 181)

The wrong medicine, dispensed at the wrong time

At first Job is annoyed with these friends. But then he becomes angry, then exasperated, replying to them with thick sarcasm. When they urge him to confess his sin, he responds that he can't confess sin that he is unaware of, and he can't think of anything he has done to offend God. Moreover, he no longer believes in justice, since their argument that the wicked always suffer simply isn't true. He further points out that many notoriously wicked people actually prosper and flourish—a fact that hasn't changed in thousands of years!

At this point, we see Job's faith sagging under the load of suffering he is called upon to bear. He says that he doesn't know what to do because God won't listen to him. He doesn't even have a chance to plead his case before God, because God hides from him and cannot be found. "If only I knew where to find him," he laments in Job 23:3–4. "If only I could go to his dwelling! I would state my case before him and fill my mouth with arguments."

Finally, in a boiling rage of confusion, bewilderment, anger, hurt, and frustration, Job yells at his friends, expressing his terror of the Almighty. "He carries out his decree against me," wails Job, "and many such plans he still has in store. That is why I am terrified before him; when I think of all this, I fear him" (Job 23:14–15). Job once thought of God as a reliable Friend. Now his Friend has seemingly turned on him. He is disoriented. Up is down. Right is wrong. White is black. Job no longer knows what to think about the God whom he has served all his life. The pain of his suffering is eating away at his mind and his emotions.

Throughout Job's trial, he is utterly and completely honest. Whatever he withstands, whatever he feels, whatever he thinks, he simply lays out the truth of it with blunt candor. He refuses to admit things he cannot accept. He dispatches the pat answers of his friends with the livid contempt that those answers deserve. Stripped as he is to his very soul, he cries out again and again with some of the deepest expressions of the human heart. Like Jacob when he wrestled with God's angel, Job is locked in a struggle with God. He is angry, he is afraid, he is confused and sick inside—but he never lets go of God. He never pushes God away. He always deals with God straight from the shoulder.

At times we see that Job's wrestling with God is rewarded. A ray of light shines in his darkness. In Job 19:25–26, Job says, "I know that my Redeemer lives, and that in the end he will stand upon the earth. And after my skin has been destroyed, yet in my flesh I will see God." Out of this man's deep distress comes a cry that will be fulfilled in the coming of Jesus Christ. He is our Redeemer who will make it possible for us to transcend the corruption of death and to stand in the flesh and see God face-to-face.

After all of Job's so-called friends have had a chance to take a verbal whack at him, the poor bruised and confused man is confronted by yet another heckler. His name is Elihu, and until now he has been a silent witness to the conversation. Now, speaking with the know-it-all air of a smug youth, Elihu clears his throat and launches into a discourse of his own. In chapter 32 we read:

"If only I could go to his dwelling! I would state my case before him and fill my mouth with arguments"

Job cries out again and again with some of the deepest expressions of the human heart

Elihu

Elihu son of Barakel the Buzite, of the family of Ram, became very angry with Job for justifying himself rather than God. He was also angry with the three friends, because they had found no way to refute Job, and yet had condemned him. . . .

So Elihu son of Barakel the Buzite said:

"I am young in years,
and you are old;
that is why I was fearful,
not daring to tell you what I know.
I thought, 'Age should speak;
advanced years should teach wisdom.'
But it is the spirit in a man,
the breath of the Almighty, that gives him understanding.
It is not only the old who are wise,
not only the aged who understand what is right"
(vv. 2–3, 6–9).

So Elihu starts by justifying himself for his outburst and for contending with those who are older (and supposedly wiser) than he. He goes on to blast both Job and his other "friends," saying, in effect, "You are all wrong. You friends of Job are wrong because you accuse him unjustly, and Job is wrong because he blames God for his difficulty. He is accusing God in order to exonerate himself." In a long-winded monologue that lasts from chapters 32 through 37, Elihu points out the weaknesses in both arguments; yet he offers nothing positive to answer the question of Job's misery.

**The answer
of the Lord**

Suddenly, in chapter 38, Job at last hears from an authoritative source: The Lord Himself answers Job out of the whirlwind. From the fury of the winds, God comes to him and says:

"Who is this that darkens my counsel
with words without knowledge?
Brace yourself like a man;
I will question you, and you shall answer me" (38:2–3).

The Lord Himself
answers Job out of
the whirlwind

In other words, "Do you want to debate with Me, Job? First, let Me see your qualifications. I have a list of questions. If you can handle these questions, then perhaps you're qualified to go head-to-head with Me in a debate." Then, in chapters 38 through 40, we find one of the most remarkable passages in the Bible. God takes Job on a tour of nature and asks him question after question, such as:

"Where were you when I laid the earth's foundation?" (38:4).

"Have you ever given orders to the morning,
or shown the dawn its place?" (38:12).

"Have the gates of death been shown to you?
Have you seen the gates of the shadow of death?" (38:17).

"Can you bind the beautiful Pleiades?
Can you loose the cords of Orion?
"Can you bring forth the constellations in their seasons
or lead out the Bear with its cubs?
Do you know the laws of the heavens?" (38:31–33).

"Can you raise your voice to the clouds
and cover yourself with a flood of water?
Do you send the lightning bolts on their way?" (38:34–35).

"Do you give the horse his strength
or clothe his neck with a flowing mane?" (39:19).

"Does the hawk take flight by your wisdom
and spread his wings toward the south?" (39:26).

"Can you pull in the leviathan with a fishhook
or tie down his tongue with a rope?" (41:1).

The answer to all these questions is obvious—and humbling. In these three chapters, the Lord paints a vast and finely detailed picture of the complex, intricately interconnected universe that He has created, from its most delicate and beautiful life-forms to its most awesome and terrifying forces, from the familiar creatures such as oxen and eagles to the distant stars in their constellations. Clearly, only a tremendous superhuman mind could embrace, comprehend, and direct the full range of Creation in all its variety, complexity, and power. At the end of this overwhelming display of God's awesome power and wisdom, Job in his smallness can only respond by falling abjectly on his face before God:

At the end of this overwhelming display of God's awesome power and wisdom, Job in his smallness can only respond by falling abjectly on his face before God

"My ears had heard of you
but now my eyes have seen you.
Therefore I despise myself
and repent in dust and ashes" (42:5–6).

✳ The essence of God's argument is that life is too complicated for simple answers. If you are demanding that God come up with simple answers to these deep and complicated problems, you are asking Him to do more than you are able to understand. Therefore, we finite human beings must take the position of trusting Him, not arguing with Him.

Ultimately, we must accept the fact that God does not exist for people but people exist for God. God is not a glorified bellboy at whom we snap our fingers, so that He scurries up to us and asks, "May I take your order?" No, we exist for Him. We are God's instruments, and we exist to carry out His purposes, some of which are so complicated and transcendent that we are hopelessly incapable of comprehending them.

As the book draws to a close, we see what the apostle James referred to when he wrote:

⭐ *You have heard of Job's perseverance and have seen what the Lord finally brought about. The Lord is full of compassion and mercy (James 5:11).*

In Job 42, God rebukes Job's "comforters" and has Job pray for these men—these stubborn, sincere, well-intentioned, misguided, self-righteous blunderers who, by their judgmental words, did far more harm than good to the body, mind, and spirit of their friend Job. Then God restores everything that Job has lost—and doubles it. He had 7,000 sheep before; God gives him 14,000. He had 500 oxen and 500 donkeys; God gives him 1,000 of each. He had 3,000 camels; God gives him 6,000. He even replaces his sons and daughters. You might say, "But no new child can replace a lost child in a parent's heart! Nothing could remove that grief!" And you are right.

Notice that Job had seven sons and three daughters before disaster struck—but God did not give him fourteen sons and six daughters afterward. God did not double the number of his offspring as He had doubled the size of his herds. Why? Because his first ten children were not lost to him forever. They were in glory with God, and he would one day be reunited with them. That was the confidence and the assurance that Job had expressed in 19:25–26, when he said, "I know that my Redeemer lives, and that in the end he will stand upon the earth. And after my skin has been destroyed, yet in my flesh I will see God."

Job had no doubt that he would survive death and corruption, and so would his children. Nothing, not even ten new children, can replace even one child who leaves this world too soon—the memories, the joys, and the sorrows remain for a lifetime in the heart of a bereaved parent. But Job knew his Redeemer, and he knew that his children, though snatched from this life, would survive death and corruption and would see God and their father Job once more.

The account closes with the words, "And so he died, old and full of years" (Job 42:17). The only answer that we are given to the question of human suffering is that all we endure takes place against a backdrop of Satan's demonic challenge to God's righteous government of creation. This answer is given to us, the reader; it is never given to Job while he lives.

At the beginning of the book you find God, Satan, and Job. At the end of the book, Satan has faded out of the picture entirely. From the beginning to the end of the book, the camera has slowly, gradually zoomed in until there are only two figures framed in the lens: God and Job. This book is the story of a genuine, dynamic relationship between two friends, a stormy relationship filled with pain and anger as well as delight and joy. God, however, never lets go of Job, and Job never lets go of God. The relationship emerges stronger than ever because of the suffering that Job endures. It is a relationship that produces change and growth in Job.

God never lets go of Job, and Job never lets go of God

The deepest note in the book is struck, I believe, when Job says—in the midst of all his pain and desolation, yet with the Spirit of God whispering within him and fanning the flame of his wavering faith—"He knows the way that I take; when he has tested me, I will come forth as gold" (Job 23:10). That is the lesson of this book. Suffering may seem purposeless, yet there is a profound lesson for us in Job's life and in the lives of so many Christians who have endured every kind of suffering: persecution, martyrdom, accidents, cancer, multiple sclerosis, financial losses, poverty, public humiliation. It is the lesson that testing purifies us and reveals the gold of God's character within us.

"I will come forth as gold."

In the New Testament, Paul rejoices, "We know that in all things God works for the good of those who love him, who have been called according to his purpose" (Rom. 8:28). That could also be the triumphant song of Job, a song of hope to live by. May it be your song and mine as well.

Songs of a Sincere Heart

S ome years ago, I went to the house of a man whom I had been counseling. The door was open, but no one answered when I called. Sensing that something was wrong, I went inside—and discovered the body of this man. He had committed suicide. It was one of the most numbing shocks of my life to find this person, whom I had known and prayed with, whom I had been trying to help—and there he was, dead by his own hand.

That night, I was so filled with grief and anguish that I couldn't sleep. Neither could my wife, Elaine. In that dark hour of desolation, we both turned to the Psalms and read some of them together. Nothing but the Psalms could calm and console our hearts in that awful hour.

Through the centuries, this great collection of Hebrew poetry has pillowed the heads of millions of Christians in times of distress and heartache. It has also given voice to emotions of gladness, joy, and hope. It has turned hearts toward God with its expressions of deep reverence and worship. All the shades of emotion that surge in the human soul are found reflected in the Psalms.

The book of Psalms is the book of human emotions. No matter what mood you may be in, you'll find a psalm to give expression to that mood. The Psalms contains exalting, exhilarating expressions of life's highs and joys. If you are happy and want some words to express your joy, try Psalm 66 or Psalm 92. If you are grateful and want to express your thankfulness

> Through the centuries, this great collection of Hebrew poetry has pillowed the heads of millions of Christians in times of distress and heartache

> **The hymn-book of the Old Testament**

For *fear* and *dread*,
Psalms 23, 56, and
91; for *loneliness*,
Psalms 62 and 71;
for *guilt* and *shame*,
Psalms 32 and 51;
for *doubt*, Psalm 119

to God, use the words of Psalm 40. If your heart is full of inexpressible praise and love for God, then turn to Psalm 84 or Psalm 116.

The Psalms also express the need of a soul that has descended into the valley of shadows. If you are troubled by fear and dread, read Psalm 56, Psalm 91, or (of course) Psalm 23. If you are discouraged, read Psalm 42. If you feel lonely, I would suggest Psalm 62 or Psalm 71. If you are oppressed with guilt, shame, or a sense of sinfulness, read Psalm 51 (written after David's double sin of adultery and murder—see 2 Samuel 11 and 12) and Psalm 32, a great expression of confession and forgiveness. If you are worried or anxious, I'd recommend Psalm 37 and Psalm 73. If you are angry, try Psalm 13 or Psalm 58. If you struggle with bitterness and resentment, read Psalm 77 or Psalm 94. If you feel forsaken, immerse yourself in the comfort of Psalm 88. If you are struggling with doubts, dwell in the heart-lifting truths of Psalm 119. Each psalm is a unique expression of our human feelings and our human experience.

These psalms were the hymnbook of ancient Israel. Many were written to be sung in public, which is why a psalm often begins with a phrase such as, "To the choirmaster." Most people assume that David wrote all of Psalms, and indeed, he is the author of more than half of them. God gave this shepherd-king the inspired gift of capturing the varied and rich emotions of his experience and setting them down in lyric form. But many were composed by other writers. Psalm 90 was written by Moses, and two other psalms were composed by King Solomon. Others were written by a group called "the sons of Korah" who were charged with leading the singing of Israel. Still others were written by Asaph, and King Hezekiah wrote ten of them.

The structure of the Psalms

There are 150 psalms in this book, the longest book in the Bible. Composed over a span of a thousand years (from about 1410 B.C. to 430 B.C.), it is really five books in one. It divides into five different sections, each with its own general theme, and each of these divisions closes with a doxology: "Amen and Amen" or "Praise the LORD!" The five divisions of the Psalms parallel the structure of the Pentateuch, the first five books of the Bible. Here, in outline form, is an overview of the structure of the Psalms.

Book 1 (Psalms 1–41)
Author and probable compiler: David
Theme: The Genesis section, dealing with humanity, creation, and human need
General content: Pleas for help and songs of praise
Probable dates of compilation: About 1020 B.C. to 970 B.C.

Book 2 (Psalms 42–72)
Authors: David and the Sons of Korah
Probable compiler: Hezekiah or Josiah
Theme: The Exodus section, dealing with deliverance and redemption
General content: The deliverance of Israel from national captivity, and the deliverance of the individual from captivity to sin
Probable dates of compilation: About 970 B.C. to 610 B.C.

Book 3 (Psalms 73–89)
Author: Asaph
Probable compiler: Hezekiah or Josiah
Theme: The Leviticus section, dealing with worship, how to approach God
General content: Songs of worship
Probable dates of compilation: About 970 B.C. to 610 B.C.

Book 4 (Psalms 90–106)
Author: Unknown
Probable compiler: Ezra or Nehemiah
Theme: The Numbers section, dealing with the wilderness wanderings, the ups and downs of life
General content: Confession of failure and expression of praise
Probable dates of compilation: Up to about 430 B.C.

Book 5 (Psalms 107–150)
Authors: David and other writers
Probable compiler: Ezra or Nehemiah
Theme: The Deuteronomy section, dealing with God's Word
General content: Hymns of exuberant praise
Probable dates of compilation: Up to about 430 B.C.

The first five books of the Bible (Genesis, Exodus, Leviticus, Numbers, and Deuteronomy) were designed by God to give us the five-step pattern of God's workings. God always follows the same pattern, whether in His dealings with an individual, with nations in history, or with the whole of creation. The Psalms follow the same five-step pattern, reflecting the reactions of the human heart to God's pattern of working in our lives.

Book 1 of Psalms, the Genesis Section. The first book of psalms contains Psalms 1 through 41, and its theme parallels the message of the book of Genesis. It is the beautiful, poetic expression of the human heart's deepest need. You will find that it follows closely the story of the book of Genesis. It begins in Psalm 1 with the picture of the perfect human being just as Genesis begins with man and woman in the Garden of Eden. Psalm 2 records human rebellion. It is a powerful psalm, opening with the words:

> *Why do the nations conspire*
> *and the peoples plot in vain?*
> *The kings of the earth take their stand*
> *and the rulers gather together*
> *against the LORD*
> *and against his Anointed One.*
> *"Let us break their chains," they say,*
> *"and throw off their fetters" (Ps. 2:1–3).*

These words of the psalmist describe human rebelliousness; Genesis provides the same description of humanity in the Garden of Eden. Throughout the rest of this first section of the Psalms, you see the anguish of humanity's separation from God, exemplified by such passages as Psalm 6:3, 6:

> *My soul is in anguish.*
> *How long, O LORD, how long? . . .*
> *I am worn out from groaning;*
> *all night long I flood my bed with weeping*
> *and drench my couch with tears.*

But it is also in this section that you see the grace and mercy of God introduced. Here, God is depicted as a defender, a refuge, a righteous judge. You see God's seeking straying human beings out in the darkness that they have created for themselves, just as He did in the shadows of the garden after Adam's sin, calling out, "Adam, where are you?" You see God's beginning to restore Adam's race to its lost estate. The first book of the Psalms is an expression of the human heart's deep-seated longing for God—and of the first echoing sound of God's answer.

Book 2 of Psalms, the Exodus Section. The second book of psalms, Psalm 42 through Psalm 72, corresponds to the book of Exodus in the Pentateuch. Here begins a new relationship between God and humanity. Exodus tells the story of Israel in Egyptian captivity, a story of sorrow and bondage; it also tells of God' great power in delivering the people from their captivity. The second book of the Psalms traces the same theme.

The first book of the Psalms is an expression of the human heart's deep-seated longing for God — and of the first echoing sound of God's answer

Psalm 45 is the psalm of God the king, concerning His sovereign rule over humanity. Psalm 46 speaks God's deliverance and help in times of trouble. Psalm 50 extols God's strength while Psalm 51 reveals God's grace toward us in our deepest sin and shame. Psalm 72, the last psalm of this section, pictures God in His almighty, conquering power—power to free us from captivity to sin.

Book 3 of Psalms, the Leviticus Section. The third book of psalms, Psalm 73 through Psalm 89, corresponds to the book of Leviticus—the book that details the tabernacle of worship and reveals how humanity is to approach a holy God. Leviticus reveals the inner workings of the human heart: its need, its deep consciousness of its own sin, and its discovery of God's remedy. In Psalms 73 through 89, the same pattern is carried out.

Psalm 75 expresses human awareness of God's judgment in the inner heart. Psalm 78 revels in the light of God's unwavering love: God loves us with tough love and holds us accountable for our own growth and benefit. He is merciful, but He is also relentless in rooting out and destroying the sin in our lives—just as He mercifully but relentlessly purified His people, Israel. When we are ready to acknowledge our sin and to agree with God's judgment concerning sin, God deals with us in grace and love. Psalm 81 describes the new strength that God offers us, and Psalm 84 portrays the continual, bountiful provision that God offers us—just as He provided for the needs of ancient Israel.

Book 4 of Psalms, the Numbers Section. Psalms 90 through 106 make up the fourth book, paralleling the book of Numbers—the wilderness book—which highlights human failure. Throughout this book you will find victory alternating with devastating defeat. Just as God steps in and delivers the Israelites in the desert—working mighty miracles and ministering to their needs, feeding them with bread from heaven, opening the rock for them so that water would flow—Israel begins to murmur and complain, precipitating an episode of defeat. This same pattern is pictured for us in the poetry of the fourth section of the Psalms.

Book 5 of Psalms, the Deuteronomy Section. The fifth section, Psalm 107 through Psalm 150, corresponds to the book of Deuteronomy, the experience of our new resource in God. These psalms picture the person who has come to the end of self and his or her own devices and who is now ready to lay hold of the fullness of God. The final section of Psalms is nothing but thanksgiving and praise, from beginning to end. It sounds one triumphant note all the way through and draws to a close with a constant "Hallelujah, praise the Lord!" It is the expression of someone so excited that all he or she can do is shout "Hallelujah!"

**Difficulties in
the Psalms**

Some Christians have difficulty with the Psalms. They have problems with passages in which David cries out against his enemies or complains about sufferings and persecutions. Particularly troubling to many tenderhearted Christians are the so-called imprecatory psalms, the psalms that speak bitter, scorching condemnation (or imprecations) against enemies, calling down God's wrath upon them and picturing them being torn limb from limb and hung from the nearest lamppost, so to speak. It is understandable that people would find these words disturbing. "This doesn't agree with the New Testament's message that we are to love our enemies!" they protest.

But I think that we can understand even these troubling psalms if we remember what the New Testament tells us about the Old Testament. As the apostle Paul says in 1 Corinthians 10:11, these things were written in the Old Testament for our instruction. If we put ourselves in the place of the psalmist, we will see that the enemies he faced then are the same enemies that we face today. The New Testament tells us that "our struggle is not against flesh and blood" (Eph. 6:12). Sometimes we forget who our real enemy is. We think that the person who opposes our plans or attacks our reputation or exasperates us in some way is our enemy. No, people may hurt us, but people are not our true enemies. It is the principles of evil, the philosophies of this world, and the spiritual forces that control this world that are the true enemy.

In many cases, the worst enemy of all is not external but internal. As Jesus said, "What goes into a man's mouth does not make him 'unclean,' but what comes out of his mouth, that is what makes him 'unclean.' . . . For out of the heart come evil thoughts, murder, adultery, sexual immorality, theft, false testimony, slander. These are what make a man 'unclean' " (Matt. 15:11, 19–20). With these words of Jesus ringing in our ears, the severe language of Psalms makes perfect sense. We must deal severely with these things. Sin has no place in a Christian's life. The tough, ruthless imprecatory psalms are a picture of the way in which we must deal with the *real* enemies of the heart.

The tough, ruthless imprecatory psalms are a picture of the way in which we must deal with the real *enemies of the heart*

**Psalms of
Jesus**

The deepest insight that you can gain into the heart of the Psalms is to understand that these songs of faith fully and beautifully reveal the work and the person of Jesus Christ. You may recall that on the road to Emmaus after Jesus' resurrection, He said to the two grieving, troubled disciples, "Everything must be fulfilled that is written about me in the Law of Moses, the Prophets and the Psalms" (Luke 24:44). Although the character, grace, and truth of Christ are presented in every psalm, several special "messianic psalms" present a clear prophetic image of Christ—including specific episodes and crises in His earthly life—though these psalms were written hundreds of years before the birth of Christ.

Psalm 2 pictures Christ as the man of destiny, the focal point of all history. God says that every nation, every tribe, every people, every individual will find its value or its lack of value in how it relates to the Son.

Psalm 22 records the Lord's anguish on the cross of Calvary. This amazing psalm takes you right to the cross itself with its opening line, "My God, my God, why have you forsaken me?" It goes on to describe the gawking crowd around the foot of the cross, looking on Him whom they pierced and numbering Him with the transgressors. It tells in detail how His tormentors took His garments and cast lots for them and pierces our hearts with its emotional description of the Lord's utter sense of abandonment by God. The words are graphic and specific, clearly prefiguring the Messiah's death by crucifixion:

> They have pierced my hands and my feet.
> I can count all my bones (Ps. 22:16–17).

Yet this harrowing, heartbreaking account of the death of the Messiah is quickly followed by the culmination of the Lord's story—the triumph of His resurrection, the glory of His second coming, and the righteousness of His future reign.

Other messianic psalms reflect the character and work of Christ and His coming reign as King over all the earth. Psalm 110, for example, clearly validates the deity of Christ—the great mystery that He is both fully human and fully God at the same time. And Psalm 118 symbolically describes Him as a stumbling block, rejected by people, yet used by God as the cornerstone of His redemptive plan on the day of the resurrection. The following table lists most of the messianic psalms and their fulfillment in the New Testament. A comparative exploration of these psalms and New Testament passages would make a rewarding, exciting, individual or group Bible study.

Psalm	Messianic Prophecy	New Testament Fulfillment
2:7	God declares Messiah as His Son	Matthew 3:17
8:6	All things placed under His feet	Hebrews 2:8
16:10	The Resurrection	Mark 16:6–7
22:1	The Messiah forsaken	Matthew 27:46
22:7–8	The Messiah surrounded by mockers	Luke 23:35
22:16	Messiah's hands and feet pierced on the cross	John 20:25, 27
22:18	Lots cast for His clothes	Matthew 27:35–36

Psalm 2: Christ the focal point of all history

Psalm 22: His anguish on the cross

Psalm 110: His deity

Psalm 118: Christ the stumbling block

Prophetic psalms and their New Testament fulfillment

34:20	Messiah's bones unbroken	John 19:32–33, 36
35:11	The Messiah accused by false witnesses	Mark 14:57
35:19	The Messiah hated and persecuted	John 15:25
40:7–8	He comes to do the will of God	Hebrews 10:7
41:9	The betrayal of the Messiah by a friend (Judas)	Luke 22:47
45:6	The throne of Messiah is forever	Hebrews 1:8
68:18	The Messiah ascends to God's right hand	Mark 16:19
69:9	His zeal for God's house (cleansing the temple)	John 2:17
69:21	Vinegar and gall upon the cross	Matthew 27:34
109:4	Messiah intercedes for His enemies	Luke 23:34
109:8	The betrayer's function is given to another	Acts 1:20
110:1	His enemies put in subjection to Him	Matthew 22:44
110:4	Messiah is a priest after the order of Melchizedek	Hebrews 5:6
118:22	Rejected stumbling block becomes the cornerstone	Matthew 21:42

All the psalms are designed to teach us how to worship God, how to have fellowship with God, how to experience the fullness and richness of God. They teach us how to honestly offer up to God the full range of our emotions. If you have a problem, don't hide it from God or from yourself. Tell Him about it. Don't put on a pious act and try to smooth it over. If you are angry with God, say so. If you are upset about something that He has done, tell Him so. If you are resentful, bring it out in the open and resolve it. If you are happy and glad, express your joy and praise to Him. That is what worship is all about—the honest expression of your heart to God.

Worship is all about the honest expression of your heart to God

As Jesus said to the woman at the well in Samaria, "God is spirit, and his worshipers must worship in spirit and in truth" (John 4:24). God is looking for that kind of worshiper. If you can be honest before God—even with all your moods, sins, failures, pain, and questioning—you will find grace to meet all your needs.

There is an old story of a miser who put his trust in Christ late in life. After his conversion, one of his neighbors sustained a serious loss. When the born-again miser heard about it, his immediate reaction was, "My friend needs help and food for his family. I'll go to my smokehouse and get a ham and take it over to them." But on the way to the smokehouse his old nature began to whisper to him, "Why give them a whole ham? Half a ham will be plenty." He debated within himself all the way to the smokehouse.

Then he remembered what he had learned in the presence of God. He remembered that, upon receiving the grace of Jesus Christ into his life, he had resolved that he would crucify his old self and stand firmly against all the old traits and habits of his pre-Christian past. Suddenly he realized where the temptation to restrain his generosity was coming from: It was the *tempter* who kept whispering, "Give him half a ham." With that realization, the old man said, "Look Satan, if you don't pipe down, I'll give him the whole smokehouse!"

Where sin abounds, grace abounds much more. And that is the purpose of the psalms: They are God's music, inspired and written to draw us to grace.

What Life Is All About

Some years ago, a man came into my study and told me a heart-breaking story. Impatient with college, eager to escape from his parents' home and get out on his own, he had left school and moved to San Francisco for the exciting life of the city. He plunged into all sorts of experiments with drugs and promiscuity, hoping to find fulfillment in life. For a while, every night was a party, but soon his lifestyle began to drag him down. He began mainlining heroin, a practice that he had once told himself he would never sink to. His experiments with hallucinogenic drugs gave him fantastic visions and left him full of fear and paranoia.

He soon became unemployable due to his drug habit, and he ended up as a procurer for prostitutes on the meanest streets of the city. Soon, nothing was able to dull the fear and shame that he felt inside—not drugs, not sex. But when he began to feel the tug of powerful suicidal impulses, he finally realized that he would end up destroyed if he didn't reach out for help from a power beyond himself. God awakened him to his need, and he took refuge at a downtown mission. He was detoxed and placed in a Christian program that enabled him to overcome his addictions; in the process, he turned his life over to Jesus Christ. In our church, he found an accepting, caring community where his faith and Christian character could grow and mature.

The horrors that this young man underwent are precisely what God, speaking to us through the book of Proverbs, wants to help us to avoid. The message of Proverbs is that life can never be fully understood nor fully lived except through a relationship with God. The complexities and perils of life are simply too big for us to handle by ourselves. In order to successfully navigate the swirling currents of our daily existence, with all of its temptations, deceptions, and risky choices, we need *wisdom*— the timeless, dependable, true wisdom of God.

The structure of Proverbs

No book of the Old Testament seems to be quite as difficult to outline as the book of Proverbs. The subject seems to change with every verse. In fact, however, the book of Proverbs is logically and helpfully constructed. If you note the divisions of it, you can easily recognize and follow the argument of this book. Here is an overview of the structure of Proverbs:

Introduction: The purpose of Proverbs is wisdom (Proverbs 1:1–1:7)
Theme: The value of wisdom

Proverbs for young people (Proverbs 1–9)
Theme: Advice about life from a father who has been there

Proverbs of Solomon (Proverbs 10–24)
The first collection of Solomon's wise sayings, compiled by Solomon himself
Theme: The principles of wisdom for godly living

Proverbs of Solomon (Proverbs 25–29)
The second collection of Solomon's wise sayings, compiled by Hezekiah
Theme: The principles of godly wisdom for healthy relationships

Proverbs of Agur (Proverbs 30)
Theme: Humility, righteous living, and learning wisdom from observations of the animal kingdom

Proverbs of Lemuel (Proverbs 31)
Theme: Wisdom learned by King Lemuel at his mother's knee
   1. Principles of godly living (31:1–9)
   2. The description of a virtuous wife (31:10–31)

A guidebook to wise choices

The book of Proverbs was written and compiled from about 950 B.C. to about 700 B.C. Proverbs begins with a brief preface in the first six verses and continues with a series of ten father-to-son discourses filled with practical exhortations on how to face the problems of life.

Beginning in chapter 10, we have a collection of proverbs of Solomon, David's son, the wise king of Israel.

When Solomon became king, he had a vision in which God asked him what his heart desired above everything else. Solomon asked for wisdom. Because he asked for the treasure of wisdom instead of riches or fame, God gave him all three. Therefore, these are the wisdom proverbs of the wisest king Israel ever had.

The second collection of Solomon's proverbs begins with chapter 25. These proverbs of Solomon were copied down by the men of Hezekiah, the king of Judah, after Solomon's death. The book closes with a postlude in chapters 30 and 31 that brings before us the words of two unknown individuals, Agur, son of Jakah, in chapter 30, and Lemuel, king of Massa, in chapter 31.

The book of Proverbs speaks to the human will, and it is primarily concerned with the choices that life sets before us. Someone has wisely said that "choices are the hinges of destiny." Our lives turn on the choices we make. To have a good life that is filled with satisfaction, abundance, and service to God, we must make good, godly, healthy choices throughout our lives. That is what the book of Proverbs is about: making wise choices. This theme is evident in the introduction to the book, which begins by telling us the title and author of Proverbs:

> *The proverbs of Solomon son of David, king of Israel.*

Then we read the purpose of the book (1:2–6):

> *For attaining wisdom and discipline;*
> *   for understanding words of insight;*
> *for acquiring a disciplined and prudent life,*
> *   doing what is right and just and fair;*
> *for giving prudence to the simple,*
> *   knowledge and discretion to the young—*
> *let the wise listen and add to their learning,*
> *   and let the discerning get guidance—*
> *for understanding proverbs and parables,*
> *   the sayings and riddles of the wise.*

In other words, this collection of wisdom is designed to meet the needs of people of all ages and stages of life, from childhood to youth to maturity. This is the practical guidebook for understanding what life is all about. It is practical and user-friendly, but it is also the key to unlocking the most esoteric mysteries of life. Reading a proverb takes seconds; memorizing a proverb takes minutes; applying a proverb takes a lifetime.

> The book of Proverbs speaks to the human will, and it is primarily concerned with the choices that life sets before us

The beginning of wisdom

The "fear of the Lord" is not the fear that God might hurt us but rather the fear that we might hurt Him

Father to son

The next verse—Proverbs 1:7—gives us the password that unlocks the Proverbs, and life. It is the summary and the conclusion of the entire book:

> *The fear of the LORD is the beginning of knowledge* [or wisdom], *but fools despise wisdom and discipline.*

The book of Proverbs approaches life from the position that God has all the answers. He is all-wise and all-knowing. Nothing is hidden from His knowledge. He understands all mysteries, sees the answer to all riddles. Therefore, the beginning of wisdom is to revere and fear God.

What does the "fear of the Lord" mean? That phrase, which is used often in Scripture, doesn't refer to a cowardly, cringing sort of fear. God does not want us to live in terror of Him; He wants us to love Him, and as we read in 1 John 4:18, "Perfect love drives out fear, because fear has to do with punishment. The one who fears is not made perfect in love." The "fear of the Lord" is not the fear that God might hurt us but rather the fear that we might hurt Him! In other words, it is the fear that something that we do might offend Him or grieve His loving heart. In this sense, "fear" really means reverence or respect, and it is this kind of loving, respectful fear that is the beginning of true knowledge and wisdom.

Notice: The fear of the Lord is not the *end* of wisdom. It is not all that is required for being wise; it is only the beginning. Once you have learned to fear and respect God, you still have to learn and experience so much to mature in godly wisdom.

Proverbs 1:8 marks the beginning of the ten discourses from a wise, loving father to his growing son. They begin with the child in the home, dealing with his first relationships. Then they move to the time when the child's experiences broaden to include a wider spectrum of friends and influences. This father offers insight regarding the powerful influence that friends can have at this age; the issue of peer pressure is as crucial today as it was three thousand years ago. It is critically important for young people to know how to evaluate and choose their friends.

In chapter 3, the father's counsel is directed toward a young man as he grows up and leaves home. When young people make their way into the city, entering college or the workforce for the first time, they are almost always confronted with pressures and temptations. Suddenly, they are free to make choices where, as live-at-home teenagers, they were limited. This father speaks delicately and yet frankly about the pressures and perils of sex and about how wrong choices can wreak destruction in a young person's life. Additionally, he warns against getting involved in unwise financial entanglements. The theme of this very practical passage is summed up in Proverbs 3:5 and 6—a passage that all Christians, young and old, would do well to commit to memory:

> *Trust in the LORD with all your heart*
> *and lean not on your own understanding;*
> *in all your ways acknowledge him,*
> *and he will make your paths straight.*

This is a proven formula for the young man or woman who wants to find the secret of life, who wants to be an authentic success. I have never met a young person who didn't want to be successful (however he or she might define *success*). In my experience, no one has ever said, "My ambition is to be a skid-row bum." The path to true success lies in trusting the Lord with all your heart, whether you seek success in business, success in raising your family, success in the performing arts, success on the mission field or in some other form of ministry. When you trust in Him and acknowledge Him, He will make your paths straight.

Chapters 8 and 9 personify the two ways of life. Wisdom is seen as a beautiful woman, calling those who follow her to come away to the place of victory and achievement and success in life. Folly or foolishness, which thinks everything it does is right, is personified as an evil woman—attractive, alluring, tempting the unwary to step aside into death.

Wisdom and folly personified

Beginning with chapter 10 we have the first collection of the wisdom of Solomon: pithy, practical words of advice covering every possible situation of life. This is a book to be read again and again, until its wisdom permeates our lives, until we have committed large blocks of it to memory, so that it will be available to us in times of pressure and decision making.

The first collection of Solomon's proverbs

This first collection is made up mostly of contrasts, in which the writer sets two things side by side and shows the good and evil results of various attitudes and actions. As you read this section note these antitheses, as in Proverbs 10:17:

Made up of contrasts

> *He who heeds discipline shows the way to life,*
> *but whoever ignores correction leads others astray.*

This collection also contains comparisons and similes that are powerfully descriptive and insightful. For example, Proverbs 11:22:

Comparisons and similes

> *Like a gold ring in a pig's snout*
> *is a beautiful woman who shows no discretion.*

What a vivid picture! Can't you just imagine a valuable, shining gold ring with the light glinting off its polished surface like brilliant stars—yet it is affixed to the swill-dripping, mud-caked snout of an ugly old porker! Gold signifies value, but here is value that has been woefully misplaced. In the same way, a beautiful woman who misuses her womanhood and her beauty has not learned to place real value on the inward beauty of the spirit. In fact, she tragically underestimates her own worth and sells herself as an adornment for filth and ugliness.

The tongue

Other notable passages in this section include Proverbs 12:16–22, which gives a powerful discourse on the tongue—on how to use it for blessing God and others instead of for cursing, defaming, gossiping, lying, lashing out, wounding, and offending.

Discipline

Proverbs 13:24 is that well-known verse for parents, "He who spares the rod hates his son, but he who loves him is careful to discipline him." Remember, however, that the rod is for guidance and discipline—not for beating or destroying a child's spirit. Parents should always recall the words of Psalm 23:4: "Your rod and your staff, they comfort me." Whenever pain, in whatever form, must be inflicted on a child—whether corporal punishment, loss of privileges, time-out in a corner, or whatever—the child should always be able to sense that you have administered the rod of correction in love, even in sorrow, not out of anger or revenge. The child should sense that when you say, "This hurts me more than it does you," you really mean it.

Proverbs 14:12 calls us to recognize the limitations of our own understanding. How often I have seen the truth of these words validated in the lives and the pain of so many well-intentioned people:

> *There is a way that seems right to a man,*
> *but in the end it leads to death.*

That is why it is so important to "trust in the LORD with all your heart and lean not on your own understanding" (Prov. 3:5).

The key to genuine success

Many people spend hundreds of dollars every year on motivational books, tapes, and seminars in order to become successful. In reality, the key to genuine success is found right in the book of Proverbs. For example, Proverbs 16:20 and 22:

> *Whoever gives heed to instruction prospers,*
> *and blessed is he who trusts in the LORD. . . .*
> *Understanding is a fountain of life to those who have it,*
> *but folly brings punishment to fools.*

Further down the page, in verse 32, we find sound instruction for managing such emotions as impatience and anger:

> *Better a patient man than a warrior,*
> *a man who controls his temper than one who takes a city.*

That verse is often quoted but seldom believed. What a change it would make in our lives if we really understood that the person who is patient and self-controlled is a greater hero than Rambo or Stormin' Norman Schwarzkopf! How do we build those qualities of patience and self-control into our lives? By asking God for maturity in those areas and by inviting the Holy Spirit to take control over our emotional lives. It also helps if we ask trusted Christian friends to observe our lives and hold us accountable in these areas. Change and maturity rarely take place overnight. They happen as God gradually gains more and more control over each aspect of our lives. As Galatians 5:22 tells us, patience, kindness, gentleness, and self-control are just a few of several fruits of the Spirit; that is, they are evidences in our lives that God has taken up residence in us, and He is cleaning house.

Proverbs 17:28 tells us that "even a fool is thought wise if he keeps silent," or as someone has said, "It is better to remain silent and let everybody think you are a fool than to open your mouth and remove all doubt!"

Proverbs 18:22 has a word for lovers: "He who finds a wife finds what is good, and receives favor from the LORD." Take it from a man who knows "what is good": Solomon had a thousand wives!

Some of the psychological insights of this book are truly astounding. For example, Proverbs 19:3 says:

> *A man's own folly ruins his life,*
> *yet his heart rages against the LORD.*

I've seen the truth of this proverb proven again and again. We err, we blunder, we sin, and then, when we reap the ruinous consequences of our own actions, our own choices, who do we blame? God! "Why didn't God stop me? Why did God allow me to be tempted? Why didn't God send those consequences away from me?" Isn't that strange? Yet it is so common. We make the choices, but we blame God for the ruin that follows.

In Proverbs 20:27, we find another insightful statement regarding the nature of human life and the human spirit:

> *The lamp of the LORD searches the spirit of a man;*
> *it searches out his inmost being.*

A more accurate rendering of that verse would be:

The spirit of man is the LORD's lamp;
it searches out his inmost being.

The Lord's lamp

That is what God made our spirits for. Our essential nature is to be indwelt by the Holy Spirit. He is the light. We are the lamp. When the lamp of the human spirit holds the light of the Holy Spirit, He searches the innermost part of a life and we begin to understand ourselves for the first time.

In Proverbs 22:6, we find yet another classic (but often misunderstood) bit of counsel for parents:

Train a child in the way he should go,
and when he is old he will not turn from it.

I believe that this should actually be translated, "Train up a child according to his way," which means, find out what is in a child, discover your child's unique character and abilities. Bring him or her up in such a way that those beautiful God-given traits can be buffed and polished into something precious and beautiful: godly, Christlike character. When those unique qualities are developed and brought out, then the child will grow to maturity and not depart from those wonderful qualities.

General discourses

The contrasting, comparing proverbs come to a close with Proverbs 22:16. Beginning with Proverbs 22:17, a different kind of proverb is brought before us. These are general discourses, two or three verses long, on various subjects such as child-rearing, relationships, getting along with neighbors, and even a pre-Christian statement of the Golden Rule: "Do not say, 'I'll do to him as he has done to me; I'll pay that man back for what he did' " (24:29).

The second collection of Solomon's proverbs

Chapter 25 begins the second collection of proverbs of Solomon—the proverbs copied by the men of Hezekiah. Verse 2 is a wonderful example:

It is the glory of God to conceal a matter;
to search out a matter is the glory of kings.

If you want to have a royal experience, I suggest you search out the glorious things that God has concealed in His Word. That is the glory of kings: to experience the thrilling adventure of discovering the riches of truth that God has hidden in the Bible.

Some of the advice in this section is mundane but ever so practical!

For example, Proverbs 25:17: "Seldom set foot in your neighbor's house—too much of you, and he will hate you." Advice like that could have come from the pen of Dear Abby or Erma Bombeck, but there it is in God's Word!

Some of us let the gossip and sneers of others destroy our happiness, but Proverbs 26:2 places the curses of others in proper perspective: "Like a fluttering sparrow or a darting swallow, an undeserved curse does not come to rest." If someone says something nasty about you and it is not true, don't worry about it. Nobody will believe it. Those who do believe it are not important. That is just one example of many helpful words in chapter 26 on how to deal with troublesome people. Verses 3 through 12 tell you how to respond to fools. Verses 13 through 16 tell what to do about lazy goldbricks. Verses 17 through 23 concern meddlers and how to handle them. And the truly hateful and vengeful people are dealt with in verse 24. In verses 25–28, you learn to watch out for smooth-tongued deceivers.

In Proverbs 28:27, we learn that no one is an island. We are all connected across lines of class, race, and income. We should not shut ourselves off from the suffering and need that surrounds us. Solomon observes:

> *He who gives to the poor will lack nothing,*
> *but he who closes his eyes to them receives many curses.*

I'm not saying that you should give money to every panhandler on the street, since in many cases you would just be subsidizing drug abuse and idleness. But there are truly needy people—adults and helpless little children—and we must not close our eyes to them. Those who say that they are too sensitive to visit the slums or reach out to the hurting are coming under the condemnation of the truth in this verse. We must recognize genuine need and help.

Chapters 30 and 31 are written by two men about whom nothing is known. Chapter 30 gives us the proverbs of Agur. He writes in a distinctly different style from the rest of Proverbs, grouping his sayings in a numerical way. For example, Proverbs 30:15–16:

Agur and Lemuel, the unknown authors

> *"The leech has two daughters.*
> *'Give! Give!' they cry.*
> *"There are three things that are never satisfied,*
> *four that never say, 'Enough!':*
> *the grave, the barren womb,*
> *land, which is never satisfied with water,*

A wife of noble
character

and fire, which never says, 'Enough!' "

Though no one knows exactly who Agur was, his counsel is practical, and it makes comparisons between spiritual truths and the wonders and processes of the created world.

Chapter 31 contains the words of King Lemuel concerning what his mother taught him about how to be a king. The epilogue, verses 10 to 31, closes the book of Proverbs on a beautiful note with a description of what a virtuous, godly wife is like. Many feel this is King Lemuel's description of his own mother—and what a woman she was! If you are a young woman looking for a godly example, I recommend this passage to you. If you are a young man looking for a model wife, I suggest you read it through and keep it in mind throughout your courtship. The woman in Proverbs 31 is a picture of strength, intelligence, competence, business acumen, industriousness, glory, and beauty. She is an example of what God intended when He created Eve—a woman who was fashioned out of Adam's rib to show (as someone has pointed out) that she is to be at his side—not on his back or under his feet! The woman of Proverbs 31 is clearly a partner and companion to her husband, not his inferior or his slave.

This, then, is the book of Proverbs: an excellent book to read and reread on a regular basis. You might even want to read it through once a month. The book of Proverbs is comprised of 31 chapters—a chapter a day in an average month! Try it, and the wisdom of its pages will seep into your soul and change your life!

The Inspired Book of Error

T he book of Ecclesiastes is unique in Scripture. No other book is like it because it is the only book in the Bible that reflects a human, rather than a divine, point of view.

This book is filled with error, yet it is wholly inspired. This may confuse some people because many feel that inspiration is a guarantee of truth. This is not necessarily so. Inspiration merely guarantees accuracy from a particular point of view: If it is God's point of view it is true; if it is a human point of view, it may or may not be true. If it is the devil's point of view, it may or may not be true; whenever Satan speaks, most of his statements are in error and even the truth he uses is intended to mislead. Inspiration guarantees an accurate reflection of these various points of view. When the Bible speaks, it speaks the truth about God's truth, and it speaks the truth about the errors of people and of Satan.

Because Ecclesiastes reflects a human, rather than a divine, point of view, it is often misused and twisted out of context by the enemies of God's Word. Ecclesiastes is the favorite book of atheists and agnostics. Many cults love to quote this book's erroneous viewpoints and give the impression that these are scriptural, divine words of God concerning life.

In order to come to such a conclusion, however, one has to ignore what Ecclesiastes very clearly states from the outset and repeats throughout the book: It draws its conclusion from appearances, from looking at the world from a human perspective. Every aspect of life that this book examines is seen as "under the sun."

That is where we human beings live. But God's perspective is much higher than ours. He can see the world from *beyond* the sun. Man views reality from a limited, horizon-level perspective, exclusive of divine revelation, and that is the viewpoint expressed throughout most of Ecclesiastes.

The author of Ecclesiastes

The book opens with this introduction (in the *New International Version*): "The words of the Teacher, son of David, king in Jerusalem." Most other translations begin: "The words of the Preacher. . . ." In context, I don't think either *Teacher* or *Preacher* is the best translation of the original Hebrew. The word can be translated in these ways, but given the context of Ecclesiastes, I think that this word would be more accurately translated as *Debater,* someone who argues a certain point of view. As you read this book you will see that it is a series of arguments set forth from a human perspective. The Debater in Ecclesiastes is Solomon, the son of David, king in Jerusalem, and the wisest individual who ever lived, according to biblical record.

Solomon was in an unusual position to undertake the experiments and investigations set forth in this book, because during the forty years of his reign there was utter peace in the kingdom of Israel. There were no neighboring tribes stirring up warfare or strife. Since he did not have to bother himself with military life, he had all the time that he needed to pursue his investigations into the meaning of life. Furthermore, he had all the wealth he needed, and he had a keen, logical mind. With these great resources of money, time, and intellect, he was free to discover what life is all about. Therefore, the value of Ecclesiastes is that it sets forth life from the standpoint of the natural person, apart from divine revelation.

Here is an outline of the structure of Ecclesiastes, the inspired book of error:

Opening Declaration: Everything Is Meaningless
(Ecclesiastes 1:1–11)

1. Introduction	1:1–1:3
2. Illustrations of human meaninglessness	1:4–1:11

Inquiries into and Demonstrations of the Meaninglessness
of Life Apart from God (Ecclesiastes 1:12–6:12)

3. Thesis of meaninglessness proved from Scripture	1:12–2:26
4. Thesis of meaninglessness proved from nature, human society, and human behavior	3–6

Counsel and Conclusion: "Fear the LORD"
(Ecclesiastes 7–12)
    5. Fearing God in a wicked, unjust world   7–9
    6. Trusting God in an uncertain, unpredictable world 10:1–12:8
    7. Conclusion: The key to meaning is the fear and
       and obedience of the Lord   12:9–12:14

As you read through the book you'll notice that everything proceeds from Ecclesiastes 1:2:

> *"Meaningless! Meaningless!"*
> *says the Teacher.*
> *"Utterly meaningless!*
> *Everything is meaningless."*

Older translations of this passage, unfortunately, tend to be confusing to modern readers, using the term "Vanity of vanities!" instead of the NIV's "Meaningless! Meaningless!" Hundreds of years ago, the average person understood *vanity* to connote "meaningless." Today, however, we think of vanity as a state of being conceited and vain regarding one's personal appearance. Someone who spends a lot of time primping before a mirror is considered vain, that is, indulging in vanity.

This kind of vanity is illustrated by the story of the woman who once whispered to her pastor, "I must confess to you, Reverend Jones, that I struggle with a terrible sin: the sin of vanity. Every morning before I leave the house, I admire myself in the mirror for an hour."

"My dear lady," the minister replied, "that is not the sin of vanity you are suffering with. It is merely an excess of imagination."

The word often translated *vanity* in English translations of Ecclesiastes is properly translated in the NIV to connote emptiness, futility, meaninglessness. The Debater has completed his survey of life, and he gives this conclusion at the beginning of the book: Everything is futile, senseless, and meaningless.

He supports this conclusion with a series of arguments that he has gleaned after sifting through the philosophies of life. Perhaps the most interesting thing about this book is that all the philosophies by which people have attempted to live are gathered together here. There is nothing new under the sun, the book says, and how true that is! Here we are, almost thirty centuries removed from the time this book was written, yet no philosopher of this or any prior era has ever produced any ideas or belief systems other than what the Debater presents here in the book of Ecclesiastes.

First we see what could be called the mechanistic view, a favorite among scientists of the past two centuries. This outlook interprets the universe as nothing but a great, grinding machine. The Debater, in his investigation of the processes of the universe, finds nothing but monotonous repetition. This is a remarkable passage, foreshadowing many of the discoveries of modern science. Ecclesiastes 1:6 states:

> *The wind blows to the south*
> *and turns to the north;*
> *round and round it goes,*
> *ever returning on its course.*

Scientists didn't discover the circuit of the wind until centuries after this was written—nor did they understand the evaporation cycle of circulating waters when these words were set down in Ecclesiastes 1:7:

> *All streams flow into the sea,*
> *yet the sea is never full.*
> *To the place the streams come from,*
> *there they return again.*

That is, the rivers run down to the sea, evaporate, come back up to the mountains again as rainfall, and run down to the sea again. The writer has discovered this in his observation of nature, and he says all this is meaningless repetition. He feels the utter weariness of this endless circuit. So what is his outlook? The universe goes on and we are lost in the endlessly turning, mindless gears of its machinery. This philosophy is very prevalent today. It is the conclusion of reductionism: the belief that life can be reduced to mere mechanistic processes. The universe is a machine. We are machines. There is no soul, no spirit, no God. Humankind is a lonely little fleck in the midst of the great, vast, uncaring universe, a tiny speck without any meaning.

"Just do it!"

In chapter 2 the writer examines the philosophy of hedonism: the pursuit of pleasure as the chief end of life. Live it up while you can, because it will all be over someday. Life is short; play hard. Grab for the gusto. Just do it. That's all there is. To these modern-day philosophers and advertising copywriters, the Debater of Ecclesiastes makes this reply:

> *I thought in my heart, "Come now, I will test you with pleasure to*
> *find out what is good." But that also proved to be meaningless (2:1).*

He goes on to itemize various pleasures: He sought the pleasures of laughter, the pleasures of gracious society. For awhile, these experiences anesthetized the meaningless of his life, but in time, even laughter and the company of others yielded a weariness of spirit. He then tried to find meaning through acquiring possessions, as so many materialists do today. In Ecclesiastes 2:9–10, he reflects:

> *I became greater by far than anyone in Jerusalem before me. In all this my wisdom stayed with me.*
> *I denied myself nothing my eyes desired; I refused my heart no pleasure.*

Yet, after giving himself to the accumulation of vast wealth and possessions, he came to the conclusion that this, too, brought only emptiness of spirit. "Live for today" may seem like a great motto, until tomorrow comes. Materialism does not satisfy our deep human longings. So where did he turn next? To the realm of ideas: the extremes and opposites of belief systems and ideologies. In Ecclesiastes 2:12–13, he writes:

"Live for today"

> *I turned my thoughts to consider wisdom,*
> *and also madness and folly.*
> *What more can the king's successor do*
> *than what has already been done?*
> *I saw that wisdom is better than folly,*
> *just as light is better than darkness.*

Wisdom is better than foolishness, he concludes, but ultimately all human wisdom and foolishness come from the same place and return to the same place. The fool and the wise person both ultimately die. As he notes in verse 14, "the same fate overtakes them both." And as far as their lives are concerned, one is as utterly insignificant as the other. It doesn't make any difference. Then, in verse 17, he comes to this shattering conclusion:

Human wisdom

> *I hated life, because the work that is done under the sun was grievous to me. All of it is meaningless, a chasing after the wind.*

Pleasure. People. Possessions. The pursuit of wisdom. It's all meaningless. In the end, says the Debater, he hated life, hated his toil, so he surrendered to despair.

Pleasure. People. Possessions. It's all meaningless

In chapter 3, the Debater views life from what we might call the *existential* viewpoint. Existentialism, as an organized school of thought, dates back to the late nineteenth and early twentieth centuries and is embodied in the philosophies of Nietzsche, Heidegger, Sartre, and others.

Existential despair

Existentialism, truly humanity's oldest philosophy, is essentially a form of fatalism. Its adherents believe that life is fatal; no one gets out of this life alive, so live for the moment.

The popularity of existentialism rose sharply at the end of World War II, when Europe was in shambles. The great cities of Europe were in ruins, and all that people had previously pinned their hopes on—the institutions of government and religion—had proven powerless to prevent the cataclysm of all-out war. At the end of the war, people were left with shattered hopes concerning all that they had believed in. They asked themselves, "What can we trust?" And they concluded that they could trust only their feelings, their experiences, their reaction to life and to events, from moment to moment to moment. Instead of living, they settled for existing.

That is where we find the Debater at this point in Ecclesiastes. He says, in effect, "I've tried that. I tried to live as a fatalist, to live in the now, to experience my present existence, knowing there is no future, no meaning, no sense to it all. But I was left empty." So, in Ecclesiastes 3:1–4, we read:

> *There is a time for everything,*
> *and a season for every activity under heaven:*
> *a time to be born and a time to die,*
> *a time to plant and a time to uproot,*
> *a time to kill and a time to heal,*
> *a time to tear down and a time to build,*
> *a time to weep and a time to laugh,*
> *a time to mourn and a time to dance . . . .*

Do we have anything deeper, anything more significant, anything more enduring than the now?

The present passes. The next moment comes and change comes with it. We cannot remain in the now. All these events described by the Debater of Ecclesiastes eventually come upon us. And what do we have left? Do we have anything deeper, anything more significant, anything more enduring than the now? Is there more to our lives than this existence, right now? If not, existentialism leads us to despair.

We cannot live only in this moment, and God did not create us to do so. Verse 11—one of Scripture's most profound passages—tells us that we were made for eternity. Solomon writes:

> *He has made everything beautiful in its time. He has also set eternity in the hearts of men; yet they cannot fathom what God has done from beginning to end.*

We never can rest with momentary explanations of our existence and the world around us. We are made to look deeper than that; deeper into time, deeper into the workings of the world, deeper into our own souls, deeper into the mind of God. Eternity is in our hearts. God placed it there. The writer of Ecclesiastes saw all this. He knew that the events of life and of death are inescapable. When life is over, all people—men and women, rich and poor, wise and foolish—face the same fate: All turn to dust.

Under the sun, from the human point of view, the future promises only futility and hopelessness, so what's the use of living?

In chapter 4, Solomon laments all the toil and oppression that he has seen in the business world: the envy and cutthroat competition, the exploitation of workers, the meaninglessness of trying to climb the ladder of success. His observations are just as timely in today's business world as they were three thousand years ago in the business world of the Middle East.

In chapter 5, he examines religion, and yes, even religion, he finds, is meaningless! Trying to live a good life and trying to be a good person is all meaningless! There's no practical value to it, no ultimate satisfaction. What's more, it's hard to tell religious and irreligious people apart! He observes that many religious people behave in unethical and even downright evil ways. They break vows to God. They oppress the poor. They are greedy and selfish. Clearly, institutional, formal religion has no power to avert wrongdoing and halt injustice. Religious formalism is empty and meaningless like everything else.

Chapter 6 reiterates Solomon's theme of the meaninglessness of riches and possessions. We spend all our efforts trying to feed ourselves, yet our hunger is never satisfied. The rich have everything they want and need, yet they still discover that they have cravings that can't be satisfied. What can you get for the person who has everything? If he or she is unsatisfied even with the wealth of a king, then he or she is no happier than a poor person. It all comes out to the same thing.

In chapter 7, Solomon views life from the standpoint of stoicism—a cultivated indifference to events. Happiness, sadness, pleasure, pain, good fortune, tragedy; it's all the same. Accept the one without rejoicing and the other without complaining. It all amounts to the same thing in the end. Accept whatever happens to you with stoic indifference. As Solomon observes in Ecclesiastes 7:15:

> *In this meaningless life of mine I have seen both of these:*
> *a righteous man perishing in his righteousness,*
> *and a wicked man living long in his wickedness.*

From the human point of view, the future promises only futility and hopelessness

Meaningless

Even religion is meaningless

Cravings that can't be satisfied

Stoic indifference

Righteousness doesn't always pay, wickedness sometimes does, at least as judged by the evidence that we can observe "under the sun," at the human level of understanding. So, from a human perspective, not God's, he concludes:

> Do not be overrighteous,
>   neither be overwise—
>   why destroy yourself?
> Do not be overwicked,
>   and do not be a fool—
>   why die before your time?

In other words, aim for a happy medium. Stop beating your brains out trying to be good. Sure, it's okay to be good, but don't be too good. Live a little, sin a little, and don't worry about it. Don't be a fanatic either way. Avoid extremes and be just a regular guy. That's the "wisdom" of the world talking, not God's wisdom.

Chapters 8 through 10 and the first eight verses of chapter 11 are a connected discourse examining what might be referred to as the wisdom of the world or the commonsense view of life. In chapter 8, anyone approaching life from this point of view is encouraged to master the power structures of the world. He says, in effect, "Try to understand who is an authority and who isn't, and do your best to be on the right side at the right time." That is a familiar philosophy, isn't it? You can find the same kind of thinking in the business and self-help sections of your local bookstore. Solomon goes on to tell you what the self-help books won't: Even if you get what you want, even if you align yourself with the power structure of the world, if you get in good with the Big Boys and start winning advances, awards, raises, the corner office, and the key to the executive washroom, it is still all meaningless.

In chapter 9, he examines the world's value judgments and points out they all come to the same thing:

> I have seen something else under the sun:
> The race is not to the swift
>   or the battle to the strong,
> nor does food come to the wise
>   or wealth to the brilliant
>   or favor to the learned;
> but time and chance happen to them all (9:11).

What difference, then, do worldly values make?

In chapter 10, he explores the value of maintaining a temperate, diligent, cautious lifestyle. Ultimately, however, this is only an expression of enlightened self-interest, a form of selfishness, and even a wise lifestyle can let you down. Sometimes, no matter how carefully and diligently we live, we end up at the bottom of the food chain. Slaves end up on horseback, while princes wind up walking off shoe leather. Fools climb to the top of the heap, while the wise end up underneath it. Despite your best efforts to live a good life, in the end life is not fair. Life throws you curve balls. Life is meaningless.

Chapter 11 talks about the work ethic—the belief that success is largely just a matter of diligence. To get something out of life, you need to work hard and apply yourself. To be as happy as possible during the brief, meaningless span of your existence, rejoice when you can, but don't expect the good times to last:

> However many years a man may live,
>   let him enjoy them all.
> But let him remember the days of darkness,
>   for they will be many (11:8).

You see? He has proved his case. Everything is meaningless. Everything comes to the same thing: Zero, naught, nada, nothing.

But before you get too depressed, I hasten to remind you: The entire book of Ecclesiastes, up to this point, has been written from a human perspective, not God's. From a human point of view, the Debater has summed up everything very well. Life lived apart from God comes to only one end: meaninglessness.

But there is another viewpoint that hasn't been expressed yet. Stay tuned; here comes the perspective that sees life from beyond the sun, not merely under it. Here comes the perspective of God.

With the final chapter, Ecclesiastes 12, comes a shift in viewpoint, a recognition that life is highly significant when God is enthroned in a human life. This is Solomon's own true conclusion to all of his findings, and it begins this way:

A new perspective

> Remember your Creator
>   in the days of your youth,
> before the days of trouble come
>   and the years approach when you will say,
>   "I find no pleasure in them."

Up to this point, we have been looking at life from a worldly, horizontal, under-the-sun perspective, and the conclusion that seems inescapable from reading the first eleven chapters of Ecclesiastes is that life is short, so live for today. The worldly philosophy that Solomon has laid out for us throughout the bulk of this book is exemplified by the "counsel" that is presented, almost satirically, in Ecclesiastes 10:19:

> *A feast is made for laughter,*
> *and wine makes life merry,*
> *but money is the answer for everything.*

It sounds practical. It seems to make sense. But it is not God's counsel, it is the world's counsel. It is all around us, in conversations around the water cooler at work, in books we read, in movies we see, on talk shows we hear. It is a devilish philosophy; it seems to make sense, but it is a snare for the arrogant and the unwary. God uses eleven chapters in Ecclesiastes to lampoon and illuminate the folly of worldly thinking. He wants us to realize, whenever we see or hear people acting and talking on the basis of "eat, drink, and be merry, for tomorrow you die," that this is all that the world, apart from God, has to offer. This is the logical conclusion of a life that has erased God from the picture.

How tragic, how blindly pessimistic. This kind of thinking denies the glory of humanness and reduces us to animals. We are born, we eke out our squalid little pleasures amid the sufferings of this life, we operate on animal instincts of hunger and sex drive and self-preservation, until one day the truck with our name on it comes along, runs us down, and leaves us in the road, as dead as if we were toads or stray cats. That is the gloomy worldview of a life that is lived without God.

Now contrast this pessimistic view with what the writer says in the last chapter:

> *Now all has been heard;*
> *here is the conclusion of the matter:*
> *Fear God and keep his commandments,*
> *for this is the whole ~~duty~~ of man.*

Notice I crossed out the word *duty?* Why? Because it does not appear in the original Hebrew text but was supplied by a translator who missed Solomon's point. Solomon was not saying that fearing and obeying God is our *duty;* he was saying that this is "the whole of man." This is what we were made for. This is our purpose in life. If we fear God and keep His commandments, then we have finally found meaning. All is no longer "vanity of vanities." Life is real, vibrant, exciting, exhilarating. This is the kind of meaning that we were meant to build our lives upon!

The secret of life is to enthrone God, and the earlier we learn this truth, the richer our lives will be. That is why chapter 12 emphasizes the

God uses eleven
chapters in
Ecclesiastes to
lampoon and
illuminate the folly
of worldly thinking

If we fear God and
keep His command-
ments, then we
have finally found
meaning

importance of remembering and obeying God "in the days of your youth." Thinking back on my own youth, I feel a great sympathy for young people today. I see in them a deep inner desire (just as I felt many years ago) not to waste their lives. Every young person wants his or her life to count for something, to have meaning. That is why I feel that the book of Ecclesiastes is such a powerful and important book for young people to understand. It touches the young heart at the very core of its emotions and struggle for significance.

I can testify that the Debater's conclusion is true: Everything is indeed vanity—pure, pessimistic meaninglessness—apart from God. But if you enthrone God in the center of your life, you will discover all that God designed you to be. Trust Him, worship Him, follow Him, love Him, and you will be able to rejoice all the days of your life.

Love Song

T he Song of Songs is regarded today as probably one of the most obscure and difficult books in the Bible. But it hasn't always been that way. Throughout the centuries, it has been one of the most read and most loved books of all. During the dark days before the Protestant Reformation, when the Albigenses fled the Catholic Church and John Hus led his small bands of Christians up into Bohemia, this book was frequently read, quoted, referred to, and memorized by the refugees. The history of another pre-Reformation group, the Covenanters of Scotland (from among whom came John Knox and the Presbyterians), shows that the Song of Songs was widely studied and quoted during their time of persecution while they were hunted like animals throughout the mountains and glens of Europe.

Like the other poetry books of the Old Testament, the Song of Songs is a book about deep yearnings, and these yearnings are expressed on two levels: the surface level of the storyline and the deeper level of symbolism. The Song of Songs completes the pentalogy (five-book series) of poetry books. Job, the first in the series, expressed the yearning cry of the human spirit for God, for answers, and for deliverance from suffering. The middle books of the series, Psalms, Proverbs, and Ecclesiastes, expressed the yearning cry of the soul in its three respective components (emotions, will, and mind). Now, in the Song of Songs, we hear the yearning cry of the body, the physical being that God has given us, the yearning for love.

> The Song of Songs is about deep yearnings expressed on two levels: the surface level of the story-line and the deeper level of symbolism

So the theme of this book is *love*. It is a Middle Eastern love song—and it is frankly and fully that. It is a revelation of all that God intended for us in the divinely given human experience of romantic sex. Sigmund Freud got many things wrong in his analysis of what makes people tick, but he was right about one thing: Sex permeates our lives, and it does so far more pervasively than we tend to realize. But sexual response and love are more than just a by-product of nerve impulses, glandular secretions, and electrical impulses in the brain. Our sexuality is intimately connected with every other aspect of our being. God made us that way. So the Song of Songs presents sex as God intended it to be: involving not just physical responses and animal drives, but our spirit and soul and body, our entire humanity.

You won't find either Victorian inhibitionism or uproarious exhibitionism in the Song of Songs. The book is amazingly candid in its portrayal of the sexual relationship between a man and a woman, but it is never pornographic. Victorianism went astray by treating sex as something to be hidden and repressed. Our modern era treats sex as something to be exploited in advertising and entertainment, as something to be indulged in obsessively, compulsively, in as many ways and with as many different partners as one desires. This is always the way Satan works: He seeks to drive our attitude toward sex in one direction or the other so that we view it from an extreme point of view, making one of God's purest and most exquisite gifts into something dirty and ugly.

This book is amazingly candid in its portrayal of the sexual relationship between a man and a woman, but it is never pornographic

God made sure that the Bible addresses sex as frankly and forthrightly as it deals with any other subject. So, first and foremost, the Song of Songs is a love song describing the delight of a husband and wife in one another's bodies. As you read through it, note how beautifully and chastely it approaches this subject.

The storyline

The Song of Songs is structured as a musical play. The characters in the play are: Solomon, the Lover, the young king of Israel in all the beauty and vigor of his youth (the book was written near the beginning of his reign); the Shulamite woman, the Beloved; and the Friends. Because it is not a narrative but a play, written for several voices, the storyline of the book can be confusing unless you know who is speaking. The various parts in this play are conveniently marked off with subheadings in the *New International Version* so that it is clear who is speaking. If you do not have a Bible that contains such subheadings, you can distinguish the different speakers in this way: The bridegroom always refers to his bride as "my love," and the bride calls him "my beloved."

A musical play

The play is set in Jerusalem, the capital of Israel. It is the story of a young woman whose family evidently rented an excellent tract of land from King Solomon in the north country of Israel. The Shulamite woman (the Beloved) is the Cinderella of the family—a simple country lass of unusual loveliness, but she was forced to spend her days in hard physical labor. Though she has two brothers and two sisters, she is charged with tending the flocks and working in the vineyard. Spending her days in the open sun has given her a deep "California tan," so she sings in 1:5–6:

> *Dark am I, yet lovely,*
> *O daughters of Jerusalem,*
> *dark like the tents of Kedar,*
> *like the tent curtains of Solomon.*
> *Do not stare at me because I am dark,*
> *because I am darkened by the sun.*

She watches the beautiful ladies of the court riding in their carriages up and down the road and envies them but is willing to remain in her quiet, humble life. One day she looks up to see a handsome stranger, a shepherd, looking at her very intently. She finds his frank gaze disturbing, but he says to her, "All beautiful you are, my darling; there is no flaw in you" (4:7). They fall more deeply in love, then he suddenly leaves. But before he goes he promises to return. Through the night, she dreams of him and wishes for him, remembering what he looks like and describing him to her friends.

The Shulamite meets the shepherd

One day there is a great commotion in the valley, caused by the announcement that the king in all his glory is coming to visit the valley. While the girl is interested in this, she is not really concerned because her heart longs for her lover, the young shepherd. Then, to the amazement of everyone, the king sends his riders to the young woman's house with the message that he desires to see her. She comes out, shy and afraid, and is brought to the royal carriage. When she looks inside she sees that the king is none other than her shepherd lover!

The shepherd is King Solomon

You may recall that, in the book of Ecclesiastes, Solomon tells us that he undertook various journeys to discover what life was like on various levels. Apparently, he once journeyed in the disguise of a simple country shepherd lad. Now, having revealed himself to his beloved as the king, he carries her away to the palace, and they live (as the saying goes) happily ever after.

Throughout the book, a chorus of singers (the Friends, referred to in the text as the daughters of Jerusalem), ask certain leading questions from time to time, punctuating various events leading to the courtship, betrothal, and marriage of Solomon and the Shulamite woman. Interestingly the word *Shulamite* is the feminine form of Solomon.

Therefore we could rightly call this woman "Mrs. Solomon." Throughout the story, we read of their courtship, the strength and delights of their love, and even the techniques of their lovemaking.

Here is an outline of the Song of Songs:

The Disguised King and the Shulamite Fall in Love (Song 1:1–3:5)
Theme: Courtship.
Events: The woman and the shepherd-king meet, fall in love, and are separated. When the woman's lover returns, he is revealed as the king. He visits her home and the wedding is planned.

The Marriage of the King and the Shulamite (Song 3:6–5:1)
Theme: United in marriage.
Events: The wedding and the sexual consummation of their love.

The Struggles of Young Married Love (Song 5:2–7:10)
Theme: Adjusting in marriage.
Events: The bride has a troubled dream in which she loses her lover. When she awakens, he reassures her of his love.

The Deepening and Maturing of Love (Song 7:11–8:14)
Theme: Coming home.
Events: The bride convinces her husband to journey with her to her country home. On the journey, their relationship deepens.

**The language
of love**

The language of the book is poetic, lyrical, and figurative. As each describes the other, you can sense the passion and the rapture of love in their words. Here is the language of love as she describes him:

> *My lover is radiant and ruddy,*
>   *outstanding among ten thousand.*
> *His head is purest gold;*
>   *his hair is wavy and black as a raven.*
> *His eyes are like doves*
>   *by the water streams,*
> *washed in milk,*
>   *mounted like jewels.*
> *His cheeks are like beds of spice*
>   *yielding perfume.*
> *His lips are like lilies*
>   *dripping with myrrh.*
> *His arms are rods of gold*
>   *set with chrysolite.*

His body is like polished ivory
> *decorated with sapphires.*
His legs are pillars of marble
> *set on bases of pure gold.*
His appearance is like Lebanon,
> *choice as its cedars.*
His mouth is sweetness itself;
> *he is altogether lovely.*
This is my lover, this my friend,
> *O daughters of Jerusalem (5:10–16).*

Solomon describes his beloved in similar language:

You are beautiful, my darling, as Tirzah,
> *lovely as Jerusalem,*
> *majestic as troops with banners.*
Turn your eyes from me;
> *they overwhelm me.*
Your hair is like a flock of goats
> *descending from Gilead (6:4–5).*

You can see how figurative this language is. If any young men were to try language like this today, they would probably be disastrously misunderstood. But in the culture in which they were first expressed, these were very sweet-sounding metaphors. This is the language of love.

The book describes married love as God intended it to be. For two people to fully give themselves to each other—trustingly, without any inhibitions, for their mutual satisfaction—they must have that complete oneness that exists only in the safe enclosure of marriage. This truth is strongly emphasized throughout the book by a threefold warning that the bride addresses to the unmarried young women—the chorus of Friends referred to as the daughters of Jerusalem. Three different times the bride, turning from her rapture and her delight with her love, gives these young women the secret of this delight:

Daughters of Jerusalem, I charge you . . .
Do not arouse or awaken love
> *until it so desires (2:7; cf. 3:5 and 8:4).*

In other words, do not rush love. Do not hurry into a sexual relationship before you are safe in the enclosure of a committed relationship. Let love come first, genuine love between a husband and his wife, then let arousal and sexual ecstasy awaken. That is the secret of true delight and satisfaction in love.

It is disturbing to watch foolish parents encourage their children to mimic adult behavior in dancing, dating, and petting as teenagers and preteenagers. This behavior stirs up adult emotions and adult behavior in children who are not prepared to handle these responsibilities, who don't appreciate the consequences. If you try to open the bud before it is ready to bloom, you will destroy it. We are seeing the results of this folly in our own society.

God has ordained that the delights reflected here be a part of the experience of men and women, but only in the relationship of marriage. Throughout this book come repeated, urgent pleas for chastity and purity in life until the time for marriage comes.

The deeper meaning

As you've surely guessed, however, we have not heard the deepest message of this song until we peer behind the surface story of romantic love, as beautiful and perfect as it is, and discover the allegory of this song. The deeper meaning embedded in this storyline is its expression of the love relationship and the redemptive relationship between God and humanity, between Christ and His church. The early Christians and even the pre-Christian Jews have recognized its allegorical sense. The preface to this song in one of the Jewish Targums reads:

> This is the Song of Solomon, the prophet king of Israel, which he sang before Jehovah the Lord.

The point of this preface is that Solomon wasn't singing a purely human love song. He sang this song before Jehovah. This was a song about his own relationship to his God, and the early church fathers also understood it in that light. It was because of this interpretation that the Song of Songs was such a comfort to the persecuted saints of the Reformation and the post-Reformation periods.

With the hindsight of the New Testament to draw on, the allegorical nature of this book becomes blindingly obvious! The love that is expressed in this book is the love of Jesus Christ for humanity and the rapturous love of redeemed believers for their Lord. The king who comes in the guise of a shepherd is King Jesus, the Good Shepherd, the Son of David. The Shulamite woman and bride, the beloved, is *us*—people who have been redeemed from the misery and sun-broiling drudgery of sin. We didn't ascend to Jesus by our own efforts; He condescended to us, coming to us peasants in the guise of a peasant. He expressed His love for us on the cross, and He went away; one day He will return for us, to sweep us away to His splendid palace in the New Jerusalem. In the meantime, like the Shulamite, we yearn for His presence and we eagerly await His coming.

After reading the Song of Songs, we gain an entirely new and magnified perspective on what the apostle Paul tells us in Ephesians 5:25–27:

> *Husbands, love your wives, just as Christ loved the church and gave himself up for her to make her holy, cleansing her by the washing with water through the word, and to present her to himself as a radiant church, without stain or wrinkle or any other blemish, but holy and blameless.*

It has been my privilege over the years to preside over many marriages. One thing that my experience has taught me is that marriage is not the product of human society. It is not something that people invented after they began living together. Marriage goes back to the very dawn of the human race. It is a God-given, integral part of human life. The physical act of consummating marriage is not the most significant aspect of the marriage but rather a picture of a deeper relationship, a spiritual and emotional bond between two people.

As you read in this book of the rapturous delight that is exchanged and experienced between the bridegroom and the bride, you are discovering a magnificent description of what God intends for the relationship between Himself and the human race. Now, perhaps, we gain a glimpse into the profound meaning of the great commandment, "Love the Lord your God with all your heart and with all your soul and with all your mind" (Matt. 22:37). In this book, we have a picture of what God will perform in the heart and life of the person who loves Him with this kind of all-consuming heart/soul/mind love. Listen to these beautiful words of the bridegroom to the bride:

> *"See! The winter is past;*
> *the rains are over and gone.*
> *Flowers appear on the earth;*
> *the season of singing has come,*
> *the cooing of doves*
> *is heard in our land.*
> *The fig tree forms its early fruit;*
> *the blossoming vines spread their fragrance.*
> *Arise, come, my darling;*
> *my beautiful one, come with me" (2:11–13).*

There is the springtime of life, but it is not past; it lies in the future. One day this whole world will experience a springtime like that. The Lord Jesus Christ, returning at last to claim His waiting bride, will greet her in words very much like these. The springtime will come, the time

There is the springtime of life, but it is not past; it lies in the future

295

of singing, the time when earth shall blossom again and the curse will be lifted and the flowers will appear on the earth. We will arise, and go with Him.

This is a beautiful, thrilling picture of what takes place in the heart and life of the person who truly falls in love with the King, Jesus Christ, and enters into His springtime. The cold winter of loneliness, sin, and pain is gone. The time of singing has come!

PART FIVE

The Promises of God

The Promises of God

During World War II, an American airman was hit during a dogfight with Japanese planes over the island of Guadalcanal. Though his plane was seriously damaged, the pilot himself was uninjured. He managed to nudge his plane away from the enemy-held main island and over a tiny neighboring island not far away. He bailed out, his parachute opened, and he floated down toward the little jungle island— a place, he recalled during his briefing, that had a reputation as being inhabited by cannibals. *Well*, he thought, *from what I hear, it's better to be eaten by cannibals than end up in one of those enemy concentration camps!*

His boots had no sooner hit the sand when a group of islanders came running toward him. *We'll soon find out if I'm on tonight's menu*, he thought. The island people surrounded him and took him back to their village. To his amazement, he discovered that a number of them spoke English; and to his relief, he discovered that they were not cannibals, they were Christians!

This American pilot was an atheist. To his mind, when the islanders had converted to Christianity after being reached by missionaries, they had simply traded their tribal myths for the Christian myths of Western society. Since he had a long wait before being rescued, he had plenty of time to talk with the islanders about their beliefs.

One day, he noticed one of the villagers sitting near a cooking fire, reading his Bible. "Do you believe the stuff in that book?" the American flyer sneered. "Why, in America we have long since learned that the stories in that book are just a lot of fables."

The villager looked up, then pointed to a big black pot that hung over his cooking fire. "If it weren't for this book," the reformed cannibal replied, "you would be in that pot."

Here is dramatic evidence of the power of the Scriptures to change the human heart. As the writer of Hebrews observed, the Word of God is "living and active. Sharper than any double-edged sword, it penetrates even to dividing soul and spirit, joints and marrow; it judges the thoughts and attitudes of the heart." God's Word is a word of power.

The purpose of the Old Testament is to prepare us to receive truth from God

In these studies thus far, we have seen that the purpose of the Old Testament is to prepare us to receive truth from God. Most of us begin our Christian experience by reading the New Testament; many of us, unfortunately, never seem to get around to reading the Old Testament. But I am convinced, after years of observation both in my own life and in the lives of others, that we can go only so far in appropriating the truths of the New Testament without beginning to understand the Old Testament. Without a firm foundation in the Old Testament, we cannot fully grasp all the riches of the New Testament.

The Old Testament begins with the Pentateuch, Genesis through Deuteronomy, five books that show the pattern of God's working in our lives. Then come the historical books, Joshua through Esther. These books vividly demonstrate the perils that confront us as Christians seeking to follow God's plan for our lives. The historical books point out the spiritual forces that oppose and oppress us, that threaten us from without and undermine us from within, and they show us how to appropriate God's power to wage a successful spiritual battle. Next come the poetical books, Job through the Song of Songs—five books that express the joys and sorrows of being human and show us how to have a genuine relationship and friendship with God.

The books of God's promises

The better we understand God's promises, the better we understand His nature and character

Having seen how the other parts of the Old Testament fit together, we now come to the last sixteen books of the Old Testament: the books of the prophets. In the prophetical books, we discover the mighty promises of God. Just as two people who come together at the altar of marriage make certain promises that bind them to each other, so God has bound Himself to us by the promises of this last section of the Old Testament. And just as a husband and wife are enabled to share themselves with each other because of the security of the promises that they have made, so God shares Himself with us by reason of the great promises of the Bible. The better we understand God's promises, the better we understand His nature and character.

The promises of God have earned the right to be trusted. They are sure, they are dependable. These promises are the foundation for our faith. Without them, we have no objective reason to trust the Bible. Because God has kept all of His promises down through history, we can believe everything else that He tells us in His Word. Let us briefly survey the prophetic books of the Old Testament in light of the promises that characterize each of these books:

The book of Isaiah records numerous promises, but the foremost promise of this book—unquestionably one of the mightiest books in the Bible—is God's promise that He will cleanse us and give us a new beginning. You see this promise in the very first chapter:

The promise of Isaiah

God will cleanse us and give us a new beginning

> *"Come now, let us reason together,"*
> says the LORD.
> *"Though your sins are like scarlet,*
> *they shall be as white as snow;*
> *though they are red as crimson,*
> *they shall be like wool" (Isa. 1:18).*

This promise is repeated and expanded in the fifty-third chapter, which presents Isaiah's prophetic vision of the Messiah hanging on a cross, "pierced for our transgressions," and "crushed for our iniquities." Here is the promise of God's atoning grace: "by his wounds we are healed" (Isa. 53:5). I have come to deeply love this book, for it declares that whenever we are mired in weakness, sin, and failure, God is able to reach in, pull us out, and set us on the road of a new beginning. The promise of Isaiah is the promise of grace, the promise of a new beginning.

The book of Jeremiah is, in many ways, the counterpoint to Isaiah. Whereas Isaiah promises the grace of God, Jeremiah promises the *absence* of God! Did you know that God promises to be absent from your life under certain conditions? Not that He is actually absent and withdrawn from us, but He makes it clear in Jeremiah that our choices and actions can cause us to lose a sense of His communion with us. The promise of Jeremiah foreshadows the New Testament promise that was delivered by the Lord Jesus to Jerusalem: "Look, your house is left to you desolate. I tell you, you will not see me again until you say, 'Blessed is he who comes in the name of the Lord' "(Luke 13:35).

The promise of Jeremiah

Desolation

The Bible repeatedly reminds us that whenever we attempt, in our egotistical pride, to match strength with the Almighty, to place our wills over His will, God will ultimately let us have our way. As a result, we end up wandering into deeper and deeper darkness, misery, and desolation of spirit, exactly as Jerusalem was left desolate after its rejection of the Messiah. Jeremiah was sent to that bleeding city to declare to the people that their city was lost and that they were going into captivity for seventy years.

But God never leaves us lost. When the heart repents and turns back, then Isaiah's promise is operative once again—the promise of a new beginning.

The promise of Ezekiel

God's presence

The promise of Ezekiel is the promise of God's presence. This Old Testament book corresponds to Jesus' promise in the New Testament: "If anyone loves me, he will obey my teaching. My Father will love him, and we will come to him and make our home with him" (John 14:23). The prophecy of Ezekiel begins with a vision of God that is the most remarkable, transcendent vision in the Bible. I have in my library an interesting pamphlet that attempts to explain the opening chapters of Ezekiel as a record of a UFO sighting! But this is very far-fetched. Ezekiel is not about a visitation from outer space but a vision of what God is like. It concludes triumphantly with a picture of the temple of God, where God is present and at rest with His people. The New Testament tells us that we are the ultimate dwelling place of God, and Ezekiel shows how God works in us to bring about His presence in the human heart.

The promise of Daniel

Illumination of the human mind

Daniel is the great predictive book of the Old Testament, setting forth the promise of God's illumination of the human mind. It corresponds to Jesus' New Testament promise, given in John 8:12: "Whoever follows me will never walk in darkness, but will have the light of life." This is one of the greatest books for teenagers to study, because it presents the story of a teenager who is standing for God in a hostile, ungodly environment—exactly what young people face in our society today. It shows how God can enable a young person to stand against the pressures of an ungodly culture, so that he or she can become God's instrument of blessing in that society. God illuminated the mind of young Daniel so that he could see through all the deceptions and phoniness of the philosophy of his day. And God operates in the same way today; that is the promise of Daniel.

The promise of Hosea

God's persistence

Hosea is one of the most beautiful books in the Bible. It is a love story but also the story of a broken marriage and of the heartache of unfaithfulness. It is a story of the persistence of God, the promise of God's persistent redemptive action. It links to the New Testament promise of Philippians 1:6: "He who began a good work in you will carry it on to completion until the day of Christ Jesus." It is the wonderful story of how God sends Hosea to marry a harlot. When she leaves him and goes back to her evil trade, God sends him back to her again to take her to himself. This woman leads Hosea through heartbreak and humiliation, but God fills Hosea's heart with love for her, until finally she is won back and restored. It is a marvelous story of the all-consuming love of God, who sought us when we rejected Him, who redeemed us when we broke His heart, and who finally won us to Himself by His great, extravagant love.

Joel shows how God is at work among the nations, shaping events and bringing about His purposes so that even the tragedies and the catastrophes that we experience become part of the fabric of history that God is weaving.

If you are troubled by what is going on in the world, read the book of Joel. It corresponds to the New Testament promise of Romans 8:28: "We know that in all things God works for the good of those who love him, who have been called according to his purpose."

The promise of Joel

God is bringing about His purposes

The promise of Amos is the promise of perfection, corresponding to that promise in Jude 24: "To him who is able to keep you from falling and to present you before his glorious presence without fault and with great joy. . . ." The message of the book of Amos is that God will never downgrade His standards. We want Him to go easy on us, to leave well enough alone. "Lord," we say, "look at the progress I've made. Isn't that enough? Don't try to improve my character any more. Just let me coast for a while." But Amos comes along and says: "No! 'Well enough' isn't good enough. God will never be content until He has brought you in line with the absolute perfection of Jesus Christ." The plumb line of God is the great theme of Amos.

The promise of Amos

Perfection

Obadiah is the promise of spiritual victory. It is the story of two men, Jacob and Esau, who symbolize two walks in life. Jacob represents walking in the Spirit. Esau represents walking in the flesh. Many of us have felt that we wanted to reach inside our hearts, take hold of the evil, and tear it out by the roots; Obadiah gives us encouragement for such times. The promise of this book links with the promise found in Romans 6:14: "Sin shall not be your master, because you are not under law, but under grace." This book declares that the flesh is always a failure, and the Spirit always triumphs. When we walk in the Spirit, we do not fulfill the lusts of the flesh. The book ends with these profound words:

The promise of Obadiah

Spiritual victory

The kingdom will be the LORD's (Obad. 21).

That is what we want for our own lives, isn't it? We want the kingdom of our lives to be the Lord's. We want Him to reign in our hearts, but we ourselves are His greatest obstacle. Obadiah shows us that God can overcome that, too. The promise of Obadiah is the promise of victory over human flesh, human self-will, and human sin.

The promise of Jonah

A second chance

The book of Jonah receives more ridicule and censure from scoffers than any other book in the Bible because this is the "fish story" of the Old Testament. But, as someone has pointed out, this is an encouraging book: If you are ever down-in-the-mouth, remember Jonah; he came out all right! It is important to remember, however, that the central theme of Jonah is not a fish story. It is a promise: the promise of a second chance, the promise of God's patience with us when we fail. You see the evidence of this promise in Jonah 3:1:

The word of the LORD came to Jonah a second time . . . .

This is why the book of Jonah is such an encouragement to our faith—it shows God's willingness to give us another chance, again and again.

The book also shows God's patience and grace toward humanity in His dealings with the city of Nineveh. Through Jonah, God told the city, "Forty more days and Nineveh will be overturned" (Jonah 3:4). Hearing this message, the entire city of over 112,000 inhabitants repented, and God gave the people a second chance. In His patience with Jonah and with Nineveh, we see God's promise of grace and patience, the promise of a second chance.

The promise of Micah

God's pardon

The prophet Micah was a contemporary of Isaiah. They both ministered to the southern kingdom, Judah. Someone has called the book of Micah "Isaiah in shorthand." Micah summarizes many of the predictions and prophecies of Isaiah and even uses some of Isaiah's wording, which is not surprising, since these two prophets labored together. The message of Isaiah, as we previously noted, is the promise of a new beginning. Micah's theme is the promise of God's pardon. Micah, by the way, is the favorite Old Testament book of political and theological liberals because of one verse—Micah 6:8—a verse Adlai Stevenson often quoted as his favorite:

What does the LORD require of you?
To act justly and to love mercy
and to walk humbly with your God.

This, to liberals, sums up God's entire requirement of humanity. And they are right, to the extent that God does indeed require justice, mercy, and humility from us all. But who can do this? No one can meet the standard of perfection that is set by God! And that is exactly the point. The obvious message of Micah is that you can't do this until you have received the pardon of God, until you have come to a place of dependence and have received His life. Only the life and the grace of God can satisfy the perfect requirements of Micah 6:8. The promise of this book is the promise of God's gracious pardon.

The brief book of the prophet Nahum gives us the promise of God's unchanging, unswerving character. He is just and holy, and He demands justice and holiness. The books of Jonah and Nahum go together because both predict the destruction of Nineveh. In Jonah, the preaching of the prophet Jonah brings forth the repentance of the entire city, and so the city was spared. A hundred years later, however, Nahum issued his prophecy of the destruction of Nineveh, and it was fulfilled to the letter.

The promise of Nahum

God's unchanging character

The combined message of these two books, Jonah and Nahum, is that God is patient, but God does not change. He can be trusted to do exactly what He says He will do. He reserves His judgment whenever people repent, but if they do not repent, God's judgment will fall. That is the promise of the book of Nahum.

Few Christians are well acquainted with the book of Habakkuk, yet it is an absolutely fascinating book. In Habakkuk, we have the answer to that eternal question: "Why? Why does God let injustice prevail? Why does He allow the poor and innocent to suffer? Why does He allow the oppressors to enjoy their riches?" Habakkuk—like Job of old—confronts the silence of God and demands to know, "Why?" God's response to Habakkuk gives us the theme for this book: God's promise of ultimate answers. God answers the prophet; His response is powerful and will stir your thinking and your emotions about these intense and very human "Why?" questions that we all ask.

The promise of Habakkuk

Ultimate answers

This book, by the way, was one of the foundational documents of the Protestant Reformation. This book contains the phrase that struck fire in the heart of Martin Luther and set in motion the wheels of the Reformation: "the just shall live by his faith" (Hab. 2:4 KJV). This book is also the thematic basis for three great New Testament books: Romans, Galatians, and Hebrews. In each of these books, the phrase is quoted: "The just shall live by faith," and each places a different emphasis on that phrase. In Romans, the emphasis is on "the just." In Galatians, it is on "shall live." In Hebrews, it is on "by faith." These books tie together

The promise of Zephaniah

God's jealous wrath

beautifully in this way, and together they underscore the promise of Habakkuk: If we live by faith, God will one day give us the answers that we seek.

The promise of Zephaniah, one of Scripture's shortest books, is the promise of God's jealous wrath. The tone of the book is overwhelmingly dark and gloomy, and it talks repeatedly of "the day of the LORD." The wrath of God is actually the flip side of His love. As we see in Zephaniah and elsewhere in Scripture, our God is a jealous God. That doesn't mean He is jealous in the way that we human beings so often are, filled with unreasoning suspicion and obsessed with possessing and controlling another person. God's love for us is a perfect love, and He hates anything that would damage us and His relationship with us. So when we say, "Lord, I want this or that," and He knows that it would be harmful to us, He says, "No, you can't have that." This seems unfair to us, but it is really God's holy, protective, perfect love for us.

God sometimes disciplines us either by directly intervening in our lives or simply through consequences and circumstances that result from our own choices. At such times, we feel the heat of God's wrath. Many people say that they can't accept the idea of a God of wrath. But you cannot believe in a God of love unless you believe that He can also become angry. If God cannot be angry with those things that hurt the ones He loves, then God cannot truly love. Our God is a God of love and a God of wrath, because His wrath is the flip side of His love. The promise of Zephaniah is the promise of God's jealous love and God's jealous wrath.

All of the prophets that we have just surveyed wrote their books before Israel and Judah were taken into Babylonian captivity. The next three books—Haggai, Zechariah, and Malachi—were written after Israel emerged from captivity. These last three books were written at about the same time as Ezra and Nehemiah, so the prophetic section of the Old Testament closes during the same era as the historical section.

The promise of Haggai

Material blessing

The promise of Haggai is a promise of material blessing. This book reveals the link between the physical and the spiritual. Haggai was the prophet to the people who had forgotten God. They had abandoned the building of the temple while they had been busy building their own houses and focusing on selfish interests. Haggai was sent to remind them that those who behave selfishly, without regard to God, are like the foolish people who killed the goose that laid the golden egg. All material prosperity comes from God and is directly related to one's decision to put God first. Those who don't put

God first will see their prosperity fade. The promise of Haggai is a promise of God's provision and abundance for those who place Him in the center of their lives.

Zechariah is sometimes called "the Apocalypse of the Old Testament." The Apocalypse, of course, is another name for the book of Revelation. Zechariah is the Revelation of the Old Testament because it has many similar features. It begins with a vision of horsemen riding out to patrol the earth and ends with the transcendent spectacle of the coming glory of God: the second coming of Jesus Christ. In this book we find the literal prediction that the Lord's feet shall stand on the Mount of Olives and that the mountain will be split in half and a great valley formed. This is where the judgment of the nations will take place. So it is a book that is intimately linked to John's vision in Revelation. The promise of Zechariah is the promise of the encouragement and comfort of God through the dark days of the end times. If it seems as though the world is falling apart and that God is about to be defeated, read Zechariah. Victory is just around the corner!

The last book of the Old Testament is Malachi. These four brief chapters give us the promise of God's responsibility. Again, this is an encouraging book, because it reveals God's answer to human failure and blindness. It opens with God's asking Israel a number of questions. To each question, Israel responds, "What?! Why?! Who?! Us?! What are you talking about?!" The people are utterly blind to what God is saying. God says, "You rob me." They say, "How do we rob you?" God says, "You have said harsh things against me." They say, "What have we said against you?" This is probably one of the most discouraging aspects of our humanity: that sense of recognizing our own blindness, hopelessness, and failure. It is a depressing state, a sense that we are always in the wrong and incapable of ever achieving God's standards.

Malachi is wonderful medicine for that condition because it shows God's answer to the blindness of our hearts. It shows that it is ultimately God's responsibility to break through the blindness and darkness. It is His job to bring us to the light.

The book closes with a magnificent view of the first coming of the Lord Jesus Christ, preceded by John the Baptist, and of what that coming will mean to the human race. Then the prophetic vision skips quickly to the Lord's second coming: the dawning of the Sun of Righteousness, who comes with healing in His wings to finally bring God's vision of glory to the earth. The promise of Jesus, of His saving power, and of His healing power—power to remove our blindness and magnify our vision—that is the promise of Malachi.

The promise of Zechariah

Encouragement and comfort in the end times

The promise of Malachi

God's responsibility

What do you do with a promise?

God's Word contains three thousand promises that are intended for our present, daily use. How many have you claimed? The answer to that question will largely determine your effectiveness, your satisfaction, and your happiness in the Christian life.

Now, what do you do with a promise? Well, you either believe it or reject it. There are no alternatives. You might say, "I won't believe God's promise. I won't reject it. I'll just ignore it." I'm afraid that option is not open to you. If you ignore His promises, then you reject them, because a promise is a demand for commitment. To ignore something or someone, you simply turn your back and walk away, but that is a rejection, isn't it? So promises must either be believed or they must be rejected. That is why I call this section of our Old Testament study, "The Promises of God."

The Gospel according to Isaiah

I saiah was the greatest of the prophets and a superb master of language. If you enjoy beautiful, rolling cadences and marvelous literary passages, then you will enjoy this book. Isaiah is the fullest revelation of Christ in the Old Testament, so much so that it is often called "the gospel according to Isaiah." The prophetic passages of Isaiah that point so clearly to Christ are some of the richest, most amazing passages of Scripture; especially when you realize that Isaiah wrote these words some seven hundred years before Christ was born! The startlingly clear prophecies of Isaiah that have been fulfilled in the life of Jesus the Messiah provide proof that the Bible is the divinely inspired Word of God.

Isaiah is exactly in the middle of the Bible and has often been called a "miniature Bible." How many books does the Bible have? Sixty-six. How many chapters does Isaiah have? Sixty-six. How many books are there in the Old Testament? Thirty-nine. In the New Testament? Twenty-seven. The book of Isaiah divides in exactly the same way. The first part of the book has thirty-nine chapters. There is a distinct division at chapter 40, so that the remaining twenty-seven chapters constitute the second part of this book.

The New Testament begins with the history of John the Baptist, the forerunner of Christ, as he came to announce the coming of the

Isaiah is exactly in the middle of the Bible and has often been called a "miniature Bible"

Messiah; it ends in the book of Revelation, with the new heaven and the new earth. Chapter 40 of Isaiah, which begins the second part, contains the prophetic passage that foretells the coming of John the Baptist:

> *A voice of one calling:*
> *"In the desert prepare*
> *the way for the LORD;*
> *make straight in the wilderness*
> *a highway for our God" (Isa. 40:3).*

John the Baptist said that he fulfilled this passage. Isaiah 66 speaks of the new heavens and the new earth. So you find here in Isaiah a remarkably close parallel-in-miniature to the entire Bible.

Isaiah: the Grand
Canyon of Scripture

The book of Isaiah is the Grand Canyon of Scripture: deep, vast, majestic, colorful, and layered with history. Visitors to the Grand Canyon are always astonished as they stand at the rim and look out over the vast, silent canyon and see the winding silver thread of the Colorado River more than a mile below. You frequently hear a tourist exclaim in amazement, "How could a tiny thing like that river carve out a huge canyon like this?"

You get a similar impression as you look out over the vast, deep expanse of the book of Isaiah. You immediately sense the grandeur and power of God. You sense the insignificance of humanity when compared with the might and majesty of God. You have to ask yourself, *How could Isaiah, just a human being like me, write a book like this?*

**The source of
the book of
Isaiah**

We know very little about Isaiah. He lived during the reigns of four kings of Judah: Uzziah, Jotham, Ahaz, and Hezekiah. His ministry was some 740 years before Christ when the ten tribes that formed the northern kingdom of Israel were captured by Sennacherib, the Assyrian invader. Judah, the southern kingdom, was plunged into idolatry toward the end of Isaiah's ministry in 687 B.C. and was carried captive into Babylon in 587 B.C.

Isaiah was a contemporary of the prophets Amos, Hosea, and Micah, and tradition tells us that he was martyred under the reign of Manasseh, one of the most wicked kings of the Old Testament. According to this tradition, Isaiah hid in a hollow tree to escape Manasseh. The king's soldiers, knowing he was in that tree, sawed the tree down. Thus, he was sawn in half. Some scholars feel that the reference in Hebrews to heroes of faith who were sawn in two includes the prophet Isaiah (see Heb. 11:37).

Isaiah was the human author of this book, and it is amazing to think that a person could write in such beautiful language and reveal the tremendous things found here. But in the same way, when visitors to the Grand Canyon go down the long trail to the Colorado River, they are no longer amazed that a river could carve out the great canyon. They can hear the grinding rocks being swept along by the force of the current, and they can sense the powerful, invisible force of this river. The book of Isaiah is like that. Here is a man carried along by an amazing force, speaking magnificent prophecies out of the depths of that force. As Peter observed in the New Testament, the prophecies of the Old Testament are not the product of human imagination but of the moving Spirit of God (see 2 Peter 1:20–21). Nothing less than divine inspiration could explain how Isaiah could speak and write as he did.

So that you can catch a glimpse of the breathtaking panorama of this deep, rich book, here is a brief outline:

Prophecies of God's Judgment (Isaiah 1–35)

1. Prophecies against Judah, the southern kingdom	1–12
A. Judah is judged	1
B. The Day of the Lord	2–4
C. The parable of the vineyard	5
D. Isaiah's commission as a prophet	6
E. Prophecy: Israel conquered by Assyria	7–9
F. Prophecy: Assyria destroyed by God	10
G. The restoration of Israel under the Messiah	11–12
2. Prophecies against the enemies of Israel (Babylon, Assyria, Philistia, Moab, Damascus, Samaria, Ethiopia, Egypt, Edom, Arabia, and Tyre; a warning to Jerusalem)	13–23
3. Prophecies of the Day of the Lord	24–27
The Tribulation	24
The blessings of the kingdom	25–27
4. Judgment and blessing among the nations (Woe to Ephraim, Ariel, Egypt, Assyria, and other enemy nations; the coming King—and the coming kingdom)	28–35

The Faith—and Folly—of King Hezekiah (Isaiah 36–39)

5. Assyria challenges Hezekiah and his God	36
6. God overthrows Assyria	37
7. God saves Hezekiah from illness	38
8. Hezekiah's foolishness: he shows off his wealth to the Babylonian envoy	39

Prophecies of Good News (Isaiah 40–66)

**A vision of
the Lord**

As you read through this book, you'll see that the prophet Isaiah was in search of something. Peter says that he was searching for the salvation that was to come from God (see 1 Peter 1:10). It is interesting, then, that the name *Isaiah* means "the salvation of Jehovah."

Isaiah lived during a time of national stress, when man's true, ugly nature was readily apparent. As the book opens, Isaiah is livid over the rebelliousness of his nation. The stupid obstinacy and disobedience of his fellow Israelites is beyond his understanding or his toleration. He angrily laments:

> The ox knows his master,
>   the donkey his owner's manger,
> but Israel does not know,
>   my people do not understand (1:3).

Even an animal knows where its bread comes from, but not Israel! His people wander stupidly, ignorantly; and Isaiah is beside himself with amazement!

Then, in chapter 6, God gives Isaiah a vision. The prophet sees God in His awesome purity and holiness:

> In the year that King Uzziah died, I saw the LORD seated on a throne, high and exalted, and the train of his robe filled the temple. Above him were seraphs, each with six wings: With two wings they covered their faces, with two they covered their feet, and with two they were flying. And they were calling to one another:
>
> > "Holy, holy, holy is the LORD Almighty;
> >   the whole earth is full of his glory."

Imagine this! As Isaiah is in the temple one day, he sees a vision of God. It is significant that this vision occurs in the year of King Uzziah's death, when the throne was vacant; for in this vision, Isaiah glimpses the throne that is *never* vacant! As you read on, you find that God has power to shake the earth to its foundations. He is an immense God, infinite

**The throne that is
never vacant**

and mighty, speaking in thunder and moving in strength. And Isaiah
responds:

> *"Woe to me! . . . I am ruined! For I am a man of unclean lips, and*
> *I live among a people of unclean lips, and my eyes have seen the King,*
> *the LORD Almighty" (Isa. 6:5).*

In other words, Isaiah wonders, *How can such an immense, holy God*
do anything but destroy the rebellious, disobedient human beings? Where is
salvation for people like us?

Isaiah's problem grows worse as, in the second part of this book, he
is made aware of human helplessness. Chapter 40 begins on that note.
Here is the prophetic passage concerning John the Baptist:

> *A voice says, "Cry out."*
> *And I said, "What shall I cry?"*
> *"All men are like grass,*
> *and all their glory is like the flowers of the field. . . .*
> *The grass withers and the flowers fall,*
> *but the word of our God stands forever" (40:6, 8).*

Humankind is temporary, just like the grass. Isaiah sees that the
human race is utterly impotent and helpless, stumbling on toward
oblivion. But that, he soon discovers, is not the end of the human story.
Woven beautifully throughout this book is the ever-growing revelation
of God's love, of Jehovah's salvation, found in the figure of Someone
who is to come: the Messiah, the servant of God. At first, the image of
Messiah is dim and shadowy, but gradually it grows brighter and clearer until, in Isaiah 52 and 53, the figure of Christ steps right off the page
and fills the whole room!

This image of the Messiah is not what we, in our limited human
imaginations, would expect. In Isaiah 52:13, we see that he "will be
raised and lifted up and highly exalted," yet in the very next verse we also
see that "his appearance was so disfigured beyond that of any man and
his form marred beyond human likeness." The pre-Christian Jews must
certainly have been puzzled by these apparent contradictions. How did
God's exalted Servant come to be so horribly marred and disfigured?
Why, as Isaiah 53 goes on to tell us, was He:

> *"despised and rejected by men, a man of sorrows, and familiar with suf-*
> *fering" (v. 3)?*

> *"pierced for our transgressions . . . crushed for our iniquities" (v. 5)?*

**ADVENTURING
THROUGH THE
BIBLE**

A contradictory
image of the
Messiah

"oppressed and afflicted, yet he did not open his mouth" (v. 7)?

*"cut off from the land of the living . . . stricken . . . assigned a grave with
the wicked, and with the rich in his death, though he had done no violence, nor was any deceit in his mouth" (vv. 8 and 9)?*

It must have baffled the ancient Jewish scholars to contemplate this
image of the Messiah: not a glorified, radiant Messiah coming in might
and power but a Messiah who "poured out his life unto death, and was
numbered with the transgressors," a Messiah who "bore the sin of many,
and made intercession for the transgressors" (Isa. 53:12). But this seemingly contradictory image is exactly the divinely inspired picture that
Isaiah was given to convey to us: The very same God of transcendent
glory—in whose presence Isaiah quaked and confessed, "I am ruined . . .
a man of unclean lips . . . and my eyes have seen the King, the LORD
Almighty"—is also the suffering, disfigured, crushed Servant whose life is
poured out for the human race. In this seemingly contradictory image,
the prophet Isaiah saw how God's love would break the back of human
rebelliousness and meet us in our hopelessness and need.

The "Revelation" of Isaiah

Ultimately, the prophet Isaiah peers beyond the darkness and gloom
of the centuries yet to come to a cloudless morning, the dawning of the
day of righteousness, when God's glory will fill the earth. Isaiah 61
announces the year of the Lord's favor, when Jesus is anointed by the
Spirit of the Sovereign Lord to "preach good news to the poor. . . . to
bind up the brokenhearted, to proclaim freedom for the captives and
release from darkness for the prisoners" (61:1). Chapter 62 proclaims a
new name and a new peace and prosperity for Zion, the redeemed and
holy people of the Lord. Chapters 63 through 66 announce God's day
of vengeance and redemption, His gift of salvation, judgment, and hope.
Also in chapter 65, we see an image of the new heavens and new earth
that is also envisioned by John in the book of Revelation. Then will be
fulfilled Isaiah's prophecy in Isaiah 2:4:

> He will judge between the nations
> and will settle disputes for many peoples.
> They will beat their swords into plowshares
> and their spears into pruning hooks.
> Nation will not take up sword against nation,
> nor will they train for war anymore.

In both Isaiah and Revelation, you see two opposite characteristics
of the Lord Jesus—His great power *and* His great humility—*together.* In

Revelation 4:2, John tells us of a mighty vision of God, a vision of a throne shining in heaven. Then he says, "I saw a Lamb, looking as if it had been slain, standing in the center of the throne" (Rev. 5:6). The throne and the Lamb, power and humility, the King and the Servant. We see these same contrasts brought together in Isaiah. In Isaiah 6:1, we see "the Lord seated on a throne, high and exalted." Then, in Isaiah 53:7, we see the Servant—who is also the Lord!—"oppressed and afflicted," and "led like a lamb to the slaughter."

This is God's plan. He doesn't solve the problem of sin on earth the way you and I probably would, with power and might and warfare, scorching and scourging the wicked human race from the face of the earth. Here we see convincing evidence of God's declaration in Isaiah 55:8–9:

> *"My thoughts are not your thoughts,*
> *neither are your ways my ways," declares the LORD.*
> *"As the heavens are higher than the earth,*
> *so are my ways higher than your ways*
> *and my thoughts than your thoughts."*

God's method is to break through human rebelliousness not by might, not by power, but by love, a costly love that suffers and endures great pain and shame. When God comes to the human race as a suffering Servant rather than as a mighty conqueror, something beautiful takes place: The human heart responds, opening to God as the petals of a flower open to the sun. And into that open heart, God pours His life, bringing to that human heart all the joy and fulfillment that He has always wanted His people to experience.

The modern kingdoms of Assyria and Babylon

The first part of the book presents the threat of the king of Assyria, the last part of the book describes the threat of the kingdom of Babylon, and the middle part of the book, chapters 37 through 39 are the filling in this historical sandwich, an interlude bridging the space between Assyria and Babylon. These two nations—Assyria and Babylon—are in the world today and have been since before the time of Isaiah. It is remarkable how up-to-the-moment the book of Isaiah truly is! Where do we see these two kingdoms today?

The king of Assyria stands for the power and philosophy of godlessness—the arrogant human assertion that there is no God; that we can live as we please, accountable to no greater moral power; that we inhabit a mindless, deterministic, materialistic universe that heedlessly grinds humanity to insignificant dust; we can do nothing in this life except enjoy this time until we die. It is the philosophy that might makes right and that humanity is accountable to no one but itself. This is the Assyrian philosophy so prominent in our own day, and it is also the philosophy behind Communism and other materialistic philosophies.

The second force that we see in Isaiah is the power of Babylon. In Scripture, Babylon is always the symbol of apostasy, of religious error and deceit. Again, this philosophy is strong today. The voice from which we should expect guidance—the voice of the church itself—is often raised against God, against the inerrant truth of His Word, against the morality and godliness that is proclaimed in the Scriptures. Today, we hear churches and religious leaders rationalizing false doctrines, justifying and defending sinful lifestyles, and ordaining to ministry people who, by their own admission, engage in behavior that should not be tolerated even among Christian laity. So we are living in the very times described in Isaiah.

The dominant characteristics of the human heart are rebellion and helplessness. I once read a newspaper account of a man who was stopped by a police officer for speeding. When the officer handed him the ticket, the man read it, tossed it back at the officer, threw his car into gear, and sped off. The officer jumped into his car and pursued the lawbreaker at high speeds. The man finally ran his car off the road and destroyed it, killing both himself and his six-year-old daughter who was in the car with him. What made him do that? Wasn't it the innate rebelliousness that arises when the human heart is confronted by authority? This man only took to a fatal extreme the same tendency that lurks within us all.

The dominant characteristics of the human heart are rebellion and helplessness

People often say to me in counseling: "I know what I ought to do, but I don't want to do it." Why not? Rebelliousness and helplessness. It is reflected in the growing despair and futility gripping so many lives today: the loneliness and apparent meaninglessness of life. Twice in Isaiah, God offers a beautiful promise to a world enslaved by rebellion and helplessness, a promise of cleansing, a promise of forgiveness, a promise of a new beginning:

> *"Come now, let us reason together,"*
> *says the LORD.*
> *"Though your sins are like scarlet,*
> *they shall be as white as snow;*
> *though they are red as crimson,*
> *they shall be like wool" (1:18).*

And:

> *"Come, all you who are thirsty,*
> *come to the waters;*

> *and you who have no money,*
> *come, buy and eat!*
> *Come, buy wine and milk*
> *without money and without cost" (55:1).*

God's message to humanity is not condemnation but grace and forgiveness. He calls out to us, "Come! The salvation of Jehovah is available to all! It is a gift; no cost, no strings attached!" And when we accept the gospel according to Isaiah, we discover the answer to our deepest need, the cure for the rebellion and helplessness of our lives, the victory over the Assyria and Babylon in our hearts, the freedom and fellowship that God intended each of us to experience with Him.

The first and last "all"

Some years ago, one of England's Bible teachers had just finished speaking at a meeting, one of a weeklong series of nightly evangelistic meetings. Following the meeting, he hurried to catch a train back to his home. At the station, just as he was about to board his train, a man ran up to him and asked to speak to him. "Sir," the stranger said, "I was in the meeting tonight and I heard you say that we can find peace with God, but I didn't understand all that you said. Could you please stay and talk with me? I need your help!"

The whistle blew, indicating that the train was seconds from pulling out of the station. "I'm sorry," said the Bible teacher. "This is the last train tonight, and I mustn't miss it. But I will tell you what to do." The teacher handed the man his battered King James Bible and said, "Take this Bible and go to the nearest lamppost. Turn to Isaiah 53:6. Stoop down low and go in at the first 'all,' then stand up straight and come out at the last 'all.'" Then he stepped onto the train, which was slowly pulling forward.

"But where . . . ?" the other man said, holding out the Bible.

"Isaiah 53:6!" the teacher repeated, shouting over the chugging of the engine and the clack of the wheels on the rails.

The man stood for a minute, watching the train pull away, puzzling over the strange instructions he had just received. Then, shrugging, he took the Bible to the nearest lamppost and opened it to Isaiah 53:6. As he read the verse, he remembered the teacher's strange advice: *Stoop down low and go in at the first "all," then stand up straight and come out at the last "all."* Then he read aloud, " 'All we like sheep have gone astray; we have turned every one to his own way.' Oh, I see! That's the first 'all'! I see what he meant! I need to stoop down low and go in at the first 'all.' I need to admit that I have gone astray, that I've turned away from God and gone my own way."

The man thought that over for a few moments, then he read further, " 'And the LORD hath laid on him the iniquity of us *all*.' Oh! Now I'm to stand up straight and come out at the last 'all'! Yes! That's it! All my sin has been laid on Him, and I don't have to carry that load of guilt anymore! I can stand up straight because He has taken my sin away!"

It was a moment of revelation and eternal insight in that man's life. The next night before the meeting, he went up to the Bible teacher, handed the old King James Bible back, and said, "Here is your Bible. I want you to know that, last night under that lamppost, I stooped down and went in at the first 'all,' and I stood up straight and came out at the last 'all.' "

That is Isaiah's message. That is the gospel we find not only in the New Testament, but here, in the gospel according to Isaiah. Let us all stand up straight and come out at the last "all."

A Profile in Courage

During the German occupation of Denmark in World War II, King Christian X was a symbol of defiant courage in the face of Nazi oppression and terrorism. One morning, the king awoke, looked out his window, and saw the hated Nazi flag flying over a public building in Copenhagen. Outraged, he called for the German commandant and angrily demanded that the flag be taken down immediately.

The commandant, amused that the king of a defeated nation would make impotent demands of the German conquerors, smirkingly refused to remove the flag. "We Germans do not take orders," he replied. "We give them."

"If you do not have that filthy flag removed this instant," growled the king, "a Danish soldier will go and take it down."

"Then he will be shot," snorted the Nazi officer.

"Fire away, then," said King Christian X. "For I shall be that soldier."

Within minutes, the Germans removed the flag. That is a profile in courage, the courage to stand up for principle, for a higher cause than life itself—the courage to take a life-or-death stand against an oppressive, hateful, murderous government. There are many profiles in courage throughout the Old and New Testaments: men and women who took a courageous, costly stand for God. Perhaps the most courageous of all was the prophet Jeremiah.

Imagine that you are Jeremiah the preacher. You live during the last days of a decaying nation, in the days of evil King Jehoiakim. You preach to the nation and call your people to repentance but no one listens; you are threatened, persecuted, and opposed at every turn. You do not have the comfort of a marriage partner, because the days are too evil and God has told you not to marry. You feel abandoned and alone; all your friends turn away.

You wish you could quit, give the job to someone else, but you can't quit. The Word of God burns in your bones, and you have to speak it regardless of the consequences. Despite the message that God calls you to deliver, despite your love for your country and your people, you see disaster looming. You see that the enemy is on the border, about to conquer and despoil your land, carrying out the judgment of God, and you seem powerless to prevent it. Instead of responding to your warnings of national destruction, the nation turns on you and seeks to destroy you, God's messenger!

Now, perhaps, you can understand why Jeremiah, of all the prophets, was the most heroic. Isaiah wrote more exalted passages and perhaps saw more clearly the coming of the Messiah. Other prophets spoke more precisely concerning future events. But Jeremiah stands out as a man of heroic courage with iron determination to speak God's message regardless of the risk or the cost.

Jeremiah was the last prophet to Judah, the southern kingdom, as the nation was crumbling, eaten from within by moral and spiritual decay. He lived about sixty years after the days of Isaiah, and he continued his ministry in Judah after the ten tribes of the north had been captured by Assyria. Jeremiah's prophetic ministry began during the reign of Judah's last good king, the boy king Josiah, who led the last revival that the nation experienced before it was captured. Tragically, this revival under King Josiah was a rather superficial matter. The prophet Hilkiah had told Josiah that the people would follow him in his attempt to reform the nation and return to God, but it was only because they loved the king not because they loved God.

Jeremiah's ministry, then, continues from the middle of Josiah's reign through the three-month reign of King Jehoahaz, the miserable reign of evil King Jehoiakim, and the three-month reign of Jehoiachin. Jehoiachin's reign was abruptly cut short when he was captured by Nebuchadnezzar and taken to Babylon. Jeremiah was still carrying on God's work during the reign of Judah's last king, Zedekiah. Then Nebuchadnezzar returned, utterly destroyed the city of Jerusalem, and took the whole nation into Babylonian captivity.

Jeremiah's ministry lasted about forty years, and during all this time the prophet never saw any sign that his ministry was even slightly successful. His message was one of denunciation and reform, and the people never obeyed him. He was called to a ministry of failure, yet he never gave up, never wavered. Despite the frustration of forty years of failure, he remained faithful to God and to his mission: witnessing God's truth to a dying, disobedient nation.

Two themes permeate the book of Jeremiah. The first is the fate of the nation, which is judgment. The second concerns Jeremiah's sorrow over his people's disobedience.

First, Jeremiah repeatedly reminds the people that their first error was their failure to take God seriously. They didn't pay attention to what God had told them, and they did what was right in their own eyes— not what was right in the light of God's revelation. As we read in 2 Chronicles 34, the nation had sunk so low that for many years, the Law of Moses was completely lost! It had been tossed into a storage room in the back of the temple—and forgotten. Decades later, Hilkiah the priest was cleaning up in the temple and he found the Book of the Law. He was astonished! For years, the nation had been completely without the Word of God, and suddenly, the Word was rediscovered!

Hilkiah took the Book of the Law to King Josiah and read it to him. Hearing the words of the Law, the king tore his clothes in grief and anguish over the years that the Law had been lost. He had the book read to the entire nation, and he made a covenant before the Lord to keep His commandments (2 Chron. 34:29–31). This rediscovery of the Word of God stimulated the great national revival led by Josiah. The rediscovery of God's Word is always the first step to revival and restoration.

It is a dangerous thing to lose contact with God's Word. When we shut our eyes and close our ears to God's voice, expressed in His Word, we invariably end up on the perilous road of doing what is right in our own eyes. Many people, of course, do what they know is *wrong* in the sight of God; that is bad enough. But it is equally dangerous to judge for ourselves what is right without consulting the Bible to see what God has already said about the matter. Without an objective source as our yardstick, how can we properly determine what we should do? The Bible is our moral and spiritual reality check. Without it, we become unrealistic and misguided, our judgment is impaired, and we easily find ourselves in the same condition of decay and deterioration that characterized the people of Jeremiah's day.

In neglecting God's Word, the kingdom of Judah gradually adopted the values of the worldlings around them. They formed political and military alliances with nearby godless nations, and soon they were even worshiping the gods of the other nations. Their idolatry and disobedience brought upon them a torrent of internal strife, external threats, perverted justice, and moral disintegration. These were the prevailing conditions when Jeremiah came to call the nation to repentance or to judgment.

Throughout the book, you see Jeremiah issuing clearly delineated prophecies, telling exactly how God would raise up a terrible and godless people who would sweep across the land and destroy everything in their path. They would be utterly ruthless, breaking down the city walls and destroying the temple, taking away all the things that the nation valued, and dragging the people themselves into bondage. Thus would God judge Israel.

But Jeremiah also made clear in these passages of judgment that God takes no pleasure in dispensing judgment. He judges with a sorrowing heart, a weeping heart. When God disciplines a nation or an individual, He does so because He is a God of love. He takes no pleasure administering the pain of discipline and judgment. He is like a loving father who repeatedly instructs his erring children in the way of obedience but who finally and reluctantly must correct them. We see His fatherly, sorrowing heart described in numerous passages, such as Jeremiah 3:19:

> *"I myself said,*
> *'How gladly would I treat you like sons*
> *and give you a desirable land,*
> *the most beautiful inheritance of any nation.'*
> *I thought you would call me 'Father'*
> *and not turn away from following me."*

Here we see that God is not so much enraged by the straying of His people as He is wounded and grieved. The Lord is gracious and merciful, but when we trample His mercy underfoot, He finally reaches the point where He must give us the discipline and judgment that we have been asking for. It is as if He is saying to us, "This is going to hurt me more than it does you." Every loving father says that to his children sooner or later, but no father ever meant it more earnestly and more deeply than God the Father.

Jeremiah is the life journal of one of the greatest prophets in the Bible recorded during the darkest, most shameful days in the history of Israel and Judah. The nation has sunk to a miserable level characterized by idolatry, immorality, apostasy, and the degeneration of worship and faith. For forty years, Jeremiah proclaims God's judgment against the erring nation of Judah. He issues prophecies that foretell events of the near future and of future millennia. Jeremiah himself lives to see many of his prophecies come true, including the destruction of Jerusalem. He will later write his feelings about that destruction in his book of Lamentations.

Here is a brief overview of Jeremiah's mighty, prophetic autobiography:

God Calls Jeremiah to the Prophetic Ministry (Jeremiah 1)

Jeremiah's Prophecies against the Nation (Jeremiah 2–25)

1.	Jeremiah's first sermon: The willful sins of the nation	2:1–3:5
2.	Jeremiah's second sermon: Repent or be judged	3:6–6:30
3.	Jeremiah's third sermon: Religious hypocrisy will be judged	7–10
4.	Jeremiah's fourth sermon: The nation's broken covenant	11–12
5.	Jeremiah's fifth sermon: The sash and the wineskins	13
6.	Jeremiah's sixth sermon: The horrors of judgment	14–15
7.	Jeremiah's seventh sermon: Why Jeremiah never married	16–17
8.	Jeremiah's eighth sermon: The potter and the clay	18–20
9.	Jeremiah's ninth sermon: The evil kings and the future righteous king	21:1–23:8
10.	Jeremiah's tenth sermon: Judging false prophets	23:9–40
11.	Jeremiah's eleventh sermon: Good figs and bad	24
12.	Jeremiah's twelfth sermon: Seventy years of captivity	25

Jeremiah's Conflicts (Jeremiah 26–29)

13.	Conflict with the nation of Judah	26
14.	Conflict with false prophets	27–29

The Distant Future of Israel, Judah, and Jerusalem (Jeremiah 30–33)

15.	The restoration of Israel and Judah	30–31
16.	The reconstruction of Jerusalem	32
17.	The restoration of the covenant	33

The Fast-Approaching Fall of Jerusalem (Jeremiah 34–45)

18.	Jeremiah's warnings to the king and the people	34–36
19.	Jeremiah imprisoned and persecuted	37–38
20.	The fall of Jerusalem	39–45

Prophecies against the Gentile Enemies
(Jeremiah 46–51)
Prophecies against Egypt, Philistia, Moab, Ammon,
Edom, Damascus, Kedar, Hazor, Elam, and Babylon

The Fall of Jerusalem
(Jeremiah 52)
Jerusalem is sacked and destroyed, and her people are
exiled to Babylon

Most of the book of Jeremiah consists of a series of prophetic sermons. The first, from Jeremiah 2:1 to 3:5, laments the willful sins of Judah. The second sermon, from 3:6 through chapter 6, warns of the judgment and destruction that will result if Judah does not repent. The third, chapters 7 through 10, expresses Jeremiah's own grief over the nation's sin and details the nation's hypocrisy and idolatry. The fourth, chapters 11 and 12, deals with the nation's faithlessness in breaking its covenant with God. The fifth sermon, chapter 13, uses a ruined sash, or belt, and wineskins to symbolize God's judgment. The sixth, chapters 14 and 15, describes God's coming judgment in terms of drought, famine, and war.

In the seventh sermon, chapters 16 and 17, Jeremiah explains why he is unmarried: Disaster is looming because of the people's idolatry, sin, and disregard for the Sabbath, and when society is disintegrating, it is better to be unmarried. In his eighth sermon, chapters 18 through 20, God speaks through Jeremiah comparing His power over Israel to a potter's control over clay. God is omnipotent, and the entire nation is as clay in His hands. He has the power to make, unmake, and reshape the Jewish nation.

In this sermon, God tells Jeremiah to go to the potter's house and watch the potter working at the wheel. The prophet sees the potter making a clay pot; as the wheel turns, the pot becomes marred and broken. The potter squashes the pot into a shapeless lump and patiently begins shaping it the second time, after which it emerges again as a pot that is pleasing to the potter.

This is one of a number of powerful word pictures or verbal visual aids that Jeremiah, inspired by God's Spirit, uses throughout this book. The potter and the clay symbolize not only God's power, but His loving intent and His desire to make something beautiful from a broken life. He takes our brokenness and deformity, the result of our past sin, and remakes it according to the creative vision of His artist's heart. Here, Jeremiah speaks not only a fateful prophecy of ruin and desolation but also of the hope and beauty of the coming days when God will reshape

Israel. We can find comfort and encouragement in realizing that the word picture of the potter and the clay applies not only to the Jewish nation but to individual human lives as well.

In his ninth sermon, chapters 21 and 22, Jeremiah speaks against the evil kings of Israel, then he predicts the coming of a righteous King, a righteous branch from David's family tree (23:1–8). This, of course, is a prediction of the righteous reign of King Jesus—and since His millennial reign is still in our future, Jeremiah is looking toward events that have not yet been fulfilled. Jeremiah's tenth sermon is an all-out attack on the false prophets of the nation (23:9–40). His eleventh sermon, chapter 24, contrasts the good people who have been exiled to Babylon with the evil leaders of Judah who remained behind, comparing them to good figs and bad figs.

In Jeremiah's twelfth sermon, chapter 25, he peers into the misty future, where he foresees seventy long years of Babylonian captivity for Judah.

As we begin to study the book of Daniel we will meet the prophet Daniel, who lived during the very Babylonian captivity that Jeremiah here foresees. In that book, Daniel reads Jeremiah 25 and discovers that Jeremiah had prophesied that the Babylonian captivity would last exactly seventy years. Thus, Daniel knew that the end of the captivity was approaching, and he could look forward to seeing the nation restored. In Jeremiah 25, the prophet looks beyond the time of captivity to the restoration of the people. Then his gaze leaps far beyond the events of the next seventy-odd years to a far-distant time, hundreds and even thousands of years ahead. He foresees the ultimate dispersion of Israel when the Jews were driven out of Palestine in the first and second centuries A.D. He also foresees the final gathering of the Jews into the land: the refounding of the state of Israel in 1948. He looks beyond even our own era to the days that will usher in the millennial reign when Israel—restored and blessed and called by God—will be the world's cultural, political, economic, and spiritual hub.

Jeremiah's twelve prophetic sermons are followed in chapters 26 through 29 by details of several conflicts that Jeremiah experienced: conflicts with his own people, the nation of Judah, and the false prophets Hananiah and Shemaiah. In this section, we see Jeremiah's boldness and courage as he opposes the civic and religious leaders of Jerusalem, prophesying the coming destruction of the city: an act of defiance against Jerusalem's corrupt human authorities. His defiance causes them to seek the death penalty against him.

In chapters 30 through 33, we come to an amazing and beautiful prediction of Jeremiah concerning the future restoration of Israel and

Daniel and Jeremiah 25

Jeremiah's conflicts

The new covenant

Judah. Not only will the city of Jerusalem be rebuilt and refurbished, but God will make a new and lasting agreement with the people of restored Israel. In Jeremiah 31:31–33, we read:

> *"The time is coming," declares the LORD,*
> *"when I will make a new covenant*
> *with the house of Israel*
> *and with the house of Judah.*
> *It will not be like the covenant*
> *I made with their forefathers*
> *when I took them by the hand*
> *to lead them out of Egypt,*
> *because they broke my covenant,*
> *though I was a husband to them,"*
> *declares the LORD.*
> *"This is the covenant I will make with the house of Israel*
> *after that time," declares the LORD.*
> *"I will put my law in their minds*
> *and write it on their hearts.*
> *I will be their God,*
> *and they will be my people."*

From the depths of those depressing and deplorable circumstances, when he was being pursued, threatened, persecuted, and imprisoned, Jeremiah was led by the Spirit of God to write this shining vision of a future time when the people of Israel would be called back into the land of promise. In this vision, God promises to be their God and to walk among them and put away their sins.

Most significant of all, it is in this passage that we find the great promise of the *new* covenant to be made with Israel. This is the same new covenant that is spoken of so powerfully in Hebrews 8 and which our Lord Himself referred to when He gathered with His disciples on the night before His crucifixion and instituted the Lord's Supper. After

The Lord's Supper

breaking the bread, which symbolized His broken body, He then took the cup and held it up to them, saying, "This is my blood of the [new] covenant, which is poured out for many for the forgiveness of sins" (Matt. 26:28). The ultimate fulfillment of the new covenant still lies in the distant future. God is fulfilling it today among the Gentile nations through His church (made up of both Jew and Gentile believers), but the final fulfillment of the new covenant for Israel will not take place until the millennial reign of Jesus the Messiah.

King Zedekiah

In chapter 37, King Zedekiah, son of good King Josiah, is installed on the throne by Nebuchadnezzar of Babylon. Unlike his father, King

Zedekiah has no regard for God. Though Zedekiah did not actively oppose Jeremiah and often listened to Jeremiah's words, he was a weak and cowardly king who lacked the will to stand up to the officials in his government who actively persecuted the prophet. First, he tacitly allowed Irijah, the captain of the guard, to arrest Jeremiah and throw him into a dungeon. Then, when the governmental officials (who supposedly owed their allegiance and obedience to King Zedekiah) approached the king, asking that Jeremiah be put to death, Zedekiah acquiesced, saying, "He is in your hands. . . . The king can do nothing to oppose you" (Jer. 38:5). So the governmental officials had Jeremiah seized and tossed into a cistern that was filled not with water but with deep, slimy mud. Only a small amount of light trickled in from above, vaguely illuminating the hole in which Jeremiah stood in ooze.

When another royal official came to Zedekiah and complained of the unjust treatment of Jeremiah, the cowardly king again changed course and sent thirty men to rescue Jeremiah from the pit. The king secretly had Jeremiah brought to him so that he could question the prophet about his own fate and the fate of the nation. The spineless king swore Jeremiah to silence concerning their conversation.

Chapters 39 through 45 tell the grim story of the fall of Jerusalem to the Babylonian invaders, just as Jeremiah had prophesied. In chapters 46 through 51, we have a series of prophecies against the various heathen nations and cities that oppose God and His people: Egypt, Philistia, Moab, Ammon, Edom, Damascus, Kedar, Hazor, Elam, and Babylon. In chapters 50 and 51, Jeremiah details the defeat and utter desolation that will ultimately swallow Babylon. Jeremiah 52 sets forth the last days of the city of Jerusalem: the capture and destruction of the city and the forced exile of its people to Babylon. Thus are the dire prophecies of Jeremiah fulfilled.

Throughout the book of Jeremiah, you see the prophet in a constant battle against discouragement. Who wouldn't be discouraged in the face of constant persecution and failure? For forty long years, he labors and preaches and ministers but never perceives even the tiniest hint of success.

We can learn a great lesson through Jeremiah's honest reactions to opposition and failure. In his public role as a prophet of God, he is as fearless as a lion. He confronts kings, captains, and murderers with utter ferocity and boldness. He looks them right in the eye and delivers the message of God, heedless of their threats or their power to have him tortured and killed.

But when he is alone, Jeremiah is just a solitary human being like you and me. When he prays he pours out the same prayer that you or I

Jeremiah is seized and tossed into a cistern

Zedekiah changes course and rescues Jeremiah

Battling the specter of discouragement

would pray in that situation: a prayer dripping with bitterness, hot with anger, twisted and tortured by discouragement, and heavy with depression. He doesn't sugarcoat his feelings. He just spreads it all out before the Lord—even his disappointment with God!—and says:

> *Why is my pain unending*
> *and my wound grievous and incurable?*
> *Will you be to me like a deceptive brook,*
> *like a spring that fails? (15:18).*

Strong words? Undoubtedly. Honest words? Absolutely. He is pouring out his true feelings. He has begun to wonder whether the trouble might be that God cannot be depended upon. He is troubled by persecution, scorn, loneliness, and discouragement. He feels forsaken.

Some people would say, "I know the trouble with this man! Jeremiah's obviously allowed himself to backslide. He's out of fellowship with God. He's fallen into disobedience." That is a quick and easy answer, a glib and superficial answer, but it is not the right answer. Jeremiah is not backslidden. He is holding fast with God and wrestling with God. He's carrying on a relationship with God—a stormy relationship at times—but a real, living, dynamic relationship. As Jeremiah prays in 15:15–16:

> *You understand, O LORD;*
> *remember me and care for me. . . .*
> *When your words came, I ate them;*
> *they were my joy and my heart's delight,*
> *for I bear your name,*
> *O LORD God Almighty.*

Clearly, this is a man who feeds on God's Word, who witnesses to God's truth, who publicly bears the name of God, the Almighty. This is not a backslidden individual, is it? Jeremiah is doing all the things that one should do in times of discouragement and depression: prayer, time in God's Word, witnessing. He does all these things, yet he is still defeated, still discouraged. What is the problem?

Simply this: Jeremiah forgot his calling. He has forgotten what God has promised to be to him. So God reminds Jeremiah that He called him to be a prophet, to speak His words. God didn't call Jeremiah to be successful. He didn't call Jeremiah to win a popularity contest. God called Jeremiah to be faithful and to be His representative, period. So why should Jeremiah be discouraged? So what if people didn't like him, if kings and captains opposed him? So what if he wasn't successful in the eyes of the world? Jeremiah needed to concern himself with only one standard of success: God's standard.

If Jeremiah was faithful and obedient, if he spoke God's words with boldness and clarity, then it didn't matter if those words produced results. It didn't matter if the people repented, if the nation came back to God or not. Results are God's department. Obedience was Jeremiah's department. As long as he kept in view the goal of obedience to God, he would be depression-proof. The same is true for you and me.

God is greater than our circumstances, our setbacks, our disappointments, and our opposition. He is bigger than anything and everything else in our lives. No matter how depressing life may seem, the God who has called us is the same great God who is able to sustain us. If we take our eyes off our circumstances and fasten them firmly on God, then we will be strengthened to rise to our task and to achieve true success: steadfast obedience to God.

God's Therapy

The full name of this book is "The Lamentations of Jeremiah." It is the second of Jeremiah's two books, containing the prophet's tear-stained reflections on the city of Jerusalem following its captivity by Nebuchadnezzar of Babylon. In the Septuagint version (the Greek translation from the original Hebrew), there is a brief notation to the effect that Jeremiah uttered these lamentations as he sat on the hillside overlooking the desolate city. Read through this book and you will get a strong impression of the foreshadowing of the Lord Jesus as He wept, centuries later, over the same city. In Jesus' last week before going to the cross, He went to the Mount of Olives and looked out over the city. With tears streaming down His face, He cried out:

> *"O Jerusalem, Jerusalem, you who kill the prophets and stone those sent to you, how often I have longed to gather your children together, as a hen gathers her chicks under her wings, but you were not willing"* (Matt. 23:37).

A weeping prophet and a weeping Messiah

The same city that had rejected the prophet Jeremiah and the word of God that he preached to that city now rejected Jesus Christ, the Word made flesh. The people of Jerusalem did not know the hour of their visitation, and so they turned their backs on their Messiah and deliverer.

You'll see other parallels between Jeremiah's lamentations and the ministry of the Lord Jesus in such passages as:

Lamentations 1:12: "Is it nothing to you, all you who pass by? Look around and see. Is any suffering like my suffering that was inflicted on me?" These words suggest the suffering of the cross and the indifference of those who watched the Savior die.

Lamentations 2:15: "All who pass your way clap their hands at you; they scoff and shake their heads." This recalls the mockery of the multitudes at the cross.

Lamentations 3:14–15: "I became the laughingstock of all my people; they mock me in song all day long. He has filled me with bitter herbs and sated me with gall." This text again suggests the mockery and the bitterness of the crucifixion.

Lamentations 3:30: "Let him offer his cheek to one who would strike him." This reminds us of the that time Jesus was brought before Pilate for judgment and was struck by the soldiers.

So this little book suggests and captures the Lord's sorrow and dying agony. He was, as Isaiah 53:3 tells us, "a man of sorrows, and familiar with suffering."

An intriguing structure

There are twenty-two letters in the Hebrew alphabet, beginning with aleph, the equivalent of our *a*, and ending with tau, the equivalent of our *t*. (The letter *z*, by the way, is near the middle of the Hebrew alphabet.) Lamentations is written in a poetic structure called an *acrostic*, a composition in which the initial letters of the lines, when read vertically, form a word, a phrase, or (as in this case) an alphabet. Jeremiah used the acrostic form to list, in order, the letters of the Hebrew alphabet. The acrostic is formed in chapters 1, 2, and 4: each chapter consists of twenty-two verses, and each verse begins with one of the twenty-two letters of the Hebrew alphabet, beginning with aleph and ending with tau.

Chapter 3 deviates from the pattern, consisting of sixty-six verses in triads. Each verse of a triad begins with the same letter of the alphabet, so that there are twenty-two groups of three: verses 1 through 3 begin aleph, aleph, aleph; verses 4 through 6 begin beth, beth, beth; then gimel, gimel, gimel; and so forth to tau, tau, tau. Chapter 5 does not follow this acrostic plan, although it does have twenty-two verses.

These chapters have been written very carefully, according to the rules of Hebrew poetry. This is certainly an intriguing structure, but the real interest of this book is in its content. It is a study in sorrow, a hymn of heartbreak. This is the kind of book that you might read when sorrow comes into your life, as it does to all of us at times. As Jeremiah was looking out over Jerusalem, he saw its desolation and he remembered the terrible, bloody battle in which Nebuchadnezzar had captured and ravaged the city, destroyed the temple, and killed the inhabitants.

These chapters have been written very carefully, according to the rules of Hebrew poetry

Each chapter stresses and develops a particular aspect of sorrow. Chapter 1 describes the depths of sorrow, the loneliness, and the desolation of spirit that sorrow wreaks upon the human heart. The people have been vanquished and taken into captivity; the city has been set on fire and totally destroyed. Jeremiah writes in verse 16:

> *"This is why I weep*
> *and my eyes overflow with tears.*
> *No one is near to comfort me,*
> *no one to restore my spirit.*
> *My children are destitute*
> *because the enemy has prevailed."*

Chapter 2 describes the thoroughness of judgment. The beginning of this chapter describes the way Nebuchadnezzar's armies utterly devastated the city. Jeremiah, however, does not attribute this destruction to the armies of Nebuchadnezzar. He attributes it to the Lord; the Babylonian army was just a tool in the hand of the Almighty. God's judgment is thorough. Everything has been destroyed, nothing is left.

In chapter 3, the long chapter of sixty-six verses, the prophet speaks of his own reaction, his personal pain as he contemplates a scene of utter devastation. He begins with these words:

> *I am the man who has seen affliction*
> *by the rod of his wrath.*
> *He has driven me away and made me walk*
> *in darkness rather than light;*
> *indeed, he has turned his hand against me*
> *again and again, all day long.*
> *He has made my skin and my flesh grow old*
> *and has broken my bones.*
> *He has besieged me and surrounded me*
> *with bitterness and hardship.*
> *He has made me dwell in darkness*
> *like those long dead (3:1–6).*

In chapter 4 we see the prophet's shocked disbelief as he recalls all that has happened. Anyone who has been through a shocking, tragic loss knows about these aspects of the grief process. First, there is a sense of utter desolation. Then comes a deep personal pain. As the pain sinks in, the mind recoils in disbelief and denial: "This can't be happening!" That is the sense we draw from this chapter:

LAMENTATIONS

Each chapter stresses and develops a particular aspect of sorrow

Chapter 1: the depths of sorrow

Chapter 2: the thoroughness of judgment

Chapter 3: personal pain

Chapter 4: shocked disbelief

How the precious sons of Zion,
* once worth their weight in gold,*
are now considered as pots of clay,
* the work of a potter's hands! . . . .*
Those who once ate delicacies
* are destitute in the streets.*
Those nurtured in purple
* now lie on ash heaps.*
The punishment of my people
* is greater than that of Sodom,*
which was overthrown in a moment
* without a hand turned to help her. . . .*
With their own hands compassionate women
* have cooked their own children,*
who became their food
* when my people were destroyed. . . .*
The kings of the earth did not believe,
* nor did any of the world's people,*
that enemies and foes could enter
* the gates of Jerusalem.*
But it happened because of the sins of her prophets
* and the iniquities of her priests,*
who shed within her
* the blood of the righteous*
*   (4:2, 5–6, 10, 12–13).*

Chapter 5: the humiliation of judgment

In chapter 5, we see the utter humiliation of judgment, the feeling that Jeremiah's people have been thoroughly disgraced. "The crown has fallen from our head," he laments in verse 16. "Woe to us, for we have sinned!" Here is an overview of the entire book in outline form:

The Destruction of Jerusalem (Lamentations 1)
1. The lamentation of the prophet Jeremiah   1:1–11
2. The lamentation of the vanquished city   1:12–22

The Wrath of God (Lamentations 2)
3. God's anger   2:1–9
4. The sorrow of the vanquished city   2:10–22

Jeremiah Seeks God's Mercy (Lamentations 3)
5. Jeremiah's sorrow   3:1–21
6. The goodness of the Lord   3:22–39
7. Jeremiah calls to God   3:40–66

The lessons of sorrow

Amid all this desolation and depression, something good emerges. In each of these chapters, an insight is revealed—a lesson God wants to teach us for all our times of pain, loss, and sorrow. This book is designed to teach us God's therapy *of* trouble and *for* trouble. All through Scripture, we are told that pain and suffering are God's instruments by which He teaches us. Through suffering comes strength of character. Do not be surprised that this is true. We read in Hebrews 5:8 of the Lord Jesus, "Although he was a son, he learned obedience from what he suffered." There were things that the Lord Jesus had to learn that could be learned only through a human experience of suffering and sorrow. If He was not exempt, why should we expect to be?

Each chapter of Lamentations reveals one particular aspect of sorrow, one specific teaching on one particular lesson of grace. Chapter 1 focuses on the sense of desolation and abandonment in spirit. As he looks out over the ruins of Jerusalem, Jeremiah suddenly realizes that this devastation is a sign that God is right, His judgment is unerring and unimpeachable. So, in verse 18, "The LORD is righteous, yet I rebelled against his command." That is the lesson of chapter 1.

Chapter 1: God's judgment is unerring and unimpeachable

Most of us are in the habit of blaming God, either directly or indirectly, for whatever happens to us. Our attitude is, "I do my best! I try hard, and still these things happen! It's not fair, and since God is in charge of justice, then it must be His fault that unfair things happen to me!" But is God unfair? The apostle Paul states the truth of the matter: "Let God be true, and every man a liar" (Rom. 3:4). It is impossible for God to be wrong. It is impossible for human beings to be more just than God, *because our very sense of justice is derived from Him!* If not for God, we wouldn't even know what justice and fairness are! It is impossible for human beings to be more compassionate than God, for our feelings of compassion come from Him. We cannot possibly judge God.

In chapter 2, Jeremiah gains more insight into this truth. He is made aware of the thoroughness of judgment, of how meticulously God has used the armies of Nebuchadnezzar to destroy everything. Is this mere cruelty on God's part? No! Jeremiah realizes that this is God's faithfulness to His own word: "The LORD has done what he planned; he has fulfilled his word" (2:17). If God says He will do something, He does it. Four hundred years earlier, in Deuteronomy, God had promised that if His people would love Him and follow Him, He would open the windows of heaven and pour out blessing; if, however, His people forsook Him and ignored the prophets that He sent to them, destruction would fall. God was patient, and He gave the people the opportunity to repent. But ultimately, God was faithful to His word.

We see evidence of God's faithfulness to His word in the precise length of the Babylonian captivity: 70 years. That is the length of captivity that Jeremiah prophesied in Jeremiah 25:11, and that was exactly how long it lasted. Why 70? What is special about the number 70? Just this: In the Law that God gave to Israel through Moses, He required the nation to allow the land to rest every seventh year. They were not to plow the soil or use it; they were to let it rest, a practical principle of agricultural management and land conservation. During the sixth year, the Lord would bless them with a superabundance of crops so that they would have enough food to carry them through that seventh year.

But Israel never obeyed that command. They continued using the land from the time they entered it. In a sense they robbed God of 70 years of rest for the land. They used it continuously for 490 years, so God sent them out of it and allowed the land to rest for 70 years.

God is utterly faithful to His promises. Many people believe that God is so loving, so tenderhearted, so indulgent, that He just gives in at the least little pressure. He won't *really* do what He says He is going to do. He won't really judge sin. He won't really hold us accountable.

Those misconceptions about God were forever laid to rest by one of the greatest verses in the Bible: "He who did not spare his own Son, but gave him up for us all . . ." (Rom. 8:32). Think of that! God did not spare His own Son! That is how unflinching He is in keeping His word. Yet that verse ends in glory: "How will he not also, along with him, graciously give us all things?" One side of this promise is as true as the other. Jeremiah learned that God is faithful by the thoroughness of judgment.

In chapter 3, where we read of Jeremiah's personal pain, we come to a tremendous passage. In the midst of a long recitation of his own grief and horror, he says:

> *Because of the LORD's great love we are not consumed,*
> *for his compassions never fail.*
> *They are new every morning;*
> *great is your faithfulness.*

> *I say to myself, "The LORD is my portion;*
> *therefore I will wait for him."*
> *The LORD is good to those whose hope is in him,*
> *to the one who seeks him. . . .*
> *For he does not willingly bring affliction*
> *or grief to the children of men (3:22–25, 33).*

This is one of the most beautiful passages in the Bible. Amid the horrors of judgment that people have brought upon themselves and their works, this passage reveals the compassion of God's heart. Judgment, as Isaiah says, is God's strange work. He does not like to do it. He does not willingly afflict or grieve the children of men. His mercies are fresh every morning. In his own pain Jeremiah remembers that behind all the desolation is the work of love. God destroyed Jerusalem because it was heading the wrong way. He destroyed it so that He could restore it later and build it up again in joy and peace and blessing. The Lord does not cast off forever. He judges, and judgment is grievous and painful, but through, below, around, and above it all is God's great love and compassion.

At the end of chapter 4, the prophet says:

> *O Daughter of Zion, your punishment will end;*
> *he will not prolong your exile.*
> *But, O Daughter of Edom, he will punish your sin*
> *and expose your wickedness (4:22).*

Chapter 3: Judgment is the work of love

The daughter of Zion is Israel. The daughter of Edom refers to the country bordering Israel that was always a thorn in Israel's flesh. The Edomites were related to Israel. They were the children of Esau, who is always symbolic of the flesh. The prophet is saying, "God will set a limit to the punishment of His own. He never drives them too far. He never disciplines them too harshly. There is a limit. The punishment is accomplished. He will keep them in exile no longer, but as to the flesh, it has been utterly set aside and Edom will be punished."

Lamentations 5:19 brings us another flash of insight:

Chapter 4: God never disciplines too harshly

> *You, O LORD, reign forever;*
> *your throne endures from generation to generation.*

Jeremiah discovers that though human beings may perish in sorrow, God endures. And because God endures, the great purpose and workings of God endure. God never does anything temporarily. All He does endures forever. Jeremiah sees that what God has taught him in his grief will have a practical use. Even if he were to die in the midst of his grief, God's purposes endure. God is simply preparing now for a work yet to come, hundreds and thousands of years hence.

God is not limited by time. He is eternal. His throne, His authority, endures to all generations. In practical terms, the prophet is realizing that after he has been through this time of grief, he will have learned a truth about God that will make him absolutely impervious to any other kind of test. He is now ready for anything. And in God's great purpose there will be an opportunity to use that strength.

I often think of those words of our Lord recorded in Luke 14, when He tells His disciples two parables about counting the cost. One involved the building of a tower: Who would begin such a large construction project without first sitting down and figuring up the cost to make sure that the job, once begun, could be completed? In another parable, He tells of a king who went out to do battle with an army of ten thousand and met an opposing king coming against him with an army of twenty thousand. Jesus said, "Will he not first sit down and consider whether he is able with ten thousand men to oppose the one coming against him with twenty thousand? If he is not able, he will . . . ask for terms of peace" (Luke 14:31–32).

We usually interpret this to mean that, before choosing to become a Christian, we should think it through and count the cost. But that's not what the Lord is saying. He is saying, "I, the Lord, have counted the cost. I don't begin to build, nor do I go out to do battle, without making sure I have what it takes to finish the job."

In this life, we are engaged in a great cosmic battle. God has landed His troops on a beachhead called Earth. You and I and everyone else in His church are camped before the gates of hell. We are carrying out His assault against Satan's stronghold, and God has promised that the gates of Satan's stronghold will not prevail against us, His church. If He sends us against such a great foe—an enemy of inhuman cleverness and ruthlessness—He must be sure that we who follow Him are soldiers He can depend on. He wants soldiers who can withstand trials and hardships, who do not wilt and fold up in the heat of battle. He has counted the cost of this cosmic war, and He has sized us up; now we are going through His boot camp, learning the lessons to prepare us for the conflict ahead.

When we learn the lessons of sorrow, when we have been emboldened and empowered by the therapy of trouble, when we have learned how to handle and grow through heartache and desolation of spirit in this limited way, then we become soldiers He can depend on. We become prepared so that nothing can overthrow us. We become unconquerable in the battle for the subjugation and occupation of the universe.

What lies ahead for you and me? What battles is He even now mapping out in the heavenly war room? Isn't God preparing us even now to do a mightier work in the future? Isn't He getting us ready to carry on a conflict that will extend to the uttermost reaches of this vast universe of ours? Of course He is. He never creates anything without intending to use it.

God can use even our pain and sorrow. As we face up to the lessons of this life, as we add our laments to the great lamentations of Jeremiah, we grow deeper and stronger in the qualities that truly count in this life and the life to come: faith, courage, obedience. God never does anything without a purpose. Praise God, you and I are a part of His plan, His purpose. Whatever our pain and grief today, we know that a day is coming when we will share in His final victory.

Flaming Wheels and Living Bones

The French philosopher Montaigne once observed, "Every man carries within himself the history of the world." In other words, history is simply a record, inscribed upon the world, of what is already written in the confines of the human heart. The history of the world is only an extension of any human life. The book of Ezekiel demonstrates this principle, telling the story of an individual man, Ezekiel, which is also the story of the nation Israel and the story of the human race. Most importantly, it is also the story of your life and mine, which is why this book is so immensely important and practical for our lives today.

The history of the world is only an extension of any human life

Ezekiel was a captive in the land of Babylon. He had been carried away by the forces of King Nebuchadnezzar when Babylon conquered and captured the nation of Judah, the southern kingdom—exactly as predicted in Jeremiah's great prophecy. Ezekiel, then, was the first of the two great prophets of the captivity (the other was Daniel). Ezekiel prophesied during the first twenty or twenty-five years of the seventy-year period of Israel's captivity.

The book begins with a tremendous vision of God, because all life starts with God. The greatest fact in human history, the greatest fact in all existence, is God. Anyone who wants to think logically about life must always begin with God. That, after all, is where the Bible begins: "In the beginning, God . . . ." The book of Ezekiel begins, then, with a vision of God. If your heart needs to be set on fire by the revelation of the character and glory of God, read Ezekiel—the prophet who saw the glory of God. Here is the structure of the book:

The Commissioning of Ezekiel
(Ezekiel 1–3)

1.	Ezekiel's vision of the glory of God— the creatures and wheels	1
2.	Ezekiel is sent to preach to Israel	2–3

The Coming Judgment against Judah
(Ezekiel 4–24)

3.	The signs of judgment against Judah	4–5
4.	Judgment against idolatry	6
5.	The coming Babylonian conquest	7
6.	Visions of coming judgment	8–9
7.	Departure of the glory of God	10
8.	The evil rulers and the faithful remnant	11:1–21
9.	Departure of God's glory from the Mount of Olives	11:22–25
10.	Signs and parables of coming judgment	12–24
	A. The signs of Ezekiel's exile and trembling	12
	B. Condemnation of false prophets	13
	C. Condemnation of idolatrous elders	14
	D. Parable of the vine	15
	E. Parable of Israel's marriage	16
	F. Parable of the eagles	17
	G. The judgment of individual sin	18
	H. Parable of the lioness and her cubs; the parable of the uprooted vine	19
	I. Review of God's past dealings with Israel and hope of future restoration	20:1–44
	J. Signs of judgment against Jerusalem	20:45–24:27

The Coming Judgment against the Gentile Nations
(Ezekiel 25–32)

The Coming Restoration of Israel (Ezekiel 33–48)

11.	Ezekiel, the watchman	33
12.	The false shepherds contrasted with the true shepherd	34
13.	The judgment of Edom	35
14.	The restoration of Israel and the vision of the dry bones	36–37

The book opens dramatically with the vision that God gave to Ezekiel by the river Chebar in the land of Babylon:

> *I looked, and I saw a windstorm coming out of the north—an immense cloud with flashing lightning and surrounded by brilliant light. The center of the fire looked like glowing metal, and in the fire was what looked like four living creatures (1:4–5).*

These are among the strangest creatures described in Scripture. Each has four faces—the face of a man, the face of an eagle, the face of an ox, and the face of a lion. These four faces looked out in all directions.

After Ezekiel saw the four living creatures, he saw wheel-shaped objects. You may recall the words of the old spiritual, which was derived from these verses: "Ezekiel saw a wheel, way up in the middle of the air; The big wheel ran by faith and the little wheel ran by the grace of God, a wheel in a wheel, away in the middle of the air." Ezekiel saw that these wheels were turning, one wheel within the other. As he watched he also saw a firmament above, shining in splendor. Higher than the firmament, as he lifted his eyes, he saw a throne. Seated on the throne was a man.

You may have already noticed the profound similarities between Ezekiel's vision and John's vision in the book of Revelation. John also saw four living creatures. He, too, saw a man on a throne (see Rev. 4:1–6). In both Ezekiel and Revelation we have visions of the greatness and majesty of God told in rich symbolic imagery.

It is only natural to wonder what all of these symbols mean. Yet, much as we would like to, we simply can't interpret all of these symbols and images because there is a mystery to the person of God. Some of these symbols can be unlocked by comparing them with other passages of Scripture; others are more difficult and obscure. But one thing is sure: In even the most obscure of these symbols, we know that Ezekiel glimpses the immensity, the authority, and the irresistible power of God.

The four living creatures illuminate God's character for us. These creatures with the faces of a lion, a man, an ox, and an eagle, represent certain qualities in Scripture. A lion always depicts sovereignty, supremacy—"the king of the beasts." A man is the picture of intelligence, of understanding, of wisdom. An ox is the symbol of servanthood, of sacrifice. And an eagle represents power and deity, soaring over all creation.

Ezekiel's revelation of Christ

In both Ezekiel and Revelation we have visions of the greatness and majesty of God told in rich symbolic imagery

Even the most obscure symbols provide glimpses of the immensity, the authority, and the irresistible power of God

It is significant that the four gospels present exactly these same qualities in their portrayal of Jesus Christ. He appears first in the gospel of Matthew as a lion, as the sovereign king. He appears in the gospel of Mark as the servant, the ox. In the gospel of Luke, He is man in His intelligence, in His insight, in His understanding of life. And in the gospel of John, He is deity, depicted here as an eagle. These four symbols, taken together, reflect the character of Jesus Christ.

Even though Ezekiel, from his limited Old Testament vantage point, cannot fully understand the significance of all that he sees, we know from our New Testament perspective that he glimpsed the glory of God as it is revealed in the face of Jesus Christ. As Paul says in 2 Corinthians 4:6, "God, who said, 'Let light shine out of darkness,' made his light shine in our hearts to give us the light of the knowledge of the glory of God in the face of Christ."

In the first three chapters, God commissions Ezekiel as His prophet by disclosing to him a powerful, soul-shattering vision of His own glory and majesty. In these opening chapters, God instructs Ezekiel and gives him a mantle of responsibility.

Human degradation

The vision of God's departing glory

Next, in chapters 4 through 24, Ezekiel moves through a series of prophecies dealing with the failure of the human race in general and the nation of Israel in particular. As the vision continues, Ezekiel sees the glory of God departing from the temple in Jerusalem, leaving the inner court and moving to the outer court (ch. 10), then rising and moving out to the Mount of Olives and toward the sky (ch. 11).

This prophecy was fulfilled when our Lord moved out of the temple, down across the Kidron Valley, up the side of the Mount of Olives, and into the Garden of Gethsemane. And later, after the Crucifixion and the Resurrection, He ascended from the Mount of Olives and departed into glory.

In chapters 12 through 24, Ezekiel tells how God struggles with His people, how He seeks to win them and awaken them to the foolishness of turning their backs on Him. They go through experiences of heartache and punishment as God seeks to bring them to their senses, to show them their need of fellowship with Him, and that without Him they are doomed to sink deeper into folly and degradation.

God charges the prophet to convey His message in various symbolic and dramatic ways. On one occasion, in chapter 4, God asks Ezekiel to lie on his left side for 390 days (more than a year!) and then to lie on his right side for 40 days. This symbolizes the 390 years that God struggled to bring this nation to its senses and the final 40 years when judgment was imminent. God kept His hand back from judgment all those years, until at last He allowed Nebuchadnezzar to come in and sweep the people away, sack the city, desolate the temple, and take the people into the land of Babylon.

When human beings choose to avoid the God who created them, He must pronounce judgment. If we neglect God, who is essential to our being, and we refuse to respond to His love and grace, the only thing left for us is to experience the consequences of turning our backs to Him.

Principalities and powers

In this prophecy, Ezekiel pronounces judgment on both visible and invisible forces. He sees through the outer appearances of people and nations to the spiritual forces that motivate and drive them. In chapter 28 we find a remarkable passage in which the prophet declares judgment upon the kingdoms of Tyre and Sidon. He speaks of the *prince* of Tyre and of a personage *behind* this prince—the king of Tyre.

Many Bible scholars have concluded that Ezekiel is talking about both the prince of the city—a ruling human being—and a sinister spiritual being that he calls the king of Tyre. This king symbolizes the principalities and powers mentioned in the New Testament: the world rulers of this present darkness who manipulate people and events on earth, producing the daily horrors we witness in our newspapers and on TV. The king of Tyre, then, is a satanic power.

Chapter 28 also contains a passage that many Bible scholars believe represents the fall of Satan himself. This is one of only two passages in the Bible that describes the fall of Satan:

> *Your heart became proud on account of your beauty, and you corrupted your wisdom because of your splendor. So I threw you to the earth; I made a spectacle of you before kings. By your many sins and dishonest trade you have desecrated your sanctuaries. So I made a fire come out from you, and it consumed you, and I reduced you to ashes on the ground in the sight of all who were watching (28:17–18).*

The reason for Satan's fall is given in Isaiah 14, where the Prince of Darkness says "I will" five times. The *will*—whether a human will or a demonic will—is the source of sin and destruction whenever it is set against the good and perfect will of God. The defiant statement "I will" is a statement of pride, and in Ezekiel 28, we see how God judges pride, the rebellious exaltation of the self above God and against God.

Dry bones

Next, the prophet turns to the grace of God, which powerfully restores the dead to life. In chapter 37, Ezekiel relates the amazing vision of the Valley of the Dry Bones. He sees the bones join together at the command of God—yet there is no breath in them. Then God breathes on them and they come to life! This is a picture of what God intends to do with the nation Israel. From God's viewpoint, Israel is a valley of bone-dry death—and it has been that way for nineteen long centuries. But a day is coming, says the Lord, when God will breathe upon this nation. Like those dry bones, Israel will receive new life, and God will use the nation of Israel as the cornerstone of His reestablished kingdom on earth.

In chapters 38 and 39, the prophet looks into the far-distant future, to the last attack upon Israel. In that battle, Israel's enemies will be met by heavenly forces. There, on the mountains of Israel, the godless nations will be judged, destroyed, and buried for all time.

Then, beginning in chapter 40, Ezekiel describes the restoration of the temple of the Lord's millennial kingdom. In this vision, the prophet is shown the temple in precise detail: The Shekinah glory of God returns to the Holy of Holies and is established there once more.

The vision of God's returning glory

The book closes with the wonderful passage in chapter 47 that describes Ezekiel's vision of God's throne. Underneath the throne comes the river of God, flowing majestically through the temple, out the eastern side, down across the land, and gently spilling into the Dead Sea to heal its waters. It is a marvelous picture of the healing, cleansing, restoring Spirit of God in the day of the millennial kingdom.

Practical meaning

The literal interpretation of Ezekiel is that it is a prophecy of Israel's restoration. But that does not exhaust the meaning of this book by any means. This entire story can be applied not only to Israel's history and future, but to our own lives in an intensely practical way. What God is doing on a large scale in the history of the world, He is also ready to do on the intimate scale of your life.

God wants to call the dry bones of your empty existence together and breathe life into your soul. He wants to reverse the process of degradation and disintegration in your life and to heal you by the grace of Jesus Christ and the power of the Holy Spirit. In addition to salvation, the forgiveness of sins, and the gift of eternal life, God wants us all to experience abundant life every day.

Through this passage, God invites us to experience the glorious ideal manhood and womanhood that He intended for us from the beginning of creation. He wants us to rise up and walk in His power, alive and energized by His Spirit, conquering His enemies by His arm of strength, showing forth His power by the way we live our lives.

Finally, in chapter 47, we see a wonderful picture of God's restored temple—and we see it restored in the lives of human beings. Now what is God's temple in us? In the New Testament, Paul says:

What agreement is there between the temple of God and idols? For we are the temple of the living God. As God has said: "I will live with them and walk among them, and I will be their God, and they will be my people" (2 Cor. 6:16).

God has chosen to dwell within the human spirit. That spirit was made to be a holy of holies in which the living God takes up residence. The secret of a rich, full, satisfying life—a life of genuine excitement and continuing significance—is to live by the limitless resources of the Holy Spirit of God. The entire thrust of the book is summed up in this passage:

The man brought me back to the entrance of the temple, and I saw water coming out from under the threshold of the temple toward the east (for the temple faced east). The water was coming down from under the south side of the temple, south of the altar. He then brought me out through the north gate and led me around the outside to the outer gate facing east, and the water was flowing from the south side.

As the man went eastward with a measuring line in his hand, he measured off a thousand cubits and then led me through water that was ankle-deep. He measured off another thousand cubits and led me through water that was knee-deep. He measured off another thousand and led me through water that was up to the waist. He measured off another thousand, but now it was a river that I could not cross, because the water had risen and was deep enough to swim in—a river that no one could cross. He asked me, "Son of man, do you see this?"

Then he led me back to the bank of the river. When I arrived there, I saw a great number of trees on each side of the river. He said to me, "This water flows toward the eastern region and goes down into the Arabah, where it enters the Sea. When it empties into the Sea, the water there becomes fresh. Swarms of living creatures will live wherever the river flows. There will be large numbers of fish, because this water flows there and makes the salt water fresh; so where the river flows everything will live" (47:1–9).

What does this passage remind you of? Don't you hear a loud, resonant echo here of the word of Jesus from John 7? For these are the words He spoke when He stood at the temple on the last day of the feast:

On the last and greatest day of the Feast, Jesus stood and said in a loud voice, "If anyone is thirsty, let him come to me and drink. Whoever believes in me, as the Scripture has said, streams of living water will flow from within him." By this he meant the Spirit, whom those who believed in him were later to receive (John 7:37–39).

This river of living water is the primary resource of the Christian life. It deserves our deeper attention and exploration.

As the prophet watches, he sees that this river of living water makes its way down past the altar, the place of sacrifice. And one of the great truths that we need to learn as Christians is that we can never drink of the river of the Spirit unless we are willing to do so by way of the cross of Calvary. Jesus was sacrificed on the altar of Calvary, and we must be willing to crucify our own fleshly desires, sins, pride, and ambitions on that same altar. We cannot receive the water of life by our own efforts or our own righteousness. It pours from a fountain called Calvary.

Second, notice the power of this river. It has quickly grown large enough to swim in, yet there is no other river adding to it. No tributary streams are coming in. It is a gushing, mighty torrent of life that comes directly from God.

Notice that God leads Ezekiel into this revelation step-by-step: Five times in this passage, he says, "He led me . . . ." Is God leading you? Have you ever had that experience? Ezekiel is led one step at a time, and each step takes him deeper and deeper.

The first step is to the place where the waters are ankle deep—a picture of the individual who has experienced only a shallow sense of God's grace and power in his or her life. This person is a Christian, but only what the Scriptures call a carnal Christian (see Rom. 8). Such a person has not learned how to live the Spirit-derived life—a life of obedience, trust, surrender, and peace. A lot of people want to wade just ankle-deep into the grace of God. They don't want to go in all the way.

But then the prophet says, "He . . . led me through water that was knee-deep." You may have experienced "knee-deep" Christianity, the place of hungering and thirsting for God, the place of seeking His face. At this stage, a Christian is not satisfied with being merely born again, but hungers for something deeper.

And Ezekiel does go deeper. "He . . . led me through water that was up to the waist." Now the waters of the Spirit are beginning to possess him. There is less of him now and more of the grace of God. The King James Version uses the word *loins*, and the loins are always the symbol of power. Ezekiel has come to a place where his own power has been swallowed up in the waters of God's power. He has grasped the fact that it is " 'not by might nor by power, but by my Spirit,' says the LORD Almighty" (Zech. 4:6) that the Christian life is lived. It is not Ezekiel's human desire to do something for God but his Spirit-led submission and dependence upon God that leads to abundant life.

But Ezekiel had not gone as far as he needed to go. He had to take the final plunge into the river of God's life: "Now it was a river that I could not cross, because the water had risen and was deep enough to swim in—a river that no one could cross." Here is a man who is utterly committed. He is in over his head. He is swept along in the current of God's grace.

Notice how this river affects the land. As the prophet is led back along the banks he says, "When I arrived there, I saw a great number of trees on each side of the river." The land has become fruitful. The barrenness of the land has been healed. Everywhere the river flows, things begin to sprout, bloom, and hum with life.

John sees the same river in Revelation: "Then the angel showed me the river of the water of life, as clear as crystal, flowing from the throne of God and of the Lamb down the middle of the great street of the city." (Rev. 22:1–2). The river flows right through the middle of life. Have you found the river of the Spirit yet?

Until we have taken that plunge, life is nothing but a plodding, dogged, difficult path full of frustrations and spiritual defeats. But when we immerse ourselves in the mighty, gushing torrent of the rivers of living water, once the Spirit of God flows through us and over us like a rushing, life-giving river, then the entire Christian life begins to make sense.

The prophet Ezekiel understands this, and he closes this beautiful book with a description of the temple (which may ultimately symbolize the resurrection body, the new temple of God). Look at the last verse of the prophecy:

> *"The distance all around will be 18,000 cubits. And the name of the city from that time on will be: THE LORD IS THERE" (Ezek. 48:35).*

May this be our
goal: to become
God's city, God's
eternal dwelling
place, God's temple
through which His
river of life flows

May this be our goal: to become God's city, God's eternal dwelling place, God's temple through which His river of life flows. May we plunge ourselves fully into the river of His Spirit, immersing ourselves in the refreshing coolness of its life-giving depths, discovering its healing power for our lives today—and the life to come.

On The Way To The Future

P eople are endlessly fascinated by Bible prophecy. The prophecies of Daniel and Revelation have been sensationalized into bestselling books and major motion pictures and have been heralded (usually in grossly distorted form) in the headlines of supermarket tabloids. People want to know what the future holds—especially if the future is filled with events as bizarre and sensational as a Japanese monster movie, as many of these books and films make it seem!

But biblical prophecy is serious business. God did not send visions to men like Ezekiel, Daniel, and John just to provide entertainment. God gave us the books of Daniel and Revelation, as well as the other prophetic books of the Bible, to unfold His program of history. They are meant not only to inform us about the future, but to instruct us for the present. God gave us these books so that we would know how to live today with tomorrow in mind. He gave them to us to sober us and ground us in His eternal perspective on human events and heavenly events.

Daniel and Revelation have not yet been fulfilled. These two books, one from the Old and one from the New Testament, remarkably complement each other in their symmetry and harmony. The book of Revelation explains the book of Daniel. The book of Daniel lays the basis for the book of Revelation. If you would like to know God's program for the future, you must first understand the book of Daniel.

God gave the prophetic books to inform us about the future and to instruct us about the present

The book of Revelation explains the book of Daniel; the book of Daniel lays the basis for the book of Revelation

ADVENTURING
THROUGH THE
BIBLE

**How to
understand
prophecy**

Knowledge of the future can be a dangerous thing. Imagine what would happen if you possessed the ability to know what will happen tomorrow or next week. Think what an advantage it would give you in the stock market, in the buying of insurance, and in other practical matters of life. But would you really want to know in advance all the sorrows and hurts that would come your way in life? Jesus had good reason for saying, "Do not worry about tomorrow, for tomorrow will worry about itself. Each day has enough trouble of its own" (Matt. 6:34).

God does not unfold the future to us in specific detail. He does not tell your individual future or mine. What He does show us in the prophetic books of the Bible is the general trend of events, the outline of His program, and the way His program is sure to end. Anyone who investigates prophecy in a careful, objective way will find significant and helpful information about both future and present events in the world. Everything that is happening is working out God's purposes on earth. We can understand the present only in light of God's prophetic program.

God has taken two
precautions in His
unveiling of the
future

God has taken two precautions in His unveiling of the future. First, He has clothed these prophetic passages in symbolic language. He has given them to us in figurative form. That is why we see such strange and even frightening images in Daniel and Revelation: startling signs in nature, strange beasts with many different heads and horns sticking out here and there, images of shattering worldwide events, and more.

1. He has clothed
these prophetic
passages in
symbolic language

These prophetic images and symbols have always puzzled people. You can't just sit down with the book of Daniel or the book of Revelation and read them through and understand them as you would a novel. You have to study them, taking the whole of the Bible into account in order to interpret the symbols in these books. This is one of the locks that God has placed on these books to keep the merely curious and sensation-seeking minds from getting into these books without an adequate background in Scripture. You cannot understand what is going on in them without first knowing a great deal about the rest of the Bible. God's program for the future is hidden from us until we spend time understanding the signs, and these books are full of signs.

2. God presents
moral teaching
before prophecy

A second precaution that God has taken in Daniel, and even more especially in the book of Revelation, is that He doesn't introduce the prophetic section first. Instead, He brings us through six chapters of moral teaching. He wants to lead us into an understanding of the moral character that He requires of us before the prophetic program can begin to make sense. To understand what the prophetic program means, you must first grasp the moral lessons of the first part of the book. There are no shortcuts.

Even more importantly, after you grasp the first six chapters intellectually, you must integrate them experientially into your life. That is the beauty of God's Word: It can't be understood by the intellect alone. It must be understood by the entire being. You can sit down with prophetic outlines of Daniel and Revelation, draw charts of future history, spend time explaining to people what all these symbols and events mean and how God's program is going to be accomplished. You can analyze eschatology and doctrine down to a gnat's eyebrow—but unless you have incorporated the spiritual lessons of the first part of Daniel into your own life, you'll find nothing in the rest of the book to enrich your life.

The Lord Jesus Himself made this clear during His Olivet Discourse when His disciples asked Him what the symbol of His return to earth would be. Jesus said, "When you see standing in the holy place 'the abomination that causes desolation,' spoken of through the prophet Daniel—let the reader understand—then let those who are in Judea flee to the mountains." In other words, "Get out of the city of Jerusalem, because horrible things will happen there. If you stay in that city, great tribulation will be upon you."

Note that when the passage says, "let the reader understand," it means, "Don't read through the prophetic passages carelessly or superficially. You have to grasp the full import of Scripture if you are to recognize the abomination of desolation when it comes." The world, in its superficial approach to truth will be uncomprehending when that day comes. People will cry, "Peace, peace!" when there is no peace, and destruction will come upon them. They will be swept away just as the people of Noah's day were swept away by the flood. Jesus does not want us to be destroyed in our ignorance, so He encourages us to seek a real understanding—practical, applied, experiential understanding of the truths of Scripture.

This book easily divides into two sections. The first six chapters, which are devoted to moral and spiritual instruction, are a history of the prophet Daniel himself and his friends in the land of Babylon. It is a story of faith lived out in the fiery crucible of a hostile world.

If you find yourself struggling to live the Christian life amid the pressures, hostility, temptation, and persecution of a non-Christian world, then the first six chapters of Daniel are must reading for you. If you work in an office surrounded by godless coworkers who take the name of the Lord in vain every few minutes or if your employer pressures you to cut corners or commit unethical acts on the job or if your friends challenge you to compromise your faith or your morality or if the law of the land tells you that you cannot be a witness to your Lord or

The structure of Daniel

read your Bible—then the first six chapters of Daniel will guide and comfort you.

These chapters are especially valuable to teenagers who must stand against peer pressure and temptation, because these chapters record the story of a group of teenagers who are taken captive by King Nebuchadnezzar and carried off to the land of Babylon. As they began their career of faith, they do so with a total lack of understanding of life and with all the insecurities that are normal for teenagers in a hostile environment. Just as today's youth must stand against peer pressure, drugs, illicit sex, and occultism, these teenagers had to take a life-or-death stand against the king himself. Daniel and his teenage friends are perhaps the strongest, most encouraging role models in all of Scripture for today's young people.

Here is an outline of the book of Daniel:

The Life of Daniel in Babylon (Daniel 1)

God's Plan for the Gentiles (Daniel 2–7)

God's Plan for Israel (Daniel 8–12)

Standing under pressure

In chapter 1, these young men—Daniel, Hananiah, Mishael, and Azariah (respectively renamed Belteshazzar, Shadrach, Meshach, and Abednego by their Babylonian captors)—are pressured to change their diet. Ordinarily, diet would not be considered as a particularly significant issue, but God had already instructed these young men as to what they could and could not eat. The foods that God had told them not to eat are the very foods that the Babylonians required them to eat as prisoners of the king of Babylon.

What could these young men do? King Nebuchadnezzar is an immensely powerful tyrant. The Bible itself records that no human king ever had or ever would command as much authority as King Nebuchadnezzar.

What kind of character did this king have? Later on in his reign, he demonstrates his absolute cruelty in killing the sons of Judah's king before their father's eyes—then having the father's eyes put out so that this horror would be the last thing those eyes would see. Nebuchadnezzar had another man roasted slowly to death over a fire. This king was an expert in torture; his cruel imagination fueled his evil deeds. And Nebuchadnezzar's word was absolute law. So these young teenagers faced this moral test knowing that they had to either comply with the king's demands or risk an unimaginably horrible death.

What could they do? Under such pressure, should they heed the advice, "When in Rome, do as the Romans do"? It's the same argument that people use today: "Everybody else is doing it." What could be so wrong with eating a ham sandwich with the Babylonians? Especially if it would save you from torture and death? Who would know? Who would care?

Yet, laying their very lives on the line, they choose to stand fast in honor of God. And God gives them the grace to maintain their stand despite that pressure. As a result, they are exalted and given positions of authority and responsibility in the kingdom of their captivity—a turn of events that reminds us strongly of the way in which God exalted Joseph when he maintained his own integrity and obedience to God.

We will see, however, that the pressure does not end for these young men. It continues and even intensifies as we proceed through the book of Daniel.

In chapter 2 we see part of the reason that God allows these young men to come under such intense testing. King Nebuchadnezzar dreams one night of a great image of a man with a strange body. The image has a head of gold, shoulders of silver, midsection of bronze, legs of iron, and feet of clay and iron. The next morning, the king calls in the wise men and asks them to tell him not only the interpretation but the dream as well.

A troubling dream

Despite the fact that the king gives ample motivation to the astrologers, soothsayers, and sorcerers—they must interpret the dream or be executed!—they are unable to come up with anything. Obviously, if the king won't tell them the dream, then they can't dream up an interpretation—and as a result, their lives are forfeit.

Though Daniel has not been asked to interpret the king's dream, he is considered one of the wise men who are now under threat of the king's death penalty. When he asks the captain of the king's guard why he and the other Babylonian wise men are to be executed, the captain explains the situation. Daniel pleads for the lives of the other wise men and asks to be brought before the king to reveal and interpret the dream. In this situation, as in chapter 1, God's man comes through, proving that he is willing to stand and obey God despite the pressures.

God is full of surprises

God is full of surprises. Mere superficial pressures never determine life's outcome. The result that seems logically inevitable as you face a situation is not necessarily what will happen if you trust in the invisible God who rules visible human affairs. That is the great lesson not only of this chapter, but of this entire book, as Daniel beautifully expresses in this prayer to God:

> *"Praise be to the name of God for ever and ever; wisdom and power are his. He changes times and seasons; he sets up kings and deposes them. He gives wisdom to the wise and knowledge to the discerning. He reveals deep and hidden things; he knows what lies in darkness, and light dwells with him" (2:20–22).*

If you are intimately linked with the living God of the universe, you don't need to worry about what the crowd is doing—or even what the king is doing. The same God who created the world is able to carry you through and to work out every situation of your life, no matter how impossible it may seem. That same theme is repeated five different times through these first six chapters.

Daniel doesn't just reveal Nebuchadnezzar's dream and its interpretation. God and Daniel have the king over the barrel, and so, inspired by God, Daniel obliges the most powerful ruler on earth to recognize the absolute, sovereign government of God.

You may not realize it, but you are in exactly the same position today that Daniel was in so long ago! The world lives with the idea that there is no God or that if He does exist He has no real power. He doesn't do anything. He doesn't change history. He doesn't affect human lives. He doesn't enter into situations and make any difference. That is the world's philosophy.

But every believer who walks faithfully—obeying what God says regardless of threats, temptations, or pressure—is eventually placed in a pivotal position and is given the privilege of opening the eyes of men and women to the fact that God exists, that He is not dead, that He is at work in the world, and that He must be reckoned with.

In chapter 3, we have the story of the fiery furnace. The young men are commanded to bow down before the image Nebuchadnezzar has erected, a prideful creation of the image in his dream. Because Nebuchadnezzar was told that he represented the head of gold, that he was the great king of earth, he proudly commanded that an image be erected on the plain. It was a huge image, as tall as some of our NASA booster rockets that send people into space.

The king gathers the whole crowd, including these three faithful young men, on the plain. All are ordered to bow down and worship the image. In order to inspire their worship, a great furnace has been erected at the other end of the plain; all who refuse to bow to the image will die in the fire. And he's provided other inducements as well.

There is a band playing a variety of instruments, many of which we do not recognize anymore: horn, pipe, lyre, trigon, harp, sackbut, dulcimer, and more. At the first chord of music from the band, all the people fall down and worship the image, just as they have been commanded.

All, that is, except the three young men—Shadrach, Meshach, and Abednego. When they are brought before Nebuchadnezzar, he orders them to fall down. They reply instantly yet respectfully that they have no need to think over their answer: They cannot obey the king of Babylon, because they must obey an even higher King. Here, in Daniel 3:17–18, we see an amazing statement not only of obedience to God, but of faith and trust in Him as well:

> *"If we are thrown into the blazing furnace, the God we serve is able to save us from it, and he will rescue us from your hand, O king. But even if he does not, we want you to know, O king, that we will not serve your gods or worship the image of gold you have set up."*

Notice those words of faith: "But even if he does not . . . ." These young men are willing to trust God to deliver them from the fiery furnace—or to take them through the fiery furnace. They leave the details of their fate to God, trusting Him for both life and death. Whatever happens, whatever the king chooses to do to them, they will not worship Babylonian gods nor the golden image that Nebuchadnezzar has erected.

These young men have learned that some things are more important than life. It is better to be dead and obedient to God than alive and disobedient to Him. An individual profits more from walking with God and dying with God than by living after disobeying Him. And God honors these men in a mighty way, taking them through the furnace and beyond the furnace. In fact, they emerge from the furnace not warmed, not toasted, not singed, and without even the scent of fire upon them!

The testimony of the king

In chapter 4 we have the conversion of Nebuchadnezzar. This chapter is, in effect, the testimony of the greatest king and tyrant who ever lived. It is the story of how God broke the pride of his heart by allowing his kingly pride to take him to the point of madness. Nebuchadnezzar actually went out and ate grass in the field for seven years. His throne was preserved, but he acted like an animal. This is what always happens to human beings when they choose to reject fellowship with the living God: they become beastly and brutish.

Then the king tells how his reason was restored to him by the grace of God. His closing word in this chapter is a great testimony of his faith, of how God humbled him and brought him back:

> Now I, Nebuchadnezzar, praise and exalt and glorify the King of heaven, because everything he does is right and all his ways are just. And those who walk in pride he is able to humble (4:37).

Who brought the great king to his senses? God, of course, yet in a very real sense, God used Daniel and his friends to win and change the heart of the greatest king of the greatest empire that the world has ever seen.

The handwriting on the wall— and more

As chapter 5 opens, we see the luxury and licentiousness of the kingdom of Babylon. Yet amid all this pleasure-seeking and selfishness, Daniel (who has lived through three empires) is still the prime minister. In this chapter, God uses him to make another crucial interpretation. As the chapter opens, King Belshazzar, son of Nebuchadnezzar, throws a party. The king, his wives and concubines, and his guests defile the gold and silver goblets that had been taken from the temple in Jerusalem by drinking wine from them and using them to toast and praise false gods. Suddenly a disembodied human finger appears and writes on the plaster of the wall, frightening the king nearly to death. The king calls for his magicians and astrologers to decipher the handwriting on the wall, and Daniel is brought before him. Daniel interprets the inscription that reads: MENE, MENE, TEKEL, PARSIN. It is a judgment on Belshazzar for his arrogance:

"This what these words mean: Mene: *God has numbered the days of your reign and brought it to an end.* Tekel: *You have been weighed on the scales and found wanting.* Peres: *Your kingdom is divided and given to the Medes and Persians" (Dan. 5:26–28).*

That night, God's judgment is carried out and Belshazzar dies; King Darius ascends to the throne.

This chapter bears out the thesis of the entire book: God is at work in human affairs, and anyone who sees beyond the visible to the invisible and acts accordingly will find that God provides all the strength and support that is required for success.

Chapter 6 is yet another demonstration of God's provision in times of pressure and even seeming hopelessness. This chapter tells of Daniel's ordeal in the lions' den. In an effort to destroy him, Daniel's jealous rivals manipulate King Darius into issuing a decree forbidding anyone to pray to any god or king except Darius. They know it is a decree that Daniel cannot obey—and when they catch him praying to God, they quickly report Daniel's crime to the king. Daniel is sent to the den of lions to die, but God sends His angel to shut the lions' mouths. Daniel is brought out again, delivered by the hand of God. As a result, King Darius issues another decree—this time exalting Daniel's God as the one, true, living God.

Daniel and the lions

The future-focused section of Daniel begins in chapter 7 with the vision of the four beasts. It is interesting that these four beasts cover the same period of time as the four divisions of the image that Nebuchadnezzar had seen in chapter 2. That image had a head of gold, symbolizing the Babylonian kingdom; shoulders of silver, for Medo-Persia; a trunk of bronze, symbolizing the Grecian empire; two legs of iron, representing the two divisions of the Roman empire; and terminating at last in a broken kingdom, characterized by feet of mingled iron and clay. This great prophetic passage outlines history from Daniel's day to a future that is still beyond our own day, to the very end of time and the return of Jesus Christ.

As the prophet watches Nebuchadnezzar's dream, he sees a stone—a stone that has been cut without a human hand—strike the image on its feet and utterly demolish it. The fragments blow away on the wind like chaff, but the stone grows to become a great mountain that fills the entire earth (Dan. 2:34–35). This indicates that when the last kingdom is shattered by a divine agency (not of human hands), it will usher in the worldwide kingdom of God and the reign of Jesus Christ.

In chapter 7, then, the four beasts represent the same kingdoms—but from God's point of view. They are not mighty powers in God's

The prophetic section begins

The vision of the four beasts

sight. They are merely beasts growling and quarreling with each other. Daniel sees these nations struggling against each other, and their struggle culminates in the powerful reign of a single individual over the entire Western world.

In chapter 8 we see the movement of Western history. The ram and the he-goat come together in battle—a picture, as we are later told in chapter 11, of Alexander the Great's conquest and the rise of the Seleucids' kingdom in Syria, in opposition to the Ptolemies in Egypt. These two families occupied the center of history for centuries after the time of Daniel—a mighty struggle between Syria and Egypt, with little Israel caught in the middle. The battle rages back and forth, and today Israel continues to be the most fought-over piece of real estate in the world. More battles have occurred in the land of Israel than in any other spot on the face of the earth, and the last great battle—the battle of Armageddon—will be fought in this region.

The ram and the he-goat

In the midst of this prophecy, in chapter 9, Daniel pours his heart out to God in prayer. The answer to his prayer, in the last section of the chapter, is one of the most remarkable prophecies in the Bible: the prophecy of the seventy weeks. This is the timetable of prophecy concerning the nation Israel. It gives us the principle called "the Great Parenthesis"—the scriptural interpretation proposing that God has interrupted His program for Israel and has inserted this present age in which we live between the first coming and the second coming of the Lord Jesus.

The Seventy Weeks and "the Great Parenthesis"

This indeterminate period, which has now spanned more than nineteen hundred years, comes between the sixty-ninth week of years and the seventieth week of Daniel's prophecy. The seventieth week, a week of seven years, is yet to be fulfilled for Israel. As you read of this, you will see that this is what the book of Revelation and other prophetic passages call "the great tribulation," the time of Jacob's trouble. It lies ahead. It has been broken off from the other sixty-nine weeks and is yet to be fulfilled.

The coming of Jesus — and final judgment

Chapter 10 illuminates the unseen things that stand behind the things that are seen. This is another great revelation of God's sovereign government in the affairs of humanity—and it is the explanation for the events of history. What causes the things that happen today? Clearly, there are unseen forces at work, and these forces are starkly revealed to Daniel.

Chapter 11 is one of the most remarkable chapters in the Bible. It records prophecy that, for the most part, has been fulfilled in detail. It foretells the struggle between the king of Syria and the king of Egypt that took place after Daniel's day—prophecy fulfilled. These historic events are described in great detail and cover two or three hundred years of history. A number of outstanding historical figures are predicted here, including Cleopatra.

We come to an interesting break at Daniel 11:35–36, in which the angel says to Daniel:

> *"Some of the wise will stumble, so that they may be refined, purified and made spotless until the time of the end, for it will still come at the appointed time.*
>
> *"The king will do as he pleases. He will exalt and magnify himself above every god and will say unheard-of things against the God of gods. He will be successful until the time of wrath is completed, for what has been determined must take place."*

Here begins a passage that deals with that seventieth week of Daniel, the tribulation period that is yet to be fulfilled—the time of the end, the last days, the ultimate arrangement of earth's kingdoms just before the return of Jesus Christ. This passage predicts an invasion of Palestine and a counterinvasion from Egypt in the south, and then the meeting of two great armies in the land of Israel and the ultimate destruction of those armies among the mountains of Israel. This event is also clearly described in Ezekiel 38 and 39 and the second chapter of Joel—and there are other prophetic references to this event.

The beginning of chapter 12 introduces the greatest event of history yet to be fulfilled: the second coming of Jesus Christ. It is revealed in symbolic language. This is what Daniel hears:

> *"At that time Michael, the great prince who protects your people, will arise. There will be a time of distress such as has not happened from the beginning of nations until then. But at that time your people— everyone whose name is found written in the book—will be delivered"* *(12:1).*

This is followed by a mass resurrection of the dead:

> *"Multitudes who sleep in the dust of the earth will awake: some to everlasting life, others to shame and everlasting contempt"* *(12:2)*

Then the final judgment of God:

> *"Those who are wise will shine like the brightness of the heavens, and those who lead many to righteousness, like the stars for ever and ever. But you, Daniel, close up and seal the words of the scroll until the time of the end. Many will go here and there to increase knowledge"* *(12:3–4).*

Many Bible scholars understand this to be an indication that as we near the last days as described in this passage, that transportation, information, and knowledge will rapidly increase. Clearly, in this jet age, this computer age, this age of mass media and advanced education and the Internet, we see the fulfillment of this prophecy.

The clash of good and evil

In this final section, chapter 12, Daniel asks certain questions of the angel who has revealed these things to him. In return, he is allowed to understand two great forces at work in the world: good and evil. You and I often hear people discussing current events, with newspaper commentators and others constantly pouring into our ears reports of terrible, frightening, tragic events. People often ask, "What is happening? What is going on in this world? Is the world situation getting progressively worse or progressively better?"

Some people make the case that humankind is progressing, that education is advancing, that technology is making life better and better. Others make an equally, if not more, convincing case that advancing technology gives us more advanced ways to kill people, to complicate life, to take away our privacy and our freedom, to strip away our humanity. Yet the book of Daniel makes it clear that we will never understand God's Word and God's work until we accept *both* of those arguments. In Daniel 12:10, Daniel is told:

> *"Many will be purified, made spotless and refined, but the wicked will continue to be wicked. None of the wicked will understand, but those who are wise will understand"* (12:10).

Today evil is more widespread than it has ever been

Today evil is more widespread than it has ever been. The twentieth century, with its two world wars and its various genocidal assaults on humanity, is the most murderous, blood-drenched century in human history—and the twenty-first promises to be no better. The evil of our age is subtle, but it is undeniably widespread and Satan-inspired.

The good of our age is also better than it has ever been

But the good of our age is also better than it has ever been before. Good is more powerful. Its effect in human society in relationship to the evil around it is far greater than it ever has been before.

Good is not going to become so triumphant that evil disappears, nor will evil completely overpower the good

These two contrasting forces are at work in human society, but neither shall overpower the other. Good is not going to become so triumphant that evil finally disappears, nor will evil completely overpower the good—at least not now. Both good and evil are headed for a final conflict: The Bible records in various passages that, at one precise moment in history, God will directly intervene in human affairs. Of the ultimate clash of these two great principles, Daniel is told:

"Blessed is the one who waits for and reaches the end of the 1,335 days.
"As for you, go your way till the end. You will rest, and then at the end of the days you will rise to receive your allotted inheritance" (Dan. 12:12–13).

Ultimately, every nation and every individual serves God—willingly or not. Even if a great king renounces God ten times over, even if he sets himself against God, relentlessly and defiantly, God is sovereign, and He works all events, all human choices, all satanic chaos, into His perfect and beautiful plan. Nebuchadnezzar, Darius, Alexander, Cleopatra, Caesar, Herod, Pilate, Stalin, Hitler, Khruschev, Saddam—none of these world leaders can resist the will of God nor interfere with the plan of God. It rolls irresistibly through time and across the face of the globe, encompassing billions of lives throughout time.

The choice that you and I have is a choice between being willing or unwilling tools in God's hand—whether we receive the blessings that come from obedience or the judgment that issues from rebellion. The good news of Daniel is that our God is a living God, and He is at work in the affairs of human beings and nations. We need not fear, even though the terrors of evil nations rise up around us. God controls everything, and we who walk with God will ultimately overcome. The lions cannot consume us, the fiery furnace cannot scorch, the will of evil kings cannot separate us from the love of King Jesus.

As we step into the last days, the days described in this prophecy, may we step boldly, triumphantly in the strength of our God.

Ultimately, every nation and every individual serves God—willingly or not

Love and The Unfaithful Bride

While in England some years ago, I met an Anglican clergyman who told me about his experiences during the Battle of Britain in World War II. "What bothered me most," he said, "were the signs in the public squares regarding conscription. They read, 'All persons must register for the draft except women, children, idiots, and clergymen.' As a clergyman, I didn't so much mind being included on that list, but I do wish they had at least placed me ahead of the idiots!"

That is the place in which the prophet Hosea finds himself. He is a preacher whose audience is polite to his face but treats him with contempt behind his back. His message is greeted with snickers of derision. He is considered nice-but-harmless, on the same list with the idiots. That's how people usually treat preachers.

But Hosea is not nice-but-harmless. He is a towering figure in Scripture, and his story and his message deserve our attention today, just as he deserved the attention of the people around him in his own day. He spoke of judgment, of the disciplining of the nation of Israel. He warned that God would send the Assyrian nation to kill and destroy the people. The people challenged him and accused him of characterizing God as a vengeful, angry deity.

Hosea tried to explain God's love to them—that genuine love is also a tough and disciplining love. This God of tough love wanted the people to see what they were doing to themselves. If the only way that He could get them to listen was to make life hard for them, He would do so. The people responded exactly as people respond today when they are told of God's tough love—they blamed God and said, in effect, "If God is really a God of love, then why does He allow things to get in such a mess? How could a God of love ever send a ruthless enemy like the Assyrians down upon our land? If God really loves us, He will excuse our sins, not discipline us." Sounds familiar, doesn't it?

Clearly, the book of Hosea is a book for today. Here is an outline of the book:

Hosea's Adulterous Wife (Hosea 1–3)

1. Hosea's marriage to Gomer	1
2. Gomer's adultery	2
3. Gomer's restoration by Hosea, the loving and faithful husband	3

God's Adulterous People, Israel (Hosea 4–14)

4. The adultery-idolatry of Israel	4–5
5. Israel's refusal to repent	6–8
6. Israel judged by God	9–10
7. Israel's restoration by her loving and faithful Lord	11–14

"Minor" Prophets are minor in length, not in importance

Hosea is the first of the twelve "minor prophets" of the Old Testament, Hosea through Malachi. They are called minor not because the messages of these prophets is unimportant, but simply because of their length. I avoid making a strong distinction between the major and minor prophets because I do not want to perpetuate the mistaken idea that these twelve short but powerful books are any less important and relevant than the other books of the Bible. Each has a powerful life-changing message for our fast-paced lives.

Hosea preached to the northern kingdom

Hosea was a young preacher in the nation of Israel, the northern kingdom. He was a contemporary of the prophets Isaiah and Amos, and he composed this book around 755 to 715 B.C. Hosea lived, as we are told in the first verse, during the reigns of Uzziah, Jotham, Ahaz, and Hezekiah—kings of Judah, the southern kingdom, and during the reign of Jeroboam, the son of Joash, the king of Israel.

Jeroboam was one of the wicked kings of Israel and the nation was going through a difficult time when Hosea preached. People were too busy living it up and enjoying the pleasures of life to give any time or thought to God. They wouldn't have put it that way themselves, of course. Instead, they would probably say what most of us say: "My life is so busy. I'd like to have more time for devotions and Christian service and fellowship with believers and Bible study—but my life is just too hectic and crowded right now. The spirit is willing but the flesh is ready for the weekend."

This is the social attitude confronting the prophet Hosea, so it is not surprising that he is discouraged as we meet him in the opening chapter of this book of prophecy. In his discouragement, he goes to God—and God gives him a very strange direction. It might have sounded something like this: "Hosea, I want you to get married." I think Hosea, being a bachelor, probably perked up a bit upon hearing that.

Then God said, "I have a woman picked out for you." When He mentioned her name, Hosea probably felt a surge of excitement because the woman whom God had told him to marry was Gomer, the most beautiful woman in Israel. Hosea was definitely interested.

But there was a downside, a catch, to this marriage. God said to Hosea, "You need to know the whole story about this woman. After you marry her, she will be unfaithful to you. But I want you to marry her anyway." Hosea must have been very puzzled by God's strange command, just as Abraham was puzzled by God's command to take his son out and kill him. God does strange things at times, things we don't understand, things that don't fit into the plans we ourselves would make. Again and again, we discover that His ways are not our ways.

"Your wife will become a common street prostitute," God went on to say, "but she will bear you three children—two boys and a girl. And when they are born I want to name them for you." Hosea then began to understand a little bit of what God was doing. He knew it was customary in Israel to teach by symbols—God often used this method of instructing His people—and he understood that names were very important. God often used the meanings of names to teach Israel certain truths. And now God was planning to use this prophet and his family as an object lesson for His people.

At about the same time, Hosea's friend Isaiah, down in the southern kingdom of Judah, was undergoing a similar experience. Isaiah also had two sons who were given highly significant names. The older boy's name was (are you ready for this?) Mahershalalhashbaz. Mahershalalhashbaz means "haste to the prey" or "haste to the spoil," and it is God's prophetic way of telling the people of Israel that they were in deep trouble. The younger boy's name was Shearjashub, which means "a remnant shall return." That was God's promise to Israel that even though the nation was being taken into captivity, a remnant would come back. Through the names of Isaiah's two sons, God gave Israel both a warning of trouble and a comforting promise that a remnant would return. In the same way, the names of Hosea's sons would also be significant.

HOSEA

God's ways are not our ways

Meaningful names

It was customary to teach by symbols

Isaiah

Jezreel, "castaway"

In obedience to what God had told him, Hosea went courting. Sure enough, Gomer was attracted to this young man and agreed to marry him. At first, their marriage was heaven on earth. Hosea loved this woman. You can't read the prophecy without seeing that. They must have been wonderfully happy together, and then they had their first child. It was a boy, as God had said. Hosea's heart was filled to bursting, and he went to God for the name of the boy. God shocked Hosea by telling him the boy's name should be Jezreel, meaning "castaway"—a name of shame in Israel.

If you turn back to 2 Kings 9:30–37, you find the story of wicked Queen Jezebel, who is judged by God, thrown from a window, and dashed to her death in a courtyard and eaten by dogs; the name of that courtyard from then on is Jezreel, a name of disgrace, and the same name as that of Hosea's firstborn son. The name Jezreel was a warning to the people to turn from their folly, sin, idolatry, and abominable practices, or they would be disgraced and "castaway." They would no longer be Israel; they would be Jezreel.

Lo-Ruhamah, "not loved"

In time, another child was born to Hosea and Gomer—a daughter named Lo-Ruhamah by God. The name means "not loved." Imagine naming your little baby girl "not loved." It meant that God would no longer have mercy and love for His people if they continued their stubborn rebellion. His patience was wearing thin. After some hundreds of years of trying to reach these stubborn people, He was now warning them that they were nearing the end of His patience. A time was coming when He would no longer offer mercy to them but would hand them over to invading armies.

Lo-Ammi, "not my people"

When this little girl was weaned, Gomer conceived again and bore a third child, a boy whom God named Lo-Ammi, or "not my people." God was warning, "You are not my people and I am not your God." God had said that He would name these children as a sign to His people, but there would come a day of restoration:

I will show my love to the one I called "Not my loved one." I will say to those called "Not my people," "You are my people"; and they will say, "You are my God" (2:23).

Even while God was pronouncing judgment, He was offering and demonstrating His love and grace.

A story of shame — and redemption

After this there were no more children in Hosea's household. Gomer began to fulfill the sad prediction that God had made when He had told Hosea to marry her. What a heartbreak it must have been to this young preacher as he heard the whispers that began to circulate about his wife and her activities when he was away on preaching trips. Perhaps his own children mentioned the men who came by the house when Daddy was away. Soon the children were left uncared for while Gomer wasted all her time running around with other men.

One day Hosea came home and found a note from Gomer: She was leaving him and the children to be with the man she really loved. You know how those notes go: "Dear John . . ."

About this time, Hosea's preaching took on a new tone. He still warned of the judgment to come and the fact that God was going to send the Assyrians across the land—but he no longer announced it with thunder. He spoke to them with tears. And he began to speak of a day when love would at last triumph, when Israel's bitter lesson would be learned, and the nation would turn back to its loving God.

The unfaithful wife of Hosea became a vivid, shocking object lesson of what was about to take place in Israel. It unfolded something like this: As Gomer passed from man to man, at last she fell into the hands of a man who was unable to pay for her food and her clothing. Her first lover had given her a mink stole, but this one made her clothe herself at the thrift shop—or from the rag pile behind the thrift shop, the stuff that was so tattered it could not be sold.

News of her miserable state came to the prophet Hosea and he sought out the man she was living with. He knew where he would find him, down at the local tavern, and when he met this man, he asked, "Are you the man who is living with Gomer, daughter of Diblaim?" The man must have said, "If it's any of your business, I am."

"Well, I am Hosea," said the prophet, "her husband." A tense moment followed. Then the man responded that he hadn't done anything wrong and didn't want any trouble. Hosea replied, in effect, "Listen, I'm not interested in causing any trouble. But I know that you are having difficulty making ends meet. I want you to take this money and buy Gomer some clothing and see that she has plenty of food. If you need any more I will give it to you." The man probably thought, *There's no fool like an old fool. If this sap wants to help pay her expenses, that's fine with me!* So he took the money and bought Gomer some groceries and went home.

You may say (along with the man in the tavern), "What a foolish thing to do!" But who can explain the motives of love? Love does not act according to reason; love has its own reasons that reason itself does not know. So Hosea acted on the basis of love. He probably watched from a distance to catch a glimpse of the woman he loved as she rushed out the door to take the groceries from this man's arms and to thank him for what he was bringing her—the gifts that true love had provided, that villainy offered, and that folly accepted.

Hosea preached with tears

The unfaithful wife of Hosea became a vivid, shocking object lesson of what was about to take place in Israel

Love has its own reasons that reason itself does not know

"Show your love for
her in the same
way that I love
Israel"

We don't know how long this situation went on. But finally, word reached Hosea that the woman he loved was to be sold in the slave market. The man she lived with had tired of her and decided to convert her into cash. The brokenhearted prophet went weeping to God, and God said, "Hosea, do you love this woman in spite of all that she has done to you? Then go show your love for her in the same way that I love the nation Israel."

So Hosea went to the marketplace and he watched Gomer as she was brought up and placed on the dock. She was stripped of her clothing and shamed in her nakedness before the crowd of gawkers. The bidding began. Somebody bid three pieces of silver and Hosea raised it to five. Somebody upped it to eight and Hosea bid ten. Somebody went to eleven; he went to twelve. Finally, Hosea offered fifteen pieces of silver and a bushel of barley. The auctioneer's gavel fell and Hosea had his wife back.

He went to her, put clothes on her, and lovingly took her home. And then follows what is among the tenderest and most beautiful verses in all the Bible:

> Then I told her, "You are to live with me many days; you must not be a
> prostitute or be intimate with any man, and I will live with you" (3:3).

He pledged his love to her anew. And that was all this poor woman could take. She had fallen to the gutter of shame, disgrace, and poverty—but the steadfast, unconditional love of Hosea broke her willful heart and raised her up again. From then on, Gomer was faithful to Hosea. In the rest of the book, Hosea goes on to tell the effect of this story on the nation of Israel. God said to the people, "How can I give you up?" He reminded them of His love for them all those years, even though they had turned their backs on Him. It is a story of God's redemptive love for a people who had sold themselves into bondage, poverty, and shame. It is the same story that would be retold in the New Testament when Jesus came and paid the price for our redemption, so that He could take His bride, the church, out of bondage and restore her to a place of honor and faithfulness.

The book of Hosea
is a story of God's
redemptive love for
a people who had
sold themselves into
bondage, poverty,
and shame

We find some remarkable predictions in Hosea. One occurs at the close of chapter 3. Right in line with the story of the personal life of Hosea and his unfaithful bride, God says of the people of Israel:

> The Israelites will live many days without king or prince, without
> sacrifice or sacred stones, without ephod or idol (Hos. 3:4).

That prophecy is being fulfilled today. The children of Israel have lived many days without a king. Ever since the destruction of Jerusalem in A.D. 70 at the hands of General Titus of Rome, Israel has been without a king or a prince, without anyone who has the undisputed right to reign over Israel.

Israel also lives without sacrifice. When the Jews of the world celebrate the Passover supper, they remember the supper instituted in Egypt when Israel was delivered from the hand of Pharaoh. God told Israel that every time they ate the Passover they were to kill a lamb. But for two thousand years the Jews have never killed a lamb. Why not? Why do they offer a bone, a burned bone for a sacrifice? God said that they would live many days without a sacrifice, and since the destruction of the temple there has never been a sacrifice in Israel, nor an ephod or idol. They would live without idolatry. God predicted that they would live exactly as we see the nation of Israel living today: as a religious people but without giving themselves to idols.

Then, after these days are ended, something exciting will happen, as the Lord predicts in Hosea 3:5:

> *The Israelites will return and seek the LORD their God and David their king. They will come trembling to the LORD and to his blessings in the last days.*

What a wonderful prophecy that is! And another one similar to it is found at the close of chapter 5:

> *"I will go back to my place until they admit their guilt. And they will seek my face; in their misery they will earnestly seek me."*
> *"Come, let us return to the LORD. He has torn us to pieces but he will heal us; he has injured us but he will bind up our wounds. After two days he will revive us; on the third day he will restore us, that we may live in his presence. Let us acknowledge the LORD; let us press on to acknowledge him. As surely as the sun rises, he will appear; he will come to us like the winter rains, like the spring rains that water the earth"* (5:15–6:3).

That is the hope of Israel—the promise that their Messiah will yet come to them, revive them, and raise them up again.

In the sorrowing, loving heart of Hosea, we see a picture of the loving, sorrowing heart of God. At the close of the book, we come to God's final plea to Israel—and to you and me:

Return, O Israel, to the LORD your God. Your sins have been your downfall! (14:1).

After all, it wasn't God who was to blame for Israel's downfall or ours. He was simply trying to get His people to see the truth. Israel needed to experience the pain of God's tough love, and so, at times, do we. The only thing that can relieve the agony of God's tough love is to return to the comfort of God's merciful love. Like the father of the Prodigal Son, God eagerly awaits our return, wanting nothing more than to restore us to the blessings of being His children. But like that father, God cannot bless us or restore us until we come back to Him.

Can you see in this beautiful story all the elements of the eternal triangle? There is the Lover, our loving God. There is the beloved, the bride, the human heart, which is tragically prone to stray from God's love. And there is the seducer, the deceptive attractiveness of the world that tries to separate us from God's love. This is your story and my story, isn't it? So many times we try to satisfy ourselves with the lying idols of self-importance or wealth or pleasure. Ours is a blindness like Gomer's that cannot distinguish between lust and love.

But the Bible tells us how to break the triangle and restore the beautiful, faithful union that God intended us to experience with Him. At Bethlehem, God entered the slave market where the whole human race had sold itself into bondage, prostituting itself, shaming itself in naked sin. At Calvary, the Lord Jesus paid the full price for our freedom, redeeming us and restoring us to a right relationship with Himself—a relationship of a beautiful bride to a loving husband. This is the story of God's love—a love that restores you and me, erasing our shame, renewing our potential, making us the full, complete, beautiful people whom God intends us to be.

The Revelation of God's Hand

J. R. R. Tolkien's three-volume fairy tale *The Lord of the Rings* is a book of momentous events executed on a vast scale. It is filled with massive battles in which the armies of powerful kings wage war against one another. Powerful spiritual forces in conflict depict a near-cosmic struggle of good against evil. Yet, when the book has ended, it turns out that all the towering events of these three epic volumes—including the fate of an entire world—hinge on the actions of the humblest, smallest creature of all, a three-foot tall hobbit named Frodo. The theme of this book is clear: Never underestimate the power of the smallest things.

The little book of Joel is only three chapters long, and it is often underestimated. That is a great mistake and a tragedy, for this is one of the most powerful books in the Word of God. Just as the fate of the world of Tolkien's *Lord of the Rings* hinged on what was going on inside a little hobbit named Frodo, so the fate of our own world hinges on what takes place inside this little book named Joel. Just as the prophecy of Hosea reveals the heart of God, the prophecy of Joel reveals the hand of God—the hand that controls destiny, the hand that moves history.

Just as the prophecy of Hosea reveals the heart of God, the prophecy of Joel reveals the hand of God

For centuries, people have searched for the principle upon which all the events of history turn. Long ago, the great Greek philosophers came up with the idea that history moves in cycles. Later philosophers

The controlling principle of life

and historians, such as Aristotle and Arnold Toynbee, agree. According to this cyclical view of history, a tyrant rises—a dictator of iron who seizes control of a nation and rules until that dynasty ends. Then control gradually passes to a ruling family or aristocracy. And gradually their power deteriorates until control passes down to the people in the form of a democracy. But a democracy also eventually deteriorates and gradually yields to the breakdown of all authority, and anarchy ensues. Out of anarchy, a tyrant again seizes control, and on goes the cycle of history. And that theory rings true. We can see evidence in our own society that democracy is breaking down and paving the way for anarchy and the emergence of a new dictator of iron, perhaps the long-prophesied Antichrist himself.

Through the centuries, other people have contributed guesses about the controlling principle of life. Thomas Jefferson thought it was political, and when he wrote the Declaration of Independence he incorporated that idea in the prologue—the belief that human governments recognize that certain inalienable rights are naturally or divinely granted to human beings, and that to preserve these rights, governments are instituted among people. A good government, said Jefferson, did not invent or confer these rights but defended the rights people already have, as given by God. Jefferson felt that the forces that shape human history and form the nations of earth are political in nature.

In the late nineteenth century, Karl Marx dipped his pen into the acid of his own embittered spirit and wrote the imposing work that has dramatically influenced our modern times. His idea was that the controlling force of history is economics: The need to meet the material demands of life shapes the course of history. He called this force dialectical materialism—the principle of materialism derived through struggle and debate, through the conflict of ideas and conflicting economic interests. This idea has so seized the people's minds today that, all over the earth and even in America, millions consider economics to be the driving force of life.

But the Bible says that all these beliefs are ultimately inadequate and flawed. The controlling principle behind human history is none other than God Himself. The hinge on which history turns is spiritual: God's Spirit is at work among people, and you cannot understand human events if you do not first recognize this fact.

God tries to win men and women to Himself by holding back the destructive forces in human events. But at last God's patience reaches an end and there comes a time—repeated throughout human history—when God says to both individuals and nations, "My Spirit shall not strive with man forever" (Gen. 6:3 NASB). And when He removes His Spirit—the controlling force of life—everything collapses. People are left alone to contend with the chaos of their own making and choosing. Catastrophe falls and judgment strikes. That is the powerful, shattering message contained in the three chapters of the little book of Joel.

Here is the structure of the book of Joel:

Past Judgment (Joel 1)
1. Disaster by locust	1:1–12
2. Disaster by drought	1:13–20

Future Judgment (Joel 2–3)
3. Judgment of Judah in the near future	2
4. The great and terrible Day of the Lord	3:1–16
5. The restoration of Judah	3:17–21

This young man Joel was a prophet to the kingdom of Judah, the southern kingdom. He was probably a contemporary of Isaiah, Hosea, and Amos. We don't know much about Joel except that he was (by God's grace) one of the most visionary people who has ever written. Joel saw far past our own day to the final stages of God's dealings in human events.

The book opens with Joel's call to the people to consider a tremendous thing that has happened in the land. He says:

> *Hear this, you elders; listen, all who live in the land. Has anything like this ever happened in your days or in the days of your forefathers? Tell it to your children, and let your children tell it to their children, and their children to the next generation (1:2–3).*

Whenever I read that verse, I am reminded of my days in the navy. Whenever the navy made an important announcement, it always began, "Now hear this." And that is the way Joel begins: "Hear this . . . ." His announcement concerns an event of such overwhelming importance that people will be talking about it for years to come. And what is Joel talking about? He is talking about the great Day of the Lord.

Back in World War II we talked about the coming of D-Day, and then V-J Day. We looked forward to the end of the war, to the day when the struggle would cease and the horrors of war would end. Here in Joel we see that God has a day, the Day of the Lord, and Joel was entrusted with the task of describing this great day to the people.

It is important to understand that, in a broad sense, what the Bible calls the Day of the Lord is not just one event in human history. We will find in this prophecy that the Day of the Lord is any event in which God moves in judgment, at any time. But judgment is building up, cycle by cycle, toward that great, final, and terrible Day of the

The Day of the Lord is not just one event in human history

Lord, the culmination of all judgment that Joel describes in chapters 2 and 3.

The great and terrible Day of the Lord is that period described by the Lord Jesus Christ as a time when there will be tribulation as has never been seen since the creation of the world, nor ever will be. And it was given to the prophet Joel to see across the intervening centuries of time to describe it and to illustrate it by events taking place in his own day.

An invasion of locusts

The event that had occurred in his day was an invasion of locusts. I was in Minnesota years ago during an invasion of grasshoppers—insects very similar to locusts. I can still remember how the sky was literally darkened by the great cloud of these insects. You could hear them descend into the standing grain of the fields like hail upon the ground and hear the continual rustling of the noise of their wings as you walked through the fields. Within moments of their descent, every blade of grass, every bit of vegetation was gone, and the fields looked as if they had never been planted. That is what happened in Israel. A locust horde descended upon the land and devoured every living thing. The crops were ruined and famine had come.

Everyone in Judah was painfully aware of this event, but they didn't understand where it had come from. So Joel said to them, in effect, "God is behind this" (see 1:10–15). This plague isn't just a freak of nature. It happened in obedience to the command of God, working through the natural laws that govern human life, and there is a lesson for us in this. God's hand allows catastrophes like this to occur in order to make people aware of the spiritual background to life. Life is not merely a cycle of eating and drinking and getting money to do so. Behind all the commonplace events of life is the controlling hand of God.

We need to wake up to the fact that God is speaking to us through the events of our lives. He wants to bless us but we will not listen. That is our problem! Has this ever happened to you? Has God ever allowed events in your life to awaken you to your need of Him? That is what God is doing in Joel chapter 1.

A vision of invasion

In chapter 2, the prophet Joel leaps over a great span of time to the end days, using this invasion of the locusts as a picture of the invasion by a great army into the land of Israel in the last days. Only by examining the whole stream of prophecy together can we detect that Joel is speaking of the future. Anyone taking this book by itself would never notice any difference, except that the prophet is now describing the invasion by an army of men instead of by an army of insects. He goes on to describe this event and again calls it the Day of the Lord:

Blow the trumpet in Zion; sound the alarm on my holy hill. Let all who live in the land tremble, for the day of the LORD is coming. It is close at hand—a day of darkness and gloom, a day of clouds and blackness. Like dawn spreading across the mountains a large and mighty army comes, such as never was of old nor ever will be in ages to come (2:1–2).

That sounds familiar, doesn't it? That is the language that Jesus used: "Then there will be great distress, unequaled from the beginning of the world until now—and never to be equaled again" (Matt. 24:21). Then the prophet describes how the land is scorched behind them as this great army advances, and he describes the army as having the appearance of horses. Now fear grips the hearts of the people as they see this invading host drawn up for battle. Nothing can resist them. The earth quakes before them. The heavens tremble. And then we come to a significant passage:

The sun and moon are darkened, and the stars no longer shine (2:10).

Anyone who spends time with the prophetic passages of Scripture learns to look for interpretational landmarks. Certain prophetic symbols occur again and again throughout various books of prophecy to give us a landmark so that we know where we are. This darkening of the sun, moon, and stars is one of these landmarks. We see this same landmark in Jesus' great discourse on the Mount of Olives. He refers to this time when the sun shall be darkened, and the moon will not give light but will turn to blood, and the stars will fall from heaven (see Matt. 24:29). We see this event in the books of Daniel, Isaiah, and Revelation. It is described in several places throughout Scripture and it always marks the same event in human history. It is an interpretational landmark pointing to the last days before what is called the great and terrible Day of the Lord.

This section, then, seems to describe the invasion of Israel that is also foretold and described by the prophet Ezekiel in chapters 38 and 39, when a great army invades the land from the north and destroys everything, capturing the city of Jerusalem. But God promises that this northern army will be dealt with in that land. Isaiah says so. Ezekiel says so. Daniel says so. Now Joel adds his voice to the chorus of prophets, and God reveals the purpose behind this great invasion:

"Even now," declares the LORD, "return to me with all your heart, with fasting and weeping and mourning."
Rend your heart and not your garments. Return to the LORD your God, for he is gracious and compassionate, slow to anger and abounding in love, and he relents from sending calamity. Who knows? He may turn

Certain prophetic symbols occur again and again throughout various books of prophecy to give us a landmark

A chorus of prophets

and have pity and leave behind a blessing—grain offerings and drink offerings for the LORD your God (2:12–14).

After all, God does not delight in judgment. That isn't what He is after. He never enjoys our pain. Rather, He seeks hearts that will listen to Him, heed Him, and open the door for the blessings that He wants to pour into our lives. In order to get a person or nation to listen and return to Him, God will permit all kinds of harsh things to occur—because these are the events that produce a repentant heart.

"Rend your heart and not your garments," He says, pleading with us in His love. He doesn't want us to simply make an external change. He wants us to change internally, through and through. But we don't like to do that, do we?

We are like the little boy whose mother told him, "Sit down!" But he wouldn't sit down. She said again, "Sit down!" And he said, "I won't." So she grabbed him by the shoulders and sat him down in the chair. Then he looked up at her defiantly and said, "I'm sitting down on the outside, but I'm standing up on the inside!" God is unimpressed by our hypocrisy, our outward show. We don't fool Him for a moment. He wants us to love Him and obey Him, on the inside and on the outside.

God's restoration

After leaping over this great span of years to the end days, the prophet returns to the event of the present hour: the locust plague in the land. He tells the people that just as God will one day deliver His people and drive away the northern armies, so today, in this present catastrophe, He will restore the land from its barren condition and its desolation:

> *The threshing floors will be filled with grain; the vats will overflow with new wine and oil.*
> [God says,] *"I will repay you for the years the locusts have eaten—the great locust and the young locust, the other locusts and the locust swarm—my great army that I sent among you" (2:24–25).*

I will never forget the agony in the eyes of a man I knew some years ago who had recently become a Christian. He looked at me with a deep sadness in his eyes and said, "It's wonderful being a Christian, yet I can't help feeling sad over the years I wasted and the things I missed during my old lifestyle. My heart gets sick as I think of all the terrible things that I used to do. If only I'd had the sense to come to the Lord before I wasted so much of my life." Here was a man who felt that he had allowed the locusts to eat up and waste the prime years of his life. But I had the joy of telling him, "Friend, God says, 'I will repay you for the years the locusts have eaten.' " That verse meant so much to him after that.

God has promised to make up for the barrenness of our lives when we turn back to Him. That is one of the most comforting promises in Scripture.

Next, Joel leaps ahead again and writes the great passage that the apostle Peter quoted on the day of Pentecost. The story of that dramatic day is recorded in Acts 2, where we see the Christians gathered in the temple courts. Suddenly a rushing, mighty wind visits the Christians. Tongues of fire appear over every head, and people begin to speak in foreign tongues. The people gathered around them hear them praising God in various languages. These people, who had come from all parts of the earth, are wonderstruck, hearing these Christians speaking in a variety of tongues, including their own. Never having seen anything like it before and groping for an explanation, these people conclude that the Christians must be drunk. Then Peter stands and speaks to the people, saying:

> *"Fellow Jews and all of you who live in Jerusalem, let me explain this to you; listen carefully to what I say. These men are not drunk, as you suppose. It's only nine in the morning! No, this is what was spoken by the prophet Joel"* . . .

And here he quotes Joel 2:28–29:

> *" 'In the last days, God says, I will pour out my Spirit on all people. Your sons and daughters will prophesy, your young men will see visions, your old men will dream dreams. Even on my servants, both men and women, I will pour out my Spirit in those days, and they will prophesy' " (Acts 2:17–18).*

Now what is this all about? As we have already seen, the prophet Joel has witnessed and prophesied events well into his own future, including the still-future invasion of Israel. Here, he sees something different, a mystery still somewhat undefined to his vision. He says that Israel's restoration will be followed by an indeterminate period when God will pour out His Spirit on all flesh, a time when no distinctions will be made between classes or ranks of people, when even servants shall speak as the voice of God. They shall speak the word of God, as God pours out His Spirit upon people everywhere.

We can identify the day that he is describing. It is the day of the Spirit in which we live, the day that began on Pentecost when God first poured out His Spirit. That same Spirit is being poured out throughout this whole age. In Acts 2, Peter also quotes Joel concerning the sign of the end of that age:

*"I will show wonders in the heaven above and signs on the earth below,
blood and fire and billows of smoke. The sun will be turned to darkness
and the moon to blood before the coming of the great and glorious day
of the LORD. And everyone who calls on the name of the LORD will be
saved" (Acts 2:19–21).*

That is Joel's description of the end of the age, which commenced
at Pentecost. Joel's prophecy of Pentecost is the sign of the beginning
of the present age. His prophecy of doom and judgment in the great
and glorious Day of the Lord is the sign of the end of this age. No one
knows how long this present age will last, but during this time, God is
pouring out His Spirit without distinction among people around the
world.

**Plowshares
and pruning
hooks**

In Joel 3, the prophet returns to the end times and beyond. All that
he sees of the age of the Spirit is the great mark of the Spirit's presence.
But beyond that he sees that God will restore the fortunes of Judah and
Jerusalem:

*"I will gather all nations and bring them down to the Valley of
Jehoshaphat. There I will enter into judgment against them concerning
my inheritance, my people Israel, for they scattered my people among the
nations and divided up my land" (Joel 3:2).*

Those who are
righteous will be
invited in to share
the Father's
inheritance, while
the unrighteous will
be sent away

Jesus said, "When the Son of Man comes in his glory, and all the
angels with him, he will sit on his throne in heavenly glory. All the
nations will be gathered before him" (Matt. 25:31–32). And then the
Son of Man will judge them and divide them, as a shepherd divides the
sheep from the goats. Those who are righteous will be invited in to
share the Father's inheritance, while the unrighteous will be sent away.
This is the valley of judgment. In preparation for this coming judgment, God instructs the nations of the world with these amazing
words:

*Proclaim this among the nations: Prepare for war! Rouse the war-
riors! Let all the fighting men draw near and attack. Beat your plowshares into swords and your pruning hooks into spears. Let the weakling
say, "I am strong!" (Joel 3:9–10).*

Did you know that the Bible says this? Many times you have heard
quoted, "Beat [your] swords into plowshares and [your] spears into
pruning hooks." That is found in Micah 4:3, but in Joel, quite the
opposite is said! And Joel's prophecy comes first; the fulfillment of Joel's

prediction comes first. That is why nations are at war. This is what God is saying to the nations today. And they will remain at war in one way or another until God says, "Beat your swords into plowshares and your spears into pruning hooks."

Jesus said: "You will hear of wars and rumors of wars, but see to it that you are not alarmed. Such things must happen, but the end is still to come. Nation will rise against nation, and kingdom against kingdom" (Matt. 24:6–7). And so it shall be until the end.

There will be wars and rumors of wars, culminating in the final gathering of multitudes in "the valley of decision," as Joel says in 3:14. Whose decision? Not our decision! Not the decision of nations or kings! The Day of the Lord will be the day that God makes *His* decision! God will enter the valley of decision and the multitudes of the nations will be gathered before Him. All the world will be there on this judgment day. At the return of Jesus Christ in power and judgment, all the nations of the world will know that the Lord is God, and the city of Jerusalem will be the Holy City once more.

The final scene in Joel 3 is a beautiful one—a scene of peace, when the final battle has been fought and won, and the judgment of God has been handed down. Then all that was wrong will be put right, and the earth will be the Eden that God originally created it to be:

> *"In that day the mountains will drip new wine, and the hills will flow with milk; all the ravines of Judah will run with water. A fountain will flow out of the LORD's house and will water the valley of acacias"* (3:18).

Water is always a picture of the Holy Spirit. Jesus said, "Whoever believes in me, as the Scripture has said, streams of living water will flow from within him" (John 7:38). He speaks of spiritual rivers of blessing to satisfy a person's thirsty soul.

Throughout the book of Joel, we have seen the hand of God—moving and shaping events, guiding His people, even clenched into a fist of war. Ultimately, we see His hand at work as the hand of an artist, reshaping the world, sculpting it into a thing of beauty once more.

Joel shows us clearly that the future is in God's hands. It isn't in the hands of mere human beings. If it were, we would certainly make a mess of it. It isn't in the devil's hands. If it were, if the devil had his own way with the future, we would all be on our way to destruction, no exceptions, no escape. The blind principle of historical determinism isn't guiding the future. If it were, life would have no meaning. The future is in the hands of One who is preparing something that eye has never seen

The valley of decision

The Day of the Lord will be the day that God makes *His* decision

The future is in God's hands

and ear has never heard. Neither has it ever entered into the heart of man or woman the wonderful things that God is preparing for those who love Him.

The future of the human race is in God's hands. We have a choice: We can confidently place our own hands in the outstretched hand of God, our trustworthy, loving, merciful heavenly Father—or we can run from Him, turn our backs on Him. But even if we flee from Him, we can never escape His hand. Someday, His hand will hold the gavel of judgment. If we have placed our hand in His, in trust and faith, we need never fear that day.

God Doesn't Play Favorites

The great coach Vince Lombardi became an American legend by spurring his Green Bay Packers football team to five NFL championships. One of his players was interviewed by a reporter who asked, "Is Coach Lombardi impartial and fair, or does he practice favoritism with some of the players?"

"Oh, he doesn't play any favorites," the Packer replied quickly. "He treats us *all* like dogs."

Well, God doesn't play favorites, either—but unlike Vince Lombardi, He doesn't treat us like dogs. He regards us as men and women of dignity and worth because we are made in His image. That is the message and theme of Amos: the impartiality of God.

The message of Amos is an immensely practical and relevant message for our times—and it is distinct from that of any of the other minor prophets. Amos tells us that God does not plays favorites; He makes no allowances for one person that He will not make for another as well. Anyone who is willing to fulfill the conditions of God's promises will find God's blessing poured out in his or her life, regardless of status, position, gender, race, or ethnicity.

Why me?

That's hard for us to believe, isn't it? We are conditioned to thinking that God reacts the way we do, that He judges on the basis of externals as we do, that He bestows extra regard and favor on those we tend to esteem. But in Amos, as throughout Scripture, we find ample proof that God's ways are not our ways. Whether we are rich or poor, whether we are powerful or powerless in this world, the message of Amos slashes across the grain of our expectations and confronts us with the fact that in God's sight no one is higher or lower than anyone else. What an encouragement for those who struggle with feelings of unworthiness, inferiority, and powerlessness!

The truths of Amos become most practical and applicable, I think, in times of crisis, loss, stress, or suffering. Our tendency in such times is to ask ourselves, "Why me?"

I'm reminded of a story that a friend once shared with me. It happened in New York City, during a summer rush hour on the subway. People jammed the subway cars as the train moved out of the station, and one man—the last man to board—was squeezed in against the door, facing outward. As the subway train moved away from the station, the walls of the tunnel passed before his eyes, moving faster and faster. The train swayed and bumped. The car was hot and stuffy and smelled a little rank. The man realized that he felt sick—and the further the train went, the sicker he felt.

Finally, the train pulled into the next stop, the door opened—and the man on the train vomited all over an unfortunate man who happened to be standing on the platform waiting to board the train. For several seconds, as the doors stood open, nobody moved. The sick man, the people on the train behind him, the unfortunate man on the platform, the others on the platform—everyone stood still and stared in horror at what had just taken place.

Then the doors of the subway car suddenly closed and the train began to move out of the station. Looking down at the mess that covered his suit, the man on the platform wailed, "Why me?!"

If we see ourselves in some privileged position with God, then that is a reasonable question: "Why me?" But if God is completely impartial, then a more reasonable question emerges: "Why not me?" If bad things happen to some people, then why shouldn't they happen to you and me as well? If God is impartial, as Amos tells us that He is, then we must expect that bad things—the kind of bad things that happen to other people—will sometimes happen to us as well.

Here is an outline of the book of Amos:

The Eight Judgments (Amos 1–2)

> against Damascus, Gaza, Tyre, Edom,
> Ammon, Moab, Judah, Israel   1–2

Three Messages of Judgment (Amos 3–6)

> 1. The judgment against Israel is just   3

If God is impartial, then we must expect that bad things— the kind of bad things that happen to other people— will sometimes happen to us as well

2. The past sins of Israel	4
3. The future of Israel	5–6

Five Visions of Judgment (Amos 7–9)

4. Locusts, fire, the plumb line	7
5. The summer fruit	8
6. The shaken pillars	9:1–10
7. Five promises of restoration	9:11–15

Amos, the shepherd-prophet

The opening verse of Amos gives us a date and setting for the book, pegging Amos as a contemporary of the prophets Hosea and Isaiah. Amos, according to the indicators in this verse, is one of the earliest of the prophetic writers:

> *The words of Amos, one of the shepherds of Tekoa—what he saw concerning Israel two years before the earthquake, when Uzziah was king of Judah and Jeroboam son of Jehoash was king of Israel (1:1).*

The book of Amos was written by a man who was not a trained prophet

One unique feature of the book of Amos is that it was written by a man who was not a trained prophet. He was an ordinary person. He is, you might say, a "cowboy preacher."

In chapter 7, Amos adds another personal note. Here is the reaction to his message as he came to the northern kingdom of Israel:

> *Amaziah the priest of Bethel sent a message to Jeroboam king of Israel: "Amos is raising a conspiracy against you in the very heart of Israel. The land cannot bear all his words. For this is what Amos is saying:*
> *" 'Jeroboam will die by the sword, and Israel will surely go into exile, away from their native land' " (7:10–11).*

A prophecy of exile

That was the burden of the prophet's message. God was going to exile Israel. God was going to judge the nation and the king. Amaziah the priest responds by saying, "Don't come to us. Go back to your hometown. Go back to the country you came from and prophesy down there." But sturdy, rugged Amos, the blunt and countrified cowboy preacher, said, "I was neither a prophet nor a prophet's son, but I was a shepherd" (7:14). Now, in saying this, Amos doesn't mean his father was not a prophet. He means that he has not been to the accepted school of the prophets. He says he is a rancher, a farmer, a cowboy who is simply going where God tells him to go and doing what God tells him to do.

Now you can see something of the opposition to the message of this man as he comes declaring the burden of the Lord in the land of Israel in the northern kingdom. The people there find his message very hard to accept.

The travels of Amos

Amos delivers God's message in a very interesting way. Comparing this account with a map of ancient Israel, you find that Amos is going around the boundaries of Israel in various directions, delivering a message concerning all the neighboring nations. He begins in chapter 1 with Damascus, in the northeast section above Israel (which we now know as Syria). He delivers to Damascus a message that God has judged Damascus, especially for the people's cruelty.

Damascus

Gaza

Next he moves down on the west coast to the ancient land of Philistia, or what is called here the land of Gaza. Once again he reminds Israel that God has judged this land. Why? Because the people have participated in an active slave trade.

Tyre

Then he moves back up the coast to the land of Tyre, on the northwest side of Israel. There he points out how God had judged this country because the people had broken their agreements.

Edom

He continues on to the far south of Israel, to the land of Edom, the ancient country of Esau, where he points out how God's judgment has fallen on this nation because of the people's unforgiving spirit and their implacable hatred of Israel.

Ammon

Amos then moves up the east side of Israel to the land of Ammon—what we now know as Jordan. Amman, the capital of Jordan, was also the capital of Ammon in Amos's day. Amos declares God's judgment against this nation because of its greed for the land held by others.

Moab

As Amos travels south to Moab, he pronounces God's judgment on Moab because that nation has hated Israel.

Judah

Next, he comes to the southern kingdom, Judah. There he declares that because Judah has despised God's law, the judgment of God had fallen on the nation. Finally, he arrives at the ten-kingdom northern nation of Israel, where he announces that God is going to judge them for corruption and for the injustice in their hearts.

Israel

An old and very overweight country elder used to sit in church Sunday after Sunday, smiling and nodding as his pastor preached about such sins as swearing, drunkenness, smoking, gossip, and arguing. But one Sunday, the minister chose to preach against the sin of gluttony— and the fat old elder was incensed. After the service, he stalked up to the preacher, shook one sausage-shaped finger at the clergyman's nose, and said, "Preacher, you have ceased to be a-preachin' and have started to be a-meddlin'!"

As you read this account, you can see that the people of Israel were quite untroubled as long as Amos was talking about *other* nations. They took this very complacently, thinking, *Well, those people got what was coming to them!* But when the prophet zeroed in on the sins of Israel, then he had ceased to be a-preachin' and had started to be a-meddlin'. The people became angry and said, "Why don't you go preach someplace else?" This inevitably happens when preachers are faithful to the message of God.

The rest of the book focuses on this northern kingdom of Israel. Beginning with chapter 3 you have the prophet's words that God addressed to this nation. He begins by pointing out to them that they were a people who have enjoyed a special, privileged position before God:

> Hear this word the LORD has spoken against you, O people of Israel—against the whole family I brought up out of Egypt: "You only have I chosen of all the families of the earth" (3:1–2).

So far, the people of Israel liked what they were hearing. God was telling them, through Amos, that they were the privileged people of God, the chosen people. They were the ones whom God Himself had chosen among all the families of the earth. You can see them swelling with pride and arrogance as the prophet says this—but Amos's next words come like a fist in the face, like a hammer blow:

> ". . . therefore I will punish you for all your sins" (3:2).

Now see their faces fall! The very source of their pride—the fact that they had been chosen by God—was the very reason that God was holding them to a high standard and subjecting them to judgment. They had received the light of knowledge of God, and light creates responsibility. Privilege exposes us to judgment. The people of Israel were chosen not because they were such wonderful people compared with any other race; God is impartial and does not show favoritism to this group or that, to this individual or that. They were chosen simply because God had a purpose for them in His eternal plan—and the fact was that they were not living up to that purpose. So, they were going to be judged and disciplined. They were going to be held responsible for the light that they had been given.

Israel was chosen simply because God had a purpose for them in His eternal plan

This is what Peter means in the New Testament when he says, "It is time for judgment to begin with the family of God" (1 Peter 4:17). It always begins there. God always starts with His people, and then He moves out to others. The prophet Joel makes this principle clear: Just because we are people of God does not mean that God's Word no longer judges our lives. On the contrary, God's Word increases our responsibility, so that we are likely to be judged even more severely, based on the responsibility that we bear because of the knowledge that we have received.

Amos describes the close relationship between God and His people as two walking together:

> *Do two walk together unless they have agreed to do so? (3:3).*

That is God's *walk* with His people. Then Amos describes God's *talk* with his people:

> *Surely the Sovereign LORD does nothing without revealing his plan to his servants the prophets (3:7).*

These were the facts that marked the Israelites' peculiar relationship and privilege before God: They walked with God. They talked with God. For this reason, the prophet Joel says, God would send judgment.

In chapter 4, Joel shows the people how God has patiently tried to awaken them through five separate acts of discipline. For years, God has been trying to awaken them, jar them, and halt their downward course. He has sent

- famine and drought (4:6–8);
- blight and mildew to destroy the gardens and vineyards (4:9);
- plagues (4:10);
- war (4:10);
- fire and natural disaster—as in Sodom and Gomorrah (4:11).

All of these terrible things happened to the people. " 'Yet you have not returned to me,' declares the LORD," God concludes in verse 11. Then comes the most ominous and frightening statement in the book of Amos—and perhaps in all of Scripture! Verse 12:

> *"This is what I will do to you, Israel, and because I will do this to you, prepare to meet your God, O Israel."*

Prepare to meet your God! The words send a chill of terror down our spines. Who of us is ready, according to our own righteousness, for such a meeting? How can we, who have accumulated such a list of sins and failings in our lives, ever hope to stand in the presence of the One who created time and space itself and whose righteousness burns like a white-hot blast furnace at the heart of the universe?!

Thank God, we are clothed in the righteousness of Jesus and not in our own righteousness. Our eternal souls are saved and secure—yet we should do everything we can in this life to make sure that we never have to endure the discipline of God—His tough love that draws us back to Him through the pain and sorrow of unpleasant circumstances.

This is not to say that when bad things happen to us, it is always the judgment of God. No, bad things do happen to good people, to God's people, to people who are walking in fellowship with Him. Even so, I have often seen Christians called to an even deeper walk with God through bad circumstances. These events shake us up, awaken us, and drive us to rededicate ourselves to godly living. Tragedies and brushes with disaster—a near-fatal accident, a cancer scare, a criminal assault, a fire, the death of someone close—these events awaken us from our preoccupation with routines, TV, superficial relationships, and church-ianity, and force us to see life as it really is.

The book of Amos is much beloved by the social liberals of our day—and Amos 5:11–15 shows why:

> You trample on the poor and force him to give you grain. Therefore, though you have built stone mansions, you will not live in them; though you have planted lush vineyards, you will not drink their wine. For I know how many are your offenses and how great your sins. You oppress the righteous and take bribes and you deprive the poor of justice in the courts. Therefore the prudent man keeps quiet in such times, for the times are evil.
>
> Seek good, not evil, that you may live. Then the LORD God Almighty will be with you, just as you say he is. Hate evil, love good; maintain justice in the courts. Perhaps the LORD God Almighty will have mercy on the remnant of Joseph.

Amos is called the prophet of social justice, the man who demanded that people deal justly and compassionately with one another. Liberals love this book because of these thundering pro-nouncements against the social evils of Amos's day—and rightly so. God is always disturbed by social injustices. But what many liberals seem to miss in this book is Amos's appeal to these people. He tells them to stop treating each other unjustly, but that isn't all he says. His core theme concerns *how* to stop doing these things, and we find it plainly stated twice in this chapter:

Thank God, we are clothed in the righ-teousness of Jesus and not in our own righteousness

Amos—the patron saint of liberalism?

God is always disturbed by social injustices

> *This is what the LORD says to the house of Israel:* "Seek me and live" *(5:4, emphasis added).*

> Seek the LORD and live, *or he will sweep through the house of Joseph like a fire (5:6, emphasis added).*

What is the answer to the wandering heart? The answer isn't just to clean up your life. It is to come back to God. It is to repent and to think again. *Seek the Lord and live!* Come back to the Lord of your salvation. Call upon Him. Ask Him to set you back on your feet and straighten out your life. That is God's appeal to us. Social action, serving the poor, seeking justice, fighting racism, showing compassion on the poor—all these are good and worthwhile activities that God has commanded us to do. But they mean nothing if our hearts are not right with God.

Over the past few decades, our society has spent trillions of dollars on programs to end racism and poverty—yet the problems of racism and poverty have grown worse not better in all that time. We have seen the failure not only of government programs but of many private, Christian, social-action programs to make a dent in the problem. Why is this? Perhaps it is because so many of our national efforts to find justice and racial harmony are rooted in seeking ideology rather than in seeking God. If we seek justice without seeking God first, we will simply become ideologues and demagogues, fighting for political causes while accomplishing nothing of eternal value in our own lives or the lives of others.

If we wholeheartedly seek God first, desiring nothing more than to be obedient to Him, to be used as tools of His eternal purpose on earth, then justice and compassion will just naturally flow from hearts that are conformed to His heart. Then and only then will the words of Amos 5:24 be realized in our lives:

> *Let justice roll on like a river, righteousness like a never-failing stream!*

The restoration to come

Amos closes his prophecy in much the same way that Joel and so many other prophets do: with a scene of beauty, peace, and glory. It reveals what God wants to produce in the world and in our lives.

> *"In that day I will restore David's fallen tent. I will repair its broken places, restore its ruins, and build it as it used to be, so that they may possess the remnant of Edom and all the nations that bear my name," declares the LORD, who will do these things (9:11–12).*

These words are quoted in the New Testament in Acts 15:16–18, in the account of the first council at Jerusalem. As the Jewish Christian leaders are wondering whether God will save the Gentiles without the Law of Moses, James stands and quotes this verse from Amos. The statement that God will restore David's fallen tent and repair it is a prophetic picture of the coming of Christ, representing the house of David. In the raising up of the Lord Jesus, the word of God goes out to all the people and all the nations. James uses this passage to show that God, as He had promised through the prophets, would bless the world through Jesus.

Then comes this beautiful scene:

> *"The days are coming," declares the LORD, "when the reaper will be overtaken by the plowman and the planter by the one treading grapes. New wine will drip from the mountains and flow from all the hills. I will bring back my exiled people Israel; they will rebuild the ruined cities and live in them. They will plant vineyards and drink their wine; they will make gardens and eat their fruit" (Amos 9:13–14).*

Compare Amos's statement that "new wine will drip from the mountains and flow from all the hills," with the concluding image from the prophet Joel: "In that day the mountains will drip new wine, and the hills will flow with milk; all the ravines of Judah will run with water. A fountain will flow out of the LORD's house and will water the valley of acacias" (3:18). Both Amos and Joel depict a glorious millennial future when Israel will at last be restored to the land—and the land will flow with luscious, delightful splendor and goodness.

Here we see God's heart of kindness and goodness toward the human race. That is why He is often so angry with humanity, which is so bent on injustice, greed, and destruction. Human cruelty makes God angry because He wants us to be kind and compassionate toward one another. Oppression stirs His wrath and brings forth His judgment because He wants people to live in love and peace, to be happy and content.

The message of this book is that God is relentless in His pursuit of our absolute best. He will not compromise with our sin, our excuses, or our hypocrisy. The word of Amos to us is that we are dealing with a God of righteousness and inflexible zeal—yet He is a God of patience, mercy, and love. He is totally impartial. He does not play favorites. If we seek Him, we will live—*truly live!* We will enjoy the blessings of peace and goodness that He truly desires to pour into our lives. If we ignore Him, if we seek lesser things, if we go our own way, then His message to us is the message of Amos 4:12—"Prepare to meet your God."

Whether we seek Him or avoid Him, we cannot escape Him. One day, one way or another, we will meet our God. If we heed the call of Amos, we will be able to meet Him confidently, because we have sought Him with all our hearts.

Both Amos and Joel depict a glorious millennial future when Israel will at last be restored to the land

Whether we seek Him or avoid Him, we cannot escape Him

Death to Edom!

W e previously noted that the little three-chapter book of Joel, despite its brevity, packed a powerful message for our times. The prophecy of Obadiah is even shorter—it is, in fact, the shortest book in the Old Testament. Yet it, too, packs a powerful wallop of importance and relevance for our lives that is greatly disproportionate to its short page count. Someone has said that less is more when it comes to getting your message across—and the prophet Obadiah seems to validate that saying!

Less is more

On one level, the book of Obadiah is a pronouncement of doom against an ancient and long-forgotten nation, the land of Edom. But this book has far greater significance than that. As with many other books of the Bible, Obadiah has important surface meaning, but diligent students mine an amazing array of rich treasures at a deeper level.

Here is an outline of the brief but powerful book of Obadiah:

Obadiah—The Story of Israel and Edom
1. Judgment pronounced against Edom	1–14
2. The result of judgment	15–18
3. Israel to possess Edom	19–21

We know little about Obadiah except that he was one of the minor prophets—that is, his book is minor in length, though hardly minor in scope or importance. Old Testament accounts of the days of Elijah and

A tale of two nations—and two brothers

Elisha include a reference to a prophet named Obadiah, so some have assumed the author of this book to be the same man. The name Obadiah, however, was a very common one among the Hebrews and it is unlikely that this is the same prophet. In this book, Obadiah mentions the day when Jerusalem was destroyed and captured by the alien armies—an event that occurs long after the time of Elijah and Elisha. Most Bible commentators believe that the author of this book was a contemporary of the prophet Jeremiah, the last of the prophets before Israel went into captivity.

The name Obadiah means "the servant of Jehovah," and he truly fulfills the role of a servant: Obadiah comes, does his work, delivers his message, then fades into the mists of history.

The book of Obadiah tells the story of two nations, Israel and Edom. The nation of Edom was located south of Israel in a region now referred to as the Negev or Negeb. The Israelites traveled through this ancient land as they escaped the slavery of Egypt and came into the land of Israel. As the Israelites passed through Edom, the Edomites persecuted them. They were Israel's enemies from its very beginning.

Underlying the story of these two nations, Obadiah tells the story of two men. Every nation in the Bible is a lengthened shadow of its founder, and the two men behind the nations Israel and Edom were twin brothers. I'm sure you recognize their names: Jacob and Esau. Jacob was the father of Israel, and Esau, his twin brother, became the father of the Edomites. In the story of these nations you also have the extended story of these two men.

Jacob and Esau were in perpetual antagonism. We read in Genesis that even before they were born, they struggled together in their mother's womb. That antagonism marked the lives of these two men, and, consequently, the lives of their descendants, the nations of Israel and Edom.

Jacob was his mother's darling and Esau was his daddy's little man. Their lives were characterized by intense sibling rivalry and conflict—a conflict that continued even after they died! Their antagonism was carried on by the nations that they founded, and all the way from Genesis through Malachi we see evidence of the struggle between them. In the book of Malachi, the last book of the Old Testament, we read:

> "I have loved you," says the LORD.
> "But you ask, 'How have you loved us?'"
> "Was not Esau Jacob's brother?" the LORD says. "Yet I have loved Jacob, but Esau I have hated, and I have turned his mountains into a wasteland and left his inheritance to the desert jackals."
> Edom may say, "Though we have been crushed, we will rebuild the ruins."

Every nation in the Bible is a lengthened shadow of its founder, and the two men behind Israel and Edom were twin brothers

Jacob and Esau were in perpetual antagonism

Their antagonism was carried on by the nations they founded, and from Genesis through Malachi we see evidence of the struggle between them

This is what the LORD Almighty says: "They may build, but I will demolish. They will be called the Wicked Land, a people always under the wrath of the LORD" (Mal. 1:2–4).

What is so important about these two men and these two nations? That is what the book of Obadiah makes clear to us. In the struggle between Edom and Israel in the Old Testament, we see a parallel with a similar struggle that is described for us in the New Testament—the Christian's struggle between the flesh and the spirit. In Galatians 5:17 we are told that the flesh lusts against the spirit and the spirit against the flesh; they are opposed to one another. God always uses pictures for us so that we can understand His truth more fully. Like children, we love to not only hear the truth but to see the picture. So God gives us many pictures of His truth—including the picture of Esau and Jacob, of Edom and Israel, which represent for us the conflict between the flesh and the spirit.

This, incidentally, is a valuable key to Bible study. Once we learn to recognize the "interpretational constants" in Scripture—the keys, symbols, images, metaphors, similes, names, and figures that consistently, repeatedly signify important truths—then many hard-to-understand biblical concepts soon become clear. For example, certain symbols have a constant meaning wherever you find them in the Old and New Testaments: Oil is almost always a symbol for the Holy Spirit; wine symbolizes joy; leaven is always a picture of evil. And these two men, Jacob and Esau, and the nations Israel and Edom, always symbolize the struggle between the spirit and the flesh.

Why does God hate Esau? Obadiah tells us:

The problem of pride

The pride of your heart has deceived you, you who live in the clefts of the rocks and make your home on the heights, you who say to yourself, "Who can bring me down to the ground?" (v. 3).

The trouble with Esau is *pride*. Pride is the basic characteristic of what the Bible calls "the flesh." Our pride wars against God's Spirit. The flesh is a principle that opposes God's purposes for humanity and continually defies what God is trying to accomplish. Every Christian has this internal struggle. Pride is the number one identifying mark of the flesh.

Proverbs 6:16 says, "There are six things the LORD hates, seven that are detestable to him." Topping that list is a proud look—a look of arrogance. Everything else that follows is merely a variation of pride. This is the fallen nature that was implanted in the human race; all who are born of Adam have this congenital twist of pride, the independent ego that evaluates everything only in terms of whether it feeds the omnipotent self. For the prideful person, the universe revolves around the self. There is no room in the universe for rivals, least of all for God. That is pride. That is Esau. That is Edom.

The prideful person says, "Who can bring me down to the ground? Nobody can touch me, nobody can stand in my way. My plans are laid out, and I will carry out everything I set out to do." This attitude of self-sufficiency and personal invulnerability is a mark of pride. The Lord answers such people in Obadiah 4:

> *"Though you soar like the eagle and make your nest among the stars,*
> *from there I will bring you down," declares the LORD.*

The reference in verse 3 to "you who live in the clefts of the rocks" is a literal reference to the nation of Edom. If you have had the privilege of visiting the Holy Land, you may have gone down into the Negev area and visited the city of Petra, the rose red city of the dead. The entry to this amazing city is a tremendous fissure that runs for a mile or more right through the rock, a narrow passage only a few yards wide that brings you at last into an open place where temples have been carved out of the living rock—giant temples with doorways some twenty-five feet high or more. That was the capital of Edom. That was the ancient city whose people felt that because of these natural defenses they were invulnerable. They lifted up their hearts in pride, and, as the Lord speaking through the prophet says, the pride of their hearts was deceived. They thought that nothing could overthrow them, but God said it would be done. Just a few years after Jesus' death, the Romans came in and destroyed the cities of Edom and captured this "impregnable" fortress. It has been in ruins ever since.

Another form of pride is found in verse 10:

> *Because of the violence against your brother Jacob, you will be covered*
> *with shame; you will be destroyed forever.*

Violence is a form of pride. What underlies the violence of the human heart? An unbroken ego, a spoiled and cowardly spirit. The person who inflicts violent pain and injury on another person pridefully believes that he or she has a right to do so—and the victim has no rights or dignity. Pride is rooted in selfishness and it strikes out against anything that dares to challenge its own supremacy. I have been in a Christian home and seen a woman with black eyes and bruises on her legs and arms because her husband—a Sunday school teacher—had beaten her. Where does this violence come from? It is from Edom. It is the pride of the flesh.

We find another form of pride in verse 11:

On the day you stood aloof while strangers carried off his wealth and foreigners entered his gates and cast lots for Jerusalem, you were like one of them.

In other words, "You just stood and watched. You were like all those gawkers who stood at their apartment windows in New York City and watched dumbly while a young woman named Kitty Genovese was tortured and murdered in front of their eyes. You were indifferent. You said, 'I don't want to get involved.' "

Indifference is a form of pride. Indifference to what is going on around you is a form of self-centeredness. "I am too important to get involved in that problem over there," says this form of pride. "My life is too important. My time is too important. My agenda is too important."

Indifference is a form of pride

The pride of indifference is a major source of marital difficulty. In my counseling experience, I have often heard the complaint, "He ignores me," or, "She pays no attention to me." This is equally true in Christian marriages and non-Christian marriages. It seems that soon after courtship and marriage, indifference moves into the relationship, sucking the romance and passion out and replacing it with selfishness and pridefulness. During the courtship, spouses ask each other, "What are you thinking about? Tell me what you would like." After marriage, it's, "Where's my dinner? What's on TV? Don't bother me!" That's Esau at work in the relationship. That's the pride of indifference.

Another form of pride crops up in Obadiah 12 and 13:

You should not look down on your brother in the day of his misfortune, nor rejoice over the people of Judah in the day of their destruction, nor boast so much in the day of their trouble. You should not march through the gates of my people in the day of their disaster, nor look down on them in their calamity in the day of their disaster, nor seize their wealth in the day of their disaster.

God charges Edom with the sin of gloating over the misfortunes of others—another manifestation of the problem of pride. Did you ever say that in your own heart about somebody? "You had it coming!" You were gloating. You hear that the boss is sick, and you say, "Nothing trivial, I hope." A business rival—or even another Christian—gets into financial or legal difficulty, and you think, "Serves him right!" Why do we do this? Why do we delight in kicking those who are down, in rubbing salt into

God charges Edom with the sin of gloating over the misfortunes of others—another manifestation of the problem of pride

open wounds? What is this perverse delight we take in finding and spotlighting another person's failures or faults? It is Esau in us. It is pride. It is the flesh warring against the Spirit of God—and it is sin, pure and simple.

This is only a partial listing of the ways of Esau, the man God hates, and it is all summed up under the heading of Obadiah 3, where He says:

The pride of your heart has deceived you.

**The trap
of pride**

Pride has a way of working out its own destruction. Pride sets a trap—and then proceeds to spring the trap on itself! Here is what Obadiah writes in verses 6 and 7:

How Esau will be ransacked, his hidden treasures pillaged! All your allies will force you to the border; your friends will deceive and overpower you; those who eat your bread will set a trap for you, but you will not detect it.

Pride deceives us. It traps us. It tricks us. It blinds us to the danger around us. We don't recognize it until too late. With a sense of invincibility, we step onto the flimsy carpet that has been spread over the pit, never suspecting that our next step is our last. Everyone else sees the danger at our feet. Some are shouting to us, jumping up and down, trying to wave us off—but we are too prideful to listen. They don't know what they're talking about! We know what we're doing!

Famous last words!

This is where we live, isn't it? We all have this problem of the flesh within. And it is absolutely crucial that we deal with and root out the pride in our lives because Edom has no place in us. God will judge Edom, and there will be no escape for the prideful. God is forever set against those who are prideful, those who live by the flesh instead of the spirit.

We see this truth illustrated for us elsewhere in the Old Testament. One of the grandsons of Esau was a man named Amalek, whose descendants opposed the Israelites on their way into Canaan. In Exodus 17:14, God says to Moses, "I will completely blot out the memory of Amalek from under heaven." That is what God is saying about the flesh. He will never make peace with it.

But for Jacob, a day of triumph awaits:

"On Mount Zion [a symbol for Jerusalem or Jacob] *will be deliverance; it will be holy, and the house of Jacob will possess its inheritance. The house of Jacob will be a fire and the house of Joseph a flame; the house of Esau will be stubble, and they will set it on fire and consume it.*

*There will be no survivors from the house of Esau." The LORD has spo-
ken (vv. 17–18).*

God sounds ruthless, doesn't He? Why must He destroy Esau and
the nation of Edom? Because Esau and Edom are equally ruthless. You
cannot make peace with the flesh, because the flesh will never make
peace with you. Try to appease Esau, try to compromise with Edom, and
they will turn and destroy you.

It is interesting that when you come to the New Testament, you find
the same two principles—Edom and Israel, flesh and spirit—personified
in the pages of the Gospels. In the last week of our Lord's sufferings, He
stands before Herod. Herod, we are told, is an Idumean. Because
Idumea is another spelling of Edom, we know that Herod is an Edomite,
a descendant of Esau. Jesus stands before Herod—the representative of
Jacob and the representative of Esau—face-to-face. King Herod the
Edomite is proud, arrogant, and rebellious; he watches the cruel mockery of the soldiers as they strip the Lord down and dress Him in His
royal robes. King Jesus, the Spirit-filled Israelite, is humble and obedient; He goes willingly to His death by torture, which is inflicted on Him
at the hands of Herod. The Gospels say that Herod plied Jesus with
many questions, but for the son of Esau there is no answer from the son
of Jacob. They have nothing to discuss. Compromise is impossible. God
has nothing to say to the flesh—nothing except judgment.

In the end, it is humble King Jesus who breaks free from the cross
and the grave, and it is prideful King Herod who ends his life in shame
and exile, a prisoner of the chains with which he as always pridefully
bound himself. The spirit is the victor. The flesh is defeated. Israel rises;
Edom falls.

Israel or Edom, spirit or flesh—on which side are you? That is the
central question of the short but towering book of the prophet Obadiah.

The Reluctant Ambassador

P robably the best known yet least understood book in the Bible is the book of Jonah. From the world's point of view, the story of "Jonah and the Whale" has become a part of our literature and our folklore—a tall tale like the story of Paul Bunyan or the legends of Greek or Roman mythology. Most people are familiar with the story, but the book itself is regarded with either smug amusement or outright ridicule—one of the "fables" of the Bible. It is not taken seriously. It is not taken historically. It is merely a big fish story.

Because of these superficial attitudes, the true message and power of this book have been obscured. Jonah was a real, living, flesh-and-blood man who lived in history, and he is mentioned in other places in Scripture. The book of 2 Kings refers to him as a historical prophet, as does Jesus in Matthew 12:40. Here is a structural overview of the book of Jonah:

God Commissions Jonah to Go to Nineveh (Jonah 1–2)

    1. Jonah's disobedience and God's discipline
       of Jonah by means of a great fish   1
    2. Jonah's prayer and deliverance   2

God Recommissions Jonah (Jonah 3–4)

    3. Jonah is obedient to God's renewed command   3:1–4
    4. Nineveh repents and judgment is stayed   3:5–10
    5. Jonah sulks, prays to die; God rebukes Jonah   4

Jonah's refusal

The theme of this story is found in the last two chapters of this little book. There you have Jonah, after his encounter with the whale (or fish)—going to Nineveh as God had originally sent him. There he proclaims the message that God gave him to proclaim. When you ask yourself, "Why did Jonah originally refuse to go to Nineveh?" you get very close to the heart of this book's message.

You know how the story opens:

> The word of the LORD came to Jonah son of Amittai: "Go to the great city of Nineveh and preach against it, because its wickedness has come up before me."
> But Jonah ran away from the LORD and headed for Tarshish. He went down to Joppa, where he found a ship bound for that port. After paying the fare, he went aboard and sailed for Tarshish to flee from the LORD (1:1–3).

It is amazing how, when you are running away from God, you can find a ship ready to take you

It is amazing how, when you are trying to run away from God, you can find a ship ready to take you. Then came the great storm and the mariners cast him into the sea, and a great fish swallowed him.

The God of mercy

In the second chapter of Jonah we find his prayer begging God to rescue him from the belly of the fish. On the third day, God answered Jonah's prayer: The fish got a terrible stomachache and vomited him up on the land. Then in chapter 3, verses 1 and 2, we are told:

> The word of the LORD came to Jonah a second time: "Go to the great city of Nineveh and proclaim to it the message I give you."

God's command contains a note of sternness. God has not changed His mind a bit. He finally has changed the prophet's mind—but God has not relented about what He wants Jonah to do and say in Nineveh.

Why was Jonah so anxious to avoid his commission? Why didn't he want to go to Nineveh? Why did he flee from God? Some Bible scholars suggest that Jonah had such a primitive idea of God that he regarded Him as just a tribal deity, for Israel alone, that he thought God could not really be interested in Nineveh, and that if Jonah could get out of the land, he would get away from God. I think that idea is dashed by Jonah's own reference to God. When the voyagers asked Jonah to identify himself, he said to them, "I am a Hebrew and I worship the LORD, the God of heaven, who made the sea and the land" (Jonah 1:9). That does not sound like the description of a tribal deity to me. No, that is not why Jonah avoided going to Nineveh.

In fact, the answer is exactly the opposite: Jonah knew God too well and that is why he did not go to Nineveh. Does that sound strange?

Well, look at the beginning of chapter 4:

Jonah was greatly displeased and became angry. He prayed to the LORD, *"O* LORD, *is this not what I said when I was still at home? That is why I was so quick to flee to Tarshish. I knew that you are a gracious and compassionate God, slow to anger and abounding in love, a God who relents from sending calamity" (4:1–2).*

Jonah knew exactly what God was like—gracious, compassionate, abounding in love—and *that's* why he would not go to Nineveh! He did not want Nineveh to repent and be spared—he wanted Nineveh to be destroyed! This is fascinating, don't you think? Jonah hated the inhabitants of this cruel, bloody city—a city that had often sent raiders into his own land killing and plundering. Jonah wanted revenge, not mercy, for the godless Ninevites!

So, in an effort to prevent God from showing mercy to his hated enemy, Jonah fled to Tarshish.

Here is amazing insight into God's character and proof that the God of the Old Testament and the God of the New Testament are one and the same God! From time to time, those who do not believe the Bible— primarily those who are educated beyond their intelligence—say that the God of the Old Testament was a vengeful, wrathful God, always zapping people with lightning and thunderbolts. But this does not describe the God Jonah knew. He views God as "gracious and compassionate . . . , slow to anger and abounding in love, a God who relents from sending calamity."

Oh, there is someone in this story who is vengeful and wrathful, who wants to see a whole city full of people get zapped by lightning from heaven. But that person is not God—it's Jonah! The judgment of human beings is always more harsh, more capricious, more angry than the judgment of God. God's judgment is just, and it is merciful. It was God— the God of the Old Testament—who invented grace and mercy and who always abounded in patient love.

So God recommissioned Jonah to go to Nineveh. Jonah still didn't want to do it, but he remembered his three-day ride in the belly of the fish. And he went.

So Jonah came at last to Nineveh, a vast city—so vast, in fact, that it took three days just to walk from one side of the city to the other. A day's journey was reckoned to be about twelve miles, so a three days' journey would be about thirty-six miles. That is a pretty good-sized city. In many ways, it was probably a cluster of towns and neighborhoods much like Los Angeles or New York City. It was gathered around the

Jonah knew exactly what God was like—gracious, compassionate, abounding in love—and *that's* why he would not go to Nineveh

It was God—the God of the Old Testament—who invented grace and mercy and who always abounded in patient love

The response of Nineveh

banks of the Tigris River and formed the capital of the great Syrian (or Assyrian) empire. Declaring God's message to such a huge city was going to take some time. So Jonah began a day's journey through the city, calling out that in forty days, God would destroy the city.

Ordinarily that kind of a message would not get much of a reception. The Bible reports that when other prophets with a similar message were being sent to wicked cities, they were laughed out of town—or worse. But an amazing thing happens in this story:

> *The Ninevites believed God. They declared a fast, and all of them, from the greatest to the least, put on sackcloth (3:5).*

And when the king heard about it

> *he rose from his throne, took off his royal robes, covered himself with sackcloth and sat down in the dust. Then he issued a proclamation in Nineveh:*
> *"By the decree of the king and his nobles:*
> *Do not let any man or beast, herd or flock, taste anything; do not let them eat or drink. But let man and beast be covered with sackcloth. Let everyone call urgently on God. Let them give up their evil ways and their violence" (3:6–8).*

And the people of Nineveh did exactly what God, through His reluctant servant Jonah, told them to do. God saw and He judged their hearts and their actions:

> *When God saw what they did and how they turned from their evil ways, he had compassion and did not bring upon them the destruction he had threatened (3:10).*

Jonah was a sign to the Ninevites

Why did the people of Nineveh listen to Jonah's message? Jesus Himself gives us a clue. In Luke 11, He refers to this account and says, "As Jonah was a sign to the Ninevites, so also will the Son of Man be to this generation" (Luke 11:30). Some Bible scholars feel that Jonah's features were changed by his experience in the whale's belly. There are some interesting, historically verified incidents of people who have been swallowed by fish or whales, much as Jonah was. I recommend Harry Rimmer's *The Harmony of Science and Scripture,* in which he tells of an English sailor who fell overboard and was swallowed by a fish. A day or two later the fish was seen floating on the surface of the water and was taken ashore. When it was opened up, the sailors, to their amazement, found their shipmate alive. He survived the experience, but his skin had turned a chalky white and remained so for the rest of his life. Dr. Rimmer talked with him and learned the details of his experience. It was clearly verified. There have been other accounts like this, probably half a dozen altogether.

If Jonah's face and body confirmed the remarkable testimony that he had been swallowed alive by a fish as a judgment from God in his own life, you can be sure that the people took him seriously when he talked about God's coming judgment upon their city. Jonah was living evidence that God meant what He said. The city repented down to the last person, and the judgment of God was stayed.

In the concluding chapter of the book, we have the encounter between Jonah and God. You might expect the story to end in chapter 3, as the city repents in sackcloth and ashes. But the fourth chapter of Jonah shows us that the focus of this book is not on the city of Nineveh but on the man Jonah—and the heart of God. We read in this chapter that Jonah was angry with God. Why? Because God did exactly what He said He would do, exactly what Jonah feared He would do: He spared the city of Nineveh. That was why Jonah ran away in the first place—to keep God from showing mercy to the enemy city. Jonah was so bitterly angry with God that he actually wanted to die.

After listening to Jonah rant and rave and demand that God slay him, God turned the tables on Jonah. He asked His servant a question:

"Have you any right to be angry?" (4:4).

Jonah didn't even answer. He sat down on the rimrock above the city and waited to see what God would do. I don't know how much time went by, but it must have been several days, because the first day, God prepared or appointed a plant. The plant grew up and covered Jonah's head, evidence of God's gracious provision.

On the second day, God prepared a worm that attacked and killed the plant. Then, when the sun came up, God prepared an east wind that blew the heat of the desert in upon Jonah. He sat there sweating and suffering until he was nearly fainting. Again, he asked that he might die, and again, God confronted him about his attitude:

God said to Jonah, "Do you have a right to be angry about the vine?"
"I do," he said. "I am angry enough to die" (4:9).

It is easy to accuse Jonah, but most of us have said something similar to God at one time or another: "Of course I'm angry with you, God. You're unfair. I don't like the way you're running things. You don't understand how I feel. You don't punish the evildoers. I have a right to be mad at you, God, because you aren't running things right."

And then God shows Jonah the ludicrous folly of his attitude. In verses 10 and 11, He points out to Jonah that he is sitting there feeling sorry for himself and he is sitting there feeling sorry for a silly plant that he hadn't even planted or labored over. Why, then, did he not feel even the slightest twinge of compassion for the 120,000 people in the city of Nineveh who were so ignorant of God and spiritual things that they were like children, not knowing their right hand from their left!

At this point, the book abruptly ends. Why? Because it has taken us right where it was supposed to take us: into the very heart of God! Most of us are so much like Jonah: We care about our own selfish wants and needs, our own agenda, our paltry possessions. With Jonah, it was a plant; with you or me, it might be a car, a job, a house, or something else. We care about things. We care about self. God cares about people, about living, throbbing, suffering human souls.

God loved these Ninevites, even though Jonah hated them. Who is your enemy today? Perhaps you would love to see God pour out His judgment on some evil world leader. Or on the cantankerous next door neighbor. Or on the person who stole your car. Or on the drunk driver who took a loved one away from you. Or on the bossy Christian who makes life miserable for you at church. But God loves that person, just as He loved the Ninevites. You want that person to suffer, but God loves that person and may even prosper him or her. You may become angry and impatient with God for delaying His judgment of that person.

But God wants us to see these people and all people the way that He sees them. He wants us to take up residence in His heart and to see the world through His eyes. God has sent us to the world to declare the word of Jonah—a word of warning and a word of mercy. All around us are unsaved people. We may find them godless and disobedient. We may dismiss them from our lives as revolting, disgusting people, deserving damnation. But spiritually, they are like children, not knowing the right hand from the left. They are the objects of God's love, mercy, and compassion, and He wants to send us to them to tell them about His love.

God has sent us to be a sign to our generation, just as He sent Jonah to be a sign to his generation

God has sent us to be a sign to our generation, just as He sent Jonah to be a sign to his generation. What is that sign? It is the sign of Jonah, the sign of resurrection, the sign of people who once were dead and who have been made alive in Jesus Christ. Our message is clear: We serve a God who can bring life from death, who can resurrect those who are swallowed up in the belly of a whale, swallowed up in sin and shame, swallowed up in depression and hopelessness.

Jonah ran from his calling. He was angry over the mercy of God. May we learn the lesson of Jonah's life. May each of us in obedience go where God wants us to go, say what He wants us to say, do what He wants us to do. Instead of being angry over the mercy of God, may His mercy fill us with joy and a sense of triumph as we declare God's message in our day.

Who Is Like God?

W hat's in a name?

In the Bible, names are often highly significant. For example, the book of Genesis contains the story of a man named Methusaleh—a famous name because Methusaleh is the oldest man in Scripture (and presumably the oldest person who ever lived). When Methuselah was born, his father, Enoch, gave him a name that proved not only significant, but prophetic: in Hebrew, it means, "When he dies, it will come." Methuselah lived 969 years, and the year in which he died, the Great Flood of Noah came.

The book of Micah is yet another example of the significance of names in the Bible. In fact, the key to this little prophetic book can be found in the meaning of the prophet's name. In Hebrew, Micah means "Who is like God?" or "Who is like Jehovah?" This is Micah's repeated question. The book indicates that "Micah" was actually a nickname given to this prophet because his oft-repeated message was, "Micah? Micah? Who is like God?"

Godlikeness—a word that has been shortened to *godliness*—is the theme of Micah. Godlikeness is also the theme of Paul's epistle to the Ephesians; it is interesting and instructive to compare these two messages, Micah and Ephesians, side by side. By doing so, we see that the Old Testament and the New Testament complement each other; they speak with a unified, consistent voice. Here again is proof of the

Micah and
Ephesians

principle that Scripture interprets Scripture; if we do not understand something in the New Testament, we can turn to the Old Testament for insight and clarification.

Micah was a contemporary of the great prophet Isaiah, and his book is similar in style. Sometimes, in fact, this book is called "Isaiah in miniature" because it is a concise presentation of essentially the same message.

The book is divided into three parts. The first three chapters describe the failure of the nation. We hear this theme in many of the prophets, but in Micah we see that the Jewish nation has particularly failed in respect to a lifestyle of godliness or Godlikeness. Chapters 4 and 5 contrast Israel's ungodliness with a vision of the One who is to come— the Godlike one. This is a prophetic section that looks forward to the coming of Christ, the Messiah. The last three chapters give us God's plea that the nation repent and return to Him.

Here is an outline of the book of Micah:

The Judgment to Come (Micah 1–3)
1. The judgment against the people	1–2
2. The judgment against the leaders	3

The Restoration to Come (Micah 4–5)
3. The kingdom to come	4
4. The Messiah to come	5

Two Appeals for Repentance (Micah 6–7)
5. God's first appeal and Micah's reply	6
6. God's second appeal and Micah's reply	7:1–6
7. The promise of salvation	7:7–20

The first chapter presents a magnificent picture of God striding forth in judgment against this nation of Judah because of the people's utter failure to be godly even though God provided them with everything that it takes to be godly. That sounds familiar, does it not? Why are we not godly? We have all that it takes, in the Holy Spirit, to be godly—yet we fall so far short. So this book meets us right where we are—in the same boat with the people of Judah.

The punster prophet

In Micah 1:10–16, we encounter an interesting facet of the text that is difficult to appreciate in the English translation. These ancient prophets were punsters, and although some people say that a pun is the lowest form of humor, the Bible has many puns in it. The problem for us as English-speaking readers is that the puns are in Hebrew! If you could read the original Hebrew, you would see pun upon pun employed in the names of these cities mentioned by Micah.

Micah tells the city of Gath not to weep—and the name of the city means "weeping." He tells Beth Ophrah (House of Dust) to roll in the dust as an act of repentance. He tells Shaphir (Beauty) that her beauty will be shamed. He tells Zaanan (Marching) that it will not march forth. He tells Beth Ezel (House of Neighbors) that it will end up being unprotected by its neighbors. He tells Maroth (Bitter Town) that it will grieve bitterly. He tells Lachish (Horse Town) to harness the horses to the chariot and get ready to get out of town.

Chapter 2 goes on to picture the utter destruction of the people, including the rulers, prophets, women, and children.

In chapter 3 we find the reason for God's judgment against Judah. Like Diogenes, lamp in hand, scouring the countryside for an honest man, Micah has been seeking godliness in the southern kingdom of Judah, and he looks where he might expect to find it—among the rulers of the nation, among the representatives of God. But there he finds only corruption, oppression, bribery, and injustice. Micah exposes the mess in Jerusalem, and he says that the reason for God's judgment upon His people is that those who have been given the authority to act in God's stead have forgotten that they are responsible to God.

This indictment touches our own lives today. For whenever we are put in a position of authority, we are told to remember that we also have an authority over us. The New Testament reminds us that masters are to remember that they have a master in heaven as well, and God holds all authority responsible and accountable to Himself (see Eph. 6:9). Anyone who forgets this is using power only for personal advantage and self-aggrandizement. And that is what corrupted the nation and brought it under God's judgment. The prophet sums it up for us in chapter 3, verse 11:

> Her leaders judge for a bribe, her priests teach for a price, and her prophets tell fortunes for money. Yet they lean upon the LORD and say, "Is not the LORD among us? No disaster will come upon us."

When you serve in a position of authority whether in government, in church, in a business or organization, or in your family, you represent God in that position. Paul declared, "Everyone must submit himself to the governing authorities, for there is no authority except that which God has established. *The authorities that exist have been established by God"* (Rom. 13:1, emphasis added). Forgetting the responsibility that we have as leaders and authorities leads to corruption, oppression, bribery, suffering—and judgment.

When you serve in a position of authority, you represent God in that position

In chapter 4, we encounter a wonderfully exalted vision. Here, the prophet lifts his eyes and looks across the centuries—past the coming of Babylon, past the rise of the great Eastern empire of Greece, past the Roman Empire and the days of the Caesars, past the Middle Ages, past the age of the Reformation and Martin Luther and John Wesley, and even past our own day. In his vision, Micah sees the coming of one who is Godlike. This is one of the most beautiful messianic passages in the Scriptures:

> In the last days the mountain of the LORD's temple will be established as chief among the mountains; it will be raised above the hills, and peoples will stream to it. Many nations will come and say, "Come, let us go up to the mountain of the LORD, to the house of the God of Jacob. He will teach us his ways, so that we may walk in his paths." The law will go out from Zion, the word of the LORD from Jerusalem. He will judge between many peoples and will settle disputes for strong nations far and wide. They will beat their swords into plowshares and their spears into pruning hooks. Nation will not take up sword against nation, nor will they train for war anymore. Every man will sit under his own vine and under his own fig tree, and no one will make them afraid, for the LORD Almighty has spoken (4:1–4).

The search for
world peace is a
forlorn hope until
the Messiah Himself
comes to impose
His rule

This passage describes a scene yet to come. The nations will never forget how to make war, never beat their swords into plowshares and their spears into pruning hooks until the One who knows how to rule in godliness comes. Though Micah's words describing a future world at peace are inscribed on the walls of the United Nations building in New York, the search for world peace is a forlorn hope until the Messiah Himself comes to impose His rule.

The rest of chapter 4 goes on to describe how Israel will be gathered and will ultimately defeat her enemies.

Chapter 5 opens with a new thought. The prophet says to Israel:

> Marshal your troops, O city of troops, for a siege is laid against us.
> They will strike Israel's ruler on the cheek with a rod (5:1).

This verse pictures the Assyrian army being gathered around the city. It is also a picture of that day when a greater Assyrian army out of the north will come against Israel. The reason it comes is given in the statement that these armies "will strike Israel's ruler on the cheek with a rod." This is a reference to the first coming of the Lord Jesus when He stood before Pilate and the rulers of the nation and they struck Him with a reed, placed a crown of thorns on His head, and mocked Him.

They struck on the cheek the ruler of Israel (see Matt. 27:27–30).

Now the prophet suddenly sees where this ruler is to come from. This is one of the great predictive passages of the Old Testament:

> *"You, Bethlehem Ephrathah, though you are small among the clans of Judah, out of you will come for me one who will be ruler over Israel, whose origins are from of old, from ancient times" (5:2).*

Remember when the wise men came out of the East looking for the newborn king of the Jews (see Matt. 2:1–6)? They said to the rulers of Jerusalem, "Where is the one who has been born king of the Jews?" And the chief priests said, "in Bethlehem." How did they know? Well, because seven hundred years before, Micah had written these words in Micah 5:2. The chief priests knew Messiah's birthplace because it had been foretold in Scripture.

This One who comes out of Bethlehem is further described in verse 4:

> *He will stand and shepherd his flock in the strength of the LORD, in the majesty of the name of the LORD his God. And they will live securely, for then his greatness will reach to the ends of the earth.*

Micah's seven-hundred-year-long vision is 20/20. He clearly sees the true nature of the Messiah, Jesus Christ, the God-man, the only godly person who ever walked on earth, the Godlike one, "whose origins are from of old, from ancient times" and whose "greatness will reach to the ends of the earth."

In chapters 6 and 7, in a passage of incredible power and beauty, Jehovah turns to plead with His people and to show them the way of Godlikeness. The prophet Micah writes:

God's plea

> *Listen to what the LORD says: "Stand up, plead your case before the mountains; let the hills hear what you have to say. Hear, O mountains, the LORD's accusation; listen, you everlasting foundations of the earth. For the LORD has a case against his people; he is lodging a charge against Israel" (6:1–2).*

That sets the stage. Now God speaks, and this is what He says:

> *"My people, what have I done to you? How have I burdened you? Answer me. I brought you up out of Egypt and redeemed you from the land of slavery. I sent Moses to lead you, also Aaron and Miriam. My*

people, remember what Balak king of Moab counseled and what Balaam son of Beor answered. Remember your journey from Shittim to Gilgal, that you may know the righteous acts of the LORD" (6:3–5).

How do the people respond to God?

With what shall I come before the LORD and bow down before the exalted God? Shall I come before him with burnt offerings, with calves a year old? Will the LORD be pleased with thousands of rams, with ten thousand rivers of oil? Shall I offer my firstborn for my transgression, the fruit of my body for the sin of my soul? (6:6–7).

God's answer is simplicity itself:

He has showed you, O man, what is good. And what does the LORD require of you? To act justly and to love mercy and to walk humbly with your God (6:8).

That is the answer, isn't it? That is the way to Godlikeness: to walk humbly with your God. After all, He is the only one who can make us Godlike. But the Israelites failed to do this, so again comes the warning of judgment, as God at last must wake them up to their folly and their sin.

Micah's question rings in our ears: Who is like God? Only the one who walks with the Messiah, Jesus the Lord, the one who patterns his or her life after the life of the Messiah, the one who acts justly (as He acted), who shows mercy (as He showed mercy), and who walks humbly (as He walked). God pleads with us, and beneath the thundering of His judgment, we hear the steady, insistent heartbeat of His love. He is merciful, and He waits for us to turn to Him for forgiveness, for restoration, for fellowship with Him, so that He can shape us and mold us to become the people for whom Micah was searching—people who are like God.

The Terrible Wrath of God

When was the last time you heard a sermon preached from the book of Nahum? The fact is, many Christians have *never* heard the message of Nahum!

The book of Nahum is generally neglected because it is so obscure, because it is so short—and, frankly, because it is not the most entertaining book to read. Yet, every portion of Scripture is indispensable and has its own contribution to make in our spiritual growth and nourishment. This is why the apostle Paul says, "All Scripture is God-breathed and is useful for teaching, rebuking, correcting and training in righteousness, so that the man of God may be thoroughly equipped for every good work" (2 Tim. 3:16–17). And this little prophecy of Nahum is no exception.

This prophecy reveals certain aspects of God's character more clearly than any other book of the Bible. The prophets unfold for us God's divine attributes, and each sees Him in a different light. As you read through the prophets, therefore, you are seeing one facet after

> Nahum is neglected because it is so obscure, so short— and because it is not the most entertaining book to read

**God's holy
anger**

Against Nineveh

Nahum means
"consolation" or
"comfort"

another of the character of an eternal God flashing like diamonds in the sunlight. We must not neglect any of these brilliant and illuminating facets.

In this book, Nahum reveals the facet or attribute of God's *anger*. No doctrine is quite as repugnant to people today as that of the anger of God. This is one doctrine many would like to forget. Some picture God as more of a Santa Claus than the Creator-Father-King-Judge He truly is. They cannot bear the thought of God's having to discipline or punish someone. They want to reshape their image of God into something more genial, more warm and fuzzy, more . . . *soft*.

While it is true that our God is loving, patient, and merciful, we should never neglect the full range of God's character. He is Judge, and judges must render verdicts and impose penalties or else they are unjust judges. He is Father, and fathers must discipline or else they do not love their children.

So it is Nahum's task to unfold the severe side of our loving heavenly Father. And he does. In this prophecy, the God of Mount Sinai flashes forth in awful fury, a God before whom humanity must stand silent and trembling. You cannot read the book of Nahum without recognizing the true solemnity and towering majesty of God.

As we begin this book, it is important to know why God is so angry—and with whom. This prophecy is directed against the city of Nineveh—yes, the very same city to which God sent the prophet Jonah. When Jonah preached in Nineveh, the city repented in sackcloth and ashes. God withheld His anger from the city and He spared it, because every Ninevite, from the king to the lowliest citizen, had turned to God and repented of his or her sins. Nahum's prophecy, however, occurs about a century after the prophecy of Jonah. During that time, Nineveh had repented of its repentance and had begun to do the same things that had called forth God's threat of judgment in the first place.

The prophet Nahum was sent to minister to the southern kingdom of Judah at the time of the invasion of the Assyrian king Sennacherib. King Sennacherib, who came from the Assyrian capital city, Nineveh, invaded Israel during the lifetime of the prophet Isaiah. It was from this great but godless city in the north that the armies of the Assyrians frequently came against the land of Judah and Israel. But God moved to protect His people, and He destroyed these enemies overnight.

Nahum means "consolation" or "comfort," and as the Assyrian army was spread out around the city of Jerusalem, the prophet was given a message of consolation. Picture the scene as the city is surrounded by armies known far and wide as ruthless warriors, without conscience about burning and destroying, raping and pillaging, killing the children, and sparing no one. Next, imagine how reassured the people of Jerusalem felt as the prophet Nahum stood and told them that God would destroy Nineveh, the proud capital of their enemies.

The book of Nahum divides into four sections, and each section is a unique description of the anger of God. Here is an outline of this book:

God's Terrible Wrath   1:1–7
Principles of God's judgment

God's Personal Wrath   1:8–15
God's judgment against Nineveh and Sennacherib

God's Thorough Wrath   2:1–3:11
The destruction of Nineveh

God's Irresistible Wrath   3:12–19
The destruction of Nineveh was inevitable

The first section could be characterized as a vision of *God's terrible wrath*, as we see described for us in chapter 1:

> The LORD is a jealous and avenging God; the LORD takes vengeance and is filled with wrath. The LORD takes vengeance on his foes and maintains his wrath against his enemies. The LORD is slow to anger and great in power; the LORD will not leave the guilty unpunished. His way is in the whirlwind and the storm, and clouds are the dust of his feet. He rebukes the sea and dries it up; he makes all the rivers run dry. Bashan and Carmel wither and the blossoms of Lebanon fade. The mountains quake before him and the hills melt away. The earth trembles at his presence, the world and all who live in it. Who can withstand his indignation? Who can endure his fierce anger? His wrath is poured out like fire; the rocks are shattered before him (1:2–6).

Section 1: God's terrible wrath

What a description that is! The prophet envisions God in His anger, looking at the hosts of Assyria. He has been patient, enduring their sins, giving them every opportunity to repent as they had done in Jonah's day. He has sent prophet after prophet to appeal to them to turn back to Him. Finally, God's patience is exhausted, and His anger comes to a full, rolling boil! Yes, He is slow to anger—but once that anger is aroused, it's a terrible thing to experience!

God is slow to anger—but once that anger is aroused, it's a terrible thing to experience

It is a dangerous thing to repent of one's repentance, as the Ninevites did. To forsake evil, then return to it—this act provokes the anger of God. His anger is not a temper tantrum. It is not vindictive, petty, or needlessly cruel. It is not capricious or unjust. It is not selfish. It is not random or chaotic. The anger of God is controlled but awesome and fearsome to behold.

Nahum uses all the Hebrew words for God's anger

In these six verses, Nahum uses all the Hebrew words for God's anger: jealous, vengeance, wrath, anger, indignation, fierceness, fury. What do these words mean?

Jealousy

God's jealousy is not like the selfish, petty green-eyed monster of human jealousy. The jealousy of God is a burning zeal for a righteous cause, an overwhelming concern for the object of God's love.

Vengeance

God's vengeance or retribution is not like the thirst for revenge that often consumes human beings. God's vengeance is rooted in justice and is an accurate assessment of what is right—and wrong. When God avenges, we know that His vengeance is proportionate, just, and true.

Wrath

God's wrath, His dark and towering anger, is one of the most awesome, terrifying aspects of God's character—and once again, it is rooted in justice and truth. The Hebrew word for wrath stems from a term that literally means "hot breathing." The wrath of God is hot and intense, and everything in its path is withered and burned away.

Indignation

God's indignation comes from another Hebrew term literally translated as "foaming at the mouth." God's indignation is not merely a stamped foot or an upturned nose. It is intense and frightening in the extreme!

Fierceness, fury

Heat is a major component of God's anger. The word *fierceness* in Hebrew literally means "heat," and the word *fury* means "burning."

You can see how picturesque these words are. Bible-believing Christians cannot possibly deny that God's attributes include a white-hot, burning, blistering anger.

Section 2: God's personal wrath

The second section, beginning with Nahum 1:8, reveals another aspect of His anger: His wrath or anger can be *personal*. The anger of God that we see in this section is directed against a single individual: Sennacherib, the pagan king and general of the Assyrian armies who plotted to destroy God's people.

Against Sennacherib

This passage parallels Isaiah 36 and 37, which describes the Assyrian army's siege of Jerusalem, taunting and mocking Judah's ruler, King Hezekiah. Isaiah tells us that Hezekiah took the enemy's messages and spread them before the Lord, asking God to save the city. That night, we are told, the angel of death went through the Assyrian hosts and slew 185,000 soldiers (see Isa. 37:36). That event is referred to in Nahum 1:12–13:

This is what the LORD says: "Although they have allies and are numerous, they will be cut off and pass away. Although I have afflicted you, O Judah, I will afflict you no more. Now I will break their yoke from your neck and tear your shackles away."

When the angel went through the camp, the Assyrian general was spared, and he returned to Nineveh. But while he was worshiping his false gods in the temple after returning from this engagement with Israel, he was murdered by his own two sons who stole the crown for themselves—an event alluded to in verse 14:

The LORD has given a command concerning you, Nineveh: "You will have no descendants to bear your name. I will destroy the carved images and cast idols that are in the temple of your gods. I will prepare your grave, for you are vile."

Years before that event took place, the prophet Nahum was told that God would deal with this man in his own temple, in the house of his gods, and make his grave there. God's anger sought him out and struck him down.

We see from this section that God's wrath *can* be directed against an individual person. Many people find this hard to accept. They want to believe that God, being a God of love, is incapable of actually punishing people. They object to the idea that God's justice demands punishment for evildoers. God's love is greater than His justice, they say, and cancels out all punishment. But, from a biblical point of view, this is a delusion. God singled out Sennacherib, the Assyrian king, for extreme punishment because his sins had reached to the skies like smoke from the cities that he had destroyed.

Chapter 2 comprises a third section that reveals still another aspect of God's anger: He is thorough. God is addressing Nineveh, the capital city of Assyria, and He says:

Section 3: God's thorough wrath

An attacker advances against you, Nineveh. Guard the fortress, watch the road, brace yourselves, marshal all your strength! (2:1).

This is framed in a dramatic fashion, as though the watchman is looking out and sees the armies of the Babylonians coming up to destroy the city of Nineveh. History tells us that the combined armies of Cyaxares and Nabopolasser, the father of Nebuchadnezzar, came up against Nineveh and this army is called the "attacker" (or, in some translations, the "shatterer"). In verse 4, God through

Nahum relates what the scene will be like as the "shatterer" invades the city:

> *The chariots storm through the streets, rushing back and forth through the squares. They look like flaming torches; they dart about like lightning.*

Nahum's prophecy fulfilled

This almost sounds like a description of the Los Angeles freeway system! In reality, it is a predictive description of the battle that Nahum foresaw raging in the streets of Nineveh as the Babylonians swarmed over the city.

Verse 6 predicts the opening of the river gates and the disarray of the palace. The Greek historian Diodorus Siculus records how the city of Nineveh fell, saying:

> There was an old prophecy that Nineveh should not be taken till the river became an enemy with the city. And in the third year of the siege, the river being swollen with continual rains, overflowed every part of the city and broke down the wall for twenty furlongs. Then the king [of Nineveh], thinking that the oracle was fulfilled and the river became an enemy of the city, built a large funeral pile in the palace and collected together all his wealth and his concubines and his eunuch, [and] burnt himself and the palace with them all. And the enemy entered at the breach that the waters had made and took the city.

The Babylonian armies destroyed Nineveh in exactly the way in which Nahum had predicted that they would. When Nineveh was destroyed, nothing remained. Earlier in this century, you could have visited the vast site of Nineveh and you never would have known that a city ever existed there. For miles around, you would have seen nothing but flat, deserted wilderness. Some years ago, archaeologists began to excavate in the area, and they unearthed shards and fragments that verify the existence of Nineveh on that site. Broken rubble is all that remains of this once-great city; it had been lost for centuries, buried under the shifting sands of the desert. This is an illustration of how thoroughly God's anger works when He moves in judgment. Nothing escapes. "Though the mills of God grind slowly, yet they grind exceedingly small."

Section 4: God's irresistible wrath

In the fourth section, Nahum chapter 3, God addresses the city of Nineveh and warns that His anger is irresistible. The tone of this section is caustic and mocking, as we see in verses 14–15:

> *Draw water for the siege, strengthen your defenses! Work the clay, tread the mortar, repair the brickwork! There the fire will devour you; the sword will cut you down and, like grasshoppers, consume you.*

In other words, "Try as hard is you may, build your defenses as strong as you can—it won't do you any good. My anger is irresistible." When a nation or an individual becomes prideful and self-sufficient, God's judgment looms. When God shows mercy and patience, only to have that nation or individual remain prideful and unrepentant, God's wrath begins to smolder and darken like a storm-cloud.

What, then, is the message of Nahum for us today? We can derive both a national and an individual application. On the national level, we should be very concerned for a nation that increasingly rewards pride and worships at the altar of the self. We should worry about the increasing immorality and dishonesty that characterizes our society, our media, and our national life.

We should also avoid being complacent about the fact that communism has fallen in many places around the world. In the Bible, the Assyrians were not only the people who were actual enemies of Israel, but they were also a type of a people yet to come—a society that would threaten the peace of the earth and play an important part on the stage of world history in the last days. Many Bible scholars see the Assyrians of this and other Bible prophecies as a picture of Russia and its allied independent states. If you want an interesting study, compare Ezekiel 38 and 39 with this prophecy of Nahum. You notice in Nahum 2:13 that God says:

"I am against you," declares the LORD *Almighty.*

And when Ezekiel opens his great prophecy against the king of the north, Gog of the Land of Magog, he opens with similar words:

"This is what the Sovereign LORD *says: 'I am against you, O Gog, chief prince of Meshech and Tubal' " (Ezek. 38:3).*

We don't know what the future holds for Russia. Today there are signs of political confusion in that formerly communist nation. Will Russia return to the totalitarianism of Marxist-Leninist government? Will Russia pursue a postcommunist path that leads to a fiercely nationalist, expansionist nation? We don't know. But the likelihood, according to Bible prophecy, is that Russia will regain her stature as a political-military force that again threatens the peace of the world. Someday, according to these prophecies, Russia will again swarm down from the north to attack Israel—and will face the final judgment of God.

We should also heed Nahum's teaching about God's anger for the sake of our individual lives. We should not presume upon God's love. Instead, we should recognize that God's anger is actually the necessary flip side of God's love! If you are a parent, you know how you feel if anyone injures or insults your child or your spouse—you become very angry! If you cannot get angry when you hear or see injury and injustice, then you do not truly love. Anger is an emotion of defense and protection toward those we love. We can even become angry with the person we love, when we feel that our loved one is engaging in self-damaging or self-shaming behavior. We become angry precisely because we love that person and want the best for him or her.

God's anger is much the same. It is unleashed in the defense of those whom He loves. You cannot preach the love of God without preaching the wrath of God, because His wrath is a manifestation of His love. As Charles Spurgeon said, "He who does not believe that God will punish sin will not believe that He will pardon it through the blood of His Son."

How, then, can we escape the anger of God? Nahum has already given us the answer in Nahum 1:7:

> The LORD is good, a refuge in times of trouble. He cares for those who trust in him.

No one who turns to God in trust will ever experience His wrath. We need not face the wrath of God. He exercises His wrath only against those who reject His love.

Years ago, when my children were small, one of my daughters and I had a disagreement about her behavior. I spanked her (yes, I believe that spanking—administered in love and sorrow, not in anger—is biblical, practical, and effective). After I spanked her, she remained defiant and unrepentant for a time—and I wondered what I should do. Should I punish her further, in an effort to break her stubborn will and bring her to repentance? I prayed for God to show me what to do.

Just then, her entire demeanor changed. Her anger and her will seemed to melt. She ran to me and threw her arms around my neck, told me she was sorry, and pleaded for forgiveness. Now, what was I to do? Continue to spank her? Of course not! She was no longer rebellious. Instead, she had taken refuge in me. She had placed her trust in me. She had come to me for forgiveness—and I freely gave it to her.

God's heart is a father's heart

That's what a father's heart is like, and God is our heavenly Father. His heart of love is always open to those who take refuge in Him and who trust Him for salvation. They will never have to experience His wrath. As the Lord Jesus put it, "I tell you the truth, whoever hears my word and believes him who sent me has eternal life and will not be condemned; he has crossed over from death to life" (John 5:24).

Not Somehow, but Triumphantly

T he prophet Habakkuk is a prophet for our times.

He lived in times very much like our own, and he struggled with one of the central questions of our age: Why does God allow bad things to happen? Habakkuk lived in a time of great national corruption when crime, hatred, and division were on the rise, when evil and immorality were flaunted openly, when ethical standards and family values were breaking down. The prophet looked out across the land and expressed his horror at what he saw in the opening lines of his book:

> *The oracle that Habakkuk the prophet received.*
>
> *How long, O LORD, must I call for help, but you do not listen? Or cry out to you, "Violence!" but you do not save? Why do you make me look at injustice? Why do you tolerate wrong? Destruction and violence are before me; there is strife, and conflict abounds. Therefore the law is paralyzed, and justice never prevails. The wicked hem in the righteous, so that justice is perverted (1:2–4).*

Habakkuk says that he cries out to God, "Violence!" and hears no answer. Here is the great problem of unanswered prayer. Here is a man who is disturbed about his nation. He sees everything going wrong. The people are living in wickedness. Civil unrest, rioting, violence, injustice, and oppression permeate the land. When issues of injustice are brought before the courts, the courts themselves are corrupt.

Why does God allow bad things to happen?

Habakkuk is greatly troubled because he is a man of God; he has taken these problems to God, and God does not answer. So in his bewilderment and pain, he cries out, "Lord, how long do I have to keep this up? When are you going to do something? When will change, revival, and healing take place?" I'm sure you've felt that way, too, as you have looked around at the many problems and injustices that wrack our society or as you struggle with your own unanswered prayers.

God's answer

Beginning in verse 5, God begins to answer Habakkuk's questions. What follows is a dialogue between God and a single hurting human heart, the heart of the prophet Habakkuk. Yet, the truth is that Habakkuk represents each of us. His questions are our questions. His pain is our pain. His perplexity is our perplexity. So the answers that God gives Habakkuk are truly aimed at your heart and mine:

> *"Look at the nations and watch—and be utterly amazed. For I am going to do something in your days that you would not believe, even if you were told" (1:5).*

In other words, God says, "I have been answering your prayer, Habakkuk. You accuse Me of silence, but I have not been silent. You just do not know how to recognize My answer. I have been answering, but the answer is so different from what you expect that you will not even recognize it or believe it when I tell you." Then God proceeds to explain His answer to the prophet Habakkuk in specific terms:

> *"I am raising up the Babylonians, that ruthless and impetuous people, who sweep across the whole earth to seize dwelling places not their own. They are a feared and dreaded people; they are a law to themselves and promote their own honor. Their horses are swifter than leopards, fiercer than wolves at dusk. Their cavalry gallops headlong; their horsemen come from afar. They fly like a vulture swooping to devour; they all come bent on violence. Their hordes advance like a desert wind and gather prisoners like sand. They deride kings and scoff at rulers. They laugh at all fortified cities; they build earthen ramps and capture them. Then they sweep past like the wind and go on—guilty men, whose own strength is their god" (1:6–11).*

He is preparing the nation of the Chaldeans

Here is God's answer to the prophet's problem: He is preparing the nation of the Chaldeans. At the time that Habakkuk wrote, the Chaldeans were not an important people. Another name for the Chaldeans is the Babylonians; these names are used interchangeably in the Old Testament.

Here is an outline of the book of Habakkuk:

Habakkuk Questions God (Habakkuk 1–2)
Question 1: Why does Judah's evil go unpunished?
Question 2: How can God punish Judah with an
even more evil nation?

Habakkuk Praises God (Habakkuk 3)
Habakkuk remembers God's mercy and trusts God for salvation

At the time that the prophet wrote, the great nation that terrified and intimidated all other nations—the superpower of the ancient era—was Assyria, whose capital was Nineveh. But here is a little nation that is beginning to rise to prominence in the affairs of the world, the Chaldean nation, and God says in effect, "I am behind this. These people are a very strange people. They are bitter, hostile, ruthless, and cold-blooded. They are going to be as powerful as any nation on earth has ever been and they will sweep through land after land, conquering everything. They will seem invincible. Their own political and military strength will be their god. They do not know Me or worship Me, but I control their destiny, and they will be the answer to your prayer."

Now that is astounding, isn't it? Evidently Habakkuk did not know what to make of this. A moment of silence interrupts here as the prophet reflects. What has he gotten himself into? By seeking a solution to the Assyrian problem, Habakkuk's prayers may have stirred up an even bigger problem—the Chaldeans!

This is what bothers many people as they look at what is happening in the world. This is what threatens the faith of many who view the problem of history. Why does God allow things to happen the way they do? Why does He permit such terrible events to occur? Why has God permitted the terrors and atrocities of ancient Rome? The tortures and persecutions of the Spanish Inquisition? The Black Death? Why does God permit the suffering caused by cancer, Alzheimer's disease, and AIDS? Why did He allow the horrors of the slave trade to take place in America? Why did He permit the Holocaust of World War II? What was God thinking of when the death-screams ascended to heaven from Auschwitz, from Pearl Harbor, from Bataan, from Dresden, from Hiroshima, from all the burning cities and sinking ships of a world at war? Why did He permit the incalculable suffering of Vietnam, Bangladesh, Cambodia, the Gulf War, Somalia, Bosnia, and on and on and on?

I once saw the results of a survey of the questions that non-Christian students were asking on campuses around our country. Number one on the list: "How can a loving God allow people to suffer? Why would God create us and then allow disease and pain and wars to enter our lives?"

For some, the answer is simple—and fatalistic. "Well," they respond, "the answer is that there is no God and it is senseless to ask why a nonexistent being would allow suffering. We live in a machinelike universe, with ponderously clanking gears, and eventually we all get ground up by those gears. There's no purpose, no point. You live for a while, try to wring as much happiness out of your miserable little life as you can, and then you die. Don't try to figure it out. The point is, there is no point."

The apparent inactivity of God leads many to conclude that He doesn't exist; that's one of the mysterious things about God, isn't it? The poet William Cowper said, "God moves in a mysterious way His wonders to perform." And the ways of God are deeply mysterious to us. One thing that you learn about God after you live with Him for a while is that He is always doing the unexpected, not because He delights in puzzling and fooling us, but because the variety of His workings are so infinite that our feeble human minds cannot grasp them.

What do you do when you are confronted with this sort of a threat to your faith? Habakkuk offers four simple steps to revive our faith relationship with God when these and other questions assail us.

What to do when your faith is challenged

Step 1: Stop and think

Avoid reacting emotionally to the problem. Don't let panic get the best of you. Use your God-given reason—and think.

Habakkuk approaches his questioning the same way: He stops and he thinks about the problem. He reminds himself of God's nature. "O LORD," he asks, "are you not from everlasting?" (Hab. 1:12). The first thing that he thinks about is that the God he knows is an everlasting God. God sits above history. He is greater than any span of human events. He created history. He is from the beginning and He is at the end. He is the God of eternity.

When these Chaldeans come, they will trust in their own might as their god. "Oh, yes," Habakkuk says, "but my God is not like that. My God is not one of these localized tribal deities. He is the God who covers history, who Himself governs these events, the everlasting God." Habakkuk's approach began with a willingness to pause and apply reason to the situation.

Step 2: Restate the things that you know about God

What should you think about? You should think about the nature of God Himself. Don't rush to resolve your dilemma immediately. Back away from the problem and begin with God. Go back to what you know about God and His character as it has been revealed to you in Scripture and by experience.

That is what the prophet Habakkuk does, reminding himself that God is the self-existent and eternal One. Notice that he uses a special name for God. He says, "O LORD, are you not from everlasting?" Whenever you find the word *LORD* in capital and small capital letters as it is here, it is a translation of the Hebrew word for Jehovah (Yahweh or YHWH). Jehovah means "I am who I am," the great name that God revealed to Moses when he was in Egypt. At that time God said to him, "I AM WHO I AM. This is what you are to say to the Israelites: 'I AM has sent me to you'" (Ex. 3:14). Do you know why Habakkuk reminded himself of this? Because there were people in his day going around saying that God was dead. This God-is-dead theology has been around since Bible times, and a God-is-dead theology pervades our society today. As Solomon has observed, there is really nothing new under the sun.

To counter this kind of thinking and to strengthen his own faith, Habakkuk went right back to what he had learned about God: God is self-existent and cannot die. It is impossible for a self-existent person to die. "I am who I am." In our own problems, perplexities, and dilemmas of faith, we must do what Habakkuk did: Back away from the problem and begin with God.

As you apply your biblical and personal knowledge of God to the problem, you will begin to see the problem more clearly. Habakkuk applies this principle by reminding himself of God's holiness. Again, verse 12:

> O LORD, are you not from everlasting? My God, my Holy One, we will not die. O LORD, you have appointed them to execute judgment; O Rock, you have ordained them to punish.

"My God, my Holy One," says the prophet, reminding himself of the holiness of God. What does *holiness* mean? I suspect that many of us use this word without any idea of what it means. To put it simply and accurately, holiness is wholeness, completeness. A holy person is a whole person. God is holy and He is whole. God is consistent with Himself. He is always what He is. He is never anything different, never a phony. He never pretends or puts on. He is never in conflict or contradiction with Himself. That is holiness.

You can find this truth reflected throughout the Scriptures—the wholeness, consistency, and unchangeable quality of God. The writer of Hebrews says, "In the beginning, O Lord, you laid the foundations of the earth, and the heavens are the work of your hands. They will perish, but you remain; they will all wear out like a garment. You will roll them up like a robe; like a garment they will be changed. But you remain the same, and your years will never end" (Heb. 1:10–12).

Step 3: Bring your knowledge of God to bear on the problem

God, like His Son, Jesus Christ, is the same yesterday, today, and forever.

After the prophet reminds himself of this, he immediately adds these words, "We will not die." What does he mean? He is thinking of the fact that God has made a covenant with Abraham. God promised Abraham that he would be the father of a nation that would forever be God's people and that Abraham's nation would never be eliminated from the earth. The prophet is reminding himself of that promise in the face of this awesome threat. The Chaldeans are going to come rolling across this land, and Habakkuk will soon see his own beloved Jerusalem ravished and captured and his people led away into captivity. But he reminds himself that God's promise stands: His people will not die. They will be chastised, but they will not be eliminated. God's faithfulness remains. He is the Rock, He is unchangeable.

In our own time, we have witnessed similar events. Within living memory, the Nazis came to power. Like the Chaldeans, their strength was their god, and their "chariots" roared across Europe, burning and destroying, killing millions of people, including six million Jews. God did not inspire the Nazis to do the horrible things that they did—but He allowed them to exercise their awful human free will before they were finally struck down by the Allied Forces. We can't fully understand all of God's purposes in allowing such horrors to take place, but we do know that as a result of these events, the western world was awakened to its selfishness, wickedness, covetousness, and moral bankruptcy. Through such terrible events, God shakes the nations and awakens people to their need of Him.

I pray that God will not have to use such drastic measures in our own society to awaken us to our spiritual and moral need—but I am not hopeful that we can escape it. As America becomes more greedy, materialistic, and morally corrupt, the probability becomes greater and greater that this pattern will be repeated.

Step 4: Be patient

Finally, if you have not come to an answer, patiently leave the problem with God and ask Him to show you the answer. Continue to act on the mustard seed of faith that you possess until God provides the answer. You will see your faith and trust in Him strengthened as you patiently wait for God to speak to your heart.

We see an inkling of this response in the prophet's words in verse 13:

Your eyes are too pure to look on evil; you cannot tolerate wrong. Why then do you tolerate the treacherous? Why are you silent while the wicked swallow up those more righteous than themselves?

Habakkuk is saying, in effect, "I can see how You are raising up this cruel Chaldean nation to punish my people, but I don't understand it. Despite the wickedness of my own people, they are not as bad as these Chaldeans. You cannot tolerate evil. How, then, can You use an evil people to punish Your own people? God, I don't understand this."

Habakkuk's mind cannot wrap itself all the way around this huge problem—so he follows the fourth step: he leaves the problem with God. Now that is a very wise thing to do because *no* human mind— not yours, not mine, not the prophet Habakkuk's—is wide enough and deep enough to understand God's purposes in these events. So, at this point we have to say, "God, I will patiently wait for Your answer."

Most people, unfortunately, lack that patience. "God, I have to understand this problem right now! If You don't explain it to me, then You must not exist. If You don't explain it to me, if You don't make this problem understandable to my finite mind, then I refuse to believe in You."

In humility, the prophet says, "Well, I don't understand this, but You are mightier than I. All I can do is patiently wait for You to reveal Your truth to me." Notice how he begins chapter 2:

> *I will stand at my watch and station myself on the ramparts; I will look to see what he will say to me, and what answer I am to give to this complaint.*

That is a wise thing to do. Habakkuk says that he is going to get away from the problem for awhile. "I am going to leave the matter with God and wait for Him to take the next step. I'll stand my watch and do my job. Later, if God in His grace gives me the answer to the problem, then I will be grateful. But that is up to God. I have gone as far as I can in my own strength and wisdom. All I can do now is be patient."

And God rewards the prophet's patience. In Habakkuk 2:2–3, we read:

> *Then the LORD replied: "Write down the revelation and make it plain on tablets so that a herald may run with it. For the revelation awaits an appointed time; it speaks of the end and will not prove false. Though it linger, wait for it; it will certainly come and will not delay."*

God is saying, "Habakkuk, the answer is coming. It won't happen immediately, but it is coming for sure, so continue to be patient and wait for it."

When Habakkuk cannot fully understand the problem, he leaves it with God

By faith

Then God goes on to state a principle that is quoted three times in the New Testament and forms the basis for the Reformation. God says,

"The righteous will live by faith."

These words are quoted in the New Testament in Romans, Galatians, and Hebrews. This is the idea that lit a fire in the heart of Martin Luther: "The righteous will live by faith." God has designed us to live *by faith* in what God has said will happen, not by circumstances, observations, or reasoning.

Everyone can be put into one of two categories: dependent on God or self-reliant

Look around and you will see that everyone can be put into one of two categories: dependence on God or self-reliance. One of the saddest things that I have seen—and I have seen it all too often—is a Christian who has chosen to live by his or her own reasoning and strength, and is doing so in the name of Christianity. We do this in so many ways. We rely on studies, surveys, and polls to direct a church's ministry. We exercise political power, pressure tactics, and clever strategies rather than spiritual authority in an effort to bring about social change. We seek the input of experts and authorities instead of seeking the face of God in trying to expand the church and evangelize the world. We are not living by faith. We are living by sight, by what we can see according to our own human reasoning ability. That is not how the Word of God says we should live.

I would encourage you to read Hebrews 11 and examine the stories of the great men and women of faith who are listed there. These are people who changed their world, increased God's kingdom, advanced God's message, and healed human hurt—and they did it all by faith in the power of God alone. They didn't hire any consultants, they didn't read books on marketing and management, they didn't analyze their situation to death. They lived by faith, and in the process, by God's power, these men and women of faith stopped the mouths of lions, subdued kingdoms, toppled thrones, won empires, and changed the course of history, to the glory of God.

Though God will use the Chaldeans to judge Israel, the Chaldeans themselves will be judged

The remainder of Habakkuk 2 reveals an interesting analysis of the Chaldeans and what God plans to do with them. God says, in effect, "Habakkuk, don't worry about the Chaldeans; it is true that I cannot tolerate evil, and it is also true that I am raising up this people to judge the nation of Israel—but be sure of this, I will judge the Chaldeans in turn. The very thing in which they trust will prove to be their downfall. Their own gods will overthrow them." God goes on to pronounce five woes on the Chaldeans—woe upon them for their thievery; woe to them for attempting to build up a false foundation for themselves, piling up material "security" without regard to spiritual security in God; woe to them for building their cities out of blood, violence, suffering, and sin; woe to them for intimidating and unjustly ruling over their neighbors; and woe to them for their idolatry, for saying to idols of wood and silver, "Come to life! Wake up!"

In chapter 3, the prophet concludes this book with a remarkable prayer. He has seen his answer. God is the God of history and everything is under His control. The problems of humanity can be solved only as human beings come into a faith relationship with God. Habakkuk prefaces his prayer with this invocation in 2:20:

The LORD is in his holy temple; let all the earth be silent before him.

Then he prays:

LORD, I have heard of your fame; I stand in awe of your deeds, O LORD. Renew them in our day, in our time make them known; in wrath remember mercy.

Habakkuk began this book by saying, "Lord, why don't you do something?" Now he says, "Lord, be careful! Don't do too much! In your wrath, don't forget to show mercy." That is all Habakkuk has to say—there is no more philosophy, no more theology, no more arguing with God.

The prayer of Habakkuk in chapter 3 is one of the most remarkably beautiful, poetic passages in all the Scriptures. Read it, and you will see how the prophet is going back and remembering what God has done in the past. That is what convinces Habakkuk that God can be trusted. He rests upon events that have already occurred, events that cannot be questioned or taken away. God has already moved in human history.

And this is where faith must rest. We do not live by blind faith. We live with a God who has acted in time and space, who has done something, who has indelibly recorded His will in the progress of human events. The prophet looks back to God's action in Egypt when Israel was in trouble and remembers how God moved in those days:

God came from Teman, the Holy One from Mount Paran. Selah. His glory covered the heavens and his praise filled the earth. His splendor was like the sunrise; rays flashed from his hand, where his power was hidden (3:3–4).

Remember how God hid His power from Pharaoh and then exploded forth in sudden acts of miraculous intervention? The prophet writes:

Plague went before him; pestilence followed his steps. He stood, and shook the earth; he looked, and made the nations tremble. The ancient mountains crumbled and the age-old hills collapsed. His ways are eternal (3:5–6).

This is the kind of God we have— a God who moves in human history to accomplish events that no human being ever could

Habakkuk remembers how the people of Israel were afflicted and wandering in the wilderness and how in the land of Midian they trembled. Then he thinks of the crossing of the Red Sea and how God made a way through the waters. He recalls how God rolled back the Jordan River when the Israelites came into the land and how at the command of Joshua (by faith in the power of God) the sun and moon stood still in the sky. This is the kind of God we have—a God who moves in human history to accomplish events that no human being ever could.

The secret of triumphant living

As the prophet considers all this, his mind goes out to the greatness of God, and he concludes:

I heard and my heart pounded, my lips quivered at the sound; decay crept into my bones, and my legs trembled. Yet I will wait patiently for the day of calamity to come on the nation invading us (3:16).

He sees the problem and he knows the calamity is coming. The horror of it grips him—but that is not all!

Though the fig tree does not bud and there are no grapes on the vines, though the olive crop fails and the fields produce no food, though there are no sheep in the pen and no cattle in the stalls, yet I will rejoice in the LORD, I will be joyful in God my Savior.
The Sovereign LORD is my strength; he makes my feet like the feet of a deer, he enables me to go on the heights (3:17–19).

Have you discovered that kind of life? Habakkuk describes a quality of joyful, triumphant living, even in the midst of pressure, problems, and stress. Even if the crops fail, even if there are no lamb chops or hamburgers for the table, yet I will rejoice in the Lord! This is the discovery that Habakkuk made, and it's the deepest, most practical truth that we can learn as children of the living, eternal God! No matter what trials come our way, even if those trials won't be removed, still we can rejoice in the fact that our God is the great eternal Lord of the universe, and all things are ultimately under His control.

I love the title of a book by Dr. Raymond Edman, former president of Wheaton College. It perfectly sums up what a Christian's attitude should be in times of trial, peril, and stress: *Not Somehow, but*

Triumphantly. We are not to say, "Well, I'll just have to get through this problem somehow," but we are to say, "God is going to lead me through this problem triumphantly!" That is the great secret of the Christian life—not that God takes all our problems away but that God takes us boldly *through* our problems, He enables us to *overcome* our problems. "In this world you will have trouble," said Jesus. "But take heart! I have overcome the world" (John 16:33).

The Day of Wrath

I f someone said, "You're so judgmental," would you consider it a compliment or an insult?

The concept of judgment has fallen into disfavor in our times. Yet the fact remains that God—the God of the Bible—is very judgmental. While our culture insists that all issues should be viewed in shades of gray, in terms of moral relativism, God insists on viewing the world and the human race in very stark terms of black and white, evil and good, sin and righteousness, wrong and right, goats and sheep, hell and heaven.

As we come to the book of Zephaniah, we encounter a very judgmental prophet who speaks for a very judgmental God. You'll find no shades of gray in the book of Zephaniah, no compromise between good and evil, no moral relativism. Although many books in the Bible deal with God as a Judge, the book of Zephaniah presents the Bible's most intense and concentrated treatment of this theme.

Many people would like to rewrite the Bible and leave out all the distasteful references to God's judgment. If such a project were ever undertaken, the book of Zephaniah would practically cease to exist! We cannot simply edit out those parts of the Bible that do not suit our delicate sensibilities. The Bible is God's truth to us, His revelation of Himself, so that we can know Him and respond to Him realistically. In order to truly know God, we must know Him in all His many magnificent dimensions. We must understand His vast love, His deep

Zephaniah: a judgmental prophet

The Bible is God's truth to us, His revelation of Himself, so that we can know Him and respond to Him realistically

mercy, His all-encompassing forgiveness—yet these concepts can have little meaning to us until we have truly understood His justice and His judgment.

Some people make the mistake of thinking that the Old Testament presents a God of judgment while the New Testament presents a God of love. The fact is, we find hundreds of references to the love and mercy of God in the Old Testament, while in the New Testament we see Jesus speaking again and again about the judgment of God. The Old and New Testaments testify in harmony and unity to a richly multidimensional God who is both just and loving, judgmental and merciful. We see these facets of God's character eloquently expressed together in Zephaniah, the book of the Day of Wrath and Judgment.

Here is an outline of the book of Zephaniah:

The Day of the Lord (Zephaniah 1:1–3:8)

1. God's judgment of the entire earth	1:1–3
2. God's judgment of the nation of Judah	1:4–18
3. God's judgment for repentance	2:1–3
4. The judgment of the nations	2:4–15
5. The judgment of Jerusalem	3:1–7
6. The judgment of the entire earth	3:8

Salvation in the Day of Judgment (Zephaniah 3:9–20)

God's promise of restoration	3:9–20

Old and New Testament prophecy

The name Zephaniah means "hidden of the Lord." The prophet speaks as a representative of the remnant of faith—those relatively few people who remain true to God and faithful to His Word through the time of trouble that is to come upon the earth. They will be hidden, as it were, by God Himself; He will watch over them to guard their faith during this time of intense worldwide upheaval and persecution. The book of Zephaniah is written about this future group of believers who live through the coming Day of the Lord—the Day of Wrath. The prophet, then, is writing as a representative of people of the distant future, people who would not be born for thousands of years.

The character of God's vengeance

In chapter 1, Zephaniah gives us the character of God's vengeance. It is not a pleasant passage. It begins after the prophet identifies himself as a great-great-grandson of one of the kings of Judah:

"I will sweep away everything from the face of the earth," declares the LORD. "I will sweep away both men and animals; I will sweep away the birds of the air and the fish of the sea. The wicked will have only

heaps of rubble when I cut off man from the face of the earth," declares the LORD.

"I will stretch out my hand against Judah and against all who live in Jerusalem. I will cut off from this place every remnant of Baal, the names of the pagan and the idolatrous priests—those who bow down on the roofs to worship the starry host, those who bow down and swear by the LORD and who also swear by Molech, those who turn back from following the LORD and neither seek the LORD nor inquire of him. Be silent before the Sovereign LORD, for the day of the LORD is near. The LORD has prepared a sacrifice; he has consecrated those he has invited" (1:2–7).

Just to make sure that there is no confusion, we should understand that there is a great deal of difference between the Day of the Lord and the Lord's Day. Sunday is the Lord's Day, the day of resurrection. What the Bible calls "the Day of the LORD" is something else altogether—like the difference between a horse chestnut and a chestnut horse.

The Day of the Lord is the day of the manifestation of God's hand of judgment in human affairs. Notice the personal pronoun all through that passage: "I will sweep away everything. . . . I will sweep away both men and animals. . . . I will stretch out my hand against Judah." God is working through events in history, working through nations and armies and calamities of various sorts. His hand is hidden in the glove of history, but all the writers of Scripture agree that a day is coming when God will intervene directly in human affairs.

Jesus refers to this time in Matthew, where He speaks of a time of great tribulation:

> *"Then you will be handed over to be persecuted and put to death, and you will be hated by all nations because of me. At that time many will turn away from the faith and will betray and hate each other, and many false prophets will appear and deceive many people. Because of the increase of wickedness, the love of most will grow cold, but he who stands firm to the end will be saved. And this gospel of the kingdom will be preached in the whole world as a testimony to all nations, and then the end will come" (24:9–14).*

As Jesus continues to describe these events, the fear-inspiring signs and horrors climax in these words:

> *"Then there will be great distress, unequaled from the beginning of the world until now—and never to be equaled again. If those days had not been cut short, no one would survive, but for the sake of the elect those days will be shortened. . . .*

The Day of the Lord is the day of the manifestation of God's hand of judgment in human affairs

Jesus speaks of it

"Immediately after the distress of those days 'the sun will be darkened, and the moon will not give its light; the stars will fall from the sky, and the heavenly bodies will be shaken.'

"At that time the sign of the Son of Man will appear in the sky, and all the nations of the earth will mourn. They will see the Son of Man coming on the clouds of the sky, with power and great glory. And he will send his angels with a loud trumpet call, and they will gather his elect from the four winds, from one end of the heavens to the other" (24:21–22, 29–31).

Paul speaks of it

The apostle Paul speaks similarly of this time, using the specific words, *the day of the Lord* in 1 Thessalonians 5:1–6. Many other passages also refer to the Day of the Lord and they all agree on certain features of that time: It will be a time when people proclaim peace but prepare for war. It will be a time when people hold to a form of godliness but deny its power. It will be a time when people declare that the problems of life have been solved when in fact the world is in greater danger than ever before. These conditions will usher in the Day of the Lord.

The Day of the Lord arrives

Hollywood has produced a number of science fiction movies that have attempted to show what the end of the world would look like. But the greatest special-effects wizard in the motion picture industry cannot hope to come close to reproducing the horrific scenes depicted for us in the word-pictures of the prophet Zephaniah:

The greatest special-effects wizard in the motion picture industry cannot hope to come close to reproducing the horrific scenes depicted for us in the word-pictures of the prophet Zephaniah

"The great day of the LORD is near—near and coming quickly. Listen! The cry on the day of the LORD will be bitter, the shouting of the warrior there. That day will be a day of wrath, a day of distress and anguish, a day of trouble and ruin, a day of darkness and gloom, a day of clouds and blackness, a day of trumpet and battle cry against the fortified cities and against the corner towers. I will bring distress on the people and they will walk like blind men, because they have sinned against the LORD. Their blood will be poured out like dust and their entrails like filth. Neither their silver nor their gold will be able to save them on the day of the LORD's wrath. In the fire of his jealousy the whole world will be consumed, for he will make a sudden end of all who live in the earth" (1:14–18).

The mind recoils from this list of future horrors. Is it easy for God to speak this way? No. God takes no delight in human death and suffering. He does not delight in judgment. Judgment, the prophet Isaiah says, is not the work that God enjoys doing. Rather, he writes in Isaiah 28:21, "The LORD will rise up . . . to do his work, his strange work, and

perform his task, his alien task." God's heart delights in mercy.
Judgment is His "strange work." But ultimately, if His will is to be
done, if humanity is to break free of the chains of sin and discover the
glorious peace, prosperity, and freedom of the golden millennial age,
the rebellion of humanity must be put down and judged. The
entrenched evil of humanity must be fully, finally dealt with. That is
why the coming day of the vengeance of our God is absolutely certain.
The Word of God speaks clearly on this, throughout both testaments.
When God's grace is turned aside, His judgment awaits.

Chapter 2 traces the extent of God's vengeance. In this passage we
read a list of nations that God will judge—and at first glance this list is
puzzling. All of these nations have already disappeared!

> *"I have heard the insults of Moab and the taunts of the*
> *Ammonites, who insulted my people and made threats against their*
> *land. Therefore, as surely as I live," declares the* LORD *Almighty, the*
> *God of Israel, "surely Moab will become like Sodom, the Ammonites*
> *like Gomorrah—a place of weeds and salt pits, a wasteland forever. The*
> *remnant of my people will plunder them; the survivors of my nation*
> *will inherit their land" (2:8–9).*

Here we have God's judgment against Moab and Ammon. Verses
12 and 13 go on to pronounce God's judgment against the Cushites
and Assyrians. These ancient nations are gone, buried in antiquity. How
can they be destroyed, then, at some future time, in the Day of the
Lord?

The answer is that these nations are used symbolically as well as
literally in the Scriptures. They were literally destroyed in the course
of history, but they are used symbolically with reference to the full
and final meaning of the Day of the Lord. Moab and Ammon, for
instance, always symbolize the flesh of humanity—our self-willed
reliance on our own resources. Ethiopia is a picture of the stubbornness or the intransigence of human beings. "Can the Ethiopian
change his skin or the leopard its spots?" the Scriptures say (Jer.
13:23). Assyria represents human arrogance and pride. God says He
is against all these things, and in the Day of the Lord, these human
evils are vanquished forever.

Chapter 3 makes it clear that God's judgment will be worldwide: | God's judgment will
be worldwide

> *"Wait for me," declares the* LORD, *"for the day I will stand up to testify.*
> *I have decided to assemble the nations, to gather the kingdoms and to*
> *pour out my wrath on them—all my fierce anger. The whole world will*
> *be consumed by the fire of my jealous anger" (3:8).*

What does God seek to accomplish by destroying the nations of the world? Does He only want to get even? Is He visiting the earth with this terrible hurricane of destruction in order to leave it nothing but a smoking ruin, barren and desolate, without inhabitants? No, that is what the human race would leave the planet after another world war—but God, the wise and loving Creator, would not destroy for the sake of destroying. He would only destroy for the sake of creating. See what follows this vision of destruction:

> Sing, O Daughter of Zion; shout aloud, O Israel! Be glad and rejoice with all your heart, O Daughter of Jerusalem! The LORD has taken away your punishment, he has turned back your enemy. The LORD, the King of Israel, is with you; never again will you fear any harm. On that day they will say to Jerusalem, "Do not fear, O Zion; do not let your hands hang limp. The LORD your God is with you, he is mighty to save. He will take great delight in you, he will quiet you with his love, he will rejoice over you with singing" (3:14–17).

The consequence of God's judgment is not destruction but a new creation

After the great and terrible Day of the Lord, a new order follows. That is why God is dealing with the human race—so that He might bring singing out of sorrow, service out of selfishness, salvation out of slavery. That is the consequence of God's judgment—not destruction but new creation filled with joy, peace, love, music, and delight.

The references to Zion and Israel in this passage make it clear, I believe, that this is specifically a picture of God's care for the remnant of Israel through the tribulation and time of judgment. I do not believe that this section refers to the church, because I believe the church will be taken out of the world before these events occur. When the time of tribulation is past and God calls the remnant of Israel to Himself, they will sing the song of the redeemed. This passage is reminiscent of that beautiful passage in the writings of Solomon:

> Flowers appear on the earth; the season of singing has come, the cooing of doves is heard in our land (Song 2:12).

After the darkness and slaughter, after the terrible destruction comes the time of the singing; none but the redeemed can join in that song

After the darkness, after the slaughter, after the terrible destruction comes the time of the singing. None but the redeemed can join in that song. That is what God is after in our lives—redemption, joy, and singing. Judgment is coming upon the world. And judgment also comes in our own lives as individual believers. We all go through painful, purifying experiences that teach us to say no to the ego and yes to God. After the pain and purification comes singing. God is able to take the pain and darkness of our lives and bring about His new creative work within us. He is able to turn our darkness and gloom to joy and gladness. The justice of God cannot be turned aside—and neither can His love.

That is the sobering yet comforting message of the book of Zephaniah.

Encouragement for Builders

The famous mystery novelist Rex Stout considered himself a very capable amateur architect and builder. In the 1930s, he designed a fourteen-room house and built it with his own hands on a picturesque hill in Connecticut. Then he invited one of the world's great professional architects, Frank Lloyd Wright, to come see it and give his opinion. He led Wright to the hill where the house stood, and Wright examined Stout's handiwork with a careful, practiced eye. Stout held his breath, hoping to hear a word of praise and encouragement from the master architect. Finally, Wright spoke. Leaning against Stout's house, he said, "Beautiful spot, Rex. Someone should tear this thing down and build a house here."

Building the Lord's house

It is not easy to be a builder. People who set out to build something of lasting value need encouragement. In the book of Haggai, we will meet a group of people who set themselves to the task of building a house—the house of God. Unlike Rex Stout, whose hopes for a word of encouragement were shattered, the builders in the book of Haggai receive a powerful word of affirmation and encouragement for their work from the greatest architect of all—the Architect of the Universe, God Himself.

The theme of the prophecy of Haggai is "get busy and build the Lord's house." Understand that when the Bible talks about the Lord's house, it does not speak merely of a building. In fact, the temple building itself is merely a symbolic picture of the *true* house of God. The true dwelling place of God is the believer—or collectively, all believers. We, as Christians, are the "house" in which God dwells, and when God talks about building His house, He is talking about building us up to be a fitting and habitable dwelling place for His Spirit.

In Haggai's day, before the New Testament was written and God revealed the true nature of His habitation, the people didn't know that the temple was actually a symbol of a greater reality. The temple was called "the Lord's house," but it actually was a symbol of God's ultimate plan to make His dwelling place among His people.

When you read the prophecy of Haggai alongside the historical books of Ezra and Nehemiah, its meaning and context become much clearer. You may recall from reading those historical books that the Babylonians invaded the land of Israel, sacked and pillaged the city of Jerusalem, put out the eyes of the king, and carried the people into bondage for seventy years (this was exactly the period of time that the prophet Jeremiah had foretold). After the seventy years were fulfilled, Daniel, who prophesied in Babylon, tells us that God began to move to bring the people back to their homeland. They came first under Zerubbabel, who is mentioned in the opening verse of Haggai. Zerubbabel, who was descended from kings, was the captain of the remnant who returned from Babylon. When they came to Jerusalem, they found the city in ruins. The walls were broken down and the temple was utterly destroyed.

Though still under the domain of the Babylonians, the Israelites had permission from the king of Babylon to begin rebuilding the temple. They started working and managed to lay the foundations and perhaps a single row of stones. It was a modest beginning for a much smaller, humbler temple than the splendid original built by Solomon. The Israelites found the work to be very difficult. In time, the workers began to lag, and after a while the project slowed to a halt. For fifteen years, nothing was done. The temple project languished.

At this time God raised the prophet Haggai to speak.

Haggai delivers four messages to the people. These prophetic messages are delivered within the space of about eighteen months, and all concern the building of the temple. But there is a deeper message, as I have already suggested—a message regarding the true temple of God, of which the humanly constructed stone temple is merely a shadow and symbol. While Haggai's immediate purpose in speaking these four messages was to encourage the people in their temple construction project, the messages also apply to you and me as the temple or great house of God—a dwelling place for God that is comprised of human hearts. So we will examine the prophet's message on two levels—on the surface level as it relates to the reconstruction of the Jerusalem temple and on the deeper level of our individual lives today.

The Reconstruction of the Temple Commanded (Haggai 1)

The Glory of the Reconstructed Temple (Haggai 2:1–9)

The Blessings of Obedience (Haggai 2:10–19)

God's Promise of Blessing (Haggai 2:20–2:23)
The future destruction of the godless nations

Each of Haggai's four messages is dated by the calendar. Each one reveals an excuse given by the people for not working on the temple— and gives the *real* reason behind that excuse. The first message is contained in chapter 1:

> *In the second year of King Darius, on the first day of the sixth month, the word of the LORD came through the prophet Haggai to Zerubbabel son of Shealtiel, governor of Judah, and to Joshua son of Jehozadak, the high priest: This is what the LORD Almighty says: "These people say, 'The time has not yet come for the LORD's house to be built'" (1:1–2).*

The prophecy was addressed to the civil governor and to the religious heads, Zerubbabel and Joshua, and in this verse the prophet repeats the excuse that the people gave for leaving the temple abandoned for fifteen years. They were saying, "The time has not yet come. There has been a mistake in calculating the seventy years that Jeremiah prophesied. There's no use doing anything now because God is not ready yet." But read the answer that God gives to their excuse:

> *The word of the LORD came through the prophet Haggai: "Is it a time for you yourselves to be living in your paneled houses, while this house remains a ruin?"*
> *Now this is what the LORD Almighty says: "Give careful thought to your ways" (1:3–5).*

In other words, God says, "Do you really mean to tell Me that it's not yet time to get to work on My house? You've certainly wasted no time building houses for yourselves—but My house remains in ruins!" God resorts to irony—almost sarcasm—and His ironic tone punctures and deflates their flimsy excuse and their hypocrisy. Obviously, they have put their own wants first and God's work second.

Clearly, the people had forgotten something important when they concocted this excuse: The fact that they were back in the land proved that God's time had come, the seventy years were fulfilled. They had simply neglected God and His house while seeking their own comfort and convenience—and there is a price to pay for doing so:

> This is what the LORD Almighty says: "Give careful thought to your ways. Go up into the mountains and bring down timber and build the house, so that I may take pleasure in it and be honored," says the LORD. "You expected much, but see, it turned out to be little. What you brought home, I blew away. Why?" declares the LORD Almighty. "Because of my house, which remains a ruin, while each of you is busy with his own house. Therefore, because of you the heavens have withheld their dew and the earth its crops. I called for a drought on the fields and the mountains, on the grain, the new wine, the oil and whatever the ground produces, on men and cattle, and on the labor of your hands" (1:7–11).

It seems that there was inflation in those days too! God is telling the people that all the labor they put out did not get them what they expected. "You are trying to become prosperous," God says to them in effect, "but prosperity eludes you. You are trying to satisfy yourself, but you never find fulfillment. There is always something missing."

An infallible rule of Scripture and of life

Why did God short-circuit all their efforts to achieve prosperity? Was it because He wanted to hurt them or punish them? No, God was trying to wake them up. He was trying to show them that there is an infallible rule that runs throughout Scripture and throughout life—a rule that human beings continually try to overturn: "Seek first his kingdom and his righteousness, and all these things will be given to you as well" (Matt. 6:33). The way to have what you need in terms of physical food and material shelter and the necessities of life is to give your major concern and interests to advancing God's work. That is why you are here. You have a Father in heaven who knows your needs, and He is willing and able to supply them.

God has called us primarily to put the building of His house first—not the brick and mortar building but the *church* of God, the *people* of God. And many of us as Christians are just as hypocritical, just as full of excuses as the people of Haggai's day. So the great question that Haggai confronts us with is this: Why are we able to find time to advance our own interests and material gain with such eagerness, yet we spend so little time advancing the cause of God? Why do we excuse ourselves from the work of building the house of God—that is, investing in the people of God—by saying, "It isn't time yet"?

A unique excitement comes into our lives when we genuinely put the affairs of God first, when we seek first His kingdom and His righteousness, without worrying about the provision of our own needs. This is why God says through Paul, "I tell you, now is the time of God's favor, now is the day of salvation" (2 Cor. 6:2).

Inspired and convicted by Haggai's hardheaded message from the Lord, the people picked up their construction tools and began to work on the temple once again. They worked and they worked—until their enthusiasm wore down and their backs began to ache. Then the work ground to a halt.

How long had they been on the job? All of three weeks! Then they put down their hammers and saws and went home.

Again, God spoke to Haggai and gave him a message for the people. In chapter 2, we read:

> On the twenty-first day of the seventh month, the word of the LORD came through the prophet Haggai: "Speak to Zerubbabel son of Shealtiel, governor of Judah, to Joshua son of Jehozadak, the high priest, and to the remnant of the people. Ask them, 'Who of you is left who saw this house in its former glory? How does it look to you now? Does it not seem to you like nothing?' " (2:1–3).

God was repeating what the people were saying. When they first began rebuilding the temple, a thrill of excitement went through the people as they thought of restoring the Lord's house to its former glory. But then something happened. Perhaps an elderly *nuhdz* (that's a Yiddish word for "meddler") came down to watch the work. Leaning on his cane, casting a critical eye on the work-in-progress, he might have said, "You call *this* a temple? Feh! I was just a little boy when the Babylonians destroyed the old temple of Solomon— but I'll never forget that beautiful building! All silver and gold, beautiful cut stones, tapestries everywhere—oy, now that was a temple!" That's the way it is with a lot of us older folks—always living in the past!

Hearing the old meddler's words, the workers may have become discouraged. "You know," they might have said, "he's right. We don't have any gold or silver. We don't have anything to make this temple beautiful like the temple of Solomon. What's the use? Why continue working just to build a second-rate temple?" So they quit.

But the Lord, speaking through the prophet Haggai, offers encouragement to the people:

" 'Now be strong, O Zerubbabel,' declares the LORD. 'Be strong, O Joshua son of Jehozadak, the high priest. Be strong, all you people of the land,' declares the LORD, 'and work. For I am with you,' declares the LORD Almighty" (2:4).

That is always God's answer. "Work, for I am with you. Don't worry about the fact that things don't look as good as they ought to." He goes on:

" 'This is what I covenanted with you when you came out of Egypt. And my Spirit remains among you. Do not fear.'
"This is what the LORD Almighty says: 'In a little while I will once more shake the heavens and the earth, the sea and the dry land' " (2:5–6).

When God says He will shake the heavens and the people and the earth, He is not speaking literally but figuratively. He means He is going to rearrange the whole historical picture:

" 'I will shake all nations, and the desired of all nations will come, and I will fill this house with glory' says the LORD Almighty. 'The silver is mine and the gold is mine,' declares the LORD Almighty. 'The glory of this present house will be greater than the glory of the former house,' says the LORD Almighty. 'And in this place I will grant peace,' declares the LORD Almighty" (2:7–9).

In other words, "Don't worry about former glories, about silver and gold. I own the whole world, and all the silver and gold in the world belongs to Me. That isn't the kind of glory that I have in mind. I am going to fill this house with a different kind of glory, so that the splendor of the new temple will be greater than the splendor of the old."

These words were fulfilled centuries later when Jesus came into the temple, which by then had become defiled by money changers and thieves. Lash in hand, He overturned the tables, drove out the money changers, cleansed the temple. The Son of God Himself strode through the temple courts and made the Lord's house a house of prayer once again. He filled it with the glory of His teaching, standing in the midst of it, saying things that people had never heard before. The words that He spoke in the reconstructed temple of Jerusalem changed the life of the nation and of every nation in the world. By His presence, He filled the temple with a glory that has never ceased, a different kind of glory than the glory of Solomon's temple.

The builders became discouraged because they compared their work with the works of the past. But God told them not to hang onto the past. Instead, He said, "Keep working, I am with you. And when I am in your midst, you don't need to worry about the outcome. Whatever new work I do through you will be better than the old work."

Emboldened and encouraged by this new word from God through the prophet Haggai, the people went back to work. But after only two months had passed, the people once again fell down on the job! As we see further in chapter 2:

> On the twenty-fourth day of the ninth month, in the second year of Darius, the word of the LORD came to the prophet Haggai: "This is what the LORD Almighty says: 'Ask the priests what the law says: If a person carries consecrated meat in the fold of his garment, and that fold touches some bread or stew, some wine, oil or other food, does it become consecrated?' "
>
> The priests answered, "No" (2:10–12).

This was in accordance with the Law of Moses. If you get into a situation where you do not know what to do, said Moses, go ask the priest to declare the appropriate principle and make an application from that. It is the same principle we are to follow as Christians today. When we get into a situation that we don't know how to handle, we should go to the Word of God, find the principle that covers the situation, and apply it in the real-life situation.

Haggai continues:

> Haggai said, "If a person defiled by contact with a dead body touches one of these things, does it become defiled?"
>
> "Yes," the priests replied, "it becomes defiled."
>
> Then Haggai said, " 'So it is with this people and this nation in my sight,' declares the LORD. 'Whatever they do and whatever they offer there is defiled.
>
> " 'Now give careful thought to this from this day on—consider how things were before one stone was laid on another in the LORD's temple. When anyone came to a heap of twenty measures, there were only ten. When anyone went to a wine vat to draw fifty measures, there were only twenty. I struck all the work of your hands with blight, mildew and hail, yet you did not turn to me,' declares the LORD. 'From this day on, from this twenty-fourth day of the ninth month, give careful thought to the day when the foundation of the LORD's temple was laid. Give careful thought' " (2:13–18).

What does God mean? If you read between the lines, you can see again what the people were saying: "Look, You said that the reason we were having such a hard time materially and financially is that we were lagging on the temple. We've been working on the temple for two months now, and life is still hard for us." In other words, the people were impatient. They wanted instant results, instant gratification. They wanted God to reward them for their work on the temple. Does that sound familiar? Does that sound like anyone you know?

A couple once came to me for marital counseling. The husband complained, "We just can't live together. She's always exploding and bawling me out about everything." After talking with both of them at length, I found that the major problem in the relationship was that the husband paid no attention to his wife. Feeling utterly neglected, she would take it for just so long—then she would blow up! He agreed with that diagnosis and immediately began to make changes in his behavior. Within a day or two, however, he called me and said, "Well, I took her out to dinner last night and we had a great time. She enjoyed it so much I was sure you were right. But this morning she blew up at me again. The thing doesn't work."

I had to say to him what Haggai said to these people: "Do you think a behavior pattern that has taken years to build up can be changed overnight? You need to be patient. It will take time for you to prove that you have changed and for her to be able to trust, at a deep emotional level, that the old ways of relating to each other no longer apply." As Paul said to the Galatians, "Let us not become weary in doing good, for at the proper time we will reap a harvest if we do not give up" (Gal. 6:9).

The fourth attempt

Once again—on the very same day, in fact—the people needed another word of encouragement to spur them on toward completion of the project. In chapter 2, we read:

> The word of the LORD came to Haggai a second time on the twenty-fourth day of the month: "Tell Zerubbabel governor of Judah that I will shake the heavens and the earth. I will overturn royal thrones and shatter the power of the foreign kingdoms. I will overthrow chariots and their drivers; horses and their riders will fall, each by the sword of his brother.
>
> " 'On that day,' declares the LORD Almighty, 'I will take you, my servant Zerubbabel son of Shealtiel,' declares the LORD, 'and I will make you like my signet ring, for I have chosen you,' declares the LORD Almighty" (Hag. 2:20–23).

The Lord sends a special word of encouragement to the leader of the people while they are yet under the authority of Babylon. Though they are back in the land and building the temple again, they are still beset by many problems. Everywhere they look, they see signs that they are a subjugated people living under the heel of a foreign power. They see chariots and soldiers in their streets, and they are weary and fearful after a lifetime in bondage. *When will we ever be free?* they wonder.

God says, in effect, "Don't worry. My program will reverse the whole order of things. I will destroy the power of this kingdom. I will bring their chariots to naught. I will break you free from bondage to these people. I will place a royal signet ring on the finger of your leader, Zerubbabel." Zerubbabel was of the royal line, the line of David, and though these words were not literally fulfilled in Zerubbabel, they were spoken of his descendent: Jesus of Nazareth. God gave His royal signet ring, His seal of authority, and placed it on the finger of Jesus. He will ultimately rule all nations of the world.

This is a word of encouragement in a day of darkness. It speaks not only to the people of Jerusalem who were building the temple, but it also speaks to us today, in our own age of darkness, as the events of the world lead us closer and closer to the climax of history, the Day of the Lord. God wants us to know that *today* is the time for building. "Rise up and act now," He says to us. "Build now. Do not wait. The work of God needs to be done today, not next year, not ten years from now. *Now.* A great harvest field is before us, here and around the world. Are you using your resources to build My house, to build human lives? Are you using your time, your home, your talent, your spiritual gifts? You can help to build God's house today: Serve in your church. Witness in your neighborhood and on the job. Go on short-term missionary ventures around the world. Invite international students to spend a year in your home. Conduct seeker-friendly Bible studies in your home and invite friends and neighbors. The possibilities are endless—but the opportunities will not remain open forever. So build now—before it is too late!"

Are you and I doing all that we can to build the house of the Lord? When all the work of human hands has crumbled to dust, when all the great civilizations of history have passed from memory, only the work of the Lord, the house of God, will stand. We are that house. We are God's eternal work. That is Haggai's encouragement to us, God's builders. Let us invest all that we are and all that we have in making ourselves a fitting and consecrated dwelling place for our God.

The Apocalypse of the Old Testament

T
he book of Zechariah has been called the "Apocalypse of the Old Testament," meaning it parallels the New Testament book of Revelation (or Apocalypse). The word *apocalypse* comes from the Greek word *apokalypsis,* which means "revelation." The New Testament book of Revelation is actually part of a long tradition of Jewish apocalyptic literature characterized by rich allegorical symbolism and the prediction of future events. In this sense, Zechariah is a forerunner of Revelation, and it is helpful to read and study the two books side by side.

The theme of Zechariah is God's program in history—which is also the theme of Revelation. The two books differ, however, in emphasis. In Zechariah, Israel is in the foreground of events and the Gentile nations are in the background. In the book of Revelation, the Gentile nations are in the foreground and the continuous thread that ties them together is the nation of Israel. We see Zechariah's focus on the nation of Israel in the first verse:

> In the eighth month of the second year of Darius, the word of the
> LORD came to the prophet Zechariah son of Berekiah, the son of Iddo
> (1:1).

Zechariah is a forerunner of Revelation, and it is helpful to read and study the two books side by side

We usually read through these opening verses without considering their significance, but remember that Hebrew names often carry a powerful weight of meaning. In this passage, we have three very significant names. Zechariah means "God remembers"; Berekiah, his father's name, means "God blesses"; Iddo, his grandfather's name, means, "at the appointed time." That is the theme of the book of Zechariah. It is a book of God's encouragement and blessing to the people of Israel, delivered at God's appointed time.

Zechariah, a contemporary of the prophet Haggai, ministered to the remnant who returned from captivity in Babylon. Although the people were back in Jerusalem rebuilding the temple and the city, they were still subjects of the Gentile nation of Babylon, and they had little hope for the future. These were dark times for the people of Israel. Zechariah came to them in the midst of their depression with an announcement that Jehovah blesses, Jehovah remembers at the appointed time. What an encouragement those names must have been!

The structure of Zechariah

At the beginning of the first chapter we find a brief outline of the book. Many books in the Bible contain these brief outlines or summaries of the book's message, usually in the opening sections. In Zechariah, the outline is broken up in a dramatic way by the name of God, "the Jehovah of Hosts"—one of the unusual names of God. The name, "Jehovah of Hosts," means "the God of the masses" or "the God of all the armies," although the *New International Version* adopts the English phrase "LORD Almighty" to convey this thought. Whether the "hosts" referred to are angel armies or human armies or the starry hosts of the heavens makes no difference. The Lord Jehovah is the sovereign God over all the masses of the universe, whether human, spiritual, or heavenly masses, and we find this name repeated three times in verses 2 and 3:

> "*The LORD* [Jehovah or YHWH] *was very angry with your forefathers. Therefore tell the people: This is what the LORD Almighty* [literally, Jehovah of Hosts] *says: 'Return to me,' declares the LORD Almighty* [Jehovah of Hosts], *'and I will return to you,' says the LORD Almighty* [Jehovah of Hosts]."

Three times that name is repeated, and each repetition marks one of the three divisions or sections of the book of Zechariah:

Section 1: "The LORD was angry with your forefathers" (1:1–6)
Section 2: "Return to me" (1:7–6:15)
Section 3: "And I will return to you" (chapters 7–14)

Here is an expanded outline of the book of Zechariah:

An Angry God Calls for Repentance (Zechariah 1:1–6)

God Says, "Return to Me" (Zechariah 1:7–6:15)
1. The vision of the watcher and the myrtle tree   1:7–17
2. The vision of four horns and four craftsmen   1:18–21
3. The man with the measuring line   2
4. Joshua, the high priest   3:1–10
5. The lampstand and the olive trees   4
6. The flying scroll   5:1–4
7. The woman in the measuring basket   5:5–11
8: The four chariots   6:1–8

God Says, "And I Will Return to You"
(Zechariah 6:9–14:21)
1. Fasting   6:9–7:3
2. Zechariah rebukes hypocrisy   7:4–7
3. Zechariah preaches repentance   7:8–14
4. Zechariah preaches the restoration of Israel   8:1–17
5. Zechariah extols Israel's bright future   8:18–23
6. Zechariah predicts the coming of the Messiah   9–14

The first section is a brief overview of God's case against His people, a statement of His displeasure with a rebellious people. This overview is as relevant to God's people in the church as it is to God's people in Israel:

Section 1: The Lord's anger

> *"The LORD was very angry with your forefathers. Therefore tell the people: This is what the LORD Almighty says: 'Return to me,' declares the LORD Almighty, 'and I will return to you,' says the LORD Almighty. Do not be like your forefathers, to whom the earlier prophets proclaimed: This is what the LORD Almighty says: 'Turn from your evil ways and your evil practices.' But they would not listen or pay attention to me, declares the LORD. Where are your forefathers now? And the prophets, do they live forever? But did not my words and my decrees, which I commanded my servants the prophets, overtake your forefathers?*
>
> *"Then they repented and said, 'The LORD Almighty has done to us what our ways and practices deserve, just as he determined to do' "* (1:2–6).

Then, beginning with verse 7, a remarkable vision is given to the prophet. This vision divides into eight scenes, all given to Zechariah

Section 2: "Return to me"

We have been invited to attend a drama in which God is the author, Zechariah is the director, and we are the audience

Act 1: A red horse in a myrtle grove

Act 2: A man with a measuring line

on the same night, and these scenes also fall into three major divisions. The three divisions are like three acts in a great drama. As we read them, we can imagine that we have been invited to attend a drama in which God is the author, Zechariah is the director, and we are the audience.

The vision covers all the time from Zechariah's day through the present, continuing on to the coming of the Lord. The first act is made up of two visions. In Zechariah 1:8–17 is a vision of a watcher astride a red horse, which is standing amid a grove of myrtle trees in a valley. Gathered behind the watcher are other riders upon horses of red, brown, and white. The angel of the Lord interprets the vision to the prophet: Israel is symbolized as a grove of lowly myrtles in a shadowed place in the valley. It is a time of despair and darkness for Israel now, but an unseen One stands among them watching, symbolically mounted in power on horseback and backed by other riders on horses, representing God's great resources to meet their needs in their hour of darkness.

The second vision, Zechariah 1:18–21, speaks of four horns and four workmen or craftsmen. Horns—such as the horns of a ram or a bull—speak of power. In this case, they refer to foreign powers that have scattered the people of Israel. The craftsmen are divine agents, probably angels, whom God is sending out to terrify the nations. This is a picture of Israel's desperate need to return to God. Israel was discouraged at the display of powers and forces that opposed, oppressed, and scattered them. The people did not see the resources that God had made available to them. They were unaware of the divine agents whom God had prepared to act on their behalf. That is what God revealed to them.

So the curtain falls at the end of act 1. In Zechariah 2, the curtain rises on act 2, which is a single vision, an act in one scene. It is a vision of a man with a measuring line in his hand. As this man went out to measure the city of Jerusalem, the interpreting angel said to the prophet:

> *"Run, tell that young man, 'Jerusalem will be a city without walls because of the great number of men and livestock in it. And I myself will be a wall of fire around it,' declares the LORD, 'and I will be its glory within' "* (Zech. 2:4–5).

This beautiful description of the coming peace of Jerusalem is followed by scenes of the days of blessing that are to come upon Israel, all of which are to be literally fulfilled as Israel is one day brought back into a place of blessing. A casual glance at the headlines on any day of the week gives proof that those days have not yet come for Israel, even in our own day—but those days will come, in accordance with God's unshakable promise when Israel returns to God.

God always promises blessing to those who return to Him. Come back to God, and blessing must flow, because God is the center of blessing. The blessings of life can come from no other source. If your life is empty, you need God, because only He can fill your life to overflowing. If you are a Christian and your life is empty, you need to return to God. The man with a measuring line symbolizes the unlimited, measureless blessing that God is ready to pour out into the life of one who comes back into a relationship with Him.

Act 3 now opens with five more visions. Here is the way to return to God, acted out for us in these five visions. The first of these visions—what I call act 3, scene 1—is found in Zechariah 3, in which Joshua the high priest is revealed standing before God. Opposed to Joshua is Satan, the Adversary. The people of Israel well knew that they had a powerful Adversary and that Satan was against them. But what they could not see was the advocate, the one who stood on their behalf and ministered for them.

In this moving vision, we see how Joshua is cleansed. His filthy garments are removed and he is clad in new, clean garments. "See," God says in 3:4, "I have taken away your sin, and I will put rich garments on you." In verses 8 and 9 we find a prophecy that looks ahead to the work of Christ upon the cross:

> " 'Listen, O high priest Joshua and your associates seated before you, who are men symbolic of things to come: I am going to bring my servant, the Branch. See, the stone I have set in front of Joshua! There are seven eyes on that one stone, and I will engrave an inscription on it,' says the LORD Almighty, 'and I will remove the sin of this land in a single day.' "

This is a prophecy of Jesus' coming, the One who would be Jehovah's servant, the Branch. The seven eyes of the stone speak of sinless perfection, and the inscription on the stone symbolizes the marks of the crucifixion. With this stone, the sin and guilt of the people will be removed in a single day. In that single day, blessing will flow out as God manifests His right and power to cleanse sinners without charging, accusing, or condemning them. Cleansing is the first step on the way back to God.

Then in chapter 4 of Zechariah, we come to act 3, scene 2. Here we see what follows the cleansing work of God: the unleashing of the power of the Holy Spirit as revealed in the vision of the lampstand and the olive tree. These symbols depict the Spirit-filled life. Oil always refers to the Holy Spirit, and here were olive trees continually dripping oil out of their branches into a lampstand that burned brightly. This image indicates that the Lord continually supplies us with inner strength through

Act 3: Joshua, the high priest opposed by Satan

The lampstand and the olive tree

the Holy Spirit and enables us to burn brightly in the midst of a dark generation.

Zechariah 5:1–4 contains act 3, scene 3—the image of a gigantic flying scroll with Scripture written on both sides and with curses against the thieves and blasphemers. It pictures God's law going forth in Israel in the midst of corruption. The people of Israel were able to see the corruption all around them, but they could not see the law. So this is God's encouragement in the hour of darkness: God was at work, imposing His judgment on lawlessness to destroy it.

The rest of Zechariah 5, verses 5 through 11, is devoted to act 3, scene 4, in which Zechariah sees a woman in an ephah or measuring basket. While the prophet and the angel watch, wings are given to this basket and it flies away to the land of Babylon. What does this strange thing mean? If you had a vision like that, you would wonder what you had been eating the night before! But the prophet knows that a meaningful vision has been given to him. As he meditates upon it, he understands it because it contains terms that are used elsewhere in the Scripture. The symbol of a woman in Scripture usually refers to a false religion or false church. Here, then, is the picture of the judgment of the false faith, the false church. John recognizes this symbol in the book of Revelation where a woman who is the false church is called Babylon the great. He knows this image represents God's judgment upon false, hypocritical religion.

In the final scene, act 3, scene 5, the prophet sees four chariots, much like the vision in Revelation of the four horsemen who ride forth to rain judgment upon the world. The curtain comes down, then, on this great drama of redemption of the future. It is God's great symbolic play, the theme of which is, "Return to God." In it, we see that the way back to God is by cleansing, then by the filling of the Holy Spirit, then by the putting away of evil in its various forms, and finally by the judgment of the entire earth as God brings the evil of human beings before the throne of judgment.

Section 3: "And I will return to you"

Chapter 7 marks a new division in the book. We find God speaking in a different way. Instead of using visions, He speaks to the prophet in a direct address. The heart of this section is expressed in chapter 8, verse 3, where the prophet announces:

> This is what the LORD says: "I will return to Zion and dwell in Jerusalem. Then Jerusalem will be called the City of Truth, and the mountain of the LORD Almighty will be called the Holy Mountain."

Here is a picture of God who is dwelling with His people. One day this is going to be fulfilled on the earth. In many ways, we see this prediction being fulfilled in the land of Israel. The reestablishment of the nation of Israel and the return of Jerusalem to Jewish control in our own century has prepared the way for the rebuilding of the temple (which was destroyed in A.D. 70) on its old site. Scripture has long predicted that this would be one of the first signs that God was about to move again to restore Israel to its place among the nations.

We read this prophetic section with great interest because it depicts something that is historically coming to pass, that is in many ways coming to pass before our own eyes, in our own time. But we can also read it with intensely personal interest because of its spiritual application to our own lives—God is living with us and in us. As God dwells in us, renewing our inner selves, then a fountain of blessing pours out in our lives, making us fruitful, effective, and a blessing to all with whom we come in contact.

Chapters 7 and 8 communicate God's plea with the people to be honest and open before Him. It is another rehearsal of their failures in His sight and a reminder that while He is unfailing in mercy and grace, He is also unchanging in His standards. He always supplies what is necessary but He never lowers His standards. The people react as people often do, in these three ways; first:

> They refused to pay attention; stubbornly they turned their backs and stopped up their ears (7:11).

That is always the first step. They ignore God by pretending not to hear. Second:

> They made their hearts as hard as flint and would not listen to the law or to the words that the LORD Almighty had sent by his Spirit through the earlier prophets. So the LORD Almighty was very angry (7:12).

They deliberately disobeyed. Third and finally, they began to play the hypocrite. The chapter opens (7:3) with a question of the people, "Should I mourn and fast in the fifth month, as I have done for so many years?" And God's answers, in effect, "Why are you doing it? Are you celebrating these feasts because you mean to worship, or simply for a religious show?" (see 7:5). Don't we do the very same thing today? Don't we use these same evasions to avoid God's will today?

I remember, years ago, that my wife told one of our daughters to put on a green dress. It was interesting to watch her response. First, she pretended not to hear. Second, after her mother repeated the request several times, she openly rebelled and said, "No. I don't want to wear that dress." Third, when it became clear that her mother was going to make her wear the dress, my daughter came up to her mother and said, "Mother, I want to wear the green dress, but it's just too dirty," which was not true at all. She followed exactly the program that is outlined here in Zechariah:

1. Pretend not to hear.
2. Deliberately disobey.
3. Be hypocritical.

This passage in Zechariah accurately portrays the human heart in the very act of deception.

Refusing to hear
God results in an
inability to hear
Him

In chapters 9 and 10, God goes on to tell us the result of our repeatedly turning a deaf ear to God's voice: We become blind to the truth. We lose our ability to see and hear what God is saying to us. In the midst of the passage, we encounter several amazingly precise glimpses of the coming of Jesus the Messiah, beginning with this prediction of Jesus' arrival in Jerusalem on the first Palm Sunday:

> *Rejoice greatly, O Daughter of Zion! Shout, Daughter of Jerusalem!*
> *See, your king comes to you, righteous and having salvation, gentle and*
> *riding on a donkey, on a colt, the foal of a donkey (9:9).*

These words were literally fulfilled in the New Testament when our Lord sent His disciples to find a colt and a donkey, and He rode the donkey in the streets of Jerusalem as the people shouted, "Hosanna to the Son of David! Blessed is he who comes in the name of the Lord! Hosanna in the highest!" (see Matt. 21:1–11) Without realizing it, the people of Jerusalem were fulfilling this prophecy of Zechariah, "Rejoice greatly, O Daughter of Jerusalem! See, your king comes to you!" They did not know Him and they did not recognize Him when He came even in such a remarkable way. That is why Jesus wept over the city as He approached it, saying:

> *"If you, even you, had only known on this day what would bring you*
> *peace—but now it is hidden from your eyes. The days will come upon*
> *you when your enemies will build an embankment against you and*
> *encircle you and hem you in on every side. They will dash you to the*
> *ground, you and the children within your walls. They will not leave one*
> *stone on another, because you did not recognize the time of God's coming to you" (Luke 19:42–44).*

That is what happens when God moves in your life and you do not listen: You lose the ability to hear and see. The judgment of blindness came upon these people. May you and I never invite such judgment.

In Zechariah 11:12–13, the Messiah speaks again through the prophet, saying these amazingly prophetic words:

> I told them, "If you think it best, give me my pay; but if not, keep it." So they paid me thirty pieces of silver.
> And the LORD said to me, "Throw it to the potter"—the handsome price at which they priced me! So I took the thirty pieces of silver and threw them into the house of the LORD to the potter.

How much did Judas contract for in betraying our Lord? Thirty pieces of silver. According to the law if a slave was gored by an ox, the man who owned the ox could settle the whole matter by paying his neighbor thirty pieces of silver. Here the Messiah says to these people, "If you want me, say so. If you do not, give me my wages. What do you think I am worth to you?" And they weighed out for His price thirty pieces of silver.

The second result of an unrepentant heart is found in Zechariah 11:15–17, where the prophet says:

> The LORD said to me, "Take again the equipment of a foolish shepherd. For I am going to raise up a shepherd over the land who will not care for the lost, or seek the young, or heal the injured, or feed the healthy, but will eat the meat of the choice sheep, tearing off their hoofs.
> "Woe to the worthless shepherd, who deserts the flock! May the sword strike his arm and his right eye! May his arm be completely withered, his right eye totally blinded!"

In other words, if you refuse the true shepherd, God will allow you to have a false shepherd. The Lord Jesus stated this principle to the spiritually blind Pharisees of His day: "I have come in my Father's name, and you do not accept me; but if someone else comes in his own name, you will accept him" (John 5:43). In a general sense, there are many false Messiahs in the world, and if we refuse the true shepherd, Jesus, we risk being led into death and darkness by a false shepherd, by the Jim Joneses and David Koreshes and other false messiahs of our age. In a more specific sense, there is a single false shepherd, of whom Paul writes:

If you refuse the true shepherd, God will allow you to have a false shepherd

> Don't let anyone deceive you in any way, for that day will not come until the rebellion occurs and the man of lawlessness is revealed, the man doomed to destruction (2 Thess. 2:3).

This man will come to Israel as their deliverer and be received as the Messiah, but he will turn out to be the anti-Messiah, the Antichrist, the false shepherd who fills the vacuum left when they reject and refuse the truth. As Paul later observes, "For this reason God sends them a powerful delusion so that they will believe the lie and so that all will be condemned who have not believed the truth but have delighted in wickedness" (2 Thess. 2:11).

The beautiful conclusion

In the last section, chapters 12 through 14, we have a beautiful picture of God as He lovingly, protectively enters the lives of those who return to Him. God says that Jerusalem will be an immovable rock and that the nations will dash themselves against her in an effort to destroy her. In that day, God will pour out on Israel and the people of Jerusalem a spirit of prayer and compassion. Most important of all, they will see Jesus Himself—and they will respond to Him in repentance and faith, as Zechariah predicts, speaking in the voice of the Messiah Himself:

> *"They will look on me, the one they have pierced, and they will mourn for him as one mourns for an only child, and grieve bitterly for him as one grieves for a firstborn son. On that day the weeping in Jerusalem will be great, like the weeping of Hadad Rimmon in the plain of Megiddo" (12:10–11).*

When Israel blindly refused her Messiah at His first coming, they never realized that God would grant them a second chance and that they would receive the One they had pierced when He would come again. His wounds on the cross are referred to again later in the prophecy:

> *"If someone asks him, 'What are these wounds on your body?' he will answer, 'The wounds I was given at the house of my friends' " (13:6).*

Then, in Zechariah 14:1–4, we have a description of the Day of the Lord, when all nations gather against Jerusalem to do battle. It will seem as if all is lost and the nation of Israel is defeated, until the Lord Himself goes forth into battle against the nations. At that moment, as verse 4 tells us, the feet of the Lord, the Messiah, Jesus Himself will stand on the Mount of Olives. This is a highly significant statement when compared with passages in the New Testament. The Mount of Olives was the place where, following His death and resurrection, Jesus stood and was taken up into heaven out of the sight of the disciples. And an angel told them:

"Men of Galilee," they said, "why do you stand here looking into the sky? This same Jesus, who has been taken from you into heaven, will come back in the same way you have seen him go into heaven" (Acts 1:11).

It is predicted that Jesus will return in the same way and to the same place—the Mount of Olives—from which He was taken. This prediction dovetails with the words of Zechariah 14:4–5:

On that day his feet will stand on the Mount of Olives, east of Jerusalem, and the Mount of Olives will be split in two from east to west, forming a great valley, with half of the mountain moving north and half moving south. You will flee by my mountain valley, for it will extend to Azel. You will flee as you fled from the earthquake in the days of Uzziah king of Judah. Then the LORD my God will come, and all the holy ones with him.

Zechariah refers to the Mount of Olives as being split in two, causing the people around to flee as from a great earthquake that occurred in the days of King Uzziah. The prophet makes reference to a fact that he could not have possibly known about when these words were written—the existence of an earthquake fault beneath the Mount of Olives in Jerusalem. This fault was discovered by geologists during our lifetime. Clearly, the very tectonic plates and fault lines of the earth have been prepared for the future fulfillment of this prophecy in Zechariah.

The concluding images of the book are images of peace, joy, prosperity, and the righteous reign of the Lord over the entire world:

> **Peace, joy, prosperity, and the righteous reign of the Lord**

On that day living water will flow out from Jerusalem, half to the eastern sea and half to the western sea, in summer and in winter.
The LORD will be king over the whole earth. On that day there will be one LORD, and his name the only name (14:8–9).

This scene pictures the glorious millennial reign of God on earth through His Son, King Jesus. The book closes then with these beautiful words:

On that day HOLY TO THE LORD will be inscribed on the bells of the horses, and the cooking pots in the LORD's house will be like the sacred bowls in front of the altar. Every pot in Jerusalem and Judah will be holy to the LORD Almighty, and all who come to sacrifice will take some of the pots and cook in them. And on that day there will no longer be a Canaanite in the house of the LORD Almighty (14:20–21).

Every cooking pot will be a sacred vessel. Every commonplace thing will be holy to the Lord. What an amazing promise—and one that applies to our lives right now! When God is the center of your life, then every moment of your life, every commonplace object of your existence, is touched with the glory of His presence. What will be visibly true some future day on earth can be vitally, spiritually true today in your life and mine. That is the message to us right now from the Apocalypse of the Old Testament, the book of Zechariah.

"I Have Loved You"

F our hundred years of silence.

This is the period of time that separates the last book of the Old Testament, Malachi, from the first book of the New Testament, Matthew. The entire history of the United States of America, from the founding of the first colonies in Massachusetts and Virginia to the present day, would fit inside that gap with decades to spare. Yet, despite the four-century gap between Malachi and Matthew, these books are linked together in a remarkable way, as we shall soon see.

But what about that four-hundred-year period? It is as if the heavens were silent. No voice spoke for God, no prophet came to Israel, no Scriptures were written. Even so, history was still being made and remarkable events were taking place in Israel and among the Jews. The New Testament opens amid the emergence of new institutions. For example, the Pharisee sect of Judaism arose in the second century B.C., and the Sadducee (or Zadokite) party arose in the first century B.C.— and both of these groups figured very prominently in the four gospel accounts of the life of Jesus. Yet none of this intertestamental activity is recorded for us in the Bible.

"My messenger"

Malachi is the last of the so-called minor prophets. Malachi is also the last prophetic voice to speak to Israel until the coming of John the Baptist and Jesus. The last three books of the Old Testament—Haggai, Zechariah, and Malachi—were written after the return of the Israelites from their captivity in Babylon.

The people did not come back from Babylon in one great big happy throng. Several groups straggled back, the first one beginning in about 535 B.C. At that time, a handful of Jews fulfilled Jeremiah's prophecy that the captivity would last for seventy years. When these pioneers were repatriated to their homeland, they found the desolated, ruined city of Jerusalem. They began to lay the foundations of the temple, but construction soon lagged, and it was Haggai's ministry fifteen years later that spurred the project on toward completion. The temple reconstruction was completed during Zechariah's ministry, at about the same time that Ezra the priest led another group back from Babylon.

During their captivity in Babylon, the Israelites' entire way of life changed. Before, they had been an agrarian culture of sheep herders. But in Babylon, they learned to be merchants and shopkeepers—which meant an urban lifestyle.

The last return from Babylon was accomplished under Nehemiah, who led a group back to Jerusalem in 445 B.C. in order to begin rebuilding the walls of the city. Shortly after Nehemiah finished this task, Malachi appears; interesting comparisons can be drawn between the book of Nehemiah and the book of Malachi. Nehemiah comes at the conclusion of the historical section of the Old Testament (Joshua through Esther). Following Nehemiah are the poetic books, and then the prophetic books. In the final prophetic book, Malachi, we come into the same era that is covered by Nehemiah.

Malachi means "my messenger"

The prophecy of Malachi was given by a man whose name means "My messenger." Indeed, this last book of the Old Testament concerns a messenger of God and the prediction of the coming of another messenger. In this, therefore, we have a direct tie between Malachi and the New Testament. Chapter 3, for instance, begins with this prophecy:

> *"See, I will send my messenger, who will prepare the way before me"*
> *(3:1).*

John the Baptist, another messenger

As you discover in the book of Matthew, that messenger was John the Baptist. He came to prepare the way of the Lord and to announce the coming of the second messenger from God. That second messenger is mentioned here in the next phrase:

> *"Suddenly the Lord you are seeking will come to his temple; the messenger of the covenant, whom you desire, will come," says the* LORD *Almighty (3:1).*

Note the phrase, "the messenger of the covenant." The Lord Jesus on the closing night of His ministry took wine and bread with His disciples. Holding the cup, He said, "This is my blood of the covenant, which is poured out for many for the forgiveness of sins" (Matt. 26:28). The messenger of the covenant is the Lord Jesus Himself.

Here is a structural overview of the last book of the Old Testament:

God's Love for the Nation of Israel (Malachi 1:1–5)

The Sin of the Nation (Malachi 1:6–3:15)
1. The sin of the priests   1:6–2:9
2. The sin of the people   2:10–3:18

God's Promises to Israel (Malachi 4)
1. The predicted coming of Christ   4:1–3
2. The predicted coming of Elijah   4:4–6

The problem with the people of Malachi's day was that they had forgotten the great and central message of God. As we go back to the beginning of Malachi's prophecy, we see that the prophet opens on that note:

> An oracle: The word of the LORD to Israel through Malachi.
> "I have loved you," says the LORD (1:1–2).

That is always the message of God's prophets: "I have loved you," says the Lord. Amazingly, the people answer the prophet with the words, "How have you loved us?" This entire book is a series of the people's responses to the challenges of God. Seven times you find them saying, "How? How does this happen? Prove it." As we go through the responses, we see how they reveal the state of this people's heart. Here is an outgoing God, a loving God—yet He deals with a callous, indifferent, unresponsive people.

God answers their question, "How have you loved us?" in verses 2 and 3. He replies by reminding them that He loved them even at the beginning of the Jewish race, in His relationship with Jacob and Esau. He says, in effect, "Take a look at history. Esau's history was disastrous and troubled, Jacob's history has been blessed. I have loved Jacob but I have hated Esau. If you want to understand My love, look at one who has not enjoyed My love. Look at Esau and see how different his story is from yours, even though Jacob and Esau were twin brothers."

That troubles many people, but you find the explanation in the New Testament, in Hebrews 12:16. There we are told that Esau despised his birthright, and thus he placed no value on spiritual matters. He treated God with indifference. He trivialized the things that God regarded as valuable. Esau's attitude caused God to say, "I have loved Jacob but I hated Esau."

If you had known these two men, you would probably have loved Esau and hated Jacob. Jacob was the schemer, the big-time operator, the supplanter, the usurper, the untrustworthy rascal. Esau was the big outdoor man; hearty, open, frank, strong, boasting in his exploits as a hunter and as a man of the out-of-doors. Of the two, he appears much the better man—yet God says, "I loved Jacob because Jacob's heart hungers for the deeper things of life; Jacob wants something more than what is on the surface." That kind of intense spiritual hunger always pleases God.

In chapter 1, the Lord, through His messenger Malachi, goes on to charge the Israelites with a series of specific failures, and after each charge their response is, "What do you mean?" He says that the people have shown contempt for His name. The people ask, "How have we shown contempt for your name?" When you ask God a question, He is happy to tell you. So God replies that the sacrifices that they have offered to Him are polluted. "How have we polluted the sacrifices?" they ask. God replies that they have sacrificed blind, diseased, inferior animals on His altars. They have not given Him their best and first, they have given Him their leftovers—sacrifices that would be an insult to serve anyone else.

Why is God insulted by their offerings? Certainly not because He has a taste for prime filet mignon. It's because God knows that when they give Him the dregs of their sacrifices, it means they are giving Him the dregs of their lives, their service, and their worship. A defective sacrifice is a symptom of a defective attitude toward God. In verse 13, God notes that the people are actually bored and weary of worshiping Him. So they have been trying to get by with shoddy, sloppy religiosity instead of pursuing a genuine faith relationship with the living God. The Lord is the God of reality, and He always cuts through the excuses and hypocrisy and gets down to the real issue.

Now what is wrong here? A relationship with the almighty Creator of the universe should be a highly charged, thrilling experience. Where has all the excitement gone? What has happened to these people? They have concluded that God is interested only in ritual, that He will be content with something less than love. They have ignored the Great Commandment, which is, "Love the LORD your God with all your heart and with all your soul and with all your strength" (Deut. 6:5; cf. Matt. 22:37; Mark 12:30; Luke 10:27). Love God; nothing else will satisfy Him. These people have been the recipients of God's love and grace for centuries, yet they have not reciprocated His love. They have ignored, insulted, patronized, and offended Him. Their love for Him has died.

God has loved these people, yet He is a lover scorned. If you have ever known the experience of intensely loving someone who would not love you back—whether in courtship or as a rejected spouse or as the parent of a rebellious child—then you know that this is one of life's most painful experiences. And God felt that pain—the pain of unrequited love.

In chapter 2, God charges that the hypocrisy has become malignant. Like a cancer, their lack of love toward God is spreading, turning others astray. Moreover, they have failed in their moral standards. They have begun to intermarry with the godless tribes around them and have forgotten that God has called them to be a special and distinct people. God is not concerned, as some might think, that the Jewish bloodline or genetic heritage might be diluted; God is not a racist. He created all the races and loves all people equally. His concern is that by intermarrying with other tribes, the Jews will become morally and spiritually polluted by the false religions and false values of the surrounding world. He is concerned that faith and obedience to God—which is the central organizing principle of the Jewish culture—would be diluted and polluted as more and more nonbelieving people were blended into the Jewish nation.

Another sign of the moral decay of the nation was that divorce was becoming prevalent throughout the land:

> Another thing you do: You flood the LORD's altar with tears. You weep and wail because he no longer pays attention to your offerings or accepts them with pleasure from your hands. You ask, "Why?" It is because the LORD is acting as the witness between you and the wife of your youth, because you have broken faith with her, though she is your partner, the wife of your marriage covenant.
>
> Has not the LORD made them one? In flesh and spirit they are his. And why one? Because he was seeking godly offspring. So guard yourself in your spirit, and do not break faith with the wife of your youth.
>
> "I hate divorce," says the LORD God of Israel, "and I hate a man's covering himself with violence as well as with his garment," says the LORD Almighty.
>
> So guard yourself in your spirit, and do not break faith (2:13–16).

I have often heard this passage—especially the line, "I hate divorce"—quoted as an indictment by self-righteous Christians against divorced people. It has been used to treat divorced people as second-class citizens in the church. But that is not the intent of this passage. Understand, God says, "I hate *divorce*," not, "I hate divorced *people*." Throughout the book of Malachi, we hear God's love expressed over and over—and this statement of God's hatred against divorce is in reality one of His strongest statements of love! God hates divorce because it brings pain and suffering to divorced people and because it is an act of vow-breaking and faith-breaking. God links divorce with violence, so that the act of divorce is seen as a kind of "nonviolent domestic violence" when it is perpetrated by one spouse against an unwilling, innocent partner.

Divorce has many causes today. It may happen because of the self-ishness or immaturity of one or both partners. Adultery by one partner may be the cause. It may be that one partner is a believer and the other is not (perhaps the believing partner came to Christ after the marriage took place); nonbelievers often want out of a marriage in which a spouse witnesses about Christ and shows the convicting evidence of a changed life. Whatever the problems in a marriage (short of abuse or domestic violence), I always encourage couples to find ways to heal the relationship and avoid divorce. But it takes two people to keep a marriage together, and if one is completely unwilling, then the other person is an *innocent* victim of the divorce. And even if a Christian is divorced because of past sins, immaturity, or failings, he or she should not be denied grace, forgiveness, and reinstatement. Yes, God hates divorce—but the reason God hates divorce is that *He loves people*, all people, including divorced people.

Next, God says that the people make Him weary—and again, this is an indictment with powerful relevance to us today:

The people weary God by calling evil good

> *You have wearied the LORD with your words.*
> *"How have we wearied him?" you ask.*
> *By saying, "All who do evil are good in the eyes of the LORD, and he is pleased with them" or "Where is the God of justice?" (2:17).*

Today's society endorses all manner of evil, calling it good. It is bad enough that moviemakers and rock stars extol the virtues of obscenity, pornography, rebelliousness, lawlessness, and degrading depictions of God and the family—but today many educators, politicians, sociologists, judges, and psychologists are equally at fault. They say that obscenity and pornography are healthy. They say that homosexual behavior is normal. They say that the "family" is whatever we want it to be, even two lesbian women or a group of homosexual men. They excuse criminals, saying that these individuals commit crimes because society doesn't understand them, not because criminals make sinful choices. While child abuse is a horrendous social ill, many godly parents have been arrested for simply spanking their children in a loving and biblically approved fashion.

We live in a culture today where, increasingly, what God calls bad, society calls good—and vice versa. And the problem is getting worse not better. There is even an organization that operates openly, calling itself a "man-boy love association." It lobbies to lower the age of sexual consent to seven, so that grown men can engage in homosexual relations with young boys. You might think, "Well, they can try, but that behavior will never be legalized in America!" But look at all the things that are happening right now in America: Gay Pride parades, pornography sold openly in neighborhood convenience stores and video rental shops, child pornography freely available on the Internet, and indecent language and sexual behavior on prime-time TV and on daytime talk shows that children can watch after school. Most of the moral horrors that surround us today were unthinkable just ten or twenty years ago. What "unthinkable" horrors await us in the next few years? Anything that is unthinkable now could easily be commonplace tomorrow.

The book of Malachi speaks loudly and clearly to the moral confusion of our own day. This is always the result when people offer anything less than a fervent love for God, when they think that ritual and external trappings will satisfy the loving heart of the Eternal.

The book of Malachi speaks loudly and clearly to the moral confusion of our day

Another issue raised in verse 17 is a question that we often hear raised today: "Where is the God of justice?" In other words, "This is a free country. You have no right to impose your God and your morality on me. There aren't any moral standards. Everything is relative. You have your truth and I have my truth—there is no objective truth! There is no God of justice who determines what is right and wrong, so no one has a right to judge or limit or criticize my behavior." We think this rebellious, amoral attitude is something new, invented in our own century—but this kind of thinking was old, even four hundred years before Christ was born.

In Malachi 3, we come to the great prophecy of the coming Messiah. Malachi lifts his eyes and sees that the heart of these people is so hardened that they cannot be awakened even by these clear and incontrovertible charges from God. They are unaware that these things are happening in their own lives, because they have nothing to measure them against. So the prophet, looking across four centuries of time, says in effect, "The Lord will take care of this. He will send Someone to you who will wake you up, one who will tell you the truth. He will be a refiner's fire. He will burn through all the hypocrisy and superficiality of your religiousness. Like strong soap, He will cleanse you and set things right. You will be able to recognize Him because a messenger will go before Him to prepare the way, and then He will suddenly come to

Prophecy of the coming Messiah

His temple." Of course, all of these words are beautifully, powerfully fulfilled in the New Testament.

Following this is another series of charges in which the Lord speaks again about their lives. Then He appeals to them:

> *"Ever since the time of your forefathers you have turned away from my decrees and have not kept them. Return to me, and I will return to you," says the LORD Almighty.*
> *"But you ask, 'How are we to return?' " (3:7).*

If you have been studying through these Old Testament prophets in order, you will no doubt remember that this was a major theme in Zechariah: "Return to Me, and I will return to you." The people respond by asking, "How shall we return? We haven't gone anywhere. We are serving You in Your temple. We bring the proper sacrifices and offerings and we go through the ritual, just as You outlined it. What do You mean, telling us to return to You?" This response indicates the utter blindness of their hearts. They do not realize that though the outward form is right, their hearts are far from God.

Next, God talks about a subject that is uncomfortable for many Christians. He accuses the people of robbing Him:

> *"Will a man rob God? Yet you rob me.*
> *"But you ask, 'How do we rob you?'*
> *"In tithes and offerings. You are under a curse—the whole nation of you—because you are robbing me. Bring the whole tithe into the storehouse, that there may be food in my house. Test me in this," says the LORD Almighty, "and see if I will not throw open the floodgates of heaven and pour out so much blessing that you will not have room enough for it" (3:8–10).*

These verses are often wrenched from this Old Testament context and used to establish a legalistic pattern of bringing all the offerings into the church as the storehouse. That is a distortion. This verse is addressed to Israel, within the limits of the system under which Israel lived in the Old Testament, yet the principle is exactly true of the church. We should never take all that God has blessed us with and use it for our own advancement. God says, "When you do that, you are robbing me. You are robbing Me of My right to use you to advance My cause."

Our purpose in life

We exist to advance God's cause. It is quite possible for Christians to perform all manner of religious obligations within the church, to spend every spare dollar and every waking minute on ministry activities yet never advance God's cause a single step. Why? Because many of us, in our various religious activities, are doing nothing but using religion to fulfill our own self-centered goals. We may write hundreds of Christian books, we may preach to millions on television and in stadiums, we may initiate scores of ministry programs in the church, but someday we will have to stand before God and be judged—and His judgment may be, "All your life you have robbed Me of My right to live My life through you and to advance My cause through you. All your life, you lived by your own religious agenda, not Mine." That is why the appeal of the New Testament is to present our bodies as living sacrifices to God. That is why we are here. If anyone wants to know, "Why am I here? What is my purpose in life?"—this is it! There is nothing that confers more significance on a human life than total service to His cause—and nothing that denotes a wasted life more than God's assessment, "You have robbed Me."

In Malachi 3:16–18, God turns a spotlight on a faithful remnant in Israel. No matter how bad things get in the world, a faithful remnant always remains, and God's searchlight always finds them:

> *Those who feared the LORD talked with each other, and the LORD listened and heard. A scroll of remembrance was written in his presence concerning those who feared the LORD and honored his name.*
> *"They will be mine," says the LORD Almighty, "in the day when I make up my treasured possession. I will spare them, just as in compassion a man spares his son who serves him. And you will again see the distinction between the righteous and the wicked, between those who serve God and those who do not."*

Body life in the Old Testament

Notice the two marks of those who are faithful in the day of apostasy. First, they talked with one another. This does not mean that they just had a conversation. It means that they opened up to each other. They shared with one another. They encouraged each other. They confessed their weak points and prayed for one another. They experienced the kind of close community and fellowship that I call *body life*.

Second, they honored the name of God. They meditated on His name. So here we see the two dimensions of biblical faith, of the lifestyle of body life: the horizontal level of relating to each other at a deep level of communion, and the vertical level of relating to God and meditating on Him at a deep level of worship. The horizontal and the vertical—both dimensions are needed if we are to grow in faith and in our ability to understand and please God.

Relating to each other and relating to God

What does it mean to honor and meditate upon the name of God? The name of God stands for all that He is, just as your name stands for

When we honor His
name, we honor all
that He is and all
that He says and all
that He does

all that you are. You sign a check and all that you are is laid on the line, up to the face amount of that check. Your name, your signature, is what gives value and meaning to that check far beyond any intrinsic value because of the paper and ink that it is made of. It's the same way with God's name. When we honor His name, we honor all that He is and all that He says and all that He does. We meditate on His character and His attributes. We seek to make His life a part of our lives, His qualities a part of our makeup.

Over the years, floods of books and seminars have claimed to tell us what is wrong with the church, analyzing its weakness and presenting some gadget or gimmick to solve the problem. The underlying failure of all these books and seminars is that the solutions that they offer are not solutions at all. They are quick fixes that do not last, Band-Aids applied to cancers. The true weakness of the church is that we have lost our ability to honor and meditate on the name of God and all that that name implies. We focus on programs and projects and fail to focus on Him. The fact is, you can take away all the props of the church—its buildings and staff, its committees and commissions, its programs and budgets, its philosophy of ministry and church-growth strategy, its experts and consultants—and if you have nothing left but some committed people who have learned to focus on the name of God, *you have not lost a thing!*

That is what this age needs to hear again.

Jesus, the Sun of Righteousness

In Malachi chapter 4, the prophet again lifts his eyes to the future and sees Jesus Christ—but this time he is not looking merely four hundred years into the future to the first coming of Christ. He is looking far into the future, across the great reaches of the centuries, beyond our own time, to the second coming of Christ, when God's program will be fulfilled:

> *"Surely the day is coming; it will burn like a furnace. All the arrogant and every evildoer will be stubble, and that day that is coming will set them on fire," says the LORD Almighty. "Not a root or a branch will be left to them. But for you who revere my name, the sun of righteousness will rise with healing in its wings" (4:1–2).*

Now that is one cause with two effects. The Sun of Righteousness shall rise. And those who refuse Him will burn. But those who receive Him will be healed. It is the same Sun, but it has a different effect on different people, depending on their relationship to that Sun.

This promise is followed by another promise regarding the reappearance on earth of the prophet Elijah:

"See, I will send you the prophet Elijah before that great and dread-ful day of the LORD comes. He will turn the hearts of the fathers to their children, and the hearts of the children to their fathers; or else I will come and strike the land with a curse" (4:5–6).

Matthew 17 describes a scene in which the disciples of Jesus are troubled by this very prophecy (this is the link between Malachi and Matthew that I mentioned earlier). "Why," they ask, "do teachers of the law say that Elijah must come first?" And Jesus' reply is twofold: Elijah will come, He says, and "will restore all things"—a reference to the return of Elijah in the future, just before the close of God's program in human history. But He goes on to add that "Elijah has already come, and they did not recognize him. . . . Then the disciples understood that he was talking to them about John the Baptist" (Matt. 17:10–13). When the angel announced the coming birth of John the Baptist, the angel said in a clear reference to Malachi 4:5–6, "He will go on before the Lord, in the spirit and power of Elijah, to turn the hearts of the fathers to their children and the disobedient to the wisdom of the righteous—to make ready a people prepared for the Lord" (Luke 1:17).

Many people identify the two witnesses mentioned in Revelation 11 as Elijah and Moses. Whether or not these two witnesses are literally Elijah and Moses returned to earth in bodily form is a matter of specu-lation. What is clear, however, is that in some remarkable way, God intends to supply a ministry like Elijah's before the return of the Lord Jesus in power and judgment.

It is significant, I think, that the last word of the Old Testament is the word *curse*. This word is not a prediction. It is a warning. This book of prophecy begins with, " 'I have loved you,' says the LORD," and it ends with the warning that if this message of love is not received, a curse will result. Now compare the last word of the Old Testament with the last word of the New Testament. Leaving out the final salutation, it is the name of Jesus: "Come, Lord Jesus" (Rev. 22:20).

That is God's answer to the curse, isn't it? He has redeemed us from the curse of the law by sending Jesus to be made a curse for us. Thus, the full answer of God is grace and love bringing us into the light and the knowledge of Christ. All the blessing wrapped up in that name is ours as we place our trust in Him and believe on His name.

The last word of the
Old Testament:
curse

God's answer to the
curse in the New
Testament: Jesus
Christ

PART SIX

Jesus: The Focus of Both Testaments

Between the Testaments

At the beginning of the previous chapter on Malachi, we discussed the four-hundred-year period of God's apparent silence between the testaments. From our human perspective, four centuries is a long time. Entire civilizations rise, decline, fall, and are forgotten in less time than that.

This does not mean, however, that no books of Hebrew history were being written then. During the period from 400 B.C. to New Testament times, a body of literature was produced that came to be called "the Apocrypha," from the Greek *apokryphos,* meaning "hidden." For a time in the earliest centuries of the Christian church, books of the Apocrypha were accepted as Scripture by some, especially in the Greek translation of the Old Testament, the Septuagint. When Saint Jerome translated the Septuagint into Latin for the Vulgate edition of the Catholic Bible (fifth century A.D.), he expressed doubts about the validity of the Apocrypha, but he was overruled by the ruling council of the church. As a result, the Roman Catholic and Eastern Orthodox Bibles contain the Apocrypha to this day. The Apocrypha was never included, however, in the Old Testament of the early Hebrew Christians and was not accepted as inspired, legitimate Scripture by Reformers such as Calvin and Luther. It was also excluded from the Authorized (King James) Version of 1611.

As historical texts, the Apocrypha sheds interesting light on the period of Hebrew history during the gap between the testaments. This was

The Apocrypha was never included in the Hebrew Scriptures or accepted by the Reformers or included in the KJV

the period during which Jewish culture was strongly influenced by Greek (Hellenistic) ideas, and the Hellenization of Israel can be clearly seen in these works. In fact, the Greek Septuagint translation of the Old Testament is a sign of the Hellenistic influence. Interesting clues to certain New Testament institutions can also be found in the Apocrypha, since the Pharisee sect of Judaism arose in the second century B.C., and the Sadducee (or Zadokite) party arose in the first century B.C. Both of these groups are crucially important in all four Gospel accounts of the life of Jesus and also figure in the life of that hardened Pharisee-turned-Christian-missionary, the apostle Paul.

The apocryphal books in the Septuagint (but not included in the Scriptures of the non-Hellenistic Jews) were:

Tobit, a book of edifying historical fiction;

Judith, a book of edifying historical fiction;

The Wisdom of Solomon, a wisdom book similar to Proverbs and Ecclesiastes;

Sirach (Ecclesiasticus), another wisdom book;

Baruch, an add-on to Jeremiah, supposedly written by Jeremiah's assistant; and

First and Second Maccabees, epic historical works.

Also included in the Apocrypha are fragmentary texts that are appended to the accepted, inspired Old Testament—additions to the Book of Esther (which appear in the Septuagint and Roman Catholic versions as Esther 10:4–10), the Song of the Three Young Men (inserted at the end of Daniel 3), the story of Susanna (which appears as Daniel 13), and the story of Bel and the Dragon (which appears as Daniel 14).

The Apocrypha makes interesting and even informative reading, but a careful examination of these books, comparing them with the accepted canon of Scripture, strongly indicates that these extracanonical books do not fit in with the overarching themes of God's Word. If you work your way through the Old Testament, book by book, as we have been doing in *Adventuring through the Bible,* you see clearly that every page of every book points clearly to Jesus, the coming Messiah. You do not see Jesus clearly, if at all, in the Apocrypha. Perhaps that is one of the factors that persuaded Saint Jerome to question their validity so many years ago. In any case, I am persuaded, as are virtually all other Protestant Bible scholars, that whatever historical or literary value the Apocrypha may have, it is not the inspired Word of God.

Jesus and His Church

Throughout the pages of the Old Testament, we have been reading about Jesus Christ. Even though He is never named in the Old Testament, He appears on every page in the form of symbols, shadows, types, rituals, sacrifices, and prophecies. As we turn to the pages of the New Testament, we encounter Him in the flesh. Here, in the form of a living, breathing human being, is the one who satisfies and fulfills all the symbols and prophecies of Genesis through Malachi. As we move from the Old Testament to the New, we find that one person, Jesus of Nazareth, is the focal point of both Testaments.

We encounter this man, Jesus Christ, through four separate portraits—Matthew, Mark, Luke, and John. Many have asked, "Why is it necessary to have four Gospels instead of just one? Why couldn't one of these writers have gotten all the facts together and presented them for us in one book?" Well, that would be like trying to use one photograph of a building to adequately represent the entire structure. One picture could not possibly show all four sides of the building at once.

The same is true of Jesus. His life, His character, and His ministry are so rich and multifaceted that a single view could not tell the whole story. God deliberately planned for four Gospels so that each could present our Lord in a unique way. Each Gospel presents a distinct aspect of Christ, and our understanding of who He truly is would be incalculably poorer if even one of these Gospels was lost to us.

The Old Testament is filled with pictures of the coming Messiah, and these pictures correspond with the portraits of Jesus, "painted" for

The fourfold image of Christ

us in the four Gospels. First, He is pictured in many prophecies—particularly those of Isaiah, Jeremiah, and Zechariah—as the coming King of Israel. For obvious reasons, the people of Israel have loved that picture—which is one of the principle reasons why Israel rejected the Lord when He came: He did not look like the King of their expectations. But Matthew, in his Gospel, saw the kingly aspects of Jesus and His ministry, and those are the aspects he emphasized. Matthew, then, is the Gospel of the King.

Second, Jesus the Messiah was portrayed in many parts of the Old Testament as the servant, the suffering one. We see these images of the suffering servant especially in Isaiah. Joseph, in the book of Genesis, is also seen as a type of the One who would come to suffer and serve. The Hebrews found these two images of the Messiah so confusing—the Messiah-King versus the suffering Messiah-Servant—that many Jewish scholars concluded that there must be two Messiahs. They called one, "Messiah Ben-david," or Messiah the son of David, and the other "Messiah Ben-joseph," or Messiah the son of Joseph. Messiah Ben-david was viewed as the kingly Messiah, while Messiah Ben-joseph was the suffering one. They couldn't imagine that the king and the servant could be the same person! But Mark understood the humble, self-sacrificing, servant nature of Christ, and that is the aspect he presents to us in his Gospel.

Third, we have frequent Old Testament pictures of Christ's coming as a man. He was to be born of a virgin, grow up in Bethlehem, and walk among human beings. He was to be the perfect human being. That is also the image presented to us by Luke in his Gospel.

Finally, we have those Old Testament pictures that speak of the Messiah as God, as the Everlasting One. For example, Micah 5:2 predicts that the Messiah will come out of the small town of Bethlehem Ephrathah—where Jesus was, in fact, born—and that Messiah's origins are from everlasting (that is, He has no beginning, He is eternal, He is God). This accords with the picture of Jesus that we derive from the Gospel of John, the Gospel of the Son of God.

So all of the Old Testament prophecies and pictures of Christ can be placed under these four Gospel headings: king, servant, human being, and God. Interestingly enough, in four places in the Old Testament (in the King James Version) the word *behold* is used in connection with one of these four pictures. In Zechariah 9:9, God says to the daughters of Zion and Jerusalem, "Behold, thy King cometh" (KJV). That prophecy was fulfilled when our Lord entered Jerusalem in triumph. Then in Isaiah 42:1, God says, "Behold my servant" (KJV). It is not "thy servant" but "my servant." Christ is not the servant of humanity but the servant of God. In Zechariah 6:12, the Lord says, "Behold, the man" (KJV). He is speaking in this passage about the Messiah. And in Isaiah 40:9, He says, "Say unto the cities of Judah, Behold your God!" (KJV). Four times that phrase is used, each time in connection with a different aspect of Christ. So we can clearly see that God has woven a marvelous and consistent pattern into His Word, both the Old Testament and the New. This pattern reveals the many facets and dimensions of Jesus the Messiah.

It is fascinating to notice all the techniques, details, and nuances used by each Gospel writer to paint his unique and individual portrait of Jesus Christ.

Unity, not harmony

Matthew, the Gospel of the King

In Matthew, the Gospel of the King, we see many evidences of His kingship: The book opens with Christ's genealogy, tracing His royal line back to David, king of Israel, and to Abraham, father of the nation Israel. Throughout the book, He speaks and acts with kingly authority: "Moses said to you so-and-so, but I say to you such-and-such." To the Jews, Moses was the great authority, so for Jesus to supersede the authority of Moses was to act as a king. He demonstrated the authority to dismiss evil spirits and command the sick to be healed and the blind to see. With kingly authority, He passed judgment on the officials of the nation, saying, "Woe to you, scribes and Pharisees, hypocrites!" The key phrase Jesus uses again and again through Matthew's Gospel is "the kingdom of heaven"—it occurs thirty-two times in Matthew. Matthew is constantly referring to the kingdom of heaven and the King. In his account of our Lord's birth, Matthew says that Christ was born King of the Jews, and in his account of the crucifixion, he says that Jesus was crucified as King of the Jews.

Mark, the second Gospel, pictures Christ as the Servant, and as you would expect, Mark does not provide any genealogy for Christ. After all, who cares about the genealogy of a servant? Nobody. In Mark's Gospel, our Lord simply appears on the scene. Again and again in this Gospel, we see the word *immediately.* That is the word of a servant, isn't it? When you give a servant an order, you want it carried out immediately, not ten minutes later. So again and again we read, "Immediately, Jesus did so-and-so." Whereas both Luke and Matthew are filled with parables on many subjects and issues, Mark, the Gospel of the Servant, contains only four parables—and each of them is a parable of servanthood. They represent Jesus as the Servant of Jehovah—the suffering servant pictured in Isaiah 53. Read through the Gospel of Mark and you will never see Jesus called *Lord* until after His resurrection—another mark of His servant role. Mark 13:32 is a verse that profoundly illustrates His servanthood—and a verse that has puzzled many. In that verse, our Lord says of His second coming:

Mark, the Gospel of the Servant

*"No one knows about that day or hour, not even the angels in heaven,
nor the Son, but only the Father."*

How could Jesus be the omnipotent God and still not know the
time of His own return? This is a total mystery until you understand the
character of Mark's Gospel. Mark describes Christ in His role as the suffering servant of God. It is not a servant's place to know what his Lord
is doing—even when that servant is the Son of God Himself.

**Luke, the Gospel of
the Son of Man**

Luke shows us Christ as human. Here we see the perfection of His
manhood—the glory, beauty, strength, and dignity of His humanity. As
we would expect, Luke also contains a genealogy of Christ. If Jesus is to
be presented as human, we want to know that He belongs to the human
race. And Luke makes this case for Christ's complete identification with
Adam's race by tracing His genealogy all the way back to Adam. In Luke,
we find Christ often in prayer. If you want to see Jesus at prayer, read the
Gospel of Luke. Prayer is a picture of humanity's proper relationship to
God—total dependence upon the sovereign, omnipotent God. In Luke,
we see His human sympathy most clearly—His weeping over the city of
Jerusalem, His healing of the man whose ear Peter cut off when the soldiers arrested Jesus in the garden. No other Gospel relates these two incidents that so powerfully show the sympathetic, human aspect of our
Lord. Luke relates the fullest account of Christ's agony in the garden
where He sweats drops of blood, so eloquently symbolic of the human
being who fully enters into our trials and pain.

**John, the Gospel of
the Son of God**

John's Gospel presents Christ as God. From the very first verse, this
is John's potent, unmistakable theme. Many people fail to realize that
John's Gospel, like Matthew's and Luke's, opens with a genealogy. The
reason so many people miss the genealogy in John is that it is so short:

*In the beginning was the Word, and the Word was with God, and
the Word was God (1:1).*

That's it! That's John's entire genealogy of Christ—two people, the
Father and the Son. Why is this genealogy so short? Because John's pur-
pose is so simple: to set forth the account of Christ's divine nature. In
John's Gospel we see seven "I am" declarations (I have listed them in
chapter 41). These seven declarations echo the great statement of the
Lord to Moses from the burning bush, "I AM WHO I AM" (Ex. 3:14).

In addition to these seven dramatic "I am" declarations, we read
about an incident in the garden where the "I am" statement of Jesus
has a powerful impact. It happens when Judas leads the soldiers to
the garden to arrest Jesus. When the soldiers tell the Lord that they
are seeking a man called Jesus of Nazareth, He responds, "I am he,"

and the force of that great "I am" declaration—a declaration of His own godhood—is so powerful that the soldiers fall back in stunned amazement (see John 18:3–8)!

In John 20:30–31, the writer clearly states that his purpose is not to set down an exhaustive biography of the Lord but to inspire saving belief in the godhood of Jesus Christ, the Son of God:

> *Jesus did many other miraculous signs in the presence of his disciples, which are not recorded in this book. But these are written that you may believe that Jesus is the Christ, the Son of God, and that by believing you may have life in his name.*

Finally, before we move on to examine these four Gospels individually, we should note that it is impossible to chronologically harmonize these accounts because they are not intended to be chronological accounts. Matthew, Mark, Luke, and John did not sit down to record a chronological biography of Jesus. They wrote to present specific aspects of the Lord's life and ministry, but none of these books claims to be a chronology of His life. The chronology of these events, of course, is hardly the most important information to be derived from the Gospels. Though we cannot precisely harmonize these events, it is possible to obtain a fairly reliable general sequence of events by comparing the Gospels, especially if we rely on John's Gospel, which appears to be the most chronologically precise of the four.

The book of Acts

You might think I've just thrown Acts into this section with the Gospels because it doesn't fit with the epistles. No, I have very deliberately included Acts with the Gospels because it continues their story. Written by Luke, it is really a sequel to Luke's Gospel, but it actually serves as a fitting sequel to all four Gospels. While the Gospels tell the story of Christ in His earthly body, in His ministry on earth, the book of Acts tells the story of the body of Christ, the church, which continues His work on earth after His ascension into heaven.

Acts, a fitting sequel to the Gospels

In many ways, Acts is the key to the New Testament. We couldn't understand the New Testament if this book were left out. The four Gospels teach us that the apostles have been sent to preach the gospel to Israel—and only Israel. But in Acts we learn of God's command that the gospel be taken into all the world, to the Gentiles as well as the house of Israel. If we leave out the book of Acts and skip directly to Paul's epistles, we find that another apostle has mysteriously been added—some fellow named Paul! Instead of talking about God's kingdom, Christians are talking about a new organization—the church. Instead of a gospel that is confined to Jews in the region around the city of Jerusalem, Christianity has spread—in the short span of a single generation—to the limits of the then-known world! We would be puzzled as to where this church and this apostle Paul came from, and we would wonder how this incredible spread of Christianity has taken place. All of this is explained in the book of Acts.

The key to understanding Acts is the realization that this book is not a record of the acts of the apostles but the acts of the Lord Jesus Christ! Notice how the book begins:

> In my former book, Theophilus, I wrote about all that Jesus began to do and to teach (1:1).

Notice Luke's choice of words! In the Gospel of Luke, he recorded what the Lord Jesus began to do. But now, in Acts, Luke gives us the record of what our Lord is continuing to do. So it is the Lord who is at work throughout both books. Luke is volume one; Acts is volume two.

During World War II, Britain's prime minister, Winston Churchill, broadcast an announcement of the victories of the allied forces when they had swept across North Africa and were about to launch the invasion of Sicily. Churchill summed up his announcement with these words: "This is not the end. This is not even the beginning of the end. But it may be the end of the beginning." That is what we have in the four Gospels. It is not the end of our Lord's ministry when He ascends into the heavens, as Luke records in Acts 1. That is just the end of the beginning. But in the rest of Acts we have the beginning of the end.

Throughout the book of Acts, we have the record of Christ's continuing ministry through the instrumentality of men and women who are just like you and me. In Luke 12:50, shortly before the cross, Jesus tells His disciples, "I have a baptism to undergo, and how distressed I am until it is completed!" That is, "How limited and shackled I am until this thing is accomplished!" Well, it has been accomplished now. Our Lord is no longer limited and shackled. When He ascended into heaven, the Holy Spirit came to us, His followers. The omnipotence of God was unleashed in the lives of ordinary men and women, enabling them to do extraordinary things in His name. That is why we have the tremendous explosion of ministry power: the book of Acts.

Acts is the one book of the Bible that is not yet finished. Notice that it ends very abruptly. The last two verses say that Paul has reached Rome:

> For two whole years Paul stayed there in his own rented house and welcomed all who came to see him. Boldly and without hindrance he

preached the kingdom of God and taught about the Lord Jesus Christ (28:30–31).

I never close this book without wondering to myself, "Well, what happened next?" The book of Acts leaves you hanging. It gives the distinct impression of being unfinished. And there is a reason for this. It is because this is the biography of a living person—Jesus Christ. The last chapter of His story has not yet been written.

I have in my library an autobiography of Dr. H. A. Ironside, and it ends on the same sort of note. It leaves you hanging. You wonder what happens next. It isn't complete because, at the time it was written, his life hadn't ended.

The book of Acts continues to be written today in the lives of men and women in the living body of Christ, the church. Even though Jesus has been taken up in the clouds, His body life goes on! It goes on in your life. It goes on in my life. It goes on and on, outliving and outlasting the lives and institutions of mere mortals, of nations, of civilizations. Rome has fallen, the empires of the Huns, the Mongols, the Aztecs, the Manchu Chinese, and the British have all risen and declined. Colonialism has collapsed in the Americas, Africa, and Asia; Soviet communism has come and gone; two world wars have been fought; we have gone from the Dark Ages to the Internet Age—and still the body life of Jesus Christ goes on, the book of Acts continues to be written. You and I are still writing the book of Acts today because it is an account of what the Holy Spirit continues to do through us today, all around the world.

We are the body of Christ. We are His miracle-working, ministering hands of service; we are His eyes of compassion and love; we are His voice of truth, calling the world to repentance and faith in Him; we are His feet, swift to carry His message around the world. His body life goes on and on and on. We are still writing the book of the Acts of Jesus Christ in the New Testament age. We haven't seen the last page yet.

So as we study the five books of His life—Matthew, Mark, Luke, John, and Acts—let us view them as a guide to our own way of life as we seek to let Him live His life through us.

Behold Your King!

Nearly a century ago, an Englishman named Greene was walking through the woods when he came upon a stranger in the path. He was startled when the stranger smiled and waved at him. "Oh, hello, Mr. Greene!" said the stranger. Obviously this "stranger" wasn't a stranger at all—but for the life of him, Mr. Greene could not place him.

Embarrassed, but unwilling to admit to a poor memory for names and faces, Mr. Greene offered his hand. "Ah, yes! Hello! Good to see you, old boy! How long has it been?"

"Well," said the other man, "it was at Lady Asquith's reception last October, wasn't it? Nearly a year, then."

Mr. Greene remembered Lady Asquith's reception and tried to recall all the people he had met. This gentleman's face looked familiar, but he just couldn't place it. Still groping for clues to this fellow's identity, Greene decided to ask a few questions. "And how is your wife?"

"Quite well," said the other man.

"And you? Still in the same business, I presume?"

"Oh, yes," said the other man, with a merry twinkle in his eye. "I'm still the king of England."

Mr. Greene, behold your king!

Astonished by the Gospels

The Old Testament was type and symbol; the New Testament is reality and substance

That is the message of the Gospel of Matthew to you and me: Behold your king! Until we have closely examined Jesus' credentials as the King of creation and Lord of our lives, as presented in this Gospel, we will not fully recognize Him in all His glory.

The Old Testament was shadow. The New Testament is sunshine.

The Old Testament was type and symbol. The New Testament is reality and substance.

The Old Testament was prophecy. The New Testament is fulfillment.

In the Old Testament, we must piece together a complex mosaic of Christ. In the New Testament, Jesus blazes from the page in three-dimensional realism.

Though the Old Testament speaks of Him on every page, it speaks in shadows, types, symbols, and prophecies that anticipate the coming of Someone. You cannot read the Old Testament without being aware of that constant promise running through every page: Someone is coming! Someone is coming!

But as we open the Gospels, it becomes clear that the long-awaited moment has come. That promised and prophesied Someone has arrived—and He steps forth in all the astonishing fullness of His glory. As John says, "We have seen his glory, the glory of the One and Only, who came from the Father, full of grace and truth" (John. 1:14).

I love the Gospels. They are the most fascinating sections of the Bible to me because they are the eyewitness accounts of the life of that wonderful Someone around whom all the rest of the Bible revolves. In the Gospels, we see Christ as He is. The Gospels confront us with the fact that what He is may not always be what we think He is or what we would like Him to be. He is startling, He is awesome. No matter how many times we have read the Gospels before, He continues to astonish us and challenge our assumptions about Him.

If you are a Christian, a follower of Christ, then all that He is, you have. All the fullness of His character and life is available to you. We learn what those resources are as we see Him as He was—and as He is. That is why the Gospel accounts are so important to us.

Jesus as He truly is

The Synoptic Gospels

Matthew, along with Mark and Luke, is one of the three Synoptic Gospels (*synoptic* means "viewed together"). Although the four Gospels, including John, complement and reinforce each other, the style, theme, and viewpoint of the Synoptic Gospels differ from that of John. Read in parallel, the three synoptics impress us with many similarities and overlapping detail, while John's approach and purpose is noticeably different. Though the three synoptics make the deity of

Christ clear, they focus on His humanity. John's Gospel, on the other hand, strongly and dramatically presents the godliness of Christ; it is the most forceful of the Gospels in its portrayal of Christ as fully God, as "from above."

As you read the Gospel accounts, I hope you experience something of the tremendous impact of the most powerful human personality in history. There is no more transforming, life-changing experience in all of life than the experience of seeing Jesus as He truly is, as He is revealed on the pages of the Gospels and by the Holy Spirit.

The first book of the New Testament is Matthew. Most people, I believe, begin reading in the New Testament rather than the Old, and most begin at the beginning of the New Testament. Matthew, then, is probably the most widely read book of the Bible. Renan, the French skeptic, called this book "the most important book of all Christendom."

The Gospel of Matthew has its critics, too. There are those who claim that this book contains nothing but the early legends of the church that grew up around Jesus but are not historical and that this book was not actually written until the fourth century A.D. Therefore, they say, we are uncertain as to how much is really true. Other critics claim that Matthew is only one of many gospels that were propagated in the early Christian era.

It is true that other "gospels" were circulated, besides the four in the New Testament. Gospels supposedly were written by Barnabas or Peter or Thomas and even Pontius Pilate! In fact, you can find more than a hundred documents called "the New Testament Apocrypha," consisting of fanciful gospels, epistles, and prophecies (the word *apocryphal* originally meant "hidden," but it has also come to mean "of doubtful authenticity"). You can find these New Testament Apocrypha at your local public library if you would like to read them, and in most cases, you can sense simply by reading them that they are absurd and far-fetched and do not belong in the accepted canon of Scripture. Many of them were generated by adherents of the gnostic heresy that was rampant during the early Christian era.

Some critics say it is mere chance that our four Gospels survived and were chosen as part of our New Testament. One legend began with a German theologian named Pappas in about the sixteenth century; he claimed that the Gospels were selected at the Council of Nicaea in A.D. 325 by gathering together all the gospels in circulation at that time, throwing them under a table, then reaching in and pulling out these four: Matthew, Mark, Luke, and John. The foolishness of such a claim is evident to anyone who reads the Gospels with thoughtfulness and care. These four books bear the fingerprints of God. The very pattern of these books reflects the divine imprint, and you cannot read them or compare them with the Old Testament without seeing that they come from an inspired source.

The first of the four New Testament Gospels was written by Matthew, otherwise known as Levi. He was a tax collector before he became a follower of Christ. Since his name means "the gift of God," it is probably a new name given him after his conversion. Perhaps it is even a name given him by our Lord Himself, just as Jesus changed Simon's name to Peter. Scholars believe that Matthew lived and taught in Palestine for fifteen years after the crucifixion, and then he began to travel as a missionary, first to Ethiopia and then to Macedonia, Syria, and Persia. Scholars also believe that he died a natural death in either Ethiopia or Macedonia, but this is not certain.

The book obviously was written at a very early date—almost certainly from the early half of the first century. It is quoted, for instance, in the well-known *Didache,* the teaching of the twelve apostles that dates from early in the second century. Papias, a disciple of the apostle John, says, "Matthew composed his Gospel in the Hebrew tongue, and each one interprets it as he is able." This was confirmed by Irenaeus and Origen, two early church fathers who were well acquainted with the Gospel of Matthew.

Even in the first century we have Jewish voices that prove the early existence of Matthew. Two Jewish people, Gamaliel the Second, a prominent rabbi, and his sister, Immashalom (which, incidentally, means "woman of peace," though she wasn't) pronounced a curse upon Christians as "readers of the evangelistic scriptures." Since the only evangelistic Scriptures extant in their day (about A.D. 45 or 50) were the Gospel of Matthew and, perhaps, the Gospel of Mark, the date of writing of this Gospel would have to be about A.D. 45 or 50. It likely was first written in Hebrew, then translated into Greek.

The Holy Spirit Himself has given the outline of the Gospel of Matthew, as He does in several other books of Scripture. The major divisions of Matthew are marked by the repetition of a particular phrase that appears twice and divides the book into three sections. First, there is an introductory section, the coming of the king, chapters 1 to 4. Then, at the beginning of the second section, in 4:17, we find the phrase "from that time on":

> *From that time on Jesus began to preach, "Repent, for the kingdom of heaven is near."*

That statement marks a major turning point in the argument and presentation of this book. We find an identical phrase occurring in 16:21, introducing the third section:

> From that time on Jesus began to explain to his disciples that he must go to Jerusalem and suffer many things at the hands of the elders, chief priests and teachers of the law, and that he must be killed and on the third day be raised to life.

That is the first mention of the crucifixion in Matthew. From this point forward, the cross is (literally) the crux of this book.

Now, there are subdivisions in Matthew, which are marked off for us by a phrase that appears five times in the book. The first is found in 7:28–29, at the close of the Sermon on the Mount:

> When Jesus had finished saying these things, the crowds were amazed at his teaching, because he taught as one who had authority, and not as their teachers of the law.

"When Jesus had finished"

In 11:1, another subdivision is indicated:

> After Jesus had finished instructing his twelve disciples, he went on from there to teach and preach in the towns of Galilee.

In 13:53–54, another subdivision is indicated:

> When Jesus had finished these parables, he moved on from there. Coming to his hometown, he began teaching the people in their synagogue, and they were amazed. "Where did this man get this wisdom and these miraculous powers?" they asked.

In 19:1–2, another subdivision:

> When Jesus had finished saying these things, he left Galilee and went into the region of Judea to the other side of the Jordan. Large crowds followed him, and he healed them there.

Notice that each of these subsections introduces a complete change of direction in the Lord's ministry and in the direction of the book. These mark the divisions of the Gospel of Matthew. Here is an outline of the Gospel of the King:

The Coming of the King (Matthew 1:1–4:16)
1. The royal genealogy   1:1–17
2. The birth of King Jesus   1:18–25

The first division is all about the preparation of the King for His ministry. "Rejoice greatly, O Daughter of Zion!" wrote the prophet Zechariah. "Shout, Daughter of Jerusalem! See, your king comes to you, righteous and having salvation, gentle and riding on a donkey, on a colt, the foal of a donkey" (Zechariah. 9:9). Matthew, then, is the Gospel of the King. The prophecy of Zechariah was fulfilled in the triumphal entry when our Lord entered the city of Jerusalem in exactly that manner.

Matthew's task is to present Jesus as the King. The book opens, therefore, with the genealogy of the King. Every king has to have a genealogy. The ancestry of a king is the most important thing about him. His right of kingship is based on his royal lineage. So Matthew opens with that exhaustive and somewhat exhausting genealogy, tracing the ancestry of Jesus from Abraham on down to Joseph, His stepfather, who was the husband of Mary. Joseph was in the royal line of David. Our Lord gets His royal right to the throne from Joseph, because He was the heir of Joseph. Jesus gets His genealogical right to the throne through Mary, who was also of the royal line of David. His legal right comes through Joseph, His hereditary right through Mary. Joseph, of course, was not His actual father, but Mary really was His mother.

The first chapter also recounts His birth. The second chapter describes events following His birth, including the escape into Egypt after Herod decreed the slaughter of the innocents in an effort to destroy this rival king, the baby Jesus. In the third chapter we read of the baptism of our Lord.

The genealogy of the King

His legal right comes through Joseph; His hereditary right comes through Mary

The first two chapters of Matthew establish the earthly connection of Jesus—His royal lineage and human birth. These chapters anchor Him in human history, in time and space. In the third chapter, His baptism establishes His heavenly connection, His heavenly credentials, and His heavenly authority. In chapter 3, the heavens open and God the Father speaks from heaven, declaring Jesus to be His beloved Son. At that moment, the royal line of Jesus is established not according to a human bloodline but according to the heavenly standard. Jesus is King by right of being the Son of the Creator-King of the universe.

The testing of Jesus, the testing of humanity

In Matthew 4, we witness the testing of the King in the wilderness, where He is permitted to be tempted by all the powers of darkness. Hungry, weary, and alone, Jesus is left in a place where hell is loosed upon Him, where Satan himself is permitted to take his best shot. The testing of our Lord is the key to the Gospel of Matthew. He is tested as a representative human being. He goes into the wilderness as the Son of Man and is tested as to whether or not He can fulfill God's intention for humanity. Humans are made up of body, soul, and spirit, and Jesus is tested in the wilderness on each of these three levels.

His *body* was tested

He was tested first on the level of the body's demands. The dominant passion of the body is self-preservation. Our Lord's first temptation came on that most basic level. Would He continue to be God's person, even when faced by an extreme challenge to His very life? For forty days and nights He had not eaten, and then the temptation came subtly to Him: "The tempter came to him and said, 'If you are the Son of God, tell these stones to become bread' "(4:3). But He steadfastly remained in the Father's will despite His great hunger and need.

His *soul* was tested

Next, Jesus was tested on the level of the soul—that is, through the dominant passion of the soul, which is self-expression. On this level, we all desire to reveal our egos, to show what we can do, to express ourselves. This is the primary drive of the human soul. It was during this testing that our Lord was taken up to the top of the temple and given the opportunity to cast Himself down and thus capture the acclaim of Israel. Such temptation plays upon the urge for status, for manifesting the pride of life. But Jesus proved Himself true to God despite the pressure that came to Him in that way.

His *spirit* was tested

Finally, He was tested in the deepest, most essential part of His humanity—the spirit. The dominant passion of the human spirit is to worship. The spirit is always looking for something to worship. That is why human beings are essentially religious beings; the spirit in them is craving, is crying out for an idol, a hero, something or someone to worship and be in awe of. It was on this level that the devil next came to Jesus:

Again, the devil took him to a very high mountain and showed him all the kingdoms of the world and their splendor. "All this I will give you," he said, "if you will bow down and worship me."

Jesus said to him, "Away from me, Satan! For it is written: 'Worship the Lord your God, and serve him only.' "

Then the devil left him, and angels came and attended him (4:8–11).

So Jesus passed the threefold test. He revealed Himself fully and adequately to be human as God intended humanity to be.

In the Sermon on the Mount, Jesus begins to put this same test to the nation Israel. Throughout the Old Testament, we see that God had chosen Israel to be His channel of communication with humanity. The people of Israel have regarded themselves as God's favored people. Now the nation is put to the test—the same test, in fact, that Jesus Himself has just passed.

This is the essence of Matthew's Gospel. He is tracing for us the way God's King came into the world, offered Himself as King of Israel—first on the level of the physical, then on the level of the soul. When He was rejected on both these levels, He passed into the realm of the mystery of the human spirit. In the darkness and mystery of the cross, He accomplished the redeeming work that would restore human beings to their Creator—body, soul, and spirit.

Redemption, therefore, begins with the spirit. The work of Christ in our own lives does not really change us until it has reached the level of our spirits, the source of our worship. We may be attracted to Christ on the level of the body, because He supplies our physical need for safety, shelter, and daily sustenance. Or we may be attracted to Him on the level of the soul, because He satisfies our need for affirmation, self-esteem, and self-expression. But if our relationship with Christ does not penetrate our lives to the deep recesses of the spirit, we have not truly been permeated and changed by His life. We must be wholly committed to Him—body, soul, and spirit.

Jesus' ministry begins, as we saw in 4:17, with the words, "From that time on Jesus began to preach, 'Repent, for the kingdom of heaven is near.' " Then follows the Sermon on the Mount, where we have the presentation of the King and the laws of the kingdom. This covers the rest of chapters 4 and 5 through 7. In these rules for life in the kingdom, laid down in the Sermon on the Mount, the obvious emphasis is on the physical life.

This is one of the most penetrating and incisive messages ever set before human beings, and it approaches us on the level of our ordinary,

Israel is tested in the physical realm

The Sermon on the Mount and the physical miracles

physical lives. Two physical sins are dealt with here: murder and adultery. The life of God is illustrated for us in the realm of giving alms and of fasting: physical acts. We see God as One who cares for us in such a way that we do not need to think of tomorrow—how to be fed or how to be clothed, the worries that come to us on the physical level. Our Lord is saying, "If you discover Me and receive Me as your King, you will discover that I am the answer to all your physical needs." He first offers Himself to the nation—and to us—on this level.

The Sermon on the Mount is followed by a section on miracles, and in chapters 8 through 12, we witness the physical miracles of the kingdom. These are illustrations of the benefits our Lord can bestow on the level of the physical life. This is not just a demonstration of Hollywood-style special effects and pyrotechnics. In fact, it is amazing how unspectacular these miracles are! There is no spectacular display of lights and fire and quadraphonic sound effects here, but rather a simple, dignified representation of our Lord's power over all forces that affect the body: demons, disease, and death. His authority in this realm is that of King—He is sovereign and supreme.

Parables of the kingdom

Following the miracles comes a section of parables of the kingdom, where the rejection of the kingdom is declared in mystery form. It is clear that the nation is going to reject our Lord's offer of Himself as King on this physical level, so a new word appears: *woe*. In chapter 11, He declares, "Woe to you, Korazin! Woe to you, Bethsaida!" Woe to those who have not believed! He pronounces judgment upon the nation on this level, the level of the physical.

The mysteries of the kingdom are found in chapter 13, where the parables are given with truth embedded within symbols—the parable of the sower and the seeds, the parable of the wheat and the weeds (or "tares"), the parable of the mustard seed, the parable of the yeast, the parable of the great catch of fish. This entire section—Matthew 13:54 through 16:20—has to do with bread. There is the feeding of the five thousand in chapter 14; the questions about what defiles a person in chapter 15; the incident of the Canaanite woman who came and asked Jesus to heal her daughter, comparing her request to begging for crumbs from His table; the feeding of the four thousand in chapter 15; and the leaven of the Pharisees and Sadducees in chapter 16.

Finally, in 16:13–20, we encounter the revelation of our Lord's person to Peter at that wonderful moment when Peter is given the first insight into the true nature of his Friend, Jesus:

> *Simon Peter answered, "You are the Christ, the Son of the living God."*

Jesus replied, "Blessed are you, Simon son of Jonah, for this was not revealed to you by man, but by my Father in heaven" (vv. 16–17).

At this point, our Lord's message takes a significant turn. Here is the transition point from the physical to the soulish, as Jesus moves beyond the bodily level of our humanity and begins to penetrate to the depths of the human soul.

The previous section—Israel's testing in the physical realm—was composed of a narrative passage detailing Jesus' ministry, followed by a group of His parables. This section is structured the same way—a narrative of the Lord's ministry, followed by His parables.

Israel is tested in the realm of the soul

Beginning with 16:21, we see the second ministry of our Lord to the nation, this time offering Himself to Israel on the level of the soul. His first revelation (16:21–18:35) is to the disciples only, for they are the nucleus of the coming church. Here is the Transfiguration and the first intimation of His death.

Next come the parables of the King. These are addressed first to the disciples, and then to the nation. All are parables presenting Him as the King who has the right to command and to judge the character of individuals. Nothing is said now about their physical lives but rather their soulish lives. Are they willing to follow Him? Are they willing to obey Him? Are they willing to let Him mold and shape their character?

Parables of the King

In Matthew 18, the Lord gives instruction in how to get along with others, how to love each other, forgive each other, and reconcile with each other. It is a masterpiece of practical instruction for everyday living and healthy relationships, and if we would only practice the principles of Matthew 18 in a faithful way in the church, the entire world would be transformed by our example.

Instruction in healthy relationships

In Matthew 19, He teaches about marriage, divorce, sexual ethics and morality, promise keeping, and truthfulness. Again, His instruction is aimed at our souls—and if we would keep His teaching, we would change the world.

Matthew 21 presents the story of His triumphal entry into Jerusalem on Palm Sunday. Triumph soon gives way to judgment as the Lord enters the city and pronounces His judgment on the sins of the nation. He strides into the temple, halts the offerings, and drives out the corrupt money changers. In Matthew 23 you hear the word *woe* pronounced with a regularity and a rhythm like the sound of a whip of punishment: verse 13—"Woe to you, teachers of the law and Pharisees, you hypocrites!" Verse 15—"Woe to you, teachers of the law and Pharisees, you hypocrites!" Verse 16—"Woe to you, blind guides!" Verse 23—"Woe to you, teachers of the law and Pharisees,

The Triumphal Entry

"Woe to you"

you hypocrites!" And again in verse 25, verse 27 and verse 29. Throughout this chapter, like the knell of death, the word *woe* rings out again and again.

This is followed by a section of instruction in chapters 24 and 25—the famous Olivet Discourse. This discourse contains the Lord's instructions to the believing remnant on what to do until He comes again. It reveals how world history is going to shape up, what will happen in the intervening years, what forces will be loosed upon the earth, how the forces of darkness will shake, test, and try God's own people. He declares that God's people can stand only in the strength of the Holy Spirit.

Finally, in chapters 26 through 28, we see the betrayal, trial, agony, and crucifixion of the Lord Jesus Christ. Willingly, He steps into the murky darkness of the valley of the shadow of death. There, alone and forsaken by His friends, He enters into a death grapple with the powers of darkness. In the mystery of the cross, He lays hold of the forces that have mastered the human spirit and He shatters them there. Amazingly, though the Gospel of Matthew presents Jesus as King, the only crown He ever wears in His earthly life is a crown of thorns; the only throne He ever mounts is a bloody cross; the only scepter He ever wields is a broken reed.

**Israel is
tested in the
realm of the
spirit**

The Resurrection

What follows the crucifixion is an event so astounding, so shattering, that it represents a complete historical break with all that has gone before: The resurrection of Jesus Christ. At the moment of Jesus' resurrection, He broke through into the realm of the human spirit; the very center of humanity's being was opened wide. As we come to know the Lord in our spirits, we discover that the worship of our hearts is given to Him there. The spirit is the key to the mastery of an entire human life.

When you get a person's spirit, you have all that he or she is. By means of the cross and the resurrection, our Lord made it possible to pass into the very Holy of Holies of our humanity—the spirit—so that God could make His dwelling place within us.

The great message of the Gospel, then, is that God is not out there, way up yonder, somewhere beyond the blue. He is not waiting in some distant judgment hall to impose His condemnation on us. He is ready and waiting to pass right into the center of a hungry, thirsty person's heart and to pour out His blessing, His character, His being, His life into that life. When the King is enthroned in a human life, the kingdom of God is present on earth. That is the message of Matthew: Repent, for the kingdom of heaven is at hand. Heaven is not someplace far out in space; it is here among us, invisible yet utterly real in the life of one where God reigns in the spirit. Where the King is, there is the kingdom. If King Jesus is enthroned in the heart, the kingdom of God has come.

The Gospel of Matthew challenges us with the most crucial and personal question facing every human being: "Is Jesus Christ King of your life?" A king is more than a savior; a king is a sovereign. King Jesus demands every corner of our lives. If we have received Jesus as the Savior of only our physical beings or the Savior of our souls, then we have not yet made Him King. He must penetrate, invade, and conquer every square inch of our lives, even the deep places of the spirit.

Has Jesus penetrated your spirit and mastered your heart? Is He the single most important person in all the universe to you? Until you meet Him and receive Him as King, you have not truly met Jesus.

May you and I respond in obedience to the message of Matthew. May we truly behold—and surrender to—our King. And may we cast out the throne of our own ego, self-will, and pride, replacing it with the bloody, glorious throne of Jesus, the cross of Calvary. Then His rule in our lives will be complete—body, soul, and spirit.

He Came to Serve

O ne of the greatest leaders of the twentieth century went about barefoot, wearing the simple clothes of the poor, traveling either on foot or in the cheapest railway class. He never lived in a palace or mansion but chose to make his home in the slums, among the poor people he loved. His name was Mohandas Karamchand "Mahatma" Gandhi, and he led a nonviolent struggle to shake off British rule and bring self-government to the people of India. He was a moral and political leader—yet he led not by political power but by an example of humble servanthood. Though he was of the Hindu religion, he studied the life of Jesus and patterned his actions after the servanthood model of Jesus.

In 1931, Gandhi went to several European nations to visit the leaders of various states. Wherever he went, he took a goat with him as a symbol of his own lowliness and humility. When he went to Rome to pay a call on the Italian dictator Mussolini, he arrived as always, dressed in old beggar's clothes, leading his goat by a rope. Mussolini's children laughed when they saw the thin, bald, powerless-looking man—but the dictator snapped at them and ordered them silent. "That scrawny old man and his scrawny old goat," he said, "are shaking the British Empire."

That is the power of a true servant: the power to shake kingdoms, the power that was first modeled for us by the greatest servant of all, Jesus Christ, the Servant-Lord.

The power of a true servant: the power to shake kingdoms

The Gospel of Mark, the second book in the New Testament, is the briefest of the four Gospels, only sixteen chapters long. It is easily read in a single sitting. Its brevity is probably the reason it is the most-often-translated book of the New Testament. The Wycliffe translators usually begin their translation work with Mark's Gospel because it so succinctly gives the whole Gospel story.

Jesus from four perspectives

Mark, like Matthew and Luke, is one of the Synoptic Gospels (*synoptic* means "viewed together"). The Synoptic Gospels impress us with many similarities and overlapping detail, though each Gospel has its own distinct atmosphere, voice, and style. The fourth Gospel, John, while differing greatly in tone and detail from the first three, provides a complementary view of the life of Christ. The Holy Spirit deliberately designed the uniqueness of each Gospel as well as the unity of the four Gospels. We make a mistake if we think these four Gospels are four biographies of the Lord, intended to be the complete life and times of Jesus Christ. They are not biographies but character sketches, intended to be different, intended to present different points of view, different dimensions of this complex and endlessly fascinating person.

Not biographies but character sketches

The Gospel of Matthew is written to present Christ as the King. The Gospel of Mark presents His character as a Servant. The Gospel of Luke presents Him as the Son of Man. The Gospel of John presents Him as the Son of God, and there you find the greatest claims for His deity.

Note that each of these Gospels was addressed to a very specific audience. Matthew wrote his Gospel primarily for the Jews, and it is filled with references and quotations from the Old Testament. Luke wrote his Gospel for the Greek mind, the philosophical mind, and it is filled with the Lord's table talk, as He sat with His disciples in intimate fellowship, exploring realms of spiritual truth—the Greeks loved this. John wrote his Gospel for the Christian, which is why the Gospel of John is dearest to Christian hearts; it not only emphasizes the deity of Christ, but unveils the teaching of the Rapture of the church, the intimacy of fellowship and communion between the Lord and His own, and the ministry of the Holy Spirit. But Mark writes his Gospel for the Roman mind; it contains the most Latin words. It is the Gospel of haste and action, which are characteristics of the Roman spirit.

Mark writes for the Roman mind

If you understand that the four Gospels were written for four different purposes, from four different perspectives, to four different audiences, you will understand why you find certain differences among these four Gospels. For example, people often wonder, *Why doesn't John's Gospel mention the struggle of our Lord in Gethsemane? You find the record of Gethsemane's agony in Matthew, Mark, and Luke, but nothing about it in John.* The answer, in light of the Holy Spirit's purpose for each unique Gospel, is clear: It is because in the Garden of Gethsemane, Jesus cried out and questioned the Father, "If it be possible, let this cup pass from me." Now, it is not Jesus in His role as the Son of God who questions the Father, because God cannot question God. It is Jesus in His humanity who does this, so the Gethsemane account is found in the Synoptic Gospels: Matthew, Mark, and Luke. They present the most complete and compelling record of His human struggle; in John, the Gospel of the Son of God, this record is omitted. This is not a discrepancy or a contradiction among the Gospels; it is simply a difference in theme and emphasis.

Another example: Matthew directs our attention to the wise men who came to offer their gifts to the baby Jesus. Luke focuses on the pilgrimage of the shepherds. Now, both wise men and shepherds came to honor the baby Jesus, but in Matthew—the Gospel of the King—the wise men brought gifts fit for a king. In Luke—the Gospel of the Son of Man—common, ordinary shepherds came to see the perfect human, the one who came to be among us, equal with us, on our level.

Why is there no account of the ascension of our Lord in Matthew and John, as there is in Mark and Luke? Because as King, Jesus came to rule on earth. Matthew's emphasis is on the kingdom on earth. The ascension is not mentioned in John, because Jesus is the Son of God, and God is always everywhere.

Why do Mark and John omit a lengthy genealogy of our Lord? You'll find a lengthy genealogy in Matthew, the Gospel of the King, because kings require royal genealogies. A lengthy genealogy opens Luke, the Gospel of the Son of Man, because human beings are interested in their ancestry, in their origins. But you'll see no lengthy genealogy in John, the Gospel of the Son of God, because God has no ancestry; He is eternal. No genealogy is recorded in Mark, the Gospel of the Servant, because no one cares about the ancestry of a servant.

All of this shows the supervision of the Holy Spirit. These Gospels are not merely copies of one another. They are each uniquely designed by the Holy Spirit of God to present special aspects of the Lord Jesus Christ.

About the writer

The writer was a young man named John Mark, who accompanied Paul on his first missionary journey and proved to be a less-than-dependable servant. He could not take the pressure and turned back to go home. Interestingly, the Holy Spirit chose this man, who had shown qualities of unreliability early in his career, to record for us the absolute dependability, reliability, and faithfulness of the Servant of God, the Lord Jesus Christ. Mark was a companion of Peter, who was one of the Lord's closest friends in His earthly ministry, so the Gospel of Mark contains many of the thoughts, teachings, and firsthand impressions of

Peter. Of the four Gospel writers, Matthew and John were disciples of Jesus Christ, Luke received his Gospel through the teaching of the apostle Paul, and Mark received his Gospel at the feet of Peter—and though Peter wrote two New Testament letters, he did not write a Gospel account.

In Acts 10, Peter gives a brief summary of all that is recorded for us in the Gospel of Mark. In the home of Cornelius, Peter stood and told the people "how God anointed Jesus of Nazareth with the Holy Spirit and power, and how he went around doing good and healing all who were under the power of the devil, because God was with him" (10:38).

If you would like to meet Mark personally, turn to Mark 14. There, in the account of Jesus' capture in the Garden of Gethsemane, just before the crucifixion, we find the only account of Mark's appearance among the disciples. In verses 51–52 we read:

> *A young man, wearing nothing but a linen garment, was following Jesus. When they seized him, he fled naked, leaving his garment behind.*

No other Gospel tells us that, and it is almost certain that this young man is Mark. He was the son of a rich woman in Jerusalem and it is very likely that his mother owned the house in which the disciples met in the Upper Room. Mark, therefore, was present at some of these events. Most Bible scholars are convinced that this incident is included in Mark's Gospel because he himself was involved.

The Gospel of the Servant

The whole gospel is summed up in a phrase from Mark 10:45: "Even the Son of Man did not come to be served, but to serve." Or, as the King James Version puts it, "not to be ministered unto, but to minister." In this short verse, you have the outline of the Gospel of Mark, because the concluding phrase of this verse goes on to say, "and to give his life as a ransom for many." From Mark 1:1 to 8:30, the theme of this book is the ministry of the Servant, Christ. From 8:31 to the end of the book, the theme is the ransoming work of the Servant.

The Ministry of the Servant   (Mark 1:1–8:30)

1. The credentials of the Servant, John
   the Baptist announces and baptizes Jesus   1:1–11
2. The testing of the Servant, temptation
   in the wilderness   1:12–13
3. The ministry of the Servant, miracles,
   healings, authority over demons and disease   1:14–2:12
4. Controversy and opposition over Jesus'
   friendship with sinners, work on the Sabbath   2:13–3:35

5. Four parables of the Servant: the soils, the lamp,
   the growing seed, the mustard seed   4:1–34
6. Four Servant miracles, the sea is stilled, demons
   cast into pigs, the raising of Jairus's daughter, the
   healing of the woman with a flow of blood   4:35–5:43
7. Increasing opposition to the Servant and the
   death of John the Baptist   6:1–8:21
8. The healing of the blind man from Bethsaida   8:22–26
9. Peter's confession of Christ   8:27–30

The Ransoming Work of the Servant   (Mark 8:31–16:20)

10. Jesus begins teaching about His impending
    death   8:31–8:38
11. Jesus is transfigured on the mountain   9:1–13
12. Jesus delivers a demon-possessed son   9:14–29
13. Jesus prepares His disciples for His death   9:30–32
14. Teachings on servanthood; death and hell;
    marriage and divorce; children; wealth; and
    the eternal reward, including the story of
    the rich young ruler   9:33–10:31
15. Jesus again predicts His death and teaches
    servanthood   10:32–45
16. Blind Bartimaeus is healed   10:46–52
17. The Triumphal Entry into Jerusalem and the
    cleansing of the temple   11:1–19
18. Instruction on prayer   11:20–26
19. Opposition from religious leaders   11:27–12:44
20. Jesus foretells the end times, the Tribulation
    and the Second Coming   13
21. The trial and crucifixion   14–15
22. The resurrection, appearances, and ascension
    of Jesus   16

In the first half of the book, from 1:1 to 8:30, two aspects of the Servant's ministry are stressed: His authority and His effect on people. Notice, first the signs of His authority.

Those who listened to Jesus were filled with astonishment. They said, in effect, "He doesn't teach like the scribes and Pharisees, but He speaks with authority and with power. What He says to us pierces our hearts like a power drill!"

Why did Jesus speak with such authority? Because, as the Servant of God, He knew the secrets of God. He reached into the treasury of

God and drew out the secrets of God, then He made those rich secrets known to human beings. Since we are human beings, we hear His words with a sense of awareness that this is reality—ultimate reality. There is a note of genuineness about what He says, and that ring of truth has the power to stop us dead in our tracks, to convict us of our sin and our need of Him. That is why the Gospels and the words of our Lord, as they are read, have power in themselves to convict human beings.

The scribes and Pharisees needed constantly to bolster themselves with references to authorities and quotations from others, but not our Lord. He never quotes anything but the Scriptures. He always speaks with the final word of authority. He never apologizes, never ventures a mere opinion, never hesitates or equivocates. He speaks always with utter authority—the same authority that once said, "Let there be light," and there was light.

In this section, His authority over the powers of darkness—the demon world—is underscored. It is a world that we take all too casually. A prime example of how seriously we underestimate the powers of darkness is our observance of a holiday called Halloween. With Halloween, we show our dim and inadequate awareness of the existence of evil spirits. We celebrate the day as an amused tribute to a pantheon of goblins, spooks, and witches on broomsticks—a distor-

tion of the true nature of evil that has succeeded in dulling our sensitivity to the reality of the spiritual world—and the realm of ultimate evil. Behind this clownish facade of Halloween is a real and deadly world of demonic power that controls human minds and influences human events.

As you read through the Gospel of Mark, you see again and again the authority of the Servant of God over the mysterious forces of darkness. The world of the occult is wide open to Him. He knows the black powers, the dark passions that work behind the scenes of history. Paul calls these demonic powers "seducing spirits" or "deceiving spirits" (see 1 Tim. 4:1). Jesus has ultimate authority over those powers, but they can do us great harm if we fail to place ourselves under the protective umbrella of His lordship.

As you read the Gospel of Mark, you see that these demonic powers influence people to do strange things—to isolate themselves in the wilderness away from the rest of humanity, to behave in lawless ways (lawlessness is always a mark of demonic influence), to torment themselves and attack others, to menace society. Mark describes one demon-possessed man as "beside himself" (see Mark 3:21 KJV; in the NIV, this verse says, "He is out of his mind"). Now, that is a significant phrase, isn't it? Imagine standing beside yourself—a split personality, alienated from your own self. That is one of the marks of demonic influence. Despite the immense power and menace of demonic powers, the Lord Jesus has complete authority and power over them all.

Mark also reveals the power of Christ the Servant over disease. The first account of that power at work is the healing of Peter's mother-in-law. That has always been a touching scene for me. People today often joke about mothers-in-law, but Peter was evidently very concerned and loving toward his wife's mother. Our Lord touched her, and her fever left her. Then all the people of the city gathered about His door, and He healed every one of them (see 1:30–34).

Authority over disease

Peter's mother-in-law

The next account is that of a leper (1:40–45). Jesus did the unheard-of thing: He not only healed the leper, but He touched him. No one ever touched a leper in those days. The Law of Moses (which was, in many ways, a law of health and hygiene as much as a law of morality) forbade that lepers be touched, and the lepers had to go about calling a warning—"Unclean! Unclean!" No one would remotely think of touching a leper, but the compassion of the Servant's heart is revealed in this story as Jesus touches the leper, heals him, and sends him to the priest. This is the first instance in all of Scripture of a leper's ever being healed according to the Law of Moses and sent to the priest, as the Law demanded.

A leper

A second major emphasis of Mark's Gospel concerns the powerful effect Jesus had on the people He came in contact with. A servant is always affecting people. As Jesus the servant performed His ministry and went about doing good, people responded to Him—and those responses were always strongly favorable or strongly unfavorable. Jesus is not the sort of person you can ignore or treat with indifference. He either inspires your devotion—or your hatred.

The Servant's effect on people

We see His effect on His own disciples after He, first, feeds the five thousand, then amazes them by walking on the water and calming the storm on the sea. In 6:51–52, we read:

His disciples

Then he climbed into the boat with them, and the wind died down. They were completely amazed, for they had not understood about the loaves; their hearts were hardened.

This hardening of the heart is characteristic of the attitudes of many toward our Lord in His ministry as a Servant.

In chapter 7, you encounter the hypocrisy and criticism of the Pharisees—but also the astonished acceptance of many who are deeply affected after seeing His miracles of healing:

The Pharisees

People were overwhelmed with amazement. "He has done everything well," they said. "He even makes the deaf hear and the mute speak" (7:37).

That is the mark of a believing heart, the heart of one who can say of Jesus, "He does all things well."

Mark 8:22–26 goes on to record a very significant act of our Lord:

> *They came to Bethsaida, and some people brought a blind man and begged Jesus to touch him. He took the blind man by the hand and led him outside the village. When he had spit on the man's eyes and put his hands on him, Jesus asked, "Do you see anything?"*
>
> *He looked up and said, "I see people; they look like trees walking around."*
>
> *Once more Jesus put his hands on the man's eyes. Then his eyes were opened, his sight was restored, and he saw everything clearly. Jesus sent him home, saying, "Don't go into the village."*

Notice the setting of this story—the village of Bethsaida. Matthew describes Bethsaida as one of those cities Jesus had pronounced judgment upon, saying,

> *"Woe to you, Korazin! Woe to you, Bethsaida! If the miracles that were performed in you had been performed in Tyre and Sidon, they would have repented long ago in sackcloth and ashes" (Matt. 11:21).*

Here is a city that has rejected our Lord's ministry and His person, and He will not allow any further testimony to go on in that city. He led the blind man out before He healed him. This is the only case where our Lord did not see an instantaneous, complete healing take place the first time He spoke. When the healing was complete, He would not even allow the healed man to go back into the village, for Bethsaida was a village under God's judgment for having rejected the ministry of the Servant of God.

In 8:27–33, we find the story of Peter's confession that Jesus is the Christ, the Messiah whose coming was prophesied in the Old Testament. This incident ends the first part of the Gospel of Mark. Beginning with the second part of the book, at Mark 8:34, Jesus increasingly begins to instruct His disciples regarding His impending death upon the cross—the ransoming ministry of the Servant.

The ransoming Servant

Now we come to the second great theme of Mark—the theme that Jesus came to give His life a ransom for many. Jesus introduces this somber theme as He begins to instruct His disciples regarding His death:

He then began to teach them that the Son of Man must suffer many things and be rejected by the elders, chief priests and teachers of the law, and that he must be killed and after three days rise again. He spoke plainly about this, and Peter took him aside and began to rebuke him.

But when Jesus turned and looked at his disciples, he rebuked Peter. "Get behind me, Satan!" he said. "You do not have in mind the things of God, but the things of men" (8:31–33).

From this point on, our Lord's face is set toward Jerusalem and the cross. He is going now to be the offering of God—the Servant who gives Himself completely as a sacrificial ransom for those He came to save and to serve. The revelation of His plan is given in this passage. He came to suffer, to be rejected, to be killed, and after three days, to rise again.

From this point on, our Lord's face is set toward Jerusalem and the cross

And who stood up to thwart that plan? Not Judas Iscariot! Not Pontius Pilate! Not some demonic spirit! No, it was Jesus' close, trusted friend—the one who had just confessed that Jesus is the Christ, the Messiah! His response to Jesus was, "Don't sacrifice yourself, Lord! Spare yourself!" That is always the way of fallen humanity. The philosophy of the world is, "Spare yourself. Serve yourself. Don't do anything you don't have to." That's the dominant philosophy of our age!

But Jesus rebuked him. "Peter," He said, in effect, "I recognize where that comes from. That is the wisdom of Satan, not God. Get that kind of talk out of My way."

Then Jesus called the multitude to Him, along with His disciples, and said to them, "If anyone would come after me, he must deny himself and take up his cross and follow me" (8:34). Sparing yourself, seeking yourself, indulging yourself is the way of the devil. Giving yourself is the way of God. This is the plan that Christ carries through to the end of Mark's Gospel—a plan of giving Himself away in a sacrificial ransom for you and for me.

The account of the Transfiguration follows in chapter 9. There, Jesus reveals His intention and His purpose:

The Transfiguration

He said to them, "I tell you the truth, some who are standing here will not taste death before they see the kingdom of God come with power."

After six days Jesus took Peter, James and John with him and led them up a high mountain, where they were all alone. There he was transfigured before them. His clothes became dazzling white, whiter than anyone in the world could bleach them. And there appeared before them Elijah and Moses, who were talking with Jesus.

> Peter said to Jesus, "Rabbi, it is good for us to be here. Let us put
> up three shelters—one for you, one for Moses and one for Elijah." (He
> did not know what to say, they were so frightened.)
>
> Then a cloud appeared and enveloped them, and a voice came from
> the cloud: "This is my Son, whom I love. Listen to him!"
>
> Suddenly, when they looked around, they no longer saw anyone
> with them except Jesus (9:1–8).

Jesus led Peter, James, and John up on the mountaintop, and there—as Jesus promised—they saw "the kingdom of God come with power." They didn't have to go through death to see the glory of the King—they saw it with their own earthly, mortal eyes. Peter refers to this event in his second letter:

> We did not follow cleverly invented stories when we told you about
> the power and coming of our Lord Jesus Christ, but we were eyewitnesses
> of his majesty. For he received honor and glory from God the Father when
> the voice came to him from the Majestic Glory, saying, "This is my Son,
> whom I love; with him I am well pleased." We ourselves heard this voice
> that came from heaven when we were with him on the sacred mountain.
> (2 Peter 1:16–18).

Why did Jesus preface this incident with the statement, "Some who are standing here will not taste death before they see the kingdom of God come with power"? Because His intention for the human race, the very purpose of His redemptive work, is that human beings should not have to taste death. He came to deliver us from the sting of death, from the awful taste of death. Christians die, but they never taste death. Death is a doorway into life. Why can the apostle Paul say with such confidence, "Where, O death, is your victory? Where, O death, is your sting?" (1 Cor. 15:55)? Because, as Hebrews 2:9 tells us, Jesus tasted death for everyone, for you and for me, so that we don't have to.

The disciples didn't understand the Lord's purpose or His words regarding life and death. In Mark 9:9–10, we read:

> As they were coming down the mountain, Jesus gave them orders
> not to tell anyone what they had seen until the Son of Man had risen
> from the dead. They kept the matter to themselves, discussing what "ris-
> ing from the dead" meant.

What did rising from the dead mean? It meant rising from the dead! Jesus couldn't have spoken any more plainly. He was going to suffer, He was going to die, He was going to rise and live again. The disciples were looking for figures of speech when Jesus was giving them literal, plain, practical truth.

In chapter 10, Jesus speaks of the family, of the children, of God's material and monetary blessings. He goes into the junkyard of human life and takes these gifts of God that people have twisted and selfishly misused—and He beautifully restores them to the purpose God intended.

In chapter 11, we have the beginning of our Lord's last week as He moves resolutely toward His rendezvous with the cross. In this chapter, we see another significant act that only Mark records:

> On reaching Jerusalem, Jesus entered the temple area and began driving out those who were buying and selling there. He overturned the tables of the money changers and the benches of those selling doves, and would not allow anyone to carry merchandise through the temple courts. And as he taught them, he said, "Is it not written:
> " 'My house will be called a house of prayer for all nations'? But you have made it 'a den of robbers' " (11:15–17).

The last sacrifice

The (second) cleansing of the temple

Now, this is not the same cleansing of the temple recorded by John in his Gospel (John 2:13–16). In John's Gospel, this incident occurred at the beginning of our Lord's ministry. But now, at the end of His ministry, for the second time, He overthrows the tables of the money changers and cleanses the temple.

In verse 16, Mark says, "and would not allow anyone to carry merchandise through the temple courts." What does that mean? The only ones who carried anything through the temple were the priests. According to the Mosaic Law, it was their duty to catch the blood of the animals sacrificed on the brazen altar in the outer court and to bear that blood into the Holy Place and before the altar. Then once a year the high priest would go into the Holy of Holies and sprinkle that blood on the golden altar of the mercy seat. It was a very significant ritual.

But our Lord stopped all this. He would not allow anyone to carry anything through the temple. In other words, He ended the sacrifices. The Jews resumed them until the destruction of the temple in A.D. 70, but they did so without divine authority. The sacrifices are meaningless from here on, because Jesus Himself now stands as the Lamb of God who takes away the sin of the world.

He ended the sacrifices

From the temple, Jesus moves right on out to the Mount of Olives, from there to the Upper Room, into the Garden of Gethsemane, and on to the cross.

The last chapters are concerned with the questions that people ask Jesus. In chapter 11, He answers the questions of the priests and the elders who come out of hatred for Him and try to trap Him with their questions. In chapter 12, He answers the questions of the Pharisees and the Herodians who likewise try to trap Him with their questions. Also in chapter 12, the Sadducees come and try to trap Him (they were the materialists, the ones who did not believe in a resurrection or a spirit life).

Finally, a scribe with an honest heart asked Him the only honest question of chapter 12: "Of all the commandments, which is the most important?" (v. 28). Immediately and forthrightly, our Lord answered him:

> "The most important one," answered Jesus, "is this: 'Hear, O Israel, the Lord our God, the Lord is one. Love the Lord your God with all your heart and with all your soul and with all your mind and with all your strength.' The second is this: 'Love your neighbor as yourself.' There is no commandment greater than these."
>
> "Well said, teacher," the man replied. "You are right in saying that God is one and there is no other but him. To love him with all your heart, with all your understanding and with all your strength, and to love your neighbor as yourself is more important than all burnt offerings and sacrifices."
>
> When Jesus saw that he had answered wisely, he said to him, "You are not far from the kingdom of God." And from then on no one dared ask him any more questions (12:29–34).

Jesus stopped all questions. That is the power of truth—it elevates the honest heart, it shames the guilty heart, it silences the lying tongue.

In chapter 13, the disciples come to Jesus asking about future events. In this chapter, our Lord unfolds the whole revelation of the age to come—the time of tribulation and the time of His return in glory.

Chapter 14 describes two acts that contrast as sharply as white contrasts with black. First, a woman named Mary comes and offers her sacrifice of expensive perfume which she pours out on His feet. Next, Judas Iscariot goes out and betrays his Lord for money. One is an act of utter selflessness, and the other an act of complete selfishness.

Beginning with chapter 15, you have the account of the cross. In Mark's account this is an act of almost incredible brutality done in the name of justice. The Lord outwardly seems to be a defeated man, a tragic failure, His cause hopelessly lost. He is ridiculed, beaten, and spat upon. As He Himself said in 8:31, "the Son of Man must suffer many things."

Finally, the Servant goes willingly to the cross and He is crucified. It seems so unlike the picture of the wonder-worker of Galilee who begins this Gospel—the mighty person of power, the Servant with authority from on high.

No wonder the high priests, as they saw Him hanging there, said of Him, "He saved others, but he can't save himself!" (Mark. 15:31). That is a strange statement. Yet it is one of those remarkable words that reveal how God is able to make even His enemies praise Him, because they are paradoxically both right and wrong. They were wrong in the sense that they were mocking His seeming helplessness; they were right in that Jesus did save others by the very act of refusing to save Himself!

As I read this account, I am impressed with the three things that they could not make our Lord do. First, they could not make our Lord speak:

They could not make Him speak

> Again Pilate asked him, "Aren't you going to answer? See how many things they are accusing you of."
> But Jesus still made no reply, and Pilate was amazed (15:4–5).

Why didn't He speak? Because He would have saved Himself if He had spoken before Pilate. The high priests were right; He saved others, but Himself He could not—would not—save.

Second, they could not make Him drink:

They could not make Him drink

> They offered him wine mixed with myrrh, but he did not take it (15:23).

Why not? Well, because He could have saved Himself if He had. The wine and myrrh were a narcotic mixture to dull the senses. Had He drunk, He would have saved Himself the full effect of the agony of the cross and the weight of the sin and pain of the world coming upon His shoulders, but He would not. He would not spare Himself.

Finally, they could not even make Him die. In the NIV we read, "With a loud cry, Jesus breathed his last" (Mark 15:37), which is not literally what the original Greek text conveys. In the Greek, this verse reads, "With a loud cry, Jesus unspirited Himself." He dismissed His spirit. He didn't die at the hands of the murderers; He let His spirit go of His own free will. Jesus Himself had said,

They could not make Him die

> "I lay down my life—only to take it up again. No one takes it from me, but I lay it down of my own accord. I have authority to lay it down and authority to take it up again. This command I received from my Father" (John 10:17–18).

Jesus could have refused to die, and the soldiers, the rulers, and the religious leaders could not have taken His life from Him. He could have even hung on the cross and taunted them with their inability to put Him to death, but He did not. He died, He unspirited Himself, willingly and deliberately.

When we come to the last chapter, the resurrection of our Lord, we learn His reason. He was silent and refused to appeal to Pilate or the crowd because He was laying the basis for a coming day when in resurrection power He would appeal to a far greater crowd, when every knee should bow and every tongue should proclaim that Jesus Christ is Lord to the glory of God the Father. He would not drink to dull His senses because He was laying a basis by which even those who stood about the cross might enter into a life so wonderful, so abundant, that the most thrilling and emotionally intense moments of life on earth would pale by comparison.

He would not let human beings take His life, but He voluntarily laid it down Himself that He might overcome humanity's greatest enemy—death—and forever deliver all who would believe in Him from the power and the sting of death. That is the gospel. He saved others, but Himself He could not—would not—save. That is the attitude of a true servant (see Phil. 2:5–7).

As we study the life of the greatest Servant who ever lived, as we seek to pattern our lives after His, may we always bear upon our lives the selfless, sacrificial imprint of the One who, by refusing to save Himself, saved others, saved me, and saved you.

The Perfect Man

K ing Canute, the Danish king of England in the eleventh century, was surrounded by a court of fawning, flattering yes-men. "O King Canute," they said, "you are the greatest, most powerful king who ever lived! You are invincible! There is nothing you do not know! You are perfection incarnate!"

A humble and realistic man, King Canute soon tired of all this empty praise. So, he commanded his palace guard to lift his throne off the dais in the throne room and carry it to the seashore. The king and all of his fawning (and now, very perplexed) yes-men followed the throne all the way to the seashore. There King Canute commanded that the throne be set down in the sand at the water's edge. The yes-men gathered around wondering what the king had in mind.

King Canute settled himself onto his throne, looking out to sea. He stretched out his arms and commanded, "Waves, be still! Tide, be stopped!" But the waves continued to roll in to the shore, and the tide continued to rise. The sea came up around King Canute's ankles, then his thighs, then his chest. Yet, he continued to command, "Waves, be still! Tide, be stopped!" Finally, a wave came crashing in that toppled the throne and cast King Canute up on the sand, gasping and sputtering.

Wide-eyed, the yes-men stared at the king whom they had called perfection incarnate, believing that he had completely lost his mind. The king stood up, wringing wet, and ordered his throne carried back to the castle. The entire entourage trudged back home. Arriving once more in the throne room, King Canute led the group of yes-men to a large carved crucifix, a statue of Jesus upon the cross. "Do you all see this man? He did what I cannot do! He stilled the waves, He commanded the sea! He is perfection incarnate. I am just a man."

Then he removed his golden crown and placed it on the brow of the statue of Jesus. The crown of Canute remained on that statue until Canute's death.

The Gospel of Luke is the Gospel of the man who was perfection incarnate, the only truly perfect human being.

The structure of Luke's Gospel

The third Gospel presents Jesus as the Son of Man. That was our Lord's favorite title for Himself—a title He used more frequently than any other name. As you read the Gospel of Luke, you meet the same person you meet in Matthew, Mark, and John. But note the differences in emphases among the four Gospels. In Matthew, the emphasis is upon Jesus' kingliness; in Mark, the emphasis is on His servanthood; in John, the emphasis is on His deity. But here in Luke, the emphasis is on His humanity.

In Luke, the emphasis is on Jesus' humanity

The essential manhood and humanity of Christ are continually underscored throughout this Gospel. The key to the Gospel is found in Luke 19:10. In fact, this verse sets forth a handy outline of the entire book:

> *"The Son of Man came to seek and to save what was lost."*

In that one sentence, you have the structure and divisions of this Gospel. *First section:* "The Son of Man came." In the beginning of this Gospel, from 1:1 to 4:13, Luke tells us how Jesus entered the human race, including His genealogy.

The Lord's earthly ministry consisted largely of seeking people out and moving into the heart of humanity, penetrating deeply into human emotions, thoughts, and feelings

Second section: "to seek." The Lord's earthly ministry consisted largely of seeking people out and moving into the heart of humanity, penetrating deeply into human emotions, thoughts, and feelings. In the middle section of Luke, from 4:14 through 19:27, we see Jesus seeking us out, putting His finger on the throbbing centers of our pain, shame, and motivations, and touching our humanity with His healing power. In this section, Jesus carries on His ministry among people. This section of the Lord's pursuit of humanity climaxes with His journey toward Jerusalem, the place where He will be sacrificed, as we read in Luke 9:51:

> *As the time approached for him to be taken up to heaven, Jesus resolutely set out for Jerusalem.*

The record of His journey to Jerusalem occupies chapters 9 through 19 and recounts a number of important incidents along the way.

Third and final section: ". . . and to save what was lost." Finally, the Lord moves into the final act of the drama of His life: to save humanity by means of the cross and the resurrection. In Luke 19:28, we read:

After Jesus had said this, he went on ahead, going up to Jerusalem.

That verse marks the close of His seeking ministry and the beginning of His saving ministry. It introduces the last section of the book, in which He enters the city, goes to the temple, ascends the Mount of Olives, is taken to Pilate's judgment hall—and then to the cross, to the tomb, and to resurrection day. Here is an outline of the Gospel of Luke:

The Coming of the Son of Man (Luke 1:1–4:13)

1.	Introduction: The purpose of Luke's Gospel	1:1–4
2.	Events leading up to the birth of Christ	1:5–56
3.	The birth of John the Baptist	1:57–80
4.	The birth of Jesus Christ	2:1–38
5.	The childhood of Jesus Christ	2:39–52
6.	The ministry of John the Baptist	3:1–20
7.	The baptism of Jesus by John the Baptist	3:21–22
8.	The genealogy of the Son of Man	3:23–38
9.	The temptation of the Son of Man	4:1–13

His Ministry—The Son of Man Seeks (Luke 4:14–19:27)

10.	The beginning of His ministry, His acceptance in Galilee, His rejection in His hometown	4:14–30
11.	Miracles demonstrating His power over demons, sickness, and paralysis; also, His calling of the first disciples	4:31–5:28
12.	Jesus and the Pharisees	5:29–6:11
13.	Jesus instructs the disciples, the Beatitudes, the Christian way of life, parables	6:12–49
14.	Miracles, the healing of the centurion's son, the raising of the widow's son	7:1–16
15.	Jesus praises John the Baptist	7:17–35
16.	Jesus dines at a Pharisee's home, a woman anoints His feet with costly perfume	7:36–50
17.	Parables and miracles, the storm is stilled, demons are cast into swine, a woman with an issue of blood is healed, Jairus's daughter is raised	8

His Death and Resurrection—The Son of Man Saves (Luke 19:28–24:53)

The lost secret of humanity

Be sure to notice the exact words Jesus uses in that key passage, Luke 19:10: "to save what was lost." He is not talking only about coming to save lost people. He has come to save what was lost. What was lost? Not just people themselves, but the essence of what people were created to be. Jesus came to save and restore our God-given humanity, which was created in the image of God. That is the secret of our humanity. We have forgotten what we were intended to be at Creation. The whole dilemma of life is that we still have, deep within us, a kind of racial memory of what we ought to be, what we want to be, what we were made to be—but we don't know how to accomplish it. The secret of our humanity was lost long ago.

A group of scientists once met at Princeton University to discuss the latest findings in astronomy. One distinguished astronomer stood and said, "When you consider the vast distances between the stars in a single galaxy, then consider the even greater distances between the various galaxies, then consider the fact that the galaxies themselves are arranged in clusters, and the clusters of galaxies are separated by even more enormous distances, we astronomers have to conclude that man is nothing more than an insignificant dot in the infinite universe."

Just then, a familiar stooped figure rose up, his head fringed with an unruly white mane, his frayed sweater bunched up around his thin frame. "Insignificant, you say?" said Professor Einstein. "Yes, I have often felt that man is an insignificant dot in the universe—but then I recalled that the same insignificant dot who is man . . . is also the astronomer."

That is the essence of humanity, that is the greatness that God created within us when He made us in His image. Yes, the universe is vast and we are small—but we are not insignificant. God has created us to seek answers and understanding of the vast questions and issues of the cosmos. There is something unaccountably grand about human beings, some hidden specialness that God placed inside us—something that was marred and distorted by sin but that still glimmers within us. It is this wonderful lost secret, this glorious and impenetrable lost mystery,

Yes, the universe is vast and we are small—but we are not insignificant

The Greek ideal
was the perfection
of humanity — an
ideal that Jesus
fulfilled

Luke and the epistle
to the Hebrews

which our Lord came to restore and to save, that we discover in the Gospel of Luke.

The author of this book is Luke, the physician, the companion of Paul. It is fitting that Luke should be the one to write this Gospel of the humanity of our Lord. He writes to another man, a Greek, about whom we know little, but who was evidently a friend of Luke (see Luke 1:1–4). Theophilus is evidently someone who had become briefly acquainted with the Christian faith, and Luke now attempts to explain it more fully to him. Luke was a Greek himself and is writing to a Grecian. This is most interesting, for the ideal of the Greek was the perfection of humanity—an ideal that Jesus fulfilled.

We cannot read the Gospel of Luke thoughtfully without noting some remarkable similarities between it and the epistle to the Hebrews. I believe (though it cannot be proven) that Luke wrote the epistle to the Hebrews. I believe Paul authored the thoughts of Hebrews, and that he probably wrote it in the Hebrew language and sent it to the Jews of Jerusalem. Then Luke, wanting to make these same marvelous truths available to the Gentile world, translated it from Hebrew into Greek, partially paraphrasing it rather than actually translating it, so that many of his own expressions are found in it. Scholars recognize the thoughts of Hebrews as being very much like Paul's, but the words and manner of expression in the Greek appear to be Luke's. If that is true, then we have an explanation of some of the remarkable parallels between Hebrews and the Gospel of Luke.

The amazing message of Hebrews is that Jesus Christ became a human being so He could enter the human condition and become our representative. Hebrews is built around the symbolism of the old covenant and especially the tabernacle in the wilderness. The epistle to the Hebrews explains the meaning of God's symbolic picture of the tabernacle. When Moses went up onto the mountain, he was given a pattern to follow explicitly in making the tabernacle, a pattern of heavenly realities that our human senses cannot perceive.

As you read Hebrews, you find that the tabernacle was a very remarkable picture of humanity. The tabernacle was built in three sections: the outer court, which even the Gentiles could enter; the Holy Place, which was restricted; and the Holy of Holies, which was highly restricted. The sacrifices were offered in the outer court. The priest took the blood and carried it into the Holy Place, where it was sprinkled on the altar. But once a year, the high priest, only under the most precise conditions, was allowed to enter behind the veil into the Holy of Holies. Apart from that single entrance, no one was ever permitted to enter the Holy of Holies on pain of death, for the mystery of the Shekinah, the strange presence of God, lived in that sacred, awesome place.

What does all this mean? It is a picture of our humanity in our fallen state. We are that tabernacle in which God planned from the beginning to dwell. We have an outer court—the body, which is made of the earth and puts us in touch with the earth and the material life around us.

We also have a Holy Place—the soul, the place of intimacy, the seat of the mind, the conscience, the memory, and other mysterious inner aspects of our humanity. It is our souls—what the Greek New Testament calls the *psuche* (or psyche), the part of us that is studied by psychology and psychiatry.

We also have a Holy of Holies—that which is behind the veil and impenetrable. We cannot enter there. We know that something more, something deeper, is hidden in the soulish aspects of our lives. Some of the great thinkers of today are recognizing the existence of this hidden dimension of our beings. It is the place where God intended to dwell— the very core of our human existence—the human spirit. Because it is largely inoperative in fallen humanity, people tend to act like intelligent animals. Hidden beneath our bodies and our souls, the spirit cannot be observed or studied, but it is real and it is the place where God wishes to live among us—the ultimate dwelling place of His Shekinah glory.

In the Gospel of Luke, we trace the coming of the one who at last penetrates into the secret place, who enters the mysterious human spirit and rends the veil, so that human beings might discover the mystery of their innermost selves—and find complete joy, peace, and fulfillment. That is what people everywhere desperately look for. There is nothing more exciting than a sense of fulfillment, of achieving the full possibilities of our personalities. We all seek it—but we have lost the key. Until that key is placed in our hands again by the Son of Man, our full possibilities remain lost.

Jesus came to seek and to save that which was lost within us. That is the good news of Luke.

The body represents the outer court—and in Luke 1:1–4:13, we see the Lord, the Son of Man, coming into the outer court of our humanity. He becomes a human being with a human body. He appears on the world stage as a baby.

Luke records three facts about His entrance into our world, our outer court: *First fact:* His virgin birth. Some people openly deny the Virgin Birth, some of them even stand in the pulpits declaring that this fact of Jesus' entrance into our world is really unimportant and unhistorical. But it is extremely important, it is supremely important. Luke (who was a doctor and, as such, put his physician's seal of approval on this remarkable biological mystery) tells us that a human being was born of a virgin.

Mary had a son, and His name was Jesus. The wonder of that mystery is given in the simple, artlessly told story that Luke presents to us.

His birth is rooted in history by means of a human genealogy. It is important to note the difference between Luke's genealogy and Matthew's. Matthew, the Gospel of the King, traces Jesus' lineage back to King David. Luke, the Gospel of the Son of Man, traces Jesus' lineage all the way back to Adam, the first human being, whom Luke calls "the son of God," since Adam had no earthly father but was directly created by the hand of God. So Luke links the First Adam with the Second Adam (Jesus Christ) in this Gospel of the Son of Man.

Second fact: Luke gives us the story of our Lord's presentation in the temple at age twelve. He tells how Jesus astounded the learned men of the law with His ability to answer questions, to ask probing questions, to understand deep issues of the Scriptures. Here is the revelation of amazing mental ability and wisdom. His mind and soul are presented to us as perfect. Just as His body was perfect and sinless through the Virgin Birth, so He is revealed as having a soul or psyche that is perfect.

Third fact: Luke gives us the story of the temptation in the wilderness, where the Lord was revealed as being perfect in the innermost recesses of His spirit. That is indicated in advance by the announcement at His baptism, when He was pronounced by the voice of God to be "my Son, whom I love; with you I am well pleased" (3:22). So we have seen Him pass from the outer court of our humanity, to the Holy Place of the soul, to the innermost Holy of Holies of the spirit. He has entered into the very center of our being, life, and thinking, where (as Hebrews tells us) He "had to be made like his brothers in every way, in order that he might become a merciful and faithful high priest in service to God, and that he might make atonement for the sins of the people" (Heb. 2:17).

This section begins with the amazing account of His visit to the synagogue in Nazareth, where the book of Isaiah was brought to Him, and He found the place and read where it was written,

> *"The Spirit of the Lord is on me, because he has anointed me to preach good news to the poor. He has sent me to proclaim freedom for the prisoners and recovery of sight for the blind, to release the oppressed, to proclaim the year of the Lord's favor" (Luke 4:18–19).*

He is declaring here what He came to do—to enter into the experience of the poor, the oppressed, the blind, the captives, and to set them free. The whole story of the following chapters is of His entering into the commonplace human experiences, where people live in darkness, slavery, and death.

Second fact: Jesus' amazing mental ability and wisdom reveal a perfect soul

Third fact: The Temptation revealed His perfection of spirit

At last, in Luke 19:28, we see Him preparing to enter as the great High Priest into the Holy of Holies of human beings, to restore that which has been lost for all these many centuries. You may remember from your study of the Old Testament that the Holy of Holies contained only two articles of furniture: (1) the ark of the covenant, with its mercy seat under the overarching wings of the cherubim, where God's Shekinah glory dwelt; and (2) the golden altar of incense by means of which the nation was to offer its praise to God. These two objects are symbolic of what is hidden in the depths of humanity.

The mercy seat speaks of human relationship with God. Hebrews tells us that it is blood alone that can make that relationship possible and acceptable:

The law requires that nearly everything be cleansed with blood, and without the shedding of blood there is no forgiveness (9:22).

> Blood alone can make possible human relationship with God

It was the blood upon the mercy seat that released God's forgiveness and grace. Our Lord now prepares to enter into the hidden spirit of humanity and offer His own blood. As we are told in Hebrews:

He did not enter by means of the blood of goats and calves; but he entered the Most Holy Place once for all by his own blood, having obtained eternal redemption (Heb. 9:12).

The altar of incense speaks of the communication between people and God—the place of prayer. Prayer is the deepest function of the human spirit. Nothing goes deeper than that. When you are driven to your knees by despair, defeat, exhaustion, or need, you discover that you have reached the rock-bottom resources of your spirit. That is what prayer is at its most fundamental level: the cry of the spirit. So the Cross of Christ enters into this deep, deep region of our humanity.

> Prayer is the deepest function of the human spirit

As you continue through Luke, you see the Lord moving from the Mount of Olives down into the city, cleansing the temple, teaching and preaching in the temple, and returning to the mount to deliver the Olivet Discourse. Next, He goes to the Upper Room and the Passover feast, where He institutes the sacrament of Holy Communion. From there He moves on to the Garden of Gethsemane, then to Pilate's judgment seat, and from there to the cross. As we come to the closing chapters, we make a startling and tremendously important discovery:

> **A burning heart**

> *It was now about the sixth hour, and darkness came over the whole land until the ninth hour, for the sun stopped shining. And the curtain of the temple was torn in two (23:44–45).*

Why was this curtain torn in two? Because the Holy of Holies was now to be opened up for the first time to human gaze! And because the Holy of Holies of the human spirit was now to be opened up for the first time to the gaze and habitation of God! When the Son of Man died, God ripped the veil wide open. He passed through the holy place, and penetrated into the Holy of Holies, into the secret of humanity—and the reality of humanity's spirit was unveiled.

Next, we have the wonder of the resurrection morning and the account that Luke gives us of the two disciples who were walking on the road to Emmaus when a stranger appeared to them and talked with them. I would pay any price to have heard the things He said—because, of course, the stranger was actually the risen Lord Himself! He opened the Scriptures to these two grieving, uncomprehending disciples—Scriptures concerning Christ and what had been predicted of Him. After Jesus left them, after they realized who He was,

> *They asked each other, "Were not our hearts burning within us while he talked with us on the road and opened the Scriptures to us?" (24:32).*

A burning heart is a heart that is caught up with the excitement and glory of a fulfilled humanity. The secret is revealed. Our humanity is fully possessed, reclaimed by our Creator. The Holy of Holies has been entered. What was lost has been saved.

The perfect parallel to the triumphant message of Luke's Gospel is found in Hebrews 10:19–20:

> *Brothers, since we have confidence to enter the Most Holy Place by the blood of Jesus, by a new and living way opened for us through the curtain, that is, his body . . . .*

That is where we stand now. The secret of humanity is open to anyone who opens his or her own heart to the Son of Man, the perfect man. He alone has penetrated the depths of the human spirit. He alone reestablishes the lost relationship with God that enables us to be what God intended us to be. He alone saves and restores what was lost in the fall of man, in the entrance of sin into the world. He alone can restore the marred, distorted image of God in our lives.

All the possibility of a fulfilled humanity is available to anyone in whom the spirit of Christ dwells. All that you deeply want to be in the innermost recesses of your heart, you can be. I'm not talking about your goals in life, such as becoming a millionaire or an Olympic gold medalist. No, I'm talking about the deepest, most inexpressible yearnings of your heart—your desire to be connected to God, to know Him and be known by Him; your desire to have your life count for something in the eternal scheme of things; your desire to be clean and whole and forgiven. Jesus makes it possible for you to fulfill God's best for you, so that you will be mature and Christlike, filled with love, forgiveness, wholeness, and good works.

Why do we act the way we do? Why do we want to do good while doing so much evil? Why are we able to accomplish such great feats of technology, engineering, medical science, athletics, art, literature, music—yet we cannot eradicate poverty, war, racism, crime, and so many other ills? Where are we heading? What is the aim of it all? The strange mystery of the ages, the great questions that have been raised by philosophers and thinkers about our great but horribly flawed human race—all this has been answered by the entrance of Jesus Christ, the Son of Man, into our humanity.

Luke has unveiled all of this to us in his Gospel, the Gospel of the Son of Man.

The God-Man

J ohn, the fourth Gospel, holds a special significance to me for many reasons but especially because it is written by the disciple closest to our Lord. When you read the Gospel of Matthew, you are reading the record of our Lord as seen through the eyes of a devoted disciple. Mark and Luke, of course, were dedicated Christians who knew and loved Jesus Christ, though they learned about Him largely through the testimony of others. But John is the beloved apostle who leaned close to Jesus at the Last Supper (13:23–25), who stood at the foot of the cross as the Lord hung dying, and who was trusted by Jesus with the care of His own mother, Mary (19:26–27). John, along with Peter and James, was of the inner circle of disciples who went with our Lord through the most intimate and dramatic circumstances of His ministry. He heard and saw more than any of the others—which is why John's Gospel is often called "the intimate Gospel."

John's Gospel opens with a startling statement, echoing the opening lines of the book of Genesis:

Who is this man?

> *In the beginning was the Word, and the Word was with God, and the Word was God. He was with God in the beginning (John 1:1–2).*

"The Word," of course, is Jesus Christ. John begins his Gospel with the astonishing statement that Jesus—this man whom John knew so well as a friend and companion—was nothing less than the Creator-God of the universe, who was there at the beginning of all things! John watched the life of Jesus more closely than any other person on earth—and John came away absolutely convinced of the deity of Christ.

Sometimes I think it is difficult to believe that Jesus is God. I've never met a Christian who has not at one time or another felt the full force of all the arguments that make Him out to be nothing more than a human being. There are times when we find it difficult to comprehend the full intent of those words, *In the beginning was the Word*.

But if we find it difficult, how much more did His own disciples! They, of all people, would be least likely to believe that He was God, for they lived with Him and saw His humanity as none of us ever has or ever will. They must have been confronted again and again with a question that puzzled and troubled them, "Who is this man? What kind of person is this who heals the sick, raises the dead, quiets the wind, and changes water to wine?" Whatever signs, miracles, power, and wisdom Jesus demonstrated, it must have been a great leap in their perceptions to move from saying of Him, "this man, Jesus," to saying, "My Lord and My God!"

I have often pictured them sleeping out under the stars with our Lord on a summer night by the Sea of Galilee. I can imagine Peter or John or one of the others waking in the night, rising up on an elbow, and as he looked at the Lord Jesus sleeping beside him, saying to himself, "Is it true? Can this man be the eternal God?" No wonder they puzzled over Him and constantly conversed among themselves about the mystery of His actions and His words.

Yet, so overwhelming and convincing was the evidence they saw and heard that when they reached the end of the story, when John began to write down the recollections of those amazing days, he began by boldly declaring the deity of Jesus. That is the theme of the Gospel of John: Jesus is God. Matthew is the Gospel of the King, Mark is the Gospel of the Servant, Luke is the Gospel of the Son of Man, and John is the Gospel of the Son of God.

The key to the Gospel of John is found in John 20. There are actually two endings to the Gospel of John. Chapter 21 reads as a postscript, an add-on, concerning events that occurred after the resurrection. But I believe that John actually ended his Gospel with these words:

> *Jesus did many other miraculous signs in the presence of his disciples, which are not recorded in this book. But these are written that you may believe that Jesus is the Christ, the Son of God, and that by believing you may have life in his name (20:30–31).*

Here we see the twofold purpose of this book: (1) John is giving us evidence why anyone in any age, in any place, can fully believe that Jesus is the Christ (or, in the Hebrew form, the Messiah, the Anointed One); and (2) John is showing that Jesus is the Son of God, so that people may have life through belief in His name.

Here is a structural overview of John's Gospel—the Gospel of the Son of God:

The Incarnation of the Son of God (John 1:1–18)

1.	His godhood, His forerunner (John the Baptist), His rejection by His own, and His reception by those called "the children of God"	1:1–13
2.	The Word made flesh	1:14–18

The Son of God Is Presented to the World (John 1:19–4:54)

3.	Jesus is presented by John the Baptist	1:19–51
4.	Jesus begins His ministry in Galilee, transforms water into wine at Cana	2:1–12
5.	Jesus in Judea, the first cleansing of the temple and His instruction of Nicodemus	2:13–3:36
6.	Jesus in Samaria, the woman at the well	4:1–42
7.	Jesus is received in Galilee, heals a royal official's son	4:43–54

The Son of God Faces Opposition (John 5:1–12:50)

8.	Jesus is opposed at the feast in Jerusalem	5:1–47
9.	Jesus is opposed during Passover in Galilee	6
10.	Jesus is opposed at the Feast of Tabernacles and the Feast of Dedication in Jerusalem	7–10
11.	Jesus is opposed at Bethany; He raises Lazarus, and the religious leaders plot His death	11
12.	Mary anoints Jesus	12:1–11
13.	The Triumphal Entry into Jerusalem, the opposition of the religious leaders	12:12–50

The Death of the Son of God Approaches (John 13–17)

14.	The Upper Room: Jesus washes the disciples' feet and announces His approaching death	13–14
15.	Jesus instructs the disciples in their relationship to Him, to each other, and to the world; He promises the Holy Spirit	15:1–16:15

The Son of God

To the Hebrews, to call someone a "son" of something was to say he is identified with, identical with, that thing or person

A great deal is made of this term *Son of God* today, as though there were a distinction to be made between God and the Son of God, but no Hebrew would ever understand it that way. To the Hebrews, to call someone a "son" of something was to say he is identified with, identical with, that thing or person. For example, the name Barnabas literally means "Son of Consolation." Why? Because he was that kind of man—an encouraging, consoling kind of fellow. His nickname meant that he was the very epitome of consolation—the living, personified expression of encouragement.

To the Hebrews, the use of this term, the *Son of God* meant, "This man is God." He was literally the personification of godhood on earth. That is why, invariably, when our Lord used that term of Himself, He was angrily challenged by the unbelieving scribes and Pharisees. Again and again, they demanded of Him, "How dare You! Who do You think You are? You are making Yourself out to be equal with God. That's blasphemy!" Of course, He described Himself as God's equal—but it wasn't blasphemy, just a simple statement of fact.

In setting out to prove this fact, John employs the principle of selection. He lets his mind run back over those amazing three and a half years he spent with the Lord. By the time John wrote his Gospel, Matthew, Mark, and Luke had already written theirs. He did not write his Gospel until the close of the last decade of the first century. He wrote it as an old man looking back on these events.

This fact, of course, has been used by critics to say that we cannot depend upon the Gospel of John, because it is the account of an old man who is trying to recall the events of his youth. Remember, however, that these events were on the heart, tongue, and memory of the apostle John every day after those events took place. He was always talking about them. He is writing now to tie together the record that Matthew, Mark, and Luke had written.

The Messiah

Notice that John underscores the fact that Jesus is "the Christ [or the Messiah], the Son of God." Jesus is the Christ—that's the first issue. Prominent figures were asking themselves, "Is this the one? Is this the Christ, the Messiah promised in the Old Testament?" It was the question on the lips of people in John's day, the question that divided the Jews. The people knew that there was a deepening sense of expectation running all through the Old Testament. In book after book, in one way or another, the Old Testament Scriptures continually repeated the refrain, "Someone is coming! Someone is coming!" At the close of the book of Malachi, you find that throbbing sense of expectation of the "sun of righteousness," the Messiah, who will rise with healing in His wings (Mal. 4:2), and that God would send "the prophet Elijah before that great and dreadful day of the LORD comes" (Mal. 4:5).

In John's day, people were stirred by the fact that John the Baptist—that fiery, Elijah-like preacher—had appeared. They asked him, "Are you the Christ? Are you the one who comes before that great and dreadful day of the Lord?" And John the Baptist said, "No, but the One you seek is coming after me." And when Jesus began to travel throughout the hills of Judea and Galilee, people wondered, *Is this the one? Is this the Messiah?*

The Lord Jesus declared again and again that He came with the authorized credentials of the Messiah. That is what He meant when He said,

> "I tell you the truth, the man who does not enter the sheep pen by the gate, but climbs in by some other way, is a thief and a robber. The man who enters by the gate is the shepherd of his sheep" (John 10:1–2).

The sheep pen was the nation Israel. Jesus is saying that there is one (Himself) who was to come by an authorized way, by the door. If anyone comes in any other way, he is a thief and a liar, but He who enters by the gate, the authorized opening, will be recognized as the Great Shepherd. He goes on to say,

> "The watchman opens the gate for him, and the sheep listen to his voice. He calls his own sheep by name and leads them out" (10:3).

"The watchman" refers to the ministry of John the Baptist, who came as the opener of the gate, the forerunner of the Messiah. Jesus goes on to offer His credentials as the one who was authorized to be the

Messiah. What were those credentials? He gives them to us Himself in the synagogue at Nazareth. In Luke 4, Jesus stood in the synagogue and read the book of the prophet Isaiah. He found the place and deliberately read to these people these words:

> *"The Spirit of the Lord is on me, because he has anointed me to preach good news to the poor. He has sent me to proclaim freedom for the prisoners and recovery of sight for the blind, to release the oppressed, to proclaim the year of the Lord's favor" (4:18–19).*

Messiah, "Anointed One"

What does the name *Messiah* mean? "The Anointed One." And what did Jesus read from the book of Isaiah? "The Spirit of the Lord . . . has anointed me." When He stopped reading and put the book aside, He actually stopped in the middle of a sentence. After the phrase, "to proclaim the year of the Lord's favor," the passage He was reading, Isaiah 61, goes on to say, "and the day of vengeance of our God." Why didn't He go on and read the rest of the sentence? Because the day of vengeance had not yet come. Jesus, in His first coming, came to fulfill the first half of the messianic mission—to preach good news to the poor, to heal the brokenhearted, to set the captives free. The second half of the messianic mission—to proclaim the day of God's vengeance—would await His second coming.

So, after Jesus stopped reading at that point in Isaiah 61, He closed the book, sat down, and said to everyone gathered in the synagogue, "Today this scripture is fulfilled in your hearing" (Luke 4:21). In other words, "This Scripture passage is about Me. I am the promised Messiah."

The marks of the Messiah

Water is changed to wine

To demonstrate the authority of Jesus as God's Anointed One, the Messiah, John selects seven events from the ministry of Jesus—seven marks of the Messiah. Let's examine them in the order in which they appear in John's Gospel:

First mark of the Messiah: the first miracle of our Lord—the changing of water into wine (John 2:1–11). That miracle was actually a visible parable. Our Lord performed a profoundly symbolic act at the wedding in Cana of Galilee. He took something that belonged to the realm of the inanimate world—water—and changed it into a living substance, wine. He took something that belonged to the realm of mere matter and changed it into something that is forever an expression of joy and life. By this act, He declared in symbol what He came to do: to proclaim the acceptable year of the Lord. He came to declare the day of grace, when God's purpose is to take human beings in their brokenness, their emptiness, and their lifelessness and to give them life.

Second mark of the Messiah: the healing of the royal official's son (John 4:46–54). The central figure in this story is not the son, who lies sick and dying, but the official, who comes to the Lord with a grief-broken heart. In his agony, the official cries out to Jesus, the Christ, and says, "Will you come down and heal my son?" The Lord not only heals the son at a distance with just a word (the same creative power that brought the world into being), but He heals the broken heart of the father. As Jesus said, He was anointed to heal the brokenhearted.

Third mark of the Messiah: the healing of the paralyzed man who lay at the pool of Bethesda (John 5:1–9). Remember, that man had lain there for thirty-eight years. He had been a prisoner of this paralyzing disease, so that he was unable to get into the pool. He had been brought to the pool in the hope that he might be healed, hoping to be set free—and the Lord singled him out of the great crowd and healed him, saying to him, "Get up! Pick up your mat and walk." Here, Jesus demonstrated His ability to set at liberty those who are oppressed and imprisoned. For thirty-eight years a man had been bound, yet Jesus instantly set him free.

Fourth mark of the Messiah: the feeding of the five thousand (John 6:1–14). This miracle appears in all four of the Gospels. Linked with it is the miracle of the walking on the water. What is the meaning of these signs? You cannot read the story of the feeding of the five thousand without seeing that it is a marvelous demonstration of the Lord's desire to meet the deepest need of the human heart, the hunger for God. He uses the symbol of bread, having Himself said, "It is written: 'Man does not live on bread alone, but on every word that comes from the mouth of God' " (Matthew 4:4). Then He demonstrates what kind of bread He means, saying, "I am the bread of life" (John 6:35). Taking the bread, He broke it, and with it fed the five thousand, symbolizing how fully He can meet the need and hunger of human souls.

Fifth mark of the Messiah: walking on water. After the feeding of the five thousand, He sends His disciples out into the storm—then He comes walking across the waves to them in the midst of the tempest. The waves are high, the ship is about to be overwhelmed, and their hearts are clenched with fear. Jesus comes to them, quiets their fears, and says, "It is I; don't be afraid" (John 6:20). The double miracle of the feeding of the five thousand and the walking on water provides a symbolic representation of our Lord's ability to satisfy the need of human hearts and deliver people from their greatest enemy, fear. This is good news! And this is one of the signs of the Messiah: He came to proclaim good news to the poor.

JOHN

The royal official's son is healed

The invalid at the pool of Bethesda walks

The five thousand are fed

Jesus walks on the waves

Sixth mark of the Messiah: the healing of the blind man (John 9:1–12). This story hardly needs comment. Our Lord said that He came "to give recovery of sight to the blind" (Luke 4:18). He chose a man who was blind from birth, just as human beings are spiritually blind from birth, and He healed him.

Seventh and final mark of the Messiah: the raising of Lazarus from the dead (John 11:1–44). This symbolizes the deliverance of those who all their lives had been held under the bondage of the fear of death. Thus, these seven signs prove beyond question that Jesus is the Messiah. He is the Anointed One, promised by God in the Old Testament.

John's theme is twofold: First, when you see Jesus in His delivering power, you are indeed seeing the promised Deliverer, the Messiah. But that is not the greatest secret to be revealed about Him. Throughout the centuries of Old Testament history, an astounding secret has been guarded. Prophets down through the ages have expected the coming of the Messiah, a great man of God—but who could have known, who could have imagined, who could have expected that this great man of God would be, in fact, the Son of God, the very person of God in human form? For that is John's second theme: Jesus is God.

When you stand in the presence of the Lord's humanity, you can see His loving eyes, feel the beating of His human heart, sense the compassion of His life poured out in service to other human beings. Yet, the amazing truth is that when you stand in His presence, you stand in the presence of God Himself! You see what God Himself is like! In the opening chapter of his Gospel, John makes this statement:

> *No one has ever seen God, but [the Son] the One and Only, who is at the Father's side, has made him known (1:18).*

"No one has ever seen God." That is a statement of fact. People hunger for God, and they are always searching for God, but no one has ever seen Him. But John goes on to say that the Son has made Him known. Jesus has unfolded what God is like. [Note: Some Greek manuscripts of John 1:18 use the word *God* in the place where I have bracketed the words "the Son." The NIV text followed those manuscripts, using the word *God* in that place. But I believe the clearer and more accurate translation is the one I have indicated, "the Son."]

The seven "I ams"

In his Gospel, John picks up seven great words of our Lord that prove his claim that Jesus is the Son of God. He bases it all on the great name of God revealed to Moses at the burning bush. When Moses saw the bush burning and turned aside to learn its secret, God spoke to him from the bush and said, "I AM WHO I AM" (Ex. 3:14). That is God's expression of His own self-consistent, self-perpetuating, self-existent nature. He says, "I am exactly what I am—no more, no less. I am the eternal I am." Seven times in John's Gospel he picks up this expression as it was used by Jesus Himself. These "I am" statements of Jesus constitute the proof that He is God.

You may have thought that Jesus' miracles establish His claim of deity. But no, they only establish the fact that He is the Messiah, the Promised One. His words establish His claim to be God. Listen to those words from His own lips:

"I am the bread of life" (6:35). In other words, "I am the sustainer of life, the One who satisfies life."

"I am the bread of life"

"I am the light of the world" (8:12). Jesus is telling us He is the illuminator of life, the explainer of all things, the one who casts light upon all mysteries and enigmas of life—and solves them.

"I am the light of the world"

"I am the gate" (10:7). Jesus states that He is the only opening that leads to eternal life. He is the open way.

"I am the gate"

"I am the good shepherd" (10:11). Jesus is the guide of life, the only one who is able to safely steer us and protect us through all the perils and chasms that yawn on every side. He is the one whose rod of discipline and staff of guidance can comfort us, give us peace, lead us beside still waters, and restore our souls.

"I am the good shepherd"

"I am the resurrection and the life" (11:25). He is the miraculous power of life, the giver and restorer of life. Resurrection power is the only power that saves when all hope is lost. Resurrection power works in the midst of despair, failure, and even death. When nothing else can be done, Jesus appears and says, "I am the resurrection and the life."

"I am the resurrection and the life"

"I am the way and the truth and the life" (14:6). That is, "I am ultimate reality. I am the real substance behind all things."

"I am the way the truth and the life"

"I am the vine. . . . apart from me you can do nothing" (15:5). I am the producer of all fruitfulness, the reason of all fellowship, the source of all identity and communion.

"I am the vine"

Seven times our Lord makes an "I am" statement, taking the great, revealing name of God from the Old Testament and linking it with simple yet profound symbols for the New Testament, using picture after picture to enable us to understand God.

John 1:14 announces, "The Word became flesh and made his dwelling among us. We have seen his glory, the glory of the One and Only, who came from the Father, full of grace and truth." The phrase "and made his dwelling among us" literally means that He tabernacled among us or He pitched His tent among us. All the glory that is God became a human being. That is the tremendous theme of this book. There is no greater theme in all the universe than the fact that we stand

Union with the Creator

John calls us to worship Jesus or to reject Him

in the presence of both the full humanity and the full deity of Jesus. He is the God-man. He shows us what God is like. He is the One who heals, loves, serves, waits, blesses, dies, and rises again—this is the ultimate human being, and this is God. That is the truth revealed in the Gospel of John.

"These are written that you may believe that Jesus is the Christ, the Son of God, and that by believing you may have life in his name" (20:31). He is the key to life. We all want to live—old and young alike. We all seek the key to life. We seek fulfillment. These are our deepest yearnings—and when we come to the end of our search, we find Jesus waiting for us with open arms. He is the goal of all our searching, all our desiring. He makes us to be all we were designed to be.

The Gospel of John does not simply present us with a story about Jesus. It does not simply inform us or even inspire us. It confronts us. It makes a demand on us. It requires a response. By forcing us to recognize the authentic deity of Christ, John calls us to either worship Him or reject Him. There is no middle ground. How can you stand in the presence of this divine mystery, in the shadow of the God-man who made the universe, then died upon a lonely hill in Palestine, and not feel your heart drawn to worship Him? As we often sing,

> And can it be that I should gain
> An interest in my Savior's blood?
> Died he for me, who caused his pain?
> For me, who him to death pursued?
> Amazing love, how can it be
> That thou, my God, shouldst die for me?
> —*Charles Wesley*

True worship

That is true worship—a recognition that Jesus is God, and that God has submitted Himself to death on our behalf! And true worship leads us to action, to service, to obedience. As in the words of the hymn, "Love so amazing, so divine, demands my soul, my life, my all."

When our hearts are filled with true worship, when our hands are engaged in true service, we are united with the one who made the entire universe, the one who is the great "I am." That is a thrilling, exalting thought.

And that is the message of the Gospel of John.

The Unfinished Story

When I was a student at Dallas Theological Seminary, each of us seminarians had to take a turn at preaching while the other students listened and evaluated. By watching and listening to these preachers-in-training preach, I could tell what great preacher had influenced each of them. Some of the young men had come from Bob Jones University, and they would stand on one leg, lean over the pulpit, shout and wave their arms just like Bob Jones. Others clearly came from a Young Life background—they would stand with their hands in their pockets, gesture with a closed fist, and drawl just like Young Life's Jim Rayburn. In seminarian after seminarian, I recognized various influences.

I also noticed something else: While these seminary students imitated the virtues of their pulpit heroes, they also tended to imitate their faults as well! That, I think, is what many Christians and many churches have done with the book of Acts. We have read the story of Acts, studied the example of the early church, and imitated that church—faults and all! So as we examine the record of the early church, as recorded in the book of Acts, we should avoid any superficial analysis. Even though our survey of Acts in *Adventuring through the Bible* will be brief and concise, we will try to make sure it is not superficial.

Acts is the book that reveals the power of the church. Whenever a church in our own century begins to lose its power, to turn dull and drab in its witness, it needs to rediscover the book of Acts. It is the story of the Holy Spirit's entering into a small group of believers, filling them

We have studied the example of the early church and imitated it, faults and all

with power and enthusiasm from on high—and *exploding* them, sending them like a shower of flaming embers around the world, igniting new fires and starting new churches. That is how the gospel spread like wildfire in the first century A.D.

The book of the revolving door

I like to think of the book of Acts as a revolving door. A hinged door is a one-way door, and people can only go in or out, one way at a time. But a revolving door is designed to allow people to go in and out at the same time: They go in one side and go out the other. The book of Acts is like that—Old Testament Judaism is going out and the New Testament church is coming in. Both are in the revolving door at the same time for a while, just as two people can be in a revolving door going in opposite directions. But don't ever try to set up housekeeping in a revolving door—you'll get knocked right off your feet! You can't live in a revolving door because it is not designed for habitation, it is designed for transition, for allowing movement.

Acts is a book of history rather than of doctrine

In the same way, we should not rely exclusively on the book of Acts for doctrine and teaching. It is not designed for that. It is a book of history, of fast-moving events, of transition—not doctrine. So it is important that we read it and compare it with the doctrinal books of the Bible. Acts is designed to stir us up and encourage us and bless us and to show us what God intends to do through the church—but it is not primarily a book of doctrine.

The book of Acts was written by Luke, Paul's beloved companion, the author of the Gospel of Luke. Unfortunately, it bears the wrong title, because in most editions of Scripture it is called the Acts of the Apostles. But as you read the book through, the only apostles whose acts are highlighted are Peter and Paul. Most other apostles go largely unnoticed in Acts. The book should really be titled the Acts of the Holy Spirit—or even more appropriately, the Continuing Acts of the Lord Jesus Christ. You find this suggestion in the introduction of the book. As Luke writes again to the same friend he addressed in his Gospel, he says,

> In my former book, Theophilus, I wrote about all that Jesus began to do and to teach . . . (Acts 1:1).

Obviously, then, Luke was volume 1 and Acts is volume 2. Acts is the sequel, the continuation of what Jesus began both to do and to teach. Luke goes on to say,

> . . . until the day he was taken up to heaven, after giving instructions through the Holy Spirit to the apostles he had chosen. After his suffering,

he showed himself to these men and gave many convincing proofs that he was alive. He appeared to them over a period of forty days and spoke about the kingdom of God. On one occasion, while he was eating with them, he gave them this command: "Do not leave Jerusalem, but wait for the gift my Father promised, which you have heard me speak about. For John baptized with water, but in a few days you will be baptized with the Holy Spirit" (1:2–5).

That is the essence of the book of Acts. It is the account of the way the Holy Spirit, moving through the church, continued what Jesus began to do in His earthly ministry. So the record of the Gospels is the story of *only the beginning* of the work of the Lord Jesus Christ. When you come to the end of the Gospels, you have come not to the end, nor even to the beginning of the end, but to the end of the beginning. In the book of Acts, the Holy Spirit now begins to fulfill the program of God. He begins to carry on His work through the reincarnated body of Jesus Christ—the church.

When Jesus ascended into heaven, He exchanged His own resurrected body on earth for a different kind of body on earth—the church, which the New Testament calls "the body of Christ." Instead of a single human body that can be in either Galilee or Samaria or Judea and that must stop every now and then to sleep, He now has a body that reaches to the uttermost parts of the earth and is active twenty-four hours a day! We now live in the age of the Spirit—an age inaugurated on the day of Pentecost, the first major event of the book of Acts.

> When Jesus ascended into heaven, He exchanged His own resurrected body on earth for a different kind of body on earth—the church

The Holy Spirit gives us the outline of the book of Acts in a very well-known verse, chapter 1, verse 8—our Lord's words to the disciples:

> **The structure of the book of Acts**

"You will receive power when the Holy Spirit comes on you . . ."

That statement encompasses the first two chapters of Acts—the chapters concerning the coming of the Holy Spirit. The Lord, in 1:8, goes on to say:

". . . and you will be my witnesses . . ."

That is the theme of the rest of Acts, chapters 3 through 28. The concluding phrase of Acts 1:8 then divides chapters 3 through 28 into several parts:

". . . in Jerusalem, and in all Judea and Samaria, and to the ends of the earth."

So the book is very plainly outlined for us. In chapters 1 and 2 we have the coming of the Holy Spirit, and in 3 through 28 we have the witness of the Holy Spirit. The divisions within the second part of Acts are:

3–7 The witness of the Holy Spirit in Jerusalem

8–12 The witness of the Spirit in all Judea and Samaria

13   The witness goes out to the ends of the earth

As we study through the book of Acts, we will see how this outline of the book, which was inspired by the Holy Spirit, is literally fulfilled by the Holy Spirit in the life of the early church. The story of Acts begins in Jerusalem, the center of the Jewish nation, and it ends in Rome, the center of the Gentile world. It carries us from the limited gospel of the kingdom at the close of the four Gospels through the spreading of the gospel of grace to the whole world at the close of Acts. With this structure as our foundation, here is an overview of the book of Acts:

The Coming of the Holy Spirit (Acts 1–2)

1.	Prologue, the resurrection, appearance, and ascension of Jesus Christ	1:1–10
2.	The promise of the Holy Spirit	1:11
3.	The appointment of replacement apostle Matthias	1:12–26
4.	Pentecost, the dramatic entrance of the Spirit	2

The Witness of the Holy Spirit from Jerusalem to the Ends of the Earth (Acts 3–28)

5.	Witness to Jerusalem	3–7
	A. Peter heals and preaches	3
	B. Peter and John minister in chains	4:1–31
	C. Early church grows and shares	4:32–37
	D. Ananias and Sapphira: don't lie to the Holy Spirit	5:1–11
	E. Miracles of the apostles	5:12–16
	F. Persecution of the apostles	5:17–42
	G. Deacons appointed, Stephen martyred	6–7
6.	Witness to Judea and Samaria	8–12
	A. Saul persecutes the church	8:1–3
	B. The witness of Philip to the Samaritans and the Ethiopian eunuch	8:4–40
	C. The conversion of Saul (Paul)	9:1–31
	D. The witness of Peter, including healings, raising Dorcas, witnessing to Cornelius, beginning of the ministry to the Gentiles	9:32–11:18

The restoration of the Twelve

In the first chapter of Acts, following the death of Judas Iscariot, the disciple who betrayed Jesus, Peter stands and says to the church, "For it is written in the book of Psalms, 'May his place be deserted; let there be no one to dwell in it,' and, 'May another take his place of leadership' " (1:20). So the church proceeds to cast lots to determine whom God wants to step into the empty slot and faithfully carry out the apostolic ministry. The lot falls to Matthias, and he is added to the eleven apostles. The number of the apostles is restored to twelve.

Then, in Acts 6, we see a problem arise. The church has been growing, including not only Christians who were converted from strictly Hebrew Judaism, but also the Hellenized Jews (Jews who have largely adopted the Greek culture). The Grecian Jews are upset because they feel that their widows and needy have been neglected in the daily distribution. So, in Acts 6:1–2, we see that the twelve apostles—the original eleven plus Matthias—are summoned to deal with the dispute. Why? Because it is upon this twelve, the complete number of the apostles, that the Holy Spirit was poured out on the day of Pentecost.

It is important and interesting to note that, in the book of Revelation, we see that the names of the twelve apostles form the foundations of the city that John saw coming down from heaven—the restored twelve, that is, including the new apostle, Matthias (see Rev. 21:12–13). There had to be twelve apostles to Israel. Judas fell, but God chose Matthias to take his place as a witness to Israel.

Interestingly, it appears that the office of Judas was actually filled by not one man but two. While Matthias became the replacement apostle to Israel, the apostle Paul became the special apostle to the Gentiles. This does not mean that the other apostles did not have a ministry to the

The place of Paul in relation to the Twelve

Gentiles, for they certainly did. In fact, it was to Peter that God gave a vision showing him that the Gospel was to go out to the Gentiles as well as to the house of Israel (see Acts 10). But while God chose Peter to be the chief apostle to Israel, Paul went primarily to the Gentiles. The other twelve apostles—the original eleven plus Matthias, were divinely chosen as a witness to Israel, and they fulfilled that ministry completely.

The pouring out of the Holy Spirit

After the full number of the apostles was restored, the great mark of the book of Acts—the pouring out of the Holy Spirit—took place. Everything else flows from this event in Acts 2. The interesting thing is to see how Christians, reading about this amazing occurrence, have focused their attention on the incidentals and neglected the essentials. The incidentals here—the rushing wind, the fire that danced on the heads of the disciples, and the many tongues or languages by which they spoke—are simply the peripheral events that took place, the signs that showed that something important was happening.

The essential, important feature of this story was the formation of a new and distinct community, the church. One hundred and twenty individuals met in the temple courts. They were as unrelated to each other as any people born in widely scattered parts of the earth might be to each other today. When the Holy Spirit was poured out on them, He baptized them into one body. They became a living unit. They were no longer related only to the Lord; they were related also to each other as brothers and sisters in Christ. They were the body of Christ.

The essential, important feature of this story was the formation of a new and distinct community, the church

As the body of Christ, they received a new program, a new purpose. With the Holy Spirit dwelling in them, they began to reach out to Jerusalem and then beyond, to Judea, Samaria, and the uttermost parts of the earth. The same body of Christ that came into existence at Pentecost is alive today and will remain alive, active, and energized until the day of the Lord's return. That is the essential and important fact of Acts 2: The birth of the body, the beginning of the church. It is this body that the Holy Spirit inhabits and into which He breathes His power and life. Through this body, the Spirit of God is active in the world today, carrying out His eternal plan.

The calling of Paul

The rest of the book of Acts deals largely with the calling and ministry of the apostle Paul—the wise master builder, the one whom the Holy Spirit selected to be the pattern for Gentile Christians. This is why Paul was put through such an intensive training period by the Holy Spirit, during which he was subjected to one of the most rigorous trials that any human being could undergo. He was sent back to his own hometown to live in obscurity for seven years, until he had learned the great lesson that the Holy Spirit seeks to teach every Christian—the lesson without which no one can ever be effective for Him. In the words of our Lord, "I tell you the truth, unless a kernel of wheat falls to the ground and dies, it remains only a single seed. But if it dies, it produces many seeds" (John 12:24).

As you trace the career of the apostle Paul, you discover that (like most of us) he didn't understand this principle when he first came to Christ. As we would have reasoned in his place, he thought that he had all it took. He believed that he was especially prepared to be the kind of instrument that could be mightily used by God to win Israel to Christ. Undoubtedly (as he reveals in Phil. 3:4–6; compare Acts 22:3), he had the background; he had the training. He was by birth a Hebrew; he was educated in all the law and the understanding of the Hebrews; he had the position; he was the favorite pupil of the greatest teacher of Israel, Gamaliel; he was a Pharisee of the Pharisees; he understood everything of the Hebrew law, faith, and culture.

Again and again in his letters, you see Paul's hungering to be an instrument to reach Israel for Christ. In Romans, he writes, "I have great sorrow and unceasing anguish in my heart. For I could wish that I myself were cursed and cut off from Christ for the sake of my brothers, those of my own race" (Rom. 9:2–3). But God had said to this man, "I don't want you to go to Israel with the Gospel. I'm calling you to be the apostle to the Gentiles, to bear My name before kings and to preach to the Gentiles the unsearchable riches of Christ."

Do you remember how he went out into the desert, and there God taught him? Then God sent him back home to Tarsus. After he tried in Damascus to preach Christ out of the energy of his own flesh and found that he was failing, he was driven out of the city and let down like a criminal over the wall in a basket. Brokenhearted and defeated, he found his way to Jerusalem and thought the apostles at least would take him in, but they turned him aside. It was only as Barnabas finally interceded for him that he was given any acceptance in the eyes of the apostles at all.

Then, going into the temple, he met the Lord, who said to him, "Go back home. Get out of the city. They won't receive your testimony here. This isn't the place I've called you to" (see Acts 22:17–21). In Tarsus, he faced up at last to what God was saying to him all the time: Unless he was willing to die to his own ambition to be the apostle to Israel, he could never be the servant of Christ. And when at last he received that commission and took it to heart, he said, "Lord, anywhere you want. Anything you want. Anywhere you want to send me. I'm ready to go." God sent Barnabas to him, and he took him by the hand and led him down to Antioch, a Gentile church, and there the apostle Paul began his ministry.

Paul believed that he was especially prepared to be the kind of instrument that could be mightily used by God to win Israel to Christ

Unless he was willing to die to his own ambition to be the apostle to Israel, Paul could never be the servant of Christ

The book ends with Paul in Rome, preaching in his own hired house, chained day and night to a Roman guard, unable to go out as a missionary. He is a prisoner—yet, as he writes to the Philippians, his heart is overflowing with the consciousness that though he was bound, the Word of God was not. One of the most amazing words in all of Scripture is given there, as he writes to his friends in Philippi and says, "Now I want you to know, brothers, that what has happened to me has really served to advance the gospel" (Phil. 1:12). These obstacles and disappointments have not stopped a thing; they have only advanced the gospel. And he gives two specific ways in which the gospel was being advanced:

The praetorian guard was being reached for Christ (Phil. 1:12–13). Paul was being guarded by the cream of the crop in the Roman army, and one by one, they were coming to know Christ. They were being brought in by the emperor's command and chained to the apostle Paul for six hours. Talk about a captive audience! God was using the emperor to bring his best men in and chain them to the apostle for six hours of instruction in the Christian gospel. No wonder Paul writes at the end of the letter, "All the saints send you greetings, especially those who belong to Caesar's household" (Phil. 4:22).

Because of Paul's arrest, all the other brethren in the city were busy taking up the slack, preaching the gospel with increased power and boldness (Phil. 1:14). "Because of my chains," Paul wrote, "most of the brothers in the Lord have been encouraged to speak the word of God more courageously and fearlessly." Ironically, the gospel was going out across Rome with even greater force and intensity since Paul had been in prison because people had stopped relying on Paul as the sole evange-list to Rome. If the job of evangelizing Rome was going to happen, other people were going to have to pick up where Paul left off and carry on in his place. And Paul said, "I rejoice in that." I have often wondered if the best way to evangelize a city might be to lock up all the preachers in jail!

Yet, there is a third advantage to Paul's imprisonment in Rome at the end of the book of Acts—an advantage that even the apostle him-self could not imagine. We can see now, with the advantage of two thousand years of hindsight, that the greatest work Paul ever did in his lifetime was not to go about preaching the gospel and planting churches, as great as that work was. *His greatest accomplishment of all was the body of letters he wrote, many of which were written in prison—*many of which would never have been written if he had not been in prison. Because of those letters, the church has been nurtured, strengthened, and emboldened through twenty centuries of Christian history.

The church has suffered for many centuries from a tragic misconception. Much of the weakness of the church today is due to this misconception that has developed within the body of Christ. For centuries, Christians have met together and recited the Great Commission of Jesus Christ to take the gospel out to the farthest corners of the earth, "Therefore go and make disciples of all nations, baptizing them in the name of the Father and of the Son and of the Holy Spirit" (Matt. 28:19). And that is unquestionably the will of God. But it is one of the favorite tricks of the devil to get Christians to pursue God's will in their own way, according to their own limited wisdom, in pursuit of their own will. It is never possible to truly fulfill God's will in a human way.

The error of the church

That is exactly what the church has been doing. We have gathered ourselves together, recited the Great Commission, and said, "Now we must mobilize all our human resources to plan the strategy for carrying out God's will." Christ is often pictured as waiting in heaven, earnestly hoping that we will get with it down here and carry out His program. According to this view, His plan for the world hinges on our strategies, our ingenuity, our effort. Without our human strength, Jesus would never get the job done. This view is a satanic deception.

According to one view, God's plan for the world hinges on our strategies, our ingenuity, our effort

Why have we become deceived? Because we have listened to only one part of the Great Commission. We have heard the first word, "Go." But our Lord (in the King James Version) spoke another little two-letter word that we have almost completely forgotten: "Lo." He says, "Lo, I am with you alway even unto the end of the world" (Matthew 28:20). It was never the intention of the Lord that Christians themselves should take over the job of planning the strategy and mobilizing the resources to take the gospel to the ends of the earth. He never intended that we should try to fulfill the Great Commission in our own strength, while He stands by and watches. He is with us always—and we must allow Him to be in charge of His own strategy for reaching the world.

God never intended that we should try to fulfill the Great Commission in our own strength, while He stands by and watches

When we come back to Him, exhausted, beaten, and discouraged—as we inevitably would be—and we cry out to Him, "Oh, Lord, we can never get this job done. We can never accomplish this," He will remind us that His program was for the Holy Spirit to accomplish this task through the church. That, after all, is what the book of Acts is about: how the Holy Spirit carried out His program and exploded ministry throughout the known world. God did not call the apostles and the early church to do all the work. Instead, the message of Acts is the message that Paul gave us in 1 Thessalonians 5:24: "The one who calls you is faithful and he will do it." It was always God's intention not only to lay the program before us, but to fulfill it in His own strength.

Philip is sent from a
citywide revival in
Samaria to one
Ethiopian in the
desert

As you read through this book, you see various aspects of the ministry of the Holy Spirit. First of all, He is visible in directing the activities of the church. It is the Spirit of God—not human beings—who takes the initiative and launches new movements in carrying out the program of God. For example, when Philip was in Samaria preaching the gospel, a great citywide revival was in progress as a result of his preaching. The whole city was swept with the spirit of revival. Human wisdom would say, "Hey, we've got something going here! Let's invest more resources in Samaria! Let's really expand our evangelistic mission in Samaria! Let's develop a big 'Win Samaria for Jesus' strategy!"

But that wasn't God's plan. Instead, in Acts 8, we see that the Spirit of God tells Philip to go to the desert and find a man—a lone Ethiopian man—and witness to him. Now, what kind of strategy is that, to leave a citywide campaign where the Spirit of God is moving in power, where multitudes are coming to Christ, only to go down into the desert to talk to one man?

But who was this man? He was the Ethiopian eunuch, the treasurer of the Ethiopian government. The account in Acts shows that this man's heart had been carefully prepared by the Holy Spirit.

As Philip came alongside the chariot of the Ethiopian, he saw that the man was reading from Isaiah chapter 53—a powerful Old Testament prophecy of the Messiah. Philip asked the man if he understood what he read, and the man answered with a rhetorical question: "How can I, unless someone explains it to me?" So Philip sat beside him and told him the story of the Messiah who had finally come, who had suffered and died, and who had been raised again. And Philip won the man to Christ on the spot. The influential Ethiopian official returned to his own country, and tradition holds that many Ethiopians were led to Christ through him, and the reach of the gospel was first extended to the continent of Africa.

That is always what
Spirit-led witnessing
is all about: The
right person in the
right place at the
right time saying
the right thing to
the right person

Saul and Ananias

That is always what Spirit-led witnessing is all about: The right person in the right place at the right time saying the right thing to the right person. This is one of the first evidences in this book of the overall directing activity of the Holy Spirit.

In Acts 9, the Holy Spirit calls a man on the Damascus road and sends another man to pray with him—Ananias, who is absolutely astounded by this commission. "Lord," Ananias prays, "you don't know what you are asking! This man is the chief persecutor of Your church!" God replies, "I know whom I have called. He's a chosen instrument of Mine." And the man whom God sent Ananias to was—of course!—Saul, the future apostle Paul.

In chapter 13, the church at Antioch fasts and prays, and in the midst of their worship, the Holy Spirit tells the church, "Set apart for

me Barnabas and Saul for the work to which I have called them" (13:2).
Later, we read,

> Paul and his companions traveled throughout the region of Phrygia
> and Galatia, having been kept by the Holy Spirit from preaching the
> word in the province of Asia. When they came to the border of Mysia,
> they tried to enter Bithynia, but the Spirit of Jesus would not allow them
> to (16:6–7).

All through this book, you find that the strategy has all been worked
out in advance not by people but *by the Holy Spirit.* As Christians are
available to the Spirit, He unfolds the strategy step by step. Nobody can
plan this kind of a program. We can only be willing to follow the overall directive activity of the Spirit of God at work in His church. That is
the divine strategy.

And how do we discover and lay hold of the divine strategy? By following the example of a "noble" group of people we find in Acts 17:

> As soon as it was night, the brothers sent Paul and Silas away to
> Berea. On arriving there, they went to the Jewish synagogue. Now the
> Bereans were of more noble character than the Thessalonians, for they
> received the message with great eagerness and examined the Scriptures
> every day to see if what Paul said was true. Many of the Jews believed,
> as did also a number of prominent Greek women and many Greek men
> (17:10–12).

If only we were more like the noble Bereans, who eagerly examined
the Scriptures, comparing Paul's words with the Word of God! If only
we would search the Scriptures for ourselves instead of allowing ourselves to be spoon-fed by this pastor or that Christian author! Even as
you and I are adventuring through the Bible together in this book, I
hope that you will never simply take my word for it on any matter of
spiritual truth. Rather, I encourage you to be like the noble Bereans.
Check God's Word for yourself, listen to the Holy Spirit's leading, pray
to God—and when you pray, listen quietly for His answer. Seek the
mind of God and the understanding that comes from His Word and His
Spirit. That is the noble thing to do!

Later in Acts, we find the Holy Spirit engaged in another aspect of
His ministry, doing what no human being can do: communicating life
to those who hear the gospel. Wherever the message of salvation is
preached, wherever the Word of God is upheld, the Holy Spirit is there
to communicate life.

All through this book, you find that the strategy has all been worked out in advance not by people but *by the Holy Spirit*

The noble Bereans

Instruments of the Spirit

Have you ever noticed who gives the altar call in the book of Acts? It is almost invariably the ones being preached to, not the preachers! On the day of Pentecost, as the Spirit of God preached through Peter to the thousands attracted by Holy Spirit's amazing miracle of the tongues of flame and the tongues of languages, Peter's audience was so convicted by the Spirit that they interrupted him in midsermon! "What must we do to be saved?" they shouted (paraphrase; see Acts 2:37). Peter didn't have to give the altar call—his audience beat him to it!

And in Acts 16, when the Philippian jailer was impressed by the singing of Paul and Silas at midnight, and then the earthquake came and shook the prison walls to the ground, who gave the altar call? The Philippian jailer himself! He came running and asked them, "Sirs, what must I do to be saved?" In case after case, incident after incident, it was the Holy Spirit, communicating to needy hearts, preparing them in advance to believe and respond when the message came to them.

Today there are many Christian groups and individuals whose sole occupation in life seems to be to defend the faith—to preserve, if they can, the purity of the church. Many of these people go so far as to corner unsuspecting pastors, inspect every sentence and clause of their sermons for hints or suggestions of unorthodox belief or faulty doctrine, then nail them to the wall for even the most minor or dubious whiff of "heresy." While it is proper to want the church to be pure and true to the Scriptures, the book of Acts shows us that it is the Spirit of God Himself who is in charge of this task.

As the church fulfills its commission to be available, to be willing instruments of the activity and life of the Holy Spirit, He is at work to preserve the purity of the church. For example, there is an amazing incident that occurs early in the book. Ananias and Sapphira's hypocrisy was revealed when they tried to attach to themselves a holiness that they did not actually possess (Acts 5:1–11). They tried to appear more committed or dedicated than they really were. They tried to gain a reputation for sanctity among their fellow Christians by appearance only. The judgment of the Holy Spirit came immediately in the form of their physical death.

I do not believe that God exercises such dramatic judgment in the church today. Rather, God used Ananias and Sapphira as an example, a pattern to indicate what the Spirit of God does on the spiritual level. In the book of Acts, He judged these two hypocrites on the physical level in order that we might see this principle at work. But whether spiritual or physical, the result is exactly the same.

Let somebody begin to use his religious standing, her Christian opportunities, to elevate his own proud reputation in the eyes of people, to pretend to a holiness she does not possess, and what happens? The

Spirit of God cuts him off from the manifestation of the life of Christ! Instantly that individual's life is as powerless, as weak and fruitless, as dead and lacking in effect, as the dead bodies of Ananias and Sapphira lying at the feet of Peter. It is a sobering principle of the Christian life, and one that every believer should consider seriously and honestly, while examining his or her own life.

Christians were the wonder and sensation of the first-century world. The message they preached and the way they lived had the entire known world in a commotion. What was it about these people that set the entire world abuzz? Only one thing: The Spirit of God was alive in them! The Spirit gave them power, energy, excitement, courage, and boldness—especially boldness!

Notice their boldness: One moment, near the end of the Gospels, you see Peter and John hiding behind locked doors, afraid to go out into the streets of Jerusalem for fear of those who hated and crucified the Lord Jesus. But now, after the Spirit of God comes upon them, they are out in the streets and temple courts boldly proclaiming the truth of Jesus Christ. When they are locked up in prison, the angel releases them and they go right back into the temple courts to pray and preach again. They are unstoppable! They are invincible! And every time they are arrested or rioted against or stoned or beaten, what do these Christians pray for? Not safety. Not protection. No, they pray for even more boldness!

That is God's program. The Holy Spirit does everything in the book of Acts. He does all the energizing, guiding, directing, programming, empowering, preparing, and communicating. He does it all. It is not up to us to do anything except to be available, to be His instruments, to go where He wills, to open our mouths and speak His words, to be ready to take advantage of whatever situation He places us in. It is the job of the Spirit to carry out that ministry. That is why this book should be called the Acts of the Holy Spirit of God not the Acts of the Apostles.

That is what the church lacks today. We want to do all the right things, but we try to do them in our own strength, according to our own wisdom, employing our own strategy, writing the Book of Our Own Acts for God rather than continuing the story of the Acts of the Holy Spirit of God. That is a tragedy that breaks the heart of God, and it should break our hearts as well.

The book of Acts concludes abruptly, with these words:

> *For two whole years Paul stayed there in his own rented house and welcomed all who came to see him. Boldly and without hindrance he preached the kingdom of God and taught about the Lord Jesus Christ (28:30–31).*

What was it about these people that set the entire world abuzz? Only one thing: The Spirit of God was alive in them

That is God's program: The Holy Spirit does everything in the book of Acts

The unfinished book

We know, of course, that this is not the end of Paul's story. In Acts 20:24 and 38, Paul talks about his approaching death. In 2 Timothy 4:6–8, he writes with an obvious sense that his days are numbered:

> *I am already being poured out like a drink offering, and the time has come for my departure. I have fought the good fight, I have finished the race, I have kept the faith. Now there is in store for me the crown of righteousness, which the Lord, the righteous Judge, will award to me on that day—and not only to me, but also to all who have longed for his appearing.*

According to tradition, Paul was executed in Rome in February, A.D. 62. The fact that Acts does not record Paul's death, nor does it refer to such important events as the persecution under Nero (A.D. 64) or the destruction of Jerusalem (A.D. 70) suggests that the book of Acts was probably written before Paul's death. In any case, the book of Acts is clearly an unfinished book. It ends—but it is not completed. Why? Certainly Luke could have gone back to the book in later years and written a postscript, even if the book was completed before A.D. 62. Why didn't he?

Because the Holy Spirit *deliberately intended* it to be unfinished!

The book of Acts is still being written. Like the Gospel of Luke, the book of Acts is yet another record of the things Jesus began both to do and to teach. Jesus isn't finished yet. He began His ministry in His human body, as recorded in the Gospels. He continued in His body, the church, through the book of Acts. He continues His ministry today through you and me and every other believer on the planet.

The book of Acts will be completed someday. And when it is completed, you and I will have a chance to read it in glory, in eternity, when the plan of God has been fulfilled. When we read it, what will my part be in that great story?

And what will yours be?

Part Seven

Letters from the Lord

LETTERS TO THE CHURCH

T he purpose of divine revelation is nothing less than the transformation of human lives. We should not merely *read* the Bible. We should *experience* it—and our contact with it should *change our lives*. If the Bible isn't changing us, then there is something drastically wrong with the way we approach this Book. The Bible is a living book with a living message that God gave us to transform the way you and I live.

It takes the entire book to do the whole job, and that is why we are engaged in this whole-Bible survey in *Adventuring through the Bible*. We have seen that the purpose of the Old Testament was to prepare us for truth, and the purpose of the New Testament was to realize the truth. In the New Testament, the Gospels and Acts go together to present us with the person and work of Jesus Christ, both in His earthly body and in His body of believers, the church. Next follow the thirteen epistles (or letters) of Paul. Following them we have the letter to the Hebrews and the letters of James, Peter, John, and Jude. These epistles are the explanation of Jesus Christ and the Christian way of living. Finally, we come to the last book of the Bible, the final chapter of biblical revelation. It is not only the story of the end of history and the culmination of God's plan, but it also contains the only letters written to us by our risen Lord—the seven letters to the first century churches.

When we come to the Epistles—which occupy the largest part of the New Testament—we are dealing not with preparation or fulfillment but with experience. These letters of the New Testament are the nuts and bolts of the Christian life. They tell us all that is involved in mastering the mystery of Christ and the Christian life. There are depths and heights in Jesus Christ that no mind can grasp—depths to understanding Him and depths to following Him. Through these letters, written by a number of apostles (though most of them were written by the apostle Paul), the Holy Spirit shows us how to discover and explore the deep truths and the deep experience of knowing and following Jesus Christ.

Christ in you: Romans to Galatians

There are three groups of epistles. The first four—Romans, 1 and 2 Corinthians, and Galatians—are grouped together around the theme, Christ in you. Although that phrase—Christ in you, the hope of glory—is found in the next group of Paul's letters, in Colossians 1:27, this phrase is really the theme of Romans through Galatians. This is the transforming principle of the Christian life. This is what makes Christians different from all other human beings on earth: Christ lives in us. These first four epistles develop this theme.

The next group consists of nine epistles—Ephesians, Philippians, Colossians, 1 and 2 Thessalonians, 1 and 2 Timothy, Titus, and Philemon. These epistles all gather around the theme, You in Christ—that is, your life in relationship to the rest of the body of Christ. Here you have the church coming into view—the fact that we no longer live our Christian lives as individuals.

When we come to the last group of eight epistles—Hebrews, James, 1 and 2 Peter, 1 through 3 John, and Jude—we will see that these all gather around one theme: How to walk by faith. So we have this great span of epistles designed to make all the mighty truths of God available to us in terms of practical experience.

We begin with the first group—Romans, 1 and 2 Corinthians, and Galatians, the books that cluster around the theme Christ in you. Romans is first not because it was written first (it was not), but because it is *the* great foundational letter of the New Testament. In this book, you find the full sweep of salvation, from beginning to end, in all its fullness. If you want to see what God is doing with you as an individual, and with the human race as a whole, then master the book of Romans.

Romans

As you study this book, you discover that it develops salvation in three tenses—past, present, and future. In other words, its themes are:

Salvation in three tenses—past, present, and future

Past: I *was* saved when I believed in Jesus;

Present: I *am being* saved as the character of Jesus Christ now becomes manifest in my life; and

Future: I *shall be* saved when at last, in resurrection life, with a glorified body, I stand in the presence of the Son of God and enter into the fullness of the truth of God.

These three tenses of salvation can be gathered up in three words that are familiar to those who have studied the Bible to any extent: *Justification* is the first word—the past tense: I was justified when I believed in Jesus Christ. Justification is that righteous standing before God that we receive when Jesus enters our lives—the state of being without spot or blemish, as if we had never sinned.

The second word—the present tense—is that much misunderstood word *sanctification*. Oswald Chambers has said, "Sanctification is the appearing of the characteristics, the perfections, of the Lord Jesus in terms of your human personality." That is a good definition of sanctification. It is a process of becoming more and more Christlike.

The third word—future tense—is *glorification.* which is the completion of this transformation when we stand in the presence of Christ in eternity.

First Corinthians contrasts carnality and spirituality—living according to the will of the flesh versus living according to the will of the Spirit of God. First, the carnality. If you have read 1 Corinthians, you know what I mean. What a mess! Here were people divided up into little factions and cliques, continually at each other's throats, dragging each other before courts of law, gossiping against each other, undermining each other, fighting with one another, and even getting drunk at the Lord's Table! The most shameful forms of immorality were parading themselves in full view of the Corinthian church. Paul, in 1 Corinthians, shows that carnal, unspiritual living is a result of a breakdown in our fellowship with Jesus Christ, but fellowship with Christ produces spirituality so that we are able to walk in resurrection power and resurrection life.

Second Corinthians is the practical demonstration of the Christian's victory under pressure. This is the great epistle of trials and triumphs, of conquering life at its rawest edge. The theme of the letter is stated in 2 Corinthians 2:14:

Thanks be to God, who always leads us in triumphal procession in Christ and through us spreads everywhere the fragrance of the knowledge of him.

For the last letter of this group, Galatians, Paul dips his pen point not in ink, but in a blue-hot flame—then he jabs us with it to wake us up and stir us to action! This is the hottest epistle in the New Testament, because Paul is angry. He is obviously and unmistakably angry. He is deeply disgusted with the Christians in Galatia, and he doesn't hesitate to say so. He is beside himself because they are so easily distracted from the truth that they clearly understood and have allowed themselves to be

1 Corinthians

Living according to the will of the flesh versus living according to the will of the Spirit of God

2 Corinthians

The practical demonstration of the Christian's victory under pressure

Galatians

The hottest epistle in the New Testament

led into a weakening, debilitating doctrine that is sapping their strength and turning them into carnal Christians. The theme of the letter is *freedom*—freedom in Christ. You find this theme stated in Galatians 5:1:

> *It is for freedom that Christ has set us free. Stand firm, then, and do not let yourselves be burdened again by a yoke of slavery.*

This book is the answer to all the dead legalism that has bound the church in so many times and places over the past two millennia. The flesh, the carnal life, brings guilt, condemnation, and failure. But the Spirit of God brings life and freedom. I love to read the book of Galatians. As you read it, you see that there is a mighty burning in the heart of the apostle, a flaming passion to see Christians set free of the chains of legalism so they can experience the fullness and richness of the Spirit of God.

All of these books, Romans through Galatians, gather around the theme, Christ in you—the greatest theme that the human mind has ever contemplated, the theme that demonstrates for us what it means to have the living God, the Creator of the entire universe, living His limitless life in us and through us. The next section of the New Testament gives a blueprint for living lives that are worthy of the fact that God lives in us. The theme that gathers up this next section is a theme I call, You in Christ.

You in Christ: Ephesians to Philemon

The whole purpose of revelation, the aim of the entire Bible, is the goal expressed by Paul in Ephesians 4, that is,

> *to prepare God's people for works of service, so that the body of Christ may be built up until we all reach unity in the faith and in the knowledge of the Son of God and become mature, attaining to the whole measure of the fullness of Christ (vv. 12–13).*

God wants us to grow up mature in Christ. He is not interested in forming chapters of the P.W.A.—the Pew-Warmers Association. He wants men and women of action, of commitment, of boldness, of passion, of enthusiasm—a body of believers who will gladly throw their bodies into the battle for His kingdom. He wants men and women who are not afraid of change but who are committed to dynamic growth. Unfortunately, all too many of us seem to think that the theme song of Christianity is "Come Blessing or Woe, Our Status Is Quo." The status quo is the last thing God wants for our lives! That is why He has given us the epistles from Ephesians to Philemon.

This group of epistles sets forth the theme of You in Christ. In John 14:20, the Lord Jesus used the formula "You are in Me, and I am in You." When we talk about Christ in us, we are talking about the indwelling life—the walk in the Spirit. When we talk about us in Christ, we are speaking of our relationship to the body of Christ—the fact that we are members of His body. Our life is incorporated in the totality of life in the body of Christ.

And we soon discover that we are not only Christians individually, but corporately as well. We belong to each other as well as to Christ. By ourselves, we can never come to fulfillment and full development in our Christian lives. We need each other in the body of Christ.

The epistles that comprise the You-in-Christ section are Ephesians, Philippians, Colossians, 1 and 2 Thessalonians, 1 and 2 Timothy, Titus, and Philemon. They are like the best books in a doctor's library. In any doctor's library we find books on physiology—the science and study of the human body. Ephesians is such a book—a careful study of the nature of the body of Christ.

The New Testament book of pathology, of the treatment of diseases of the body of Christ, is Philippians. In this letter, Paul takes a very practical approach to the problems and diseases that threaten the health of the body. As we read through this book, we see that the maladies that afflicted the first-century church are the same maladies we see in the church today. If you find your spiritual health and well-being disturbed by pressure, discouragement, weariness, and pain, read the epistle to the Philippians for the cure. If you find yourself in conflict with other Christians, or if someone in the church has wounded you in some way, read Philippians. If you find yourself drawn to some new spiritual teaching and you wonder if it is of God—or if it is a deception—study Philippians.

There is a New Testament book of biology—the fundamental study of life itself, what makes the cells of the body function and live; that New Testament epistle is the book of Colossians. Here we see what powers and energizes the body of Christ and gives it life. We discover the force that binds Christians together.

There are even a couple of New Testament books of good mental health—the two letters to the Thessalonians. These books show us how to treat depression and despair within the body of Christ. When you (like the Thessalonian Christians) feel troubled and pessimistic about your present circumstances, when you are stricken with grief or fear, turn to Thessalonians. These books look into the future and set forth the certainty of Christ's second coming. Paul wrote these letters to fearful, distressed, depressed people who believed they might have missed Christ's return, who were heartsick over the deaths of loved

Ephesians

A careful study of the nature of the body of Christ

Philippians

A practical approach to the problems and diseases that threaten the health of the body

Colossians

The force that binds Christians together

1 and 2 Thessalonians

How to treat depression and despair within the body of Christ

ones. Paul wanted these people to know that when Jesus returned, no believer would be missed. The entire church would be together with Him. The key to 1 and 2 Thessalonians is found in 1 Thessalonians 5:23:

> May God himself, the God of peace, sanctify you through and through. May your whole spirit, soul and body be kept blameless at the coming of our Lord Jesus Christ.

Notice that God wants to give us peace, and He wants us to be whole and faultless in our entire being—not only the body and spirit, but the soul, the psyche, the mental and emotional being. That is the thrust of these two crucial letters of Paul.

1 and 2 Timothy

In Paul's two letters to Timothy, the young man who had accompanied him on his travels, we have the New Testament analogy to neurology—the study and science of the nervous system. In the body of Christ, you find certain people who have been specially gifted by God to act as the nerve centers, pathways, and stimulators of the body, carrying the message from the Head to the body. This special gift is suggested in Ephesians 4, where Paul says that Christ has given apostles, prophets, evangelists, and pastor-teachers to the church in order to build up the believers so that they can carry out the work of the ministry. Here is one of those gifts to the church—a young man named Timothy. Paul invests in him special instructions about how to stimulate, activate, and mobilize the body, how to instruct its leaders, how to probe and prod and correct and rebuke where need be. The first letter is a message of instruction and encouragement for a young pastor ministering under fire, while the second letter offers specialized instruction in view of growing apostasy and decline in order to keep a church from losing its life and vitality.

Special instructions about how to stimulate, activate, and mobilize the body, how to instruct its leaders, how to probe and prod and correct and rebuke

Titus

A book about physical conditioning and general fitness

When you come to the epistle of Titus, you find a similar discussion of the workings of the body. Here, however, the emphasis is not so much on the ministry of the nervous system of the body as on the body itself, on the muscle tone and fitness of the body. You might think of Titus as a book on physical conditioning and general fitness. It shows the kind of disciplined training that the body must be subjected to on a regular basis in order to keep the body in fighting trim. We see this emphasis on discipline and training in the key passage of the book, Titus 2:12–13:

> [The grace of God] *teaches us* [some translations say "trains us"] *to say "No" to ungodliness and worldly passions, and to live self-controlled, upright and godly lives in this present age, while we wait for the blessed hope—the glorious appearing of our great God and Savior, Jesus Christ.*

The concluding letter of Paul is like a physician's book of good nutrition. The body of Christ needs good nutrition in order to live, and the nutrients that we find throughout Paul's epistles—but especially in the letter to Philemon—are love, grace, acceptance, and forgiveness. Without these nutrients, the body of Christ withers and dies. Philemon, one of the shortest books in the Bible, places a beautiful emphasis on the unity of the body. The thrust of the book concerns a slave, Onesimus, who has run away from Philemon, his master. Onesimus has found Paul in Rome and has been led to Jesus Christ. Now Paul sends Onesimus back to Philemon, urging the man to accept Onesimus back—not as a slave but as more than a slave, as a beloved and forgiven brother in Christ. In this epistle, more than any other, we see that the ground is level at the foot of the cross; all distinctions between Christians are done away with in Christ. As Jesus said, in Matthew 23, there is only one Master, the Lord Jesus, and under His lordship we are all brothers and sisters—equals.

This is life and health in the body of Christ. This is what it means to be in Christ and to have Christ living in us. Now, let us open these epistles, one by one, and begin building their rich and powerful truths into our lives.

The Master Key to Scripture

A church I know of in Montana was once regarded as the most liberal church in the city of Great Falls. The pastor happened to be in Chicago one weekend, so he decided to visit Moody Church to see what the fundamentalists were saying. He was looking, quite frankly, for something to criticize. There, he listened to Dr. Ironside teaching from the book of Romans—and to his own amazement, this theologically liberal pastor found his heart gradually being challenged and won over by the message.

After the service, this pastor went forward and talked with Dr. Ironside, who gave him a copy of his lectures on Romans. This man read the book of sermons on the train back to Montana. By the time he reached Great Falls, he was a transformed man. He went into his pulpit and began to proclaim the truths of the book of Romans, and the church was soon transformed. With my own eyes, I saw this church completely changed from a dead, liberal theology to a vibrant evangelical testimony in the space of a few years—and that transformation took place by the power of the book of Romans.

The book of Romans was written to the Christians in Rome by the apostle Paul. He was spending a few months in Corinth before going up to Jerusalem to carry the collection of money that had been gathered by the churches of Asia for the needy saints in Jerusalem. We do not know how the church in Rome was founded, though it may have been started

The power of Romans

by Christians who had been converted at Pentecost and returned to the imperial capital. Paul was writing to them because he had heard of their faith, and he wanted to fulfill it to the utmost. He wanted them to be soundly based in the truth. So this letter constitutes a magnificent explanation of the total message of Christianity. It contains almost every Christian doctrine in some form, and it is a panorama of the marvelous plan of God for the redemption of humanity.

If you had no other book of the Bible than this, you would find every Christian teaching at least mentioned here. That is why I call this book The Master Key to Scripture. If you really grasp the book of Romans in its totality, you will find yourself at home in any other part of the Scriptures.

In the introduction, contained in the first seventeen verses, Paul writes to us about Christ, about the Roman Christians, and about himself. As in every good introduction, he declares here the major themes of the letter. The letter itself is divided into three major divisions:

Chapters 1 through 8—doctrinal explanations of what God is doing through the human race and His redemption of our total being: body, soul, and spirit.

Chapters 9 through 11—Paul's illustration of the principles of the first eight chapters, as demonstrated in the life and history of the nation Israel.

Chapters 12 through 16—Practical application of these mighty truths to everyday human situations.

These three divisions grow naturally out of one another, and these three sections, taken together, cover all of life. If you will remember this simple outline, you will have a key to the book of Romans. Here is a structural overview of the book:

God's Righteousness Revealed (Romans 1–8)

1.	Introduction	1:1–17
2.	The problem: our guilt before God	1:18–3:20
	A. The guilt of the Gentiles	1:18–32
	B. The guilt of the Jews	2:1–3:8
	C. Conclusion, all are guilty	3:9–20
3.	Justification: covered by God's righteousness	3:21–5:21
4.	Sanctification: God's righteousness demonstrated in our lives	6–8

Lessons in God's Righteousness from the Nation of Israel (Romans 9–11)

5.	Israel's past: chosen by a sovereign God	9:1–29

6. Israel's present: Israel seeks the "righteousness" of works, rejects the righteousness of Christ — 9:30–10:21
7. Israel's future: the nation will ultimately be restored by God — 11

The Nuts and Bolts of Righteousness: Practical Application of the Principles of Romans (Romans 12–16)

8. Christian duties and responsibilities — 12–13
9. Principles of Christian liberty — 14:1–15:13
10. Conclusion, benediction, personal greetings — 15:14–16:27

This letter moves in such a logical development that the best way to gain an appreciation of it is to trace Paul's argument, without getting bogged down in details, so that we might see the devastating logic by which the apostle develops his theme. When we are through, we will see how magnificently he has captured all the mighty truths of the gospel for us.

To begin with, in chapter 1, we have the central affirmation of the letter to the Romans: the power of the gospel of Jesus Christ:

> *I am not ashamed of the gospel, because it is the power of God for the salvation of everyone who believes: first for the Jew, then for the Gentile (1:16).*

This statement demonstrates Paul's clear understanding of what the gospel truly is: God's dynamic power. After all, who could be ashamed of possessing the infinite power of God, the greatest force in the universe? The powerful gospel of Jesus Christ can change lives, heal relationships, and rescue lives from addiction, depression, desperation, and despair. That is the power of God at work. That is the gospel.

Next, Paul explains the power of the gospel by quoting from Habakkuk as he lays out his core theme in the letter to the Romans:

> *In the gospel a righteousness from God is revealed, a righteousness that is by faith from first to last, just as it is written: "The righteous will live by faith" (1:17).*

This is the verse that burned its way into Martin Luther's heart, touching off the Reformation. That is Paul's theme: the righteousness of God that is revealed in the gospel.

In the rest of chapter 1, on into chapter 2, and through most of chapter 3, Paul looks at the world around him. He analyzes the state of humankind and sees two apparent divisions of the human race.

The power of the gospel

Someone has well said, "There are only two classes of people, the right-eous and the unrighteous, and the classifying is always done by the righteous." I've seen the truth of that statement in my own backyard. When my children were very small, I stepped into the backyard one day and found that someone had taken a piece of chalk and had drawn a line down the center of a panel of the backyard fence. One side of the fence was headed Good People, and the other side, Bad People. Under the heading Bad People were listed the names of the neighbor children. On the other side were the names of my children. It was obvious who had drawn up these classifications: The righteous, of course!

The wrath of God is revealed

The apostle Paul starts his argument with the Bad People, the unrighteous, the evildoers:

> *The wrath of God is being revealed from heaven against all the godlessness and wickedness of men who suppress the truth by their wickedness (1:18).*

Against the Bad People

That verse says a great deal. It says, for instance, that the problem with people is that they have the truth, but they will not look at it; instead, they suppress it. If you want proof of that, I suggest you look at your own life for a while and also at the lives of those around you. Isn't the power of denial strong in us all? Isn't it true that, if there is an unpleas-ant or unwelcome truth confronting us, our first impulse is to attack it, argue with it, or simply shove it down into our subconscious minds? This is why people keep so busy in the rat race of life, never wanting to be alone, never wanting to stop and reflect on the deep issues and questions in life. As long as we stay busy, we don't have to face the truth. Suppression of the truth is the central problem of human existence.

Because of the suppression of His truth, the wrath of God is con-tinuously pouring out upon humankind. His wrath is described for us as this chapter develops. It turns out not to be lightning bolts from heaven flung at wicked people who step over God's boundary lines. Rather, God is saying to us, "Look, I love you, and because I love you, I don't want you to do certain things that will bring harm, shame, pain, and destruction to you. But I have also given you free will. I will not control your choices. If you insist on doing these harmful, shameful, self-destructive acts, then I won't stop you—but you will have to accept the consequences. You can't make a choice to live any way you please while avoiding the consequences of that choice."

The way God's wrath of works, "God gave them over"

Three times in this chapter we see how the wrath of God works as Paul repeats the phrase, "God gave them over." The wrath of God results in this condition:

They have become filled with every kind of wickedness, evil, greed and depravity. They are full of envy, murder, strife, deceit and malice. They are gossips, slanderers, God-haters, insolent, arrogant and boastful; they invent ways of doing evil; they disobey their parents; they are senseless, faithless, heartless, ruthless (1:29–31).

That is the condition of the rebellious people who display their hostility toward God and suppress of the truth of God by flagrantly disobeying Him, observing no standard, living as they please, and doing what they like. The result is moral decay and the perversion of the natural drives of life. Even the sexual drives become perverted, so that men give themselves to men and women to women, as this chapter describes. This is exactly what is taking place in our society today—open moral rebellion and open sexual perversion. God does not hate the people who do such things; He truly loves them—but He will not remove either their free will nor the consequences of their actions.

In chapter 2, the apostle turns to the other side, the Good People, the so-called moral and religious people who are by this time very delightedly pointing the finger at the Bad People who are guilty of so much open and vile wickedness. Paul says to the righteous people, "Wait a minute! You Good People don't get off that easy!" He writes:

Against the Good People

You, therefore, have no excuse, you who pass judgment on someone else, for at whatever point you judge the other, you are condemning yourself, because you who pass judgment do the same things (2:1).

Do you see what Paul is doing? He is casting a net that draws us all in—even you and me! At first, we think Paul is just talking about those Bad People over there. Then we discover that he is talking about us too! We may not go in for sexual immorality, and we may not be major lawbreakers, and we may see ourselves as good people—but in the end, we are forced to admit that we are as guilty as anyone else. No one has any reason to see himself or herself as more righteous than anyone else.

Those who point the finger at the homosexual or the drug addict must face the truth about themselves: The sins of so-called Good People are many, and they include such acts as hatred, malice, gossip, slander, deception, and more. The Good People may be more adept at covering up their sin, but inside them, their hearts are filled with envy, lies, and evil.

So Paul has held up a mirror to each of us—and the image we see is not pleasant. God has judged us all to be equally guilty, apart from His own righteousness.

Next, the Jew comes in and says, "What about me? After all, I am a Jew and have certain advantages before God." Paul examines this claim and shows that the Jew is in exactly the same boat as the others. Despite being a descendent of Abraham and Jacob, despite being a member of the chosen people, in terms of righteousness, Jews are no better off than the Gentiles. So Paul's conclusion is that all of humanity stands, without exception, in need of a Redeemer.

This dismal diagnosis of the human condition serves to prepare the way for the gospel, as we see in Romans 3:19–20:

> Now we know that whatever the law says, it says to those who are under the law, so that every mouth may be silenced and the whole world held accountable to God. Therefore no one will be declared righteous in his sight by observing the law; rather, through the law we become conscious of sin.

We are all guilty

The law of God has condemned us all, without exception, because all, without exception, have sinned as Romans 3:23 tells us:

> For all have sinned and fall short of the glory of God.

Or, as the J. B. Phillips paraphrase renders it, "All have sinned and missed the beauty of God's plan." So we stand condemned according to the *law* of God—but the *grace* of God stands ready to rescue us and redeem us! We see this redemption take form in Romans 4. In fact, Paul outlines three phases of redemption for us:

1. Justification
2. Sanctification
3. Glorification

Three phases of redemption

Beginning in the closing verses of Romans 3 and continuing into Romans 4, Paul illustrates for us the meaning of justification. He begins by showing us that justification means that God gives us a righteous standing before Him on the basis of the work of Christ. Another One has died in our place. Another One has met our need. We could never do it ourselves, for we are totally incapable of pleasing God in our own strength with our own shabby righteousness. As a result, righteousness is not something we can earn; it only comes to us as we accept the gift of God in Jesus Christ. That is justification.

1. Justified

Justification means that God gives us a righteous standing before Him on the basis of the work of Christ

Justification involves the entire human being—body, soul, and spirit. God begins with the spirit, the deepest part of our humanity. There, He implants His Holy Spirit. The Spirit seals our righteous standing before God. Justification is therefore a permanent, unchangeable thing. It is far more than forgiveness of sin, although it includes forgiveness. It is—and this is truly amazing—*the condition of standing before God as if we had never sinned at all!* It is Christ's righteousness imputed to us, reckoned to your account and to mine. When this takes place we are delivered from the penalty for sin.

Paul illustrates this truth for us in chapter 4 where he says that both Abraham and David were justified on this basis, the basis of God's free gift of grace, accepted by faith—not on the basis of circumcision or obeying the law or by any of the things people do to please God. No religious hocus-pocus, no striving to obey an unreachable moral standard would be adequate in God's sight. Only God's grace, flowing forth from the cross, is adequate. And God's grace can be appropriated only by faith.

Abraham looked forward and saw the coming of the Messiah (Christ) and believed God; as a result, he was justified by his faith. David, although he was guilty of the twin sins of adultery and murder, believed God and was justified so that he could sing about the person "to whom God would not impute iniquity." So, these men are examples from the Old Testament of how God justifies.

Unfortunately, many Christians stop right there. They think that is all salvation is about—a way to escape hell and get to heaven. But there is more to the human life than the spirit and far more to the Christian life than the salvation of the spirit. We are also made up of a soul and a body—and the soul and body must be delivered also. So, beginning in chapter 5, Paul sets forth God's plan to deliver the soul (that is, the mind, the emotions, and the will).

The soul of humanity, born of Adam, is under the reign of sin. The flesh (if you want to use the biblical term for it) rules us. The life of Adam possesses us, with all its self-centered characteristics. Even though our spirits have been justified, it is quite possible to go on with the soul still under the bondage and reign of sin. So, though our destiny is settled in Christ, our experience is still as much under the control of evil as before we were Christians. That is why we often experience up-and-down times with the Lord—sometimes looking to Him as our Savior, living for Him as our Lord, while at other times slipping back into the terrible bondage of sin.

What is God's solution to this yo-yo existence we find ourselves in? Sanctification. The word *sanctify* means to "dedicate to God" or to "set apart for God." It comes from the same root word from which we get the word *saint*—because a saint is nothing more or less than a person who is dedicated or set apart for God. All genuine Christians, all committed followers of Christ, are saints, sanctified and set apart for His service. God intends to see us not only saved, but free—free from the

In Adam

In Christ

His death for us produced our justification; our death with Him produces our sanctification

reign of sin in our lives. Paul outlines the program of sanctification for us in Romans 5. He takes the two basic divisions of humankind—the natural being in Adam and the spiritual being in Christ—and contrasts them side by side.

"Look," he says, "when you were in Adam, before you became a Christian, you acted on the basis of the life that you had inherited from Adam. You did things naturally, and what you did naturally was wrong, it was self-centered. Sin is the natural heritage you have received from your father, Adam. But now, when you become a Christian, God does something to that old life. He cuts you off from this life in Adam. You are no longer joined to fallen Adam, but you are joined to a risen Christ, and your life is now linked with him. He wants to express His life through the new you, just as Adam once expressed his life through the old you."

When you learn the process of sanctification, it becomes easier to be good in Christ, just as it was once easier and more natural to be bad in Adam. But it takes time to put our sanctification into practice. You do it feebly at first and you struggle with it. Perhaps it will take you quite a while to really see what Paul is talking about, but when you do, you will discover that where sin once reigned over you, chaining you under the power of death, Christ now reigns over you to life. Right now, in this life, you can experience victory in Christ where once you experienced only defeat in Adam.

Romans 6 begins to show us how to experience victory and sanctification in our everyday lives. Here Paul declares that God, through the death of Jesus, not only died for us, but *we also died with Him*. His death for us produced our justification; our death with Him produces our sanctification. That is a great truth. When God says He set us free from the life of Adam and linked us to the life of Christ, He really did! We don't always *feel* linked to Him— but feelings are variable and often deceptive. Feelings can be altered by so many factors—circumstances, chemical imbalances in the brain, blood-sugar levels, medications, chronic problems such as clinical depression, or even the weather. Feelings change—but our relationship to Jesus does not change with our moods. When God promises to weld a life to His, it stays welded, and we must believe God's promise, whatever our feelings.

God wants us to know that He now empowers us to be as good in Christ as we were once bad in Adam. Day by day, as you come into situations of pressure and temptation, remind yourself that what God says is true and act on it, even though you do not feel like it. You will not feel dead with Christ. In fact, you will probably feel as if this evil within you is very much alive and that it has control over you. The thought will come to you that if you live a sanctified Christian life, you will be missing out, you will be at odds with the world around you, and you will lack satisfaction in life. These are the lies of the flesh. Instead, trust the truth of the Spirit that comes from God.

When pressures and temptations come, whom will you believe? The One who loves you? The One who gave Himself for you? If you believe Him, He will prove that His Word is true in your life, and He will lead you safely to a place of liberty and deliverance.

Romans 7 introduces the issue of our inner struggle, the warfare that goes on between our old Adam nature and our new Christ nature, between the flesh and the spirit. It is a lifelong, frustrating struggle that virtually all Christians wish would simply go away. Paul writes:

> I do not understand what I do. For what I want to do I do not do, but what I hate I do. And if I do what I do not want to do, I agree that the law is good. . . . What a wretched man I am! Who will rescue me from this body of death? (7:15–16, 24).

You can hear the anguish of Paul's soul as he describes the inner conflict in which he wrestles with himself. What is wrong? The problem is that we usually try to be good according to the strength of the flesh—and the flesh is weak and ineffectual against evil and temptation. The flesh is the Adam in us. The best good that the flesh can do is still hopelessly bad in the eyes of God. So what is the solution? Fortunately, Paul shares the solution with us in the next few verses:

> Thanks be to God—through Jesus Christ our Lord!
> So then, I myself in my mind am a slave to God's law, but in the sinful nature a slave to the law of sin.
> Therefore, there is now no condemnation for those who are in Christ Jesus, because through Christ Jesus the law of the Spirit of life set me free from the law of sin and death. For what the law was powerless to do in that it was weakened by the sinful nature, God did by sending his own Son in the likeness of sinful man to be a sin offering (7:25–8:3).

There is nothing we can do for God—but He intends to do everything through us. When we come to that realization, we come into deliverance. That is when we begin to fully realize what it means to have our minds, emotions, and wills brought under the control of Jesus Christ. That is when we experience the glorious, triumphant power that He has made available to us. That is the process (and it truly is a process, not an instantaneous event!) of the sanctifying of the soul.

The warfare between flesh and spirit

There is nothing we can do for God—but He intends to do everything through us

We have looked at the justification of the spirit and the sanctification of the soul. But what about the body? Romans 8 gives us the answer. Here Paul shows us that while we are still in this life, the body remains unredeemed. But the fact that the spirit has been justified and the soul is being sanctified is a guarantee that God will one day *redeem and glorify the body* as well. When we enter at last into the presence of Christ, we shall stand perfect in body, soul, and spirit before Him. That is the exultant thought that erupts into a great, tremendous anthem of praise at the close of this chapter:

> *In all these things we are more than conquerors through him who loved us. For I am convinced that neither death nor life, neither angels nor demons, neither the present nor the future, nor any powers, neither height nor depth, nor anything else in all creation, will be able to separate us from the love of God that is in Christ Jesus our Lord (8:37–39).*

Election and predestination

In chapters 9 through 11, Paul answers many of the questions that naturally arise from a careful consideration of his argument in the first eight chapters. In Romans 9, he deals with the issue of God's sovereignty, including the paradoxical fact that human beings have free will at the same time that God in His sovereignty chooses us—the question of election and predestination. We tend to think that God is unfair if He does not choose to save all people, but the fact is that our entire race is already lost in Adam; we have no right to be saved, no right to question God's choices, no rights at all. It is only God's grace that saves us, and we have no right to complain to God that some are saved while others are lost.

The sovereignty of God and human freedom

In Romans 10, Paul links the sovereignty of God with the moral responsibility and freedom of man. God chooses, but so do we—and the great spiritual paradox of free will and predestination is that while God has chosen us, we have also chosen Him. All people have the same free will, which operates in harmony with God's sovereignty and predestination in some mysterious way that is beyond our understanding. Salvation is a choice of faith. As Paul observes:

> *The righteousness that is by faith says: "Do not say in your heart, 'Who will ascend into heaven?'" (that is, to bring Christ down) "or 'Who will descend into the deep?'" (that is, to bring Christ up from the dead). But what does it say? "The word is near you; it is in your mouth and in your heart," that is, the word of faith we are proclaiming: That if you confess with your mouth, "Jesus is Lord," and believe in your heart that God raised him from the dead, you will be saved. For it is with your heart that you believe and are justified, and it is with your mouth that you confess and are saved (10:6–10).*

You need not climb up into heaven to bring Christ down or go down into the grave to bring Him up from the dead—which is what you would have to do in order to be saved by your own efforts. It can't be done. The word is already in your mouth that Jesus is Lord; only believe in your heart that God has raised Him from the dead, and you will be saved.

In Romans 11, Paul shows us that even as God set aside Israel for a time, in order that grace might do its work among the Gentiles, so God has completely set aside the flesh, the fallen nature, so that we might learn what God will do for us and through us. When we freely admit that without Christ we can do nothing—and when we live our lives accordingly, totally dependent upon Him—then we discover that *we can do all things* through Him who strengthens us (see Phil. 4:13). And what an amazing discovery that is!

Pride, therefore, is our greatest temptation and our cruelest enemy. Someday, even our flesh will serve God by His grace—our glorified flesh. In the day when creation is freed from its bondage to sin and the sons of God stand forth in resurrection bodies, then even that which was once rejected and cursed shall demonstrate the power and wisdom of God.

A living sacrifice

The final section, chapters 12 through 16, begins with these words:

> *I urge you, brothers, in view of God's mercy, to offer your bodies as living sacrifices, holy and pleasing to God—this is your spiritual* [or reasonable] *act of worship (12:1).*

The most reasonable, intelligent, thoughtful, purposeful, spiritual thing you can do with your life, in view of all these great facts that Paul has declared to you, is to give yourself to God and to live for Him. Nothing else can fulfill you to any degree. Therefore, give yourself to Him as a living sacrifice. It's the only reasonable thing to do!

How do we do that? How do we offer our bodies as living sacrifices to God? That's what the rest of Romans is about: Practical application of these truths in our everyday lives. When you follow these principles, you will find your life being changed in all your relationships. First, it is changed with regard to your Christian brothers and sisters, as Romans 12:3–13 shows. Presenting your body as a living sacrifice affects your life in the church.

Relationships among Christians

Next, as we see in Romans 12:14 through the end of chapter 13, Paul shows how this way of life affects our relationships to the governing powers and to society in general. Even your inner attitudes will be different, as Paul tells us in Romans 14 and 15. Your attitudes toward

Relationships to government and society

those who disagree with you and hold different values than you will be changed. Also, your attitude toward the lost will be transformed. You will feel a burning passion to reach those who are lost and live apart from Christ.

There is no more powerful way to close this brief survey of the master key to Scripture than with the same words Paul uses to conclude this powerful epistle, Romans 16:25–27:

> *Now to him who is able to establish you by my gospel and the proclamation of Jesus Christ, according to the revelation of the mystery hidden for long ages past, but now revealed and made known through the prophetic writings by the command of the eternal God, so that all nations might believe and obey him—to the only wise God be glory forever through Jesus Christ!*

The Epistle to the 21st Century

O
urs is a society devoted to sensualism and pleasure, where hardly any sexual deviation is too extreme to be censored or forbidden. It is also an information-oriented society, devoted to the rapid transmission and endless analysis of events, ideas, and philosophies. That sounds like a description of America at the brink of the twenty-first century—but it is also a description of the city of Corinth in the first century.

Paul's first epistle to the Corinthians is important and extremely relevant to us today because it so thoroughly captures the problems that we face as Christians living in a postmodern, post-Christian age—an age of tabloid TV, radio talk shows, rampant prostitution, pornography, homosexuality, and child pornography. Of all the cities we find in the New Testament, Corinth is the most typically American. It was a resort city, the capital of pleasure-seeking in the Roman Empire. Located on the Peloponnesian peninsula, Corinth was a beautiful city of palms and magnificent buildings.

Corinth was a gathering place for the great thinkers and speakers of Greece. They would come together in the public forums and talk endlessly about various ideas and issues, from politics to philosophy, from economics to metaphysics, from entertainment to morality. These were the low-tech forerunners of our mass-media public forums today— Oprah and Rosie, Rush Limbaugh and Larry King, America Online and

Corinth: like society today

the Internet. The city of Corinth was the cultural heir of the great thinkers of the Golden Age of Greece; Socrates, Plato, and Aristotle all had their devoted followers within the city of Corinth.

The city was also devoted to the worship of the goddess of sex. In the city of Corinth, there was a temple dedicated to the Greek goddess of love, Aphrodite, and part of the worship of the Greek goddess was the performance of certain religious ceremonies involving sexual activity. The priestesses of this temple were actually prostitutes, and some ten thousand of them served in the temple. The city was openly given over to the most depraved forms of sexual activity, and then—as now—unrestrained sensualism and obscenity were not only tolerated, but approved by the leaders and opinion-makers of society.

A problem church but a commendable church

Into this city comes the apostle Paul. You remember the story from the book of Acts. Paul had come down through Thessalonica and had been driven out of that city by an uprising of the Jews against him. From there he passed briefly through the little city of Berea and then went down into Athens. Walking through Athens, he noted the many temples to various pagan gods, and he went to preach to the Athenians on Mars Hill. When he left Athens at last, he came down across the little isthmus into Corinth. There he stayed for a period of about a year and a half to two years, preaching the gospel and making tents for a living.

Paul with Aquila and Priscilla

In Corinth, Paul found a couple who had come from Rome named Aquila and Priscilla who were also tentmakers, and he stayed with them and led them to Christ. He formed a church in their home and the gospel spread throughout the city from that first Corinthian church. Many Corinthians on hearing the gospel believed and were baptized and became members of this church. This was the church to which Paul wrote his letter. As you read it, you see that the Corinthian church was a problem-plagued church—probably the biggest problem church in the New Testament!

But although there were a great many things wrong with the Corinthian church, there were also many commendable aspects of the church. As Paul begins his letter to them, he affirms these commendable aspects. He begins by reminding them of their calling to be sanctified and holy, set apart for God's service:

> To the church of God in Corinth, to those sanctified in Christ Jesus and called to be holy, together with all those everywhere who call on the name of our Lord Jesus Christ—their Lord and ours:
> Grace and peace to you from God our Father and the Lord Jesus Christ (1 Cor. 1:2–3).

He goes on to talk about some of the reasons why the Corinthian believers are what they are: followers of the Lord Jesus Christ. He talks about the great themes of the Christian faith, which the Corinthians have believed and put into practice. He notes that they have received Christ by faith and by grace, and so they have entered into a new life. Soon, Paul comes to the key statement of this entire letter—the statement around which every other point in this letter is built:

God, who has called you into fellowship with his Son Jesus Christ our Lord, is faithful (1:9).

That is the central truth of the Christian life: We are called to share the life of the Son of God. That is what fellowship is: *sharing.* Fellowship with anyone is a sharing time, and that is what God has called us to. Everything that follows in this letter gathers about this verse and this concept of sharing and fellowship with Jesus.

The letter to the Corinthians falls into two major divisions: first, a section dealing with what we might call "the carnalities," chapters 1 through 11. Then, in chapters 12 through 16, we have what Paul himself calls "the spiritualities." The carnalities include everything that is wrong with the Corinthian church. The spiritualities include everything the church needs to do to correct it.

The carnalities versus the spiritualities

**The Carnalities—What Is Wrong
(1 Corinthians 1–11)**

**The Spiritualities—How to Correct
What Is Wrong (1 Corinthians 12–16)**

As you read this letter through, you will see not only the problems of the Corinthian church but you will recognize the problems of the church in America today. We, like the first-century Corinthians, suffer today from all the carnalities—at least in principle. And in order to set our lives straight, we need the spiritualities.

So this letter is directed especially to those (such as we Americans at the brink of the twenty-first century) who live in a sex-saturated atmosphere, dominated by the constant ebb and flow of ideas and information. It is directed to Christians who are living in the midst of pressures and temptations of the kind you and I face every day.

Three major problems

In the first section, Paul addresses the problems of this church in trouble, and he identifies three major problem areas: First, there is the problem of divisions within the church. Second, there is the problem of scandals in the church. Third and finally, he takes up certain questions that the Corinthian Christians have asked him about. All of these issues are brought together under the major heading, The Carnalities, the things that were troubling the church.

1. Healing the divisions

The first problem—divisions—is the result of the surrounding culture infecting the church. And this is a problem we contend with today. You hear it again and again: "The church is lagging behind! The church is out of step! We need to catch up with the times in which we live!" While I would never want the church to be stodgy and resistant to change, I would be even more horrified to see the church become indistinguishable from the world around us! When a church begins to reflect the spirit of the age in which it lives, it ceases to reflect Jesus Christ, it ceases to be sanctified, set apart, and distinct from the culture. When that happens, the church loses its power—and that is what had happened to the church at Corinth.

The Corinthian Christians had allowed divisions over human philosophies to come into the church. They had chosen certain religious leaders to gather around, and so now they were divided into factions, saying, "I follow so-and-so, and his insights are better and truer than the foolishness you and your leader believe!" Sects, factions, and cliques had arisen so that some were following Peter, some Apollos, and some were gathering about the teachings of Paul himself. There was even an exclusive little group who claimed to be the purest of all—they said they followed Christ alone! And they were the worst troublemakers of all because of their spiritual pride!

Paul answers this problem with a tremendous word in which he shows that human wisdom is useless. Paul sets it aside completely and says that in the church human insights are always partial and untrustworthy to a great degree. The Corinthians will never learn anything, he insists, until they give themselves to the wisdom of God. "For since in the wisdom of God the world through its wisdom did not know him," he writes in 1 Corinthians 1:21, "God was pleased through the foolishness of what was preached to save those who believe." The deep issues of God and the life of the spirit cannot be settled by a popularity contest or by philosophical debate. They can only be settled by the Word of God.

The deep issues of God and the life of the spirit can only be settled by the Word of God

That is still true today. The church will never solve its problems as long as it constantly pursues this writer and that teacher, this pastor or that speaker. Insight comes from the Spirit of God, speaking to us through His Word. I would frankly be horrified if you were to read this book, then go around quoting Ray Stedman! I intend for this book to be a guide, a kind of road map in your own personal study of God's Word. If you emerge from our adventure together through the Bible better equipped to go out and say, "This is what the Bible says about that," then I will be pleased, I will feel I have done my job. If you quote me, I will have failed.

The apostle Paul answers the factions and divisions in Corinth by confronting the Corinthian church with the word of the cross—the word that presents the cross of Christ as the instrument by which God cuts off all human wisdom, not as being worthless in its own narrow realm, but as being useless in solving the major problems of human beings. Paul writes,

The cross cuts off all human wisdom

> The message [or word] of the cross is foolishness to those who are perishing, but to us who are being saved it is the power of God (1:18).

When we understand this, we realize that we will never begin to learn until we first learn that we do not know anything. When we come to appreciate the word of the cross, we understand that upon the cross of Jesus Christ, God took His own Son, a completely perfect human being, made like us in every way, and nailed Him up to die. That is the word of the cross. That is why it looks so foolish to the natural man and woman.

The cross of Christ operates on a totally different principle than worldly wisdom; in fact, it is like a saw that rips across the grain of the wisdom of this world. Once we understand and accept that fact, says

Paul, we begin to discover that true, secret, hidden wisdom that unwraps the problems of life and answers them, one by one. We begin to understand ourselves and to see why this world is the way it is and where it is heading and why all the confusion and problems of life exist.

Paul is saying, in effect, "I'm not going to waste time arguing with you about the philosophies of Socrates or Plato or Aristotle or the wisdom of any other human being. They have their place, but when it comes to solving the deep-seated problems of human nature, there is only one wisdom that can touch it, and that is the word of the cross." This becomes, then, one of the mightiest answers of all time to the intellectualism that constantly hounds the Christian church and attempts to undermine it. God designed us to learn, inquire, and wonder—but He never intended that all our knowledge should come from worldly sources. He designed us to learn from Him, to seek our answers from Him. And He provided the answers in the form of revelation in Scripture. Our knowledge must have a right foundation, so He calls us back to the principle He laid down in the Old Testament:

> The fear of the LORD is the beginning of wisdom, and knowledge of the Holy One is understanding (Prov. 9:10).

That is the true source of knowledge and wisdom. That is where we begin.

What is the source of all the divisions in the Corinthian church? It's not what you might think or what the Corinthians thought—differences of human points of view. No, you can have many points of view on many issues in a church and still have unity and fellowship. The source of these divisions was carnality, pride, the fleshly desire to have preeminence and to be idolized and praised. Paul tells them that while carnality is at work in their lives, they will remain spiritual infants. They will never grow.

So it is with you and me. All that we do in the flesh is wood, hay, and stubble, fit only to be burned. All the praise we crave and seek from others is worthless—no, worse than worthless, for when we crave it and seek it, we bring division and destruction to God's work. God's judgment is true and it is relentless; He is not the least bit impressed by the works we do in the flesh. Only what is done in the Spirit will last. The word of the cross must come in and cut off the flesh before we can experience growth and maturity. Until that happens, division and conflict will reign in the church and in our lives.

Next, Paul turns to the matter of the scandals that were occurring in this church. These were, of course, also the effects of the carnality of the

The source of division was carnality, pride, and the fleshly desire to have preeminence and to be idolized and praised

2. Dealing with the scandals

Corinthian church. There was, first of all, an intolerable case of sexual immorality in the church—and this case was being openly regarded with acceptance and tolerance! Paul's response: This sin must be dealt with! Whenever sin breaks out openly and there is no repentance, the church must act in discipline—yet the Corinthian church had failed to act! As a result, immorality was eating away at the ranks of the Corinthian church.

Here again we see a parallel to the church today. It is frightening to see certain leaders of the church openly advocating sexual immorality, encouraging young people to sleep together and live together, and commending people in openly immoral relationships for the ministry. Today, as in first-century Corinth, we are surrounded by a culture that accepts immorality as normal, even healthy. But we in the church must stand for the fact that the violation of God's laws of sexual conduct are, in fact, a violation of the humanity of the individuals involved.

It is not just the wrath of God that burns when there is sexual sin, it is truly the love of God that burns. God loves us too much to allow us to hurt ourselves and each other by abusing one another sexually, joining ourselves body and soul to those with whom we have no lifelong, God-honored relationship, and using each other for self-gratification rather than honoring one another other as brothers and sisters in Christ. It is not only God's law but God's love for us that is transgressed when we sin sexually against one another.

If we want young people to keep themselves sexually pure, we must help them to understand that sex is more than just a matter of "thou shalt not." They need to understand that their bodies are the temples of the Holy Spirit. The Son of God Himself dwells in us, and we are never out of His presence. Everywhere we go, He goes with us and is in us. Everything we do is done in the presence of the Son of God Himself. Would we drag Jesus into a house of prostitution, into the presence of pornography, or into the backseat of a car? What a horrible thought! If our young people can learn to practice His presence and to consciously take Him wherever they go, they will be better equipped to withstand the pressures and temptations that come their way.

Marriage and other matters

Beginning with chapter 7, Paul turns to the four major questions they had written to him about—marriage, meat that had been offered to idols, women's hats, and the Lord's Table.

On marriage

On marriage: The Corinthians had asked Paul if it was right to be married, in view of the pressures that surrounded them. They wondered if, perhaps, they should give themselves completely to the service of God in an ascetic lifestyle. Although Paul himself was not married, nevertheless he told them in this section that it is best, if possible, for men and women to be married, that marriage is a perfectly proper way of life.

Each man should have his own wife and each woman her own husband; that was in view of the Corinthian conditions.

Then he went on to say that it is also right to have a single life if God grants this as a special calling to any individual. Singleness, too, is a perfectly honorable way of life. Marriage is not a necessity, though it is often an advantage. But marriage can also be a problem. Paul deals very thoughtfully, helpfully, and carefully with this whole question of marriage.

About meat

Second, the Corinthians had written Paul about meat that had been offered to idols. They were worried about offending God and about offending the conscience of the weaker Christian in this matter. Although we are no longer troubled by the problem of whether we ought to eat meat offered to idols or not, we are still confronting this same principle. We have Christian taboos about many issues that are not directly addressed or stated to be evil in Scripture: smoking, social drinking, dancing, and many other issues.

It is interesting that Paul was an apostle, with all the authority of an apostle, but he absolutely refused to make up any rules along this line. This is because the weak, immature Christians always want somebody to put them under law, but if you put Christians under law, then they are no longer under grace! And Paul knew that Christians must learn to deal with what he calls "the law of liberty." The fact is that all things are right; nothing is wrong in itself. No urge or desire is wrong in itself; we are at liberty in these things.

But with this law, he links two other laws. One he calls the "law of love"; that is the law that says, "I may be free to do it, but if I am really putting a stumbling block in somebody else's path, I won't do it." This limitation is not imposed by my conscience but by another's conscience—and by my Christian love for that person. I set aside my rights in order to avoid offending the person whose conscience is more legalistic or fragile.

The other law Paul appeals to is the "law of expediency"; that is, everything is legal and lawful, but not everything is helpful or expedient. There are a lot of things I could do, and many directions I could go as a Christian, but if I spend all my time doing all the things I am free to do, I no longer have any time to do the things I am called to do. That is not helpful or expedient.

About women's hats

Third, the Corinthians had written Paul about women. Specifically, there was a problem with women's hats. Hats? Yes, hats! It sounds silly to our culture, but it was a big issue in that time and place—and not as silly as you might think. This particular church had a problem because of the local culture. If a woman was seen bareheaded in Corinth, she was immediately identified as a prostitute, one of the temple priestesses, and that is why Paul writes to these people in Corinth and says, "You women, when you come to church, put a hat on! It is a sign that you are a Christian woman subject to your husband" (my paraphrase; see 1 Cor. 11:3–16).

The fourth problem they wrote Paul about concerned the Lord's Table. There were certain ones who were partaking of the Lord's Supper in a mechanical way, seeing no meaning and having no insight into what they were doing. So the apostle had to show them that everything the Christian does must be done realistically, with a clear understanding of the meaning of the Lord's Supper and with a recognition that it must be done as to the Lord.

In chapter 12 through the rest of the book, Paul deals with the great spiritualities, the correction to these carnalities. You do not correct these problems by just trying to straighten yourself out by your own efforts. You must begin with a recognition of the ministry of the Holy Spirit in your life.

Notice that chapter 12 begins with that very word *spiritualities,* as we see in verse 1:

Now about spiritual gifts, brothers, I do not want you to be ignorant.

Where was the word *spiritualities?* The English translation here uses two words, "spiritual gifts," but in the original Greek language, there is only one word here, and it is a word that might most literally be interpreted "spiritualities."

Paul says he does not want the Corinthians to be uninformed concerning the spiritualities. Why not? Well, because the spiritual realm, even though invisible, is the realm of ultimate reality. The spiritualities make all other realms of life work. It is the presence of the Spirit that makes Christ real to us, and the gifts of the Spirit—the spiritualities—are designed to make the body of Christ function effectively and in a healthy way. As the church performs its function, it reaches out and affects society on every side, carrying out the eternal plan of God.

We have missed so much of the great richness of the provision of Christ for His church. We know so little about the gifts of the Spirit. What is your gift? Do you know? Have you discovered it? Are you using it? Or do you need the same spiritual prodding that Paul gave Timothy:

For this reason I remind you to fan into flame the gift of God, which is in you through the laying on of my hands (2 Tim. 1:6).

The body of Christ functions by the exercise of its gifts, and every Christian has *at least* one gift. There are many different gifts; we do not all have the same gift. That's why we need each other in the body of

Christ: No two Christians are alike, and no one Christian is expendable. If one Christian fails to exercise his or her gifts, the entire body of Christ suffers.

This is a beautiful chapter, clearly showing us that we must not despise or offend one another because of a difference in gifts. One of the most beautiful—and convicting—passages in this chapter is the passage that clearly defines the church as a body made up of many indispensable parts:

> *God has arranged the parts in the body, every one of them, just as he wanted them to be. If they were all one part, where would the body be? As it is, there are many parts, but one body.*
>
> *The eye cannot say to the hand, "I don't need you!" And the head cannot say to the feet, "I don't need you!" On the contrary, those parts of the body that seem to be weaker are indispensable, and the parts that we think are less honorable we treat with special honor. And the parts that are unpresentable are treated with special modesty, while our presentable parts need no special treatment. But God has combined the members of the body and has given greater honor to the parts that lacked it, so that there should be no division in the body, but that its parts should have equal concern for each other (1 Cor. 12:18–25).*

The Love Chapter

As we live in unity, carrying out our functions in the church and in the world by exercising our spiritualities, our spiritual gifts, in the power of the Holy Spirit, the world will be rocked on its heels by the force of our love and our witness. The proof that God is real and active in the world is the proof that we demonstrate in our lives. We demonstrate God's reality and power when we have learned the secret set forth in the next chapter, the famous Love Chapter of the New Testament, 1 Corinthians 13. The most startling aspect of Paul's description of love—considering how the word *love* has come to be defined in our culture as a warm-fuzzy feeling or even as sex—is the way he defines love not as an emotion but as a *decision* and as an *act of the will:*

> *Love is patient, love is kind. It does not envy, it does not boast, it is not proud. It is not rude, it is not self-seeking, it is not easily angered, it keeps no record of wrongs. Love does not delight in evil but rejoices with the truth. It always protects, always trusts, always hopes, always perseveres. Love never fails (vv. 4–8).*

Then in chapter 14, Paul takes up another problem that was causing confusion in the church: the misuse of one of the gifts, the gift of tongues. The presence of the false use of tongues is a problem in our society today as it was when Paul addressed it in this chapter. To correct these abuses, Paul attempts to focus this section on the importance of the gift of prophecy. It is always amazing to me how many read this chapter and entirely miss the apostle's point. The whole purpose of the chapter is to encourage those with the gift of prophecy to exercise it. But you hardly ever hear anything about that today. These days, we hear a lot about tongues but very little about prophecy. Paul was trying to play down the gift of tongues and play up the gift of prophecy. The gift of prophecy is simply the ability to explain and expound the Scriptures, to speak comfort and edification and encouragement from the Scriptures.

Chapter 15 places great emphasis on the Resurrection. What would any of these truths be worth if we did not have a living Christ to make them real? The Resurrection is the great pivot upon which the entire Christian faith balances. Without the Resurrection, all else that is Christianity collapses. If Jesus Christ was not raised from the dead, then, as the apostle says in this chapter, we are hopeless, and not only that, we are the most to be pitied of all people—we are nuts, we are fools, we ought to be locked up somewhere if Christ was not raised from the dead.

But praise God, the Easter event was a real event that occurred not in someone's imagination but in history, in time and space! Jesus is alive! And that is why Paul can close chapter 15 with this word of confidence and encouragement:

> My dear brothers, stand firm. Let nothing move you. Always give yourselves fully to the work of the Lord, because you know that your labor in the Lord is not in vain (v. 58).

Chapter 16 is Paul's postscript in which he catches up on certain matters that the church needed to know about, such as the need to take a regular collection, the commending of certain missionaries, Paul's personal plans, and a few last-moment words of encouragement:

> Be on your guard; stand firm in the faith; be men of courage; be strong. Do everything in love (vv. 13–14).

Like the first-century Corinthians, we live in a world of pressures, temptations, and constant spiritual and moral battles. But you and I have everything we need to win the victory. We have the spiritualities of God—and these are more than enough to make us super-conquerors over the carnalities of the flesh and Satan.

The gift of tongues

The Resurrection

The Resurrection is the great pivot upon which the entire Christian faith balances

Paul's P.S.

When I Am Weak, I Am Strong

S ome years ago, I visited the city that Paul addresses in this epistle. Visiting the ruins of the city of Corinth was a tremendously moving experience for me. There is very little left standing of the original city because it was destroyed by the Romans a few short years after Paul's visit there. It has been in ruins ever since. Some temple columns remain, as well as the marketplace and other public areas of the city. The actual pavement of the judgment hall of the Roman proconsul is well preserved.

It wasn't hard for me to imagine the apostle Paul as he came down from Athens into this city which was, at the time, a center of pleasure, a center of public discourse and philosophical debate, and a great commercial city. It was certainly a city of great beauty, with many richly adorned temples to pagan gods and goddesses. It had gained a reputation as the center of lascivious worship—the worship of the goddess of love, Aphrodite. Her temple was the site where some ten thousand prostitutes (for that's exactly what a priestess of Aphrodite was) carried on their trade. Corinth represented a sex-saturated society, much like our own. You can see indications of this in Paul's letters to the Corinthian church.

As I stood among the ruins of the city of Priscilla and Aquila, where Paul had preached and labored for God while supporting himself as a tentmaker, I couldn't help thinking of certain phrases that come right

Corinth: a sex-saturated society much like our own

The background of the letter

A group of people who wanted to reintroduce hard-line, legalistic Judaism into Christianity caused a great deal of trouble in the church

out of this letter of Paul's. Reading through Paul's second letter to the church at Corinth made me aware that this is one of the most personal and emotional of all his letters.

To understand 2 Corinthians, it's important to grasp the background and context in which it was written. After Paul had established the church there and labored in the city for almost two years, he left and went to the city of Ephesus on the Asian mainland. From there he wrote his first letter to the Corinthians. Its purpose was to correct some of the divisions that had arisen in the church at Corinth as well as some of the scandals that had rocked the church. After Paul had written that first letter, a group of people who wanted to reintroduce hard-line, legalistic Judaism into Christianity caused a great deal of trouble in the church and gained a great deal of influence over the people. This group was headed by a teacher who opposed Paul and had probably come over from Jerusalem, infecting the church and teaching the people that they had to observe the Law of Moses. Calling themselves the "Christ party," they represented themselves as the only true followers of Christ and the law of God, and they claimed that the great themes of grace taught by Paul were not authentic Christianity. Paul makes reference to these people who claim to follow only Christ in his first letter (see 1 Cor. 1:12).

After Paul had written the first letter, this faction apparently took over the church in Corinth, so Paul revisited Corinth for a short time and apparently was rebuffed by the church leaders. The very church Paul had planted had become so permeated with false Christianity that Paul himself was not welcome there! So Paul returned to Ephesus. From there he wrote a short, sharp, emotional letter, rebuking and reproving the Corinthian Christians for allowing themselves to be misled—but that is not this letter. That letter has been lost to us. It is clear that Paul penned a letter that was not preserved—perhaps because Paul, writing in anger, may have said things that went beyond what the Holy Spirit intended. Or perhaps that letter simply dealt with temporal matters of the Corinthian church—matters that would not be meaningful to us today. In any case, that lost letter certainly did not have the force of Scripture. If God had wanted that letter saved, it would not have been lost.

That letter was sent by the hand of Titus. While Titus took the letter to the church at Corinth, the apostle remained in Ephesus, anxiously waiting to hear what the Corinthians' response would be. This is the chord that was struck in the opening verses of 2 Corinthians. Paul tells them that he has been troubled about them. He has undergone intense suffering while waiting in Ephesus for word from them. In chapter 1, verses 8–9, he writes,

> *We do not want you to be uninformed, brothers, about the hardships we suffered in the province of Asia. We were under great pressure, far beyond our ability to endure, so that we despaired even of life. Indeed, in our hearts we felt the sentence of death. But this happened that we might not rely on ourselves but on God, who raises the dead.*

Then he tells them how anxious and concerned he was about them in chapter 2, verse 4,

> *I wrote you out of great distress and anguish of heart and with many tears, not to grieve you but to let you know the depth of my love for you.*

So he was waiting in Asia for a response from the Corinthian church—but while he was waiting, trouble arose in the Ephesian church. This trouble is recorded in Acts 19. There, the silversmiths caused a great commotion in the city, and Paul was threatened with being dragged before the Roman judges. He escaped and decided to go on to Macedonia to meet Titus, who would be coming up through Macedonia on his return from Corinth, and because his anxiety over the Corinthians was so great, he could wait no longer for news. He also intended to raise money there for the relief of the Christians in Jerusalem, who were suffering from a famine. With these two concerns weighing heavily on his heart, Paul went to Philippi in Macedonia.

There Paul met Titus and received word that the sharp letter he had written to the Corinthians had accomplished its work. The majority of the Corinthian Christians had repented of their rejection of his ministry and had begun to live again the life of Jesus Christ. A minority was still unyielding, however, and continued to rebel against the authority of the apostle. So, from the city of Philippi, Paul wrote this letter, 2 Corinthians, a letter that expresses so much of the anxiety and agitation of heart that he experienced.

With that background you can understand something of the passion of the apostle as he writes. Out of his tears and heartache come the great spiritual themes embodied in this letter:

The themes of 2 Corinthians

1. Ministry within the church (chapters 1–4);
2. Giving and service, or ministration by the church (chapters 5–10); and
3. Authority, wise exercise of church leadership (chapters 11–13).

Here is a structural overview of Paul's second letter to the church at Corinth:

Ministry within the Church (2 Corinthians 1–4)

1.	Introduction	1:1–11
2.	Paul's change of plans, inability to come to Corinth	1:12–2:4
3.	Forgive and restore the repentant sinner	2:5–13
4.	Christ causes us to triumph	2:14–17
5.	Paul's ministry, a ministry of changed lives, a ministry of the new covenant, a ministry of Christ	3:1–4:7
6.	The trials of ministry	4:8–15
7.	Our motivation for serving God	4:16–18

Giving and Service Ministration by the Church (2 Corinthians 5–10)

8.	Our future reward for serving Christ	5:1–16
9.	The ministry of reconciliation	5:17–21
10.	Giving no offense to others	6:1–10
11.	Paul's appeal for reconciliation in the church and separation from harmful influences	6:11–7:1
12.	Paul and Titus	7:2–7
13.	The Corinthians' response to 1 Corinthians	7:8–16
14.	Paul's collection for needy Christians and principles of godly giving	8–9
15.	Paul answers accusations against him	10

Authority, Wise Exercise of Leadership (2 Corinthians 11–13)

16.	Paul's own apostleship and authority	11:1–12:6
17.	Paul's thorn in the flesh and God's sufficient grace	12:7–10
18.	The signs of Paul's authority as an apostle	12:11–13
19.	Paul discusses his plans for a future visit	12:14–13:10
20.	Conclusion	13:11–14

In the opening chapters, we discover a declaration of what true Christian ministry ought to be. As Paul states in chapter 3, for instance, it is not the ministry of the old covenant but of the new. In other words, the message is not the demand of the law upon people to compel them to follow certain rules and regulations. When Christianity becomes a set of do's and don'ts, it always becomes a deadly, stultifying, *dangerous* thing. At that point, it is no longer a living relationship with a loving Lord but a grim determination to cross all the *t*'s and dot all the *i*'s of the law. These are demands made upon the flesh. As

Paul says, the old covenant, exemplified by the Ten Command-ments, makes its demands upon us but without an accompanying dynamic to fulfill it. It is a ministry of death. As he writes in 2 Corinthians 3:6:

> *He has made us competent as ministers of a new covenant—not of the letter but of the Spirit; for the letter kills, but the Spirit gives life.*

Next, Paul traces the history of the new covenant. This is the new arrangement for living not the old grim determination to clench your fists and set your teeth and try to do what God demands—that is not true Christianity. The new covenant relationship is the realization that He has provided the Holy Spirit to minister the life of a risen Lord in your life. The same power that raised Him from the dead is available to you as strength and grace to do all that life demands of you. That is the new arrangement for living. Here we find the exciting resources of the Christian life. What are these resources?

First resource: the Word of God. The business of a minister of Jesus Christ (and remember, *all* Christians are called to be His ministers—not just pastors and teachers) is to declare the Word of God. Notice how Paul puts it:

> *Since through God's mercy we have this ministry, we do not lose heart. Rather, we have renounced secret and shameful ways; we do not use deception, nor do we distort the word of God. On the contrary, by setting forth the truth plainly we commend ourselves to every man's con-science in the sight of God (4:1–2).*

Here we see not only the failure of the first-century church, but of today's church in so many areas—clever, subtle tampering with the Word of God, undermining its authority, subverting its message, ignor-ing its witness, refusing to act upon its truth.

Second resource: the mysterious indwelling treasure of the Spirit of God. Paul addresses this resource in 2 Corinthians 4:7:

> *We have this treasure in jars of clay to show that this all-surpassing power is from God and not from us.*

Victorious living does not come from a charming personality or by being clever or educated. Victorious Christian living comes from this treasure hidden inside the earthen vessel of our lives. The power of a vic-torious life comes from the Spirit of God, not from us. This is the secret by which God's power is released in our lives.

The Christian's resources

The Word of God

The indwelling Spirit of God

Third resource: hope. Paul goes on to declare the great hope of the believer:

> *We fix our eyes not on what is seen, but on what is unseen. For what is seen is temporary, but what is unseen is eternal (4:18).*

We know that we have a body that cannot be destroyed—"an eternal house in heaven," as 5:1 tells us, "not built by human hands." God has a great future ahead for us. The life we now live is the preparation for that life that is to come. The present is but a prologue to the future.

Chapter 5 also reveals to us the radical transformation that takes place when we commit ourselves to Christ. In verse 17, Paul writes:

> *If anyone is in Christ, he is a new creation; the old has gone, the new has come!*

We are new in Christ, and as a result, God has given us a new ministry and a new message: the ministry and message of reconciliation:

> *All this is from God, who reconciled us to himself through Christ and gave us the ministry of reconciliation: that God was reconciling the world to himself in Christ, not counting men's sins against them. And he has committed to us the message of reconciliation (5:18–19).*

That is our theme. That is our banner headline, unfurled before all the people of the earth: You can be reconciled to God through faith in Jesus Christ. With that as our message and ministry, we have become what Paul calls ambassadors for Christ, His representatives to the world:

> *We are therefore Christ's ambassadors, as though God were making his appeal through us. We implore you on Christ's behalf: Be reconciled to God. God made him who had no sin to be sin for us, so that in him we might become the righteousness of God (5:20–21).*

That is the gospel in a nutshell.

Giving and service: The ministration of the church

In chapters 8 and 9 we have Paul's declaration of the ministrations of the church. Because of the great famine in Jerusalem, Paul was taking up a collection for the physical relief of the saints in that city. Giving, said Paul, is the proof of genuine Christian love. Paul appeals to the Corinthian believers to open their hearts to give, just as they have received from Jesus Christ:

For you know the grace of our Lord Jesus Christ, that though he was rich, yet for your sakes he became poor, so that you through his poverty might become rich (8:9).

Here, as in many place in Scripture, we see a spiritual paradox at work: Christianity operates in poverty, making many rich. Jesus, the Creator of the universe, set aside His riches and entered into His creation in a state of poverty in order to enrich us all by His grace. He is our pattern. We are to give in order to enrich others with the grace of Jesus Christ. This passage is not a justification for high-pressure financial campaigns or efforts to shame Christians into giving. Under God's economy, nobody is to be put under any compulsion. We are to give as each one has made up his or her own mind, according to personal conscience. As Paul writes:

> *Remember this: Whoever sows sparingly will also reap sparingly, and whoever sows generously will also reap generously. Each man should give what he has decided in his heart to give, not reluctantly or under compulsion, for God loves a cheerful giver. And God is able to make all grace abound to you, so that in all things at all times, having all that you need, you will abound in every good work (9:6–8).*

Have you dared to put God's economic plan to the test? His Word is as true in our century as it was in the first century.

Authority — wise exercise of church leadership

In chapters 10, 11, and 12, Paul's tone changes. He begins to speak to that rebellious minority of Christians in Corinth who were still refusing the authority of his ministry among them. He wasn't confronting their disobedience to *him,* but to the *truth of God.* From this situation in the Corinthian church comes a great dissertation on the basis of authority in the Christian life. These false teachers had exalted themselves before the people on the basis of their lineage, their background, and their education. They were prideful and arrogant—and the apostle Paul takes on the entire basis of their arrogant claim to be leaders of the people.

Paul's personal credentials

In an ironic, almost sarcastic fashion, Paul shows these pretentious leaders the true basis of authority—and he does so by contrasting the credentials they care so much about (status, background, university degrees) with the credentials God gives (the knowledge of God). Paul is saying, in effect, "If you insist upon being impressed by these worldly symbols of authority, well I could boast before you too. If I did, I would be a fool. But since you are so impressed by such things, very well, I'll play your foolish game and boast a little. I'll tell you what God has done through me."

And then there comes this great passage in chapter 11:

> *What anyone else dares to boast about—I am speaking as a fool—I also dare to boast about. Are they Hebrews? So am I. Are they Israelites? So am I. Are they Abraham's descendants? So am I. Are they servants of Christ? (I am out of my mind to talk like this.) I am more. I have worked much harder, been in prison more frequently, been flogged more severely, and been exposed to death again and again. Five times I received from the Jews the forty lashes minus one. Three times I was beaten with rods, once I was stoned, three times I was shipwrecked, I spent a night and a day in the open sea, I have been constantly on the move. I have been in danger from rivers, in danger from bandits, in danger from my own countrymen, in danger from Gentiles; in danger in the city, in danger in the country, in danger at sea; and in danger from false brothers. I have labored and toiled and have often gone without sleep; I have known hunger and thirst and have often gone without food; I have been cold and naked. Besides everything else, I face daily the pressure of my concern for all the churches. Who is weak, and I do not feel weak? Who is led into sin, and I do not inwardly burn?*
>
> *If I must boast, I will boast of the things that show my weakness (11:21–30).*

Incredible credentials! Yet these, he is quick to add, are mere foolishness, idle boasts! "This is not where my authority lies," he is saying. "If you really want to know where my authority lies and where true spiritual power comes from, let me tell you how I began to learn the lesson. This is not going to sound very impressive, but I want you to know that I am telling you the truth. This is the event I boast about more than anything else in my life—the moment when I began to learn the secret of genuine power."

And, beginning with 11:31, Paul describes the time he had to be let down over the city wall of Damascus, just so that he could slink away into the darkness from the pursuing guards of King Aretas—as if he were a common thief! This is not a story of great victory and valor—it's a story of defeat and discouragement. Yet this is the story, Paul says, of the day he learned the secret of effective, victorious Christian living: "When I am weak, then I am strong."

He goes on in 12:6–10 to describe his thorn in the flesh, some ugly, painful aspect of his life—perhaps some physical affliction—and how he prayed earnestly three times that God would remove it. But God knew best, and God allowed Paul to keep his thorn in the flesh. God's message to Paul was:

"My grace is sufficient for you, for my power is made perfect in weakness." Therefore I will boast all the more gladly about my weaknesses, so that Christ's power may rest on me. That is why, for Christ's sake, I delight in weaknesses, in insults, in hardships, in persecutions, in difficulties. For when I am weak, then I am strong (12:9–10).

That is the secret of true Christian strength: not outward impressiveness; not great prestige, pomp, and favor; not degrees and honors and awards. No. Spiritual power never lies in the place of human pride and might. Neither does it lie in a brilliant, impressive personality nor in ability to speak with eloquent oratory. Spiritual power is found in the heart of the humble human being who fully recognizes his or her dependence on the living Lord within. The weaker you are, the stronger Christ can be.

In an epistle rich with meaning, this is perhaps the richest truth of all: *Out of weakness comes strength.*

So Paul closes the epistle by addressing the people at Corinth as he addresses us today,

Examine yourselves to see whether you are in the faith; test yourselves (13:5).

Do you truly believe and trust God, even in your times of trial and weakness? Are you counting on His strength rather than your own? Are you walking boldly into situations and going out on limbs for Him—not foolishly, but trustingly, knowing that He has led you there and wants to use you in your weakness, so that His might and power might be demonstrated to a watching world? That is the great secret of true Christian living:

Our weakness—His strength!

> Spiritual power is found in the heart of the humble human being who fully recognizes his or her dependence on the living Lord within

How to Be Free

T wo of the great leaders of the American Revolution in 1776 were the American-born Benjamin Franklin and the Englishman Thomas Paine. Once, as these two men were discussing their passionate belief in the concept of liberty, Franklin commented, "Wherever liberty is, there is my country."

Paine replied, "Wherever liberty is *not,* there is *my* country." In other words, Paine was committed to going wherever there was oppression and injustice and seeking to bring liberty to those countries. And he did so, passionately working for liberty—at great personal cost—in England, America, and France.

Paine's attitude is much like that of the apostle Paul, as expressed in his great epistle to the Galatians. Seeing both political and religious oppression on every hand, seeing people bound up and held down by laws and rules and legalism, the apostle Paul saw a large part of his mission as one of going wherever liberty is *not,* in order to bring freedom to people whose spirits and souls are in chains.

Galatians is probably the most colorful epistle in the New Testament. It is filled with vivid, forceful language. It is closely related to the epistles to the Romans and Hebrews. These three New Testament letters—Romans, Galatians, and Hebrews—form what might be regarded as an inspired commentary on a single verse from the Old Testament book of Habakkuk:

Our spiritual "Emancipation Proclamation"

The goal of this
epistle is that
Christians might
discover the liberty
of the children of
God in accordance
with all that God
has planned for
humanity in the
way of freedom
and enjoyment

The righteous will live by his faith (2:4).

All three of these New Testament letters quote this verse, and each of them offers a different aspect or dimension of this verse. In Romans, Paul places the emphasis on the words, "the righteous." Paul details what it means to be righteous and how a person becomes justified before God and declared righteous in Christ. It was the epistle to the Romans that delivered Martin Luther from his terrible legalism and showed him the truth of God's grace through faith.

In Galatians, Paul places the emphasis upon the words "shall live." His intention is to show us the source of life for a righteous person, justified in Christ. This is the letter of Christian liberty, the fullest expression of life and faith.

In Hebrews, you find an emphasis on the last words: by . . . faith. This is the great New Testament treatise on faith, culminating in that memorable section on the heroes of the faith in Hebrews 11, demonstrating that salvation by faith has always been by grace through faith, both in the Old Testament and in the New.

Galatians comes to grips with the question of what real Christian life is like. The answer can be framed in a single word: *liberty.* As Christians, we are called to liberty in Jesus Christ. The goal of this epistle is that Christians might discover the liberty of the children of God in accordance with all that God has planned for humanity in the way of freedom and enjoyment. Paul wants us to experience freedom to the utmost in our spirits, restrained only as necessary to be in harmony with the design of God. So it is with good reason that this letter has variously been called the Bill of Rights of the Christian Life, or the Magna Carta of Christian Liberty, or Our Spiritual Emancipation Proclamation—emancipation from all forms of legalism and bondage in the Christian experience.

Here is an overview of the structure of Paul's epistle to the Galatians:

The Gospel of Liberty (Galatians 1–4)
1. Introduction—Why have the Galatians departed from this gospel of liberty? 1:1–9
2. The gospel of liberty came directly from God 1:10–24
3. The gospel of liberty affirmed in Jerusalem and by Paul's rebuke to Peter 2
4. Salvation comes by faith, not works or the Law 3–4

How to Live Freely (Galatians 5–6)
5. Stand fast in your liberty 5:1–12

6.	In liberty, love one another	5:13–15
7.	Walk in the Spirit, not the flesh	5:16–21
8.	The fruit of the Spirit	5:22–26
9.	Live free, do good to all, care for one another	6:1–10
10.	Conclusion, including a curse upon those who impose their legalism on believers under grace	6:11–18

This is not a letter written to a single church as in the cases of the letters to Corinth and Ephesus. This letter is addressed to a number of churches. In the introduction of the letter we read:

The unique identity of the Galatians

> *Paul, an apostle—sent not from men nor by man, but by Jesus Christ and God the Father, who raised him from the dead—and all the brothers with me,*
> *To the churches in Galatia (1:1–2).*

Who were these Galatians? You find the background of the Galatian churches described in Acts 13 and 14. These churches were begun by Paul on his first missionary journey, when he traveled with Barnabas into the cities of Antioch, Iconium, Derbe, and Lystra. In Lystra, he was first welcomed and honored as a god—then he was later stoned and dragged outside the city and left for dead. In fact, he experienced persecution in every one of the cities in the region of Galatia.

The name of the province comes from the same root as the word *Gaul*, the ancient Roman name for France. I remember years ago studying Julius Caesar's *The Gallic Wars*, which begins with the Latin phrase, *Gallia est omnis divisa in partes tres*—"Gaul as a whole is divided into three parts." About three hundred years before Christ, Gauls from what is now France had invaded the Roman Empire and sacked the city of Rome. Then they crossed into northern Greece and continued across the Dardanelles straits into Asia Minor (modern Turkey). At the invitation of one of the kings of the area, these Gauls settled there.

So the Galatians were not Arabs or Turks or Asians. They were a Celtic race, of ancestry similar to that of the Scots, the Irish, the Britons, and the French. Since many Americans are also of that ancestry, this letter is particularly pertinent to us, as you will recognize when you read Julius Caesar's description of the Gauls: "The infirmity of the Gauls is that they are fickle in their resolves, fond of change and not to be trusted." Or, as another ancient writer put it, "They are frank, impetuous, impressionable, eminently intelligent, fond of show but extremely inconstant, the fruit of excessive vanity." Doesn't that sound like Americans? Certainly, much of the world would agree with that assessment!

The residents of Galatia were members of a Celtic race

On his second missionary journey, accompanied this time by Silas instead of Barnabas, Paul set out to return through these Galatian cities and visit the churches that had been established. On this second journey, he spent a considerable time in various cities of the region because he became sick. He refers to this illness in a rather oblique manner in this letter. Evidently it was some kind of serious eye trouble, for he says to the Galatians:

> Even though my illness was a trial to you, you did not treat me with contempt or scorn. Instead, you welcomed me as if I were an angel of God, as if I were Christ Jesus himself. . . . I can testify that, if you could have done so, you would have torn out your eyes and given them to me (4:14–15).

Some Bible scholars feel he had inflamed eyes that made him seem repulsive. Yet, these Galatians received him with great joy, treating him as though he were an angel of God or even Christ Jesus Himself. They reveled in the gospel of grace he brought because he had disclosed to them—with brilliant, vivid clarity—the glory and the work of the crucified Lord. As a result, they had entered into the fullness of life by the Spirit and had received the love, joy, and peace that Jesus Christ gives when He enters the human heart.

An apostle's anger

"Wolves"— Judaizers—had come among them

To these Gentile believers, who had just received from Paul the liberating gospel of Jesus Christ, these wolves declared a gospel of bondage, a gospel of laws, rules, and rituals

But as he writes this letter to the Christians in the region of Galatia (he is probably writing from the city of Corinth), something has happened. Certain people, whom Paul labels in another place "wolves" (see Acts 20:29), had come among them. Who were these wolves? They were Judaizers—hardened legalists who had come down from Jerusalem with what Paul calls "an alien gospel," a mixture of Christianity and the practices of Judaism. The gospel of the Judaizers was not a totally different gospel, but a perversion of the true gospel. To these Gentile believers, who had just received from Paul the fresh, liberating gospel of Jesus Christ, these wolves declared a gospel of bondage, a gospel of laws, rules, and rituals. In order to become *genuine* Christians, they claimed, the Gentiles would have to become circumcised, keep the Law of Moses, and obey all the Old Testament regulations. These legalists were trying to impose all the restrictions and the ceremonial obligations of the Law of Moses.

What about Jesus Christ and His complete work upon the cross? Well, these Judaizers hadn't set Jesus Christ aside—like most false gospels, the false gospel of the Judaizers maintained an outer shell of Christianity. But the heart of this false gospel was not grace and faith; it was works. The Lord Jesus Christ was given a secondary place in this gospel. Keeping the rules and rituals of the old Law of Moses was paramount.

Moreover, the Judaizers challenged the apostolic authority of Paul. They challenged him for being (in their view) independent, undependable, and overly enthusiastic. They even claimed he had graduated from the wrong seminary! So they were trying to get the Galatians to reject his authority as an apostle.

Paul was greatly disturbed by this news. As you read this letter you can see that he is agitated to the max! Listen to some of the expressions he uses:

> *Even if we or an angel from heaven should preach a gospel other than the one we preached to you, let him be eternally condemned! (1:8).*

To put it bluntly, Paul is saying that anyone who preaches a different gospel than the one he has already preached should be damned to hell! That should leave no doubt about the strength of the apostle's feelings on this matter! He repeats the same curse in the very next verse:

> *As we have already said, so now I say again: If anybody is preaching to you a gospel other than what you accepted, let him be eternally condemned! (1:9).*

When we hear such words as *damned,* we think of curses and insults—but Paul is not being gratuitous, profane, or indecent. He is simply facing the fact that any who come with a different gospel have already damned themselves. Such people have rejected the truth of the grace of Jesus Christ. Those who reject His grace and seek to work their own way to God through rituals or their own righteousness are accursed, as the full range of the New Testament makes clear. At the close of the letter, Paul's emotions are stirred against those who preach circumcision and legalism instead of the liberating grace of Jesus:

> *As for those agitators, I wish they would go the whole way and emasculate themselves! (5:12).*

In other words, "Since the Judaizers are so zealous to put Christians under bondage to circumcision, I wish that, while they're at it, they would *completely* remove their manhood!" You can see some of the fire that flashes throughout this letter. The apostle is deeply disturbed. He is armed for battle, and he is taking no

To put it bluntly, Paul is saying that anyone who preaches a different gospel than the one he has already preached should be damned to hell

prisoners! In fact, Paul is so intense and full of passion that he can't even wait for a secretary to take dictation. Despite his poor eyesight, he painfully, indignantly scrawls this epistle out in his own large-lettered hand.

Why is the apostle so angry with these Judaizers? Because they have perverted the purity of the gospel! And in doing so, they have attempted to reenslave those who are just becoming free through the grace of Jesus Christ! They are undoing everything Paul himself is trying to accomplish by preaching the gospel of salvation by grace through faith in Jesus Christ. The gospel is simplicity itself: First, Christ gave Himself for our sins—that's *justification.* Second, Christ gave Himself to deliver us from this present evil age—that's *sanctification.* All of it is by grace and not by works. It is the assault upon these truths that has so deeply disturbed the apostle. He knows that injecting legalism into Christianity kills the very heartbeat of the gospel and leads people back into bondage, failure, and misery.

These two issues of the gospel—justification and sanctification—make up the basic outline of the letter to the Galatians. Chapters 1 through 4 deal with the issue of justification by faith. Christ died for our sins—that's the basic declaration of the gospel, the good news that Christ has borne our sins. So Paul spends Galatians 1 defending this good news.

Paul's gospel

First he shows that it was revealed by Jesus Christ directly to him. He didn't get it from anyone, not even from the apostles. Christ Himself appeared to him and told him this good news. Paul writes,

Revealed to him by Christ

> *I want you to know, brothers, that the gospel I preached is not something that man made up. I did not receive it from any man, nor was I taught it; rather, I received it by revelation from Jesus Christ (1:11–12).*

Acknowledged by the apostles

Second, it was acknowledged by the other apostles as being the same gospel they received. Some people have claimed that Paul preached a different gospel than Peter, James, John, and the others—that Paul's gospel is superior to theirs. But Paul himself in this letter says that fourteen years after his conversion, he went up to Jerusalem and had an opportunity to compare notes with the other apostles. When he did so, the other apostles were amazed to discover that this man, who had never been a part of the original twelve, knew as much about the truth of the gospel as they did.

In fact, he knew what had gone on in the secret, intimate gatherings that they had had with the Lord Jesus Christ. You can see an example of this in 1 Corinthians, where the apostle describes the Lord's Supper. He says:

I received from the Lord what I also passed on to you: The Lord Jesus, on the night he was betrayed, took bread, and when he had given thanks, he broke it and said, "This is my body, which is for you; do this in remembrance of me" (1 Cor. 11:23–24).

How did Paul know all of this? He received it *directly* from the Lord Jesus. So when Peter, James, and John heard that this man knew as much about what had gone on in that Upper Room as they did, they recognized that here indeed was a man called of God. His apostleship, which came directly from Jesus Christ, rested upon that fact.

Third, it was not only revealed to him by Christ and acknowledged by the other apostles, but it was vindicated when Peter came to Antioch. Peter, the ostensible leader of the apostles, was in error in Antioch. You can read the story in Galatians 2:11–21. The difficulty between Peter and Paul was the matter of eating kosher foods versus Gentile foods. Peter had been a Jew, raised to eat nothing but kosher foods, but when he became a Christian, he ate with the Gentiles and thus indicated the liberty he had in Christ. But then, when certain men came down from Jerusalem, he began to compromise and went back to eating only with Jews, thus denying the very liberty that he had formerly proclaimed. This is what stirred up Paul and made him angry with Peter—publicly and to his face. Think of that! This maverick apostle challenged Peter the Rock! And he vindicated the gospel as he did so.

In chapters 2 through 4, Paul goes on to show us that the gospel is about salvation by faith and not by works. Jesus has done everything to secure our salvation; we can do nothing to secure our salvation. Moreover, our salvation is the result of a promise and not by law. This promise predates the Law of Moses, having been given to Abraham four hundred years before Moses was born. The Law, therefore, cannot change the promise. The promise of God stands true whether the Law comes in or not.

Paul also shows that those who are in Christ are children, not slaves. They are no longer servants but they are part of the family of God. In this connection, he deals with the great allegorical passages concerning Hagar and Sarah, the law, and the mountain of grace (Jerusalem that is above; see Gal. 4:25–26). From these passages he declares the great fact of justification by faith.

This was the truth that delivered the soul of Martin Luther. More than 450 years ago, the monk of Wittenburg strode up and nailed his Ninety-Five Theses to the door of the castle church and thereby began what we call the Protestant Reformation. Here was a man who had tried his very level best to find his way to heaven according to the pathway of works. He had done everything the church of his day suggested. He had tried fasting, indulgences, the sacraments, the intercession of the saints, penances, and confessions. He had endured nightlong vigils and heavy days of labor. He had done everything he could, but the harder he worked, the more his inner distress increased.

Finally, in complete desperation, he went to the head of the Augustinian order, of which he was a monk, and asked for some kind of release. The dear old man who headed the order knew little about the Word of God—so miserable was the condition of the organized church at that time—yet, he did tell Luther one thing: "Put your faith not in yourself but in the wounds of Christ." A dim ray of light broke through to Martin Luther's soul. But it wasn't until he was in his little room in the tower, preparing lectures on the Psalms for his students, that the full light suddenly shone upon his awareness. He was struck by a verse in the Psalms:

> *In you, O LORD, I have taken refuge; let me never be put to shame; deliver me in your righteousness (Ps. 31:1).*

This verse gripped Martin Luther's heart. It suddenly struck Luther that the righteousness of God was to him a terrible thing. He saw it as an unbending righteous judgment by which God would destroy everyone who failed in the least degree to measure up to the full expectation of the holiness of God. Luther said that he even hated the word *righteousness.*

But then as he began to investigate the Word, it led him to the epistle to the Romans where he read the words, "The righteous shall live by faith." That struck fire in his heart, and he saw for the first time that Another had already paid the penalty for sin so that he himself didn't have to. Christ had entered the human race and carried our guilt so that God might, in justice, accept us—not according to our merits or righteousness, but according to His. Martin Luther was never the same man again. This discovery led him to challenge the system of indulgences and all the other legalistic practices that kept people in bondage to the organized church and moved him to nail the theses to the door.

The unique gospel

It is interesting, as someone has pointed out, that every single religion known to humanity is a religion of works—*except the gospel of Jesus Christ!* Hinduism tells us that if we renounce the world and relate ourselves to the "spirit of the universe," we will at last find our way to peace. Buddhism sets before us eight principles by which human beings are to walk and thus find themselves on the way to salvation. Judaism says we must keep the Law absolutely and inflexibly and then we will be saved. Islam says that a person must pray five times a day and give alms and fast during the month of Ramadan and obey the commands of Allah. Unitarianism says that people are saved by having good character. Modern humanism says salvation is achieved through service to humankind. All are ways of works. In every case, salvation is said to be attained by something *we* must do.

But the good news of the gospel is that Jesus Christ has done it all! He *alone* has done what no one can do for himself or herself.

And He has set us free.

In Galatians 5 and 6, Paul turns to the second and equally important aspect of this great truth, summarized in the words I have emphasized below:

> [The Lord Jesus Christ] *gave himself for our sins* to rescue us from the present evil age, *according to the will of our God and Father (1:4).*

Christianity is not merely about going to heaven when you die (justification). It is also living now in this present life (sanctification). It is being set free from bondage to the world and its ways, its evil and wickedness. It is being liberated in the here and now. This, too, is by the gift of Jesus Christ. He came not only to deliver us from death, but also from this present evil age. How does He deliver us in the here and now? By living His life through us. That is the key to sanctification. We know that this age is evil. We feel its pressures to conform, to lower our standards, to believe all the lies shouted at us by TV, films, popular music, and the people around us.

But we fall into the trap of thinking that we can deliver ourselves! So we set up our Christian programs, we fill our days with activity, we teach Sunday school, we sing in the choir, we join a Bible study or a Christian club—and we think that we are free. These are all good things, of course, but they do not save us. If we think we are saved by all the good religious things we do, we are still in bondage. We are sunk to our eyeballs in Galatianism. We have fallen into the same bondage that had crept into the Galatian churches. We are living by works— not by faith.

In the closing two chapters of Galatians, we see that the whole point of our Christian walk is to repudiate the life of the flesh with its self-centeredness and to rely upon the work of the Spirit of God to reproduce in us the life of Jesus Christ. This is all gathered up for us in one of the best-known verses of the entire letter:

I have been crucified with Christ and I no longer live, but Christ lives in me. The life I live in the body, I live by faith in the Son of God, who loved me and gave himself for me (2:20).

The old self-centered "I" has been crucified with Christ so that it no longer has any right to live. Your task and mine is to see that it doesn't live, that it is repudiated, that it is put aside, along with its determination to express what Paul calls "the works of the flesh"—such acts as those listed in 5:19–21: sexual immorality, impurity, and debauchery; idolatry and witchcraft (a word that, in the original Greek, is linked to abuse of drugs for mind-altering, mood-altering purposes); hatred, discord, jealousy, fits of rage, selfish ambition, dissensions, factions, and envy; drunkenness, orgies, and the like. All of these ugly characteristics are the works of the flesh—the old self-centered life that, Paul declares, was judged and cut off at the cross, to be replaced by the life of Jesus Christ shining through us.

Instead of being controlled by the flesh, our lives are to show a growing evidence of control by the Spirit of God. The evidence that God is gradually sanctifying us and taking control of more and more of our lives is found in Galatians 5:22–23, in a list of character qualities that Paul calls "the fruit of the Spirit"—love, joy, peace, patience, kindness, goodness, faithfulness, gentleness, and self-control.

Now this is where Christian liberty enters in. You haven't begun to live as God intended you to live until the fruit of the Spirit is a consistent manifestation in your life. Anything less is the bondage of legalism, with its frustration, fear, and failure.

In Galatians 6, Paul describes how being filled with the Spirit enables us to experience true fellowship with each other in the body of Christ. When our lives show evidence of the indwelling of God's Spirit, we begin doing the things that lead to wholeness, health, and unity in the body of Christ: We begin bearing one another's burdens, restoring one another in meekness and gentleness. We begin giving generously and freely to meet one another's needs, and we begin sowing to the Spirit instead of to the flesh.

Paul's personal P.S.

Finally, Paul closes with one of the most intensely personal postscripts in the entire New Testament. He writes,

See what large letters I use as I write to you with my own hand! (6:11).

Painfully scrawling each letter, hampered by poor eyesight, he says in effect, "I do not glory in my flesh like these Judaizers do. They love to compel people to be circumcised because to them, each person circumcised is another scalp they can hang on their belts as a sign they have done something tremendous for God. That is not my glory. I glory only in the cross of Christ—and the cross cuts off that kind of living. The cross destroys the 'old man' with all his arrogance, ambition, and self-glorification."

Paul knows that his strong words in this powerful epistle will rub some people the wrong way. It will stir up anger and even opposition. And he is ready for it. He writes:

> Let no one cause me trouble, for I bear on my body the marks of Jesus (6:17).

In other words, "If anyone wants to oppose me or make life hard for me—don't even think it! I want you to know that living this kind of life has been costly for me. I have earned the hatred and persecution of many. I bear in my body the scars of serving the Lord Jesus."

If you challenge the world and its ways—and even if you challenge worldliness in the church—you will be resented, even hated. Some will be ready to burn you at the stake for defying the status quo. Your life judges theirs by shining the light of God's truth upon them—and they resent it. But the apostle Paul says, in effect, "It doesn't make any difference to me. I am scarred and battered and beaten, but I glory in the Lord Jesus Christ who has taught me what true liberty is. Wherever liberty is *not*, wherever people are being held in bondage and ignorance and oppression, wherever the grace of Jesus Christ is being subordinated to rituals and rules, that is where I will go. In the name of Jesus Christ, I will go where He sends me and say what He tells me to say, and I will point the way to liberty."

The Calling of the Saints

T he epistle to the Ephesians is, in many ways, the crowning glory of the New Testament. It would probably surprise you, however, to learn that this letter probably shouldn't be called "Ephesians"! The fact is, we don't really know to whom it was written. The Christians at Ephesus were certainly among the recipients of this letter, but undoubtedly there were others. In many of the original Greek manuscripts, there is actually a blank where the *King James Version* and the *New International Version* insert the words "at Ephesus." That is why the *Revised Standard Version* does not say, "To the saints at Ephesus," but simply, "To the saints who are also faithful in Christ Jesus."

In Colossians 4:16, Paul refers to a letter he wrote to the Laodiceans. Since our Bible does not include an epistle to the Laodiceans, many have assumed that this Laodicean letter was lost. Many other Bible scholars, however, feel that the letter to the Laodiceans is actually this very letter, the epistle to the Ephesians. Ephesus is located not far from Laodicea in Asia Minor (modern Turkey), and it is possible that Ephesus and Laodicea were two among several cities in the region that this letter was addressed to. This explanation may account for what would otherwise seem to be a lost letter from the apostle Paul to the Laodiceans.

The theme of this epistle is a grand and exalting theme, and Paul sets it forth in a way that is unique to this letter among all his letters in

Ephesians: the crowning glory of the New Testament

the New Testament. It is the theme of the nature of the true church, the body of Christ.

Here is an outline of the epistle to the Ephesians:

Our Position as Christians (Ephesians 1–3)

1. Introduction: we are redeemed by the Son, sealed by the Spirit — 1
2. Our position before God: once dead, now alive in Christ — 2:1–10
3. Our position in the church: Jews and Gentiles reconciled — 2:11–22
4. The mystery of the church revealed — 3

Our Lifestyle as Christians (Ephesians 4–6)

5. Unity in the church — 4:1–6
6. One church, many spiritual gifts — 4:7–16
7. Put off the old self, put on the new — 4:17–29
8. Do not grieve the Holy Spirit, but be filled with the Spirit — 4:30–5:21
9. Christian submission: husbands and wives, children to parents — 5:22–6:4
10. Service in the workplace — 6:5–9
11. Spiritual warfare: the armor of God, praying for boldness — 6:10–20
12. Conclusion — 6:21–24

You in Christ

As we discussed in chapter 54, "Letters to the Church," the first four letters of the New Testament—Romans, 1 and 2 Corinthians, and Galatians—develop the theme, *Christ in you,* teaching us what the indwelling life of Christ is intended to accomplish in us. But beginning with the letter to the Ephesians, the overarching theme of the epistles changes from Christ in you to *you in Christ.* In Ephesians through Philemon, we are to discover and understand what it means for us to be *in Christ* and to share the body life of the Lord Jesus Christ. Here is the great theme of this letter—the believer in Christ, and the believer in the body of Christ, the church. Paul sets the tone for his epistle in Ephesians 1:3:

> *Praise be to the God and Father of our Lord Jesus Christ, who has blessed us in the heavenly realms with every spiritual blessing in Christ.*

The heavenly realms

It is easy to misunderstand this phrase *the heavenly realms,* which appears several times in this letter. If you take this only as a reference to heaven after we die, you will miss the main thrust of Paul's message in Ephesians. While this phrase includes the fact that we are going to heaven someday, it speaks primarily about the life you are to live right now, here on earth. The heavenly realms are not off in some distant corner of space or on some planet or star. They are simply the realms of invisible reality in which the Christian lives right now, in contact with God and in conflict with the satanic realms in which we are all daily engaged. The heavenly realms are the seat of Christ's authority and power. In Ephesians 2:6, we are told,

And God raised us up with Christ and seated us with him in the heavenly realms in Christ Jesus,

But in Ephesians 3:10 we learn that in the heavenly realms are also found the headquarters of the principalities and powers of evil!

His intent was that now, through the church, the manifold wisdom of God should be made known to the rulers and authorities in the heavenly realms.

The nature of our conflict in the heavenly realms is disclosed in Ephesians 6:12:

For our struggle is not against flesh and blood, but against the rulers, against the authorities, against the powers of this dark world and against the spiritual forces of evil in the heavenly realms.

So you can see that when Paul talks about the heavenly realms, he is not talking about heaven at all but about an invisible but very real realm here on earth. He is talking about a spiritual kingdom that surrounds us on all sides and constantly influences and affects us, whether for good or evil, depending upon our own choices and our relationship to these invisible powers. In this realm, where every one of us lives, the apostle declares that God has already blessed us with every spiritual blessing. That is, He has given us all it takes to live in our present circumstances and relationships. Peter says the same thing in his second letter:

> When Paul talks about the heavenly realms, he is talking about a spiritual kingdom that surrounds us on all sides and constantly influences us, for good or evil

His divine power has given us everything we need for life and godliness through our knowledge of him who called us by his own glory and goodness (2 Peter 1:3).

That means that when you receive Jesus Christ as Lord, you have already received all that God ever intends to give you. Isn't that remarkable? The weakest believers hold in their hands all that is ever possessed by the mightiest saints of God. We already have everything, because we have Christ, and in Him is every spiritual blessing and all that pertains to life and godliness. Thus, we have what it takes to live life as God intended. Any failure, therefore, is not because we are lacking anything, but because *we have not appropriated what is already ours.*

You are the church

Most of us have a tendency to think of the church as something we go to, something we attend, something separate from us that we give a donation to. But Paul, in this powerful letter to the Ephesians, wants us to understand that we are the church and the church is us!

Every once in a while, when I was in the pastorate, someone would come to me and say, "The church ought to do such-and-such." And I would reply, "Well, you are the church; go do it." The person would always look at me with a bit of astonishment—and then say, "Okay, I will!" When someone would say, "The church ought to be more friendly," I would say, "All right, you and I are the church—let's be more friendly." When someone would say, "The church needs to do more to reach out to the community," I would say, "All right, you and I are the church—let's think of some things we can do to have a more effective ministry in the community." Invariably, that thought struck people as a breakthrough, a revelation—and it changed the way people lived their lives as members of the body of Christ.

The church is people. Every believer is a member of the body of Christ—the church—so I would prefer to go through this letter using the word *church* interchangeably with the word *Christian,* because every believer is a small replica of the whole church. If we understand that God lives within the church, then we must acknowledge that He also lives within each believer. Each one of us, as a believer in Jesus Christ, is a microcosm of the whole body. We can, therefore, go through this whole epistle relating what Paul says not to the church in some institutional sense, but to each one of us as individual believers.

Each one of us, as a believer in Jesus Christ, is a microcosm of the whole body

Metaphor 1: The church is a body

In Ephesians, Paul uses six metaphors to explain the nature of the church—and of the Christian—in relationship to Jesus Christ. In the first of these metaphors, he refers to the church as a body:

> *And God placed all things under his feet and appointed him to be head over everything for the church, which is his body, the fullness of him who fills everything in every way (1:22–23).*

The first chapter is entirely devoted to the wonder and amazement that we as ordinary, flawed, sin-drenched human beings should be called by God in a most amazing way to become members of that body. It is a tremendous declaration! The apostle Paul never got over his amazement that he—a bowlegged, baldheaded, half-blind former persecutor of the church should become a member of the Lord's own body, called by God before the foundation of the earth, blessed and equipped for everything that life could demand of him. That is what it means to belong to the body of Christ.

What is the purpose of the body? It is to be "the fullness of him who fills everything in every way." What a mighty phrase that is! Do you ever think of yourself that way? Do you ever dare think of yourself the way God thinks of you—as a body to be wholly filled and flooded with God Himself? If that were truly our perspective on ourselves as Christians as we go through our daily lives, I believe our lives would be transformed by that realization.

So the body of Christ is "the fullness of him who fills everything in every way." In other words, the body is the expression of the Head. That is what your own human body is for. It is intended to express and perform the desires of your head. The only time a healthy human body does not do that is when some secondary nervous center is artificially stimulated. For example, if you hit your knee in the right place with a hammer, your leg will kick up in the air without your even willing it. Even if you choose not to kick, it will react. I sometimes wonder if some of the activity of the church isn't a lot like that—an involuntary reflex action in which the body acts on its own without direction from the head.

Next, Paul uses the metaphor of a temple to describe the nature of the church:

In him the whole building is joined together and rises to become a holy temple in the Lord. And in him you too are being built together to become a dwelling in which God lives by his Spirit (2:21–22).

Here is a picture of a holy temple. When all the worthless products of human endeavor have crumbled into dust, when all the institutions and organizations we have built have been long forgotten, the temple that God is now building—His church—will be the central focus of attention through all eternity. That is what the passage implies. God is using us as His building blocks—shaping us, edging us, fitting us together, placing us in His design, using us in His plan, placing us in His temple in the place where we can be the most effective for His purpose. We are to be His temple, His house, His dwelling place, where He can enter in and say, "I'm home. This is where I am comfortable. This is where I am pleased to dwell."

> What is the purpose of the body?

> The body is the expression of the Head

> **Metaphor 2: The church is a temple**

> The temple that God is now building— His church— will be the central focus of attention through all eternity

Metaphor 3: The church is a mystery

Ephesians 3 introduces the third metaphor. Here we learn that the church is a mystery, a sacred secret:

> *Although I am less than the least of all God's people, this grace was given me: to preach to the Gentiles the unsearchable riches of Christ, and to make plain to everyone the administration of this mystery, which for ages past was kept hidden in God, who created all things. His intent was that now, through the church, the manifold wisdom of God should be made known to the rulers and authorities in the heavenly realms (3:8–10).*

The purpose of the mystery of the church is to make known the wisdom of God to the spiritual rulers of those invisible realms

There are wonderful intimations here that God has had a secret plan at work through the centuries—a plan He has never unfolded to anybody. But He has had a goal and a purpose in mind that He intends to fulfill, and the instrument by which He is doing it is the church. Paul is saying that, through the church, the manifold wisdom of God—all the many levels of God's knowledge and all the depths of His limitless wonders—will now be made known to all the principalities and powers that inhabit the heavenly realms. The purpose of the mystery of the church is to educate the universe—to make known the wisdom of God to the spiritual rulers of those invisible realms.

Metaphor 4: The church is a new self

In chapter four, the apostle uses a fourth metaphor:

> *Put on the new self, created to be like God in true righteousness and holiness (4:24).*

The church is a new being, a new self with a new nature, because every Christian in it is a new self. This metaphor is linked with Paul's statement in another letter:

> *Therefore, if anyone is in Christ, he is a new creation; the old has gone, the new has come! (2 Cor. 5:17)*

God is building up a new generation, a new race of beings, a new order of souls or selves the likes of which the world has never seen before

The present creation, which began at the beginning of the heavens and the earth, has long since grown old and is passing away. The world with all its wealth and its wisdom belongs to that which is passing. But God is building up a new generation, a new race of beings, a new order of souls or selves the likes of which the world has never seen before. It is a generation that is even better than Adam, better than the original creation—it is a new creation! In Romans, we learned that all we lost in Adam has been regained in Christ—and more!

For if, by the trespass of the one man, death reigned through that one man, how much more will those who receive God's abundant provision of grace and of the gift of righteousness reign in life through the one man, Jesus Christ (5:17).

Also in Romans the apostle Paul says that the whole creation is standing on tiptoe (that is the literal meaning)—craning its neck to see the manifestation of the sons of God, the day of the unveiling of this new creation (see Rom. 8:19). But remember, this new creation is being made right now, and you are invited to put on this new self, moment by moment, day by day, in order that you might meet the pressures and problems of life in the world today.

That is why the church is here. The church is a new self, and the purpose of the new self is to exercise a new ministry. In this same chapter of Ephesians, we read,

But to each one of us grace has been given as Christ apportioned it (4:7).

This new self in each of us has been given a gift (that is what is meant by the word *grace* in this verse) that we never had before we became Christians. Our task, our reason for existence, is that we might discover and exercise that gift. The reason the church has faltered and failed and lost its direction is that Christians have lost this great truth, and the gifts He has given us have gone undiscovered and unused. The risen Lord has given a gift to you, just as the lord in the parable gave the talents to each of his servants, entrusting them with his property until his return (see Matt. 25). When our Lord comes back, His judgment will be based on what you did with the gift He gave to you.

Ephesians 5 introduces another metaphor to describe the true nature of the church: The church is a bride:

Husbands, love your wives, just as Christ loved the church and gave himself up for her to make her holy, cleansing her by the washing with water through the word, and to present her to himself as a radiant church, without stain or wrinkle or any other blemish, but holy and blameless (vv. 25–27).

And then Paul quotes the words of God in Genesis:

"For this reason a man will leave his father and mother and be united to his wife, and the two will become one flesh." This is a profound

Creation is standing on tiptoe

When our Lord comes back, His judgment will be based on what you did with the gift He gave to you

Metaphor 5: The church is a bride

mystery—but I am talking about Christ and the church (Eph. 5:31–32).

The church is a bride, and Paul says Christ's intention in preparing the church as a bride is that He might present the church to Himself. Isn't that what every bridegroom desires—that his bride shall be his and his alone? During their early days of courtship she may go out with some other fellows, but when they are engaged she has promised to be his and they are both waiting for the day when that can be fully, finally realized. Then at last the day comes when they stand before the marriage altar and promise to love, honor, and cherish one another until death shall part them. They then become each other's—she is his and he is hers, for the enjoyment of each other throughout their lifetime together. That is a picture both of the church and of the Christian, in relation to Christ, the bridegroom.

Do you ever think of yourself this way? My own devotional life was revolutionized when it dawned on me that the Lord Jesus was looking forward to our time together. If I missed our time together, He was disappointed! I realized that not only was I receiving from Him, but that He was receiving from me, and that He longed and yearned for me. When I met with the Lord after that it was with a new sense that He loved me and delighted in our time of fellowship.

**Metaphor 6:
The church is
a soldier**

The last metaphor of the church that Paul paints for us in the epistle to the Ephesians is the metaphor of a soldier:

> *Therefore put on the full armor of God, so that when the day of evil comes, you may be able to stand your ground, and after you have done everything, to stand. Stand firm then, with the belt of truth buckled around your waist, with the breastplate of righteousness in place, and with your feet fitted with the readiness that comes from the gospel of peace. In addition to all this, take up the shield of faith, with which you can extinguish all the flaming arrows of the evil one. Take the helmet of salvation and the sword of the Spirit, which is the word of God (6:13–17).*

We are soldiers

What is the purpose of a soldier? To fight battles! And that is what God is doing in us and through us right now. He has given us the great privilege of serving on the battlefield upon which His great victories are won.

We are the
battlefield

In fact, there is actually a very real sense in which we are the battlefield! That is the essence of the story of Job. This man who dearly loved God was struck without warning by a series of tragedies. All in one day, he lost everything that mattered to him, everything he prized, even his entire family except his wife. Job didn't understand what was happening, but God had chosen Job to be the battlefield for a conflict with Satan. God allowed Satan to afflict Job physically, mentally, and materially, because God knew that Job was the perfect battleground upon which to win a mighty victory against the great invisible powers of the heavenly realms. Job was a soldier in a great spiritual battle—and so are you and I.

In his first letter, the apostle John writes to his young Christian friends:

> *I write to you, young men, because you are strong, and the word of God lives in you, and you have overcome the evil one (1 John 2:14).*

In other words, John is telling his young friends, "You have learned how to fight, how to move out as soldiers in a spiritual war, how to throw off the confusing restraints of the world, how not to be conformed to the age in which you live, how to move against the tide of the culture—and in so doing you have overcome Satan and you have glorified God!"

I love the story of Daniel who, as a teenager, was a prisoner in a foreign land. He was trapped in a pagan culture and had to fight the battle day by day, counting solely upon God's faithfulness to defend him when everything was against him. The pressures brought to bear upon him were incredible. Yet Daniel and his friends met the tests again and again. They won the battles, defeated Satan, and gave God the glory. In a tremendous spiritual battle, Daniel was a faithful soldier.

This is the privilege to which God is calling us in this day of world unrest and increasing darkness. This is the battle God calls us to as our world slips closer and closer to the mother of all battles, Armageddon. God is calling us to be soldiers, to walk in the steps of those who have won the battle before us. They have shown us how to remain faithful—even unto death. Battered, bruised, and bloodied, they have counted it a badge of honor to serve in God's army, to be wounded in service to the King.

God is calling us to to walk in the steps of those who have won the battle before us; they have shown us how to remain faithful—even unto death

This, then, is our sixfold calling. God has equipped us with every spiritual blessing, with every gift we need, so that we might become a body, a temple, a mystery, a new self, a bride, and a soldier for Jesus Christ. That is quite a calling. The ultimate exhortation of this letter is contained in Ephesians 4, where Paul writes,

> *As a prisoner for the Lord, then, I urge you to live a life worthy of the calling you have received (v. 1).*

Ephesians gives us an exalted picture—a series of pictures, in fact—to reveal to us the grandeur of the church in God's plan and the crucial importance of every believer in God's sight. Never lose sight of what God is doing through you, through the church. The world cannot see it, because the world is unaware of the heavenly realms. The world has no idea what is taking place through you and me, through the church. But you know what God is doing through you. His power surges through you. His love for the world flows out of you. His courage for the battle emboldens you. So do not lose heart. There's a war on—and you are on the winning side!

Christ, Our Confidence and Our Strength

T he letter to the Philippians has been called the tenderest of all Paul's letters. It is also the most delightful to read. It brims over with expressions of praise, confidence, and rejoicing, despite the fact that this is one of Paul's prison epistles, written from his confinement in Rome. We find the background for this letter in Acts 16, which tells of Paul's visit to Philippi and the founding of the Philippian church, and Acts 28, which tells the story of Paul's house arrest in Rome.

The founding of the Philippian church took place during the exciting and danger-filled days when Paul and Silas journeyed together on the second missionary journey. Arriving in Philippi, they first met a group of women having a prayer meeting by the riverside, and they shared the gospel with these women. One of them, Lydia, a seller of purple goods (one who dyed garments for royalty and the wealthy), invited Paul and Silas into her home, and her name has been known throughout the centuries because of her kindness and hospitality to the apostle Paul. The Philippian church had its beginning in Lydia's home.

Philippians: the tenderest of Paul's letters

Paul's preaching throughout the city stirred up a great deal of reaction. It aroused the resentment of the rulers so that Paul and Silas were arrested and severely flogged, then thrown into jail and their legs fastened in stocks. That same night, as Paul and Silas were praying and singing hymns to God and the other prisoners were listening to them, an earthquake struck—a quake so violent that the foundations of the prison were crumbled and broken. The prison doors flew open, and all the prisoners' chains came loose. The Philippian jailer, seeing that all the prisoners were free to escape, pulled his sword and would have fallen upon it when Paul shouted, "Don't harm yourself! We're all here!"

The jailer rushed in, fell at the feet of the two missionaries, and asked, "What must I do to be saved?"

"Believe in the Lord Jesus," they replied, "and you will be saved—you and your household."

Paul later went on to the cities of Thessalonica, Berea, Athens, Corinth, and other places in Greece. Years later, finding himself a prisoner of Nero in Rome, Paul thought back on his beloved friends in the church he had founded at Philippi—and he wrote a letter, the epistle to the Philippians. Although he was allowed to stay in his own rented house, awaiting trial before Emperor Nero, he was chained day and night to a Roman soldier. Paul knew his life could easily be forfeited when he appeared before Nero, yet this epistle glows with radiance and joy, confidence and strength.

If you are going through times of pressure and trial, I urge you to read this little letter. It will encourage you greatly, especially if you remember the circumstances out of which it comes.

The letter to Philippians is divided into four chapters that represent four natural divisions within the text. One of the abiding frustrations of many Bible teachers is the arbitrariness of the chapter divisions throughout Scripture. These divisions, of course, were not part of the original Scripture text but were added much later. In many passages of Scripture, chapter divisions are inserted right in the middle of a thought, chopping up the text and obstructing the flow of the writer's argument. But amazingly, the chapter divisions in Philippians all make excellent sense and help to organize the message of this encouraging and instructive New Testament book. Here's an overview of the four divisions of Paul's epistle to the Philippians:

Paul's Current Afflictions (Philippians 1)

1. Paul's thankfulness that his afflictions
   serve to spread the gospel   1:1–26
2. Paul encourages others who are afflicted   1:27–30

Have the Mind of Christ (Philippians 2)

Christ Our Confidence (Philippians 3)

Christ Our Energizer (Philippians 4)

The theme of this letter is Jesus Christ's availability to us for the problems of life. The church at Philippi to which Paul wrote was not troubled by serious doctrinal or behavioral problems like some of the other churches. It experienced only the normal problems of everyday life—Christians who have trouble getting along with each other, growing pains, ministry stresses, disturbances by certain persons whose beliefs and practices were not in full accord with the true Christian faith.

Life in Christ—living the adventure

To deal with these problems, Paul designed this epistle as a guide for ordinary living. The recurring refrain throughout the letter is one of joy and rejoicing. Repeatedly the apostle uses phrases such as, "Rejoice"; "Rejoice with me"; "Rejoice in the Lord." Rejoice in your sufferings, rejoice in your afflictions. This becomes, then, a letter in which we are instructed how to live victoriously and joyously in the midst of the normal difficulties of life.

The four chapters present Christ in four different aspects. The themes are caught up for us in four key verses that appear in these chapters. He is presented in Philippians 1 as our life, as we see in the key verse of chapter 1, verse 21:

For to me, to live is Christ and to die is gain.

I think we often treat this verse as a statement of Christian escapism. We put the emphasis at the end of the sentence, "to die is gain," and we think, *Yes, it would be great to get away from all the pressures and pain and struggles of life.* But that's not what Paul is saying. Look closely and you see that he is really saying, "I don't know which to choose. To me to live is to have Christ—but on the other hand, to die is to gain heaven! I enjoy living the adventure of life—but I long to experience the next adventure in the life to come." Paul was certainly not fed up with life! He loved living, because he wanted Christ to have every opportunity to live through him!

How could Paul be so excited about life when he was forced to live it under prison conditions? Because he saw what God was doing through him even while he was in chains. A unique evangelistic enterprise was occurring in Rome, the like of which may never have been seen before or since. And Paul—chains, guards, house arrest, and all—was at the hub of this evangelistic enterprise. God had a plan for reaching the Roman Empire that Paul had never dreamed of. And do you know who God placed in charge of all the arrangements for this great evangelistic outreach in Rome? Emperor Nero! As Paul himself explains,

> It has become clear throughout the whole palace guard and to everyone else that I am in chains for Christ (1:13).

If you read between the lines, you can see what was happening. Nero, the emperor, had commanded that every six hours one of the finest young men in the whole Roman Empire, from the elite who constituted his personal bodyguard, would be brought in and chained to the apostle Paul. Nero's purpose was to keep a fresh guard on this dangerous man. But God had a higher purpose than Nero's: He used Nero to send a succession of Rome's best and brightest in to be instructed by Paul in the things of Christ!

Isn't that amazing? One by one these young men were coming to Christ—because they could see the reality of Jesus Christ living through this amazing man, Paul. If you doubt that, look at the last chapter of the letter, where in the next to last verse Paul says:

> All the saints send you greetings, especially those who belong to Caesar's household (4:22).

No human mind could have conceived such a unique plan for evangelizing the Roman Empire—only the mind of God! But that is the kind of God whom Paul served, and that is why he could say, "To me, to live is Christ. I don't know what He is going to do next but whatever it is, it will be interesting and exciting!" That is what life in Christ means.

In chapter 2, Paul deals with the problem of the disunity that was threatening some of the saints at Philippi. Certain ones among them were quarreling, and there were divisions within the body of the church. This is constantly happening in almost any church. People get irritated with each other, they get upset over the way other people do things. They do not like someone's attitude or tone of voice. Then cliques and divisions, which are always destructive to the life and vitality of a church, begin to develop. So Paul points out to these people that Christ is our example in settling difficulties and problems. The key passage in this section is verse 5:

Your attitude should be the same as that of Christ Jesus.

Then he immediately proceeds to explain what the attitude of Jesus, the mind of Christ, was like:

Who, being in very nature God, did not consider equality with God something to be grasped, but made himself nothing, taking the very nature of a servant, being made in human likeness. And being found in appearance as a man, he humbled himself and became obedient to death—even death on a cross! (2:6–8).

That was the self-condescension of Jesus Christ. It was the emptying out of all that He held of value in His life. This, says Paul, is the mind of Jesus Christ. In your disagreements with one another, have this attitude toward each other: Do not hang onto your rights at all costs. How apropos this is in these days when we hear so often about insisting on our rights! How different is Christ's example!

Dr. H. A. Ironside used to tell a story that took place when he was only nine or ten years old. His mother took him to a church business meeting. The meeting erupted into a quarrel between two men. One of them stood and pounded the desk, saying, "All I want is my rights."

Sitting nearby was an old Scotsman, somewhat hard of hearing, who cupped his hand behind his ear and said, "Aye, brother, what's that you say? What do you want?"

The angry gentleman replied, "I just said that all I want is my rights, that's all!"

The old Scot snorted, "Your rights, brother? Is that what you want, your rights? Well, I say if you had your rights, you'd be in hell. The Lord Jesus Christ didn't come to get His rights, He came to get His wrongs. And He got 'em."

The fellow who had been bickering stood transfixed for a moment—then he abruptly sat down and said, "You're right. Settle it any way you like."

In a few moments the argument was settled—and it was settled when the combatants were challenged to take on the mind of Christ, the attitude of the One who never demanded His rights but who, uncomplaining, took His wrongs, humbling Himself, becoming obedient to death, even the death of the cross. But don't stop there. What was the result of Jesus' self-effacing humility and sacrifice?

> *God exalted him to the highest place and gave him the name that is above every name, that at the name of Jesus every knee should bow, in heaven and on earth and under the earth, and every tongue confess that Jesus Christ is Lord, to the glory of God the Father (2:9–11).*

Jesus placed everything He had in the hands of God the Father—and the result was that God the Father vindicated Him

When He willingly surrendered His rights, God gave Him every right in the universe. Jesus placed everything He had, everything He treasured, in the hands of God the Father—and the result was that God the Father vindicated Him. This is what Paul is saying to quarreling Christians: Give up your rights. Don't insist on them. With Christ as your example, lay aside your rights and absorb your wrongs. Replace selfishness with humility, and trust God to vindicate you. That is the mind of Christ. If we would truly put that admonition into practice, we would be different people. There would be no quarreling within churches and no divisions among Christians if we all truly followed our Example and patterned our minds after His.

Christ our confidence

What more confidence do we need than to have the Creator of the universe living within us and empowering all we do?

Chapter 3 sets forth Christ our confidence, our motivating power. He is the One who moves us to boldly, obediently step out in faith, believing that we can achieve the task God has set for us. And isn't that what most of us lack and what is in such short supply today? Everywhere you look, you see books, tapes, and seminars offering us a motivational boost, advertising that they can build our confidence so that we can achieve our goals. If we truly understood what it means to be in Christ and to have Christ living in us, we would possess all the confidence and motivation we need to achieve any godly goal. What more confidence do we need than to have the Creator of the universe living within us and empowering all we do? What greater motivation could we possess than to know that Jesus is on our side, and that with Him as our encourager and our coach, there's no way we can lose!

All that is lacking in us is the true knowledge of what we already possess in Christ. That is why Paul says, in Philippians 3:10:

> *I want to know Christ and the power of his resurrection and the fellowship of sharing in his sufferings, becoming like him in his death.*

The power of Christ our confidence stands in stark, black-and-white contrast to the power most of us place our confidence in: the power of the self. In Philippians 3:3, Paul defines a Christian as one who worships by the Spirit of God, who glories in Christ Jesus not in the self, and who puts no confidence in the flesh, in human pride and power. Compare that statement with all the best-selling books and late-night infomercials that try to get us to discover the power within us, trying to build up our confidence in our own minds and our own flesh.

If anyone had the right to glory in the flesh, it was the apostle Paul. In this chapter, he lists all his credentials and qualifications for having confidence in his own flesh.

> *I myself have reasons for such confidence.*
> *If anyone else thinks he has reasons to put confidence in the flesh, I have more: circumcised on the eighth day, of the people of Israel, of the tribe of Benjamin, a Hebrew of Hebrews; in regard to the law, a Pharisee; as for zeal, persecuting the church; as for legalistic righteousness, faultless (3:4–6).*

What a lot of reasons to have confidence and pride in his own flesh! Perfect ancestry, as purebred and highborn as they come; perfect ritual and religious observance; perfect religious zeal and morality; perfect performance in the strictest sect of the Hebrew religion! Yet despite all this perfection, all these reasons for human pride, Paul set it all aside, he counted it as worthless next to the confidence that Jesus Christ gives. In verse 7, he writes,

> *Whatever was to my profit I now consider loss for the sake of Christ.*

You've seen him a thousand times: The pink Energizer bunny, with the big drum in front of him and the Energizer batteries on his back—while the announcer says, "He keeps going and going and going. . . ." In Philippians 4, Paul tells us that we are like that little pink bunny! With Christ living in us, energizing us and empowering us, we can keep going and going and going in service to Him, fulfilling His will, reaching out to people in His name.

I can think of few tortures more horrible in life than to have a great desire—but not the ability to fulfill it. That is a recipe for frustration. In Philippians 4, Paul tells us that God has not only given us the desire to live our lives in service to Him and others, but He supplies our strength and energy so that we also have the power to fulfill the great desire He has given us! Here in this chapter, we find that great declaration that has been such an inspiration to believers down through the centuries:

The problem of getting along with others

I can do everything through him who gives me strength (4:13).

Is this statement mere wishful thinking or idealism on the apostle's part? Or is it a practical, reliable truth?

Practical! Absolutely practical! In fact, just to show how down to earth and trustworthy Christ's energizing power really is in our everyday lives, Paul addresses just such a situation. The problem he deals with is the problem of getting along with others. Did you ever hear of such a problem in a church before? No? Well, what church do you go to? The Philippian church had such a problem—two women, named Euodia and Syntyche. In our churches today we still have no lack of people who delight in trampling the feelings of others, and those whose feelings are quickly bruised. But the apostle Paul begs these people to end their disagreement and be of the same mind in the Lord.

But how? Isn't Paul asking the impossible? No! The answer is found in verse 13: "I can do everything through him who gives me strength." Even put up with odious people? Positively! Even get along with touchy people? Absolutely! When Christ is our energizer, we can get along with people, and we can keep going and going and going along with them, loving them, accepting them, and forgiving them for the sake of the unity of the body of Christ.

The problem of worry

Next, Paul addresses the matter of worry. In Philippians 4:6–7, Paul—a man with every rightful reason to worry, a man in chains, a man facing a possible death sentence from Rome's erratic ruler, Nero—writes:

Do not be anxious about anything, but in everything, by prayer and petition, with thanksgiving, present your requests to God. And the peace of God, which transcends all understanding, will guard your hearts and your minds in Christ Jesus.

What a recipe for mental peace and serenity Paul has just served up! Paul is not minimizing worries and problems and the cares of life. He is simply telling us not to be ruled by them. He doesn't suggest that we live in denial and try to suppress our anxieties and pretend they aren't there. He is saying that we should present those anxieties to the Lord and allow the Lord to give us His peace—a peace beyond our ability to understand. We don't know where that peace comes from or how it works, but believer after believer can tell you it is real.

I can personally testify to many times in my own life when I was low or worried or fearful, and after sharing those feelings with God, I felt my soul suddenly flooded with peace and a sense of well-being in the Lord. Here again, it is a case of the Lord Jesus Christ's energizing power, flooding our lives with His strength, enabling us to keep going and going and going, even amid our fears and worries.

Finally there is the matter of poverty and material blessing. Paul has known both, and he wants to convey to the Philippian Christians—and to you and me—what a Christlike attitude toward these conditions should be:

> *I am not saying this because I am in need, for I have learned to be content whatever the circumstances. I know what it is to be in need, and I know what it is to have plenty. I have learned the secret of being content in any and every situation, whether well fed or hungry, whether living in plenty or in want (4:11–12).*

What is Paul's secret of contentment? In verse 19, he passes that secret on to the Philippians and to us:

> *And my God will meet all your needs according to his glorious riches in Christ Jesus.*

That is our Lord Jesus Christ, our strength, our energizer, supplying all our need, enabling us to keep going and going and going.

The letter to the Philippians embodies the soul and the life-secrets of a man who ran the full course, who fought the good fight, who kept the faith, who kept going and going for God. This little power-packed book contains Paul's road map for a life lived with power, enthusiasm, and a sense of adventure. We who live at the transition point from the second to the third millennium, facing all the perils, anxieties, and unforeseen challenges of the new century, need to discover and appropriate the Lord's power for our lives.

In truth, we are no different from Paul. The same One who lived through Paul now lives through us. Christ is our life; Christ is our example; Christ is our confidence; and Christ is our energizer and our strength.

Power and Joy!

Paul wrote most of his letters to churches that he himself founded. He did not establish the church at Rome, however, nor did he begin the church to which this letter was written. We can't verify who established the church at Colossae, in Greece, but it likely was Epaphroditus (also known as Epaphras), a man mentioned in some of Paul's other letters. This letter mentions that he was from Colossae. We don't know where he heard the gospel, but after hearing and believing, he apparently took the gospel back to his hometown, where he began to proclaim Christ. The church to which this letter was written is very likely the result of the bold hometown witness of Epaphroditus. These believers had never met Paul face-to-face.

Colossians was written at about the same time as Philippians, and you will notice that its structure and content are similar to Paul's letter to the Ephesians. All were written at about the same time, during Paul's first imprisonment, and are therefore called the Prison Epistles.

The Colossians had a problem, and that is Paul's focus in this letter. The Colossian Christians were on the verge of losing their understanding of the power by which the Christian life is lived. This letter, then, is Paul's great explanation of the power and joy that God provides for living the Christian life.

Paul expresses the theme of Colossians in his introductory prayer:

We pray this in order that you may live a life worthy of the Lord and may please him in every way: bearing fruit in every good work, growing in the knowledge of God, being strengthened with all power according to his glorious might so that you may have great endurance and patience, and joyfully giving thanks to the Father, who has qualified you to share in the inheritance of the saints in the kingdom of light (1:10–12).

Paul's prayer is that Christians *might be strengthened with all power* (that's why he wrote the letter) *according to God's glorious might* (the central issue of this letter). Beginning on this note, Paul then sets forth the *source* of all power in the Christian life: Jesus Christ. How can Jesus—a man who was born as a baby, lived as a man, and died on a cross—be the source of all power? Simple. Jesus is God. Paul makes this point in a powerful way in verses 15–20:

He is the image of the invisible God, the firstborn over all creation. For by him all things were created: things in heaven and on earth, visible and invisible, whether thrones or powers or rulers or authorities; all things were created by him and for him. He is before all things, and in him all things hold together. And he is the head of the body, the church; he is the beginning and the firstborn from among the dead, so that in everything he might have the supremacy. For God was pleased to have all his fullness dwell in him, and through him to reconcile to himself all things, whether things on earth or things in heaven, by making peace through his blood, shed on the cross.

Anyone who claims that Jesus is not truly God has at least two big problems. One is the gospel of John, a book entirely devoted to the subject of the deity of Christ. The other is this passage, which is an absolutely clear and unambiguous statement of the deity of Christ. Of course, the deity of Christ is a theme that is woven throughout Scripture, but John and Colossians make the case in terms that are direct and unassailable.

Here is an outline of Paul's letter to the Colossians:

Christ, the Head of Creation and the Head of the Church (Colossians 1–2)

1.	Introduction and prayer for the Colossians	1:1–14
2.	Christ, the Head of creation	1:15–17
3.	Christ, the Head of the church	1:18–2:3
4.	Our freedom in Christ	2:4–23

Submission to Christ the Head (Colossians 3–4)

Firstborn is a term that confuses some people. Twice in Colossians 1, Paul refers to Jesus as the firstborn. It does not mean, as some people have understood it, that Jesus had a beginning—that He is not truly eternal. Here, the word *firstborn* refers not to the chronology of Jesus Christ but to His role or position. In the culture to which Colossians was written, *firstborn* was understood to mean the heir, the first in line as the owner or master. This phrase, "firstborn over all creation," means that the Lord Jesus stands in relationship to all creation just as an heir stands in relationship to a parent's property. Jesus is not part of the created order. Rather, He owns it and rules it as the heir of the Father.

In this passage, Paul declares Jesus Christ to be the Creator, the One who brought all the worlds into being with a word, the One who, being God the Son, was present in the beginning with God the Father. Note Paul's statement in verse 17:

He is before all things, and in him all things hold together.

One of the continuing puzzles of science is the question of what holds the universe together. We know that everything is made up of tiny atoms that consist of electrons buzzing around a nucleus. Why doesn't the centrifugal force of those orbiting electrons cause atoms to fly apart? Scientists talk hopefully of a "grand unified theory" of forces that they hope will someday explain what holds the universe together, but scientists are still a long way from such a theory. Moreover, as the great physicist-mathematician Stephen Hawking has pointed out, testing such a theory would require a particle accelerating machine "as big as the solar system," and such a machine is "unlikely to be funded in the present economic climate" (Stephen Hawking, *A Brief History of Time* [New York: Bantam Books, 1988], 74).

What holds our universe together? Science cannot answer and can only point to unnamed, undiscovered, unknown forces. The predicament of science in its pursuit of the unknown force reminds me of Paul's experience in Athens where he encountered an altar to "AN UNKNOWN GOD." It is the unknown God that science is struggling with today: His name is Jesus of Nazareth. He is the Grand Unifying Force of the universe. All power in the natural world comes from Him, He is before all things, and in Him all things hold together.

Jesus the firstborn

What holds the universe together?

Jesus is the Grand Unifying Force

In verse 18, Paul goes on to say that the One who created the universe and holds it together is also the One who created the church and holds it together:

> He is the head of the body, the church; he is the beginning and the first-born from among the dead, so that in everything he might have the supremacy.

Notice, again, that term *firstborn*. Jesus, says Paul, is "the firstborn from among the dead." What does that mean? First, it does not mean that Jesus was the first person ever to be raised from the dead, because Scripture records others who preceded Him. In fact, Jesus Himself raised some of them. What Paul means is that Jesus is the heir, the Lord of all the new creation. He is the Head of the new creation, as the apostle tells us, and we are part of a new body, the new body of men and women that God is forming—a body called the church. Jesus is the Head of that body, and from Him flows all power—the power He demonstrated on the first Easter: *resurrection power.*

I am becoming increasingly convinced that the problem with most Christians is that we do not understand what the Bible teaches about resurrection power. If we had any idea what this power is and how it functions, we would never again live as we live now.

Resurrection power is quiet. It is the kind of power that was evident in the Lord Jesus. He came silently from the tomb—no sound effects, no pyrotechnic visual effects. There was only the quiet, inexorable, irresistible power of a risen life. The stone was rolled away—not to let Jesus out but to let people in, so they could see that the tomb was empty.

This is the same power that God has released to us. His quiet but irresistible power changes hearts and lives and attitudes, recreating from within. That is resurrection power. It flows to us from the Head of the new creation, the risen Christ, the source of all power.

Next, Paul goes on to show for whom God intends this power:

> Once you were alienated from God and were enemies in your minds because of your evil behavior. But now he has reconciled you by Christ's physical body through death to present you holy in his sight, without blemish and free from accusation (1:21–22).

In this passage, Paul is addressing you and me, as well as the Colossians. We too were once estranged, enemies of God because of sin—but now God has reconciled us through the physical death of Jesus, unleashing His resurrection power in order to make us holy and guiltless in His sight.

Then Paul goes on to give us a demonstration from his own life of this power. He says that God called him and put him in the ministry to proclaim a mystery:

I have become its servant by the commission God gave me to present to you the word of God in its fullness—the mystery that has been kept hidden for ages and generations, but is now disclosed to the saints. To them God has chosen to make known among the Gentiles the glorious riches of this mystery, which is Christ in you, the hope of glory (1:25–27).

In other words, you will not find this mystery explained in the Old Testament. It was experienced there but never explained. Now, however, it has been disclosed to the saints, to the followers of Jesus Christ. What is this mystery? "Christ in you, the hope of glory."

It is Christ living in you. This is the supreme declaration of the Christian church. You have never preached the gospel until you have told people not only that their sins will be forgiven when they come to Christ, but that Jesus Himself will indwell them and empower them! That is the transforming power of the gospel: Jesus lives in us and through us, giving us the creation power, the resurrection power, to do all God expects us to do and all He designed us to do and all He created us to do.

Jesus died for us so that He might live in us. That is the ultimate glory of the Christian gospel.

Plugged into the source

Paul goes on to describe what it means to live by the power of Christ. In Colossians 1:28–29, he writes:

We proclaim him, admonishing and teaching everyone with all wisdom, so that we may present everyone perfect in Christ. To this end I labor, struggling with all his energy, which so powerfully works in me.

What does Paul mean when he talks about "struggling with all his energy, which so powerfully works in me"? Well, just think about the life that Paul lived and the work that he accomplished. Think of this amazing apostle, with his indefatigable journeying night and day, through shipwreck and hardship of every kind, working with his hands, enduring persecution, stonings, beatings, and opposition as he carried the gospel from one end of the Roman Empire to the other. Some of us think that we can barely make it from weekend to weekend in our 9-to-5 jobs—but this man was spending himself day and night, seven days a week, for the sake of Jesus Christ. He could not do that in his own strength, his own energy. He plugged into an outside power source, the ultimate power source, and he allowed that power to surge through him, performing the will of God.

In other words, Christ in you! The hope of glory!

If Christians would only understand the power that God has made available to us we would never again be the same. We would never have to plead with people in the church to perform needed ministries or roles. We would never have a shortage of workers for our neighborhood ministries, or of people to act as advisors on youth mission trips to Mexico or the inner city. We would never have a shortage of Sunday school teachers, Bible-study leaders, youth advisors, or visitation volunteers. We would not be giving the excuse, "Oh, I just don't have the strength to do it. I don't have the energy," because we all have the energy available to us. The source is Christ, the extension cord is the Holy Spirit, and we are the little electrical appliances that God wants to enliven with His resurrection power and to use according to His eternal plan.

Hidden treasures of wisdom and knowledge

And there are even more depths to this mystery of Christ. He is not only the source of energy, but the source of understanding, wisdom, and knowledge. In chapter 2, Paul continues his exploration of the mystery of Christ:

> *My purpose is that they may be encouraged in heart and united in love, so that they may have the full riches of complete understanding, in order that they may know the mystery of God, namely, Christ, in whom are hidden all the treasures of wisdom and knowledge (2:2–3).*

Paul also warns us about certain false powers that would woo us away from the true power that Christ has given us

Paul also warns us about certain false powers that would woo us away from the true power that Christ has given us. These warnings are as valid and relevant today as they were when Paul wrote them. More than ever before, people today are in search of power—power to achieve goals, wealth, status, success. Thousands of people are spending millions of dollars dialing up psychic hotlines, buying videotape series, or going to seminars that are actually high-pressure sales pitches—all in search of the power to get what they want or to become their idealized self. All that searching for false power—yet the true Power is right in front of our noses in the person of Jesus Christ.

If Jesus lives in us, we don't need any more power than we already possess

If Jesus lives in us, we already have what it takes. We don't need any more power than we already possess. We don't need more of Jesus; He just needs more of us. Now that we have the power, our job is to live by that power on a daily basis. As Paul tells us in 2:6–7,

Just as you received Christ Jesus as Lord, continue to live in him, rooted and built up in him, strengthened in the faith as you were taught, and overflowing with thankfulness.

It is not enough simply to receive Jesus. We must live in Him. When we truly do, an attitude of thankfulness permeates our lives. To look at some Christians, you would think that our Bibles translate this verse "overflowing with grumbling." But Paul underscores the need for thankfulness in our lives. What robs us of a spirit of thankfulness? Primarily, it's the idea that power comes from human knowledge, as Paul shows us in verse 8:

See to it that no one takes you captive through hollow and deceptive philosophy, which depends on human tradition and the basic principles of this world rather than on Christ.

I have seen this principle tragically played out in so many lives. I have seen young people from Christian homes—full of faith and enthusiasm—go into a college or university and come out with their faith destroyed, their enthusiasm turned to cynicism. Why? Because they have been exposed to the wily, subtle teachings of human wisdom. No one warned them—or perhaps they ignored the warnings they received—about the deceitfulness of this world's wisdom. They fell prey to human knowledge.

This statement may seem to imply that the gospel is anti-intellectual. But the Bible is not against knowledge. It is against knowledge that does not come under the judgment of God's Word. Certainly, not all of the knowledge of this world is false knowledge. Much of it is good and true and cannot be found in Scripture—medical knowledge such as the secret of penicillin and techniques of surgery; technical knowledge such as how to build a computer or a space shuttle; historical knowledge such as the defeat of Napoleon at Waterloo or events of the Civil War. All of this is human knowledge, and it is valuable.

The Bible is not against knowledge; it is against knowledge that does not come under the judgment of God's Word

But Paul wants us to understand that there is a deceptive knowledge that comes from false sources—traditions and philosophies that have built up, idea upon idea, over the centuries. Many of these traditions and philosophies mingle truth and error in such a way that the two become indistinguishable. Those who accept these ideas uncritically are bound to accept as much error as they do truth. It will lead them, therefore, into mistaken concepts and erroneous and injurious ideas—ideas such as these: "The human spirit is recycled again and again through reincarnation." Or, "As a human being, you have totally unlimited power and potential to be your own god, to make up your own morality." Or, "A

Paul wants us to understand that there is a deceptive knowledge that comes from false sources

human being is just a mound of molecules that is born, lives, and dies—there is no afterlife, no purpose for living, so enjoy yourself, forget faith and morality, eat, drink, and be merry for this moment, because that's all there is." These philosophies are prevalent today, and all are false—completely contrary to the true knowledge of Scripture. They depend, as Paul says, "on human tradition."

But Paul goes on to say that there is also deceptive knowledge that is built on "the basic principles of this world rather than on Christ." What does he mean? Paul is referring here to the dark powers that (as he brings out in other letters) rule this world, govern the minds of men and women, darken the human intellect, and lead human beings into self-destructive error. Much of what human beings consider to be "knowledge" is actually demonic deception.

Human knowledge, then, is rudimentary, elementary, and basic to the fallen nature of this world. It stays on the periphery of truth, never getting to the real heart of spiritual reality. That is why our nation's university community, its entertainment community, its information and news community, and its political establishment have become so saturated with those who profess the highest levels of human knowledge yet who are filled with vileness, corruption, immorality, lawlessness, drug abuse, suicide, and every evidence of moral decay and spiritual deterioration. Today, all of these institutions in our society are permeated—if not dominated—by a philosophy called *deconstructionism,* a worldly philosophy that teaches that words have no objective content, and therefore words have no truth. Today's liberal theology has become deeply infected with the disease of deconstructionism, and it fosters two very destructive beliefs.

First, if truth cannot be assigned to words, then we can make words mean anything we want them to. We no longer have to be concerned with objective truth, with true truth. Each of us can invent our own truth, our own reality. I can lie and call it truth if it gets me what I want.

Second, the Bible—the Word, or Logos of God—can be deconstructed, emptied of all truth. These words of Jesus make no sense to deconstructionists: "Sanctify them by the truth; your word is truth" (John 17:17). While Jesus says God's Logos is truth, the wisdom of this world cancels out the Logos of God, portraying the Word of God as empty and meaningless. "You have your truth," says the wisdom of this world, "and I have my truth—so don't you dare impose your truth on me!"

Even at its very truest and most pure, human knowledge does not address the heart of reality as the Word of God does. The truth of this world, when it is validated by God's Word, can complement the truth of Scripture (as when archaeological discoveries verify biblical accounts). But human knowledge can never supersede, contradict, or invalidate

God's Word. The wisdom of God always stands above any so-called knowledge of this world.

Paul goes on to indicate another false source of power, which also leads many people astray:

> *Do not let anyone judge you by what you eat or drink, or with regard to a religious festival, a New Moon celebration or a Sabbath day. These are a shadow of the things that were to come; the reality, however, is found in Christ. . . .*
> *Since you died with Christ to the basic principles of this world, why, as though you still belonged to it, do you submit to its rules: "Do not handle! Do not taste! Do not touch!"? These are all destined to perish with use, because they are based on human commands and teachings (2:16–17, 20–22).*

What is this false source of power? It is found under many names: unrestrained zeal, legalism, religious extremism, judgmentalism, pharisaism. This false source of power manifests itself in the keeping of days and special feasts and regulations and ascetic practices—flogging the body, wearing a hair shirt, laboring long hours out of zeal for the cause. All these practices look like sources of spiritual power. Sometimes we cannot help but admire the zealousness of individuals who get themselves all wrapped up in a cause. But, says the apostle, they are deceiving themselves. They do not discover real power (2:23):

> *Such regulations indeed have an appearance of wisdom, with their self-imposed worship, their false humility and their harsh treatment of the body, but they lack any value in restraining sensual indulgence.*

You see, you can wear an outfit made of burlap and be filled with lust. You can beat your body black and blue and still be always guilty of lascivious thinking. These outward legalistic, ascetic trappings provide no check to the indulgence of the flesh. Therefore, they do not generate the power to lead the kind of life that we must live.

In this passage, Paul also mentions a third source of false power—one of the most deceptive sources of all!

> *Do not let anyone who delights in false humility and the worship of angels disqualify you for the prize. Such a person goes into great detail about what he has seen, and his unspiritual mind puffs him up with idle notions (2:18).*

What does Paul mean here? He is talking about a spiritual deception that is as real and perilous today as it was in the first century A.D. It is the belief that if we can contact invisible spirits or the dead and get messages from them, we can access hidden spiritual power and knowledge. The Colossian Christians were troubled with these influences, just as we are. Today, we see a growing influence of the New Age, occultism, astrology, satanism, magic, seances, and more. All of these practices are deceptive, satanic substitutes for the indwelling power of Jesus Christ.

True power

In chapter 3, the apostle turns to the true manifestation of power and how to lay hold of the power of Christ:

> Since, then, you have been raised with Christ, set your hearts on things above, where Christ is seated at the right hand of God. Set your minds on things above, not on earthly things (vv. 1–2).

Let your desires be shaped by the Word of God

Paul is not saying that we should go around constantly thinking about heaven. There is nothing super-pious about this. He is simply saying, "Don't let your desires and your attitudes be governed or directed by desires for earthly fame or power. Instead, let your desires be shaped by the Word of God." We are to exhibit love, truth, faith, and patience—the qualities that mark the life of the risen Lord. We are to manifest heaven in our everyday situations. Paul gives us the recipe for carrying out this mission:

> Put to death, therefore, whatever belongs to your earthly nature: sexual immorality, impurity, lust, evil desires and greed, which is idolatry (3:5).

God has already sentenced the earthly nature to death on the cross. When it manifests itself in us, we must treat it like a guilty prisoner under the sentence of death from God. We are not to compromise with any of these practices. We are to put them away. That is step number one. Step two is found in verses 12 through 14:

> As God's chosen people, holy and dearly loved, clothe yourselves with compassion, kindness, humility, gentleness and patience. Bear with each other and forgive whatever grievances you may have against one another. Forgive as the Lord forgave you. And over all these virtues put on love, which binds them all together in perfect unity.

What does Paul mean by this? He is telling us that Christ already dwells in us. Since He lives within us, the challenge to us is simply to get ourselves out of His way and allow His life to be manifest in us. We are to allow these Christlike characteristics to bubble forth in our lives. His life in us will make them authentic not artificial. Paul goes on to list certain areas in which these characteristics are to show forth in us:

> *Wives, submit to your husbands, as is fitting in the Lord.*
> *Husbands, love your wives and do not be harsh with them.*
> *Children, obey your parents in everything, for this pleases the Lord.*
> *Fathers, do not embitter your children, or they will become discouraged.*
> *Slaves, obey your earthly masters in everything; and do it, not only when their eye is on you and to win their favor, but with sincerity of heart and reverence for the Lord. . . .*
> *Masters, provide your slaves with what is right and fair, because you know that you also have a Master in heaven (3:18–22; 4:1).*

All of our relationships, from family relationships to our relationships with those under our authority and over us in authority, must exhibit the character and love of Jesus Christ. His life is to shine through our lives.

Paul concludes with these practical admonitions:

The basis for joy

> *Devote yourselves to prayer, being watchful and thankful. And pray for us, too, that God may open a door for our message, so that we may proclaim the mystery of Christ, for which I am in chains. Pray that I may proclaim it clearly, as I should. Be wise in the way you act toward outsiders; make the most of every opportunity (4:2–5).*

Then Paul continues with personal greetings from those who are with him. He concludes the letter, as was his custom, by taking the pen in his own hand and writing:

> *I, Paul, write this greeting in my own hand. Remember my chains. Grace be with you (4:18).*

The key verse to the entire book of Colossians, however, is found in chapter 1, where Paul writes:

> *We pray this* [for knowledge of God's will, for wisdom, for understanding] *in order that you may live a life worthy of the Lord . . . being strengthened with all power according to his glorious might (1:10–11).*

What a tremendous truth! Don't we all want that? Don't we, as Christians, want to see Christ's power, Christ's life, manifested in us? Not so that we can dazzle people with miracles or see our names in the papers, but so that we can experience everything that God intended for us: "joyfully giving thanks to the Father, who has qualified you to share in the inheritance of the saints in the kingdom of light" (1:11–12). And what He intends for us to experience is nothing less than joy!

The world cannot produce joyful living. The world can give us excitement, thrills, highs—a whole range of intense, fleeting emotions—but the world cannot give us genuine joy. The world cannot help us endure trials with courage or accept hardships with faith and patience. As far as the world is concerned, this takes an unknown kind of power—the power that Christians know can be found only in Jesus Christ. This power will transform our hardships and our difficulties into joyful experiences, not just phony, superficial manifestations of feel-good happiness. True joy enables us to learn and grow through trials.

If our hearts are right with Christ, if we are putting off the old and putting on the new, then we can go through tough times—experiences that would produce grumbling, griping, and despair in others—and we can find joy! Genuine, lasting, dependable, reliable, supernatural joy! That is what Paul means when he writes, "Christ in you, the hope of glory." That is the message of Colossians.

Hope for a Hopeless World

S ome years ago, a team of archaeologists was digging in an ancient part of the Greek city of Thessaloniki—also called Salonika or Thessalonica—a port city in Macedonia, northeastern Greece. As they excavated, the archaeologists uncovered a Grecian cemetery dating back to the first century A.D. Among the pagan tombstones, they found one that was inscribed in Greek with these words: No Hope. How ironic, then, that as we examine Paul's first letter to the Christians who lived in that same city during that same era we find that his theme is the *hope* of the believer!

As we adventure through the book of 1 Thessalonians, we will see that these Christians lived during a time of great upheaval, great persecution, great peril. The world around them was coming apart at the seams. Yet Paul's message to them was, "Take heart! Have hope! Jesus is returning, God is in control, and He knows what He is doing!"

The background and structure of the letter

Many of the cities where Paul preached and founded churches have long since crumbled into ruin, but Thessaloniki is still a thriving, bustling metropolis. A Roman province in Paul's day, the city of Thessaloniki or Thessalonica has had a troubled history. It was occupied by the Saracens in the tenth century, by the Normans in the twelfth, by the Turks from 1430 to 1912, and by the Nazis in World War II.

This letter was written about A.D. 50, making it the first of Paul's epistles. In fact, it may well be the first written book of the New

Testament, though some Bible scholars believe the gospels of Matthew and (perhaps) Mark can be dated as early as A.D. 43 to 45. This letter was written to a struggling yet vigorous church that was only a few months old at the time. The Thessalonian church was made up of Christians who had just come to Christ under Paul's ministry. This is a delightfully personal letter, revealing the heart of the apostle toward these new Christians. This letter also shows the intense struggles that the early Christians were undergoing in that city.

The first letter to the Thessalonians divides very simply into two major sections. In the first three chapters, the apostle pours out his heart concerning his relationship to them. In the final two chapters, Paul gives them practical instruction in how to live and experience the believer's hope amid the pressures of life.

Here is a brief overview of 1 Thessalonians:

Paul's Personal Relationship with the
Thessalonian Christians (1 Thessalonians 1–3)
1.	Paul affirms the Thessalonians for their growth	1
2.	How Paul founded the Thessalonian church	2:1–16
3.	How Timothy strengthened the church	2:17–3:10
4.	Paul's desire to visit the Thessalonians	3:11–13

Paul Gives the Thessalonians Practical Instruction—
and Eternal Hope (1 Thessalonians 4–5)
5.	Instructions for growth	4:1–12
6.	The dead in Christ will be raised	4:13–18
7.	The coming Day of the Lord	5:1–11
8.	Instructions for righteous living	5:12–22
9.	Conclusion	5:23–28

The account of Paul's founding of this church is recorded in Acts 17. After Paul and Barnabas were thrown into prison in Philippi for preaching the gospel, an earthquake shook the prison, breaking the prison doors and freeing the prisoners—but, fortunately for the Philippian jailer (whose life was forfeit if any prisoners escaped), none of the prisoners fled. Paul was then officially set free by the Roman magistrates; he left Philippi and went to Thessalonica.

From the account in Acts, we learn that Paul was there for only about three weeks when persecution arose, forcing him to leave the city for his own safety. He went down to Athens and from there he sent Timothy back to see how the Christians were doing. He was very concerned about them, fearful that the persecution they were undergoing would harm their newborn faith.

Two major sections,
one personal,
one practical

He went on to Corinth, where he founded another church after several months of difficult labor. Later, Timothy returned to him at Corinth, bringing word of how the Thessalonians were doing and of some of the problems they were facing.

As we read this letter, we may relate to the problems of the Thessalonians. Today, we live in a culture that is becoming increasingly hostile toward Christianity. As we move into a new century, a new millennium, it is not hard to imagine that, even in America, Christians soon may be actively persecuted for our faith—by the increasingly godless society around us, and even by the government.

Familiar-sounding problems

That was the environment of Paul and the Thessalonian Christians. For one thing, wherever the apostle Paul went, he was hounded by a group of Jews who told others that he was not a genuine apostle because he was not one of the original twelve. And the Thessalonian Christians were severely persecuted by the pagans of Thessalonica, who threatened them, abused them, and seized their property. Here were new Christians—some were only days or weeks old in the faith—and they were being called upon to endure extreme hardship for their newfound Lord.

New Christians were being called upon to endure extreme hardship for their newfound Lord

Also, just as we live today in an age of heightened sexual permissiveness and promiscuity, so did the people of first-century Greek society. Their religion sanctioned sexual promiscuity. The priestesses of the pagan temples were often prostitutes, practicing their trade right in the temples. Those who practiced moral purity were regarded as laughable freaks. New Christians felt enormous pressure to fall in line with the common sexual practices of their day.

Another major problem in this church was confusion over the second coming of Jesus Christ. The apostle had evidently told them about the Lord's eventual return, but they had misunderstood part of his teaching. Some expected Christ to come back so soon that they had actually stopped working for a living; they were simply waiting for Him to come and take them away. Since they weren't earning a living, somebody had to take care of them and they had become leeches on the rest of the congregation. Also, there were developing tensions between the congregation and church leaders to resolve. Finally, some of them were somewhat indifferent to the Holy Spirit's work among them, and to the truth of God proclaimed in the Scriptures.

Confusion over the Second Coming

Do those problems sound familiar? We can't deny our likeness to the Thessalonian church.

In the first section of the letter, chapters 1 through 3, Paul pours his heart out for these early Christians. He is afraid that they might have misunderstood his leaving Thessalonica as though he had abandoned them to avoid persecution; so, he reminds them that he had just come through a terrible time of persecution in Philippi and that his own heart was deeply concerned for them. The key to Paul's heart is found at the beginning of this section:

> We always thank God for all of you, mentioning you in our prayers. We continually remember before our God and Father your work produced by faith, your labor prompted by love, and your endurance inspired by hope in our Lord Jesus Christ (1:2–3).

Those three qualities marked the Thessalonian believers: their work of faith, their labor of love, and their endurance in hope. These are detailed more clearly later in this chapter where we read:

> They tell how you turned to God from idols [that was the Thessalonians' work of faith] to serve the living and true God [that was their labor of love], and to wait for his Son from heaven, whom he raised from the dead—Jesus [that is their patience, evidenced by their waiting in hope for His Son from heaven], who rescues us from the coming wrath (1:9–10).

Interestingly enough, those three qualities of the Thessalonians serve as a brief outline, built right into the text, to guide our understanding of the first three chapters of the book. The work of faith, the labor of love, and the patience of hope: chapter 1, chapter 2, chapter 3.

In chapter 1, Paul reminds them that the word he spoke to them when he founded the Thessalonian church was not the mere word of human beings:

> Our gospel came to you not simply with words, but also with power, with the Holy Spirit and with deep conviction. You know how we lived among you for your sake (1:5).

The work of faith

The gospel that Paul preached came not only in word but also in power and in the Holy Spirit. When the Thessalonians believed in his word and turned from their former devotion to idols, they performed the work of faith. Suddenly, these people who once lived in a condition of powerlessness had power. These people who once lived in a condition of hopelessness had hope. They had a reason for living, they had purpose, and they had the Holy Spirit living out His life through them.

In chapter 2, Paul gives us a wonderful description of the labor of love. This is not only the labor of the Thessalonians, but Paul's labor as well. In verses 9 through 12, we have a powerful description of Paul's ministry, his labor of love:

> Surely you remember, brothers, our toil and hardship; we worked night and day in order not to be a burden to anyone while we preached the gospel of God to you.
> You are witnesses, and so is God, of how holy, righteous and blameless we were among you who believed. For you know that we dealt with each of you as a father deals with his own children, encouraging, comforting and urging you to live lives worthy of God, who calls you into his kingdom and glory (2:9–12).

This was Paul's labor of love. And the Thessalonians evidently did what Paul exhorted them to do, for in verse 14 he goes on to say:

> You, brothers, became imitators of God's churches in Judea, which are in Christ Jesus.

This is the service, the labor of love of the Thessalonians.

Chapter 3 is an account of how Paul sent Timothy to them, and Timothy brought back word of the persecution they were undergoing—and especially of their patience and endurance amid the persecution. Here is a powerful description of the patience of hope, which enabled the Thessalonian Christians to endure trials with joy.

The patience of hope

Chapters 4 and 5, the practical section of this letter, are divided into four brief sections that address the problems that this church confronted. The apostle's first exhortation is to live cleanly in the midst of a sex-saturated society. These words have great application to us who have to live in the same kind of society today. Paul begins by reminding them that he has already taught them how to live:

Practical advice

Live cleanly in a sex-saturated society

> Brothers, we instructed you how to live in order to please God, as in fact you are living. Now we ask you and urge you in the Lord Jesus to do this more and more (4:1).

He had not taught them, as many people think Christianity teaches, that they ought to live a good, clean life. Buddhism teaches that. Islam teaches that. Most religions advocate a moral lifestyle—and Christianity certainly does, but that's not its sole emphasis. The Christian faith teaches you how to live a good, clean life. Christianity is not so much concerned with rules and laws but with a relationship. Because we have a living, love relationship with God through Jesus Christ, we naturally want to please God.

Now, what one quality of life is essential to pleasing God? Faith! Without faith it is impossible to please God. You cannot please God by your own efforts, struggling to live up to a self-imposed standard or one that someone else has imposed upon you. You can please Him by depending on Him alone and, by faith, allowing Him to live His life through you.

This kind of life produces behavior that is morally pure. This is not to say that we will be perfect, but we will be making progress, and perfection in Christ (not our own strength) will be our continuous goal. If Christians are characterized by impurity, that is a clear sign that we are not living a life of faith. As Paul says,

> It is God's will that you should be sanctified: that you should avoid sexual immorality; that each of you should learn to control his own body in a way that is holy and honorable, not in passionate lust like the heathen, who do not know God; and that in this matter no one should wrong his brother or take advantage of him. The Lord will punish men for all such sins, as we have already told you and warned you. For God did not call us to be impure, but to live a holy life. Therefore, he who rejects this instruction does not reject man but God, who gives you his Holy Spirit (4:3–8).

We are clearly told how to live a pure and holy life. That is what God expects of those who are in a living, faith relationship with Him.

Live honestly and productively

The second problem Paul takes up is the matter of living honestly and productively. As he says in 1 Thessalonians 4:9–12, we are to show love toward one another, and the practical manifestation of that love is for all to get busy and work with their hands so they won't have to depend upon somebody else for support. God does not want us to enable laziness or subsidize unproductive people, as our society does to such a great degree. Rather, Paul tells each person

> to mind your own business and to work with your hands, just as we told you, so that your daily life may win the respect of outsiders and so that you will not be dependent on anybody (4:11–12).

Our present and future hope

In verse 13, we come to the major problem—and the crowning theme—of this book: the Thessalonians' misunderstanding about the coming of the Lord and their reason to hope. These Thessalonian Christians had gotten the idea that when Jesus Christ returned to earth the second time to begin His millennial kingdom, those who were alive would enter with Him into this kingdom. They were expecting the Lord's return within their lifetimes. But what about those who had died in the meantime? Wouldn't they miss out on all the benefits and the blessings of the Millennium?

This sort of thinking probably arose because of a misunderstanding of the doctrine of resurrection. They were thinking in terms of one resurrection, a single event that would occur at the end of the Millennium, when the dead would be raised, good and evil alike, to stand before the judgment seat of God. And there are passages, of course, that do speak of a resurrection to come at the end of the Millennium. Paul points out that the resurrection does not proceed as a single event but that groups of believers are resurrected at various times. Notice his argument:

> Brothers, we do not want you to be ignorant about those who fall asleep, or to grieve like the rest of men, who have no hope. We believe that Jesus died and rose again and so we believe that God will bring with Jesus those who have fallen asleep in him (4:13–14).

In other words, those who have died are going to be raised again; and they'll come back with Jesus when He comes to establish His millennial reign. But this presents another problem: How will they come back with Jesus in bodily form when their bodies have been placed in the grave? What reassurance can believers have that this claim is true? "Ah," says the apostle Paul, "let me give you a revelation I received from the Lord!" And this is what Paul says:

> According to the Lord's own word, we tell you that we who are still alive, who are left till the coming of the Lord, will certainly not precede those who have fallen asleep. For the Lord himself will come down from heaven, with a loud command, with the voice of the archangel and with the trumpet call of God, and the dead in Christ will rise first. After that, we who are still alive and are left will be caught up together with them in the clouds to meet the Lord in the air. And so we will be with the Lord forever. Therefore encourage each other with these words (4:15–18).

Paul is describing an aspect of the Lord's coming that takes place before His return to establish the millennial-kingdom reign. He is coming for His people, to gather those who are His to be with Him, in His presence, before His return to establish the kingdom. This first return is called the Parousia in Greek. It does not refer to the second coming of Christ. At this first return, this Parousia, the dead in Christ will be raised, so that we all will be with Him when He is ready to establish His kingdom. So you see how this doctrine answers their problem? The Thessalonians who have lost loved ones need not grieve over those who have died; those who have died in Christ will actually precede those who are alive when the Lord comes for His own.

By comparing this passage with other passages of the Old and New Testaments, we know that between that Parousia and the Lord's coming to establish the kingdom will come a seven-year period of great worldwide tribulation. Paul goes on to speak of this period in chapter 5:

> Brothers, about times and dates we do not need to write to you, for you know very well that the day of the Lord will come like a thief in the night (vv. 1–2).

Nobody can set a date for this event. It's going to come suddenly, quickly. When the Lord comes in the Parousia, two great chains of events will be set in motion. The Lord will begin one series of events in which all believers will be caught up to be with Him, and at the same time, He will begin another series of events on earth known as the Great Tribulation—or, as it is called in the Old Testament, the Day of the Lord.

There are two "days" that we need to distinguish in Scripture: the Day of the Lord and the Day of Christ. They both begin at exactly the same time, but they concern two distinct bodies of people. The Day of Christ concerns believers, while the Day of the Lord refers to what is happening to unbelievers during this time. It is my personal conviction, from my study of Scripture, that when the Lord comes for His own, when the dead in Christ rise, and when we who are alive are caught up with them to be with the Lord, we don't leave this planet at all! We stay here with the Lord, visibly directing the events of the tribulation period as they break out in great judgmental sequences upon the ones who are living as mortals upon the earth. The terrible scenes of that day are vividly portrayed in the book of Revelation.

The apostle Paul says to the Thessalonian believers that no one knows when this is going to happen:

> While people are saying, "Peace and safety," destruction will come on them suddenly, as labor pains on a pregnant woman, and they will not escape.
>
> But you, brothers, are not in darkness so that this day should surprise you like a thief (5:3–4).

This day will surprise the people of the world like a thief—but it needn't surprise you like a thief, because you are looking forward to it!

Paul tells us that we should not go to sleep as others of this world do—we should stay awake, sober, and on alert. We should never assume that life is simply going on as usual. We must be aware of what God is doing throughout history and eternity—and we must act accordingly. These signs are given us in Scripture so that we can be spiritually prepared and not caught unaware, as Paul tells us:

> *Let us not be like others, who are asleep, but let us be alert and self-controlled. For those who sleep, sleep at night, and those who get drunk, get drunk at night. But since we belong to the day, let us be self-controlled, putting on faith and love as a breastplate, and the hope of salvation as a helmet (5:6–8).*

Paul is not talking here about salvation from hell. He is referring to the salvation to come—that is, salvation from the wrath of God during the time of the judgment. He goes on to add,

> *God did not appoint us to suffer wrath but to receive salvation through our Lord Jesus Christ. He died for us so that, whether we are awake or asleep, we may live together with him. Therefore encourage one another and build each other up, just as in fact you are doing (5:9–11).*

Here was the complete answer to the Thessalonians' distress! They did not need to be discouraged or frightened. Rather, they could go on about their lives, confident that God was in charge of all matters pertaining to life, death, and beyond. And although times were extremely perilous, they could busy themselves about the work of the Lord, knowing that they were investing themselves in a certain future.

The concluding section speaks not only of living confidently, but of living peacefully in the midst of troubled and uncertain conditions:

Live peacefully

> *We ask you, brothers, to respect those who work hard among you, who are over you in the Lord and who admonish you. Hold them in the highest regard in love because of their work. Live in peace with each other (5:12–13).*

Animosity was developing toward some of the church leaders, and Paul says, "Remember that these people are concerned about your souls' welfare, and although they may have to speak rather sharply at times, it's not because they want to hurt you, but to help you. Therefore, remember that and live at peace with them and with each other. Love your leaders, because they serve you."

Parting words

Above every other virtue, the virtue of forgiveness characterizes the gospel

He follows this with admonitions against idleness, encouragement for the fainthearted, help for the needy, and patience for all. Then comes the most important admonition of all:

> *Make sure that nobody pays back wrong for wrong, but always try to be kind to each other and to everyone else (5:15).*

Without a doubt, this is one of the most frequently broken commands in Scripture. A famous bumper sticker says, "Don't get mad, get even!" But most of us, when someone offends, usually do both! We get mad—and we get even. This is tragically true even in the church. But this is worldly thinking. It has nothing to do with the grace, truth, and love of Jesus Christ. Above every other virtue, the virtue of forgiveness characterizes the gospel.

He goes on to enjoin rejoicing, continual prayer, and the giving of thanks. After various other admonitions, his final prayer for the Thessalonian believers—and for all believers who read this powerful letter, including you and me—is a beautiful prayer:

> *May God himself, the God of peace, sanctify you through and through. May your whole spirit, soul and body be kept blameless at the coming of our Lord Jesus Christ (5:23).*

Those words sum up the great overarching theme of 1 Thessalonians, for they sum up the hope of all believers: One day we shall all stand before God—and the whole spirit, soul, and body shall be blameless in that day, thanks to what Jesus Christ has done for us. What a blessing—and what a hope—to correct certain misunderstandings they had about the Day of the Lord, a time of unequaled trouble and tribulation for the world.

Holding Back Lawlessness

CHAPTER 63: 2 THESSALONIANS

B efore Jesus Christ left this earth, He said that He would return—but before His return, there would be a time of trial, persecution, and widespread lawlessness. The seams of society would be ripped apart, and violence would become so widespread that people's hearts would literally fail them for fear of coming events. It would be a time of global tribulation, said Jesus, "unequaled from the beginning of the world until now—and never to be equaled again" (Matt. 24:21).

As the Christians of Thessalonica were going through their time of trial, many thought they were experiencing that foretold time of tribulation. The apostle Paul wrote this second letter to correct certain misunderstandings they had about the Day of the Lord, a time of unequaled trouble and tribulation for the world.

This letter is comprised of three chapters, and each one is a correction of a very common attitude that many people, even today, have about troubled times. Here is an outline of the three chapters of the book of 2 Thessalonians:

The Day of the Lord

Paul's Encouragement for a Time of Trial
(2 Thessalonians 1)
    1. Paul's thankfulness for the Thessalonians   1:1–4

Encouragement for trials and persecution

The first chapter is devoted to the attitude of discouragement in times of trial. These Christians were undergoing persecutions and afflictions. Though they were bearing up remarkably well, many were becoming weary and discouraged. "Why try any more?" they groaned. "There's no justice. Everything is always against us."

To counteract this attitude, Paul reminds them that a day is coming when God will set everything right and repay them for their sufferings. In 1 Thessalonians 1:4–10, Paul writes:

> *We know, brothers loved by God, that he has chosen you, because our gospel came to you not simply with words, but also with power, with the Holy Spirit and with deep conviction. You know how we lived among you for your sake. You became imitators of us and of the Lord; in spite of severe suffering, you welcomed the message with the joy given by the Holy Spirit. And so you became a model to all the believers in Macedonia and Achaia. The Lord's message rang out from you not only in Macedonia and Achaia—your faith in God has become known everywhere. Therefore we do not need to say anything about it, for they themselves report what kind of reception you gave us. They tell how you turned to God from idols to serve the living and true God, and to wait for his Son from heaven, whom he raised from the dead—Jesus, who rescues us from the coming wrath.*

The day may come when we, too, will have to choose between standing for our faith and life itself

We in America have not undergone much persecution during the two-hundred-plus years of our history—although today we see indications that a time of persecution may be looming. Our culture, media, courts, and government increasingly challenge our religious liberty, as well as our Christian faith and morality. In some parts of the world, Christians suffer and die for the sake of their faith—and the day may come when we, too, will have to choose between standing for our faith and life itself. If that day comes, we will fully appreciate the meaning of Paul's words in this letter.

Paul reminds the Thessalonians that God has not forgotten them, that He is going to straighten out the world at last. When people go through a time of great persecution, they say, "Isn't there going to be a time when this injustice is corrected? How can a man like Hitler get away with killing so many Jews? How can a man like Stalin get away with killing so many of his own people? Why does a man like Saddam Hussein stay in power? Why doesn't God punish these horrible evil-doers now? Why does He wait so long to straighten things out?"

But Paul says, "Have faith! Be patient! A day is coming when a three-fold repayment will be made: First, believers will be repaid for their sufferings, because these trials build their endurance and make them worthy of the coming kingdom of God. Second, the unbelieving will be repaid for their unbelief and the misused opportunities in life; they will face the righteous Judge who knows their hearts, and He will exclude them from His presence. Third, the Lord Himself will be repaid, for He will "be glorified in his holy people and . . . marveled at among all those who have believed" (2 Thess. 1:10). Notice, Paul does not say that God will be glorified *by* His people, but *in* His people when He takes sinful, fearful, powerless, self-centered human beings and infuses His character qualities, His love and joy, into their lives for all the world to see. It is not a question of praise being offered to God from our lips but of God's receiving glory in the world as His personality is lived out through the quiet example of our lives. That is one of the most powerful ways in which God is glorified.

A day is coming when a threefold repayment will be made

Before we examine chapter 2, let's take a closer look at the payment the unbelieving will receive. That payment is what the Bible calls "hell."

Hell, the payment of the unbelieving

Hell is widely thought of as a fiery furnace where people in chains experience the torment of being continually, unrelentingly burned with fire. The Bible does use symbols of hell that support this idea, but I believe that the most literal understanding we can have of hell is that it is a condition of being forever excluded from the Lord's presence. God is the source of everything good: beauty, truth, life, love, joy, peace, grace, strength, forgiveness. All those things come only from God, and if someone chooses sin and self-will over these good things, God finally says to that person, "I've been trying to give you My best, but you prefer the worst. Have it your own way." When that person gets what he or she has demanded throughout life, it will be the last thing that person wants.

Paul opens the second chapter of 2 Thessalonians by addressing the fears of the Thessalonian Christians. In verses 1 and 2, we read:

The Day of the Lord explained

Concerning the coming of our Lord Jesus Christ and our being gathered to him, we ask you, brothers, not to become easily unsettled or alarmed by some prophecy, report or letter supposed to have come from us, saying that the day of the Lord has already come.

The Thessalonians—who were already undergoing a time of terrible persecution—had evidently received a letter from somebody signing Paul's name, telling them that the day of the Lord had come, and times were going from bad to worse. Their minds are becoming unsettled by all that is happening around them. Paul tells them, in effect, "Don't be shaken out of your wits by what is happening or by people who are trying to get you rattled."

Paul reminds them that he has already explained the difference between the Day of the Lord and the time of the Lord's coming to gather His people to be with Him. When the Lord comes for His people, He will descend from heaven with a shout and the voice of the archangel and the trumpet of God. The dead in Christ will be raised, and we who remain will be caught up together with them in the clouds to meet the Lord in the air. That is our gathering together to Jesus.

But the Day of the Lord, the terrible time of judgment, is a different event altogether. Having introduced the subject of the Day of the Lord, Paul goes on to tell them what it will be like and how they can tell it's coming:

> *Don't let anyone deceive you in any way, for that day will not come until the rebellion [or departure] occurs and the man of lawlessness is revealed, the man doomed to destruction. He will oppose and will exalt himself over everything that is called God or is worshiped, so that he sets himself up in God's temple, proclaiming himself to be God (2:3–4).*

The departure of the church

I believe the word *rebellion* used in this translation is misleading. Literally translated, the original Greek word means "a departure." Many translators have taken this to suggest a departure from faith—that is, rebellion. I don't agree. I believe this departure refers to the departure of the church, when Jesus comes to gather His people to Himself.

I find this to be an amazing passage, especially when we link it together with the rest of Scripture, such as the Gospels. When Jesus was here, He offered Himself to the Jewish people as the promised Messiah, and most of them rejected Him. That is what John says in the opening verses of his gospel: "He came to that which was his own, but his own did not receive him" (John 1:11). That is what Jesus said to the people: "I have come in my Father's name, and you do not accept me; but if someone else comes in his own name, you will accept him" (John 5:43). Who is this person whom Jesus is talking about—this "someone else" who would come in his own name and be accepted where Jesus Himself was rejected? That is the person whom Paul talks about, the one Paul calls "the man of lawlessness . . . , the man doomed to destruction."

Who is this man of lawlessness? Well, Paul tells us that this character will be an utterly godless individual, yet so remarkable that people will actually accept him as a divinely empowered being who could deliver them from their difficulties. He will have extraordinary powers of communication and persuasion, and people will see him and believe that evil is good, that black is white. The world is hungry to follow such a leader. Even today's diplomats, politicians, and leaders are looking for a single leader of leaders who can unite the world and bring us into harmony and peace. This man of lawlessness will be manifest, says Paul, in the temple of God in Jerusalem.

When Paul wrote this letter in about A.D. 52, the temple in Jerusalem was still standing, but in A.D. 70 it was destroyed, and it has never been rebuilt. In fact, a great Islamic mosque, the Dome of the Rock, now squats on the site where the temple used to be. Scripture predicts that, somehow, the Jews will find a way to reconstruct another temple on the site in Jerusalem where the Dome of the Rock is now. And it is in that future temple that Paul says the man of lawlessness will take his seat. In 2 Thessalonians 2:5–8, Paul goes on to say:

> Don't you remember that when I was with you I used to tell you these things? And now you know what is holding him back, so that he may be revealed at the proper time. For the secret power of lawlessness is already at work; but the one who now holds it back will continue to do so till he is taken out of the way. And then the lawless one will be revealed, whom the Lord Jesus will overthrow with the breath of his mouth and destroy by the splendor of his coming.

This mystery, "the secret power of lawlessness," has baffled our world's leaders and thinkers all through the centuries. As Philippine ambassador to the United States Carlos Romulo once said, "We have harnessed the power of the atom, but how can we bridle the passions of men?" The spirit of lawlessness, of sinfulness, of self-willed rebellion against authority and lust for power poses the greatest danger to any nation. Indeed, in this age of weapons of mass destruction, it is a threat to the existence of the entire human race.

But Paul says that something is restraining the power of lawlessness, preventing total anarchy. Jesus has made it clear what that restraining force is: "You are the salt of the earth," He said. "You are the light of the world" (Matt. 5:13–14). Salt prevents corruption from spreading. Light dispels darkness. So it is the presence of God's people on earth that restrains the secret power of lawlessness and evil—but before we become proud, we should understand this: It is not we who hold back the darkness, but the Spirit of God, living in us, acting through us. So we must make sure that the Holy Spirit has all there is of us so that He can be fully present in the world, guarding against corruption, illuminating the dark corners of this world.

The power of lawlessness released

"The secret power of lawlessness is already at work," says Paul, "but the one who now holds it back [the Holy Spirit] will continue to do so till he is taken out of the way." Paul says here that the restraint that holds back the darkness is going to be removed, and then the whole flood of human evil will be let loose upon the earth. When Jesus comes to gather His people out of the world, the Holy Spirit—who lives in all of us who follow Jesus Christ—will be removed from the world. The restraining force will be gone. Lawlessness will reign on earth—but only for a brief period of time. At the end of that period, the man of lawlessness—who is also called the Antichrist—will be defeated and the worldwide reign of evil will come to an end. As Paul writes:

> The lawless one will be revealed, whom the Lord Jesus will overthrow with the breath of his mouth and destroy by the splendor of his coming. The coming of the lawless one will be in accordance with the work of Satan displayed in all kinds of counterfeit miracles, signs and wonders, and in every sort of evil that deceives those who are perishing. They perish because they refused to love the truth and so be saved. For this reason God sends them a powerful delusion so that they will believe the lie and so that all will be condemned who have not believed the truth but have delighted in wickedness (2:8–12).

God has planted truth inside every human being—yet some choose to believe the lie. So God gives them over to a powerful delusion, so that those who willfully delight in wickedness remain mired in the lie, until their self-deception and self-destruction is complete. The lie, and all those who believe it, will be destroyed by the coming of Jesus, the Son of Man, who will destroy the destroyer.

The conduct of believers under pressure

Chapter 3 deals with the conduct of believers in the face of difficulty and pressure. Certain people in Thessalonica were saying, "Why not just wait until Jesus comes back for us? Why should we concern ourselves about making a living? Let's just live and enjoy ourselves and wait for His coming." So Paul says to them:

> In the name of the Lord Jesus Christ, we command you, brothers, to keep away from every brother who is idle and does not live according to the teaching you received from us (v. 6).

Paul's statement is occasioned by facts that he describes in verses 11 through 13:

> *We hear that some among you are idle. They are not busy; they are busybodies. Such people we command and urge in the Lord Jesus Christ to settle down and earn the bread they eat. And as for you, brothers, never tire of doing what is right.*

As we get nearer to the time of His coming, Paul says, remember that your responsibility is to keep on living normally and working with your hands, taking care of your responsibilities. The Christian life is a normal, natural life, which involves fulfilling all the responsibilities that God places upon us. So, Paul rejects the irrational fanaticism that says, "Let's just drop everything and wait for Jesus to take us away." That is not reasonable, realistic, or even spiritual. It is just lazy and foolish. No one knows when Jesus is coming for us. Although many signs seem to indicate that His return is imminent, He may not come for another thousand or ten thousand years. Only God the Father knows the day and the hour of the Lord's return.

Our responsibility is to keep on living normally and working with our hands, taking care of our responsibilities

Many of the Thessalonian believers had been fooled once before by a forged letter purporting to be from Paul. To make sure this can't happen again, he gives them a sample of his own handwriting:

> *I, Paul, write this greeting in my own hand, which is the distinguishing mark in all my letters. This is how I write.*
> *The grace of our Lord Jesus Christ be with you all (3:17–18).*

With these words, Paul closes a very practical, powerful, and timely letter—timely even in our own day and age. The practical application of this letter to each heart is this: God's people are called to be restrainers of lawlessness, but in order to do so, we must allow God to have complete reign in our lives. If we operate in even the smallest degree by lawlessness, how can we restrain the lawlessness of this world? The measure in which you have dealt with and vanquished the lawlessness of your own heart will determine how effectively God can use you to restrain the lawlessness of this world.

After all these years, the hope of the church has not grown dim. The very events that Jesus and Paul predicted are beginning to be fulfilled in our own time. We are rapidly moving toward the end of the age. Jesus is coming again—and our task is to patiently work, watch, wait, and hope until we hear the shout of triumph and see Him coming for us in the clouds.

After all these years, the hope of the church has not grown dim

How to Build a Church

What happens when Christians gather together at church? Charles Swindoll answers that question in this passage from his book *Come Before Winter and Share My Hope*:

> See you Sunday. That's when the Body and the Head meet to celebrate this mysterious union, . . . when ordinary, garden-variety folks like us gather around the pre-eminent One. For worship. For encouragement. For instruction. For expression. For support. For the carrying out of a God-given role that will never be matched or surpassed on earth—even though it's the stuff the world around us considers weird and weak (Charles R. Swindoll II, *Come Before Winter and Share My Hope* [Wheaton, Ill.: Tyndale, 1985], 403–4).

The world considers the church "weird and weak"

Yes! Though the world truly does consider the church to be "weird and weak," we know that the church is the most powerful instrument in the world. Jesus Himself has said, "On this rock I will build my church, and the gates of Hades will not overcome it" (Matt. 16:18).

In Paul's first letter to Timothy, we are given a set of detailed instructions, a blueprint that shows us how to build a church. Jesus Himself is the architect, the master builder, but we are the carpenters and bricklayers, painters, and carpet layers. So if we want to build His church in a way that pleases Him, we had better read the blueprint He has given us—the blueprint of 1 Timothy.

The authority of an apostle

Paul wrote two letters to Timothy. The second was unquestionably the last letter we have from his pen. The first was written a few years earlier, probably immediately after the apostle Paul was imprisoned in Rome for the first time. After he was released, he wrote this letter to the young man whom he had won to Christ when he preached in Timothy's hometown of Lystra. Timothy was probably no more than sixteen years old at the time he found Christ (he is probably in his late twenties or early thirties at the time this letter is written). He accompanied Paul on his second missionary journey and was a faithful minister and son in the faith to Paul for the rest of Paul's life.

This is one of three pastoral letters in the New Testament, letters written from a pastor's viewpoint; the other two are 2 Timothy and Titus. In these letters, Paul expresses his intimate thoughts to the young people he was mentoring in the ministry, ones who frequently accompanied him on his journeys. Paul had sent Timothy to Ephesus, the great commercial and pleasure resort on the shores of the Mediterranean in Asia Minor.

Despite their close teacher-mentor, father-son relationship, Paul begins both of his letters to Timothy with very similar words. In 1 Timothy 1:1, he writes:

> Paul, an apostle of Christ Jesus by the command of God our Savior and of Christ Jesus our hope.

The letters were not to Timothy only

Timothy certainly did not need this reminder that Paul was an apostle of Christ Jesus; he knew Paul's position well. But Paul expected these letters to have a wider readership than Timothy alone. His previous letters had frequently been circulated among the churches, and he knew these letters would also be circulated. So it is with the authority of an apostle that Paul begins these two letters.

The apostles were commissioned by the Lord Himself

The apostles were men with a unique ministry—men who were commissioned by the Lord Himself and given the task of speaking authoritatively on doctrine and practice in the church. In the first century, some people spoke disparagingly of Paul—just as people sometimes do today. You've probably heard, just as I have: "Well, you know, Paul wrote some things that we cannot take as authoritative. He was a confirmed old bachelor, and what he said about women is not really significant." But to say such a thing is to deny the apostolic office and to refuse the authority that the Lord Jesus gave His apostles, including Paul.

Paul's first letter to Timothy concerns the ministry of the church itself: its character, its nature, and its function in the world. His second letter pertains to the message that the church is to convey to the world—

the gospel of Jesus Christ and Timothy's relationship to that gospel. Here is a structural overview of 1 Timothy:

True and False Doctrines (1 Timothy 1)
1. The danger of false doctrine; teach the truth — 1:1–17
2. Fight the good fight, hold onto faith — 1:18–20

Church Worship (1 Timothy 2)
3. Rules for public worship; the role of women — 2

Church Leadership (1 Timothy 3)
4. Qualifications of church leaders (bishops and deacons) — 3:1–13
5. Conduct in God's household — 3:14–16

Warnings against False Teachers (1 Timothy 4)
6. False and true teachers contrasted — 4:1–10
7. Do not neglect the gift of God — 4:11–16

Church Discipline (1 Timothy 5)
8. Treatment of all people — 5:1–2
9. Treatment of widows — 5:3–16
10. Treatment of elders — 5:17–20
11. Avoid prejudice in church discipline — 5:21–25

The Motives of a Church Leader (1 Timothy 6)
12. Exhortations to servants — 6:1–2
13. Godliness with contentment is gain — 6:3–16
14. Exhortation to the rich — 6:17–19
15. Guard what has been entrusted to you — 6:20–21

Two themes intertwine throughout 1 Timothy: the true nature of the Christian church and the true nature of Christian love. A powerful expression of this first theme, the true nature of the church, is found in 1 Timothy 3:14–15:

Although I hope to come to you soon, I am writing you these instructions so that, if I am delayed, you will know how people ought to conduct themselves in God's household, which is the church of the living God, the pillar and foundation of the truth.

The true Christian church and true Christian love

What does Paul mean when he talks about "the church of the living God." Clearly, he is not talking about a *building*. He is talking about *people.* In fact, he is talking about a family, God's household. One of the great weaknesses of present-day Christianity is that we tend to think of the church as a building. Paul wanted Timothy to know how to conduct himself in the ministry and the relationships of the body of Christ, the church of the living God.

We find a powerful expression of this second theme, the true nature of Christian love, in 1 Timothy 1:5:

The goal of this command is love, which comes from a pure heart and a good conscience and a sincere faith.

This is a more personal theme. While the first theme is that of the church and its ministry, the second theme concerns the individual's relationship to the world, to other Christians, and to God. As the apostle puts it, this second theme states that the Christian's relationships are to consist of "love, which comes from a pure heart and a good conscience and a sincere faith."

Actually, we always begin with the last of these qualities—a sincere faith. That is how we came into the Christian life—by believing God's Word; by exercising faith in what He says. Then, we are led to a good conscience and a pure heart that loves in obedience to His Word. We all come to God in need of being purified by the washing of the Word of God and the cleansing of the blood of Christ. But if you have a good conscience about your faith, it will result in a pure heart, and from that pure heart will flow an unceasing stream of love.

True and false doctrines

In 1 Timothy 1, Paul gives us the background of his counsel to Timothy. Understand that Timothy was pastoring the church in Ephesus, a city largely given over to the worship of a pagan goddess, Diana (also called Artemis), the love goddess of the Greek world. Timothy's task was to minister to the church that was opposing the blind idolatry and superstition of this spiritually dark city—much as our task is to oppose the spiritual darkness and idolatry that surrounds us today.

So the first note the apostle strikes is that Timothy is to oppose false teaching. Apparently, the Ephesian church was being infiltrated by false teachers. The early church had its share of heretics, as does today's church. And Paul warns Timothy about them:

As I urged you when I went into Macedonia, stay there in Ephesus so that you may command certain men not to teach false doctrines any longer nor to devote themselves to myths and endless genealogies. These promote controversies rather than God's work—which is by faith (1:3–4).

Paul added that one of the problems in the church was a wrong understanding of the law. Some church leaders tried to control the conduct of the Ephesian Christians through regulations—in other words, legalism. These legalists who were infecting the church did not understand the power of the indwelling life and grace of the Lord Jesus Christ.

Using the law to control people, says Paul, is wrong. The law is intended for a specific and valid purpose—yet these legalists were abusing the law:

> They want to be teachers of the law, but they do not know what they are talking about or what they so confidently affirm.
> We know that the law is good if one uses it properly. We also know that law is made not for the righteous but for lawbreakers and rebels, the ungodly and sinful, the unholy and irreligious; for those who kill their fathers or mothers, for murderers, for adulterers and perverts, for slave traders and liars and perjurers—and for whatever else is contrary to the sound doctrine that conforms to the glorious gospel of the blessed God, which he entrusted to me (1:7–11).

The law, says Paul, is made for the unrighteous, not the righteous. If you have come to Christ, and your heart is intent upon pleasing Him, why do you need the law? You certainly don't need it to keep you from doing wrong—love will take care of that! But remember that love is interpreted by the law. We understand what love is only when we see it spelled out for us in terms of the law: Do not lie, steal, kill, commit adultery and so forth. These laws describe how true love behaves.

In chapter 2, Paul turns to instructions for public worship. He begins by differentiating between the roles of men and the roles of women in public worship. Men, he says, are to lead in prayer, praying for kings and those in authority, so that citizens might live in peace and godliness. Then he turns to the role of women in the church—and this passage is sometimes used (usually by men) to suggest that women have an inferior position in the church.

We must understand the significant difference between someone's *role* and someone's *importance*. In the church, we all have different roles, but we are all equally important. As Paul tells us in 1 Corinthians 12, the eye can't say to the hand, nor the head to the feet, "I'm the important one here. The body does not need you as much as it needs me." All are necessary, all are equally important—but each has a different role to play. Paul differentiates between the role of men and the role of women in the church in these verses:

These legalists who were infecting the church did not understand the power of the indwelling life and grace of the Lord Jesus Christ

Who needs the law?

Church worship

Roles of men, roles of women

All are necessary, all are equally important—but each has a different role to play

I want men everywhere to lift up holy hands in prayer, without anger or disputing.

I also want women to dress modestly, with decency and propriety, not with braided hair or gold or pearls or expensive clothes, but with good deeds, appropriate for women who profess to worship God.

A woman should learn in quietness and full submission. I do not permit a woman to teach or to have authority over a man; she must be silent. For Adam was formed first, then Eve. And Adam was not the one deceived; it was the woman who was deceived and became a sinner. But women will be saved through childbearing—if they continue in faith, love and holiness with propriety (1 Tim. 2:8–15).

Paul is not saying that women have no right to minister and pray in public like men, although some have misunderstood this passage that way. Rather, he is saying that women are not to teach men authoritatively. They are not to be the final word in the church as to doctrine or teaching, and Paul gives two reasons. First, he says, Adam was formed first, then Eve. Second, the woman was deceived and therefore fell into transgression. It is interesting to note that Eve's sin was primarily that of trying to arrive at a theological conclusion apart from the counsel of her husband.

In a verse that has been somewhat garbled in translation and greatly misunderstood, the apostle goes on to show that women have a wonderful ministry. Women, he says, will be saved through bearing children, if they continue in faith and love and holiness, with modesty or propriety (v. 15). It is important to note, by the way, that the pronoun *they* refers to the children, not the women.

What does Paul mean when he says that women will be saved through bearing children?

Now what does Paul mean when he says that women will be saved through bearing children? I have struggled long with this passage. Late in life, I have come to believe that we can understand the principle of this difficult passage through Paul's exhortation to Timothy in 1 Timothy 4:16:

Watch your life and doctrine closely. Persevere in them, because if you do, you will save both yourself and your hearers.

What does Paul mean by the word *save?* Timothy was already saved; he had been a Christian for many years. And certainly other people were not saved by Timothy's obeying the truth. What does he mean, then? Paul is using the word *salvation* in a different sense than we usually think of it. In fact, Paul uses the word *saved* or *salvation* similarly in several other letters. For example, in Philippians, Paul tells us to "work out your salvation with fear and trembling"—that is, work out the solutions to the problems you confront with fear and trembling, because "it is God who works in you to will and to act according to his good purpose" (Phil. 2:12–13). So here in 1 Timothy, I believe the meaning is that the woman "will be saved" in the sense that her desire for a ministry will be fulfilled and problems will be resolved through childbearing if the children continue in faith and love and holiness with modesty.

Next, Paul turns to the qualifications of church leaders. These leaders fall into two major categories: bishops (or elders) and deacons. Broadly defined, bishops or elders are authorities or decision makers in the church. Deacons are men and women who perform a special task or function in the church, such as caring for the sick and aged, working in an outreach ministry, or teaching a Sunday school class.

Church leadership

Paul begins by stating three crucial qualifications for bishops or elders. First, they are to be "blameless," so as to avoid being disapproved. Second, they are to be pure; that is, they are to be people of proven integrity who understand how to tell the difference between good and evil and who live according to God's Word. Paul gives this requirement of purity so as to avoid pride. The great risk in placing a spiritually immature person in leadership is that he or she may be lifted up with pride and fall into the trap of the devil (pride is always a trap). Third, these people were to be of good repute, to avoid public scandal that would bring the whole ministry of the church into disgrace.

Qualifications for elders

Deacons are treated somewhat similarly, but Paul adds one major instruction concerning deacons: they are first to be tested, to be given work to do on a trial basis. If they perform it well, they are recognized as people who can be trusted with responsibility in the work of the church. The importance of this charge is that it all relates to the fact that the church is linked with the mystery of Christ. Christ is the greatest figure in the universe—everything relates to Him. Paul quotes a first-century hymn to set forth what he means:

Qualifications for deacons

> *Beyond all question, the mystery of godliness is great: He appeared in a body, was vindicated by the Spirit, was seen by angels, was preached among the nations, was believed on in the world, was taken up in glory (3:16).*

Paul puts the church in its proper perspective. We must select the leaders of the church very carefully, because the church represents Jesus Christ to the world.

**Warnings
against false
teachers**

In chapter 4, Paul turns to the subject of apostasy. Before going on, let's clarify our terms. Though the terms are often confused by Christians today, an *apostate* is not the same thing as a *heretic*. A heretic is a misguided Christian—one who basically accepts and knows the Lord Jesus Christ, but who tends to go wrong in some particular doctrinal issue. But an apostate has never been a Christian, although an apostate testifies that he or she is a Christian. As John tells us in his first letter, "They went out from us, but they did not really belong to us. For if they had belonged to us, they would have remained with us; but their going showed that none of them belonged to us" (1 John 2:19).

*Jesus said these
good and bad
plants would grow
up together until
the harvest*

In Matthew 13, the Lord tells the story of the sower who went out to sow the good seed of the kingdom. In the middle of the night, an enemy came in behind him, sowing weeds in the same fields. The good grain and the weeds came up together. Jesus said these good and bad plants would grow up together until the harvest, which is why we will never get rid of the apostates within the church. Apostate attitudes arise when people follow doctrines of demons, deceitful spirits. Apostasy is not rooted in twisted human ideas, but rather from deliberately deceitful ideas of wicked spirits who sow spiritual "weed seed" in order to pollute the kingdom and lead people astray.

Paul goes on to say that only when the evil of the apostates becomes evident is Timothy to excommunicate them, not before. His first priority is not to weed out evil and deception but to preach the truth. His next priority is to set an example for the people in his own personal life.

Until I come, devote yourself to the public reading of Scripture, to preaching and to teaching. Do not neglect your gift, which was given you through a prophetic message when the body of elders laid their hands on you (4:13–14).

*Jesus and Paul tell
us that the best
guarantee against
the weed of
apostasy is to keep
the garden as
strong and weed-
resistant as it can
possibly be*

Unfortunately, too many Christians have forgotten the message of Jesus and of Paul regarding apostasy. They see their ministry in the church as that of being a Christian weed-whacker, like one of those whirring garden implements that mows down weeds with nylon fishing line. Unfortunately, such Christians also whack down a lot of fruit-bearing plants as well! Jesus and Paul tell us that the best guarantee against the weed of apostasy is not to go around whacking weeds but to keep the garden as strong and weed-resistant as it can possibly be. That means informing the congregation of the dangers, setting a positive example, and continually expounding the Scriptures.

**Church
discipline**

In chapter 5, Paul discusses specific church issues and problems, including how to treat younger and older people within the church and advice to women on various practical matters. Then he takes up the official problem of how to handle accusations against the elders. Finally, he discusses certain personal issues involving Timothy, including an exhortation to remain pure and advice for the care for his chronic stomach problems.

Chapter 6 deals with certain social problems, beginning with the issue of slavery and human rights. This is an especially pertinent passage for us to examine in our own day, given the issues we wrestle with from racial tensions to materialism. We cannot deny that in our times, in our own society, people have been degraded and deprived of basic human rights and dignity. Paul addresses this section of his letter to Christian slaves, and he reminds them that they should consider their masters worthy of respect so that God's name and Christian teaching will not be slandered.

Next, Paul exhorts Timothy to walk honestly and steadfastly in the sight of God until the day that the Lord calls him home.

Having begun by addressing the poor, Paul concludes by assigning Christian responsibilities to the rich and the learned. They are rich, he says, because they have been blessed by God so that they could be a blessing to others—not so that they could indulge themselves and their own desires. They have a responsibility, he says, to be rich in good deeds and generosity, laying a foundation for the future so that they can take hold of the truly abundant life right now—not abundant in material possession but abundant in the things of God (see 1 Tim. 6:18–19).

In closing, Paul entrusts to Timothy a word of warning to be delivered to those who trust in human knowledge:

> *Timothy, guard what has been entrusted to your care. Turn away from godless chatter and the opposing ideas of what is falsely called knowledge, which some have professed and in so doing have wandered from the faith.*
> *Grace be with you (6:20–21).*

Here is a letter for our own times, our own churches. It provides an objective standard against which to measure our modes of worship, church leaders, beliefs and doctrines, and cultural attitudes. In short, it is a set of clear, profound instructions from God in how to build a church. Truly, 1 Timothy is a letter for the twenty-first century as well as the first! God grant us eager, obedient hearts to read it, understand it, and live by it.

Closing admonitions

To slaves

To Timothy

To the rich

Sturdy Christians in a Collapsing World

I n A.D. 68, an old man sat in a filthy, rock-walled, circular cell in a Roman prison. This man, who had once traveled the world, telling thousands of people how to find an intimate relationship with the Creator of the universe, was now confined in a dingy space about twenty feet in diameter. From that prison cell, he put pen to paper and wrote a letter to a young man far across the Aegean and Adriatic Seas in the city of Ephesus. The subject of his letter: How to remain strong in the midst of a collapsing civilization. That is the theme of 2 Timothy.

Roman society in the first century was in rapid decline. Likewise, America stands at the threshold of the twenty-first century as a sin-soaked, crumbling society permeated with moral disintegration, pornography, abortion, child abuse, crime, poverty, satanism, occultism, and racial division. So Paul's wisdom in 2 Timothy is as applicable today as it was when he wrote it some two thousand years ago.

In 2 Timothy, Paul writes to his son in the faith—a young man who is troubled by a weak constitution (a weak stomach, to be exact), a fearful spirit, and a timid outlook on life. Understand, Timothy had much to be fearful about! He was surrounded by intense persecution. His friend and mentor Paul was in prison for his faith and facing a possible sentence of death. The world was in political crisis and social chaos. Sound familiar?

Paul's last will and testament

Paul knew that he was about to depart and be with the Lord, and he wanted to pass the torch to this younger man. He does so in this letter—a letter that, in fact, is the last letter we have from Paul's pen. This is his farewell message, his final words of exhortation and friendship, his legacy, his last will and testament.

This letter centers on four challenges that Paul wants to communicate to Timothy, his young son in the faith. These timeless challenges apply to today's Christians as well:

1. Guard the truth.
2. Be strong in the Lord.
3. Avoid the traps and pitfalls of life.
4. Preach the Word.

If I had to write to a young person today, I am sure I could never find anything better to say. Here is a structural overview of this letter:

A Christian's Responsibility in a
Collapsing World (2 Timothy 1–2)

1.	Paul expresses thanks for Timothy's faith	1:1–5
2.	Timothy's responsibility as a pastor	1:6–18
3.	The job description of a faithful pastor	2
	A. Teacher-discipler	2:1–2
	B. Soldier of God	2:3–4
	C. Athlete who competes by the rules	2:5
	D. Patient, hardworking farmer	2:6–13
	E. Diligent worker	2:14–19
	F. Instrument for God's use	2:20–23
	G. Gentle servant-teacher	2:24–26

The Christian's Strength in a
Collapsing World (2 Timothy 3–4)

4.	The coming time of apostasy	3
5.	Preach the Word	4:1–5
6.	Paul approaches the end of his life; parting words	4:6–22

Paul begins by reminding Timothy that God has committed to Timothy a deposit of truth, which is his responsibility to guard:

Guard the good deposit that was entrusted to you—guard it with the help of the Holy Spirit who lives in us (2 Tim. 1:14).

Paul then suggests certain ways to carry out this commission. While this letter is addressed to someone who is a pastor, Paul's challenge should be taken to heart by all Christians. Timothy lived in a pagan, secularized society, just as we do today. Paul impressed upon him his responsibility to strengthen the defenses of the Ephesian church—a church that was imperiled by the pressures, temptations, and persecutions of the evil society around it.

Like Timothy, you and I have been given this same deposit of truth—the fundamental revelation of the Scripture concerning the nature of reality: what the world is like, what God is like, what people are like, and what we need to do in order to be saved from our sin condition. From Timothy's day until now, people have wondered: *What makes the world operate the way it does? Why does it fall apart all the time? Why does nothing good seem to prosper and everything evil seem to reign unchallenged?* The answers are found in the deposit of truth that has been given to us through Jesus Christ, and we must guard it. Paul suggests three specific ways to do this:

- Guard the truth by exercising the spiritual gift God has given you.
- Guard the truth by suffering patiently.
- Guard the truth by following the pattern of sound teaching (read and trust the Scriptures).

Paul addresses the first of these ways to guard the truth in 2 Timothy 1:6–7:

1. Exercise your spiritual gifts

> *I remind you to fan into flame the gift of God, which is in you through the laying on of my hands. For God did not give us a spirit of timidity, but a spirit of power, of love and of self-discipline* [or a sound mind].

Over the years, my parishioners have come to me during various world crises and asked, What is going to happen in the world? What does it mean that communism has collapsed and the Berlin Wall has fallen? What does it mean that America is getting involved in a war in the Persian Gulf? What is going on in the Middle East? What is going on in Russia? What is going to happen at election time? Though I've studied Bible prophecy, I have no crystal ball (nor would I want one!). I don't think it's very useful or wise to try to match this or that headline with this or that specific verse in Scripture. We definitely see that the pattern of history and current events matches the pattern of prophecy, but I don't know how this event or that election fits into God's eternal plan. The truth is, no one can say for sure that there will even be another election in this country!

As someone has wisely said, we don't know what the future holds, but we know who holds the future. Even more importantly, we know that God has not given us a spirit of timidity and fear. If we are anxious and troubled about what is going on in our nation and in the world, it does not come from God. The Spirit of God is the Spirit of power who prepares us for action. He is the Spirit of love who enables us to respond to people in a way that produces healing and grace. He is the Spirit of a sound mind who enables us to be intelligently purposeful in all we do. The way to discover this Spirit is to exercise the spiritual gifts that God has given us.

If you are a Christian, the indwelling Holy Spirit has given you a special ability. If you are not putting that spiritual gift to work, you are wasting your life. In the judgment of God—truly the only judgment that counts—all you accomplish outside of His will and His strength will be counted as so much wood, hay, and stubble, fit only to be burned.

What work has God given you to do? What spiritual gifts has He given you? Do you know? Have you discovered your purpose in life? Do you know what to look for? Do you know how to find it? When you have discovered your gifts and you begin to use them for His purpose, you will find that God does not give a spirit of fear but of power and love and a sound mind. That is Paul's first word to Timothy about how to guard the truth.

You might ask, "How does that work? How can using my spiritual gifts help to guard the truth?" It's simple: When you exercise your spiritual gifts, you literally unleash the truth and set it free to work in the world. The truth is not some fragile, brittle thing; rather, it is powerful, robust, vigorous, active. And the most effective way to guard God's truth is to unleash it in the world!

Charles Spurgeon was exactly right when he said, "Truth is like a lion. Whoever heard of defending a lion? Turn it loose and it will defend itself." That is what we need to do with this truth. We do not need to apologize for it with theological, exegetical arguments. We do not need to fend off attacks on the truth. We merely need to set the truth free in the world, act on it, live it, use our spiritual gifts, and the truth will take care of itself!

Second, Paul says that we should guard the truth by suffering patiently. He reminds Timothy that every Christian, without exception, is called to suffer for the gospel's sake.

> *Do not be ashamed to testify about our Lord, or ashamed of me his prisoner. But join with me in suffering for the gospel, by the power of God (1:8).*

Later in this same letter, Paul makes a related statement:

When you exercise your spiritual gifts, you literally unleash the truth and set it free to work in the world

2. Suffer patiently

In fact, everyone who wants to live a godly life in Christ Jesus will be persecuted (3:12).

You might say, "Well, that doesn't include me! I haven't been physically tortured or imprisoned for my faith." Really? Well, then you are certainly in the minority! Most Christians around the world see persecution and peril as a normal condition of being a Christian! More Christians have been tortured and put to death for Christ's sake in the twentieth century than in any other. Worldwide trends indicate that the twenty-first century will likely be far worse. Expect to see increasing hostility toward believers around the world—and in America. Don't think that living in a country with a constitution and two-hundred-plus years of religious liberty will protect you.

The suffering that we will face will likely be not only physical, but mental and emotional as well. It is the kind of suffering that we endure when our faith is ridiculed, when we are excluded from various events because of our moral and spiritual stand, when we are treated with open contempt or disdain, when our values and Christian lifestyles are mocked and laughed at. These are all forms of suffering for the gospel, and we are to accept this suffering with patience, says Paul. Again, when we do so, we unleash the truth of God in the world, and without even defending ourselves, we guard the truth of God.

One of the reasons that the gospel is not widely accepted in many places today is that Christians have been impatient in suffering. Instead of patiently withstanding the abuse of this world, we have either been offended and outraged by persecution or we have given in and gone along with the crowd to escape having to suffer for the Lord's sake. You cannot challenge the sin and corruption of the world without getting the world mad at you. Obviously, you don't go out of your way to offend people, but the truth alone will bring about offense and backlash enough. The Scriptures make it clear that God is able to use our patient suffering for His truth as a tool for expanding the influence of His truth in the world. Our patient suffering is a potent, powerful way of guarding the truth of God.

The third way in which Paul says we guard the truth is contained in Paul's admonition to Timothy, "What you heard from me, keep as the pattern of sound teaching" (1:13). In other words: Listen to, trust, and live out the Word of God. I love that phrase, "the pattern of sound teaching." There are so many today who are departing from the pattern of sound teaching. They believe that some secular writer, out of the blindness and darkness of his or her own heart, has more insight into the problems of life than Scripture does. When they repeat these arguments, or live according to this philosophy, they soon find themselves engulfed

More Christians have been tortured and put to death for Christ's sake in the twentieth century than in any other

You cannot challenge the sin and corruption of the world without getting the world mad at you

3. Read and trust the Scriptures

The pattern of sound teaching

in neuroses, psychoses, and other problems—and they can't understand why. If we live as Paul tells Timothy he should live—guarding the truth that God has entrusted to us by exercising our gifts, suffering patiently, and trusting the Scriptures—God will guard us, protect us, and keep us secure in the faith, even amid this crumbling, collapsing world.

Be strong in the Lord

Paul's second exhortation: "Be strong in the Lord." You never tell someone to be strong unless that person is capable of carrying it out. Obviously, Paul knew that Timothy had the capacity for strength—and you and I do as well. It is not a strength that we manufacture within ourselves but a strength that comes from trusting in the infinite power of Jesus Christ. There is a saying, "When I try, I fail. When I trust, He succeeds." Not I. He. His strength, remember, is perfected in our weakness (see 2 Cor. 12:9–10). That is the central truth about how the Christian life is to be lived.

Dedicated, like a soldier; disciplined, like an athlete; diligent, like a farmer

Paul uses a number of word pictures to describe what it means to be strong in the Lord. First, we are to be strong as a soldier is strong—that is, we are to be utterly dedicated to the task. Second, we are to be strong as an athlete is strong—that is, we are to be disciplined and we are to abide by the rules of the Christian life so that we can compete to the utmost. Third, we are to be strong as a farmer is strong—and that means we are to be diligent in our work, not slowing down or slacking off, because we know that only if we work hard planting and cultivating will we be able to harvest. Dedication, discipline, and diligence—these are the keys to strength as described by Paul in this visual job description of the Christian.

He closes this second challenge with a reminder of the strength of the Lord. We are not merely to be strong, but to be strong *in the Lord.* He writes:

> *Remember Jesus Christ, raised from the dead, descended from David. This is my gospel (2:8).*

Paul wants Timothy to remember two things about Jesus: (1) He is the risen Christ, the Messiah, alive and powerful to be with us, completely unlimited by the constraints of space and time; (2) He is a human Christ, the Son of David, the one who has been where we are and who has felt what we feel—our pressures, our fears, our temptations, and our pain. He is the Son of God and the Son of Man—and He is the source of our strength in a crumbling, collapsing world.

Avoid the traps

Paul's next challenge is found in 2:14–3:17. Here, Paul tells us to avoid the traps and pitfalls that lie in wait for us along the Christian life. He then describes some of those traps.

The first trap: battles over words. Have you ever seen the way Christians often get all upset over some little word in Scripture? over, say, a particular mode of baptism, or the exact timing of the Millennium? I've seen it many times—Christians dividing up into camps and choosing up weapons and battling it out. Paul says we must avoid this kind of conflict over words. These are stupid and useless controversies, dividing Christian from Christian, and they spread like gangrene. I'm not saying that such matters as baptism and the Millennium are unimportant—these are clearly areas of important biblical and scholarly inquiry, and Christians may engage in a robust discussion of such issues. But Christians should never separate over such issues.

Avoid stupid and useless controversies

The second trap: dangerous passions and temptations. Here is a word to a normal red-blooded young man who must have felt the urgings of a normal sex drive and who lived in a sex-saturated society much like ours.

Avoid dangerous passions and temptations

> *In a large house there are articles not only of gold and silver, but also of wood and clay; some are for noble purposes and some for ignoble. If a man cleanses himself from the latter, he will be an instrument for noble purposes, made holy, useful to the Master and prepared to do any good work (2:20–21).*

Paul uses a beautiful word picture, depicting the whole world as a great house. In that house are instruments or vessels, representing people, and God uses these different instruments or vessels for either noble purposes or ignoble purposes. In other words, some people are like beautiful vases and crystal goblets. Others are like brick doorstops and brass spittoons. One way or another, God will use us for His purposes. It is completely up to us what kind of vessel we choose to be. God uses committed Christians to tell the world about His love, to draw others to faith in Him, to actively care for the hurting and the needy. But He also uses ungodly people.

Some years ago, a young man and a young woman were living together, unmarried, living a completely hedonistic lifestyle involving drug abuse. The young woman reached a point where she realized she was unhappy with her life, and she told the young man, "I don't know what it is, but I'm unhappy all the time." He replied, "I know what your problem is. If you want to be happy, you should ask Jesus Christ to come into your life. I know, because I was raised in a Christian home." When the woman asked why he didn't live according to Christian principles, he replied, "I want to live my life without rules, without morality. So I want nothing to do with Jesus—but if you really want to be happy, that's what you have to do." And the young woman accepted Christ, broke up with the young man, moved out, got involved in a church, and got her life straightened out. She became a noble vessel, willing to be used by God; he was an ignoble vessel, unwilling—but used by God nonetheless!

Our goal as Christians is to be our best, most noble, most beautiful vessels for God. To be used for a noble purpose rather than ignoble, says Paul, we must separate ourselves from the things that would destroy our lives:

> *Flee the evil desires of youth, and pursue righteousness, faith, love and peace, along with those who call on the Lord out of a pure heart (2:22).*

One of the great destructive forces of our time—sexual immorality

One of the great destructive forces of our time—especially in this age of AIDS—is sexual immorality. Deadly sexually transmitted diseases are only the most visible harm this behavior causes. Sexual promiscuity destroys families, wounds the emotions and the psyches of men, women, and adolescents, and tears the fabric of our civilization. Most people in our society seem to be blinded to this fact. But Christians have been instructed and warned: Flee evil desires, pursue purity before God. Then He will be able to use you for noble purposes, not ignoble.

The third trap: a rebellious attitude.

Avoid lawless people

> *Mark this: There will be terrible times in the last days. People will be lovers of themselves, lovers of money, boastful, proud, abusive, disobedient to their parents, ungrateful, unholy, without love, unforgiving, slanderous, without self-control, brutal, not lovers of the good, treacherous, rash, conceited, lovers of pleasure rather than lovers of God—having a form of godliness but denying its power. Have nothing to do with them (3:1–5).*

First, understand that the phrase "last days" refers to the final end time of the church on earth. It includes the entire period of time between the first and the second comings of Christ. From the very day that our Lord rose from the dead, these were the last days. During these last days in which we now live, says Paul, there will come recurrent cycles of distress.

Demonic forces are at work stirring up divisions

We are experiencing such times right now when people long for peace but are beset with anxiety about the future. Demonic forces are at work in the world, stirring up divisions, wars, racial strife, intergenerational tension, and even unprecedented warfare between men and women. Today we see characteristics that Paul describes: self-centeredness, greed, arrogance and pride, abuse, disobedience, and disrespect. These are characteristics of rebellion—an attitude of lawlessness. People—even Christians—easily assume such an attitude. Paul says, "Avoid such people. Do not join them in their lawlessness."

In the closing part of chapter 3, Paul shows Timothy the twofold way out of all these snares: (1) patience in suffering, and (2) persistence in truth. "Remember the way I behaved," he says to Timothy. "You've seen how I've endured all the trials that came my way. Remember that if you're quietly patient in suffering and continue in the truth holding to the Scriptures and to what God has said, you will find your way safely through all the perils and the pitfalls of the collapsing world."

In chapter 4, Paul gives Timothy his final challenge:

> *In the presence of God and of Christ Jesus, who will judge the living and the dead, and in view of his appearing and his kingdom, I give you this charge: Preach the Word; be prepared in season and out of season; correct, rebuke and encourage—with great patience and careful instruction (4:1–2).*

In other words, do not merely believe the Word but share it with others. Declare the great truth that God has given you. And there are three dimensions to declaring God's truth: Correct, rebuke, and encourage all who will listen to the truth, in order to counteract the corrupting influence of this dying age. For, as Paul adds in verse 3, a time is coming when people will not endure sound teaching.

Paul closes this commanding letter on a personal, poignant, yet triumphant note:

> *I am already being poured out like a drink offering, and the time has come for my departure. I have fought the good fight, I have finished the race, I have kept the faith. Now there is in store for me the crown of righteousness, which the Lord, the righteous Judge, will award to me on that day—and not only to me, but also to all who have longed for his appearing (4:6–8).*

That triumphant statement is all the more astounding when you remember the setting in which it is written. Here is the apostle in a tiny little stone-walled cell, cramped and cold, writing in semidarkness by the light of a sputtering oil lamp. He knows his fate is sealed. He has already appeared once before Nero, that monster in human flesh, and he must appear before this Roman emperor once more. Paul knows what will

Paul shows Timothy the twofold way out of all these snares: (1) patience in suffering, and (2) persistence in truth

Preach the Word

Paul's parting words

happen next. He knows how evil Nero is. Paul fully expects to be taken outside the city wall and, with a flash of the sword, to lose his head.

But notice where Paul's gaze is fixed—not upon the moment of his death, but beyond death, to the crown of righteousness that awaits him. Death is but an incident to one who truly believes. Beyond death, victory beckons.

Yet, mingled with this intensely passionate shout of triumph, we hear a chord of strong human emotion—especially the emotion of loneliness:

> *Only Luke is with me. Get Mark and bring him with you, because he is helpful to me in my ministry. I sent Tychicus to Ephesus. When you come, bring the cloak that I left with Carpus at Troas, and my scrolls, especially the parchments (4:11–13).*

We can admit our
feelings to God, and
He fully accepts
them; there is
nothing sinful about
normal human
emotion in times
of trial

Though Paul could look beyond his present circumstance to the glory of God that awaited him, see how human he is. This is normal. This is acceptable to God, because He knows what we are made of. He knows that it is hard for a human being to remain hopeful when feeling lonely, cold, isolated, and bored. We can admit these feelings to God, and He fully accepts these feelings. There is nothing sinful about normal human emotion in times of trial.

I have often thought about that appearance of Paul before Nero. Paul's only concern at that moment was that he be able to proclaim God's message boldly and fully:

> *At my first defense, no one came to my support, but everyone deserted me. May it not be held against them. But the Lord stood at my side and gave me strength, so that through me the message might be fully proclaimed and all the Gentiles might hear it. And I was delivered from the lion's mouth. The Lord will rescue me from every evil attack and will bring me safely to his heavenly kingdom. To him be glory for ever and ever. Amen (4:16–18).*

Today, people name
their sons Paul—
and their dogs Nero

When Paul stood before Nero, the name of Nero was honored and praised throughout the known world. Who was Paul of Tarsus? A little bald-headed, bowlegged man with weak eyes, poor speech, and a strange faith in a crucified Jew. But two thousand years later, the tables are turned. Today, people name their sons Paul—and their dogs Nero.

Paul closes with some personal words to his friends, familiar names like Priscilla and Aquila, and some lesser known names as well.

What a powerful letter this is—and how young Timothy's heart and life must have been affected by it. I would love to have gotten a letter like that from Paul, wouldn't you? Yet, in a real sense, that's exactly what this letter is: a letter to me and you from the heart of Paul—and from the heart of God. Paul and God want us to know how to stand firm and be strong, even though the world seems to be collapsing all around us. No matter how bad this sorry world gets, we know that God enables us to be faithful in a world that is false, for He has not given us a spirit of timidity and fear, but of power, of love, and of a sound mind.

Hope for the Future, Help for Today

Alvin Toffler's best-seller *Future Shock* describes the kind of stunned emotional reaction that people would experience as the world changes all too rapidly around them. People would experience "future shock" as they began to see the future as a reality that was moving at the speed of light, leaving them behind. Amazingly, the future shock of which Toffler wrote in the early 1970s did begin to take into account our present age of personal computers, Stealth fighters and cruise missiles, the Internet, cellular phones, the demise of communism, and so much more.

Our world has changed—and continues to change—even faster than a futurist like Toffler could have imagined. As a result, many people have given up on the future and have settled into a state of despair. But in Paul's letter to Titus, we find a powerful antidote to future shock. Paul calls this antidote "our blessed hope." Even though the world is changing, even though our heads are spinning as we try to keep up with the dizzying pace of new developments in our society, we have a hope that anchors our future and enables us to feel secure . . .

Titus: Antidote to future shock—"our blessed hope"

while we wait for the blessed hope—the glorious appearing of our great God and Savior, Jesus Christ (Titus 2:13).

Jesus will appear in glory to set right all the things that are wrong in this world. That is our hope. That is the cure for our future shock. That is one of the themes that Paul weaves into his letter to Titus.

Titus and the character of the Cretans

Titus was one of the young men who accompanied the apostle Paul on many of his missionary journeys. Titus was a Greek who came to Christ in the city of Antioch. At the time this letter was written, he was on the island of Crete, just south of Greece.

The church in Crete likely was begun by Paul and Titus after Paul's first imprisonment in Rome. Apparently, Paul was released from that imprisonment, as recorded in the book of Acts. You may recall that Paul had expressed the desire to go to Spain, and many scholars believe that after his journey to Spain, he and Titus went to the island of Crete and began the church there. According to this letter, he left Titus there to "straighten out what was left unfinished and appoint elders in every town, as I [Paul] directed you" (1:5). This letter provides an interesting insight as to what occurred in the early church as Paul traveled and sent these young men as apostolic delegates to do special work for him in various places.

Paul's letter to Titus is short and practical, rich in instruction and encouragement. As we look at it, we will not go through it chapter by chapter, verse by verse. The themes of this little book are interwoven throughout, so we will explore it theme by theme. Thus, we may seem to jump from, say, chapter 3 to chapter 1 and back again—but I believe that you will find this method to be a helpful way to examine the truths of this book. Here is an overview of the structure of Paul's letter to Titus:

Church Leadership (Titus 1)

1.	Introductory remarks	1:1–4
2.	The qualifications of elders (church leaders)	1:5–9
3.	Dealing with false teachers in the church	1:10–16

Christian Living in Difficult Times (Titus 2–3)

4.	Teach sound doctrine	2
5.	Commit to good works	3:1–11
6.	Conclusion	3:12–15

In one of the most unusual passages in the New Testament, Paul quotes from one of the ancient writers of his day, a secular Greek poet who characterized the people of Crete, among whom young Titus lived and labored:

Even one of their own prophets has said, "Cretans are always liars, evil brutes, lazy gluttons" (1:12).

This is obviously Paul's private message to his son in the faith, Titus; Paul wants him to understand the formidable problem that he must resolve. Paul warns Titus that he is dealing with dishonest, brutish, lazy, and gluttonous people. He underscores this by adding, "This testimony is true" (v. 13). As we move through the letter, Paul amplifies and explores these characteristics of the Cretan people. For example, Paul says,

To the pure, all things are pure, but to those who are corrupted and do not believe, nothing is pure. In fact, both their minds and consciences are corrupted. They claim to know God, but by their actions they deny him. They are detestable, disobedient and unfit for doing anything good (1:15–16).

This was the kind of wicked, morally corrupt society in which the church of Titus existed. These Cretans' minds and consciences were corrupted. They professed to know God, but they denied Him by their deeds.

Paul also called the people of Crete evil brutes, because they were like rabid animals in their attitudes toward one another. This theme is amplified in chapter 3:

Avoid foolish controversies and genealogies and arguments and quarrels about the law, because these are unprofitable and useless. Warn a divisive person once, and then warn him a second time. After that, have nothing to do with him. You may be sure that such a man is warped and sinful; he is self-condemned (vv. 9–11).

These words refer primarily to those who profess to be Christian but whose lives reflect the attitudes of the evil world around them. The purpose of the church is to invade the world with the love of Jesus Christ. When the church is beset with problems, it is usually because the world is invading the church, not because the church is invading the world! The gospel was given to be a disturbing element in the world, because society never changes for the better unless it is disturbed. Whenever the church is true to its authentic message, it stands against the status quo. The church is a revolutionary body—and the revolution it brings is one of love and purity that challenges the wicked, brutish status quo.

These Cretans' minds and consciences were corrupted

When the church is beset with problems, it is usually because the world is invading the church, not because the church is invading the world

**The needs of
the Cretans —
and of us all**

What would you do with factious people who acted like animals, snarling and biting at one another, engaging in stupid controversies and quarrels over the law? What would you do with people who were characterized further as lazy gluttons—easygoing, pleasure-loving people? In chapter 3, Paul speaks not only of Cretans, but also of himself and of all human beings as we were before becoming Christians. Here is a description of the world as God sees it:

> *At one time we too were foolish, disobedient, deceived and enslaved
> by all kinds of passions and pleasures. We lived in malice and envy, being
> hated and hating one another (v. 3).*

Sound doctrine

This is the kind of a world into which the apostle Paul sent young Titus, with the power of the gospel. What did these people need? Several times throughout this letter, we read the phrase *sound doctrine.* Paul knew that in order to change society, people must be told the truth. People walk in darkness and act like animals, tearing one another apart and hating one another, for one of two reasons: Either they have rejected the truth—or they have never heard the truth. So you begin by teaching them the truth.

Good deeds

Another basic need: good deeds. This phrase appears five times in Titus. Chapter 1 ends with a description of those who are "unfit for doing anything good" (1:16). Chapter 2 says, "In everything set them an example by doing what is good" (2:7). The chapter closes with the idea that Jesus gave Himself "to purify for himself a people that are his very own, eager to do what is good" (2:14). In chapter 3, Paul says, "those who have trusted in God [should] be careful to devote themselves to doing what is good" (v. 8), and adds that Christians "must learn to devote themselves to doing what is good" (v. 14). Sound doctrine alone is not enough. The world is looking for good deeds that back up our good doctrine.

Sound doctrine
alone is not
enough; the world
is looking for good
deeds that back up
our good doctrine

We keep trying to change the way people are and the way they behave. We try to change people with education, or with tougher laws, or with inducements and rewards—but nothing works. People are people, and human nature is the same today as it ever was. As someone has well said, "If you bring a pig into the parlor, it won't change the pig, but it will certainly change the parlor!" And that is the problem. It's not enough to try to change people's behavior. You have to change what people intrinsically are. You have to transform their nature. That's what the truth of salvation is all about—and that is the truth Paul says is desperately needed—by all people in every era. In chapter 3, he says,

> *At one time we too were foolish, disobedient, deceived and enslaved
> by all kinds of passions and pleasures. We lived in malice and envy, being*

hated and hating one another. But when the kindness of God our Savior appeared, he saved us, not because of righteous things we had done, but because of his mercy. He saved us through the washing of rebirth and renewal by the Holy Spirit (3:3–5).

Good deeds are not enough; our greatest need is not merely to become nicer people. We need to be turned inside out and shaken! We need to be completely changed! We need to be saved! That's what Paul means when he talks about "the washing of rebirth and renewal." He says that God completely makes us over from the inside. God does not patch us up from the outside like an old inner tube. He completely melts us down and remolds us in His own image, by the washing of regeneration and renewal in the Holy Spirit. The supreme message of the church is to proclaim this great good news—"the hope of eternal life" (v. 7).

Understand that when the Bible speaks of hope, it does not use the word in the same way we usually do today, meaning a faint glimmer of a possibility: "I hope I win the Irish sweepstakes," or, "I hope that clattering sound in the engine doesn't mean what I think it does!" When the New Testament speaks of hope, it speaks of a *certainty:* The hope of eternal life rests upon the One who came to give us eternal life, and we are justified by His grace. This is rock-solid reality!

Here is our shock-proof hope for the future, our bullet-proof shield against the uncertainty of tomorrow. The world is changing rapidly. We witness morality crumbling, deviant behavior being called normal, moral values being redefined as "repressive." We see good being called evil, and evil, good. Arrogance, extremism, and hedonism are celebrated and applauded in our society; humility, moderation, and virtue are ridiculed. If we do not have a rock-solid hope in the midst of such rapidly shifting, dizzying, sickening changes, we will succumb to despair. Paul describes the hope that God has given us in Titus 2:11–13:

> *The grace of God that brings salvation has appeared to all men. It teaches us to say "No" to ungodliness and worldly passions, and to live self-controlled, upright and godly lives in this present age, while we wait for the blessed hope—the glorious appearing of our great God and Savior, Jesus Christ.*

This is the answer to future shock and present despair—our blessed hope, the glorious appearing of our great God and Savior, Jesus Christ. In this passage Paul clearly identifies Jesus as *God*. Many people today try to escape this truth of Scripture. We see it clearly stated throughout the gospel of John, in Philippians 2, and in Titus 2:13. And wherever it is not stated with such unambiguous, obvious clarity as we see here, it is always implied throughout the Old and New Testaments: Jesus the Messiah is the eternal God in human flesh.

Another major issue that Paul addresses in this book is the issue of church leadership. The Cretans needed to understand how an orderly Christian church should function, so in the opening chapter, Paul describes the qualifications for church leaders (the word *elder* refers to the individual holding the leadership office; the word *bishop* refers to the office itself). Paul writes:

> *An elder must be blameless, the husband of but one wife, a man whose children believe and are not open to the charge of being wild and disobedient. Since an overseer is entrusted with God's work, he must be blameless—not overbearing, not quick-tempered, not given to drunkenness, not violent, not pursuing dishonest gain. Rather he must be hospitable, one who loves what is good, who is self-controlled, upright, holy and disciplined (1:6–8).*

Where do you find such people? Paul expected Titus to find them in Crete. He expected God to raise up people of proven character, faith, and spiritual gifts from among those who had once been characterized as liars, evil brutes, and lazy gluttons. The gospel effects such transformation. Properly understood, the church is a community of change, a family in which God's grace and the love of His people bring about radical healing, therapy, and redirection. That is what a church was created to accomplish.

Paul also tells Titus that he needs to teach the Christians in Crete about civic responsibility:

> *Remind the people to be subject to rulers and authorities, to be obedient, to be ready to do whatever is good, to slander no one, to be peaceable and considerate, and to show true humility toward all men (3:1–2).*

Paul exhorts the church to recognize that the authorities are in a real sense God's ministers (whether or not they see themselves and offer themselves to God as such). God has ordained government to maintain order in human society, so we should be respectful and obedient to the law in every area except those in which government opposes God's law.

How practical this letter is! And how relevant to our own lives today. As Paul gives these guidelines, he is quietly injecting into the Cretan community a power that, if followed, would transform the national character of Crete, just as it will transform the national character of our own society.

Paul closes his letter with some personal words of admonition and advice, giving us a penetrating glimpse into his own life. He writes:

> As soon as I send Artemas or Tychicus to you, do your best to come to me at Nicopolis, because I have decided to winter there (3:12).

Nicopolis was on the western shore of Greece, just across the Adriatic Sea from the heel of the Italian boot. Paul, probably writing from Corinth in Greece, was sending two young men down to replace Titus in Crete, so that Titus could rejoin Paul. Later we read that Titus went on up to Dalmatia, on the northern coast, sending Zenas, the lawyer, and Apollos on their way (perhaps to Alexandria, which was Apollos's home), and Paul admonishes Titus to make sure that they lack nothing.

Paul closes the letter by bringing it full circle with the opening verse. He began the letter with this statement:

> Paul, a servant of God and an apostle of Jesus Christ for the faith of God's elect and the knowledge of the truth that leads to godliness (1:1, emphasis added).

He closes with these words:

> Our people must learn to devote themselves to doing what is good, in order that they may provide for daily necessities and not live unproductive lives.
>
> Everyone with me sends you greetings. Greet those who love us in the faith.
>
> Grace be with you all (3:14–15, emphasis added).

Truth leads to godliness. Sound doctrine and good deeds go hand in hand. We must know the truth—and then we must do it. The basis of the truth of the gospel that transforms our lives and our behavior is (as Paul says in Titus 1:2) "the hope of eternal life, which God, who does not lie, promised before the beginning of time."

The promise that Paul talks about is found in Genesis, where God promised before Adam and Eve were driven out of Eden that a Redeemer would come and bring life to humanity (see Gen. 3:15). That Redeemer has come; His name is Jesus. That hope is now. Our hope is not just the expectation of heaven, but the strength for living in these troubled times. We are living out our eternal lives right now, today, as we live in reliance upon Him.

A Brother Restored

C lara Barton, the founder of the American Red Cross, was once painfully betrayed by a coworker. Years later, a friend reminded her of the incident. "I don't remember that," replied Miss Barton.

"You don't remember?" asked the astonished friend. "But you were so hurt at the time! Surely you must remember!"

"No," Clara Barton insisted gently. "I distinctly remember forgetting that ever happened."

As we are about to see in our adventure through Paul's letter to Philemon, this is the true nature of forgiveness: It's a deliberate decision to forget wrongs suffered. Christlike forgiving grace is the strongest force in the universe. It is the power to restore broken relationships, to heal shattered churches, to make families whole once more. It is the heart of the gospel. It is the key to the book of Philemon.

The structure of this short, one-chapter book is very simple:

Paul's Appeal to Philemon (Philemon 1–25)

1.	Paul gives thanks to God for his friend Philemon	1–7
2.	Paul asks Philemon to forgive Onesimus	8–16
3.	Paul's promise to Philemon	17–21
4.	Personal remarks, greetings from others, benediction	22–25

Slaves and brothers

This is the fourth of Paul's personal letters (following the two letters to Timothy and the letter to Titus), and it differs from all of Paul's other letters in that it contains no instruction that is intended for the church as a whole or as foundational doctrine. Instead, this is a letter that applies, in a powerful, practical way, all the tenets and values contained in Paul's other writings: love, acceptance, forgiveness, grace, and Christian brotherhood.

The background of this letter is interesting. The epistle to Philemon was written when the apostle Paul was a prisoner in the city of Rome for the first time. Philemon, who lived in the Greek city of Colossae, was a friend whom Paul had won to Christ. Philemon apparently had a young brother whose name was Onesimus. Though many believe that there was no blood relationship between Philemon and his slave, Onesimus, I am strongly convinced that they were brothers because of what Paul says in verse 16—a statement the King James Version renders:

a brother beloved, specially to me, but how much more unto thee, both in the flesh, and in the Lord?

What else could a brother "in the flesh" be but a brother by birth—a distinction Paul seems to underscore when he adds that Onesimus is also a Christian brother, a brother "in the Lord." This distinction is blurred in the NIV, which reads:

He is very dear to me but even dearer to you, both as a man and as a brother in the Lord.

Though the NIV is an excellent translation, I believe the KJV is more accurate than the NIV on this point.

Given the view that Onesimus was Philemon's brother in the flesh, we find some powerful applications in this letter that we can use in relating to each other not only as Christians but within our families. As you probably know, one of the hardest places to apply lessons of love, acceptance, and forgiveness is right at home, within our own family relationships. So many of us seem to have a huge blind spot in our closest relationships: We treat family members in ways we wouldn't think of treating even a rude stranger on the street.

I believe that what probably happened in the relationship between these two brothers, Onesimus and Philemon, is that Onesimus got into some sort of financial trouble. Perhaps he was a gambler—or perhaps some other issue in his life brought him into financial disgrace. In those days, people in financial trouble could not appeal to bankruptcy court to bail them out. But they could sometimes get someone to redeem them by selling themselves to that person as slaves. Perhaps Onesimus got into debt and went to his brother, Philemon, and said, "Phil, would you mind going to bat for me? I'm in trouble and I need some cash."

Philemon might say, "Well, Onesimus, what can you give me for security?"

Onesimus would reply, "You know I haven't got a thing but myself—so I'll become your slave if you'll pay off this debt." That may or may not have been how it occurred, but it is one likely scenario.

If irresponsibility got Onesimus into this jam, it is easy to see why this young indebted slave might choose to run away from his responsibilities to his brother. Onesimus packed up and fled, taking refuge in Rome. Onesimus apparently found Christ while under Paul's instruction in Rome, during Paul's first imprisonment there. Philemon may well have been a Christian for some time when this letter was written—we know that in Colossians 4:9, he is commended as a faithful and beloved brother who had been of great service to Paul and to the gospel.

Why would a faithful Christian be a slave owner? This question naturally occurs to us because the issue of slavery seems so strange and abhorrent to us today. Slavery, however, was an accepted part of the Roman culture. Ultimately, it was such Christian principles as the belief in human equality, love, grace, and our Christian duties to one another that eventually broke down those cultural attitudes and ended slavery in the Roman world. And hundreds of years later Christian principles ended slavery in America. We see the approaching end of slavery in this very letter where—even though slaves continue to serve their masters—both slaves and masters are challenged to see each other as kindred, and to worship together in the church on an equal footing. In Paul's other epistles we see these admonitions to slaves and masters.

> *Slaves, obey your earthly masters with respect and fear, and with sincerity of heart, just as you would obey Christ. Obey them not only to win their favor when their eye is on you, but like slaves of Christ, doing the will of God from your heart (Eph. 6:5–6).*

> *Slaves, obey your earthly masters in everything; and do it, not only when their eye is on you and to win their favor, but with sincerity of heart and reverence for the Lord (Col. 3:22).*

> *Teach slaves to be subject to their masters in everything, to try to please them, not to talk back to them (Titus 2:9).*

> *Masters, treat your slaves in the same way. Do not threaten them, since you know that he who is both their Master and yours is in heaven,*

Why would a faithful Christian be a slave owner?

To slaves

To masters

and there is no favoritism with him (Eph. 6:9).

> *Masters, provide your slaves with what is right and fair, because you know that you also have a Master in heaven (Col. 4:1).*

In the cultural context of the Roman Empire, a slave's life was usually extremely harsh, cruel, and unforgiving. If a slave ran away from his master, he could either be put to death or shipped back to his master for punishment—and there were virtually no limits to the amount or severity of punishment and torture that could be applied. When Onesimus ran away, he apparently compounded his problems by stealing money from Philemon. He found his way to Rome, was converted to Christ through Paul's ministry, and became an assistant to Paul. But Paul was determined to send him back to Philemon so that Onesimus could clear his conscience of all past transgressions against Philemon. So, Paul wrote this gracious little note that has been preserved to us in Scripture, and he sent it back in the hand of Onesimus himself.

The return of Onesimus

Imagine the scene at Philemon's home when this letter arrives. Philemon stands on his porch one morning looking down the road, and he sees someone approaching. He says to Mrs. Philemon—his wife, Apphia—"Dear, doesn't that look like my ne'er-do-well runaway brother?" Sure enough, it's Onesimus himself—the black sheep has returned. All the old anger floods back to Philemon's face. As Onesimus comes within earshot, Philemon growls, "So you've come home at last! What brings you back?"

Without a word of defense, Onesimus reaches out and hands his brother a scroll—the letter we are now studying. Philemon takes it and reads,

> *Paul, a prisoner of Christ Jesus, and Timothy our brother,*
> *To Philemon our dear friend and fellow worker, to Apphia our sister,*
> *to Archippus our fellow soldier and to the church that meets in your home:*
> *Grace to you and peace from God our Father and the Lord Jesus Christ (vv. 1–3).*

Philemon says to Apphia, his wife, "Yes, this is from Paul all right. That's the way he always begins his letters. I don't know how my brother got this letter, but it is authentic."

People gathered together in Philemon's home to study and pray together

Note the interesting reference in these opening verses: "and to the church that meets in your home." People gathered together in Philemon's home to study and pray together. This is the church that Paul greets—not a building of stone walls, stained glass, and wooden pews, but merely a home in which people gathered to study God's Word, to pray together, and to share their struggles and their strength.

Philemon goes on reading:

> *I always thank my God as I remember you in my prayers, because I hear about your faith in the Lord Jesus and your love for all the saints. I pray that you may be active in sharing your faith, so that you will have a full understanding of every good thing we have in Christ (vv. 4–6).*

Philemon says, "Imagine, Paul has been praying for us, even from prison. Isn't that amazing!" He reads on, and in verses 8 through 10, he sees that Paul gets down to the nub of the issue:

> *Although in Christ I could be bold and order you to do what you ought to do, yet I appeal to you on the basis of love. I then, as Paul—an old man and now also a prisoner of Christ Jesus—I appeal to you for my son Onesimus, who became my son while I was in chains.*

Paul says, in effect, "I could order you to do this by my authority as an apostle, but instead I will appeal to you on the basis of your own Christlike love." He goes on to describe Onesimus as one "who became my son while I was in chains." I think the tears probably came to Philemon's eyes as he read this. Here was dear old Paul, who had led him to Christ, sitting in that lonely prison, writing, "Philemon, old friend, would you do me a favor? I'm appealing to you, even though I could command you. I'd appreciate a special favor from you while I am here in prison." How could Philemon's heart not melt at these words?

I imagine Philemon's turning to Apphia and saying, "Look! It says here that Paul, the apostle who led me to the Lord, has had the same influence on my brother and slave, Onesimus. Not only do we have the same father in the flesh, but now Paul is a spiritual father to us both!"

In the next verse, we encounter an interesting play on words:

> *Formerly he was useless to you, but now he has become useful both to you and to me (v. 11).*

What's in a name?
A play on words

Clearly, Onesimus was worse than useless to Philemon—he'd stolen from Philemon and run away. Useless? He was a nuisance! He was trouble! He was bad news! And what is truly ironic in this is that the name Onesimus literally means "useful" or "profitable." Paul has a wonderful sense of humor and (like Shakespeare) enjoyed a good, well-aimed pun now and then. He is saying, in effect, "Mr. Useful may have been Mr. Useless to you once, but he's now Mr. Useful once more!" And so, as he adds in verse 12, he is sending Mr. Useful back to Philemon, where he can live in a way that is worthy of his name.

He sends Onesimus, in fact, because Paul views Onesimus's service to Philemon as service to himself. Though Paul would like to keep this useful young man with him, he would much rather see Onesimus repay his debt to Philemon, whom he has wronged.

The key to this little letter is in the sixteenth verse. Paul says to Philemon that he is sending back Onesimus

> *no longer as a slave, but better than a slave, as a dear brother. He is very dear to me but even dearer to you, both as a man* [or, brother in the flesh] *and as a brother in the Lord.*

Paul erases the line of distinction between slave and free. The rigid boundaries of cultural views are transcended by love and kinship in Christ. Regardless of position—slave or master, according to Roman customs—both are slaves of one Master, Jesus Christ. This must be your view and my view as we approach the people around us. Instead of labeling people according to economic status, political views, race, or any other characteristic, we must begin to see one another as people for whom Christ died, people of whom Christ is Lord.

As he reads, Philemon's heart is beginning now to turn toward his black sheep brother. I can imagine that he says to his wife, "If Paul found Onesimus so dear to him, maybe we ought to forgive him for all the things he has done. Maybe the fellow has been changed. Let's see what else Paul has to say." And he reads verse 17:

> *If you consider me a partner, welcome him as you would welcome me.*

"Well," Philemon might have said, "this puts quite a different slant on things! I was going to take Onesimus back—as a slave! I was going to house him in the slave quarters and put him back to work—but now Paul says I've got to receive Onesimus as if he were Paul himself!"

Apphia says, "Well, we surely would never send Paul down to the slave house. We would give him the very best guest room in the house. So if we are going to receive Onesimus as we would receive Paul, we'd better give him the best room."

Don't you hear in this story an echo of the story of the loving father and the Prodigal Son (see Luke 15)?

So Philemon says, "All right, Dear, go get the guest room ready—but just a moment! Hold everything! He never paid back the money he took!"

But Paul addresses this issue, too. In verses 18 and 19, he writes,

If he has done you any wrong or owes you anything, charge it to me. I, Paul, am writing this with my own hand. I will pay it back—not to mention that you owe me your very self.

That is grace. That is the gospel. It exemplifies what God has done for us through Jesus Christ. The debt we owe has been paid by another. Here is the doctrine of acceptance and the doctrine of substitution wonderfully portrayed for us in a living object lesson. In fact, Martin Luther once observed, "All of us were God's Onesimus." We were slaves. We were debtors. We were sinners. We merited nothing. On our own, we stand naked and wretched before a God who is righteous and holy, yet the Lord Jesus says to the Father, "If this one has done anything wrong, or owes you anything, charge it to my account. I will pay it." That is what Paul says here.

We were slaves, debtors, sinners

Philemon's heart must have been completely melted by this amazing expression of grace from Paul's heart as he wrote from the solitude of his cold prison cell. Paul had nothing—no money with which to repay the debt of Onesimus—yet he wrote, "If he owes you anything, put it on my tab. I'll pay it myself when I come."

"I will pay it back"

That, I think, was the crowning touch of Paul's entire appeal. With that, I believe Philemon's heart broke, he opened his arms, hugged Onesimus to himself, and forgave him. The kinship of the family was restored once again. Paul understood that the two brothers could not live together as family when one was a slave and one was a master. Both had to be free of the chains that bound them—Onesimus of the chains of his debt to Philemon and Philemon of the chains of his cultural blindness, which saw mastery over his brother Onesimus as his legal right. In the end, those chains were broken not by the force of law; they were dissolved by the free-flowing waters of love and grace.

As this brief letter draws to a close, Paul makes this affirming statement:

Confident of your obedience, I write to you, knowing that you will do even more than I ask (v. 21).

Here we see how far grace can reach in affecting human lives, relationships, and behavior. Paul has appealed to Philemon on the basis of grace. If he had chosen instead to impose demands on Philemon on the basis of law, on the basis of his authority as an apostle, he would have said, "Philemon! As the holy apostle of the holy church, I command you

The far reach of grace

to receive back this young man and to give him back his job!" That is as far as law can go. Philemon would have obeyed such a legal demand. But grace reaches so much farther than law. Grace not only restored Onesimus to his job in the household of Philemon, but restored him to a relationship, to a place of love and belonging in the family of Philemon! Grace breaks down all the barriers, smooths out the friction, cleanses the bitterness, and heals the pain of the past.

Paul closes with some personal references and requests:

> *And one thing more: Prepare a guest room for me, because I hope to be restored to you in answer to your prayers (v. 22).*

Here we see that the apostle expects to be released—but how? "I hope to be restored to you *in answer to your prayers*" (emphasis added). We know that God did indeed grant these requests. Paul was released, and he preached the Word of God for several years before he was incarcerated for the second time.

Finally, Paul includes greetings from some of those who were with him. Epaphras was well known in Colossae; he had founded the church there. But now as a fellow prisoner with Paul in Rome, he sends greetings. So does Mark, author of the gospel of Mark, and Aristarchus, one of Paul's disciples. Demas was a young man who later forsook Paul (as we discover in the last-written letter of Paul) because "he loved this world" (2 Tim. 4:10). Luke, author of the gospel of Luke and the book of Acts, also was with Paul in Rome and sent greetings to Philemon.

Paul closes with words so characteristic of the apostle of grace: "The grace of the Lord Jesus Christ be with your spirit." Here is the theme of Philemon, the theme of the apostle Paul, the theme of the entire Word of God to human beings, who are lost in sin: Grace is the answer to all our problems, all our pain. It is the answer to our guilt and sin. It is the answer to our troubled relationships. It is the answer to our fear of death.

Grace is the answer

God's grace has been shed upon us through the Lord Jesus Christ. And His grace calls us to show the same Christlike quality of grace to those grace-starved souls around us, the Onesimus-like people we meet every day and especially those in our own homes. May God give us grace to represent His gracious character every day.

Part Eight

Keeping the Faith

All About Faith

L arry King, the famous CNN interviewer, once found himself in an unusual position—being the interviewee instead of the interviewer. He was appearing on the David Letterman show, and during their conversation, Letterman asked King, "If you could interview any person from history, who would it be?"

Instantly, King replied, "Jesus Christ."

Letterman was so surprised, it took him several seconds to ask a follow-up question: "Well, what would you ask Him?"

"Oh, a lot of questions," King responded, "but my first question would be, 'Were you really born of a virgin?' The answer to that question would define history."

That's really true, isn't it? The answer to that question really *does* define history. If Jesus was truly born of a virgin, if Jesus was truly born of God, the Word made flesh, then we have something tremendous to believe in, to place our faith and trust in. If not, then faith is meaningless, life is meaningless. Truly, our faith must be rooted in reality—the reality of the incarnation, life, death, and resurrection of Jesus Christ—or we have nothing to live for.

Faith is not a magical power or potion. It is not a feeling. It is not a set of doctrines or creeds. Faith is trusting in the Ultimate Reality of the universe. Faith is the key that opens the door to God. Without faith we cannot reach God or receive salvation from God. So it is vitally important for us to discover what faith truly is. That is the theme of the epistles of Hebrews through Jude. They tell us all about faith—where faith comes from, what it rests on, how to lay hold of it, and how to live it out in our everyday lives.

Time after time during my many years as a pastor, I have heard people make excuses for either failing to receive Jesus as Savior or for failing to appropriate His power to live the Christian life, and the number one excuse is this: "I just can't believe. I just don't have faith." Yet believing is precisely what human beings are designed to do! The proof is found in this well-known passage:

Without faith it is impossible to please God, because anyone who comes to him must believe that he exists and that he rewards those who earnestly seek him (Heb. 11:6).

In other words, this is the very minimum level of faith: If we do not draw near to God, we cannot be saved. If faith is truly impossible for any human being, then that person is beyond the reach of salvation and redemption—but we know that this is not true. Every human being can believe. That is what we are made for. We were made to be dependent creatures, to seek our life from and place our trust in Someone or Something much bigger and more powerful than we are.

We continually place our trust in the things around us. We accept by faith that the chair we sit in will support us or that the roof over our heads will not cave in on us. Faith is the automatic response of the human spirit. The problem is that we so easily place our faith in things that let us down. We place our faith in people or systems or false gods and philosophies that lead us to grief or even to destruction.

The great comedy team of Stan Laurel and Oliver Hardy once made a movie called *Big Business* in which the comedians completely demolished a house for hilarious effect; they put furniture through windows, battered down a door, destroyed the chimney, smashed vases with a baseball bat, uprooted trees and shrubs. In order to carry out such mayhem on the screen for a reasonable cost, the producers had to locate a house that was already slated for demolition. They found a suitable old house in the Los Angeles area, and the owners were pleased that their house would be used by the famous comedy team to make one of their exceptionally popular movies.

On the appointed day, the film crew and cast arrived, found the house unlocked, set up their cameras, and started rolling. Within a few hours, they managed to make a complete shambles of the house while the camera operator captured every smash, clatter, and crash on film. As they were almost finished filming, the owner of the ruined house arrived—and flew into a rage. The house Laurel and Hardy were supposed to destroy was the house next door!

The entire film crew sincerely believed that they were destroying the right house. But their misplaced faith resulted in a very costly mistake.

It is not enough to have sincere faith. We must have faith that is rooted in truth.

But how do we know that the Bible is the truth? Many books have been written on *apologetics,* the body of evidence that verifies biblical truth by means of reason and historical research. The evidence for our faith is there, it is real, and it is compelling. Clearly, the Christian faith is a reasonable faith, because we serve a logical God who says, "Come now, let us reason together" (Isa. 1:18). However, I believe that very few people who come to faith are really brought there by reason, rational evidence, and argument. I believe most people come to faith and grow in faith through *personal experience.*

Some people say that seeing is believing, but I suggest it is much more accurate to say that believing is seeing. When you believe in Jesus Christ and act on your belief, you begin to experience confirmation of the validity and trustworthiness of your beliefs—and your faith grows stronger and deeper as a result. The more of Jesus you experience, the more clearly you see Him. Believing truly is seeing. It is the principle expressed by the father who asked Jesus to heal his epileptic son:

Believing is seeing

The more of Jesus you experience, the more clearly you see Him

> *Immediately the boy's father exclaimed, "I do believe; help me overcome my unbelief!" (Mark 9:24).*

You begin with the little particle of faith you have, however weak, however small, and you offer it to God. Honestly say to Him, "Lord, I scarcely have any faith at all, but what little there is, I offer to You and I will act upon it. Help me to know the truth and believe the truth. Reveal Your truth to me."

As we adventure together through these epistles, the books of Hebrews through Jude, we will learn all about faith.

The theme of Hebrews is, "What is Faith?" And the writer to the Hebrews illustrates the meaning of faith through a series of capsule biographies of Old Testament heroes of the faith: Moses, Joshua, Melchizedek, Aaron, and more. All of these stories demonstrate that faith is simply an awareness of certain invisible realities that cannot be perceived by the five senses but which are verified through daily experience with God. As we become increasingly aware of these realities, God expects us to grow in our testing of them and our reliance upon Him. If we don't grow in our faith, we shrink from it. Hebrews warns us not to draw back but rather to plunge fully into our faith in Him.

Hebrews: The roll call of faith

In Hebrews 11, we encounter the roll call of faith, the great record of men and women who lived by faith and accomplished amazing things for God. These were ordinary people (like you and me) who did extraordinary things by plugging into the power of God by the simple act of faith. They started out with small faith, acted on their tiny mustard seeds of faith, and nurtured that faith into full bloom by putting it to the test. We see how the faith of these Old Testament people was exercised and stretched until they were able to obey God without having any idea what He had planned for their lives:

> By faith Abraham, when called to go to a place he would later receive as his inheritance, obeyed and went, even though he did not know where he was going (11:8).

This event in Abraham's life demonstrates the principle stated in the theme verse of Hebrews:

> Now faith is being sure of what we hope for and certain of what we do not see (11:1).

Here is the key principle of faith: Faith is not a matter of being sure of all the factual, logical, footnoted, photographed, notarized evidence that our senses can confirm. It is a matter of being certain of what we do not see! How is that possible? What brings us to the conviction of faith? Simply this: As we act on our little bit of belief, as we grow in our experience of God's reality in our lives, His Word sounds a bell in our hearts. It rings true. Our experience aligns with the truth of God's Word.

Our experience aligns with the truth of God's Word

James: The work of faith

The epistle of James is an extremely practical book. You can apply its truths to your life continually, in all of your interactions and relationships. James sets forth what faith does, in an active, visible way. The key to James is this famous verse:

> As the body without the spirit is dead, so faith without deeds is dead (James 2:26).

Faith isn't really faith until you act upon it

In other words, faith isn't really faith until you act upon it. Saying, "I believe" while living as if you don't believe is the same as not believing. Many people think that faith is an attitude or an agreement with a certain statement or doctrine. That's not faith at all. Genuine faith changes us. It affects our behavior. It controls our actions. Faith that is nothing more than a mental attitude is worthless, dead, of no effect. Faith must venture out, take risks, and change our lives.

According to James, genuine faith is active, stands up to temptation, shows no prejudice, is kind and responsive to human needs, speaks blessing and love rather than cursings, spreads peace instead of strife, and teaches patience and prayer. These are the deeds of genuine, active faith that we read about in James.

1 and 2 Peter: Strength for the trial of faith

Peter was the apostle whose faith failed in the fire of trial, when his Lord was being taken to the cross. Though Peter had brazenly declared before his fellow disciples that he would never deny Jesus even if all the other disciples failed Him, it was Peter who ultimately denied Him three times, including one denial with a vile curse. As he crept away into the night, having failed his Lord, he heard the words of Jesus as they burned a hole in his heart: "When you have turned back, strengthen your brothers" (Luke 22:32).

In Peter's two letters, we find the apostle doing exactly that: strengthening other Christians for times of trial and persecution. Christians who truly exercise their faith will find their faith tested and tried, and that is the theme of these letters.

Suffering makes faith tremble. Catastrophe provokes our deepest questions. We ask, "Why?" In these two letters, Peter answers that question. Our faith in Christ joins us to the life of Christ, including the suffering of Christ. To reach people in a lost and rebellious world will inevitably cause us pain and persecution. When we become a part of Christ, we become instruments for fulfilling His work in the world.

> To reach people in a lost and rebellious world will inevitably cause us pain and persecution

The key verse of all three of these letters, 1 John 3:23, shows the link between a life of faith and a life of Christian love:

1, 2, and 3 John: Faith lived out in love

> *This is his command: to believe in the name of his Son, Jesus Christ* [that's faith], *and to love one another as he commanded us* [that's the life of the believer].

That is how faith works. It believes, and that belief produces love. To have faith in God means to manifest the life of God—and God is love. How can we say that we truly have faith in God if we do not love one another as God, in Christ, loved us?

The three intertwined themes of 1 John are walking in the light, manifesting love, and reflecting the life of Christ—light, love, and life. In 2 John, the theme again is love, but here the beloved apostle shows us that love is lived out through obedience to God's truth:

> *This is love: that we walk in obedience to his commands. As you have heard from the beginning, his command is that you walk in love (v. 6).*

In 3 John, the apostle addresses a problem in the church—the problem of people who want to be church bosses. John contrasts those who

ADVENTURING
THROUGH THE
BIBLE

**Jude:
Protecting
our faith**

love one another in the body of Christ versus those who love to be first in the church. So faith and love are intertwined—a person of faith is a person who demonstrates faith through love for others.

The book of Jude addresses the perils that threaten our faith. Jude outlines a plan to guard our faith against those subtle forces that try to undermine faith, including the desire to have our own way, the lure of immorality, the trap of greed, the dangers of false authority, divisiveness, and worldly influences. Near the close of his book, Jude gives us an admonition that is very timely for us today:

> *Build yourselves up in your most holy faith* [this is the key] *and pray in the Holy Spirit* [that's the exercise of faith]. *Keep yourselves in God's love* [again, the exercise of faith] *as you wait for the mercy of our Lord Jesus Christ to bring you to eternal life (vv. 20–21).*

To protect our faith,
we must exercise it

To protect our faith, we must exercise it. Like the human body, faith must be exercised to keep it from becoming flabby and unhealthy. We exercise our faith by venturing out, by trusting God and daring great things for Him, by stepping out boldly in service and ministry for Him, by discovering and putting to use those hidden resources of spiritual power and spiritual gifts that God has made available to all those who have faith in Him.

Faith is an adventure—a grand, bold, exciting, thrill-a-minute journey. That is what we discover as we adventure through these books, Hebrews through Jude, and learn all about this daring enterprise that we call faith. By living in these books, we learn to trust in things unseen, to love and serve in ever deeper ways, to guard our faith and exercise our faith—and in so doing, we add our names to that glorious roll call of those faithful men and women who have placed their trust in God since the beginning of the world.

The Roll Call of Faith

Baseball has its Hall of Fame in Cooperstown, New York. Football has its Hall of Fame in Canton, Ohio. Basketball has its Hall of Fame in Springfield, Massachusetts. But do you know about the Hall of Fame for heroes of the Christian faith? It's found in the book of Hebrews. We will explore the Hebrews Hall of Heroes when we reach chapter 11 of this rich epistle of faith.

The theme of Hebrews is faith. In fact, Hebrews is one of the three New Testament commentaries on a single Old Testament verse, Habakkuk 2:4, which tells us that "the just shall live by his faith" (KJV). This verse opened the eyes of Augustine and inspired him to become a mighty man of faith. This is the Old Testament verse that ignited a fire in the heart of Martin Luther and began the Protestant Reformation some five hundred years ago. It still ignites our hearts today, and we find this idea explored and amplified in the New Testament books of Romans, Ephesians, and Hebrews. Each of these epistles emphasizes a different aspect of that statement, and all three, viewed together, help us to appreciate the rich and multifaceted applications of that statement, "the just shall live by his faith."

The book of Romans talks about "the just" and tells us what it means to be justified, to be accepted as righteous in Jesus Christ. The book of Ephesians emphasizes the words "shall live," and it tells us how to live as justified people—how to walk in the Spirit, how to allow the

The theme of Hebrews is faith

**The object
of our faith**

The quantity of
faith is not the
important thing,
the object of faith is

**The
mysterious
origin of
Hebrews**

life of Jesus to live in us. The book of Hebrews takes up the words, "by . . . faith," and shows us how to lay hold of the life by which we are justified.

We must understand that faith in itself is meaningless and power-less. Many people have faith in things that not only cannot save, but can actually bring about their destruction. The power of faith derives not from faith itself but from the One in whom we invest our faith, the object of our faith, Jesus Christ. This is a source of great confusion among many Christians. I often hear people say, "If I only had enough faith, I could do such and such," as though faith were a commodity sold by the pound.

Jesus has already made it completely clear that the quantity of faith is of no significance. "I tell you the truth," He said, "if you have faith as small as a mustard seed, you can say to this mountain, 'Move from here to there' and it will move. Nothing will be impossible for you" (Matt. 17:20). It is not the quantity of faith that is important; it's what your faith is fastened to. If it is fastened to Jesus Christ, you have all the power you need to carry out God's will in your life. If it is fastened to anything other than Jesus Christ, then your faith is meaningless.

The book of Hebrews is about faith—but even more importantly, it is about the object of our faith, Jesus Christ. As you read it, you will find that Hebrews is the most Christ-centered book in the New Testament. It focuses on the character and redemptive power of Jesus Christ—which is why it is one of the most healing books to read in times of discouragement, defeat, or depression. If we see Him as He is, we cannot help but be strong in faith.

The King James Version titles this book, The Epistle of Paul the Apostle to the Hebrews. However, Paul likely would not have written this epistle, and the oldest and most reliable manuscripts refer to it as simply, To the Hebrews. We do not know when it was written or to whom. Internal evidence shows it was written to Jewish Christians with the intention of keeping them from slipping back into the rites and legalism of Judaism, but we don't know whether those Christians lived in Palestine, Asia Minor, Greece, or Rome. The list of prospective authors for Hebrews is long, and it includes Paul, Barnabas, Luke, Clement of Rome, Apollos, Silas, Philip, and Priscilla.

While there are some similarities between Hebrews and Paul's epis-tles—similarities of language and theology—the contrasts are even greater. In Paul's other epistles, the apostle always signs his name, usu-ally at both the beginning and near the end of each letter:

Paul, called to be an apostle of Christ Jesus by the will of God . . . (1 Cor. 1:1).

I, Paul, write this greeting in my own hand (1 Cor. 16:21).

Paul's name appears nowhere in the book of Hebrews, as it does in all of his other letters. Moreover, the overall style of the Greek language used throughout Hebrews tends to be more polished and learned than the often colloquial and personal tone of Paul's recognized epistles. Throughout his epistles, Paul claims to be an apostle and eyewitness of Jesus Christ (due to his experience on the road to Damascus), whereas the writer of Hebrews refers to the gospel as having been "confirmed to us by those who heard" Jesus (Heb. 2:3). Paul, as an eyewitness of Christ, did not need to have the gospel confirmed to him by another person. Also, the author of Hebrews quotes only from the Greek Old Testament (the Septuagint), whereas Paul often quoted from the Hebrew Old Testament.

What does all of this mean? Certainly, the book of Hebrews does not have to be written by Paul to be recognized as powerful, authoritative, and inspired by the Spirit of God. We find God's heart expressed on every page. Whoever wrote this magnificent book did so under the inspiration of God—and ultimately, it is only His authorship that truly matters.

Now, let's take an overview of the entire book of Hebrews, so that we can see the flow of the argument of the book at a glance:

> Whoever wrote this magnificent book did so under the inspiration of God—and ultimately, it is only His authorship that truly matters

Christ, the Object of Our Faith (Hebrews 1:1–4:13)

1.	Christ, before and above all the prophets	1:1–3
2.	Christ, before and above all angels (His deity and humanity)	1:4–2:18
3.	Christ, before and above Moses	3:1–6
4.	The challenge to enter into God's rest	3:7–4:13

The Superior Work of Christ (Hebrews 4:14–10:18)

5.	The priesthood of Christ versus the priesthood of Aaron and the priesthood of Melchizedek	4:14–7:28
6.	The superior covenant of Christ	8:1–13
7.	The superior sanctuary and sacrifice of Christ	9:1–10:18

The Christian's Walk of Faith (Hebrews 10:19–13:25)

8.	Hold fast to the faith you have received	10:19–39
9.	The definition of faith (key verses of Hebrews)	11:1–3
10.	The role call of faith (the Hebrews Hall of Heroes) Abel, Enoch, Noah, Abraham and Sarah,	

In this corner, the challengers . . .

From Hebrews 1:1 to 10:18, Jesus Christ is compared to a number of other leaders and systems and religious values in which recipients of this letter once trusted. The contrast between Christ and these other people and systems is presented much like an athletic contest or an elimination match where contestants vie for a championship. Again and again, a challenger rises to confront the hero, Jesus Christ, and one after another, the challenger is vanquished. Again and again, the hero emerges triumphant, superior to all comers. Throughout this letter, Christ, the object of our faith, is compared with all the lesser things in which people place their faith—and every challenger is found wanting. Christ alone is supreme.

The first challengers: the Old Testament prophets

> In the past God spoke to our forefathers through the prophets at many times and in various ways, but in these last days he has spoken to us by his Son, whom he appointed heir of all things, and through whom he made the universe (1:1–2).

The writer of Hebrews recalls the prophets who meant so much to the Hebrew mind and heart—the great names of Hebrew history such as Isaiah, Jeremiah, Ezekiel, Daniel, Hosea, and Habakkuk. These prophets lived at the same time as great secular philosophers such as Socrates, Plato, and Aristotle, yet their views of truth and reality far outstripped the thinking of their secular contemporaries. God spoke *to* them and *through* them in the past, "but in these last days he has spoken to us by his Son."

Immediately, the writer of Hebrews dismisses the prophets as having no equality with Jesus Christ. After all, they were merely spokesmen and instruments, but Jesus is God Himself, enthroned as King of the universe. His life defines the boundaries of history and He upholds everything by the word of His power. How can a mere prophet compare with Him?

The second challengers: the angels

The next challengers are the angels. In the Greek world of the New Testament church, angels were regarded as very important beings. The Greek gods and goddesses were virtually the equivalent of angels in the eyes of the Greeks—powerful supernatural beings who were flawed and limited. The Greek pantheon of deities did not contain a single, all-powerful, all-knowing, all-loving supreme being—only a bunch of sub-deities much like the angels of Judeo-Christian theology.

In this passage, the writer to the Hebrews considers the question of who is greater, the angels or the Son of God. He points out immediately that the Son, the Lord Jesus, is superior to any angel:

> *To which of the angels did God ever say,*
> *"You are my Son; today I have become your Father"?*
> *Or again,*
> *"I will be his Father, and he will be my Son"?*
> *And again, when God brings his firstborn into the world, he says,*
> *"Let all God's angels worship him."*
> *In speaking of the angels he says,*
> *"He makes his angels winds, his servants flames of fire."*
> *But about the Son he says,*
> *"Your throne, O God, will last for ever and ever, and righteousness*
> *will be the scepter of your kingdom" (1:5–8).*

God never said to any angel, "You are my Son; today I have become your Father." The Son is superior to the angels—and what's more, the angels worshiped and obeyed Him! The angels themselves confess that Jesus is superior.

The angels themselves confess that Jesus is superior

The second Adam

In chapters 2 and 3, the writer of Hebrews presents Jesus as the true man, the Second Adam. Jesus came to fulfill the destiny of human beings—a destiny lost when Adam threw it away through the first sin. God created human beings to be creatures of splendor and authority; how heartbreaking to think of how much of God's image was lost in the Fall! We were originally made to be rulers, king and queens in the universe, a fact that is reflected in Psalm 8:

God created human beings to be creatures of splendor and authority

> *When I consider your heavens, the work of your fingers, the moon*
> *and the stars, which you have set in place, what is man that you are*
> *mindful of him, the son of man that you care for him? You made him a*
> *little lower than the heavenly beings and crowned him with glory and*
> *honor.*
> *You made him ruler over the works of your hands; you put every-*
> *thing under his feet (vv. 3–6).*

That is God's design for humanity, but our fallen state keeps us from fulfilling it. But Jesus—"the son of man"—is here in this passage, fulfilling our original destiny, living out our unfallen potential, sitting at the right hand of God. He is the true man—humanity as God intended us to be. We are higher than the angels, because God created us to be higher than the angels. God said of humanity, "Let us make man in our image." He did not say that about any angel—only of men and women, you and me. So Jesus—the Son of Man, the perfect human being, the Second Adam—is superior to the angels.

The book of Hebrews contains five warnings, and at this point we encounter the first one:

> We must pay more careful attention, therefore, to what we have heard, so that we do not drift away. For if the message spoken by angels was binding, and every violation and disobedience received its just punishment, how shall we escape if we ignore such a great salvation? This salvation, which was first announced by the Lord, was confirmed to us by those who heard him (2:1–3).

If Jesus is greater than the prophets and greater than the angels, says Hebrews, then we ought to listen to Him. If prophets have affected the stream of history as much as they have, and the angels are the invisible agents of God working through all of history, then surely we ought to listen to the Son. Do not neglect to listen!

The next challengers: Moses and Joshua

The next challengers who move into the picture are Moses and Joshua—great people of God whom God greatly used. The Hebrew people almost idolized them as supreme examples of people mightily used of God. In chapter 3, Jesus is compared to Moses; in chapter 4, He is compared to Joshua. What is the writer's argument? Simply this: Moses was a servant in the house of God. Jesus, however, is the Son to whom the house belongs and for whom it is built. Obviously, He has the supremacy.

As a boy in Montana, I was invited to visit a ranch owned by a wealthy family. The invitation came not from the family but from one of the hired hands. He drove me to the ranch, and as we drove toward the imposing two-story ranch house, he turned toward the bunkhouse out back.

"What's it like in that big house?" I asked.

"I dunno," the ranch hand said. "Never been in there. That house belongs to the owner and his family. I can't take you in there."

Sometime later, I saw a beautiful palomino horse in the pasture, and I said, "Gee, I'd sure love to take a ride on that horse."

"Sorry, boy," said the ranch hand. "You can't ride that horse. It belongs to the family." All day long I was frustrated, because everything I wanted to do he couldn't let me do, because he was only a hired worker.

Later, I got to know the son of that family, a boy my own age, and everything changed! We rode that palomino horse all over, and we went into the house and had the complete run of the place! We even went into the kitchen and helped ourselves to the refrigerator! We made ourselves at home. Why? Because a son has greater liberty than a servant.

Moses was just a servant, but Jesus was the Master. Moses led the people of God out of Egypt toward the land of Canaan, which symbolized the place of God's rest—the rest and peace God wants all of us to experience through faith in Jesus Christ. Moses led his people toward a symbol of the rest of God, but Jesus leads all people into the actual place of rest.

That rest is defined for us in Hebrews 4:9–10:

> *There remains, then, a Sabbath-rest for the people of God; for anyone who enters God's rest also rests from his own work, just as God did from his.*

The point of this passage is this: If you stop depending upon yourself and your own effort, you have learned to enter into rest, because you start depending on God's work in you. That is the lost secret of humanity. That is the secret that Adam and Eve lost in the Garden of Eden and the one Jesus Christ came to restore to us. When we learn to live by the work of God in us instead of by our own work, we experience lives that are peaceful, calm, trusting, powerful, and undisturbed by circumstances, so we can accomplish great things for Christ's sake. The paradox of this principle is that nothing is more active, effective, and powerful than a life that is lived in God's rest.

Joshua tried, but he could not take the people into real rest. He merely took them into the symbol of rest, the land. Only Jesus can give us real rest. Hebrews tells us, "Let us, therefore, make every effort to enter that rest" (4:11), so that we avoid the downfall of those in the wilderness who, through disobedience, fell away and lost out on God's will and blessing for their lives.

The second warning is in Hebrews 3:12–15:

Second warning

> See to it, brothers, that none of you has a sinful, unbelieving heart that turns away from the living God. But encourage one another daily, as long as it is called Today, so that none of you may be hardened by sin's deceitfulness. We have come to share in Christ if we hold firmly till the end the confidence we had at first. As has just been said:
> "Today, if you hear his voice, do not harden your hearts as you did in the rebellion."

Remember and heed this warning: Do not harden your heart and resist God's leading. Do not say to yourself, "I'm all right the way I am.

I'm doing okay. I don't need to make any progress in my relationship with God. I don't need to listen to Him anymore. I don't need to enter into His rest." No, do not harden your heart. Do not resist what God is saying. Let God lead you into His rest.

The next challenger to the superiority of Christ is Aaron, the high priest of Israel, along with the whole system of the priesthood. A great deal of this letter has to do with the subject of priesthood. This is very significant, because priests have great value. In the Old Testament, the priests had two very important functions: to relieve guilt and to relieve confusion. In Hebrews 5:1–2 we read:

> *Every high priest is selected from among men and is appointed to represent them in matters related to God, to offer gifts and sacrifices for sins.* [That is relief of guilt—to lift the load and burden of sin.] *He is able to deal gently with those who are ignorant and are going astray, since he himself is subject to weakness.* [That is the relief of confusion—to deal gently with the ignorant and wayward.]

The priesthood of Christ is far superior to any other priesthood because Jesus is instantly available, He is eternal, and He provides us with His own infinite power and strength

The writer of Hebrews symbolizes Jesus Christ's higher priesthood through a man named Melchizedek. Melchizedek appears in the Old Testament in a very mysterious way. He steps out of the shadows for a moment and deals with Abraham, then returns to obscurity and is never heard from again. The Old Testament refers to Melchizedek several times, but he is a figure of mystery until you read the New Testament. Here in Hebrews, we see what this strange man signified. Melchizedek's characteristics were those of the priesthood Christ has today:

He was instantly available. The story, recorded in Genesis 14, tells of Abraham meeting the king of Sodom, after Abraham's defeat of the five kings. Although he did not know it, Abraham was in trouble. The king of Sodom planned to make him a very subtle offer that would derail Abraham in his walk of faith. He could not possibly have detected the subtlety of this offer—but then Melchizedek suddenly appeared. He was instantly available.

He was a king without father or without mother. This is as far as the record goes in the Old Testament. Here is an Old Testament picture of Christ in His eternal relationship to God.

He provided the strength of Christ to Abraham, symbolized by the elements of holy communion. Melchizedek strengthened Abraham; likewise, Jesus Christ strengthens us. Melchizedek strengthened Abraham by the offering of bread and wine, which in the communion service are the symbols of the body and the blood, the life of the Lord Jesus.

Here in Hebrews, the image of Melchizedek is summoned to represent the priestly ministry of Jesus Christ. The priesthood of Christ is far superior to any other priesthood because Jesus is instantly available, He is eternal, and He provides us with His own infinite power and strength.

In this connection, we find a third warning—the warning against delay. This is one of the most serious warnings in the book:

> *Let us leave the elementary teachings about Christ and go on to maturity, not laying again the foundation of repentance from acts that lead to death, and of faith in God, instruction about baptisms, the laying on of hands, the resurrection of the dead, and eternal judgment. And God permitting, we will do so.*
>
> *It is impossible for those who have once been enlightened, who have tasted the heavenly gift, who have shared in the Holy Spirit, who have tasted the goodness of the word of God and the powers of the coming age, if they fall away, to be brought back to repentance, because to their loss they are crucifying the Son of God all over again and subjecting him to public disgrace (6:1–6).*

Although we may have tasted the outward experiences of Christianity and seem to have much that is real in our Christian lives, we must press on into this place of rest and of trust in Jesus Christ or these external evidences of Christianity are of no value to us. Here is a sobering warning: If you trust too long in the untrue, the unreal, the unreliable, a day of desperation will come when you will look for the true, and you will not be able to find it.

The tabernacle and the law are two more things that people trust in—buildings and self-effort (represented by the law). The writer of Hebrews draws a sharp contrast between the tabernacle and the law on the one hand and Christ on the other. He takes the old tabernacle in the wilderness and says, "That's just a building symbolizing the real house of God, which is a human life—a man, a woman, a boy, a girl. God doesn't want to live in buildings, He wants to live in us!"

I like the story of the little boy who was chewing gum in a church building, and a woman said to the pastor, "Look at that boy chewing gum in church. Do you let children chew gum in the house of God?"

"My dear lady," the pastor replied, "it's the house of God that's chewing the gum!" And he is exactly right.

So the old tabernacle, or the temple in Jerusalem, or a cathedral, or a church, is nothing but a building. The true house of God is you. We are His house. He dwells in us: "Christ in you, the hope of glory" (Col. 1:27).

Intimately linked with the Old Testament tabernacle is the Old

Testament law: the Ten Commandments and the other laws, rites, and restrictions of the Law of Moses. The Ten Commandments are wonderful, flawless guidelines for human conduct. They fail in practice not because they are flawed but because we are flawed. We are weak and powerless to keep the law's demands. Even when we try our best, all we can achieve is an outward external obedience to avoid punishment—but the heart within is still wrong and we know it.

The Lord Jesus has a solution to this: *He writes the law on your heart.* He puts the Spirit of God within you to prompt you to love—for love is the fulfillment of the law.

Fourth warning

Here we encounter yet another warning: Do not deceive yourself. Do not allow sin to establish a deceitful foothold in your life. If you presume on God's grace this way, the writer of Hebrews says, there will be nothing left for you but a certain end of evil:

> *If we deliberately keep on sinning after we have received the knowledge of the truth, no sacrifice for sins is left, but only a fearful expectation of judgment and of raging fire that will consume the enemies of God. Anyone who rejected the law of Moses died without mercy on the testimony of two or three witnesses. How much more severely do you think a man deserves to be punished who has trampled the Son of God under foot, who has treated as an unholy thing the blood of the covenant that sanctified him, and who has insulted the Spirit of grace?* (10:26–29).

Think of it! At infinite cost—the cost of His own Son—God has provided a way to be righteous before Him, a way to be strengthened within, a way to be preserved strong and pure in the midst of all the decadent influences and adverse circumstances around us. How could we even think of setting all this aside and saying, "No, God, I'm going to make it on my own"? Could anything be more insulting to God? So the writer of Hebrews warns us not to presume on God's grace.

The Hall of Heroes

In the final section of the letter, the writer of Hebrews states the means by which we obtain all that God makes available to us. That means is called faith. In chapter 11, we can learn what faith is, how it behaves, and how to recognize it. The key verse of the entire book of Hebrews is found right here:

> *Now faith is being sure of what we hope for and certain of what we do not see (11:1).*

People are always looking for evidence for the Christian faith. And it is available because Christianity is a reasonable faith, based on the historical fact of the life of Christ and the reality of the Resurrection.

But the real evidence for faith comes not from an archaeological dig in Palestine nor from the Hubble space telescope or from the pen of a great theologian. It comes from experience. Faith is not a matter of being sure of all the evidence we can see. Faith is a matter of being certain of what we do not see! How do we become certain of something we do not see? By experiencing the reality of God's love and friendship in our daily lives. Seeing is not believing. Believing is seeing. When we make a decision to live by faith—even if we think our faith is weak or nearly nonexistent—God meets us, shows Himself to us, and increases our faith through a daily relationship with Him.

In the rest of chapter 11, the writer of Hebrews presents the roll call of faith. And as you read through the wonderful chapter that lists the heroes of faith, you find that faith anticipates the future, acts in the present, evaluates the past, dares to move out, and persists to the end. As you read through this roll call of God's Old Testament faithful, you read the stories of:

• Abel, who by faith made a better sacrifice than his brother Cain;

• Enoch, who did not taste death because of his faithful service to God;

• Noah, who saved his family from the flood of God's judgment because of his faith in God's word;

• Abraham and Sarah, who followed God by faith, not knowing where God would lead them;

• Isaac, who blessed his sons by faith;

• Jacob, who blessed Joseph's sons by faith;

• Joseph, who foresaw by faith the exodus of Israel from Egypt to the Land of Promise;

• the parents of Moses, who by faith hid their child, the future leader of Israel, from the wrath of Pharaoh;

• Moses, who chose by faith to identify with the suffering of his people, even though he could have chosen the pleasures, wealth, and security of sinful Egypt;

• Joshua, who by faith called down the walls of Jericho;

• Rahab, the prostitute who received Israel's spies because of her faith in Israel's God;

• and others—Gideon, Barak, Samson, Jephthah, David, Samuel, the prophets, and many other saints unnamed but remembered forever by God for battling by faith to the end of their lives, enduring incredible persecution while trusting in God to provide for them a better resurrection.

As you read through the wonderful chapter that lists the heroes of faith, you find that faith anticipates the future, acts in the present, and evaluates the past

The walk of faith

When you read the stories of Abraham, David, Moses, Barak, Samson, Martin Luther, John Wesley, D. L. Moody, Jim Elliott, and C. S. Lewis, you will be inspired; when you look to Jesus, you will be not merely inspired, you will be empowered

It is an incredible record of faith, an inspiring list of heroic accomplishments—ordinary people of faith doing extraordinary things by faith. It is a list of people who, by faith, allowed God to live out His life through theirs.

The final two chapters tell us how faith is produced in our lives and how God makes us strong in the faith so that we can walk the daily Christian walk. First, we are made strong by looking to Jesus:

Let us fix our eyes on Jesus, the author and perfecter of our faith, who for the joy set before him endured the cross, scorning its shame, and sat down at the right hand of the throne of God (12:2).

When you read the stories of Abraham, David, Moses, Barak, Samson, Martin Luther, John Wesley, D. L. Moody, Jim Elliott, and C. S. Lewis, you will be inspired. But when you look to Jesus, you will be not merely inspired, you will be empowered! That is why we are told to fix our gaze steadily upon Jesus, the author and the finisher of faith, because He alone can make us strong in our time of weakness.

The writer of Hebrews goes on to say:

In your struggle against sin, you have not yet resisted to the point of shedding your blood. And you have forgotten that word of encouragement that addresses you as sons:
"My son, do not make light of the Lord's discipline, and do not lose heart when he rebukes you, because the Lord disciplines those he loves, and he punishes everyone he accepts as a son."
Endure hardship as discipline; God is treating you as sons. For what son is not disciplined by his father? (12:4–7).

Faith grows through times of trouble—the disciplining season of our lives. God does not enjoy our pain, but He does use pain as a disciplining hand to teach us to exercise our faith. If you never had any problems, how could you exercise faith? If you never experienced lean times and losses, how could you ever learn to depend solely on God? That is why you can be sure you'll have trouble in this life!

But that's not the only way we exercise our faith. We also exercise our faith by encouraging one another in the shining hope that awaits us:

You have not come to a mountain that can be touched and that is burning with fire; to darkness, gloom and storm; to a trumpet blast or to such a voice speaking words that those who heard it begged that no further word be spoken to them, because they could not bear what was

commanded: "If even an animal touches the mountain, it must be stoned." The sight was so terrifying that Moses said, "I am trembling with fear."

But you have come to Mount Zion, to the heavenly Jerusalem, the city of the living God. You have come to thousands upon thousands of angels in joyful assembly, to the church of the firstborn, whose names are written in heaven. You have come to God, the judge of all men, to the spirits of righteous men made perfect, to Jesus the mediator of a new covenant, and to the sprinkled blood that speaks a better word than the blood of Abel (12:18–24).

The first paragraph in this passage speaks of the harshness of the law. The law is so strict and so terrifying that no one can bear the weight of it. Even Moses is terrified of it. But we have not been brought to Mount Sinai, a mount of law and fire, smoke and judgment, storm and fear. We have been brought to Mount Zion, a shining city of light, a place of grace and joy where people have been made perfect and where Jesus reigns as the mediator of the new covenant. Isn't that a beautiful word picture of our future with Him? Doesn't that encourage your faith? It does mine.

But linked to this powerful word picture of encouragement is a warning:

Fifth warning

See to it that you do not refuse him who speaks. If they did not escape when they refused him who warned them on earth, how much less will we, if we turn away from him who warns us from heaven? At that time his voice shook the earth, but now he has promised, "Once more I will shake not only the earth but also the heavens." The words "once more" indicate the removing of what can be shaken—that is, created things—so that what cannot be shaken may remain (12:25–27).

I believe we are in those times when everything that can be shaken is being shaken. What does this world depend upon? Governments, politics, education, legislation? All of these things are the fundamentals of history, the institutions people invest their hopes in—yet every one of these human institutions is something that can be shaken and will be shaken. Even now, we are facing the times when God is going to allow everything to be shaken that can be shaken. In this entire, vast universe of ours, only one thing exists that cannot be shaken:

Since we are receiving a kingdom that cannot be shaken, let us be thankful, and so worship God acceptably with reverence and awe, for our "God is a consuming fire" (12:28–29).

The kingdom of God, His rulership over our hearts, the lordship of Jesus Christ in our lives, can never be shaken. What is being shaken and tested today is phoniness and deception. What cannot be shaken is truth and faith. These days we see many people who claim to be Christians, who outwardly seem strong in the faith, turning away, falling away, renouncing or betraying their faith when they are shaken or exposed. But the things that cannot be shaken will remain, even while all else crumbles and falls.

A prayer and a
blessing

A few verses toward the end of Hebrews sum up the meaning of this letter for our lives in these perilous times, at the threshold of a new millennium:

> *May the God of peace, who through the blood of the eternal covenant brought back from the dead our Lord Jesus, that great Shepherd of the sheep, equip you with everything good for doing his will, and may he work in us what is pleasing to him, through Jesus Christ, to whom be glory for ever and ever. Amen (13:20–21).*

These words are both a prayer and a blessing. May we carry the peace of our great Shepherd with us no matter where we go, no matter what we face, as we walk the walk of faith.

Faith in Action

T he epistle of James has presented a number of problems to Bible scholars over the years. For example, Martin Luther had trouble accepting James as inspired Scripture, calling it "an epistle of straw." His problem, and the problem of many theologians over the years, has been James's emphasis on works as well as faith. Three times in this letter, James makes a statement such as this one:

> As the body without the spirit is dead, so faith without deeds is dead (2:26).

Some see these words of James as clashing with the emphasis on grace in Paul's epistles, typified by this statement:

> It is by grace you have been saved, through faith—and this not from yourselves, it is the gift of God—not by works, so that no one can boast (Eph. 2:8–9).

Some look at Paul on the one hand and James on the other and say, "Who should we believe? Is salvation by grace through faith alone—or is faith truly dead without works?" The fact is, this is a false dichotomy. Paul and James are both correct. The epistles of Paul and the epistle of James do not contradict each other—they supplement each other. Paul is saying that good works cannot save us. Rather, only the grace of God, appropriated by our faith, can save us. James would never argue against Paul's assertion that God's grace alone saves; he presupposes that the reader understands these doctrines that are so clearly stated in Paul's letters.

Faith involves commitment that is expressed through action

But James goes a step further. He wants us to also understand a principle that is fully accepted and understood in Paul's letters: Faith means more than simply agreeing with a set of doctrines. Genuine faith involves commitment that is expressed through actions. If we do not demonstrate behavior that is consistent with what we say we believe, then what good is our supposed faith? Faith that is not demonstrated by action is dead indeed! Works cannot save us, but works demonstrate that we do have a saving faith.

The book of James—far from being an epistle of straw—is the practical application of all the doctrines that Paul sets forth on faith. James is where the rubber meets the road. James is where our faith is expressed in tangible ways through our actions. This epistle is indispensable to our understanding of what our faith is all about and how the Christian life is supposed to be lived. Properly understood, this is one of the most powerful, inspired, life-changing books of the Bible! It is the road map for the walk of faith.

**James:
Witness to
the deity of
his half
brother, Jesus**

The book of James is a book of unique significance to us because it comes from the one who probably knew more about the Lord Jesus than any other human being—James, the half brother of our Lord. The apostle James was raised in the same home in Nazareth by Joseph and Mary with Jesus. He grew up with the Lord Jesus, saw Him through all those silent years of which we have no record, and joined with His three other brothers—Joseph, Simon, and Judas—in opposition to the Lord Jesus during the early days of His ministry. James was converted to faith in Christ, his half brother, by the unmistakable evidence of the Resurrection. The apostle Paul tells us that after the Resurrection, the Lord appeared to James (1 Cor. 15:7)—what greater evidence could James have asked for than to see the risen Lord in person?

Some people question whether James the brother of Jesus was the same James who wrote this letter. But if you look carefully into the background of this letter, you'll find sufficient evidence. In the early days after the Resurrection, James the Lord's brother became the acknowledged leader of the church in Jerusalem, and he was regarded by all, even the Jews, with reverence and respect, so that he gained the title, "James the just one."

Tradition tells us (as does Eusebius, an early church father and respected historian) that James was finally martyred for his faith by being pushed off the pinnacle of the temple of Jerusalem. The pinnacle was the point in the wall around the temple that jutted out over the Kidron Valley. From the top of that wall down into the valley is a drop of about a hundred feet. I once stood on that wall, on the pinnacle of the temple, and as I looked down I realized that this was the very place where the devil took Jesus and tempted Him to jump off.

Eusebius tells us that in about the year A.D. 66, James the Just, the brother of our Lord, was pushed off this pinnacle by the Jews who had become angered with him for his Christian testimony. According to Eusebius, the fall did not kill him, and he managed to stumble to his knees to pray for his murderers. So they finished the job by stoning him to death, and he joined the roll call of martyrs, a hero of the faith.

If you lay this letter of James alongside Jesus' Sermon on the Mount, you'll see more than a dozen exact parallels. So, it is evident that James, the writer of this letter, listened to the Lord Jesus and heard these messages, even though he may have struggled with them at the time. This letter, like the teaching of the Lord Himself, also contains many figures of speech taken from nature—word pictures of the waves of the sea, the animal kingdom, the forests, the fish, and more—just as Jesus Himself did so frequently.

James begins his letter with a tremendous testimony to the deity of Christ:

> *James, a servant of God and of the Lord Jesus Christ,*
> *To the twelve tribes scattered among the nations:*
> *Greetings (1:1).*

It is amazing that a man who grew up with Jesus Christ, who had known Him all his life and had once opposed Him, would now address Jesus in this way: "the Lord Jesus Christ." James wrote with a reverence and a respect for the person of the Lord that is unequaled in the New Testament. It is a tremendously powerful and practical message from someone who not only had seen and heard the Lord Jesus, but had known Him intimately.

Here is a structural overview of the epistle of James:

The Testing of Faith (James 1:1–18)
1.	The purpose of testing	1:1–12
2.	The source of temptation	1:13–18

The Operation of Genuine Faith (James 1:19–5:6)
3.	Genuine faith is obedient	1:19–27
4.	Genuine faith is not prejudiced	2:1–13
5.	Genuine faith is demonstrated by good works	2:14–26
6.	Genuine faith controls the tongue	3:1–12
7.	Genuine faith demonstrates wisdom	3:13–18
8.	Genuine faith demonstrates humility	4:1–12
9.	Genuine faith demonstrates reliance on God	4:13–5:6

The letter of James and Jesus' Sermon on the Mount share more than a dozen exact parallels

Faith Hopes, Cares, and Triumphs (James 5:7–20)

**How faith
grows**

The theme of this letter is faith. Without faith, the book of Hebrews tells us, it is impossible to please God (Heb. 11:6). Faith, therefore, is the channel by which all God's blessings come to us, and without faith, all you can do is sin. "Everything that does not come from faith," says the apostle Paul, "is sin" (Rom. 14:23). If your actions are not consistent with your Christian faith, then what you are doing is distasteful and disgusting to God, even though people may applaud you.

In this letter, then, the apostle James tells us several things about faith. James 1 answers the question, "What makes faith grow?" Jesus said that it takes very little to constitute faith. If you have faith like a grain of mustard seed—just the tiniest particle of faith—you have enough faith to act upon. Even if your tiny particle of faith is hemmed in with doubts, when you are committed enough to act on that tiny particle of faith, it is enough. Your faith will move mountains.

1. Trials

Two forces in life make faith grow. The first is trials. "Oh, no!" you may be thinking. "Not that!" But it's true. Trials are the fertilizer that makes faith grow. So James 1 is a wonderful chapter for those who are facing trials. James writes,

> *Consider it pure joy, my brothers, whenever you face trials of many kinds, because you know that the testing of your faith develops perseverance. Perseverance must finish its work so that you may be mature and complete, not lacking anything (1:2–4).*

You need trials. This is a biblical truth. James goes on to describe how to take trials: Accept them, he says, as from God. And that's very hard. It takes a lot of wisdom to be able to accept the trials of life and to know that God wants to use those trials to produce good in our lives. Where does that wisdom come from? James replies:

> *If any of you lacks wisdom, he should ask God, who gives generously to all without finding fault, and it will be given to him (1:5).*

And what is the result of enduring trials while seeking comfort and wisdom from God to withstand those trials? Blessing!

Blessed is the man who perseveres under trial, because when he has stood the test, he will receive the crown of life that God has promised to those who love him (1:12).

What kinds of trials was James talking about here? Stonings, beatings, imprisonment, death, derision, the destruction of entire families—and for what? For something we take for granted in our own society: saying, "Jesus is Lord." Just think of the kinds of "trials" that can absolutely ruin a day today: crabgrass in the lawn or getting cut off in traffic.

Trials teach us lessons we could never learn otherwise. Without the buffeting of trials in our lives, we would be weak, spindly, incomplete Christians, unable to take on the great responsibilities that will be placed upon us in the day we enter into the Lord's kingdom and into the fullness of His service. We see this principle in nature. Butterflies must struggle to break out of their cocoons and chicks must struggle to break free of their eggs. If we break open the cocoon or the eggshell, thinking we are doing that creature a favor, the butterfly or the baby chick will be weak, sickly, and incomplete for having been spared the struggle of fully emerging through its time of trial. So it is with us.

So trial is the first instrument God uses to help us grow. The second instrument God uses to produce growth is His Word.

Do not merely listen to the word, and so deceive yourselves. Do what it says. Anyone who listens to the word but does not do what it says is like a man who looks at his face in a mirror and, after looking at himself, goes away and immediately forgets what he looks like. But the man who looks intently into the perfect law that gives freedom, and continues to do this, not forgetting what he has heard, but doing it—he will be blessed in what he does (1:22–25).

James reminds us that it is the Word of God that makes our faith grow, particularly as the Word is expressed in our actions. Faith comes by hearing, says the apostle Paul, and hearing by the word of God (see Rom. 10:17). The only way to know the great thoughts of God, the deep things of God, the underlying secrets of life, is to spend time with the book that reveals them. So let your faith grow by rejoicing in trial and by understanding and acting on God's Word.

In chapters 2 and 3, James shows us how to take something as intangible and invisible as faith and make it solid and visible. He gets down to practical realities and suggests three indications that a person's faith is real.

Without the buffeting of trials in our lives, we would be weak, spindly, incomplete Christians

2. God's Word

Making faith visible

First, there must be no partiality, nor prejudice. If a person is prejudiced against others, because of the color of their skin or the state of their bank accounts, he or she has no real faith. If a person treats others as unimportant because of their low social status or lack of influence, then that person has no real faith. James writes,

> My brothers, as believers in our glorious Lord Jesus Christ, don't show favoritism. Suppose a man comes into your meeting wearing a gold ring and fine clothes, and a poor man in shabby clothes also comes in. If you show special attention to the man wearing fine clothes and say, "Here's a good seat for you," but say to the poor man, "You stand there" or "Sit on the floor by my feet," have you not discriminated among yourselves and become judges with evil thoughts?
>
> Listen, my dear brothers: Has not God chosen those who are poor in the eyes of the world to be rich in faith and to inherit the kingdom he promised those who love him? But you have insulted the poor (2:1–6).

Prejudice destroys faith. Faith destroys prejudice. The two cannot coexist in a church or an individual Christian.

The turbulent racial tensions of the 1990s have been, in many respects, a replay of the racial divisions of the 1960s.

I remember being invited to speak on the subject of racial violence at a state college campus during the sixties. I pointed out that one of the tragic causes of the racial conflict in our land is the church of Jesus Christ. This statement shocked many people, for they expected that I, a pastor, would defend the record of the church in race relations. Instead, I went on to say that if the church had been what it should have been, if Christians in both the North and the South actually received African-Americans and other minorities as fully equal brothers and sisters in Christ Jesus, this whole conflict would long since have disappeared.

The church has an enormous impact on the attitudes in society. If the church practices bias and discrimination, then prejudice takes root like a weed in the soil of our society.

Second, faith is made visible by deeds of mercy. James was eminently practical, and he sets forth some eminently practical scenarios for us so that we can see his point with inescapable clarity:

> What good is it, my brothers, if a man claims to have faith but has no deeds? Can such faith save him? Suppose a brother or sister is without clothes and daily food. If one of you says to him, "Go, I wish you well; keep warm and well fed," but does nothing about his physical needs, what good is it? In the same way, faith by itself, if it is not accompanied by action, is dead.

But someone will say, "You have faith; I have deeds."

Show me your faith without deeds, and I will show you my faith by what I do (2:14–18).

Notice, James is not saying that we can be saved by good works. He is clearly saying that only faith, not works, can save us—but genuine faith is validated by action. What good is it if we tell a starving person, "I feel for you, I'll pray for you," yet we do nothing to alleviate his hunger? That's not faith. That's just a pious display. Can you imagine Jesus Himself treating someone that way? Real faith doesn't just talk, it acts. See Matthew 25:42–43.

3. Controlled tongue

Next, James devotes all of chapter 3 to the third way by which faith is made visible and recognizable: a controlled tongue. He uses a series of vivid figures of speech to describe the tongue: It is "set on fire by hell." You can tame every beast and bird and reptile, but no one can control his or her tongue. The tongue, James says, is the member of our body most closely linked to our real nature. It shows what is motivating us, and therefore, what you say reveals what you are! James wants us to understand that if we claim to be Christians and to have faith in Jesus Christ, our tongues must submit to His control.

This is not to suggest that Christians should never reprove or confront one another, but any confrontation of a brother or sister in Christ should be gentle, loving, and humble—not caustic, humiliating, and bitter. As Paul says in Ephesians, we are to speak the truth, but we are to speak the truth in love.

When faith fails

In chapter 4 and most of chapter 5, James answers the question, "What happens when faith fails? What if we fail to demonstrate our faith by the way we live and speak?" Answer: War breaks out. These wars and fights among Christian brothers and sisters are the result of prayerlessness, which is itself a demonstration of faithlessness. Faith is evidenced through prayer, and prayer produces love and peace. When faith fails, prayer fails; then fighting, arguments, hatred, and distrust break out. James writes:

When faith fails, prayer fails; then fighting, arguments, hatred, and distrust break out

You want something but don't get it. You kill and covet, but you cannot have what you want. You quarrel and fight. You do not have, because you do not ask God (4:2).

That is the trouble! We fight with each other because we do not ask God for anything. We do not take from Him the nature of love and compassion He offers us. We choose not to receive from Him that sweetness of tongue that will turn away hostility and produce peace. Instead, we lash out and fight with one another.

The next thing is that the love of the world comes in and pollutes our relationship with God. James writes:

> *You adulterous people, don't you know that friendship with the world is hatred toward God? Anyone who chooses to be a friend of the world becomes an enemy of God (4:4).*

James also addresses the practical issue of the way we judge each other and speak about one another:

> *Brothers, do not slander one another. Anyone who speaks against his brother or judges him speaks against the law and judges it. When you judge the law, you are not keeping it, but sitting in judgment on it (4:11).*

People who criticize others have put themselves above the Word of God and have assumed God's role as judge. Instead of letting the Word judge themselves, they become the judges of others.

Another result of lack of faith is being presumptuous about our plans, and not allowing God to be sovereign over our lives and our future. James writes:

> *Listen, you who say, "Today or tomorrow we will go to this or that city, spend a year there, carry on business and make money" (4:13).*

This is not to say that we should not make plans or set goals for our lives. Of course we should. But we should never become arrogant or presumptuous. We should never think we own our lives or that we control our own destinies.

A college student once said to me, "I don't need Christianity. I've got all it takes to live my life. I don't need any help from God."

"Oh?" I said. "Well, tell me—how do you keep your heart beating and your lungs functioning?"

"What do you mean?"

"Well," I said, "your heart is beating away and your diaphragm keeps moving up and down, forcing air in and out of your lungs. How do you do that?"

He seemed flustered. "I . . . I don't know. It just takes care of itself, I guess."

"No, it doesn't," I countered. "Nothing takes care of itself. Someone's operating the involuntary processes of your body, keeping you alive from moment to moment."

Then I told him the story of my friend who was back in Washington, D.C., during World War II. He wanted to fly from

Washington to New York during those days when you needed a priority for air travel. So, he went into the ticket office and said to the woman at the desk, "I want a ticket for New York."

"Do you have a priority?" she asked.

"I didn't know I needed one," he replied. "How do I get a priority?"

"Well," she said, "if you work for the government or for the airlines, I could give you one."

"I don't work for either of them," my friend replied. "But I'll tell you who I do work for. I work for the one who owns the air that your airline flies its planes through!"

She looked at him strangely. "Well, I don't think that's good enough to get you a priority."

He leaned over and said, "Did you ever think what would happen if my boss shut off your air for ten minutes?"

She blinked perplexedly, then said, "Just a minute, I'll see what I can do." She was gone for a few moments, then returned—with a priority in hand. "You can go right aboard," she said. She recognized that my friend served the highest authority of all!

God is the ultimate authority over our lives—not us. We should never become arrogant or presumptuous about our plans for the future. The more we respect His sovereignty over our lives, the better equipped we will be to adjust to the unforeseen circumstances that come our way. Time is in God's hands, not ours.

In chapter 5, James paints a beautiful word picture of authentic Christian community. This image of communion revolves around four qualities: confession, prayer, honesty, and love. James writes:

> *Confess your sins to each other and pray for each other so that you may be healed. The prayer of a righteous man is powerful and effective (5:16).*

Christian fellowship requires us to talk openly with trusted Christian brothers and sisters about our problems and to pray for each other for insight and healing of those problems. True Christian intimacy takes place as we come out from behind our masks, as we quit trying to be something we are not and simply become what we really are. As we confess our faults and pain with each other and pray for one another, we live out the honesty and truth of God. Immediately, the grace of the God of truth, the God who loves truth, will flow through us—individually and as a family of faith. We will become a true community—and the world will press its nose against the glass, trying to get what we have, trying to become what we are.

I am convinced that this is the missing element in society today: genuine fellowship and community—what the Greek New Testament calls *koinonia*. It is missing even in many (if not most) of our churches, where we have a lot of Christians living in little isolation cells not willing to let anyone into their lives, not willing to let anyone see who they truly are. You ask them how things are going, and they respond automatically, "Oh, great!" But they are not great at all, and this kind of hypocrisy must end. James says that God will be in your midst if you take down the fences, join hands with other Christians, pray together, and be honest with one another.

In and through and around and above and below it all, binding our community together, must be genuine Christlike love, expressed in an intense concern and caring for one another—a concern that dares to tell the truth to one another and a concern that will not let a brother or sister go. The closing verses of James give us the pattern:

> *My brothers, if one of you should wander from the truth and some-one should bring him back, remember this: Whoever turns a sinner from the error of his way will save him from death and cover over a multitude of sins (5:19–20).*

Here we have a wonderful glimpse into the life of the early church—and into the church as it should be today. No wonder these Christians turned the city of Jerusalem upside down! Under the leadership of this man James the Just, the church grew until there was a vast multitude of believers who lived by mutual confession, prayer, honesty, and love. The world today aches for Christians who will return to this pattern, who will become a genuine *koinonia* community, a family of faith, modeling the character of Christ.

That is the claim of the Christian faith upon our lives. That is the call of this gospel we claim to believe in. That is the message of the epistle of James to you and me at the brink of a new millennium. If we truly believe it, let's live it! And let's turn the world upside down for Jesus once more!

Living Stones

I n July of the year A.D. 64, a great fire broke out in the city of Rome. Soon, the entire city was engulfed in flames. Hundreds of public buildings burned to the ground, thousands of houses were destroyed, and most of the city's inhabitants were left homeless. History concludes that Emperor Nero set that fire to destroy the ramshackle buildings of Rome and make room to erect marble palaces and other monuments to his name. This event gave rise to the saying, "Nero fiddled while Rome burned"—even though the violin had not yet been invented. Historians of the time claim that Emperor Nero was seen looking over the city and enjoying the fire.

The people were incensed to the point of revolution, so Nero created a scapegoat to blame for the fire: a group of people called "Christians." These Christians followed a man named Christ, about whom strange things were said. He had supposedly been crucified— then was raised to life again! There were wild rumors about the strange practices of His followers. These Christians were considered cannibals, because they talked about meeting in houses, drinking the blood and eating the body of their Master. They spoke about "agape-love feasts," where they greeted one another with a holy kiss and shared their innermost problems with each other. These stories became the basis for rumors of wild sex orgies. Christians were already subject to suspicion, so when Nero blamed them for the burning of Rome, the people of Rome believed him.

With the people's support, Nero initiated a series of persecutions against the Christians. Christians were dipped in tar and burned alive as torches to light Nero's gardens when he threw an outdoor party. They

The context of 1 Peter: the persecutions under Nero

were tied to chariots and dragged through the streets of Rome until dead. They were thrown to the lions. They were sealed up in leather bags and thrown into water so that when the leather bags shrank, the Christians inside were squeezed and suffocated to death. In a hundred other cruelly inventive ways, Nero exploited satanically inspired hatred against Christians and used them to satiate his own sadistic lusts.

This time of unbelievably harsh persecution of Christians in Rome was the context for the epistle of 1 Peter.

A letter for trials and pressures

Most Bible scholars believe that Peter wrote his first letter from the city of Rome. He begins with these words:

> Peter, an apostle of Jesus Christ,
> To God's elect, strangers in the world, scattered throughout Pontus, Galatia, Cappadocia, Asia and Bithynia, who have been chosen according to the foreknowledge of God the Father, through the sanctifying work of the Spirit, for obedience to Jesus Christ and sprinkling by his blood:
> Grace and peace be yours in abundance (1:1–2).

Later in this epistle, Peter writes:

> She who is in Babylon, chosen together with you, sends you her greetings, and so does my son Mark (5:13).

Peter was not talking about the ancient city of Babylon on the Euphrates River. Most scholars agree that Peter was undoubtedly using the term that was common among first-century Christians. They often referred to Rome as "Babylon" because the idolatry, blood lust, and open immorality of ancient Babylon had infected the capital of the Roman Empire. His greeting from "she who is in Babylon" suggests that Peter himself was in Babylon, or Rome, at the time.

Peter probably wrote this letter from the city of Rome in about A.D. 67. He addressed it to Christians scattered about the cities of the northeast province of Asia Minor (present-day Turkey). They were being hounded and persecuted all through the empire because of Nero's proclamation against them, so the apostle Peter wrote to encourage them and embolden them to face the deadly persecution of the Roman state.

This letter is especially helpful to anyone undergoing trial or suffering of any kind. If you wonder what God is doing in the world, and how to withstand the pressures and pain, become intimately acquainted with 1 Peter.

Here is an outline of Peter's first letter:

Our Salvation as Believers (1 Peter 1:1–2:12)

Our Submission as Believers (1 Peter 2:13–3:12)

Our Suffering as Believers (1 Peter 3:13–5:14)

The letter begins with the greatest fact in the life of any Christian: our relationship to Jesus Christ through the miracle of the new birth:

A living hope

> *Praise be to the God and Father of our Lord Jesus Christ! In his great mercy he has given us new birth (1:3).*

As a boy, I would hear Christians give their testimonies. They would say, "The greatest thing that ever happened to me was the day I met Jesus Christ." Well, I was a Christian, but deep down in my heart, I didn't really believe it was the greatest thing that had ever happened to me. In fact, it seemed to be a rather minor incident in my life. I didn't have a shattering emotional experience at my conversion. The windows of heaven didn't open up and flood my soul with light. I was ten years old when I asked Jesus into my life, and though it was a precious experience and one I did not discount, it didn't compare to some of the other experiences and important decisions of my life.

But now as I look back over the decades of my Christian life, I can say that beyond a shadow of a doubt that decision was the greatest decision of my life. Everything else that has happened to me has been related to that one turning point in my life at age ten.

The reason that the experience of the new birth is so important is not only that we have a hope of heaven when we die, but that we have a living hope to carry us through this life. What an important word for us in this hopeless age! Peter writes:

In his great mercy he has given us new birth into a living hope through the resurrection of Jesus Christ from the dead, and into an inheritance that can never perish, spoil or fade—kept in heaven for you, who through faith are shielded by God's power until the coming of the salvation that is ready to be revealed in the last time (1:3–5).

Here is an expression of the hope of heaven—a place in eternity that is already reserved for us. But that is not all. Peter says that we not only have a living hope for the future and eternity, but we have present power—right now, today! We are kept and sustained by that power, guarded through faith for a salvation that is ready to be revealed.

A rejoicing love

Peter also reminds us of another benefit that we enjoy because we have received Jesus as Lord and Savior—a benefit that can carry us through times of trial—a rejoicing love:

Though you have not seen him, you love him; and even though you do not see him now, you believe in him and are filled with an inexpressible and glorious joy (1:8).

I hope you know what Peter is talking about—the kind of quiet joy that fills your heart simply because you know Jesus in an intimate, personal way. This joy is not the result of anything He does for you, but simply the result of who He is and of the fact that He loves you and you love Him. Even though you cannot see Him you love Him.

Peter goes on to say that the plan of salvation has been predicted by the Old Testament prophets. Peter writes:

Concerning this salvation, the prophets, who spoke of the grace that was to come to you, searched intently and with the greatest care, trying to find out the time and circumstances to which the Spirit of Christ in them was pointing when he predicted the sufferings of Christ and the glories that would follow (1:10–11).

This is not some new invention or wild fable. The birth, life, death, and resurrection of Jesus Christ—which is our hope of salvation—was planned since the beginning of time and was predicted throughout the Old Testament.

Peter sets forth three marks as distinctives that every Christian should bear. *First mark: "Be holy"* (see 1 Peter 1:14–16).

What do you think of when you hear that word *holy?* Do you think of someone who has been stewed in vinegar? Someone so piously sour that he or she is always mouthing righteous-sounding words, speaking a super religious language? Is this what holiness means to you? If so, then you have missed the biblical meaning of the command, "Be holy."

The Old Testament talks about "the beauty of holiness." Obviously, a sour-pickle personality is not what you would call "the beauty of holiness." A truly holy person is a person with an attractive, beautiful personality. At base, the word *holiness* truly means "wholeness." A holy person is a whole person. Holy people are whole-minded, whole-hearted, whole-spirited. They are dedicated to God, committed to loving, accepting, and forgiving others, and focused on living righteously and joyfully. They have the healthiest personalities you can imagine. Their talk is godly, and their lifestyle mirrors their talk. There is no conflict between their words and their walk. They are at rest. They are adjusted. They are content, because their trust is in God. That's what holiness truly is.

I love holy people. I wish we were all holy in the church—it would be so much fun going to church! When churches experience fights, splits, and discord, it is because God's people are not living holy lives.

Second mark: the right kind of fear. In 1 Peter 1:17–19, Peter says, "Be fearful." Fearful?! Yes, God does indeed want us to be fearful—but that word *fearful* needs some explanation. Peter is not saying we should be timid or terrorized or paralyzed with dread. Rather, Peter challenges us toward what he calls reverent fear:

> *Since you call on a Father who judges each man's work impartially, live your lives as strangers here in reverent fear. For you know that it was not with perishable things such as silver or gold that you were redeemed from the empty way of life handed down to you from your forefathers, but with the precious blood of Christ, a lamb without blemish or defect (1:17–19).*

The kind of fear that Peter describes is really an honest and profound respect for God. Peter says, in effect, "Remember whom you are dealing with. You are not dealing with another human being who can be fooled by your actions and attitudes. You are dealing with one who knows you better than you know yourself. He is no respecter of persons. So conduct yourself with fear, awe, and respect for the eternal, omnipotent, all-knowing God of the universe. Be honest with God and with yourself, remembering that you are not your own, you have been bought with the precious blood of Jesus Christ."

1. Beautifully holy

2. Reverently fearful

Third mark: "Be priests." In 1 Peter 2:4–5, the apostle writes:

> *As you come to him, the living Stone—rejected by men but chosen by God and precious to him—you also, like living stones, are being built into a spiritual house to be a holy priesthood, offering spiritual sacrifices acceptable to God through Jesus Christ.*

3. A royal priest

Here is the answer to a question people often ask: "What did Jesus mean when He said to this apostle, 'I tell you that you are Peter, and on this rock I will build my church'?" (Matt. 16:18). We know that the name Peter means "rock," and the Roman Catholic Church tells us that Jesus meant He was going to build His church upon Peter. But Peter says, "No." He was there. He ought to know. He says, "Jesus is the Rock." And every believer who comes to Christ is like a stone built upon that Rock, that great underlying Rock upon which God is erecting the institution called the church.

What is the goal of building us up as "stones" upon the Rock? He is building us up as a priesthood—as a people dedicated and offered to God, special and holy, set apart for God. Peter writes:

> *You are a chosen people, a royal priesthood, a holy nation, a people belonging to God, that you may declare the praises of him who called you out of darkness into his wonderful light (2:9).*

God wants us to declare to the world what He has done for us

That is what God wants: He wants us to declare to the world what He has done for us. As we do so, we offer to God a sweet-smelling offering and a savor of worship to Him. So these are the three distinctives Peter says should mark the life of every Christian: Be holy. Be reverently fearful. And be a priesthood, set apart to God.

Practical advice

Peter then deals with the more practical aspects of life, with how we should live our lives, whether as citizens of the Roman Empire or of the United States of America. Though they lived under persecution, the first-century Christians still had certain obligations. Today, many of us see our own government behaving in ways we disapprove of, ways we feel are unrighteous and even harmful to us—yet we still have certain obligations as citizens. Peter writes:

> *Dear friends, I urge you, as aliens and strangers in the world, to abstain from sinful desires, which war against your soul. Live such good lives among the pagans that, though they accuse you of doing wrong, they may see your good deeds and glorify God on the day he visits us.*

Submit yourselves for the Lord's sake to every authority instituted among men: whether to the king, as the supreme authority, or to governors, who are sent by him to punish those who do wrong and to commend those who do right. For it is God's will that by doing good you should silence the ignorant talk of foolish men. Live as free men, but do not use your freedom as a cover-up for evil; live as servants of God. Show proper respect to everyone: Love the brotherhood of believers, fear God, honor the king (2:11–17).

Honor the king? But the king Peter refers to is Nero! He is the one who drags Christians behind his chariot and burns them as living torches in his garden! Honor *him?* Surely, Peter must be out of his mind! Yet that is God's word to us: As citizens, we owe honor to those in authority over us.

Then Peter talks about servants:

Slaves, submit yourselves to your masters with all respect, not only to those who are good and considerate, but also to those who are harsh. For it is commendable if a man bears up under the pain of unjust suffering because he is conscious of God. But how is it to your credit if you receive a beating for doing wrong and endure it? But if you suffer for doing good and you endure it, this is commendable before God. To this you were called, because Christ suffered for you, leaving you an example, that you should follow in his steps.

"He committed no sin, and no deceit was found in his mouth" (2:18–22)

So servants are to obey and respect their masters—and I might add that the principle is clear that employees are to obey and respect their employers. If an employer or master is unjust, we are not to behave unjustly in return, we do not return insult for insult. We commit ourselves to the Lord.

Next, Peter moves into the Christian home, encouraging Christians to honor one another and behave justly and considerately (3:1–7).

Then he addresses the entire church, encouraging the family of faith to live together in unity, loving one another as brothers and sisters, behaving tenderly and humbly with one another. This is the mark of our Christian fellowship and community (3:8–14).

Peter tells us to always be ready to share the Good News of Jesus Christ with those around us. He writes:

In your hearts set apart Christ as Lord. Always be prepared to give an answer to everyone who asks you to give the reason for the hope that you have. But do this with gentleness and respect, keeping a clear conscience, so that those who speak maliciously against your good behavior in Christ may be ashamed of their slander (3:15–16).

Notice that Peter expects Christians to live such positive, hopeful, exemplary lives that people will be eager to know why. He says, in effect, "When people ask you why you're such an optimistic, cheerful, righteous person, have an answer ready for them. Be prepared to tell them that Jesus is the answer." Saint Francis of Assisi understood this principle well; he always taught his disciples that they should spread the gospel through the way they lived and loved. "Preach the gospel at all times," Saint Francis advised. "If necessary, use words."

A difficult passage

Then comes a difficult passage about spirits in prison and baptism—passages many Christians have struggled with. But the key to 1 Peter 3 is verse 18:

Christ died for sins once for all, the righteous for the unrighteous, to bring you to God. He was put to death in the body but made alive by the Spirit.

Jesus suffered in order to bring us to God. He came in the flesh. He died in the flesh. He did all this that He might accomplish the great goal of God's plan—bringing us to God.

Peter recalls the way the gospel was preached in Noah's day, and how the Spirit of Christ, speaking through Noah, preached to the people of his day so that he might bring them to God. But they refused—so the ark becomes a symbol of the life of the Lord Jesus Christ, carrying us over the floods of judgment and bringing us to God. Baptism, which is also a picture relating to the ark, saves us just as the ark saved Noah. Baptism is that which now saves us—but Peter is very clear at this point that he is not talking about water baptism:

This water [the water of the Genesis flood] *symbolizes baptism* [the baptism of the Holy Spirit] *that now saves you also—not the removal of dirt from the body* [which is what water baptism accomplishes] *but the pledge of a good conscience toward God* [which is accomplished by salvation]. *It saves you by the resurrection of Jesus Christ (3:21).*

The baptism of the Spirit occurs at the moment of salvation and puts us into the ark of safety, our Lord Jesus. Water baptism is the visible symbol of the real baptism that saves us, the baptism of the Holy Spirit. Salvation removes the stain of guilt and sin from our lives, replacing it with a clear conscience through the resurrection of Jesus Christ. If you read the passage in that light, I believe you will have no difficulty with it.

Peter then concludes his discussion of the issue of suffering, encouraging us as Christians to remember that we are not to live as the worldly, the Gentiles, who return evil for evil. Rather, we are to return good for evil. We are not to be concerned about our own satisfaction and our own rights. We are to be concerned about living after the pattern of Jesus Christ, the suffering Servant. When we begin to insist on our rights, even in small ways, we nullify our witness. We cease to resemble Christ.

A young boy once became very concerned about all the chores he had to do around the house. He began to feel exploited, so he decided to demand his rights. He did this by presenting a bill for all the chores he had done:

Mowing the lawn	$1.00
Making my bed	.50
Vacuuming the rug	.50
Pulling weeds	1.00
Taking out the garbage	.50
Cleaning up after the dog	.50
Washing the dishes	1.00
	$5.00

The next morning, the boy placed the bill beside his mother's breakfast plate. She read it. She did not say anything. But the next morning he found a list beside his plate. It read:

Washing your clothes	no charge
Fixing your meals	no charge
Providing shelter	no charge
Driving you to soccer and baseball practice	no charge
Helping you with your homework	no charge
Trip to Disneyland	no charge
Teaching you right from wrong, and telling you about Jesus	no charge
Etc., etc., etc.	no charge
	Absolutely no charge, done out of love

He read it—and he hugged his mom, then did all his chores without complaint.

We are to do what this mother did—return good for evil. She could have lectured the boy on his ingratitude and selfishness. Instead, she showed him how much she loved him—and he responded to that love.

The end of all things

The closing section of the letter deals with life in the church, the body of Christ. Peter writes:

> *The end of all things is near. Therefore be clear minded and self-controlled so that you can pray. Above all, love each other deeply, because love covers over a multitude of sins. Offer hospitality to one another without grumbling. Each one should use whatever gift he has received to serve others, faithfully administering God's grace in its various forms. If anyone speaks, he should do it as one speaking the very words of God. If anyone serves, he should do it with the strength God provides, so that in all things God may be praised through Jesus Christ. To him be the glory and the power for ever and ever. Amen (4:7–11).*

Here is the Lord's program for the end of the age—and He plans to carry it out through you and me in the church. As the end draws near and the world slouches toward Armageddon, He expects His church to stand in stark, shining contrast to the world's darkness. He intends our lives, both individually and as a body, to be characterized by agape love so wide and so deep that it covers any sin or wrong that is done to us; by generosity and gracious hospitality toward our brothers and sisters in Christ; by the exercise of our spiritual gifts so that we can show God's grace to one another and to the world; by speaking truthfully and gently to one another; by serving one another to the nth degree, so that Jesus will be exemplified and God will be praised and glorified. This is God's plan. It may not look like a very impressive plan in the eyes of the world, but in the eyes of heaven, this is a powerful plan that will accomplish the will of God.

Peter goes on, in 4:12–19, to speak of suffering as a privilege, because we have an opportunity to share Christ's sufferings—not suffering as wrongdoers but rejoicing in the fact that God is at work through our suffering.

In chapter 5, Peter then speaks of the mutual ministry of the elders to the members, and of the members one to another. Then he returns one final time to the matter of suffering in verse 10:

> *The God of all grace, who called you to his eternal glory in Christ, after you have suffered a little while, will himself restore you and make you strong, firm and steadfast.*

As the end draws near and the world slouches toward Armageddon, He expects His church to stand in shining contrast to the world's darkness

Rejoice that God is at work through our suffering

This present suffering is just for a little while—then Christ Himself will restore us to strength and health, a strength that can never fail, a vitality that can never fade, reserved for us in heaven. The world is temporal, more temporal than we human beings are. For God will bring an end to the world, but we will go on forever with Him. This is God's plan.

As we see the end approaching, as we suffer and endure for Jesus' sake, the words of 1 Peter are a blessing and a comfort. "Peace to all of you who are in Christ," Peter says in the very last line of his letter. Amid our trials and sufferings, amid a world that is crumbling all around us— peace! That is the encouraging message of 1 Peter.

God will bring an end to the world, but we will go on forever with Him

Faith in the Face of Falsehood

I t almost seems that 2 Peter was written to us at this crucial time, at the threshold of a new millennium. Every word of this book is so pertinent, so contemporary, so full of practical advice for today; that it confirms two truths:

1. The Bible is relevant, fresh, and vital; it never goes out of date.

2. History has come full circle; we live in days very similar to those of the first century, and we face conditions similar to the ones faced by the early church.

Whereas the theme of 1 Peter was how to rejoice in the face of suffering, the theme of 2 Peter is how to maintain faith in the face of falsehood—how to detect error, how to avoid the lure of deception, how to know and do what is right in a world gone wrong.

Second Peter can be outlined neatly. Each of its three chapters portrays a different facet of the main theme. Here is an overview of 2 Peter:

The theme of 2 Peter: How to know and to do right in a world gone wrong

What the Christian Life Is All About (2 Peter 1)

1.	Peter's greeting	1:1–2
2.	How we grow in Christ	1:3–14
3.	The basis of our faith	1:15–21

Warning against False Teachers (2 Peter 2)

4.	The danger of false teachers	2:1–3
5.	The destruction of false teachers	2:4–9
6.	The description of false teachers	2:10–22

The Certainty of Our Lord's Return (2 Peter 3)

7.	Scoffers in the last days	3:1–7
8.	The arrival of the day of the Lord	3:8–10
9.	How to live in expectation of His return	3:11–18

It's a simple outline for a very practical letter—just as you might expect from a practical, hardheaded Christian like Peter.

Mighty apostles or ordinary believers

This letter was probably written from Rome, as was 1 Peter. In fact, Peter may have been a prisoner of Emperor Nero. From this letter we know that Peter is, at the very least, in great danger.

Peter says that he feels the time is drawing near when he is to put off his body—what he refers to as his tent, his habitation—to go and be with the Lord. He says the Lord Himself showed him this, as recorded for us at the close of the gospel of John. In John 21:18, Jesus had told Peter that a time would come when someone would bind his hands and lead him where he did not want to go. Peter understood this to mean that he was to suffer and die as our Lord died, on a cross. Tradition tells us Peter was indeed crucified, and that he was so humbled by the fact that he was counted worthy to die the same death as his Lord that he begged his captors to crucify him upside down.

Peter opens his second letter with these words:

> Simon Peter, a servant and apostle of Jesus Christ,
> To those who through the righteousness of our God and Savior Jesus Christ have received a faith as precious as ours:
> Grace and peace be yours in abundance through the knowledge of God and of Jesus our Lord (2 Peter 1:1–2).

The weakest believer enjoys all that the mightiest saint ever possessed

Note that phrase: "To those who . . . have received a faith as precious as ours." Think of that! Christians today are tempted to think of the apostles as mighty men of sterling character and superhuman faith. Notice, however, that the apostles never thought of themselves that way. Truly, the weakest believer holds in his or her hands all that the mightiest saint ever possessed. That is the theme of Peter's opening chapter. Listen to these words:

> His divine power has given us everything we need for life and godliness through our knowledge of him who called us by his own glory and goodness (1:3).

All of us who have genuinely come to Jesus Christ—without exception—have everything we need to handle life and to manifest godliness (which literally means "God-likeness").

Do you understand and truly believe that this statement by Peter applies to your life right now? A lot of people do not. They are always looking for something more—some new experience, some transforming new truth, some further revelation, some elevating emotional high—and they think that without these things they can never be the kind of Christians they ought to be.

Peter says, in effect, "You don't need any new experience or revelation. You already have all you need to be spiritually empowered and energized to serve God, please God, and imitate God in your lifestyle. If you have come to Christ, you have all there is to have of Him, and you have all He has to give you. You have all power and all things that pertain to life and godliness though the knowledge of Him. If something is missing, it's not because you need any more of Christ. It may be that Christ needs more of you. You simply need to turn more of your life and your will over to Him."

If something is missing, it's not because you need any more of Christ; it may be that Christ needs more of you

If what Peter says is true (and it is), then we have no excuse for failure. If we have everything in Christ, we only need to know more of Him and to yield more to Him, and our problems will be solved. To me, the great thing about being a Christian is that in Jesus Christ I really am finding practical answers to every problem that confronts me. Obviously, coming to Christ does not automatically enable us to know everything. But we do gain insight and understanding to handle the difficulties, heartaches, and problems of life. We do gain the power to live godly, Christlike lives. God's power is already granted to us, and it comes to us through two channels: (1) His promises, and (2) putting our faith into practice. First, the promises. Peter writes:

Two channels of God's power

1. His promises

Through these he has given us his very great and precious promises, so that through them you may participate in the divine nature and escape the corruption in the world caused by evil desires (1:4).

These are not just glowing words, not just so much theological twaddle. These are sure guarantees that God has given us, and He will honor them with all His power and authority as the Creator-God of the universe. His very nature, His very character is at stake in these words.

So the first thing we need to do is to learn what He has promised—and that means we must acquaint ourselves with those promises, as contained in the Scriptures. You cannot possibly find fulfillment and victory in your life and really discover the kind of person God wants you to be unless you study and understand God's Word.

As we come to know and rely on God's promises, we become strengthened and empowered to "escape the corruption in the world

2. Our practice

caused by evil desires." So much evil and corruption surround us. Our airwaves, cable TV, radio, books, magazines, and even our workplaces and social arenas are polluted by the evil of this world. We see sexual corruption, greed, materialism, ambition, pride, and selfishness. You cannot escape from such pervasive corruption unless you have armored yourself in the truth of God.

The second means of receiving God's power for our lives is found in 1:5–7:

> *For this very reason, make every effort to add to your faith goodness; and to goodness, knowledge; and to knowledge, self-control; and to self-control, perseverance; and to perseverance, godliness; and to godliness, brotherly kindness; and to brotherly kindness, love.*

In other words, once you have faith, you must put it into practice. You must begin growing and applying your faith, from moment to moment, from deed to deed, one day at a time. Whenever you identify a new area of your life that needs to be dealt with—a problem with anger, a lack of self-control, harshness in dealing with others, a timidity and lack of perseverance—then you work to bring that area of your life in line with your faith. It's important to understand that faith is not an event, it's a process. As we grow and mature in Christ, He gradually opens our eyes to different aspects of our characters that are not under His control. As we make ourselves available to Him in obedience, He gradually chips away at our imperfections, helping us to become more and more like His own perfect character.

Faith is not an event, it's a process

And what is the result of putting our faith into practice on a daily basis? Peter writes:

> *If you possess these qualities in increasing measure, they will keep you from being ineffective and unproductive in your knowledge of our Lord Jesus Christ (1:8).*

A recipe for success as a Christian is right here in this passage: faith and obedience. Knowledge of God's promises coupled with the willingness to apply those promises in the specific situations of life is what enables Christians to be effective. And what of those who do not know and apply God's promises? Peter replies:

> *If anyone does not have them, he is nearsighted and blind, and has forgotten that he has been cleansed from his past sins (1:9).*

Christians who fail to live according to their faith are blind. Their conversion experiences seem to have little or no effect on them. They leave themselves open for doubt, backsliding, and even self-destruction through sin. Therefore, writes Peter in verses 10–11:

> *Be all the more eager to make your calling and election sure. For if you do these things, you will never fall, and you will receive a rich welcome into the eternal kingdom of our Lord and Savior Jesus Christ.*

When the Lord calls you home, the trumpets will blare in glory at your entrance into the kingdom, because you have found the secret of successful living, and you have been effective in your service to God.

Peter reveals two guarantees that support the faith he commends to us: (1) his own eyewitness account of the life of the Lord Jesus Christ, and (2) the voice of the Old Testament prophets. He writes:

Two guarantees

> *We did not follow cleverly invented stories when we told you about the power and coming of our Lord Jesus Christ, but we were eyewitnesses of his majesty. For he received honor and glory from God the Father when the voice came to him from the Majestic Glory, saying, "This is my Son, whom I love; with him I am well pleased." We ourselves heard this voice that came from heaven when we were with him on the sacred mountain (1:16–18).*

Peter refers to the event cited in Matthew 17 and Mark 9, where Jesus was transfigured on the mountain, when His face shone and His clothes became as white as light. Peter says, "We were eyewitnesses of his majesty." And that is where Christian faith rests: on the credible eyewitness accounts of men and women who were there and who simply reported what they saw and heard Jesus do.

1. Eyewitness accounts

Peter goes on to state the second guarantee. Our faith is confirmed, he says, by another voice—the voice of the Old Testament prophets. He writes:

2. Old Testament prophets

> *We have the word of the prophets made more certain, and you will do well to pay attention to it, as to a light shining in a dark place, until the day dawns and the morning star rises in your hearts. Above all, you must understand that no prophecy of Scripture came about by the prophet's own interpretation. For prophecy never had its origin in the will of man, but men spoke from God as they were carried along by the Holy Spirit (1:19–21).*

These men did not write their own opinions. They wrote under instruction from the Spirit of God, and they accurately predicted events that were to occur centuries later. Two guarantees—eyewitnesses and fulfilled prophecy—support our faith.

A warning against false teachers

In chapter 2, Peter sounds a warning against false teachers—and his words are as relevant today as they were when the ink was still wet on the page:

> There were also false prophets among the people, just as there will be false teachers among you. They will secretly introduce destructive heresies, even denying the sovereign Lord who bought them—bringing swift destruction on themselves. Many will follow their shameful ways and will bring the way of truth into disrepute (2:1–2).

Today we see these words fulfilled in many ways. We see cults in which the leaders claim to be Jesus Christ—and in which members are sometimes destroyed through horrible mass suicides. Those are extreme cases. But there are also more subtle cases where false teachers introduce destructive heresies into individual churches—or even into entire denominations.

These teachers claim to be Christians and profess to love the Lord Jesus, yet their teachings deny everything He stood for

Notice that Peter says, "They will secretly introduce destructive heresies, even denying the sovereign Lord who bought them"—which tells us that these false teachers are not mere atheistic antagonists of Christianity. These teachers claim to be Christians and profess to love the Lord Jesus, yet their teachings actually deny everything He stood for!

As a result of these false teachers, says Peter, the truth of the gospel will be brought into disrepute. People will look down on those who believe the Bible; they will consider believers simple-minded, ignorant folk from the Dark Ages—or worse—narrow-minded bigots.

God will judge them

In 2:3–9, Peter assures us that God will surely judge these false teachers just as He dealt with the rebellious angels, just as He dealt with the sinners of the ancient world whom He judged with a flood, and just as He dealt with the sinful cities of Sodom and Gomorrah. Peter says that the godly will be rescued from trial, just as Noah was saved from the flood and Lot was saved from the destruction of Sodom.

False teachers described

In verses 10–22, Peter gives a vivid description of the characteristics of these false teachers. They are:

• presumptuous; eloquent with impressive words about issues of life, salvation, and spirituality—but actually ignorant of God's truth

• like animals, creatures of instinct; reviling matters about which they are ignorant

- shameless; they encourage licentiousness and sexual misconduct
- greedy; for the sake of money, they will teach anything people want to hear
- boastful and full of folly
- slaves of corruption, even while they promise freedom (much like those today who advocate drug abuse and sexual depravity)
- aware of what the Scriptures say, yet deny its truth and power, choosing instead to follow their own delusions

Encouragement for the last days

In chapter 3, Peter encourages us not to be discouraged by this prevailing atmosphere of error. Remember that Jesus is returning, and He will set matters right. Even though the scoffers and false teachers may say that the universe is stable and unchanging, never affected or invaded by divine power, we know that the universe is actually temporary and it is passing away. God has intervened in the past and will intervene in the future. The flood of Genesis occurred in the past, but it points to a day in the future when the world will be destroyed again—not by water, but by fire. In verse 10, Peter writes:

> *The day of the Lord will come like a thief. The heavens will disappear with a roar; the elements will be destroyed by fire, and the earth and everything in it will be laid bare.*

It may well be that the vivid description Peter sets down in this verse suggests the awful power of nuclear devastation, or of an asteroid or comet collision with the earth. All that keeps life functioning on our world at all is the Word of God, the authority of God, and the will of God. All He needs to do is to alter some aspect of our physical universe and the whole mechanism of the universe collapses.

All that keeps life functioning on our world at all is the Word of God, the authority of God, and the will of God

Many of us look around at all the evil of the world, and we get impatient. We wonder why the Lord doesn't come and clean house right now. Why does He delay? We need to remember that a day with the Lord is as a thousand years, and a thousand years is as a day. Our concept of time is not the same as His. We also need to remember that God has a purpose in delaying, for which we ought to be grateful. Once God's judgment commences, it can't be stopped. He waits to give men and women a chance to think things through and reconsider their ways. He delays judgment in order to give us all a chance to repent.

Peter then confronts us with a searching question:

> *Since everything will be destroyed in this way, what kind of people ought you to be? (3:11).*

Peter's own answer to that question is clear:

> *You ought to live holy and godly lives as you look forward to the day of God and speed its coming. That day will bring about the destruction of the heavens by fire, and the elements will melt in the heat (3:11–12).*

Three means of hastening the Lord's coming

Notice that Peter says that as we live holy, godly lives, we not only wait expectantly for the day of God, we actually *speed its coming!* How do we hasten the coming of the Lord Jesus Christ? How do we help bring about the end of global evil and help God to realize the hope that humankind has dreamed of for centuries—a world at peace, a world of plenty, a world of blessing and joy? In three ways:

Our prayers. Remember what the Lord Jesus taught us to pray? "Our Father in heaven, hallowed be your name, *your kingdom come*" (Matt. 6:9–10, italics added). That is a prayer for hastening the day of God. Remember John's prayer at the end of the book of Revelation? "Come, Lord Jesus" (Rev. 22:20). We are to pray for the end of this world system and the coming of the Lord's kingdom on earth, because that is the only way this world's ills and suffering will ever be ended.

Our witnessing. The gospel of the kingdom must be preached to all the nations, and then the end will come, says the Lord Jesus, in Matthew 24:14. Whenever we share the good news of Jesus Christ with one other person, we bring the return of Jesus Christ a little bit closer.

Our obedience. The Jews say that if all of Israel would obey the law fully for one day, the Messiah would come. God is looking for men and women who will be obedient, who will truly be His. The only freedom we have is the freedom to serve either God or the devil. There is no middle ground, no third alternative. The "freedom" offered by sin and Satan ultimately leads to despair and enslavement. But the *genuine* freedom that comes with being a slave to Christ leads to *abundant* life and *eternal* life.

So, in view of the approaching return of Jesus Christ and the approaching end of this corrupt world system, Peter concludes, "make every effort to be found spotless, blameless and at peace with him" (2 Peter 3:14).

In a final postscript, verses 15 and 16, Peter says that Paul agrees that prayerful, obedient waiting for the Lord's return means salvation when the day of God appears—not eternal salvation, but being ready, not being caught unaware and unprepared, when the dire end-of-the-world events begin to take place. When the rest of the world trembles with fear and despair, we who have prayed and worked to hasten that day will stand, expectant and unafraid.

Peter adds another warning against false teaching, this time in regard to those who twist and distort Paul's teachings, just as they do the other Scriptures. Do not listen to them, Peter warns. Don't be fooled.

The final two verses include a final warning—and a final blessing and encouragement:

> *Dear friends, since you already know this, be on your guard so that you may not be carried away by the error of lawless men and fall from your secure position. But grow in the grace and knowledge of our Lord and Savior Jesus Christ. To him be glory both now and forever! Amen (3:17–18).*

We have all the facts we need for faith and for defending ourselves against falsehood. We have the unchangeable truth of Jesus Christ. Let's be on our guard so that we are not carried away or undermined by the false teachers who want to steal our faith. Though our faith is under attack, though truth is continually on the scaffold, we have the victory in hand. The Lord is coming soon, and we are praying, witnessing, and obeying Him in order to hasten that day. Amen! Come, Lord Jesus!

Authentic Christianity

Jesus had two disciples whom I particularly wish I could have known. One is Peter, the other is John. I love to read about these two. They are very different from each other in character and personality, yet both were so close to Jesus Christ. Simon Peter was erratic, impulsive, and brash. Whenever he entered the scene, it was with a crash and a thud. Yet, the Lord chose to make him a steady, stable, dependable "rock" (which is what his name, Peter, literally means). He became a rallying point for first-century Christians in those days of intense persecution.

John was another disciple who was dramatically transformed by his encounter with Jesus Christ. He was a young man when he began following Christ. In fact, many Bible scholars believe he was a teenager at the time, perhaps seventeen or eighteen years of age. The gospel record shows that he was a hotheaded young man, given to sharp and impulsive speech and a tendency toward blowing off steam—hence Jesus' nickname for him, "Son of Thunder." That was our Lord's gentle way of labeling John's problem. He just kept the thunder rolling all the time. So, our Lord called John and his brother James "Sons of Thunder."

Amazingly, however, "Thundering John" ultimately became the "apostle of love." He became known not for his thundering but for his gentleness and goodness. We have no record that he ever married; history indicates that he devoted himself to a life of loving and serving Jesus.

A Son of Thunder became an apostle of love

John, the apostle of love, authored these three letters—1, 2, and 3 John. First John was among the last of the New Testament books to be written, and it may have been written after the gospel of John. It was penned near the close of the first century, in the city of Ephesus, where John spent his later years. John wrote this epistle to Christians who are facing the dangers and trials of living in a godless world in which any selfish or sexually perverse practice is okay. It was written, in short, to people just like you and me.

Here is a structural overview of 1 John:

The Basis of Authentic Christianity (1 John 1:1–2:27)

1.	Introduction	1:1–4
2.	Walking in the light, loving one another	1:5–2:14
3.	Avoid the love of the world, the spirit of antichrist	2:15–2:27

The Behavior of Authentic Christianity (1 John 2:28–5:21)

4.	Practicing truth, righteousness, and love	2:28–5:3
5.	Victory over the world	5:4–5
6.	Assurance of salvation	5:6–13
7.	Confidence in prayer	5:14–17
8.	Victory over habitual sin	5:18–21

Three aspects of authentic Christianity

John's principle concern in this letter is authentic Christianity. He reminds us of the three aspects of our faith that make the Christian life vital and effective: truth, righteousness, and love. These are his focus in 1 John 2:18–4:21.

Truth, righteousness, and love

But first, John describes the relationship with Jesus Christ from which flows those three personal qualities—it's a relationship of oneness with Him, a synchronization of our lives with His. Apart from that relationship, we cannot live lives characterized by truth, righteousness, and love.

This world has enough good advice—but the power to do what we know we should do is in painfully short supply

The wisdom of Socrates, Aristotle, Plato, Confucius, and Buddha contain the same advice for living that you find in the New Testament. In other words, if all you need is good advice, you do not need the Bible. You can get plenty of good advice from these other philosophers and religious leaders—but one thing these leaders and philosophers do not give you is the power to live out their wonderful advice. This world has enough good advice—but the power to do what we know we should do is in painfully short supply.

We all know the Golden Rule of our Lord Jesus—Do to others as you would have them do to you—and though it is also expressed in other religions, Jesus goes a step further and empowers us to live by the

Golden Rule. How does He do that? By showing us the secret of unity with Him! Fellowship with the Lord Jesus gives us the power to live out the advice He gives us. As Paul wrote in Colossians 1:27, "Christ in you, the hope of glory." The indwelling presence of Jesus, the most intimate relationship in human experience, gives us the power to live out the precepts of our faith.

Throughout this letter, John emphasizes this fact: Jesus appeared in history. The first theme John talks about under the heading of truth is that Jesus is God and man. This message was diametrically opposed to a prevalent philosophy called *gnosticism*. The nearest thing to gnosticism today is Christian Science, which is almost pure gnosticism. Gnostics believe that matter is evil and spirit is good and that the good human spirit is imprisoned in an evil material body. They say that the purpose of life is to teach us how to rise above the evil of our bodies and release the good spirit from it, the material body, to achieve a form of nirvana or heaven or spiritual perfection.

First aspect: Truth

Jesus is God and man

John says, in effect, "Don't be deceived by gnostic heresy, because Jesus has come in truth. He is the God-man, eternal Spirit bonded to a human body, and anyone who denies this truth about Jesus Christ is a liar." First John was not written to refute those who were bent on destroying Christianity. No, the deception John opposed in this letter was much more subtle and crafty than any outright, fire-breathing opposition. The gnostics simply wanted to "improve" upon Christianity. So they played down the truth of Jesus' humanity; they made subtle twists and distortions in their teaching so that their image of Jesus fit their gnostic beliefs.

Against gnosticism

This process is still going on today. John says: Do not be deceived. Don't be tricked by distortions in the gospel story. You will end up following a lie further and further into error, until you finally end up spiritually destroyed.

Truth is important, but it takes more to be a Christian than simply mentally assenting to a certain doctrine or creed. To our truth we must add righteousness.

Second aspect: Righteousness

Truth is meaningless if it doesn't change our behavior. The message of John is this: If you really have Jesus Christ living in you, you can't go on living in sin, doing what is wrong, lying and stealing, and living in sexual immorality. You must change your way of life. But the gnostics said in effect, "Look, if spirit is good and matter is evil, then the only thing that counts is the spirit. What you do with your material body doesn't matter. If you want to indulge your lusts, go ahead. It won't affect your spiritual standing with God." John responds to this error in 1 John 3:9:

No one who is born of God will continue to sin, because God's seed remains in him; he cannot go on sinning, because he has been born of God.

You cannot allow sin and the Holy Spirit to inhabit the same body. If you profess to be a Christian while living an unholy life, you are (John states bluntly) a liar.

Third aspect: Love

Truth and righteousness are difficult to master—yet these first two aspects are relatively easy compared with the third, love. Many Christians can say, "I know the truth and I stand on it. My doctrine is sound. And what's more, I've given up the sins and attitudes of the world. I used to drink and carouse and cheat in my business dealings and read the worst kind of magazines and see the worst kind of movies, but I don't do those things anymore." We should never minimize the changes in the life of a person who becomes truly committed to Jesus Christ, upholding His truth and forsaking sinful behavior.

But if truth and righteousness are the extent of your testimony, you'll soon find that most of the people in this world are completely unimpressed by that. Most of the things you don't do anymore are things people in the world love to do and don't want to give up, so if your gospel consists of, "I have the truth, and I don't drink and smoke anymore," you'll find that most people shrug and turn away. They'll say, "That's nice for you, but I like drinking and smoking, so I don't want your faith." Truth and righteousness are only two of the three aspects of an authentic Christian life.

The world is not impressed by what you *don't* do; the world is impressed by what you *do* do

The world is not impressed by what you *don't* do. That's negative. The world is impressed by what you *do* do. That's positive. And the positive action that impresses the world and makes our gospel attractive to the people out there is our love. That is why John says that the third mark of a genuine Christian is *love*—a special kind of love, what the New Testament Greek language calls agape love—love that is based on our will, not our emotions. It is a love that is based on a decision to seek the good of others, not on the fact that other people are lovable. In fact, agape love is precisely aimed at those who are hard to love!

Anyone can love someone who is lovable. It takes a special effort to love those who hate you, mistreat you, ignore you, attack you. It takes a special effort to love those who are wretched, suffering, smelly, dirty, poor, needy, unsightly, and unpleasant to be near. It's not hard to love those beautiful people who invite you to a lavishly catered garden party. But it takes an effort to love the toothless derelict, smelling of cheap wine, holding his paper plate in line at the downtown mission. Yet that's the kind of love God calls us to, the kind of love 1 John teaches us. It's the same kind of love that Jesus demonstrated when He reached out to the lepers, the prostitutes, the tax collectors, the poor, and when He forgave those who pounded the nails into His hands and feet, as well as the crowds who jeered Him in His dying moments. That is why John writes:

> *We love because he first loved us. If anyone says, "I love God," yet hates his brother, he is a liar. For anyone who does not love his brother, whom he has seen, cannot love God, whom he has not seen. And he has given us this command: Whoever loves God must also love his brother (4:19–21).*

Fellowship and oneness with the Lord Jesus means that we will gradually experience an opening of our hearts, like the opening of a flower in the morning sunlight. As His love shines on us, we will become more open to others, allowing the fragrance of love to drift out and attract those around us. As the power of Jesus changes us, we will grow not only in truth and righteousness, but in love toward our Christian brothers and sisters and in our love toward those who are outside the faith.

The letter closes on a note of assurance: What God has told us is true and unshakable. What He has revealed about the world is absolutely certain. Three consecutive verses—1 John 5:18, 19, and 20—begin with the confident phrase, "We know." John writes:

> *We know that anyone born of God does not continue to sin; the one who was born of God keeps him safe, and the evil one cannot harm him. We know that we are children of God, and that the whole world is under the control of the evil one. We know also that the Son of God has come and has given us understanding, so that we may know him who is true. And we are in him who is true—even in his Son Jesus Christ. He is the true God and eternal life (5:18–20, emphasis added).*

We know, John says, that we are of God, that we possess the very nature and being of God, and that the whole world is in the power of the evil one. That is why the world cannot engage in agape love. The world talks about love and hungers for love, but it doesn't understand the very thing it seeks, and it lacks the power to practice it because the world does not know the One who is love personified. God is love. Since we are of God, John writes, He has given us the understanding to know Him and the power to experience eternal life.

What a declaration that is! We live in an age of moral relativism, where people claim we cannot know anything for sure, where uncertainty and confusion abound. But we know. We have been given an

Our assurance: "We know…"

understanding, an assurance. We are people who can stand firm and secure in a world that is falling apart.

Here is John's final word—and at first sight, it may seem irrelevant in our high-tech, sophisticated age:

Dear children, keep yourselves from idols (5:21).

Modern-day idolatry

We don't have wooden or stone gods in our homes today, do we? We don't have to worry about idols today, do we? The fact is, we are more imperiled by idolatry today than ever before! We so easily give our devotion to things that are lower than God. Idolatry is loving anything other than God. If you took an hour to go through the register of your checkbook and your credit-card statements, you could find out what some of your idols are. What do you spend your money on and what do you save your money for? What do you spend your time on? What do you think about when you wake up in the morning and when you go to bed at night? What is most important to you? Whatever it is, that is your god. If your god is not God Himself, you are practicing idolatry.

For some of us, our god may be Narcissus, the god of self-love, of self-centered ambition, of self-admiration, of obsession with success or self-beautification or self-exaltation, of having others admire us or desire us or envy us for our beautiful possessions. For some of us, our god may be Venus, the goddess of love and sex, or Bacchus, the god of revelry and pleasure, of eating and drinking, of substance abuse and mind-altering, mood-altering drugs—as if fun and pleasure were the only reasons for living. For some of us, our god may be Mars, the god of war and competition, of vanquishing the opposition, of winning at all costs, of cutting the throats of those who oppose us, whether in business or in the church.

Prayer of deliverance

Our prayer of deliverance from these forms of idolatry must be, "Lord, deliver me from these false gods that would rob me of my faith, of my love for humanity. Make me fall more truly in love with the Lord Jesus who alone is the only true God, who has come to give me an understanding of myself and the world around me, and has come to teach me truth, righteousness, and love." The danger of idolatry is no less real for us today, at the threshold of the twenty-first century, than it was for Christians in the first century, and we need to be vigilant against the taint of idolatry in our own lives.

You have found the true God, John says, so keep yourselves from these secondary idols, these substitute gods that demand your attention. Give yourself completely to the One who can fulfill all your heart's desires.

The Vital Balance

S econd John is the only letter in the New Testament that was
written to a woman. We gather from the letter itself that it was
written to a mother with several children, perhaps a widow, to answer
her questions regarding specific problems that had arisen. In those days
the people were dependent on the apostles and church leaders for truth
and for answers to problems. Of course, a question then arises: How do
we know if a certain leader who claims to speak for God actually speaks
the truth? How do we distinguish between *God's* prophets and *false*
prophets?

Evidently some who claimed to be prophets had come to this
woman's home, probably in the city of Ephesus, and they had raised certain doctrinal matters that disturbed her. Not knowing how to evaluate
their opinions, she wrote to John and asked for his counsel. The letter
we now know as 2 John is his response to her question. As we go through
this letter, we will see how it also answers many questions we have
today—especially the question of how to deal with people who teach
spiritual concepts that are not in line with God's truth.

Here is an outline of 2 John:

Truth and Love (2 John 1–6)

1.	John's greeting	1–3
2.	Walk in the truth of Christ	4
3.	Walk in the love of Christ	5–6

Second John
explains how we
distinguish between
God's prophets and
false prophets

CHAPTER 74: 2 JOHN

The Danger of False Teachers (2 John 7–13)

A balance of truth and love

The first six verses of the letter present the problem—and John's approach in answering it:

> *The elder,*
> *To the chosen lady and her children, whom I love in the truth—and not I only, but also all who know the truth—because of the truth, which lives in us and will be with us forever:*
> *Grace, mercy and peace from God the Father and from Jesus Christ, the Father's Son, will be with us in truth and love.*
> *It has given me great joy to find some of your children walking in the truth, just as the Father commanded us. And now, dear lady, I am not writing you a new command but one we have had from the beginning. I ask that we love one another. And this is love: that we walk in obedience to his commands. As you have heard from the beginning, his command is that you walk in love.*

Here John sets the stage for the answer to this woman's problem. He is highlighting two factors that must be taken into consideration when facing a problem of this kind: truth and love. Notice how he links these two factors in verse 3:

> *Grace, mercy and peace from God the Father and from Jesus Christ, the Father's Son, will be with us* in truth and love *(emphasis added).*

Truth and love: These two qualities ought to characterize our lives as Christians. These are the same qualities that Paul commends to us in Ephesians 4:15—"speaking the truth in love." The great challenge we face in the Christian life is the challenge of learning to keep truth and love in balance.

Saltshakers and sugar bowls

Someone once said that a well-balanced Christian life contains salt and sugar. Salt is truth. Sugar is love. Some Christians want only the salt, and so these salty Christians go around scattering their salt wherever they go. They are all truth, no love. They are full of doctrines, dogmas, opinions, tenets, and laws. They are cold and judgmental, having no concern for the feelings, needs, or hurts of others. They defend the truth at the expense of love. In fact, they have no problem whatever speaking the truth in *cruelty!* The truth is all that matters. These people are nothing but religious saltshakers.

Others are sugar bowls. They are all love, no truth. They would never confront anyone caught in sin because that would involve telling a hard truth to that person—even if it were for that person's own good and for the good of the church. We also know of people who want to receive only sugar from their brothers and sisters; they run from the salt of truth. They say, "Give me grace, love, acceptance—but don't hold me accountable, don't confront me when I stray. If I sin, say, 'That's okay. Don't feel bad. You're okay.' Don't tell me I have to change—that's too judgmental! Don't be honest with me. Don't tell me the truth. Just be nice to me. You can keep your salt. All I want is your sugar."

Our goal as Christians should be to keep truth and love—salt and sugar—in balance. The Lord Jesus provides our perfect example. He walked in truth and love. He dealt tenderly with sinners and outcasts and truthfully with arrogant Pharisees. When He met the Samaritan woman at the well in John 4, Jesus truthfully told her all the sins she had committed—yet He dealt lovingly with her and offered living water for her thirsty soul. In John 8, after He lovingly saved the adulteress from being stoned and assured her that He did not condemn her, Jesus truthfully confronted her with her need to change. "Go," He said, "and sin no more." Jesus spoke the truth in love. He kept truth and love in perfect balance. And so should we.

In the next section, John answers to the woman's question regarding the reliability of those who claim to be spiritual teachers and leaders:

> Many deceivers, who do not acknowledge Jesus Christ as coming in the flesh, have gone out into the world. Any such person is the deceiver and the antichrist. Watch out that you do not lose what you have worked for, but that you may be rewarded fully. Anyone who runs ahead and does not continue in the teaching of Christ does not have God; whoever continues in the teaching has both the Father and the Son (vv.. 7–9).

Deceivers and antichrists

Two statements in this passage describe the two fundamental forms of false teaching. All Christian error and heresies arise from one of these two forms of falsehood:

Deception regarding the person of the Lord Jesus. He is the one who came from God into the world and became human; He is the only Messiah. The Incarnation is an essential doctrine of Christian faith. If you trace someone's origin from birth and you discover that this person entered the stream of humanity through the normal reproductive process yet claims to be the Savior sent from God, you can disregard this

Two forms of falsehood

1. Deception regarding the person of the Lord Jesus

person's claims. Many such false christs are in the world today, and John clearly warns us not to believe them.

Also, many people distort the truth about Jesus. One of the most common distortions is the claim that Jesus was a good person, a good moral teacher, but not truly God. This sounds nice, because it's an affirmation that Jesus had many good things to say. But such a claim ignores the central message of Jesus, which was the message of Himself: He claimed to be both God and human. Anyone who denies either His divinity or His humanity makes Him a liar. Anyone who denies the incarnation of the Son of God is a deceiver and does not speak for God. Such a false teacher may not be intentionally deceptive; he or she may be a deceived deceiver—but John minces no words: That person is an "antichrist," opposed to the truth about Jesus.

1. Deception regarding the teaching of the Lord Jesus

Deception regarding the teaching of the Lord Jesus. John says that anyone who does not continue in the doctrine or teaching of Christ does not know God (v. 9). This revealing statement addresses people who say that the Bible is not an adequate revelation of God and that we need some additional revelation from some additional teacher, guru, or book. These people may be very persuasive and sincere, but if they do not agree with the teaching of Jesus Christ, they do not know God.

The danger of falsehood

Now notice the danger in these two forms of falsehood: "Watch out that you do not lose what you have worked for, but that you may be rewarded fully" (v. 8). What do you lose, as a Christian, if your faith becomes polluted by cults, heresies, and the watered-down liberal theology that is so prevalent today? Will you lose your salvation? Not if you are truly born again, of course. Salvation rests upon the work of Christ. You are not going to lose your place in heaven nor your redemption nor your part in the body of Christ. But you will lose a great deal, as John makes clear. You will lose the value of your life spent here. You will have wasted the time God gave you to serve Him effectively and obediently. Your religious activity will be revealed as nothing more than wood, hay, and stubble to be consumed in the fire of God's searching judgment. You will lose your reward.

The response to false teachers

How, then, should we respond to those who approach us with false doctrines and heresies regarding the Lord and His teaching? John replies:

> *If anyone comes to you and does not bring this teaching, do not take him into your house or welcome him. Anyone who welcomes him shares in his wicked work (vv. 10–11).*

As we read this, remember what John has said about truth and love. Christians who are concerned about the doctrinal matters of Scripture can easily forsake the courtesy and charity that should characterize every believer. We interpret a passage like this to mean that we are to slam the door in the face of anyone who comes to the door with a cultish tract or that we order people out of the house if they bring up some heretical teaching. If that were the case, it would be impossible even to invite neighbors, coworkers, foreign students, and the like into our homes.

John is not suggesting that our hospitality be subject to some doctrinal litmus test. We would be very offensive people if that were the case, and we would certainly have little impact in our witnessing. After all, who would we witness to if we could talk only with those who are doctrinally pure?

What, then, does John mean? He is telling us that truth should be spoken in love, and love should be bounded by truth. In other words, we are not to receive deceivers in such a way that we appear to be authenticating or accepting their teaching. In John's day, itinerant preachers and teachers stayed in private homes. The homes that received these preachers and teachers, then, served to support and subsidize their messages—thus, whoever you opened your home to was someone whose doctrine you endorsed. John is saying that we should never allow ourselves to be placed in a position where we appear to entertain, support, endorse, or subsidize the teaching of antichrist.

John underscores the importance of his warning against receiving false teachers in verse 12, where he writes:

> I have much to write to you, but I do not want to use paper and ink. Instead, I hope to visit you and talk with you face to face, so that our joy may be complete.

In those days, mail was slow and uncertain, and I suppose John, like most of us, found it difficult to sit down and write letters. So he said, in effect, "I have a lot to tell you later, when I see you in person, but this matter of false teachers is so important it couldn't wait. I just had to write now to warn you about these deceivers and antichrists." Then he concludes with greetings from the Christian family he is evidently staying with, underscoring the need in Christian life for both truth and love.

Truth and love together—that is the vital balance we must seek in the Christian life. It is not only Christian balance, it is Christian sanity. A person who practices truth without love or love without truth does not have a Christian worldview. To be spiritually unbalanced is to be, in a very real sense, spiritually insane. John's goal in this brief but powerful letter is to restore us to a sane balance.

We are not to receive deceivers in such a way that we appear to be authenticating or accepting their teaching

Believers and Bosses

T hird John gives us an intimate glimpse into the life of the early church. It is a delightful accompaniment to the second letter, which was written to a Christian woman about how to deal with false teachers. This letter was written to a Christian man about how to care for the true teachers who traveled widely to minister God's Word—and how to deal with a troubling personality type that is as common in the church today as in the first century A.D. Thus, we see both a contrast and a similarity between 2 John and 3 John.

Third John gives us insight regarding the problem of personalities in the church, as illustrated by three people: Gaius (to whom this letter is written, a Christian of grace and generosity), Diotrephes (a problem personality), and Demetrius (a trustworthy and truthful Christian). These three people represent three kinds of Christians found in the church in any age.

Here is an outline of 3 John:

Third John profiles three personalities in the church

Gaius Is Commended (3 John 1–8)
1. John's greeting   1
2. The grace (godliness) of Gaius   2–4
3. The generosity of Gaius   5–8

Diotrephes Is Condemned (3 John 9–11)

Gaius, a Christian of grace and generosity

He was strong of soul

He lived what he professed

He was generous

Demetrius Is Praised (3 John 12–14)

4.	Demetrius is trustworthy and truthful	12
5.	Conclusion and benediction	13–14

First, let's get to know this good man named Gaius. He may be one of three Gaiuses mentioned elsewhere in the New Testament, although Gaius was a common name in New Testament times. John evidently knew him and addresses him in a warm and friendly way. This letter portrays Gaius as a gracious and generous individual. Note three things John says about him. First, Gaius was strong of soul. John writes:

> *Dear friend, I pray that you may enjoy good health and that all may go well with you, even as your soul is getting along well (v. 2).*

That is a wonderful thing to say about someone, isn't it? "I wish you may be as strong in body as you are in your soul." It would be interesting to apply this test to people today. If your physical appearance reflected your spiritual, mental, and emotional state, what would you look like? Would you be a robust individual—strong and vital? Or would you be a doddering weakling, barely able to lift your head? Well, Gaius was the spiritually vigorous sort of person about whom John could say, "I hope your physical life is as strong as your spiritual life."

Second, Gaius was a consistent person, a man of integrity. His life matched his profession of the truth. John observes:

> *It gave me great joy to have some brothers come and tell about your faithfulness to the truth and how you continue to walk in the truth (v. 3).*

Gaius demonstrated the truth of Jesus Christ through the way he lived. He did not preach cream and live skim milk. He walked in the truth.

Third, Gaius was generous in his giving. John writes:

> *Dear friend, you are faithful in what you are doing for the brothers, even though they are strangers to you. They have told the church about your love. You will do well to send them on their way in a manner worthy of God (vv. 5–6).*

One of the signs that a person has been genuinely touched in the heart by God is that the pocketbook loosens up. He or she becomes a cheerful giver. John says that Gaius was "faithful" in his giving. This means he was a regular and systematic giver. He gave not just when his emotions were moved, but he made a conscious habit of giving. So, Gaius is commended as an open-hearted believer, full of grace and generosity.

Next we come to the problem personality in Gaius's church, a man named Diotrephes. John writes:

> *I wrote to the church, but Diotrephes, who loves to be first, will have nothing to do with us. So if I come, I will call attention to what he is doing, gossiping maliciously about us. Not satisfied with that, he refuses to welcome the brothers. He also stops those who want to do so and puts them out of the church.*
>
> *Dear friend, do not imitate what is evil but what is good. Anyone who does what is good is from God. Anyone who does what is evil has not seen God (vv. 9–11).*

This is the first example in the New Testament church of a church boss—someone who feels it is his or her job to run everything and everybody in the church. Today, a church boss could be an elder, a deacon, a pastor, or a layperson who has no official role in the church. Often, it is a wealthy, influential person, respected or even feared in the community and in the church.

You may be familiar with such movies as the David Niven-Loretta Young classic, *The Bishop's Wife*, in which the church boss is a wealthy old widow who controls the church—and the pastor—with her money and her cantankerous temperament. Or you may recall the Frederic March film, *One Foot in Heaven*, in which the church bosses are a clique of powerful businessmen. Church bosses often represent the real but hidden power base of a church; while the pastor and church board may be the official leaders of the church, they may all kowtow to the person or people who really call the shots. That, of course, is not how the church of Jesus Christ is supposed to function.

The early church of Gaius apparently had some kind of a membership roll. If Boss Diotrephes did not like somebody, he would scratch that person's name off the list and put him or her out of the church. This, says John, is dead wrong. Diotrephes, he explains, was guilty of four particular wrong attitudes and actions.

First and worst, Diotrephes was arrogant, selfish, and domineering. He insisted on being first in the church, an attitude which is a dead giveaway that he was acting in the flesh. This is always the demand of the flesh: "Me first." In doing that, he robbed Jesus Christ of His prerogative in the church. Jesus had the right to preeminence—but it was Diotrephes who claimed the honor and glory. Unfortunately, we see plenty of people in churches today who have the spirit of Diotrephes.

One wonders if these modern versions of Diotrephes ever read 3 John, and if they recognize themselves in John's description. If they do, how do they live with themselves? Dr. H. E. Robertson, an outstanding leader among the Southern Baptists and a great Greek scholar, once wrote an editorial about Diotrephes in a denominational publication. The editor of the magazine reported that twenty-five individuals from various churches wrote to cancel their subscriptions, feeling they had been personally attacked! If only such people would cancel their bossy ways instead!

Second, the apostle says Diotrephes slandered John and rejected his authority as an apostle. "Diotrephes . . . will have nothing to do with us," says John, adding that he is continually "gossiping maliciously about us."

The apostles had a unique role in the history of the church. They were to lay the foundations of the church and were given authority to settle all questions within the church. This apostolic word—the responsibility to speak God's message to God's church—was invested in the New Testament, which is why the New Testament is so authoritative to Christians. The apostles are no longer with us, but their Spirit-inspired words have been handed down to us in God's Word. When Diotrephes slandered John and rejected his apostolic authority, he was slandering the Holy Spirit's message as spoken through John.

Third, Diotrephes refused to welcome the brethren who came in the name of the Lord speaking the truth of the Lord. Diotrephes would have nothing to do with them. He turned them aside and refused to allow them to speak in the church.

Fourth, Diotrephes put out of the church people who would have taken these men in. He indulged in what we would call today "secondary separation." He objected not only to the missionaries who came to the church, but he objected to those who would have received them. This has been one of the curses of the church ever since. Because of this tendency to refuse fellowship to someone who likes someone you do not like, the church is still a church divided and lacking in the power that oneness in Christ brings.

How, then, should we deal with church bosses? John's twofold counsel is as timely now as it was in John's day. First, church bosses should be confronted and exposed for their own good and the good of the church. "If I come," says John, "I will call attention to what he is doing, gossiping maliciously about us." The church must exercise its legitimate authority to deal with sin and pride in its ranks. If pastors or elders behave arrogantly, they must be confronted by the other elders. If lay members behave as bosses, the church leadership must attempt to show them their error and restore them, gently and lovingly but firmly and uncompromisingly—even if it means risking the wrath of very wealthy donors! This is a matter of faith and principle, and churches must not capitulate on the basis of pragmatism, power, or dollars.

The process for confronting sin in the church is found in such passages as Proverbs 27:5–6, Matthew 18:15–20, 1 Corinthians 5 and 2 Corinthians 2:1–11 (these Corinthian passages are linked and should be studied together), and Galatians 6:1–3. Although these passages don't deal specifically with the problem of church bosses, the principles are valid regardless of the nature of the sin that must be confronted.

Most important of all is John's principle of dealing with the matter openly: "I will call attention to what he is doing." Church bosses tend to operate in the shadows; when their deeds are brought into the light, they lose their power to intimidate and control.

The second word of counsel John gives Gaius is to avoid becoming like Diotrephes. He does not advise Gaius to organize a split away from the church or to attempt to wrest power from Diotrephes through subtle strategies or hidden agenda. He doesn't suggest a whisper campaign against Diotrephes. Instead, he counsels Gaius to avoid becoming contaminated by the attitude and spirit of that: "Do not imitate what is evil but what is good." If you become like Diotrephes, then he has defeated you. He has turned you away from becoming like Christ and caused you to become like him. Remember, Christ was not a boss; He was a servant.

Avoid becoming like Diotrephes

The third personality we discover in 3 John is a man named Demetrius, of whom John writes:

Demetrius, a Christian of trust and truth

> Demetrius is well spoken of by everyone—and even by the truth itself. We also speak well of him, and you know that our testimony is true (v. 12).

John writes as an apostle with the gift of discernment. He says, in effect, "I want to underscore what everybody thinks about Demetrius. Here's someone you can trust. He is a person of the truth." Demetrius was apparently the mail carrier, the bearer of this letter to Gaius, and likely was one of those missionaries who traveled from place to place. John characterized such missionaries (whom he calls "the brothers"):

> Dear friend, you are faithful in what you are doing for the brothers, even though they are strangers to you. They have told the church about your love. You will do well to send them on their way in a manner worthy of God. It was for the sake of the Name that they went out, receiving no help from the pagans. We ought therefore to show hospitality to such men so that we may work together for the truth (vv. 5–8).

Missionaries like
Demetrius have left
the comforts of
home, and they
have embraced a
high calling

These words describe the first group of traveling missionaries, and Demetrius was evidently one of this group. As they went from place to place, they would enjoy the hospitality of various churches. They labored as church-supported evangelists in each area, reaching out into places where the church had not yet gone.

John says three things of these missionaries: First, they have gone out; they have left behind the comforts of home. Second, they have given up income and security to obey a higher calling. Not everyone is called to missionary work. Some are called to this special task on behalf of the Lord Jesus. Others, such as Gaius, are to stay and support those who are sent out.

And third, why were people like Demetrius sent out into the world? John replies, verse 7, "It was for the sake of the Name that they went out." Literally, for the sake of the name of Jesus. The name of Jesus is very special to these Christians.

In Old Testament times, the Jews treated the name of God in a unique way. That name, Jehovah, appears throughout the Old Testament and is referred to as the Ineffable Tetragrammaton. *Ineffable* means indescribable or unutterable. *Tetragrammaton* means four letters (YHWH). Whenever the Jews encountered these four Hebrew letters for God, they did not dare speak them, so holy was the name. Even the scribe who wrote the Tetragrammaton would change pens and continue writing with a different pen. Scribes also changed their garments in reverence for God's name before they would write it. When they wrote the words of Deuteronomy 6:4—"Hear, O Israel: The LORD our God, the LORD is one"—the Tetragrammaton occurs twice, so a scribe would have to change clothes twice and change pens four times to write that one line!

In the New Testament, a high measure of respect and devotion is reserved for the name of Jesus. The apostle Paul says,

> *God exalted him to the highest place and gave him the name that is above every name, that at the name of Jesus every knee should bow, in heaven and on earth and under the earth, and every tongue confess that Jesus Christ is Lord, to the glory of God the Father (Phil. 2:9–11).*

They are motivated
by love for the
name of Jesus

Love for the precious name of Jesus has been the motive for sacrificial missionary efforts ever since the first century. Men and women have suffered and died for the beautiful name that people all over the world need to hear. Love for Jesus' name motivates you and me to evangelize our neighborhoods and workplaces. Even people who are not called to go out into the world can still do a great deal to glorify and spread that name to a needy world. We can be witnesses for Jesus wherever we are, and we can be partners with the missionaries who are telling His story around the world. John says, in verse 8:

> *We ought therefore to show hospitality to such men so that we may work together for the truth.*

Now John closes his letter with a very warm and personal conclusion, verses 13 and 14:

> *I have much to write you, but I do not want to do so with pen and ink. I hope to see you soon, and we will talk face to face.*
> *Peace to you. The friends here send their greetings. Greet the friends there by name.*

So ends a very powerful, very intimate little letter. It seems as though it came not only from John, but from the Lord Himself. Whenever I read these words, I feel as if I am hearing the Lord Jesus Christ say to me and to His entire church, "There is much that I'd like to say to you, but I'd rather not write it in a letter. Instead, I'm coming soon. We'll talk face-to-face then. In the meantime, I leave my peace with you. Love, your friend, Jesus."

Contending for the Faith

A clash of cymbals! A boom of tympani! A cannon blast and a cascade of fireworks! That is what the letter of Jude is like. The words of this apostle thunder from the page. Who is Jude, you ask? In the opening verse, he refers to himself simply as:

Jude, a servant of Jesus Christ and a brother of James.

That clearly identifies him to the first-century reader, for Jude's brother James was very well known as a leader in the early church in Jerusalem. This is the same James who wrote the epistle of James. Note that Jude, the brother of James, was also a physical half brother of the Lord Jesus! He grew up in the town of Nazareth, as did Jesus. Notice, however, that he says nothing about being physically related to the Lord. You would think that would be a credential worth putting up in neon lights—yet Jude calls himself a brother of James and a servant of Jesus Christ. Why?

I believe we can safely surmise that Jude had learned to see Jesus no longer as "my brother Jesus," but as He truly was: God poured into human flesh, the Son of God, the Savior of the world. Jude and James had a unique perspective on Jesus: They worshiped and were disciples of the One with whom they had grown up.

> Jude expresses a unique perspective

As in so many other passages of the Bible, we find here yet another clear testimony of the deity of the Lord Jesus. If anyone would be in a position to refute His claim to be God, it would be Jesus' brothers. Although Jude, like James, did not come to believe in Jesus until after the Resurrection, this statement at the beginning of Jude's letter is yet another seal that confirms the deity of Jesus of Nazareth.

Here is a structural outline of Jude's epistle:

Introductory Remarks (Jude 1–4)

The Danger of False Teachers (Jude 5–16)

1.	God's past judgment of false teachers	5–7
2.	How to detect a false teacher	8–13
3.	God's future judgment of false teachers	14–16
4.	How to deal with false teachers	17–23

Benediction (Jude 24–25)

In his introductory remarks, the apostle Jude tells us how he came to write this letter:

> *Dear friends, although I was very eager to write to you about the salvation we share, I felt I had to write and urge you to contend for the faith that was once for all entrusted to the saints (v. 3).*

He had started out to write a letter containing certain insights and understandings of the faith, and perhaps others had urged him to write his memoirs as a brother of the Lord. Then he learned about an outbreak of some false and very distasteful teaching. So Jude felt constrained by the Holy Spirit to set aside his planned treatise and to write a short, toughly worded tract instead. We don't know if the other treatise was ever written; however, this tract has become a powerfully important part of the New Testament. Here, Jude urges his readers to "contend for the faith that was once for all entrusted to the saints."

That brief statement is a powerful directive for Christians. Jude is telling us: (1) Our faith was not fabricated by people. (2) It is a single body of consistent facts. (3) It has been entrusted to the apostles whose authority is indisputable because they are inspired by God. (4) This faith was delivered once and for all; it is complete as is.

This little letter is a dynamic, authoritative response to the claims of the cults and false doctrines of today. I believe that Jude's epistle answers every false doctrine that has ever been taught. For example, Mormonism teaches that new books, new revelations, were added since the close of the New Testament, but Jude says clearly that we are to contend for this faith that has already been delivered to us, once and for all.

Why do we need to contend for the faith? Because false teachers have crept into the church. Jude writes:

Certain men whose condemnation was written about long ago have secretly slipped in among you. They are godless men, who change the grace of our God into a license for immorality and deny Jesus Christ our only Sovereign and Lord (v. 4).

Jude is especially disturbed that these false teachers were attacking the church from within. These teachers were people who professed to be Christians. They had arisen within the church and were doing two things: (1) changing the grace of God into license to live an immoral, sexually degraded life; (2) saying that the grace of God is so broad that He will forgive anything you do—the more you sin, the more grace abounds, so go to it! This same destructive idea also pervades our society. Many people today, even within the church, claim that if you "love" someone, anything you do with that person is justified. This is not some "new morality"—it's an old heresy! And Jude rightly condemns it.

How does Jude view the problem of false teachers? First, he states that God's judgment is certain. God will not ignore those who twist His truth. Jude provides biblical evidence to support his view: (1) God brought the people out of captivity in Egypt—over a million people, in fact. Some were believers, some were not, but God brought them all through the Red Sea and the wilderness, showing them miracle after miracle of divine protection and provision. Those who murmured and complained against God were judged; they perished in the wilderness. Those who lived by faith in God entered the Promised Land. (2) The angels lived in God's presence, ministering before Him; yet some followed Satan in his rebellion. They, too, were judged. Even angels are not beyond God's judgment when they submit to pride and lust. (3) The cities of Sodom and Gomorrah, at the southern end of the Dead Sea, had fallen into vile, open homosexual practices. When God's angels visited Lot, the men of the city surrounded Lot's house and ordered Lot to send his guests out to them so that they might indulge their lusts. God judged that city for its sin.

Jude reminds us that God does not take sin and rebellion lightly. He judges it. Judgment may come suddenly, as in the case of Sodom and Gomorrah—or it may be delayed, as in the case of the angels. It may even occur in the natural course of events, as in the case of those who came out of Egypt. But, whether swift or slow, God's judgment is always sure.

God's judgment against false teachers is certain

The example of the Old Testament

The example of the angels

The example of Sodom and Gomorrah

False teachers sin against God in three ways, as Jude says in verse 8:

> *In the very same way, these dreamers pollute their own bodies, reject authority and slander celestial beings.*

**The threefold
sin of false
teachers**

In verses 8 to 13, Jude expands upon these three forms of sin, taking them in reverse order. He explains how the false teachers (1) slander the "celestial beings" or angels, (2) reject authority, and (3) pollute their own bodies.

1. They slander
celestial beings

First, they slander celestial beings. Jude refers to an incident unrecorded in our Bible. It comes from a book called the Assumption of Moses, which was familiar to readers of the first century. Many Christians have been troubled by this reference, because they think Jude refers to a book that has been lost from the Bible. But the book has not been lost—it still exists. It simply is not part of the accepted canon of Scripture. You can find the Assumption of Moses in most public libraries and in virtually all seminary libraries. That book, like many other non-canonical books of that time, contains a mixture of truth and error. If a New Testament writer refers back to one of these so-called lost books, a book that is not inspired Scripture, then he does so under the inspiration of the Holy Spirit, and we can be assured that the incident cited from that "lost book" is true and reliable, even if that lost book, taken as a whole, is not reliable and inspired.

Jude's use of
apocryphal
literature

Jude 14–15 includes a quotation from another lost book, the Book of Enoch, which can also be found in seminary libraries. The quotation Jude uses is valid and reliable. The entire lost book from which it was taken is not reliable; it is not Scripture.

Here is the story that Jude cites from the Assumption of Moses: When Moses died, the archangel Michael, highest of angels, disputed with the devil over the body of Moses. The devil's claim on the body of Moses was twofold: (1) Moses was a murderer, he'd killed an Egyptian; and (2) the body of Moses was part of the material realm, over which the devil was lord. Michael disputed the devil's demand, claiming the body for the Lord; Scripture says our bodies are important to God, and He has a plan for them as well as for our spirits.

Jude's point is this: Even so great a being as the archangel Michael would not address Satan directly but simply said, "The Lord rebuke you!" Jude's argument is that if the great archangels respect the dignity of a fallen angel, then how dare human beings speak contemptuously of the principalities and the powers in high places? Worldly people behave presumptuously when they sneer at the existence of angels or demons in Scripture.

Second, the false teachers reject authority:

Woe to them! They have taken the way of Cain; they have rushed for profit into Balaam's error; they have been destroyed in Korah's rebellion (Jude 11).

Here, Jude traces the way sin—especially the sin of rebellion—develops in a human life. He cites three biblical individuals as personifications of human rebellion: Cain, Balaam, and Korah. He speaks of "the way of Cain," which was essentially selfishness. Cain was the man who thought only of himself, who had no love for his brother, but put him to death. Selfishness is the first step to rebellion.

The second step is the "error of Balaam." The Old Testament contains two stories about Balaam. In one story (Num. 22:21–35), a pagan king hired him to curse the children of Israel. As he rode along on a donkey to do this, the donkey balked because it saw the angel of God blocking the way. Balaam could not see the angel, and finally the donkey had to speak with a human voice in order to rebuke the sin of this prophet. In the second story (Num. 31:15), Balaam again takes money, this time for sending pagan women into Israel's camp to seduce the army and introduce idol worship and sexual rites. Balaam would do anything to gain money, even curse Israel and lead Israel into sin and judgment. His sin is greed and leading others astray. That is the error of Balaam. Teaching someone else to sin results in multiplied judgment on oneself.

> *Jesus said to his disciples: "Things that cause people to sin are bound to come, but woe to that person through whom they come. It would be better for him to be thrown into the sea with a millstone tied around his neck than for him to cause one of these little ones to sin" (Luke 17:1–2).*

From the selfishness of Cain to the sin of Balaam—greed and leading others into sin—false teachers descend to the sin of Korah: defiant rebellion. Korah and his followers opposed Moses and Aaron in the wilderness. In Numbers 16:1–3 we read:

> *Korah . . . and certain Reubenites . . . became insolent and rose up against Moses. With them were 250 Israelite men, well-known community leaders who had been appointed members of the council. They came as a group to oppose Moses and Aaron and said to them, "You have gone too far! The whole community is holy, every one of them, and the LORD is with them. Why then do you set yourselves above the LORD's assembly?"*

Korah blatantly challenged the God-given authority of Moses and Aaron. In response, God told Moses and the rest of the people to separate themselves from Korah and his band. When Moses and the people

---

2. They reject authority

The way of Cain

The error of Balaam

The rebellion of Korah

had moved a safe distance away, the ground opened beneath Korah and the other rebels, and they went down alive into the pit. This was God's dramatic way of warning against the grievous, damnable sin of defiance of God-given authority.

Third, the false teachers defile the flesh.

As you read along in this letter, you hear Jude getting more and more worked up, like a backwoods preacher on revival night. At this point, the apostle really begins to thunder! He growls that these false teachers are blemishes on the Christians' agape-love feasts that lead the people into riotous carousing. The agape-love feasts were actually potluck suppers where the early Christians would gather and bring food with them to the Sunday worship service. After the service, they would all partake together; they called this a love feast. What a blessed name! I love potluck suppers, but I would much rather we returned to the original Christian name for them: love feasts!

These feasts were wonderful times of fellowship, but they began to deteriorate as people divided into cliques. Some kept the bucket of finger-lickin' chicken for themselves, others kept the angel food cake, and soon there was division. Instead of love, these feasts began to celebrate selfishness. The false teachers were the most selfish of all—taking and partaking, giving nothing, looking only after themselves.

As Jude goes on, he adds imagery upon imagery, much as James does in his epistle and as Jesus does in His parables. In verses 12 and 13, Jude describes these useless teachers as waterless clouds (promising rain, delivering nothing), fruitless trees (promising fruit, producing nothing), twice dead (dead not only in Adam, but dead in Christ as well, since they have rejected Him), wild waves of the sea, casting up the foam of their own shame, and wandering stars in the eternal darkness.

In verses 14 and 15, Jude quotes Enoch, from the lost Book of Enoch that I mentioned earlier, predicting the judgment that is coming upon the false teachers. In verse 16, Jude describes them as grumblers, malcontents, following their own passions, loud-mouthed boasters flattering people to gain advantage. These words sting us, because we see aspects of ourselves in this description, don't we?

Finally, after thundering, shouting, and pounding the pulpit, Jude comes to a pause. As the echoes of his last shout fade in the air, he drops his voice, leans close to us, and says softly,

Dear friends, remember what the apostles of our Lord Jesus Christ foretold. They said to you, "In the last times there will be scoffers who will follow their own ungodly desires." These are the men who divide you, who follow mere natural instincts and do not have the Spirit.

But you, dear friends, build yourselves up in your most holy faith and pray in the Holy Spirit. Keep yourselves in God's love as you wait for the mercy of our Lord Jesus Christ to bring you to eternal life (vv. 17–21).

In other words, "The apostles predicted these deceivers would rise up among you and try to divide you. This comes as no surprise. So, my friends, what are you going to do about it?"

Jude goes on to commend four responses to us. The first way we respond to false teachers is: Build yourselves up in the most holy faith—*know the truth.* We have to learn what the truth is, and that means we must study the Bible. Notice, Jude doesn't call for a counterinsurgency against the false teachers. He doesn't call for an inquisition or a lynching of these deceivers. His solution is not a negative—it's a positive. He says, "Fight lies with the truth! Know the truth, and the lies will never harm you."

The second way we must respond to false teachers is: *Pray in the Spirit.* To pray in the Holy Spirit means to pray according to His teaching and in His power, depending upon God. Study and learn what prayer is, follow the teaching of Scripture about it. Obey the Holy Spirit in your prayer life.

The third way we respond to false teachers is: *Keep ourselves in the love of God.* Jude is saying to us, "God's love is just like the sunshine, constantly shining on you. But you can put up barriers to shade yourself from His love. Don't do that! Keep yourself in the bright sunshine of His love! Keep walking in the experience of His goodness!" We must constantly purge sin from our lives through confession, allowing His love and forgiveness to continually flow through our hearts, filling our lives. When we choose to hide in the shadows, His love is out there—but we remain dark and cold by our own choosing. He loves us whether we are in fellowship with Him or not, but when we walk in communion with Him, we experience and feel the warmth of His love.

The fourth and final way to respond to false teachers is: *Wait for the mercy of our Lord Jesus Christ to eternal life.* This refers to our expectation of the second coming of Christ. We must keep our hope bright and alert, looking for Jesus to intervene in history, bringing to an end the age of sin and suffering. Our prayer of expectation is, "Your kingdom come, Your will be done in earth as it is in heaven." Come, Lord Jesus.

Jude concludes his letter with some practical instruction in how to meet the spiritual needs of those around us:

**Conclusion:
Show mercy
to those
around you**

Mercy mixed
with fear

*Be merciful to those who doubt; snatch others from the fire and save
them; to others show mercy, mixed with fear—hating even the clothing
stained by corrupted flesh (vv. 22–23).*

What does Jude mean, "Be merciful to those who doubt"? He wants
us to be understanding, not judgmental, toward those who struggle in
their faith. A person who has questions or doubts about the Christian
faith should not be treated as an unbeliever or an enemy of the faith, nor
as a person who is sinning. So don't condemn such people. Instead,
answer their questions, reason with them, love them.

He then addresses the problem of Christians who have become a
danger to themselves because of sinful attitudes and behavior. These we
must snatch from the fire—if possible. We must love them enough to try
to pull them back from the brink of disaster—if possible. But note that
Jude says our mercy should be "mixed with fear—hating even the clothing stained by corrupted flesh."

We must always remember that it is easier for a falling person to pull
us down than for us to pull that person up. Risk is involved when we
reach out to someone who is tumbling into the fire, and it is not always
possible to save someone who is determined to continue the slide into
sin and judgment. We cannot save a person who chooses not to be saved.
If you feel that person pulling you into the fire, you must let go and save
yourself. You are not responsible for another person's bad choices. Save
the falling brother or sister if possible—but if it is not possible, at least
save yourself.

Jude closes with these words:

*To him who is able to keep you from falling and to present you
before his glorious presence without fault and with great joy—to the only
God our Savior be glory, majesty, power and authority, through Jesus
Christ our Lord, before all ages, now and forevermore! Amen (vv.
24–25).*

A glowing—and
sobering—
benediction

This is one of the most glowing benedictions in the New
Testament. It is also a sobering benediction. Jude states that God is able
to keep us from falling—but this very statement suggests the possibility that we could fall if we choose to. He is able to keep us from falling—
but He does not guarantee that we will not fall. The choice of whether
to fall or stand is ours. If we will only obey God, He will keep us from
falling.

Jude also states that God is able to present us without fault and with
great joy. God has so completely dealt with sin that He is able to wipe
our sins completely away and to present us faultless before His glory.

Finally, Jude exalts the only God, our Savior, the Lord Jesus Christ, and offers to Him glory, majesty, power, and authority from before all time and now and forever. All majesty and dominion belong to God from before Creation to beyond the end of the world. The entire universe, all of time and space, gathers about Him and worships Him. That is the God we serve and trust. That is the faith for which we contend.

PART NINE

SIGNS OF THE TIMES

The End—and a New Beginning

W hat is it that makes us want to read the last chapter of a book first? For some reason, many people begin reading the Bible with the book of Revelation—and that's usually a mistake. While it is vivid, dramatic, and exciting, this book plunges you into a confusing swirl of dragons and trumpets, vials and seals, symbols and Old Testament imagery. Someone who begins with Revelation might well give up the whole Bible in frustration over trying to make any sense of Revelation. Without a background in both the Old and New Testaments, this book will certainly leave you baffled.

But the book of Revelation is not impossible to understand. Someone who is familiar with the rest of the Bible will be able to relate events in Revelation to the entire prophetic pattern of God's Word; with careful, patient study, it will make sense. Revelation is the capstone of the Bible, strategically placed at the end of the Bible. It is the climax of the entire revelation of God to His people. It is also the lens through which human history and Bible prophecy begin to come into focus and make sense. This book shows us how all the events of the past several thousand years are actually moving toward a single event: the return of Jesus Christ to establish His kingdom.

The book of Revelation is the only prophecy book in the New Testament. However, other New Testament books do contain prophetic passages. The Gospels contain prophetic utterances of Jesus, and the

Revelation shows how the events of history are moving toward the return of the Lord Jesus Christ

prophetic revelations given to Paul are found primarily in his letters to the Thessalonians. Nonetheless, Revelation is the only book in the New Testament that is primarily devoted to prophecy.

The title of the book is contained in the first line:

The revelation of Jesus Christ . . .

That's the title page of this book. Notice, it is not "Revelations," plural. This is a singular revelation of a singular person, Jesus Christ. John continues:

. . . which God gave him to show his servants what must soon take place. He made it known by sending his angel to his servant John (1:1).

God the Father gave this revelation to Jesus Christ. Jesus then revealed it to John through an angel. The purpose of this revelation is to show the Lord's servants—that's you and me and all other followers of Christ—what must soon take place. This book was written by the apostle John when he was a captive on the island of Patmos in the Aegean Sea. It dates from about A.D. 95. John says that he was in the Spirit on the Lord's Day and he began to see visions of things that must soon come to pass. So this is clearly a predictive book.

Why did God use symbols?

Notice that statement at the end of 1:1—"He made it known by sending his angel." The words, "He made it known" are a translation of a Greek word that means, "He signified it." Notice that the word *signified* can be broken down this way: "He sign-ified it." That is, God made this revelation known by signs, by symbols.

Why did God use symbols? Why didn't He reveal the future in plain language? One reason is that He was dealing with future events, which were beyond the imagination and understanding of men and women of the first century: nuclear warfare, worldwide plagues, biological warfare, information technologies, and space technologies. How could these concepts be explained to a generation who knew nothing about computers, missiles, nuclear energy, Stealth fighters, or helicopters?

Another helpful thing to understand about these symbols is that they are consistent with symbols found in other prophetic passages of the Bible. They are part of the overall prophetic tapestry of Scripture. So, if you want to understand Revelation, you should begin by comparing Revelation with Daniel, Ezekiel, and other parts of the Old and New Testaments.

I believe the Holy Spirit knew that this book would be difficult for many, so we find these words at the beginning of the book:

To explain modern technologies to a generation who knew nothing of computers, nuclear energy, helicopters, and so forth

They are consistent with symbols found in other prophetic passages of the Bible

Blessed is the one who reads the words of this prophecy, and blessed are those who hear it and take to heart what is written in it, because the time is near (1:3).

We who seek God's blessing on our lives and who want to understand the shape of things to come are eager to understand the symbols and the substance of God's book of Revelation.

The book of Revelation is addressed, first of all, to the seven churches in Asia Minor (present-day Turkey). The first section of the book consists of seven letters to these seven churches. There were more than seven churches in that region, of course, but these seven churches were selected because they are representative of the churches of every era, including ours. These letters come not from the apostle John, but from the triune God who has inspired these words. In Revelation 1:4–5, John sets forth the triune nature of the divine author of these letters—although it must be read carefully to be understood:

> *John,*
> *To the seven churches in the province of Asia:*
> *Grace and peace to you from him who is, and who was, and who is to come* [that's God the Father], *and from the seven spirits before his throne* [signifying the Holy Spirit in His sevenfold plenitude of power], *and from Jesus Christ* [the Son], *who is the faithful witness, the firstborn from the dead, and the ruler of the kings of the earth.*

Father, Son, and Holy Spirit jointly gave to seven churches—and to us—these seven letters, as well as the amazing prediction that follows. As is the case with most modern books, the ancient book of Revelation contains a dedication:

> *To him who loves us and has freed us from our sins by his blood, and has made us to be a kingdom and priests to serve his God and Father—to him be glory and power for ever and ever! Amen (1:5–6).*

The book is dedicated to Jesus Christ, the One who laid the foundation for all human blessing. Next, the theme of the book is introduced:

> *Look, he is coming with the clouds, and every eye will see him, even those who pierced him; and all the peoples of the earth will mourn because of him. So shall it be! Amen (1:7).*

The background of the book

John sets forth the triune nature of the divine author of these letters — although it must be read carefully to be understood

Dedication

This is a book about the second coming of Jesus Christ—how it will be accomplished, the events on earth that accompany this event, and what will happen afterward. The Lord then adds His personal signature as the book's author:

> *"I am the Alpha and the Omega," says the Lord God, "who is, and who was, and who is to come, the Almighty" (1:8).*

John's audience needed to hear that all of history, including their time of suffering, was under God's control

This book was written during a time of intense persecution of the church, during the reign of the vicious Roman emperor Domitian, who declared himself lord and god of the Roman people. The Christians of the time were desperate for encouragement and assurance, so they welcomed this message from the Lord, the one who is the Alpha and the Omega, the beginning and the end. They needed to hear that all of history, including their time of suffering, was under His control.

A framework for the book is given in verse 19, where John records what the Lord told him:

> *"Write, therefore, what you have seen, what is now and what will take place later."*

Let's look at the three divisions of the book of Revelation: (1) the things John saw—chapter 1; (2) current conditions as expressed in the seven letters to seven churches—chapters 2 and 3; and (3) things that will take place later—chapters 4 through 22. I believe that the phrase "what will take place later" refers to the events following the departure of the church. While chapters 2 and 3 cover the entire present age (from John's time to our own), all of the chapters that follow concern the culmination of human events. Elsewhere in the Bible this startling event is called the Great Tribulation, or the time of the end, or Daniel's Seventieth Week. All the frightening turbulence of our own day is moving toward this event.

In our overview of Revelation, we will touch briefly on some of the highlights of this unfolding of God's plan. Here is a brief structural overview of this amazing book:

What You Have Seen (Revelation 1)
1.	Introduction	1:1–8
2.	The Revelation of Christ	1:9–20

What Is Now (Revelation 2–3)
3.	The Lord's letter to Ephesus	2:1–7
4.	The Lord's letter to Smyrna	2:8–11

In chapters 2 and 3, we have the letters to the seven churches. These letters should be viewed on three levels. First, they are addressed to actual churches and deal with actual problems in those churches. Second, these churches symbolize individual churches during any time in history; your own church undoubtedly fits the pattern of one of these churches. Third, these churches represent the seven stages in the process of the history of the church, from the first century until today.

Let's look at each of these letters and churches.

The church in Ephesus was outwardly successful, but was beginning to lose its first love—that driving motivation so necessary for effectiveness in the Christian life. When we look at this letter from the viewpoint of church history, we see that many churches began to lose their first love during the period immediately following the death of the apostles. The "Ephesian" period of church history covers the years from A.D. 70, when the temple at Jerusalem was destroyed, to

Seven letters to seven churches

Letter 1, *Ephesus* (2:2–7): losing its first love

about A.D. 160. During that time, literally hundreds of churches had drifted from their warm, compassionate ministry to the world toward a formal, unloving institutional religion. The church became rife with conflict and theological arguments.

The word *Smyrna* means "myrrh," a fragrant spice or perfume obtained when the tender bark of the flowering myrrh tree is pierced or crushed. It is a fitting name for the first-century church of Smyrna, which gave off a fragrance of Christ throughout the region because it was a church that was often afflicted. Historically, the church in Smyrna represents a period called the Age of Martyrs, which lasted from about A.D. 160 to the rise of the first so-called Christian emperor, Constantine the Great, in A.D. 324. To call this period the Age of Martyrs is not to suggest that this was the only time in history when Christians have been martyred, but these particular Christians were persecuted with unequaled cruelty.

Pergamum means "married." This church had married the world; it was trying to cohabitate with the godless world system. All the attitudes and value systems of an unbelieving world had infiltrated the processes of the church. The Pergamum stage of church history is that period of time between the accession of Constantine the Great in A.D. 324 to the sixth century, when the era of the popes began. This was the time of the first "marriage" between church and state, when Constantine made Christianity the official religion of the Roman Empire. During this time in its history, the church was enjoying considerable popularity. It had come to be viewed not so much as a family of faith but as a formal worldly kingdom, much like any other kingdom. As the church's political influence grew, its spiritual influence waned.

The church in Thyatira was going through a period of spiritual adultery. It had lost its purity and needed to purify itself lest the Lord Himself purify it through a painful process of discipline. It was the most corrupt of the seven churches and symbolized a dark and corrupt period in Christian history—the Dark Ages, a period when the church lost its zeal and purity, when it became infiltrated with superstition and paganism. The Dark Ages lasted from the seventh century to the sixteenth century, when the Reformation began.

The church in Sardis had rediscovered the truth, but it lacked vitality. The church had built up a good reputation, but it was really dead and corrupt inside. Today, we would call the Christians at Sardis "nominal Christians"—*nominal* from the root word for "name." The Christians at Sardis were Christians in name only. Jesus told them, "You have a reputation, a name for being alive—but you are dead!" Apparently, the church at Sardis was largely made up of people who outwardly professed Christ, but who possessed no real spiritual life.

This is a picture of the period of the Reformation, from the sixteenth century to the eighteenth century. Although the Reformation churches began in a flaming fire of zeal, they soon died down to the whitened ashes of a dead orthodoxy.

The church of Philadelphia is a wonderful church. The Lord has no criticism whatsoever of this church. He commends the Philadelphia church because it is true and faithful to the Word. It has a little strength, He says, speaking of the quiet inner strength of the Holy Spirit, as contrasted with the overt power of the world's political structure. This church typifies the church age of the nineteenth century, the great evangelical awakening, when the Christian church focused less on acquiring political power and more on obeying its inner strength, the Holy Spirit. The church of this era was stirred to action and it expanded into the far corners of the earth in a great missionary movement.

REVELATION

Letter 6, *Philadelphia* (3:7–13): true and faithful to the Word

The church of Laodicea, the rich church, says, "We don't need anything at all from God. We've got money, influence, power—that's all we need." And God says, "You blind fools! Don't you know you don't have anything—that you are wretched and poor, pitiable and blind? Buy from me gold refined by fire." The Lord pictures Himself standing outside the door of the church, knocking for admittance. "You are neither cold nor hot," says the Lord. The Laodiceans were not like the church at Sardis, which was as cold as death. Nor were they like the church at Philadelphia, which was hot, alive, and vital. They were merely lukewarm.

Letter 7, *Laodicea* (3:14–22): materially rich but spiritually poor

Each of the seven churches of Revelation represents a specific time in church history. Looking back across twenty centuries of church history, we can see how accurate each of these prophetic symbols has been. As both history and prophecy clearly confirm, Laodicea symbolizes the church of the last age—our own age! Yes, the fact is that we live in Laodicean times, when the church considers itself rich but is poor, when it is lukewarm, neither hot nor cold.

As both history and prophecy clearly confirm, Laodicea symbolizes the church of the last age — our own age

Of course, this is a generalization—we see many vital, alive Christians, even in our lukewarm age. Our challenge and our task is to make sure that we live as Philadelphian Christians even in this Laodicean age. Even if every other church around us seems infected with Laodiceanism, we can still choose to burn brightly and hotly, giving off the light of Jesus in this twilight age of the church. If we do so, then Jesus says that the concluding promise of Revelation 3 is ours:

"To him who overcomes, I will give the right to sit with me on my throne, just as I overcame and sat down with my Father on his throne.

ADVENTURING
THROUGH THE
BIBLE

What will
take place
later

He who has an ear, let him hear what the Spirit says to the churches"
(3:21–22).

The book takes a sudden turn at chapter 4. Notice the key phrase in verse 2: "in the Spirit." This phrase occurs four times in Revelation: in 1:10, where John is on the isle of Patmos and hears the trumpet-like voice that introduces this entire vision; here in 4:2; in 17:3, when an angel carries him into the desert where he sees the woman sitting on the scarlet beast; and also in 21:10, when John is carried to a mountain and shown the Holy City, the New Jerusalem, coming down out of heaven. Each time John is "in the Spirit," it signals that something highly significant is happening.

At once I was in the Spirit, and there before me was a throne in heaven with someone sitting on it (4:2).

Heaven

This juncture is significant because the scene shifts now from earth to heaven. By "heaven," I don't mean somewhere out in space. In the Bible, heaven is the realm of the invisible—another dimension, if you like, wherein God reigns hidden from our eyes but present among us. It is a spiritual kingdom that surrounds us on every side, but one we cannot taste or touch or see—yet it is utterly real, more real than this plane of existence that we call "real life." What we think of as "reality" is a mere vapor compared with the reality of the heavenly realm.

This kingdom of heaven was opened to John, and he saw a throne and the One who sat upon it. Immediately he knew who it was—he did not need to be told. It was the throne of God, and God was in control of all history. John saw a remarkable vision of the powerlessness and the weakness of humanity contrasted with the vast might and authority of God.

The Lamb turned Lion

John then saw a Lamb standing in front of the throne—a Lamb with its throat cut. That may seem a strange symbol for the Son of God, but it is a very apt one—a slaughtered innocent lamb, a sacrifice. As John watched, the Lamb turned into a Lion, and John saw that this Lamb-turned-Lion was also the King of all. He stood before the One upon the throne, who held in His hand a little book. This little book is enormously significant in the book of Revelation: It is God's program for the establishment of His kingdom on earth. In heaven, God rules unchallenged; on earth, His will is constantly being challenged by puny people who dare to lift their fists against the Creator-God of the universe. But God is going to change all that, and He is going to do so by means of the Lamb who is the Lion—

the one who alone has the right to take the book (actually, a scroll) and open it.

And as the seven seals of this book are loosened, the scroll unrolls until at last its text is plain to all. John weeps as he first sees the scroll because he thinks that no one has the right to open it. But then he sees the Son of Man, and he knows that Jesus alone is entitled to unfold the scroll that will produce God's kingdom on earth.

As the scroll unfolds, we see that there are seven seals. Notice that the number seven appears frequently in this book; it is always a significant number. We have already seen the seven churches. Now we see seven seals, each one revealing a new power at work on earth. These are followed by seven trumpets, and then seven vials (or bowls) full of God's wrath.

In Revelation 6, we witness the beginning of this seven-year period that, the prophet Daniel tells us, is the culmination of history. All the worldwide events of our present day are moving toward this seven-year period called the Great Tribulation. This cataclysmic event will be ushered in by a worldwide preaching of the gospel, as we learn from our Lord's talk to the disciples on the Mount of Olives:

> *"This gospel of the kingdom will be preached in the whole world as a testimony to all nations, and then the end will come" (Matt. 24:14).*

The book of Revelation first considers the church as a unit, then turns to historical events concerning the rest of the world. In light of this, I believe that the church is caught up to be with the Lord prior to the period of the seven-year tribulation. The first event of that age is the worldwide preaching of the gospel, symbolized by the first of these seven seals:

> *I looked, and there before me was a white horse! Its rider held a bow, and he was given a crown, and he rode out as a conqueror bent on conquest (6:2).*

White always symbolizes divinity and deity; it represents purity and holiness. The bow represents conquest. This is a picture of the gospel's conquest of the world.

The second seal means war. John writes:

> *Another horse came out, a fiery red one. Its rider was given power to take peace from the earth and to make men slay each other. To him was given a large sword (6:4).*

The opening of the scroll

The seven seals

The beginning of the Tribulation

The first seal

The second seal

Could that great sword symbolize the terrible power of nuclear weapons? Or even conventional warfare on a previously unimagined scale?

The third seal

The third seal and the third horseman symbolize famine, which is inevitable in the wake of worldwide war.

The fourth seal

The fourth seal and the fourth horseman bring calamitous death—death by four means—sword, famine, plague, and wild beasts:

> *I looked, and there before me was a pale horse! Its rider was named Death, and Hades was following close behind him. They were given power over a fourth of the earth to kill by sword, famine and plague, and by the wild beasts of the earth (6:8).*

In the second, third, and fourth seals, John describes the forces at work in humanity to produce the events of history in the last days. Human power is therefore prominent throughout this time, and we see that God allows the sinful human race to unleash horrible events.

The fifth seal

The fifth seal is an expression of the inward power of humanity, the prayer of the martyrs. This is followed by cosmic disturbances, which provide a key to the entire book:

> *I watched as he opened the sixth seal. There was a great earthquake. The sun turned black like sackcloth made of goat hair, the whole moon turned blood red, and the stars in the sky fell to earth, as late figs drop from a fig tree when shaken by a strong wind. The sky receded like a scroll, rolling up, and every mountain and island was removed from its place (6:12–14).*

The sixth seal

The earthquake in this passage gives us a clue to understanding this book. The final event previewed here in the sixth seal is marked by a great earthquake, hail, and fire. This event signals the end of the seven-year period Jesus described when He said, "Immediately after the distress of those days 'the sun will be darkened, and the moon will not give its light; the stars will fall from the sky, and the heavenly bodies will be shaken'" (Matt. 24:29). This will happen just before Jesus Christ returns with His church.

The seventh seal

The seventh seal summarizes the events of the last half of this seven-year period, unfolded in Revelation 10 and 11, where we again encounter the earthquake when the seventh trumpet sounds:

> *Then God's temple in heaven was opened, and within his temple was seen the ark of his covenant. And there came flashes of lightning,*

rumblings, peals of thunder, an earthquake and a great hailstorm (11:19).

Chapters 12 through 14 introduce to us larger-than-life characters who act out the drama on earth. First, a woman (easily recognizable as Israel) brings forth a manchild, whom history has already informed us is the Son of God. Against Him in a great conflict are arrayed the angels of the devil and the great dragon called Satan. As John watches, a beast rises up out of the sea, and John recognizes that the beast is a form of human government linked to Rome, the fourth great world kingdom spoken of by Daniel. In some form, the Roman Empire is to exist until the end of time.

The woman, the beast, and the dragon

If you look at our western world, you can see how true that is. Every nation of the western hemisphere was settled by a member nation of the Roman Empire. We are Roman to the core; the whole western world is Roman in its thought, philosophy, and attitude. Associated with this beast out of the sea is another beast, or religious leader, who rises out of the earth and whom many link with the antichrist.

Chapters 14 through 16 largely deal with the description of the vials of God's wrath, which are exactly the same as those terrible judgments of which Jesus spoke when He said the sun would be darkened, the moon turned to blood, and God's wrath would be poured out upon the earth.

The vials of God's wrath

In the latter part of chapter 16 and continuing through chapters 17 and 18, you find the judgment of the great religious harlot called "MYSTERY BABYLON THE GREAT." Babylon was the source of ancient idolatry, and is used as a symbol of what we might call "religious godlessness"—something that looks godly and spiritual but is essentially godless. It is a religion that exercises political power through religious authority.

The judgment of Babylon the Great

If you read this passage carefully, you will see that this mystery Babylon is not any one system, institution, or denomination but rather an attitude that permeates the entire church. Wherever you find anyone acting religiously, trying to gain political power or authority, you have mystery Babylon, and it is found in all churches. As Jesus said, referring to the weeds planted among the good wheat, "Let both grow together until the harvest" (Matt. 13:30). And in Revelation 19, you have the harvest (as predicted in chapter 14):

This mystery Babylon is not any one system, institution, or denomination but rather an attitude that permeates the entire church

I looked, and there before me was a white cloud, and seated on the cloud was one "like a son of man" with a crown of gold on his head and a sharp sickle in his hand. Then another angel came out of the temple

The harvest

and called in a loud voice to him who was sitting on the cloud, "Take your sickle and reap, because the time to reap has come, for the harvest of the earth is ripe" (14:14–15).

This harvest occurs when Jesus Christ returns to earth:

> *I saw heaven standing open and there before me was a white horse, whose rider is called Faithful and True. With justice he judges and makes war. His eyes are like blazing fire, and on his head are many crowns. He has a name written on him that no one knows but he himself. He is dressed in a robe dipped in blood, and his name is the Word of God. The armies of heaven were following him, riding on white horses and dressed in fine linen, white and clean. Out of his mouth comes a sharp sword with which to strike down the nations. "He will rule them with an iron scepter." He treads the winepress of the fury of the wrath of God Almighty (19:11–15).*

Armageddon

By this time, all the nations of the earth have gathered in that battlefield called Armageddon, in the land of Israel, and this is where the Son of God appears with the armies of heaven. Now at last, all the supernatural forces—forces that human beings have so long and arrogantly denied—suddenly reveal themselves to human eyes in such a way as to eliminate all the opposition of entrenched evil against the will and authority of God.

A new heaven and a new earth

The book closes as the Son of God sets up His kingdom on earth, as He had promised. After the judgment of the dead comes a new heaven and a new earth, and the city of God, the New Jerusalem, descends from heaven. There, God makes His habitation with the human race. It is the fulfillment of the prayer Jesus taught us to pray: "Your kingdom come, your will be done on earth as it is in heaven" (Matt. 6:10).

The entire universe is at last cleansed of human rebellion, and there is nothing to be feared

This city is astoundingly beautiful. John sees no temple in it, for it does not need a temple, nor does it need the sun or moon to shine upon it. The light within it is the presence of God Himself. Its gates shall never be shut by day or by night. The entire universe is at last cleansed of human rebellion, and there is nothing to be feared. All the beautiful dreams of the prophets are fulfilled at this time. Swords are transformed into plowshares and spears into hooks for pruning the fruit-laden trees. War no longer exists.

At the end of the book, we are admonished to wait for the coming of Jesus—and to work for it, to be diligent and faithful and obedient until the Son of God comes. You may be surprised to know that this is a book of extreme optimism. Although Revelation is better known for its scenes of death, horror, upheaval, and mass destruction, it truly does not stop there. Revelation looks beyond the Tribulation, beyond Armageddon, all the way to the final victory of God, more sure than tomorrow's sunrise. C. S. Lewis writes this commentary on that glorious coming day:

REVELATION

Revelation is a book of extreme optimism

> God is going to invade, all right: but what is the good of saying you are on His side then, when you see the whole natural universe melting away like a dream and something else—something it never entered your head to conceive—comes crashing in; something so beautiful to some of us and so terrible to others that none of us will have any choice left? For this time it will be God without disguise; something so overwhelming that it will strike either irresistible love or irresistible horror into every creature. It will be too late then to choose your side. There is no use saying you choose to lie down when it has become impossible to stand up. That will not be the time for choosing: it will be the time when we discover which side we really have chosen, whether we realized it before or not. Now, today, this moment, is our chance to choose the right side. God is holding back to give us that chance. It will not last for ever. We must take it or leave it (*Mere Christianity*, [1943; reprint, New York: Macmillan, 1960], 66).

"God without disguise"

Revelation is filled with encouragement. It is a book that will either inspire your faith—or fill you with fear. It will give you great comfort and encouragement if you know the Lord of all time and all space. But it is also a solemn book designed to make us understand that the One who unrolls the scroll is the One who was once here, the One who died on Calvary's cross, the Lamb led to slaughter so that He might win the right to be the Lion, the King of all the earth.

The Lord is coming—and it won't be long now. Those who know Him welcome that day and work and pray to hasten it. People who don't know Him either scoff at that day—or dread it. The book of Revelation concludes with this promise of Jesus Himself:

> *He who testifies to these things says, "Yes, I am coming soon."*
> *Amen. Come, Lord Jesus.*
> *The grace of the Lord Jesus be with God's people. Amen (22:20).*

Index

message of, 33, 52, 60–61, 73
outline of, 61–62
overview of, 50–52
principle themes of, 47–48
Gibeonites, 137–38, 172
giving, 590–91, 762
gloating, 397–98
glorification, 72, 555, 570
gnosticism, 751
God
 absence of, 301–2
 adequacy of, 54
 anger of, 145–46, 414, 416, 453
 belonging to, 92–93
 character of, 305, 403
 compassion of, 336–37
 enjoyment of, 91
 eternality of, 337–38
 faithfulness of, 335–36
 grace of, 145, 146
 holiness of, 87, 425
 image of, 65, 87
 impartiality of, 383–84
 involvement of, 429–30
 jealousy of, 306, 416
 judgment and, 322, 337, 433–34
 justice of, 335
 love of, 370, 371–72, 465–66, 775
 mystery of, 424
 name of, 472, 766
 nature of, 82, 424–25
 patience of, 304
 persistence of, 302–3
 power of, 356–57
 presence of, 302
 purpose of, 16–18
 response to, 90–92
 responsibility of, 307
 righteousness of, 563, 602
 severe mercy of, 181
 sovereignty of, 363, 570
 trusting in, 87–88
 vengeance of, 416